VIETNAM

The Valor and the Sorrow

Best regards to
Morton Mc Donald,

Tom Butter
August 15, 1992
Baltimore

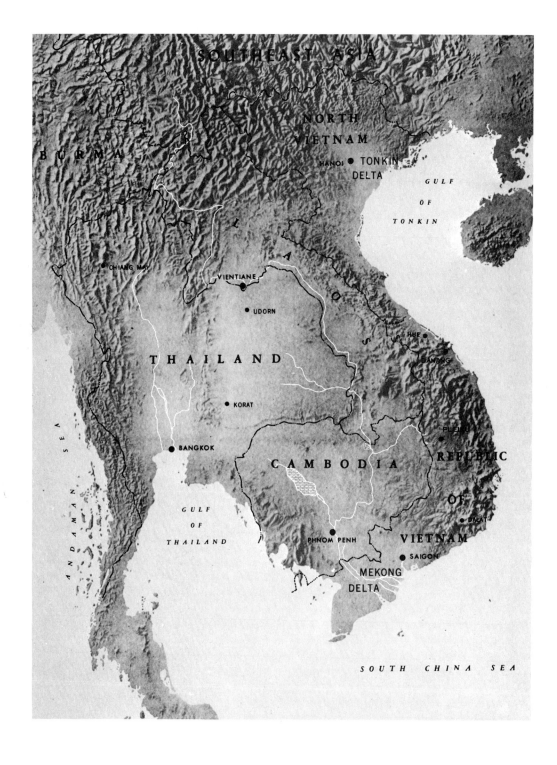

VIETNAM
The Valor and the Sorrow

From the home front
to the front lines
in words and pictures

Thomas D. Boettcher

Little, Brown and Company

Boston-Toronto-London

For Pam and my parents

Acknowledgments

This book which I was privileged to write benefited from the efforts of many people. Beth Rashbaum, my editor, provided expert guidance and effort in my behalf, as did copy editor Mike Mattil. Beth's assistants, Debra Roth and Skye Gibson, and Claude Lee and Jeannie Abboud from the production department, helped make the process of creating this book both possible and pleasant. Phil Jordan designed and thereby enhanced these pages. Ronnie Harlowe, Clarence Harlowe and Joe Vicino supervised the typesetting. At the beginning, Larry Ashmead liked my idea and introduced me to my agent, Don Cleary, who ably represented me and found a distinguished publisher. My wife Pam was patiently supportive during the entire process. I also want to thank my brother Fred.

Furthermore, I wish to acknowledge the work of other authors, especially that of David Halberstam, Joseph Buttinger, Godfrey Hodgson, James Aronson and Bernard Fall. I hope that in the same way my work will be of benefit to other writers' examination of this important period of our history.

Contents

Foreword

In 1969, at Tan Son Nhut Air Base near Saigon, I met with a classmate from the Air Force Academy. His name was Bob Henderson. Bob had just arrived for duty in the war zone. I had been there almost a year, so, referring to all the fighting and dying in Vietnam, he asked, "Is it worth it, Tom?" He had good reason to ask; he had orders to fly a small observation plane while serving as forward air controller, an extremely dangerous mission. In the years since, I've often recalled our conversation and his question, because several weeks later he was dead.

Hundreds of thousands of other young men sent to Vietnam asked the same question. In an undeclared war, in which there is no public affirmation of the worth of the cause for which he is fighting, each soldier must work out the answer for himself. Vietnam was the first war in foreign territory to put American soldiers to that test. Though there had been no declaration of war in Korea, either, American soldiers ordered there were bolstered substantially by knowledge that their contribution was part of an official United Nations action. Even so, the Korean war commitment was constitutionally one of the legal close calls that tend to make bad precedent. It was, however, a precedent that a series of presidents seemed generally comfortable with, though in 1965, as the air war on North Vietnam heated up, even Lyndon Johnson felt compelled to ask his attorney general, "Don't I need more authority for what I'm doing?"

What gave Johnson second thoughts was the very carefully worded statement in Article I, Section 8, Clause 11 of the Constitution that "The Congress shall have power . . . To declare war." The first draft of the Constitution presented to the Convention of 1787 by its Committee of Detail empowered Congress "to make war." But James Madison and others foresaw problems with that wording. Madison noted in his journal that he and "Mr. Gerry moved [on the floor of the Convention] to insert 'declare' striking out 'make' war; leaving to the Executive the power to repel sudden attacks." Their motion was adopted by the Convention.

Their opinion that Congress should officially declare a state of war, even when hostilities had already commenced, was grounded in their experiences during the Revolutionary War, still fresh in their minds. The colonies had won not because they had had the superior army, but because their citizens believed they had the better cause. These men understood that wars were primarily tests of national will not of weaponry. Therefore, as they envisioned it, congressional debate about whether there should be a declaration of war would be the essential test of public support.

Thomas Jefferson, while president, adhered to a strict interpretation of Congress's power to declare war when he dealt with the Bey of Tripoli in 1801. Though Tripoli had declared war on the United States and its ships were attacking American commercial vessels, Jefferson ordered the commander of a squadron sent to the Mediterranean to take defensive action only. As a result, after U.S. warships had disabled an attacking Tripolitan cruiser, the American squadron commander allowed it to return to port. To have captured it at that point, argued Jefferson, would have been a declaration of war, a power reserved for Congress by the Constitution.

By 1964, when North Vietnamese torpedo boats attacked American destroyers in the Gulf of Tonkin, such restraint was entirely absent. President Johnson seemed almost eager to go to war and Congress allowed him to do so without asserting its constitutional authority. The president and his advisers conducted themselves more like attorneys looking for loopholes in an ordinary contract than like caretakers of the public trust in need of all the guidance they could get. And what better guidance could they have found than the Constitution, which during almost two hundred turbulent years had required so few changes? It had, in fact, become much more than the country's fundamental body of laws. Its enduring quality had caused it to become the center of the national psyche.

The reactions of Jefferson and Johnson reflected not just differences in their personalities, but differences in the politics of their times. Johnson was very much the product of the political environment that evolved after the Second World War. How and why this evolution occurred is one of my major concerns in this book. The consequences of that evolution, specifically as they affected the way the president and the Congress dealt with the Constitution, in effect ignoring it and committing U.S. troops to combat without a declaration of war, are the second of my concerns.

Generally speaking, a series of administrations after the Second World War were blinded by arrogance, paranoia and cultural parochialism. Specifically, the Kennedy, Johnson and Nixon administrations worked first to convince the American public that U.S. soldiers weren't really involved in a war; then, that it was just a small war which we were winning; and, finally, that the soldiers would be coming home soon anyway. The political method which allowed this to happen was insidious. Soldiers were plucked one by one from their communities across the country. During the First and Second World Wars and even during the Korean war, there were huge troop sendoffs, rituals of a sort that should not be construed as celebrations of war but rather as public affirmations of confidence and support. Whole units were called up together and shipped off together. This was very deliberately avoided during Vietnam. Instead, young men, with orders in hand, individually reported to an embarkation point such as Travis Air Force Base, California. There was no parade, no marshaling orders, not even a banner. The experience was so lacking in ceremony that for me, at least, that day has almost slipped from memory. We just lined up, received our seating assignment on a chartered jet, climbed the ramp and were on our way to South Vietnam. By then, each of us should have understood that this war was going to be a long, long way from Tipperary.

Thomas D. Boettcher

Washington, D.C.
February 1985

VIETNAM

The Valor and the Sorrow

1 Colony of Cruelty

The French in Vietnam

As he worked among the peasants in Vietnam in 1963, Major Herb Brucker had reason to regret his idea ten years earlier that the Special Forces wear the green beret.

"As far as they were concerned, the French had come back," he says, recalling the local farmers' reaction to him and other American Special Forces soldiers assigned there in the early 1960s to train the South Vietnamese army to fight the Viet Cong. "We looked exactly the same."

The intimidating height. The foreign language. And the clincher — the uniforms topped off with those berets. Who else could these "round eyes" be? Yes, they must be French all right, and the black ones were their colonial troops.

And so it went. Since we Americans immediately followed the French, even looked like the French, many Vietnamese initially thought we were the French. It was not a good beginning.

The French had been unwelcome since 1847 when their navy sent cannonballs instead of calling cards into the 908-year-old kingdom of Vietnam. And they did nothing during the following ninety-six years of their occupation to alter that first impression.

They expropriated the land; destroyed a system of almost universal education; supplanted stable, local government with an inept colonial administration; and taxed millions of Vietnamese into starvation-level poverty.

No wonder the French were forced to spend forty years wrestling the Vietnamese into submission. Nor is it any wonder that in 1954 the French were finally forced to leave. By that time, almost all Vietnamese — rich and poor, Buddhist and Catholic, capitalist and Communist, Ngo Dinh Diem and Ho Chi Minh — shared a fierce determination to kick them out.

The Second World War gave the Vietnamese the chance. Just as dislocation wrought by the First World War destroyed the old order in Europe, dislocation wrought by the Second World War destroyed the old order in European colonies throughout the world. Kings lost their crowns because of the First; countries lost their colonies because of the Second.

Governor General Albert Sarraut and Emperor Khai Dinh, the father of Vietnam's last emperor, Bao Dai.

Colonialism— *In their own words.*

Everything here tends toward ruin.— Admiral Rigault de Genouilly, commander of the first French forces to establish control over a portion of Vietnamese territory, reporting on the fact that more French soldiers died of diseases than in fighting; in 1859.

I did not believe it possible that as strange and absurd a concept of colonial government as that created in Cochinchina could exist.—Charles-Marie Le Myre de Vilars, the first civilian governor of Cochinchina; in 1880.

The worst insult you inflict on a European in Indochina is to call him a lover of the natives.—Chamber of Deputies member Maurice Violette; in 1912.

Très bien! Continuez!—Governor General René Robin, on being told that French soldiers were killing all prisoners taken during a peasant rebellion in northern Annam; in 1934.

It can be taken as established that the population lives at the borderline of famine and misery.—Pierre Gourou, the leading authority on the living conditions in Tongking; in 1936.

In the wake of the Second World War, only two superpowers remained, the United States and the Soviet Union. Both were actively concerned about which political wing of the local citizenry in each of the newly emancipated colonies would come to power. The United States was drawn into Vietnam because of this concern. Though our objectives were in part strategic—we worried that all Southeast Asia might emerge as a bloc hostile to the U.S.—we couched them in almost purely ideological terms, as the once-secret *Pentagon Papers* clearly reveal.

In 1961 President Kennedy told the National Security Council our purpose was to prevent Communist domination of South Vietnam. In 1964 Secretary of Defense Robert McNamara called it "a test case of U.S. capability to help a nation meet a Communist 'war of liberation.'" In 1965 McNamara agreed with John McNaughton, assistant secretary of defense for international security affairs, that our objective there was "NOT—To 'help friend,'" but primarily "To avoid a humiliating U.S. defeat (to our reputation as a guarantor)." The emphasis and words in parenthesis were McNaughton's.

These intentions, however myopic they may have been, were different from those of the French. We did not go to Vietnam to colonize. But billions of American dollars and thousands of American soldiers proved insufficient to establish the point. Too many Vietnamese associated our intentions, as well as our berets, with those of the French, so that our efforts there were probably doomed from the start.

The land mass that was eventually to become French Indochina was composed of five "states." Three covered the land area later known to Americans as North Vietnam and South Vietnam. The other two French Indochinese states were Laos and Cambodia, the latter now known as Kampuchea.

Cambodia, a thinly populated state, was almost inadvertently acquired in 1883 while the French navy was continuing its vain search for a water route to China by way of the Mekong River. Laos, also a sparsely populated kingdom covered with jungle, was added in 1893 for strategic purposes. Laos and Cambodia were of neither much interest nor trouble to the French. The real fight was for the bigger prize, Vietnam, whose conquest preceded that of Laos and Cambodia and required the years from 1858 to

1883 to achieve. In fact, guerrilla fighting and trouble with Chinese pirates continued in northern Vietnam for yet another fourteen years.

The three French states in Vietnam were won in stages, as the French progressed from south to north. The first to fall was Cochinchina, consisting of the Saigon region with its fertile Mekong Delta plains. Annam, comprising the central highlands and their coastal regions, including the imperial capital of Hue, was next. Tongking, the Red River region of the far north with its principal city of Hanoi, was the last to be completely controlled. Each step of the way, the Vietnamese offered stiff resistance. The major part of Cochinchina fell only after five months of pitched battles against the armies of the

Each city of sizable population had a French quarter, clearly demarcated by its European architecture. This photo, taken in early 1955 shortly after French withdrawal from the north, is of Campha, one of three ports in the Hanoi area.

Vietnam sends an envoy to President Grant . . .

In 1873 Emporer Tu Duc sent an emissary to Washington to seek the assistance of the Grant administration in staving off the French conquest of Vietnam. Might the president entreat his European friends to stop? the envoy asked.

Unfortunately, hardly anyone in Washington knew where Vietnam was. The answer was no, the U.S. could not help.

On his return trip, the envoy stopped in Yokohama, Japan, to visit the American consul there, who was a close friend. They both agreed that one day the U.S. would be greatly involved in Asian affairs. As a farewell gift to the American, the Vietnamese composed a poem that expressed his thoughts regarding their two countries. "Spiritual companion," it read, in part, "in what year will we be together in the same sampan?"

In March 1967 President Johnson recounted this story at the conclusion of the Guam Conference on Vietnam. Answering the question posed almost a century before, he said, "Today we know the answer. We are together. And we know our destination."

emperor of Vietnam. To win Annam and Tongking, the French were forced to storm Hue and Hanoi. Since the French encountered different political and military obstacles in each of the three regions, and overcame them at different times, it followed that the nature of French administration was to take different forms in Cochinchina, Annam and Tongking.

Cochinchina, the first acquired, was administered directly by the French. In 1862 a French admiral forced the Vietnamese emperor, Tu Duc, to cede that part of his territory by treaty. The French governed this land not as a protectorate region but as their own territory.

Though French guns forced the Vietnamese leader to relinquish Cochinchina, they could not force his subjects to collaborate with the French in administering it. Mandarins who for centuries had been responsible for Vietnamese affairs of state—administrative, fiscal, legal, educational and military—on all levels, from the villages to the royal court, faded into the countryside. Consequently, the French ran Cochinchina from Saigon by direct military rule. Young French officers, ignorant of the language and local customs, replaced the mandarins and, in fact, exceeded their native predecessors in power. A French admiral became the chief local authority.

The military continued to run Cochinchina until 1879, when civilian control was reestablished and the first governor general was appointed, but of course the civilians in power were not Vietnamese. By that time real political power was in the hands of local French business interests. They governed themselves through a legislative body known as the Colonial Council of Cochinchina, constituted in 1880. The colons, as these business people were called, even elected a delegate to France's Chamber of Deputies.

By 1883 the French presence was established enough to support the conquest of Annam and Tongking. In August of that year the French attacked Hue and Hanoi, and within days the Vietnamese surrendered. A treaty was signed August 25. Old Tu Duc was spared this humiliation, however. He died of natural causes the month before, heartbroken by the imminent demise of his kingdom and cursing the French to his last breath.

This time the mandarins did not abandon their posts and remove themselves to the countryside as they had after Cochinchina's conquest. They continued with their duties of state. In

The commander of the French force that arrived off the Vietnamese coast at Tourane on August 31, 1858, hoped to sail up a river and attack the imperial capital of Hue. But the river was too shallow for his ships, so he settled for shelling Tourane, as this early engraving shows, before departing for Saigon.

The Vietnamese fought hard to keep the French out of their country. In 1861 the French army, supported by overwhelming firepower, defeated the soldiers of Emperor Tu Duc outside Saigon. The following year, the French forced the ruler to cede Cochinchina, which included Saigon, to France.

"Old Ironsides" in Vietnamese waters . . .

The captain of the U.S.S. *Constitution*, "Old Ironsides," played an unwitting part in a series of events that led to the first French military action against Vietnam. While on a trip to Asian waters in 1845, the *Constitution* was docked at the port of Tourane, Vietnam's principal harbor near the imperial capital of Hue. Word of the ship's presence reached a French priest, Bishop Dominique Lefebvre, who was in a Hue prison.

Lefebvre, a zealous missionary, had for ten years been preaching to the Vietnamese, trying, with some success, to convert them to Catholicism. The emperors opposed such activity, but for the most part limited their reprisals to booting the priests out of the country. Lefebvre exceeded Emperor Thieu Tri's tolerance, however. He conspired with other priests to have Thieu Tri overthrown in favor of another ruler more supportive of his proselytizing efforts.

Thieu Tri uncovered the plot and at first condemned Lefebvre to death. By the time the *Constitution* arrived, the death sentence had been commuted.

From his cell Lefebvre managed to have a message calling for help smuggled to the *Constitution*'s captain, John Percival, who at that instant was hosting several Vietnamese mandarins.

Percival's Occidental loyalties immediately overwhelmed all the constraints of good diplomacy. He held the mandarins hostage, pending Lefebvre's release.

But Thieu Tri refused to negotiate. Left with no option, save sailing off with three new crew members, Percival eventually released them and departed without Lefebvre. Shortly thereafter, the U.S. government disavowed Percival's action and apologized to Thieu Tri.

At that point the emperor decided the priest was potentially more dangerous in prison than free, so he deported

recognition of this apparent cooperation and their own military limitations, the French did not force Tu Duc's heir to cede the two regions; Annam and Tongking became military protectorates of France, not colonies, administered by Vietnamese, though the French reserved for themselves ultimate authority on all matters. Or, at least, they tried to.

About a year after the treaty was forced upon them, the mandarins, under the royal banner, began a vigorous resistance that lasted until 1895. Determined to allow nothing to interfere with their cause, they engineered the quick demise of three successive emperors within a year of Tu Duc's death because each was afraid to fight the French. Finally, the mandarins found a twelve-year-old of royal blood named Ham Nghi who agreed to resist and whom they therefore crowned emperor.

In the meantime, the mandarins had been building a secret capital in the jungles of Quang Tri Province, from which they planned to execute their campaign. Tan So was fortified and filled with provisions, from rice to guns. In June of 1885 the mandarins secretly transported all the gold and silver in the royal treasury to Tan So. The next month the fighting began. Vietnamese soldiers attacked the French garrison at Hue.

Western military equipment proved superior, however. The Vietnamese soldiers were forced to withdraw to Tan So. Along the way they killed thousands of Vietnamese peasants in Catholic villages, accusing them of compromising the Vietnamese cause by sharing the religious faith of the French.

The mandarins' bold move in Ham Nghi's name stirred the citizenry of Annam. On their own initiative, they attacked French convoys pursuing the Vietnamese army. A royal proclamation urged them on. The emperor asked "of the rich their wealth, of the mighty their strength and power, and of the poor their limbs, that the country might be retaken from the invader."

In spite of this, Tan So fell soon thereafter, the French confiscating the twenty-five hundred gold and six thousand silver bars found there. But Ham Nghi escaped, and it was not until late 1888 that he was captured, a victim of treachery by fellow Vietnamese. He was deported to Algeria.

Various persistent mandarins continued fighting, leading guerrilla bands against the French. Gradually they were pushed deeper and deeper into the jungles and toward the Laotian border. The last of these great mandarin resisters, Dr. Phan Dinh Phung, died of dysentery in 1895, after ten years of fighting. Though sporadic guerrilla activity continued even after Governor General Paul Doumer arrived in 1897, resistance under the royal banner ended with Phung. All his followers were beheaded, though the French had promised a pardon if they surrendered.

The first French civilians in Vietnam arrived concurrently with their troops. They sold supplies to the soldiers. Next came traders, farmers, land speculators, exporters, developers, all sorts of business people including bankers, publishers and doctors, and, of course, government functionaries.

Virtually all came to serve themselves, not France. Many became very rich. In time Vietnam became their colony, not France's. Most of the governors general who arrived thinking otherwise never finished their five-year terms. Dealing with entrenched French interests became so difficult that many capable and honest administrators simply avoided the assignment.

As the problems and politics confronting any governor general in Vietnam became more complex, debates in the French Chamber of Deputies concerning the appointment became so intense that sometimes the slot remained open two years awaiting a nomination. The colons welcomed this condition, the absence of authority from France giving them even greater latitude. Because of the colons' provincial attitude and their power, France never really developed a long-term policy regarding Vietnam, except one of general tolerance for the self-serving interests

him to Singapore. Unfortunately for the Vietnamese, the wily Lefebvre reentered the country, once again forcing Thieu Tri through the cycle of capture, sentencing and deportation.

This time, in March 1847, two French warships sailed into Tourane to rescue Lefebvre, their commander unaware the priest was already back in Singapore. Lefebvre's presumed peril was just the pretext France had been looking for to begin moving into Vietnam. They demanded his release and the free exercise of faith of all Catholics in Vietnam.

For two weeks the unwelcome guests remained at anchor awaiting reply. As is so often the case concerning the initiation of hostilities, accounts differ as to what happened next. The French commander apparently mistook the movement of some Vietnamese vessels for prelude to an attack. Whatever the case, both French warships opened fire on the vessels and on Tourane's fortress, sinking five of the former and also killing a large number of Vietnamese in the city. All prospects of negotiation thus ended, the two ships sailed off.

As reprisal, Thieu Tri threatened to kill all priests in the country, but never killed a single one. In fact, Lefebvre himself again returned to Vietnam, where he lived and preached another twenty years.

The only known photograph of the U.S.S. *Constitution,* "Old Ironsides," under sail; taken in 1846.

✸ In precolonial Vietnam, eighty percent of the population could read and
write to some degree. In 1954, at the
end of French colonialism, eighty percent could not.

Frenchmen in a Vietnamese bordello.

Those posted to Vietnam enjoyed a
pampered life, as the number of male
domestics who worked in this home of a
French officer serving in Phuc Yen
Province indicates.

of their colonial citizenry.

The Frenchmen who filled government administrative posts in Vietnam were typically those
who could not win such appointments at home.
Each owed his job to patronage. Generally of
marginal talent and low income, they were emi-
nently corruptible, thus amenable to bribes from
the colons to facilitate business deals.

Responsibilities often overlapped or duplicated each other. The more centralized administration imposed by Paul Doumer in the late
1890s, for instance, usurped duties previously
performed by state-level officials, but the latter
retained their posts. Other governors general
also enlarged staffing levels by bringing their
own preferred officials with them, without sending an equal number home.

The colony became such a haven for sinecures
that one early critic, a Frenchman named Girau-
deau, wrote in 1897, "The English have colonies
in order to do business; we have them in order to
give positions to bureaucrats." Sometimes so
many arrived at once, all assured of a job by
politicians back home, that they had to spend
months in Saigon or Hanoi waiting for a position to be created. The British ruled 325 million
Indians with fewer officials than the French
employed to rule 30 million Vietnamese.

The cost of this bureaucracy was enormous,
and made much worse by French reluctance to
hire Vietnamese. Even lowly officials who sold
postage stamps were transported five thousand
miles from France to do the job. Moreover, they
were paid at least six times as much as the
highest-salaried Vietnamese in government. In
1906, labor costs made up seventy-five percent
of the postal budget for Indochina. In 1911, the
cost of the administrative staff for the state of
Tongking made up eighty-five percent of its
budget; public works took only ten.

Such gross inefficiency created a heavy tax
burden, of course, but not one borne by the
French living in Vietnam. For many years it was
their compatriots back home who were taxed to
cover whatever costs were not absorbed by the
taxes imposed on the Vietnamese. Eventually,
this drain on the French treasury contributed to
a determination in Paris to send, at last, a
strong administrator for the troubled French
territories.

Paul Doumer was a former minister of finance in
his thirties when in 1897 he became governor

general of French Indochina. Both friend and foe supported his nomination, such being the nature of the job and the man. Friends deemed him a genius in matters of administration and finance, and thus the most capable for the difficult task. Foes wanted him removed from the domestic political scene, and expected that failure in Vietnam would inevitably put an end to his career. All previous governors general had failed. Indochina was still not a profitable colony for France.

The French had looked to the region for inexpensive raw materials and agricultural products for their businesses and for new sources of tax revenue for the state. Vietnam had instead been a drain on the treasury for forty years. Furthermore, the frustrating conclusion of most members of the Chamber of Deputies was that fighting the Vietnamese had become a permanent state of affairs.

Doumer was determined to reverse this pattern. His initial objectives were to centralize administrative control, balance the books and force an end to the sporadic guerrilla activity. He then planned to launch a massive public works program to construct roads, bridges, railroads and waterworks.

In miraculous fashion, Doumer achieved his initial objectives in one year, using such worldly means as brutal force and guile. France's Chamber of Deputies, overwhelmed by his success, granted him immediate support for his public works program. The colony was awarded a 200-million-franc loan to begin. So ambitious were his projects and so great were his organiza-

Paul Doumer put French administration on a course followed for decades.

✳ In 1919 there were only six schools for secondary education in all Indochina —three were reserved for children of the French, three for the children of millions of Vietnamese, Laotians and Cambodians.

Frenchmen beheaded Vietnamese who opposed their rule or were guilty of serious crimes.

Johnson warns Kennedy about following French colonialists into Vietnam ...

In May 1961, President Kennedy sent Vice-President Lyndon Johnson to India, Pakistan and various Southeast Asian nations to draw upon the insight of leaders there and to assess our options in Vietnam. Johnson's report included the following statement: "Asian leaders —at this time—do not want American troops involved in Southeast Asia other than on training missions. American combat troop involvement is not only not required, it is not desirable. Possibly Americans fail to appreciate fully the subtlety that recently-colonial peoples would not look with favor upon governments which invited or accepted the return this soon of Western troops." However, in the same report, he warned Kennedy that "the battle against Communism must be joined in Southeast Asia with strength and determination" because "Without this inhibitory influence, the island outpost—Philippines, Japan, Taiwan—have no security and the vast Pacific becomes a Red Sea."

---

tional skills, that Doumer's program determined the course of French policy regarding Vietnam from his own time until the fall of France there in 1954.

Ironically, the scope of his achievement and the brutality with which it was brought about made inevitable the day the French would finally be forced to leave. He brought the fighting to an end not by compromise but by repression. His centralized administration removed all traces of local government so thoroughly that there was no viable Vietnamese infrastructure with which to negotiate an accommodation later on. His balancing of the books was achieved at the expense of the Vietnamese, whose taxes became unbearable.

When Doumer set out to centralize authority in the office of the governor general, he correctly anticipated more resistance from the colons of Cochinchina than from the Vietnamese. The colons resisted centralized authority for two reasons. First, they wanted to confine the authority of the governor general to Annam and Tongking so that they could continue running Cochinchina without interference. Paul Doumer was correctly perceived by them as a representative of the interests of France and not of their own selfish interests. They saw a French-oriented colonial policy as an intrusion into their private domain.

Second, they recognized that a centralized authority would necessitate a general budget to which they might be required to contribute. They insisted that what few francs they paid in taxes should be spent on projects in Cochinchina. They saw no reason why they should contribute to the development of the other four states.

Doumer moved first against the Vietnamese-administered states of Annam and Tongking. In Tongking especially the emperor's authority had already been weakened by mandarin-led guerrillas and marauding Chinese pirates. French troops were assigned to Tongking to do battle with the guerrillas and pirates, and the position of viceroy was created to tighten authority. The viceroy of Tongking was a Vietnamese chosen and controlled by the French. But soon Doumer decided he wanted even more direct control over Tongking. He unilaterally abolished the office of viceroy and installed a Frenchman in the newly created position of resident superior, who would report directly to himself.

Centralizing French authority in Annam was Doumer's next goal. There the emperor had ruled for years through a body known as the Secret Council, composed of Vietnamese. In late 1897 Doumer replaced it with a new council in which every Vietnamese member had a French counterpart. He then appointed a French resident superior for Annam who replaced the emperor as chairman of the council.

A short time later Doumer removed the final remnant of Vietnamese authority in Annam and Tongking by taking the tax-collection duties away from the mandarins. To mollify the emperor, by then only a puppet who owed his elevation to the French, he guaranteed him a large yearly allowance. The mandarins became low-paid employees of France.

Three months after firming his grip on those two provinces, Doumer moved against the entrenched colons and their allied government functionaries in Cochinchina. There his moves were only slightly less subtle. He began by establishing a body called the Superior Council of Indochina, whose membership included the resident superiors of not only Annam and Tongking but also Laos and Cambodia, as well as the lieutenant governor of Cochinchina, Doumer's own deputy.

The Superior Council was initially without power because no general budget existed with which to support a united administration and pay for projects leading to the five states' general development. Doumer was moving in that direction, though, as his council's name very clearly indicated. The message was not lost on the colons. They recognized that Doumer planned to make his council superior in authority to their Colonial Council of Indochina and, as a consequence, to diminish their influence.

Doumer then created what he called the General Services of Indochina, within which he initially established two administrative units, one to coordinate agriculture and commerce, the other to handle customs and indirect taxes.

With this framework of general authority and administration in place, Doumer next petitioned the government in France for authorization for a general budget—exactly the move the colons dreaded. Their reaction was immediate. They condemned the idea in the strongest terms and petitioned Paris to reject his proposals.

A protracted political battle ensued. A measure of the colons' influence is that Doumer's

✳ In 1926 only one Vietnamese boy in twelve was literate. Only one girl out of a hundred attended school of any kind.

Mandarins were the key figures in running pre-colonial Vietnamese society; they achieved their positions through education and merit.

Vietnamese society is diverse, ranging from Chinese immigrants to Montagnard tribesmen, such as this boy with his bow.

Colons enjoyed a life of royalty. A huge labor pool provided every imaginable creature comfort.

proposals, so obviously needed for France to reap a sufficient return on its Indochinese investment, required a full eight months for approval. By decree Paris finally granted Doumer authority for a general budget as well as for expansion of his General Services. In Doumer's words, these actions, on July 31, 1898, "consecrated the birth of Indochina." And he was right. At the same time, he became more dominant over the affairs of Vietnam than the local emperors had ever been.

Doumer's vision for Indochina, particularly Vietnam, was to make it France's richest colony —not rich in the sense that its native people would prosper through growth in agriculture and industry, but rich as a source of wealth for France. Doumer naturally wanted industries to develop in Vietnam, but only in a way that would allow France to reap for itself the maximum return on its investment in the region.

The building of the infrastructure—the railroads, bridges, roads and waterworks that would be the focus of his public works—was crucial to Doumer's master plan. After he centralized control of Indochina, the Chamber of Deputies gave him virtual carte blanche to pursue his public works plan, and the 200-million-franc loan he had requested to make it a reality.

Doumer responded like a man possessed. With the huge loan, he initiated simultaneous construction of projects throughout Indochina, ninety percent of which were planned for Vietnam. Hundreds of French engineers and foremen were brought over. Thousands of peasants were or-

dered from their villages. Together they built on a scope and at a pace Southeast Asia had never before witnessed.

Doumer seemed everywhere, and everywhere in motion. No slothful functionaries or obdurate colons would miss his measure. He defied the odds of human endurance in the tropics. He worked late and he worked hard.

He started his biggest projects first, knowing that the wheels of bureaucracy, once set in motion, would ensure their completion. Thus, he succeeded in imposing his vision of Vietnam's future on governors general for the next fifty years. Their success was measured by how far along they pushed Doumer's projects. For years his allocation of resources among these projects was not even questioned—sixty-two percent for railroads, bridges and roads, nineteen percent for hydraulic agriculture, seven percent for maritime ports, seven percent for civil buildings, two percent for city sanitation, and the remaining three percent for miscellaneous expenditures. Consequently, long after it was obvious that the massive railroad construction plan was a huge mistake, tracks were still being laid. The primary effort, it later became obvious, should have been to develop all varieties of waterworks.

Regrettably, Doumer's genius for administration and fiscal matters did not extend to economic planning. Few of the projects were commenced on the basis of need. They presumed a degree of development in the Indochinese economy that did not exist. No feasibility studies had been done, so planning was no more sophisticated than the impulse to connect points on a map.

The Trans-Indochinese railroad connecting Saigon and Hanoi is an example: It never paid for itself because its narrow-gauge tracks too severely limited cargo weights and because it essentially duplicated an existing, cheaper route. To make matters worse, Doumer also built a highway along the coast, connecting the same two cities. Thus, two enormous state projects competed with one another, and lost out to a preexisting alternative.

Generally speaking, Doumer's projects were a bonanza only for the contractors, many of whose charges were later found to be grossly inflated. Even the highways proved unsuitable for the Vietnamese. They found no reason to divert their oxen carts from traditional routes connecting villages and later found it dangerous to do

A French bridge becomes a symbol of North Vietnamese resistance . . .

The crown jewel of French Governor General Paul Doumer's public works program was a spectacular bridge near Hanoi spanning the high dams that hold back the turbulent Red River. With great fanfare, it was dedicated by Doumer himself in 1902, a short time before his return to France.

Ironically, this bridge named for a Frenchman became a symbol of North Vietnamese resolve in fighting the Americans. U.S. aircraft targeted the Doumer Bridge for destruction because it carried the principal rail and truck traffic from China to Hanoi. Hundreds of bombing sorties were directed at it. The bridge area was one of the most heavily defended in the history of air warfare, bristling with anti-aircraft missiles and guns.

The superstructure of this durable bridge is made of iron girders cast in Paris beginning in 1889. Its pillars hoist the bridge forty feet above the river and descend through one hundred feet of water to the riverbed. More than a mile long, it was, at least until the mid-1960s, the largest such structure in Asia.

Many suspicious Vietnamese advised the original French builders against trying to cross the Red River there, believing that the structure would disturb the realm of a dragon that lived in its depths. Many French opposed building the bridge there with equal fervor, but for more mundane reasons—the difficult terrain and the scope of the project being the major ones.

The bridge still stands, though it now lists slightly due to overuse. It is so clogged with traffic by day that trucks are allowed to use it only at night.

✳ In 1937 coal accounted for sixty-three percent of the value of all mineral exports from Vietnam. Almost all this production was controlled by the Bank of Indochina.

Saigon became known as the Paris of the Orient. Frenchmen created for themselves the amenities of Europe, such as in Saigon this opera house and the Continental Palace Hotel. Years later, during the Vietnam war, Americans sipped drinks on this veranda.

so because of auto traffic. For the most part, the roads became avenues for tourists.

The monetary and human costs of these projects were enormous. The Trans-Indochinese railroad required forty years to complete instead of the predicted ten. And because these projects could not pay for themselves by generating more revenue, the French government was forever underwriting more construction loans, which were repaid by more taxes on the Vietnamese population. All this work, all this investment, actually reduced the net worth of the colony's resources.

Furthermore, Doumer's public works extravaganza cost thousands of lives. The dangers of building over mountains and rivers and through jungles exacted a terrible toll. Of the eighty thousand employed to build one frightful three-hundred-mile stretch of railway in Tongking, twenty-five thousand died of accidents, malaria and other sicknesses.

Doumer's successors were like engineers at the controls of a huge train without brakes, chugging up the slope of a steep mountain. The prospect of getting over the top was nil, but there seemed no safe alternative to continual forward motion. Millions of francs ceaselessly fueled Doumer's public works engine.

Had the Vietnamese known the scope of Doumer's ambition and had the power to act on that knowledge, they would have opposed him with even greater vigor than the colons did. It was the Vietnamese who would pay for Doumer's schemes — and errors.

Even before Doumer arrived, the French had greatly increased taxes. During the 1860s, while French soldiers were still stabilizing control, Vietnamese in Cochinchina paid taxes amounting to about one-half million francs. By the 1880s, the amount increased to 20 million. By 1887, the amount was 35 million. Doumer's increases came on top of those. At the same time, French citizens residing there, who controlled almost all the wealth and were in many cases making huge fortunes, paid virtually nothing. The pattern thus established endured throughout the French occupation. The wealthiest Frenchman living in Cochinchina paid taxes on his income at a 0.33 percent rate. The poorest Vietnamese peasant paid an average twelve percent.

In 1897 Doumer reserved for his newly authorized general budget all indirect tax revenues,

Roads constructed by the French with Vietnamese labor were of greater use to tourists than the local population, who preferred smaller trails and paths. (Left) For decades, a military assignment to Vietnam entailed more ceremony than action. The mere presence of French troops kept the population passive.

Though the French kept Vietnam their private business preserve, many of the world's wealthy took advantage of the country's extraordinary geography, some yachting along the coast, others hunting wild game in the jungles.

※ In precolonial Vietnam, the export of rice was forbidden. Surplus rice was stored to feed the people during bad years.

such as those from customs duties and taxes on items like mineral oil, cinnamon, tobacco and matches. Indirect tax revenues also included profits from the state monopolies for the production, distribution and sale of opium, alcohol and salt. Doumer allotted to the five states all direct tax revenues, such as personal income taxes and head taxes, the latter being the same for the wealthiest Frenchman and the poorest peasant.

The states' budgets immediately went into the red because Doumer was siphoning off revenues they had relied upon. However, within three years, all were in the black because they too increased taxes on the native populations.

Doumer's indirect taxes, especially the monopolies, were the greatest burden on the Vietnamese. His predecessors had created them, but it was Doumer who mined them. It was the only fuel on which his public works engine would run. The monopolies accounted for seventy percent of all general budget revenue. Even hungry peasant families had to contend with them on a daily basis. The indirect tax resulting from the salt monopoly, for example, meant that a starving family would eat even less. Salt was necessary for food preservation, and *nuoc mam*, a liquid

extract of fermented fish and salt, was indispensable in Vietnamese food consumption. Thus, any increases in the price of salt were immediately felt by all Vietnamese.

All producers of salt—even the backyard variety—had to sell their product to the government at a price set by the government. Obviously, they would have to buy a portion of it back for their own use. They customarily paid six to eight times more for it than what they received.

On average the monopoly increased the price the Vietnamese paid for salt fivefold. Fisherman frequently discarded their catches because they could not afford the salt to preserve them. The frustration and hatred that welled up within them can easily be imagined. Salt marshes were often within sight of their boats, but they were prohibited from drawing upon such readily available sources. And those who did went to jail. Not surprisingly, there was a proliferation of jails. Eventually there were three for every school in the country.

Though continually increasing taxes for the Vietnamese, the French did nothing to increase Vietnamese income potential. Vast new rice-farming regions were opened up, but no portion

Vietnamese traditionally made salt by spreading ocean water on flats to dry. The French made the mineral much more expensive by forcing the population to buy it from a monopoly.

✳ Rice was the principal export commodity of the French. By the Second World War, Vietnam was the third largest exporter of rice in the world, behind Burma and Thailand.

✳ The average Vietnamese peasant landowner had less land in 1930 than he did before the French colonized, even though the latter had opened up enormous new farming areas.

✳ In 1905 the French cultivated only one-quarter of the farmland they owned in Vietnam, the remainder lying fallow.

Some active opposition to the French began reemerging in the early 1900s. But the French delayed reforms, underestimating the barely disguised contempt for them.

of them went to the poor, as had been the traditional practice for centuries in Vietnamese society. Instead, wealthy landowners got all the land at little or no charge. These policies, in time, exceeded even the vexatious taxes as an underlying source of discontent. A piece of land, however small, gave the poor a small measure of hope for the future. The typical rural peasant family shared a rickety shack with a few small farm animals and worried about its next meal.

French administrators frequently pointed to increases in rice production as proof that Vietnamese, though still poor, were indeed enjoying an improved standard of living because of the French presence. But the true measure of whether Vietnamese were eating better was not how much rice was produced but how much remained in the country for consumption. During the years 1900 to 1937, while the Vietnamese population increased eighty percent, total rice consumption actually declined thirty percent. A study in 1942 confirmed the resulting state of hunger among Vietnamese. "It is only in periods of intense agricultural labor, which means during one-third of the year and particularly during the harvest, that the people have enough to eat," it read.

Exploring rugged Vietnamese territory was stimulating diversion, a challenge even with guides. Fighting in it would be difficult.

Vietnamese who were employed by the French on public works projects, in the mines or at one of the rubber or rice plantations fared no better. The working and living conditions were, in fact, worse. They slept stacked together, elbow to elbow in long barracks, worked ten to twelve hours daily, prepared their own meager twice-daily meals, and fended for themselves when sick.

Furthermore, they were separated from their families, sometimes by hundreds of miles. They worked during the monsoon rains and tropical heat. But they were forced to keep working until they dropped. Fines were imposed on those not working hard enough, sickness being an unacceptable excuse. Physical abuses such as kicking were acceptable forms of supervision.

Peasants obviously wanted to avoid such employ, making conscription necessary. It was technically against the law, but colons and administrators such as Doumer ignored this constraint until the 1930s when the Depression, which hit Indochina particularly hard, encouraged enforcement of the law.

Most of the unemployed lived in Tongking and Annam, states that were even poorer than Cochinchina because of overpopulation and limited farming lands. Vietnamese agents were hired to bring these unfortunate souls south by force so that they could be put to work on large plantantions and public works projects all over Indochina.

This was essentially a slave market. The agents earned sixteen piasters for each worker signed up to the usual three-year contract. No

✳ French plantation owners made virtually no effort to increase their yields per acre because additional land to increase their gross output was made available so cheaply to them. Therefore, by 1954 Vietnam had the lowest yield per acre of any of the world's major rice-growing countries.

These men in stocks were part of a 1908 plot to poison French officers of the Hanoi garrison and take control of the city. Such early rebellions failed for lack of sound planning and organized involvement of the population.

4. TONKIN — Criminels inculpés dans le complot des Empoisonneurs (Juillet 1908) à la barre de Justice, dans la prison

(Top) French missionaries preceded their country's colonizing efforts. Priests and nuns eventually converted a large number of Vietnamese to Catholicism. (Bottom) Littering was a crime taken very seriously. Those in jail helped sweep streets.

one had the right to decline. Once signed, those who ran away from the job were treated like military deserters. To avoid such service, men abandoned their families and went into hiding for long periods whenever the conscription agents were active in their areas.

A Frenchman named Bazin controlled these agents, a new set of Vietnamese mandarins whose ascendance was due not to education and training, as before, but rather to their willingness to do a Frenchman's bidding.

The conscription process was perpetually in motion. In order to keep manning levels constant on the plantations, agents had to recruit two peasants for every one actually working, because the rate of attrition due to death, desertion and refusal to re-sign a contract was so high. Recruitment quotas were even higher for some public works projects, especially railroad construction.

Indochina could have been profitable for France without such devastation. France could have formulated an economic policy for Indochina that would have improved the lot of the desperate millions of Vietnamese, while still generat-

ing francs for the French till. Factories could have been built in Vietnam to take advantage of the abundant quantities of raw materials such as latex and lumber; sources of energy such as coal and water; and the vast supply of cheap labor. Consumers in France would have benefited. French workers, in turn, would have had another market for their goods, as conditions for the Vietnamese improved. As it was, the average Vietnamese peasant had only two to six piasters per year of disposable income. But, of course, the French never colonized Vietnam to improve the living standard of Vietnamese; nor, for that matter, to make Vietnam a source of inexpensive manufactured products for Frenchmen, or even a market for the goods of France. France cared only that Vietnam remain a source of tax revenue, raw materials and agricultural products.

The abuses of French colonialists in Vietnam had not gone unreported. During the nineteenth century, various writers noted them in books and newspapers. Some enlightened politicians even spoke out about them on the floor of the Chamber of Deputies. But the political power of those with financial interests in Vietnam dominated French thinking right up to the time French troops departed. Early on, the Socialist Party was probably the most ardent proponent of colonial reform, and was sensitive enough to pleas for corrective action to invite Ho Chi Minh, then unknown, to their party congress at Tours in 1920, when he was living in France. Nevertheless, the Socialists were not disposed to see reform in terms of independence for Vietnam, which is why Ho joined a group of Socialists that broke away from their party after Tours. This splinter group became the French Communist Party; one of its founding precepts was independence for Vietnam.

In spite of agitation by the French Communists, there was never a serious movement to reevaluate the role of Vietnam in the economic life of France until shortly before the Second World War, for a brief period, when it was too late. The French government was either unwilling or unable to encourage such a reevaluation, usually because of the political obstruction of powerful business interests who preferred the status quo. The business environment of Vietnam was not laissez-faire, though; it was tightly controlled. But the control was in the hands of powerful businessmen, not the government. This was the

The green beret: a case of mistaken identity . . .

The green beret, which caused some Vietnamese peasants to think early arrivals of American soldiers were actually the French reclaiming their colony, had a much-beleaguered early history. It began with a scratch-pad sketch by then-Captain Herbert Brucker and ended with a visit by President Kennedy.

Brucker, an army officer and former OSS agent in China during the Second World War, was one of the first assigned to the newly formed, elite Special Forces unit constituted in 1952. As a team leader, he was given the opportunity to design a distinctive outfit for his men. He came up with camouflage fatigues topped off with green berets.

He managed to procure the fatigues from the U.S. Marine Corps, the army not having such uniforms in those days. The berets proved more difficult. Brucker and Captain Roger Pezzelle, another Special Forces officer, contrived as justification on their army requisition form the excuse that the berets were needed for "test purposes."

Months passed without word from army supply. In the meantime, Brucker and Pezzelle were transferred from Fort Bragg, North Carolina, to another Special Forces unit in West Germany.

Then one day a box full of green berets from Canada arrived at Fort Bragg. An accompanying form said something about testing. Brucker and Pezzelle's order had been processed. Thinking that the Department of the Army had ordered them, the soldiers began testing them. They dipped them in gasoline and water, stretched them every which way, and wore them all the time. Being cheap cotton models, most shrank. They looked terrible.

The commanding officer of Fort Bragg soon lost patience. He ended the "testing." He and other generals especially despised the foreign look the berets gave American soldiers.

Unfortunately, the troops loved them as much as the generals hated them, so berets kept popping up around the post. Finally, it became a court-martial offense to wear one.

Brucker and Pezzelle were completely unaware of what had happened until one day they noticed a story in *Stars and Stripes*, the newspaper for servicemen overseas. "They Fight for the Green Beret," the headline read. The story incorrectly implied that berets were temporarily being allowed for wear by the Special Forces, pending final approval.

With their unit commander's blessing, the two set about outfitting the thousand Special Forces soldiers in Germany. Each one voluntarily agreed to pay for his own.

Brucker took hat sizes while Pezzelle searched for a source of supply. He began by driving to Baden-Baden, where a unit of French troops was assigned. There he found a snappy, tailored, velvet model owned by a French officer. Borrowing an extra, he and Brucker found a German tailor who duplicated the design in green a thousand times.

Word later reached Germany that the hat had, in fact, not been approved; quite the contrary. But true to their resourceful nature, the Special Forces soldiers there avoided trouble by carrying other headgear in their pockets. They had standing orders to be ready to change from the beret in an instant. Years passed without incident.

In 1961 four hundred Special Forces soldiers were ordered to Vietnam by President Kennedy. Some were assigned from Germany; they took their green berets. Soon every Special Forces soldier there was wearing one.

Somehow word of the unauthorized item got back to Kennedy. He wanted to see one. Lieutenant David Weddington was ordered to the White House, hat in hand.

It so happened Kennedy was planning a trip to Fort Bragg. The Special Forces attracted his interest because their training and versatility seemed

legacy of the French colons.

Ironically, it was Doumer's centralized control over the colons that in the end gave that group control not just of Cochinchina but of all Indochina. They gradually took control of his centralized government after his departure, thus extending their control beyond Cochinchina. As it happened, Doumer's reforms were only a temporary setback for them, that in the long run actually enhanced their power. In 1875 the colons' influence had been institutionalized in the form of the Bank of Indochina. Not surprisingly, it was said in later years that the Bank of Indochina either held a part of or otherwise closely controlled the capital of almost every business enterprise in Indochina.

These investors invariably put short-term profits ahead of long-term potential, and themselves ahead of Vietnam or France. Initially their focus was on agriculture—rice farming first, then coffee, tea and latex. Since virtually no capital investment was necessary to gain control of the land, and as the labor to work it was so cheap, fortunes were made quickly.

Expropriation of mineral interests later followed the same pattern. It made no difference that the long-term investments—usually in manufacturing—would have generated yields that were high by normal business standards.

A good example of the failure to develop was the cotton mill in Nam Dinh, the second largest factory in Vietnam, which, even before the First World War, employed five thousand. Its initial capitalization of 5 million francs was quickly recovered so that during the 1920s it distributed dividends to investors at a rate of more than 50 million francs per year. In spite of this extraordinarily high dividend rate, the firm managed to increase the value of its capital and reserves to 80 million francs by 1940. Such balance-sheet numbers spoke eloquently of the potential available through expansion, yet the plant was never enlarged, nor was another built. Presumably, the reasons for not acting were fourfold. First, investors favored short-term profits in the form of large dividends. Second, within the larger scheme of things, the colons did not want to spur industrialization. There was an underlying feeling that a factory worker was potentially more politically dangerous than one who toiled in the fields. Third, unbelievable as it may seem, even more spectacular profits could be made elsewhere. Fourth, since virtually all outside investment groups, including those of Frenchmen not established in Vietnam, were kept out, those inside this privileged business enclave were not driven by competitive forces.

The development of entire manufacturing industries was ignored for these same reasons. The rubber industry was a prime example of such lost opportunity. The rubber plantations produced latex in abundance, but factories were never constructed in Vietnam to process this raw product. Instead, the latex was shipped back to France where it was processed.

Had rubber factories been built in Vietnam, France would have been in a strong position to compete with its rubber goods in the vast Asian market. Rubber-industry workers in France would not have been adversely affected because the products of their work were never competitive in Asia anyway due to transportation costs and higher labor costs.

Steel manufacturing was another industry ignored, this in spite of the presence in Vietnam of coal located near deposits of high-quality iron ore.

Quite obviously, the sins of the French colonialists were of omission as well as commission. And by 1940, the time to pay for them was at hand.

JFK meets General William Yarborough in 1961.

perfectly suited to "brush fire" wars like Vietnam. Perhaps because of his own highly developed sense of style, Kennedy thought the green beret projected the distinctive image he wanted them to have.

To the consternation of a few generals and the delight of the troops, Kennedy ordered that all Special Forces soldiers at Fort Bragg stand in review wearing green berets during his visit. Thus, the Green Beret became the informal and famous name for the Special Forces and, in time, the symbol of early American involvement in Vietnam.

Early in this century, pleasurable adventure was the lure of Vietnam for some Americans who could afford the trip, as these. One of the party is a Roosevelt, perhaps related to the famous family.

The Diplomatic Puzzle

A New World Order

During the Second World War Franklin D. Roosevelt was convinced the British Empire was a greater threat to postwar peace than the Soviet Union. His vision of the future was shaped by the world order that had endured for the preceding hundred-odd years. For most of that time Russia had been a provincial monarchy; indeed, she came close to missing the Industrial Revolution. Her perceived power was more historic than real. Britannia ruled the waves, as well as lands that touched all the seven seas. She harvested rice in Burma, sorghum in Sudan, grapes in Cyprus, tea in India, sugarcane in Jamaica; mined bauxite in Malaya, diamonds in Sierra Leone; and drilled for oil in Nigeria, to name just a few of her colonies and products. Her wealth and power were the envy of the world, which was what worried Roosevelt. He thought British colonies, not Russian Communism, the more likely cause of future fighting.

Roosevelt's thinking was first revealed by his son Elliott in 1946 in the book *As He Saw It*. Historians discounted Elliott's account until recent years when classified government archival material and private papers in the U.S. and Great Britain, made public for the first time, confirmed what he wrote.

Roosevelt saw colonies as nothing more than private business reserves. Nations that controlled them kept others out. Their businesses used colonies as almost exclusive and thus cheap supply sources for raw materials and food.

The French concept of colonialism went one step farther: Colonies were not simply regions under French control; the French thought they held title to their colonies, a notion that mystified Roosevelt. "How do they belong to France?" he asked Elliott. "Why does Morocco, inhabited by Moroccans, belong to France? Or take [sic] Indochina?"

Roosevelt put independence for colonial peoples high on his postwar agenda. He was motivated by a number of factors. Foremost among them was the need to defuse international tensions. He viewed colonies as a major cause of the Second World War. Japan coveted the raw resources of Southeast Asia; so its armies

Surrender ceremonies on the battleship *Missouri*, September 2, 1945.

During his world tour in 1942, Wendell Willkie reviews Chinese troops with Generalissimo Chiang Kai-shek.

In October 1940, during negotiations between Governor General Jean Decoux and General Nishimura, France granted Japan military use of Indochina.

invaded the Dutch East Indies, British Malaya, French Indochina and other colonies to supplant the colonial dominance of European rivals.

Roosevelt was further motivated to push for colonial independence for domestic political reasons. Anticolonial feelings ran deep in this country. Americans had a natural empathy for the plight of colonial subjects because of their own colonial history. Furthermore, American business interests complained about how Europeans monopolized the raw resources of their colonies.

Woodrow Wilson was the first American president to popularize the anticolonialism issue here. During the First World War he "identified the struggle for overseas markets and raw materials as a cause of war. At American insistence, the former German colonies and parts of the Ottoman Empire were not annexed as colonies but administered as mandated territories under the League of Nations." This arrangement at least opened up these regions as markets for raw goods, though it did not make them independent states.

Roosevelt took Wilson's anticolonial thinking to its logical conclusion: He wanted colonies eliminated, not just reformed. The idea had bipartisan support, so popular the notion had become in the U.S. between the wars. In 1942, for example, Wendell Willkie, Roosevelt's Republican opponent in the 1940 elections, traveled throughout the world speaking against colonialism. Once home he wrote a book entitled *One World* in which he proposed that all the world unite to end colonialism after the war.

With respect to Roosevelt's particular animus against the colonial policy of the French, he was probably motivated by a desire for revenge. According to William Roger Louis in his scholarly work *Imperialism at Bay*, "Decadent is not too strong a word to sum up [Roosevelt's] estimate of the people who not only collaborated with the Germans in Europe but also gave the Japanese the airfields in north Indo-China in 1940. To Roosevelt the French were corrupt. France could no longer be counted among the great powers." In fact, during the war, French colons and administrators continued to run Indochina just as profitably for Japan as they had previously done for France.

Last but not least, Roosevelt was motivated by concern for the best interests of colonial peoples. Roosevelt recognized that colonialists managed their subject peoples in different ways, but to him, this distinction only amounted to varying degrees of mistreatment. He thought the British and Dutch treated their colonial peoples best, the French and especially the Portuguese, worst.

During the Cairo and Teheran conferences of 1943, he managed to confer individually with Chiang Kai-shek and Joseph Stalin. They discussed trusteeship for colonies after the war. Roosevelt talked about Russia, China, Great Britain and the United States serving as joint trustees for colonies, or some sort of united nations group serving that purpose.

He followed up those talks upon his return to Washington by calling to his office representatives from the governments of China, Egypt, Turkey, Russia and Great Britain. He told them he was "working hard" to end French colonization of Indochina. Britain's Lord Halifax reported Roosevelt's words:

"The poor Indochinese had nothing done for them during a hundred years of French responsibility, no education, no welfare. They were just as poor as they had ever been, and there was no reason why this state of affairs should be allowed to go on."

The British, of course, understood the implications for themselves of Roosevelt's anti-French colonial policy. Permanent Undersecretary of the Foreign Office Sir Alexander Cadogan wrote, "I have heard the President say that Indo-China should not revert to France, and he is on record as saying that the French, in that region, 'were hopeless'. I have not had the advantage of hearing him develop the theme. We'd better look out: were the French more 'hopeless' in Indo-China than we in Malaya or the Dutch in the E. Indies?" Foreign Secretary Anthony Eden agreed with these remarks.

Thus, the British and French cases merged. During the war, Britain took it upon herself to argue the French case. Churchill's assessment was that Indochina was the focus of Roosevelt's intentions because the French were not in a position to defend themselves, France being occupied by Germany. He hoped the Free French would eventually argue their own case, at which time Great Britain would give them strong support.

The two allies did not mince words. "The British would take land anywhere in the world, even if it were only rock or a sand bar," Roose-

The Diplomatic Puzzle— ❢*In their own words*❢

❢*The king rules but does not govern.*❢— Governor General Jean Decoux to Emperor Bao Dai, as the French persisted in their policy of denying aspirations for self-government, despite mounting insurrection in the Cochinchina countryside; in late 1940.

❢*Bring in troops, more troops, as many as you can.*❢—General Douglas MacArthur to General Jacques Philippe Leclerc, the first commander of French Indochina forces after the Second World War, on how to reestablish French control of the region; during Japanese surrender ceremonies on the U.S.S. *Missouri* on September 2, 1945.

❢*I beg you to understand that the only way to safeguard French interests and the spiritual influence of France in Indochina is to recognize frankly the independence of Vietnam and to renounce any idea of reestablishing French sovereignty or administration in whatever form it may be.*❢—Emperor Bao Dai in a (never-answered) letter to Charles de Gaulle three days after Japan agreed to an unconditional surrender and about two weeks prior to Bao Dai's abdication in favor of Ho; on August 18, 1945.

❢*. . . keep in mind that we are determined to fight to the end if forced to.*❢—Ho Chi Minh to a French journalist who asked what would happen if Ho's new government and France were unable to negotiate an acceptable compromise; on January 6, 1946.

✳ The day after Marshal Henri-Philippe Pétain asked Germany for an armistice, Japanese officials handed the French governor general of Indochina an ultimatum to close off the border with China. The Japanese were fighting the Chinese army and wanted to halt supplies reaching them through Indochina via Doumer's old Haiphong–Yunnan railroad. Within forty-eight hours General Georges Catroux complied. This Japanese demand was the first of several to which the French acceded without a fight, though fifty thousand French troops were posted in Indochina and another eighty thousand Vietnamese troops were under French command. The Japanese never had more than thirty-five thousand troops stationed in Indochina.

Japanese troops bicycle into Saigon in 1940 to take control.

velt told Churchill. "Never would we yield an inch of the territory that was under the British flag," Churchill told the American ambassador to China. "Our victory must bring in its train the liberation of all peoples. . . . The age of imperialism is ended," spoke Undersecretary of State Sumner Welles. "I did not become the King's First Minister to preside over the liquidation of the British Empire," countered Churchill.

British feelings were intensified by two factors. First, many British officials, including Churchill, believed Roosevelt wanted to create an American empire at British expense. Some even believed the U.S. delayed entering the war so that it could pick up the pieces after Great Britain and Germany had fought it out.

The empire Churchill thought Roosevelt envisioned was not of the colonial variety, but rather an informal, economic one that would achieve the same purpose. American businesses, unlike those of almost every other large nation, would, by all estimates, emerge from the war untouched. British thinking was that these businesses would compose an overwhelming competitive force that would drive other nations' businesses out of markets just as surely as

colonial barriers did. Furthermore, many Britons anticipated that the burgeoning U.S. economy would have an insatiable appetite for the resources of European colonies in Asia. Gerard Gent, the head of the Eastern Department of the British Colonial Office, voiced this sentiment. He concluded that the raw materials of British Malaya and the Dutch Indies were "responsible for a good deal of hopeful thinking in New York and Washington." The French, of course, shared the same misgivings. Following the British lead, all Allied colonial nations resisted Roosevelt's trusteeship ideas as tactics to keep them from retaking their colonies. They deemed American phrases such as "Open Door" and "Free Trade" euphemisms for American economic imperialism.

British feelings were also intensified by worries that the U.S. could easily impose its will in Asia after the war, since only the U.S. would be strong enough to dislodge the Japanese from the vast empire they were wresting from European colonial powers.

The most important of the Asian colonies to fall was Singapore, a sort of Hong Kong and Gibraltar rolled into one, long a symbol of the indomitable presence of the British Empire and

The British colonial empire, the world's largest, never recovered from the fall of Singapore, marked by the surrender of General Arthur Percival (extreme right) on February 15, 1942.

the superiority of the white man over his Asian subjects. After the Japanese overran its defenses and forced the surrender of its 130,000 defenders on February 15, 1942, European colonial dominance in Asia never recovered. The image of European superiority was shattered. Nationalists in dozens of colonies were encouraged to seek their independence because the continuity of control had been broken—by fellow Asians, no less. The Vietnamese in particular were encouraged. For years the Japanese had granted political asylum to various Vietnamese nationalist leaders because they shared a hatred for European powers. Some Vietnamese thought Japan might liberate them eventually, not replace the French as colonialists.

The stakes were too high for the British to acquiesce to U.S. government will on the colonial question. One tactic the British employed was to try to sway American public opinion. By far the most persuasive was Lord Hailey. During the war he lectured at Princeton, Yale and Columbia, wrote articles for *Reader's Digest* and *Foreign Affairs,* and met with influential leaders such as Willkie. Perhaps his most memorable effort for the good of the Empire was at a conference in Mont Tremblont, Canada, in December 1942, sponsored by the Institute of Pacific Relations. Representatives of all Allied Pacific powers attended the conference in an unofficial capacity. The U.S. sent a delegation of college professors pressed into State Department duty during the war. The urbane Hailey's performance was extraordinary. In a patient, pleasant and precise way, he created the impression that Great Britain stood for progress in colonial affairs. A representative of the British Colonial Office made this observation, which though biased was accurate in its portrayal of the impact Hailey had on his audiences:

"I was lost in admiration at the whole ten-day performance and many times as I watched him cross swords with the American 'Professors' and gracefully prick one balloon after another, I thought what a stupid tragedy it would be to take the management of great affairs from men like Hailey and given them over to the boys with thick-lensed glasses, long hair and longer words nasally intoned."

Hailey convinced the conferees that the American concept of trusteeship was essentially no different from that which the British practiced

❋ A graphic example of how far French attitudes lagged behind the emerging aspirations of the Vietnamese is the set of meager reforms instituted by Governor General Jean Decoux during the Second World War. To "win the hearts of the Annamite," Decoux decreed that henceforth Frenchmen would quit using the deprecating *"tu"* when addressing Vietnamese and would cease whipping Vietnamese in public.

and which in fact was supported by American case law. He cited *The Cherokee Nation v. The State of Georgia,* which defined the trusteeship position of the federal government. With exceptional skill he applied such examples to the British case, concluding that his country was dealing in the same manner with its dependent peoples.

This line of reasoning was so persuasive that other British officials later elaborated on its theme. Questioning the rationale that Indochina should be taken from the French for the sake of "the poor Indochinese," one Foreign Office official observed, "I have never heard that the Indo-Chinese were any more unhappy than the share-croppers of the Southern United States."

Even Stanley K. Hornbeck, the U.S. State Department's adviser on the Far East, was troubled by the comparison. "The average negro does enough work to get enough to live on and no more," he said. "Peoples of the South Seas are similar. He [sic] is not interested in property or culture and you have to impair his freedom to make his economic standards higher." And in a conclusion that would have pleased a conservative Oxford don as much as his earlier statements would have delighted any local racist, Hornbeck, a Rhodes Scholar, said, "There are some things to be said in favor of imperialism."

In January 1945 British Colonial Secretary Oliver Stanley, armed with the same arguments, traveled to Washington. During a dinner hosted by British Ambassador Halifax and attended by Vice-President-elect Harry Truman, Justice Felix Frankfurter and Walter Lippmann, he planned to use them to great advantage.

Expecting to run roughshod over the Americans' arguments, he asked, "Just what is meant by trusteeship?" He did not anticipate an answer, and paused for effect before continuing with what he intended to be a defense of the notion that the British could serve as trustees of their own colonies, not needing third-party trustees. As that point, according to one account, "Justice Frankfurter took over. The Justice pointed out that trusteeship had a very definite meaning in Anglo-Saxon law; that the basic principle of trusteeship was that the trustee did not judge its own acts. He reiterated this several times as Stanley tried to make a case that the British were the trustees of their own colonies. Stanley for the first time appeared to be on the defensive. He evaded direct questions of Frankfurter and

Stanley K. Hornbeck

Justice Felix Frankfurter

Teddy White in Hanoi in 1940...

In 1940 Theodore H. White became one of the few Americans to visit Vietnam during the days Japanese and French troops jointly occupied the country. At the time, Europe was engulfed in war—Hitler's forces had already overrun Belgium and France—so *Time's* editors decided to send White, their China reporter, on a three- to four-month fact-finding trip throughout Southeast Asia before fighting engulfed that region too.

White would later be famous as a journalist and historian, but in 1940 he was still a wide-eyed twenty-five-year-old not too many years out of a Boston ghetto. He remembers thinking it was a great way to travel: first class and at company expense.

Hanoi was an important stop on his itinerary. While there he booked into the Hotel Metropole, enjoying the amenities of this grande dame of colonial comfort while writing "local color" pieces. He became part political reporter, part anthropologist, and part travel writer.

He admired the beauty of the Vietnamese women whose figures and beautiful features he described as the product of "the mingling of the Malaysian and Chinese strains." In words which he would later regret, he dismissed the Vietnamese men as "a whining, cringing, gutless mass of coolies, part mule, part goat, part rabbit," who would "sit on their haunches, chew betel nuts, and do nothing" for hours on end. He abhorred the brutish behavior of arrogant Japanese soldiers who sat around the Metropole in brown undershirts where they would "grunt and spit on the floor, courteous to no one, as they demanded of the French colonials that three air bases in northern Indo-China be given to their air force for bombing South China." He denounced the French army as one "of oppression—seven

appeared to be purposefully evading the issue."

Frankfurter's arguments did not change British attitudes, but they clearly show Roosevelt was on firm legal footing in demanding third-party trusteeship for colonies. The idea was not a foreign or frivolous proposition but one grounded in English common law. American mistreatment of blacks and Indians did not militate against its application, though it certainly raised legitimate questions about the sincerity of our concern for downtrodden colonial subjects, given our failure to rectify domestic inequities.

Events, as well as allies, conspired against Roosevelt in his attempts to negotiate a period of trusteeship leading to independence for Indochina. By 1944 it was becoming clear that China, torn by revolution, would not emerge as a world power on a par with the U.S., the Soviet Union and Great Britain. Roosevelt's vision of "Four Policemen" who would conspire to keep the peace faded. After the war, when the decline of the British Empire saw the number of superpowers dwindle to two, all chance of cooperation died.

Events within Indochina also conspired against trusteeship. On March 9, 1945, French administrators and troops there, who had been cooperating with the Japanese for almost five years, decided the time was ripe for overwhelming them. Their real purpose was to rid themselves of the taint of collaboration before the anticipated arrival of American troops and to impress Charles de Gaulle, the head of the provisional French government. Unfortunately for them, they acted prematurely. The Japanese crushed the rebellion before it could really get under way, killed seventeen hundred French soldiers, and for the first time took administrative control of Indochina from the French. Consequently, the U.S. could not very well discourage the intrigues of the French and British to get more French troops back into Indochina. To do so was very awkward politically; it would appear that this country favored Japan over France.

Events in Europe likewise worked against Roosevelt. The U.S. State Department and the military began thinking that strategic considerations there outweighed idealistic designs for Indochina. A revived France friendly to this country was deemed of paramount importance. Differing with Roosevelt's assessment that Russia would be cooperative after the war, the U.S.

military agreed with Churchill that Russia would, in fact, be the primary threat to European security. France must, therefore, become an essential link in the Western alliance. The State Department's Advisory Committee on Post-War Foreign Policy recognized the problem. "It is possible that at the end of the war if Cochin China is taken from France, it would give an added political strength to the anti-American trend of conservative circles in France," said James T. Shotwell, a noted historian who was a committee member.

The State and War Departments were also troubled by whether insistence on international trusteeship for Indochina would affect U.S. control of islands captured from Japan. International trusteeship was by then considered the only feasible form, the Four Policemen idea having been all but discarded. High-minded ideas about trusteeship could boomerang, Hornbeck pointed out.

For example, U.S. military planners deemed it absolutely necessary to keep the Marshall, Caroline and Mariana Islands, collectively known as Micronesia. Though they compromised only 830 square miles of land area, they covered a vast region of the northern Pacific. These small islands, one of which was Iwo Jima, were the equivalent of anchored aircraft carriers forming a security belt around Guam and the Philippines. Whatever nation held the islands of Micronesia could, depending on its designs, either threaten or assure the security of Guam and the Philippines. Should these islands, like Indochina, be subject to trusteeship and scheduled for independence? Residents there might think so, someone pointed out. And the French, if relieved of their colonies, would certainly be inclined to agree.

The State Department was similarly concerned that the universal application of the trusteeship idea would raise questions about Alaska, the Hawaiian Islands, Puerto Rico and Guam, all U.S. possessions.

The fact that the war was approaching a foreseeable end exerted great pressure on Roosevelt to resolve the trusteeship question. Throughout the war, contrary to his true intentions, he had publicly promised French freedom fighters—the underground and de Gaulle's Free French—that he supported reestablishment of French control there. He was encouraging them to fight the

thousand Frenchmen, three thousand Foreign Legionnaires and scores of thousands of black African colonial troops, Moroccans with their fezzes, Algerians in distinctive uniforms." He observed that the colons "made money out of Indo-China" but "despised the people who lived there"; and concluded that "nothing could obscure the prime political fact that all politics in this white man's colony revolved around hate."

Some images would remain indelible in his memory. Years later he remembered seeing, for the first time, a white man slap a native, a rickshaw driver whose offense was to complain that he had not been fairly paid. He vividly recalled the tiny replica of the Statue of Liberty some Frenchmen had erected in Hanoi—perhaps not officially—"a sublime act of hypocrisy," as he would later call it. Nor could he forget what the French called the "tableau," a favorite game staged by Frenchmen who would climb into separate rickshaws and race each other to a bordello. The Vietnamese pulling them usually collapsed upon arrival, but for one of the rickshaw men, at least, the game was not over. The French took the winner inside and hired him a prostitute. "They enjoyed observing his servitude and even more when he showed inability to achieve erection with the girl they had paid to please him," he wrote.

Not surprisingly, when White left Vietnam in 1940 he was convinced that America should not engage itself in the affairs of that country. "On Vietnam I was then an isolationist, and I should have remained so forever," he wrote many years later after the last American combat troops had been pulled out.

Germans. Now he was being forced to show his hand.

Throughout early 1944 de Gaulle, taking up the French argument from the British, had been insisting that the U.S. formally commit to French colonial control of Indochina. And duplicating earlier English efforts, he actively worked to shape public opinion in the U.S. The Brazzaville Conference of January–February 1944, attended by French colonial administrators and governors general, was one such attempt. The group resolved to allow colonies to seek "their own identity." The conference had a positive effect on American public opinion. The press misread the rhetoric (as they were intended to do) to mean that France would put its colonies on the road to independence.

For Charles de Gaulle, Indochina was the most important topic of his dis cussions with President Roosevelt on July 6, 1944. Also present were Secretary of State Cordell Hull and Roosevelt's daughter, Anna Boettiger.

No one in government was fooled, however. Both Roosevelt and Churchill saw through the machinations, and Churchill became deeply concerned about how the colonial question would be resolved at war's end because he fully understood how committed Roosevelt was to eventual independence for Indochina. In May 1944 he wrote Eden, "Before we could bring the French officially into the Indo-China area, we should have to settle with President Roosevelt. He has been more outspoken to me on that subject than on any other Colonial matter, and I imagine it is one of his principal war aims to liberate Indo-China from France."

July 1944 was a propitious time for de Gaulle to settle with Roosevelt. By that time American troops were fighting Germans on French soil. The liberation of Paris (August 26) was at hand. Amid this spirit of goodwill, de Gaulle met with the president at the White House. Indochina was at the top of the agenda. Ironically, France's military weakness and political instability worked in de Gaulle's favor. Roosevelt wanted to revive France as quickly as possible; he did so by accommodating de Gaulle, its leader at the time. After the meeting de Gaulle announced that Roosevelt would not bar French reentry into Indochina. In exchange, Roosevelt secured a vague commitment that France would grant Indochina a degree of independence after the war. France was gradually to put Vietnamese into positions of authority in Vietnam; independence would follow, perhaps. Roosevelt and de Gaulle did not like or trust one another, so both men probably did not feel particularly committed to what was said.

Whatever the case, Roosevelt was gradually yielding to the realities of the situation. Without China, the Big Four trusteeship idea for Indochina was no longer feasible. And for all practical purposes, the U.S. could do little to keep the French out, short of firing on French troops once they showed up in Indochina, which of course was out of the question. The American plan, as it evolved under these pressures, was only a vague strategy aimed at putting whatever obstacles we could in the way of France's efforts to reestablish a strong presence in Indochina before the war ended. The weaker the French presence at war's end, the better the chances of imposing on France this country's vision of the future for Indochina.

In the meantime, American troops in the

✳ Between one and a half and two million people died of starvation in Tongking during 1944-1945 because of exceptionally poor harvests. The shortfall was not satisfied by shipments from the south because of transportation problems and a "lack of real concern for the fate of the people" by the French and the Japanese, says Joseph Buttinger.

✳ During the Second World War, crews of Major General Claire Chennault's Fourteenth Air Force bombed railways and roads in Vietnam as well as various strategic targets such as Saigon's port facilities. Flying out of China bases, these crews were trying to hinder the Japanese war effort. Navy planes flying off U.S. carriers also participated in this campaign. Some were shot down, of course. Ho helped many escape, but at war's end there were 214 Americans among the 4,549 Allied POWs in the Saigon area.

Smoke spirals from a Japanese ship in Saigon Harbor attacked by U.S. planes.

Ho and Giap worked closely with U.S. forces during the Second World War, providing a stream of accurate intelligence.

Southeast Asia–China Theater were ordered not to assist either side if fighting broke out between French soldiers and Ho Chi Minh's nationalist revolutionaries. Some French soldiers, on de Gaulle's orders, had managed to slip back into the country, though others had been captured and killed by Ho's guerrilla forces.

Unlikely as it may seem in light of later events, American soldiers favored Ho's men over French troops, for they owed the former many a debt of gratitude. During the war Ho's troops repeatedly rescued downed American pilots and funneled a steady stream of accurate intelligence on Japanese operations in Indochina to American commanders headquartered in Chungking, China. Ho's forces had a reputation with the Americans for being the only nationalist group in Indochina to fight back against the Japanese, and they were considered excellent fighters. In fact, American officers preferred the company of Ho's soldiers to de Gaulle's on joint guerrilla missions against the Japanese. As a result, American officers in China stated openly that they believed France should be denied Indochina after the war.

In full agreement with the sentiments of his field commanders, Roosevelt in March 1945 ordered the senior American officials in Asia — the ambassador to China, Patrick Hurley, and General Albert Wedemeyer — to keep close watch on British and French intriguing, since he knew the two countries supported each other's recolonizing aims in the region. In response, Wedemeyer reported to Roosevelt that British Admiral Lord Mountbatten was making illegiti-

mate use of American-supplied Lend-Lease equipment in Asia. Such material had been provided to bolster British national survival, not to reestablish colonial dominance halfway around the world.

Shortly before his death Roosevelt was working to form a unified command of the Allied forces in Asia, with Wedemeyer in control. He reasoned that if Mountbatten had to report to the American general, the English lord would be unable to airlift French troops into Indochina or otherwise assist the French effort without American permission. On April 12 Roosevelt died and, with him, the impetus toward colonial trusteeship.

The founding conference of the United Nations convened two weeks later in San Francisco. Concurrently, de Gaulle launched a propaganda campaign to justify French recolonization of Indochina. His foreign minister, George Bidault, decried what he called "a campaign of ignorance and calumny" against the French colonial empire. And defiantly he announced that "France would be her own trustee."

For two reasons, policy under the new Truman administration began to shift to a more pragmatic approach that had been evolving within the State Department. First, no one was able to come up with an acceptable plan to keep the French out. Second, the frightening degree to which the war had destabilized former European

Roosevelt ordered the U.S. ambassador to China, Patrick Hurley, to be watchful of French intrigues to reenter China, while trying to mediate among opposing factions in China. Here Hurley meets with Mao Tse-tung.

General Albert Wedemeyer (standing) tried to block Lord Mountbatten's support of French reentry into Indochina. Seated: Mountbatten between U.S. Generals Sultan and William J. Donovan.

Delegates gathered at the first plenary session of the United Nations, held in San Francisco on April 25, 1945, listen to a radio speech by President Truman marking the occasion. At subsequent sessions the U.S. fostered agreements intended to lead to independence for colonies.

colonial regions was now becoming clear. Strong independence movements were emerging in many colonies. The worry was that all Asia would be in turmoil once the Japanese surrendered. Where that condition might lead, no one knew. The better course of action, it now seemed, was for the U.S. to support French reoccupation, but at the same time mollify nationalists such as Ho by committing the French to self-government and eventual independence for Indochina. The conference in San Francisco presented the Americans with their first opportunity to propose this plan.

Primarily as a result of American initiatives the delegates to the convention adopted Chapters XI and XII of the United Nations charter. The first concerned non-self-governing territories

such as Indochina. In that chapter the delegates endorsed the principle of "self-government" for such territories and recognized the responsibility of controlling nations such as France to promote the economic, political, social and educational advancement of local populations, but nowhere did it make mention of the word "independence."

Chapter XII dealt with the International Trusteeship System. Its explicit objective was "the progressive development towards independence."

According to William Roger Louis, the American delegation, "in putting forward these provisions that had matured after years of consideration in the State Department, regarded the trusteeship system as a mechanism to promote independence. They hoped that, as colonies became self-governing under Chapter XI, the administering authorities would then place specific territories under Chapter XII for preparation for independence. This proved to be a false trail. Only later did the State Department learn that the British, for example, had no intention of placing any of their colonies under trusteeship." Nor, of course, did the French. On May 15, while the conference was going on, de Gaulle wired Truman about the "very important political, moral and military consequences" of American opposition to French control.

By that time de Gaulle most likely was already aware of the shifting American position. At San Francisco, Undersecretary of State Edward Stettinius told a French representative that the U.S. had never "even by implication" questioned French sovereignty over Indochina, which, of course, was not true, but now served American purposes. Secretary of State Dean Acheson said the same thing several months later. The U.S. had "no thought of opposing the restoration of French control," he said.

This more accommodating American attitude was as great a relief to the British as it was to the French. By the middle of May, Mountbatten notified Wedemeyer that British pilots would be flying twenty-six sorties into Indochina to support French guerrillas. The American vigorously objected, not yet having been informed of the changed policy of his government. He asked for assurances that the true mission of these troops was fighting the Japanese, not the Vietnamese nationalists. Mountbatten ignored Wedemeyer's objection and abruptly ordered

Ho's visa application to enter the U.S....

Ho Chi Minh might have become an employee of the U.S. Office of War Information, broadcasting Annamese translations of American propaganda releases against Japan from a station in San Francisco, had he and an American OWI officer in China had their way. On August 28, 1944, William R. Powell, the OWI air liaison representative in Kunming, filed a visa application in Ho's behalf with William R. Langdon, the American consul general there. Langdon told Powell he would grant the visa only if Ho could get a Chinese passport—which he knew to be a remote possibility because it was a known fact that Ho was born in Indochina. Langdon imposed this bureaucratic barrier because he was concerned that French authorities would be "greatly disquieted" if "Ho Ting-ching" (U.S. officials were still having problems with Ho's name) were granted a visa. The visa application was sent on to the embassy in Chungking, thence to Washington, D.C., where it languished and died a quiet death in the tangles of bureaucracy.

Any possibility that some sort of trusteeship arrangement would replace colonial control of regions such as Indochina ended with President Roosevelt's death on April 12, 1945. Above, thousands along Pennsylvania Avenue use mirrors to view his funeral cortege.

✳ Wendell Willkie visited China in October 1942, when Ho Chi Minh was in the Tienpao prison. Willkie was researching *One World,* the book he would write upon return from his trip. The anticolonial pronouncements Willkie made during his visit were published in Chinese newspapers, which Ho managed to read and from which he took heart, for the light they shed on the American-French-British rift on the colonial question. Ho later told American OSS officers that Willkie's comments heartened him in his campaign to win the favor of U.S. officials in China.

British planes into the air with the French.

The impact of Roosevelt's death on U.S. Indochina policy was acknowledged by Mountbatten himself about five months later when French General Jacques Leclerc, on his way to Saigon to take command, visited him in Ceylon. Mountbatten told Leclerc that if Roosevelt were still alive, the French could not have returned to Indochina. He felt certain that if Roosevelt had lived to attend the Potsdam Conference in July, he would have proposed that Chinese troops occupy all of Vietnam after the Japanese surrender. Truman did not do so. Thus, Stalin, Truman and Clement Attlee, who had replaced Churchill as prime minister during the conference, agreed that China would occupy Vietnam above the sixteenth parallel; Great Britain would occupy the rest.

Scholars differ as to what would have happened if Roosevelt had lived and installed the Chinese throughout Vietnam. Joseph Buttinger believes France could not subsequently have returned to Vietnam because, as it turned out, the Chinese did accept the Vietnamese national revolution, thus allowing Ho's Viet Minh to establish a foothold in the north, and would presumably have done the same in the south. The British, of course, did not recognize the independence movement and allowed the French back in almost immediately.

Arthur Schlesinger, Jr., wrote in 1966 that had Roosevelt's objectives been carried out "the world might have been spared much bloodshed and agony."

Louis disagrees. His view is that China's internal chaos and other hard realities of post-war power politics make trusteeship schemes seem in retrospect "more and more like a pipe-dream."

Ho realized that the days immediately following the Japanese surrender would be critical for his planned revolution. His objective was to seize control before Allied troops arrived.

Ho spent most of the war in China in exile with other nationalist-movement leaders, most of who were non-Communist. China was a safe haven for two reasons. China and the Vietnamese nationalists were united in their opposition to the Japanese and the French colonials who had preceded them. The presence of the Americans (as chief sponsors of Chiang Kai-shek) in China was a further guarantee of safety. The U.S. even advanced funds to nationalists, including Ho, to encourage them to fight the Japanese.

Vo Nguyen Giap was Ho's top man in Vietnam during the war. Exposing himself to great danger, he traveled the country organizing cadres of Vietnamese who would be ready to move when Ho issued the call for national revolution.

Vietnamese nationalists of the full spectrum, from Ho to Diem, realized even sooner than the Allies that the war would be their great opportunity to achieve independence. In 1941 no single faction could claim the general support of the people; there was no obvious choice of a local leader to take control. Thus they all jockeyed for power during the war, uncertain how to position themselves because the final war scenario was itself uncertain. When would the war end? Would Japan and the U.S. negotiate a truce? Would American troops actually land on Vietnamese beaches to fight the Japanese? Would Vietnamese nationalists have to fight Japan or France or both to achieve independence? Would the U.S. impose its will on Vietnam at the expense of the French?

Ho recognized more quickly than the others that Japan would lose the war. Acting accordingly, he curried the favor of the U.S. by ordering his men to rescue American pilots and provide intelligence to American officers. At the same time, he distanced himself from the French

Cal-Texaco's agent in Vietnam...

Ho Chi Minh was not the U.S.'s only source of intelligence about Japanese activities in Vietnam during the Second World War. Another was a worldly Cal-Texaco employee named Laurence Laing Gordon, a British subject born in Canada. Gordon was director of operations for Cal-Texaco in Haiphong until 1940, when he moved with his family to California because of Japanese troops being assigned to Vietnam.

In 1941 Cal-Texaco induced him to return to Southeast Asia to look after its interests. A semiofficial cover was arranged by Sir William Stephenson, the head of the British Security Coordination Office, later renowned as the man called "Intrepid." Gordon was commissioned a captain in the British Secret Service. His travels took him first to India, then China and eventually Vietnam, where he roamed Cochinchina, Annam and Tongking on the pretense of being a free-lance oil agent. While in China, he convinced the OSS to finance his activities in Vietnam, where he set up a network of spies, many of them Vietnamese who had worked for Cal-Texaco.

Two Americans somehow living unmolested in the bizarre environment of Vietnam during the war years joined the team—Harry V. Bernard, a former Cal-Texaco employee living in Saigon, and Frank ("Frankie") Tan, a Bostonian of Chinese extraction. The group became known to the OSS as the GBT group, an acronym for their last names. By 1943 the three had set up listening posts and radio stations throughout Vietnam and were providing indispensable information to Major General Claire Chennault's Fourteenth Air Force operating out of China and various navy aviation units.

and Japanese who together were running Vietnam. He thus avoided the taint of collaboration that would haunt other Vietnamese nationalist leaders.

Little changed in Vietnam during the war for the French living there or for the native population. The Japanese did not really occupy Vietnam. The docile colons did not make that necessary. Japan merely stationed troops there. French administrators continued to run the colony as if it were still their own. Colons did a booming business, with Japan replacing France as their almost exclusive business client. French Indochina even joined Japan's Greater Asian Co-Prosperity Sphere. French soldiers, still armed, manned garrisons, keeping the local citizenry in line. And agents of the French Sûreté ruthlessly pursued nationalist revolutionaries such as Giap.

This all changed in March 1945 when French leaders in Indochina decided the time was ripe to fight the Japanese. U.S. forces had landed on Iwo Jima, only six hundred miles from Japan, on February 19, and had reoccupied Manila on February 24. The French mistakenly believed U.S. ships would soon appear off the Vietnam

✳ The earliest known reference to Ho Chi Minh by name (or something approximating his name) in the files of the OSS (now the CIA) is dated December 31, 1942. A cable from Clarence C. Gauss, U.S. ambassador to China, talked about the arrest of "an Annamite named Ho Chih-chi(?)" by the Chinese. The earliest known reference to Ho by name in State Department files is a letter dated October 25, 1943, addressed to Gauss and forwarded by him to the State Department, in which associates of Ho requested American assistance in getting him released.

Because of Iwo Jima, Frenchmen in Indochina were convinced that U.S. forces would soon storm Vietnam's beaches. This belief had profound consequences.

coast to unload Marines.

The Japanese uncovered the French plot before it could be executed, however, They then staged a coup, taking control of the administration of Indochina for the first time. Though some French units fought hard, the whole French army was disarmed within hours. The Japanese proceeded to jail seven hundred and fifty French civilians. Ironically, they threw them into jails built for Vietnamese. Because of overcrowding .and disease, four hundred died during incarceration.

The Japanese announced that they had acted against the French to liberate the country for Vietnamese self-government, though in fact the coup had been staged for preemptive purposes. They further announced that an independent government of local representatives would be appointed by Emperor Bao Dai. But no one was really fooled into thinking the Vietnamese were now masters of their own country; Japan was. Still, the appointments did present an opportunity for some Vietnamese to emerge as leaders after the war.

Diem was the initial Japanese choice to form a government. However, at the last possible instant,

Major General Marcel Alessandri, here with his aide, was forced to flee Vietnam after the aborted March 1945 fight with the Japanese.

Some of Alessandri's legionnaires prepare to cross the Red River into China.

"Yours Sincerely, Claire L. Chennault"...

Ho Chi Minh's guerrillas rescued their first downed American pilot, Lieutenant Shaw, in early 1945. At the time, they had no cooperation agreement with the U.S., but a shared political cause because both they and the U.S. were fighting the Japanese. Eager to enhance the potential political significance of the rescue, Ho ordered some of his men to escort Shaw all the way back to China. Later, Ho tried to make the most of the episode at the OSS and OWI offices in Kunming.

When the Japanese coup of March 6, 1945, ended the GBT team's target intelligence work for Army Air Corps Major General Claire Chennault, Lieutenant Charles Fenn was sent to find Ho: Perhaps Ho would put his intelligence operation to work for Chennault's Flying Tigers? Fenn found Ho, who agreed to go to work in exchange for "recognition of his group (called Vietminh League or League for Independence)," as Fenn later wrote. Though no such promise was made,

Major General Claire L. Chennault

the Japanese decided he would be too difficult to control. Diem had briefly served as Bao Dai's minister of interior in 1933 after the young emperor disbanded the council of mandarins. But Diem had soon resigned in protest, charging that the French retained all real authority. Thus, the Japanese in 1945 named a more docile Vietnamese, history professor Tran Trong Kim.

The Japanese overthrow of French administrators aided Ho and Giap immeasurably. Giap could now roam the full length of the country with virtual impunity. French soldiers were disarmed and agents of the Sûreté were in jail. Since the Japanese had used Vietnamese independence as the pretext for the coup, they did not take action against nationalists such as Giap. In fact, for tactical military reasons, the Japanese did not even deploy troops into the northern provinces, which, because of their proximity to the safe haven of China, had been the area Giap and the Viet Minh had most actively organized. Thus, by June 1945 Ho's men actually controlled six Vietnamese provinces between the Chinese border and Hanoi.

Ho returned to Vietnam in October 1944 to direct operations personally. Other rival nationalist leaders in exile in China were pleased to turn over the task and its dangers to him. They complacently assumed that the political struggle for independence would not begin in earnest until after the world war ended; they did not know how actively Ho's followers had been laying the groundwork in Vietnam.

Ho's objective was to be in a position to disarm the Japanese in Vietnam once Tokyo had ordered its forces to quit the fight. Unlike the French in Vietnam, he somehow knew that American forces would bypass Vietnam while bringing the war to an end. He therefore understood that he would have a few days after the Japanese surrender before Allied troops arrived. During that short period he planned to form a government and greet the Allies as Vietnam's leader in place. He miscalculated only how quickly the war would end. He could not have known that the U.S. was developing the atomic bomb.

The first and only test of the A-bomb occurred July 16 about sixty miles from Alamogordo, New Mexico. Truman, in Potsdam, Germany, negotiating with Churchill and Stalin, was notified that morning, as was Churchill. Truman, in turn, informed Stalin that the U.S. had developed "a new weapon of unusual destructure force."

Eight days later, on July 24, Truman tentatively approved dropping it. A message was then broadcast by Truman, Churchill, and Chiang Kai-shek to the Japanese, warning that they surrender or face "prompt and utter destruction." This message, which became known as the Potsdam Declaration, offered the Japanese a "new order of peace, security and justice" and "participation in world trade relations." The Japanese ignored the fuzzy warning and on August 6 the *Enola Gay,* piloted by Colonel Paul W. Tibbets, Jr., dropped the bomb over Hiroshima.

The Japanese again failed to respond. On August 9 Stalin declared war against Japan and Russian forces invaded Manchuria. Later that day a second atomic bomb was dropped on

operational details of the cooperative venture were worked out, stipulating that Ho would return to Indochina to put OSS radios and OSS-trained Vietnamese operatives to work.

During a meeting with Fenn, Ho asked if he could meet Chennault. Fenn agreed to arrange it if Ho "agreed not to ask him for anything: neither supplies nor promises about support. Ho agreed."

On March 29, 1945, Ho was escorted into Chennault's office by Fenn and Harry Bernard, formerly of the GBT team. According to Fenn, Chennault told Ho how grateful he was for Shaw's rescue and Ho responded by expressing great admiration for Chennault and his Flying Tigers. That Ho was familiar with the famous flying group pleased Chennault very much.

After a pleasant meeting, Ho was being escorted to the door when he stopped, turned to Chennault, and asked for one small favor. Could he have a photograph of the great American general?

In short order, a folder with about ten glossies was produced.

"Take your pick," said Chennault.

Ho carefully selected one and then, ever so deferentially, asked if the general would be so kind as to sign it. With good humor, the American officer quickly complied: "Yours Sincerely, Claire L. Chennault."

For Ho, of course, the signed photo would prove to have much more than sentimental value. According to OSS officers, the photo helped convince many skeptical Vietnamese that the Viet Minh represented the mighty United States of America when they entered Hanoi on August 19, 1945.

Ho Chi Minh greatly benefited when the *Enola Gay* dropped the atomic bomb on Hiroshima, which ended the war much sooner than expected. Of all Vietnamese independence movements, his was the best organized to act quickly.

General Jacques Leclerc signed for France at surrender ceremonies aboard the *Missouri*, where he sought MacArthur's advice. Leclerc's next assignment was to reestablish French control of Indochina.

Nagasaki. On August 10 Emperor Hirohito, against the advice of many Japanese military leaders, accepted the Potsdam Declaration. On August 14 the Japanese people, hearing the emperor's voice for the first time, were ordered, via a taped radio broadcast, to cease hostilities. On August 28 the U.S.S. *Missouri* sailed into Tokyo Bay with General Douglas MacArthur on board to accept the Japanese surrender.

The day after Hiroshima was bombed, Kim resigned as the Vietnamese leader of Japan's puppet government in Vietnam. This action was of great significance to the Viet Minh. Now they would not have to remove an existing Vietnamese government, however illegitimate; they could simply move to fill the vacuum.

Ho began acting quickly as planned. Of the independence-movement factions, only his was prepared. And as the result of Giap's efforts, cadres of supporters had been organized throughout Vietnam. On August 13 he gave orders for the national uprising to begin. Pamphlets promoting independence and proclaiming the Viet Minh the new leaders of Vietnam were distributed in all provinces. Where possible, rallies were organized to evidence popular support. Even before these actions, the Viet Minh had emerged as the best known of the independence movements.

On August 16 the first detachment of the Viet Minh army, formally organized the December before, entered Hanoi, with orders to avoid fighting with Japanese soldiers if at all possible. The Japanese, no longer having the will or the mandate to fight, merely watched, guarding only the Bank of Indochina. The Viet Minh occupied all other public buildings in the city. The French, disarmed in March, were likewise powerless to do anything but watch.

This show of popular support and power impressed Bao Dai, ensconced in his palace in Hue. On August 25 he abdicated and publicly endorsed the Viet Minh, no doubt in the hope that he would win favor with the Allies as well as with his own people, since Ho's troops were perceived as a pro-U.S. force. Though Bao Dai was nothing more than a figurehead, his endorsement was important because he remained to many a symbol of Vietnamese independence a hundred years before and was, according to tradition, heir to a divine right of leadership.

Four days later Ho formed his first government and on September 2, before a Hanoi rally of half a million people, he formally declared Vietnam's independence. "Vietnam has the right to be a free and independent country—and in fact it is so already," he said.

Even though the Potsdam Agreement had British and Chinese troops sharing occupation duties in Vietnam, Ho realized that in the end France alone would determine Vietnam's future status. The Potsdam Agreement did not take Indochina away from France; it merely provided that British forces would temporarily occupy southern Vietnam, and Chinese forces, the northern part. Implicit in the agreement was that France would work out its own methods for regaining control. Potsdam neither prohibited nor supported that effort. The U.S. position was one of neutrality. OSS officers adhered to this directive, though some French officials complained of their partiality to the Viet Minh. Jean Sainteny, who would later negotiate with Ho,

Only ten days after the second atomic bomb blast, Ho's Viet Minh staged this huge Hanoi rally.

At Potsdam, Stalin, Truman and Attlee agreed that British and Nationalist Chinese forces would temporarily occupy Indochina after the war.

Surrender ceremonies occurred at all levels of command. MacArthur accepted the surrender of all Japanese forces. (Right) Mountbatten accepted the surrender of the commander of all Japanese troops in Southeast Asia. (Opposite, top) Gracey delegated to a Gurkha officer the privilege of accepting the surrender of the top Japanese officer in southern Vietnam. (Opposite, bottom) Japanese officers lay down their swords during Saigon ceremonies.

Ho's declaration of independence...

One week after flying from Kunming, China, to Hanoi to serve as the American liaison for the Japanese surrender in Vietnam and to coordinate the release of Allied POWs, OSS Major Archimedes Patti was delivered the personal calling card of Ho Chi Minh with the following message scribbled by Ho himself on the back: "Urgent we meet before 12 noon today. Please come if you can. HOO." The Vietnamese leader was apparently then uncertain of the English spelling of his name.

A car was sent for Patti and by 10:30 he had arrived at Ho's residence on Hang Ngang Street. The place was abustle with activity. Vietnamese in an almost euphoric mood hurried about. The great day was at hand. In four days, on September 2, Ho would officially declare Vietnam's independence from France and present his government to a huge gathering in Hanoi. Preparations were being made, and that was why Ho wanted to talk to Patti.

The two men had had a pleasant dinner meeting several days before, and on this day too, Ho greeted Patti warmly, extending his thin hand for a firm handshake. First they talked about

accused American soldiers of keeping him under house arrest when he first arrived in Hanoi. (In truth, it was the Viet Minh who did so; Americans had nothing to do with it.) Sainteny, a French intelligence officer who was the principal agent in Hanoi for Charles de Gaulle's provisional government during a short period immediately after the war, had accompanied a small contingent of OSS personnel sent to Saigon and Hanoi soon after Hirohito ordered Japanese troops to stop fighting.

The first British mission arrived September 2, landing in Saigon. That day also marked the first outbreak of violence against French citizens living in Saigon since the world war ended. A large parade and rally got out of control. Three French citizens were killed. By September 12, when the first contingent of British troops under General Douglas Gracey arrived, Saigon was in chaos.

Gracey supposedly had been ordered by Mountbatten to remain neutral, but his remarks and actions indicated unequivocal support of the French, a support that merely echoed the obvious intentions of the British government. On August 13 and 22, British aircraft had dropped small groups of French soldiers into Vietnam. And Gracey, even before departing India for Vietnam, had made public his views. "The question of the government of Indochina is exclusively French," he said. "Civil and military control by the French is only a question of weeks."

Gracey viewed Vietnam's self-proclaimed leaders with disdain. "They came to see me," he later

recalled, "and said 'welcome' and all that sort of thing. It was an unpleasant situation and I promptly kicked them out."

Restoration of order was, understandably, Gracey's first concern, though his primary mission was to disarm the Japanese. Within days he banned all Vietnamese newspapers, ordered martial law, and made the Vietnamese police force an auxiliary of the British army. All his restrictive actions were taken against the Vietnamese. His mistake was not to put the French under similar constraints, for it would be they who plunged Saigon into chaos.

On September 22 Gracey rearmed some French paratroopers the Japanese had captured, as well as fourteen hundred French soldiers who had

Bao Dai. Ho had heard from his representative in Hue who had personally seen the emperor's Act of Abdication; the next day it would be made public. Ho was elated. Then they talked about the Chinese occupation forces, whose forward elements were just then crossing the border into Vietnam, where they would disarm the Japanese in the northern part of the country and accept their surrender. Ho was concerned about them, but confident that somehow his government could please them.

At that point, Ho got to his real purpose. He said he wanted Patti to be the first to learn details of festivities scheduled for the next few days. Patti remembers being impressed with the thoroughness of his planning, right down to the writing of the oaths of office for public officials. But Ho said he needed some help polishing the speech in which he was to proclaim Vietnamese independence from France. Patti agreed to look it over, whereupon a young man handed him a typewritten document with extensive editing and numerous notes in the margin. Ho himself had evidently been much involved in its preparation.

Unfortunately, Patti could not read or speak Vietnamese, so Ho quickly ordered a translator to read it aloud. Patti was stunned by the familiarity of the first few sentences and the frank attribution that followed: "This immortal statement was made in the Declaration of Independence of the United States of America in 1776."

Patti stopped the translator and turned to Ho in amazement, asking him whether he was really going to read it. Patti later confessed to the feeling that Ho was violating some sort of proprietary right.

Ho was not the least bit discomfited by Patti's reaction. He settled back in his chair, bringing his palms together in prayerful fashion, his fingertips touching his lips ever so lightly. His pleasant, almost quiet response embarrassed Patti. "Should I not use it?" he asked.

Patti asked the translator to read the words again.

"All men are created equal," he intoned. "They are endowed by their Creator with certain unalienable rights; among these are liberty, life, and the pursuit of happiness."

Patti again stopped the translator, noting the transposition of the words liberty and life. "Why, of course," said Ho, immediately understanding Thomas Jefferson's progression of thought. "There is no liberty without life, and no happiness without liberty."

Ho pressed Patti for more quotations from the American document, but Patti could not remember any. Furthermore, he had the feeling that he was being cleverly drawn into at least the appearance of formulating policy, and he was under strict orders not to do so. At meeting's end, Ho told Patti he would be honored by his presence at the Vietnamese Independence Day celebration.

On Sunday, September 2, 1945, half a million people crowded into Ba Dinh Square. In some cases, entire villages had made the trek to Hanoi to witness the great event. Men, women and children wore their best clothing. All were in a festive mood. Signs were everywhere: "Viet Nam to the Vietnamese," "Woe to the Oppressors," "Welcome American Delegation." Ho had not overlooked a single detail, thought Patti. Deference was also made in subtle ways to all the various religious faiths. The day coincided with the Feast of Vietnamese Martyrs for Catholics, for example.

Precisely at noon, whistle blasts and military commands for hundreds of troops in formation launched the proceedings. An honor guard appeared and the dignitaries on the high platform walked forward to be seen. All were dressed in white suits, except Ho himself, who wore a high-collared khaki tunic. After preliminary ceremonies, a speaker walked to the microphone and introduced Ho as the "liberator and

been kept under guard near Saigon since the March uprising. They immediately went on a rampage through Saigon, taking over police stations and public buildings, and arresting dozens. They were joined by French civilians who began beating up almost any Vietnamese found in the streets. This riot of sorts lasted two days. The result was a coup. The French were once again in control of Saigon, though tenuously.

The Viet Minh ordered its counterattack on September 23. They sabotaged Saigon's electrical works and ordered a general strike. Some scholars consider this date the first day of the fight for national liberation for Vietnamese.

Viet Minh control of Saigon, shaky at best from the start, now disintegrated. Different factions of the nationalist movement fought free-lance wherever possible in the Saigon area. Hoodlums joined the melee, taking advantage of the disorder. Mobs attacked the French and Eurasian sections of the city killing one hundred and fifty, including women and children, many in horrible fashion.

Reacting to the turmoil, Gracey on September 27 arrested Marshal Terauchi, the commander of Japanese forces, and threatened to try him as a war criminal if his troops did not help restore order. Terauchi's troops complied and began firing on Vietnamese guerrillas and rioters taking advantage of the turmoil. The action greatly aided the French cause and was deemed such a grave violation of the Potsdam Agreement that Mountbatten reportedly almost fired Gracey.

Order was restored, however. On October 2, a truce was arranged, Gracey now eager to visit with nationalist leaders. Three days later the first French troops from France arrived under the command of Leclerc. Meanwhile, back in England, French Ambassador Massigli concluded an agreement on October 9 with British Foreign Minister Ernest Bevin, which stated that the only authorized administration south of the sixteenth parallel was that of France.

Following the truce, Leclerc bought time by negotiating with the Viet Minh, while more French troops poured in from three locations outside Indochina. By February Leclerc had thirty-five thousand under his command. But fighting again erupted October 11. This time French, British and Japanese fought side-by-side against the Vietnamese. The British air force provided aircover. Within two weeks the Saigon area was completely under French control and the city was calm.

Leclerc's next objective was to establish control of the countryside south of the sixteenth parallel. Acting only with French troops this time, his armored columns thundered into the larger towns, quickly taking charge. But fighting in the villages and along the Mekong River was much more difficult. What was expected to take four weeks took four months. The experience of these battles was a harbinger of future difficulties. "If we departed, believing a region pacified," wrote author Philippe Devillers, who accompanied Leclerc, "they would arrive on our heels and the terror would start again."

On March 4 the British began departing Vietnam, leaving the French in charge, though not necessarily in control.

While the British army was occupying the south, Chiang Kai-shek's Chinese army entered northern Vietnam in September 1945. Though the occupation of the north was peaceful, it was not without human cost. The Chinese army, estimated at fifty thousand, was a ragtag outfit that had to forage for almost every meal. Food was confiscated from Vietnamese, themselves on short rations.

The Chinese generals, actually warlords who operated almost independently of Chiang's control, were as rapacious as their soldiers. Their appetite was for profit, however. They devalued the piaster to ridiculously low levels relative to the worthless Chinese dollar and made the latter legal tender. They then bought up land and all sorts of business interests, including mines, shops and factories, whether owned by the Vietnamese or the French. And they used whatever pressure necessary to effect transactions.

Ho's Viet Minh did not share in the profiteering, but acquiesced in it because they wanted the Chinese to tolerate their government, which the Chinese did. In fact, Ho actively encouraged acceptance by direct payoffs. He conducted a "gold week" in which Vietnamese donated as a "patriotic contribution" jewelry and other items made of gold. Some of the eight hundred pounds of gold collected was used to defray the cost of running Ho's government, but some of it (how much is unknown) went directly to Chinese generals as bribes.

The Chinese were inclined to support the Viet Minh for unselfish reasons, too, their own experiences with colonials weighing heavily with them.

savior of the nation." Spurred by what Patti says were Communist Party members interspersed throughout the throng, the people began chanting "Doc-Lap, Doc-Lap"—independence—over and over for several minutes. Ho stood there behind the microphone, smiling, exhilarated by the thunderous chant. Finally he raised his hands, and the crowd fell silent.

Ho delivers his independence speech.

"All men are created equal," he said. "The Creator has given us certain inviolable Rights; the right to Life, the right to be Free, and the right to achieve Happiness."

Suddenly he stopped. And with perfect confidence and timing, he asked the audience: "Do you hear me distinctly, fellow countrymen?"

"Yes!" they roared.

From that instant on, says Patti, they hung on his every word, Ho's voice being "quiet and clear, warm and friendly."

"These immortal words are taken from the Declaration of Independence of the United States of America in 1776," Ho continued. "In a larger sense, this means that: All the people on earth are born equal; all the people have the right to live, to be happy, to be free."

The first American killed by Ho's troops...

Saigon was in chaos in late September 1945. No one was in control—not the Japanese, whose troops were still in the city; not the British, who had come to disarm them and accept their surrender; not the French, who were trying to rearm and reorganize; not the Viet Minh, who had set up a provisional government. The end of the Second World War in the Pacific had uncorked hatreds that had long been bottled up. French and Vietnamese took turns killing one another.

After the French coup against the fledgling Viet Minh administration in Saigon on September 22-23, French men and women struck out against any Vietnamese they saw, sometimes even breaking down their doors to get at them. "No one they found was spared— men and women, young and old, even children were slapped around, spanked and shaked. For most victims, the beatings were severe; some were maimed for life." The number of victims reached into the "high hundreds and probably into the thousands." French and British troops watched all this with apparent amusement.

Foreign correspondents did not, and their reports began appearing in papers throughout the world. Major A. Peter Dewey, twenty-eight, the American OSS chief in Saigon, the son of a Republican congressman from Chicago and the nephew of New York Governor Thomas Dewey, was another who recoiled at the sight of this orgy of violence. He tried to protest the French action to Major Douglas D. Gracey, the commander of the British occupation forces, but Gracey refused to see him. Dewey then complained to senior members of the general's staff and various French officers, who all told him it was none of his business. Gracey decided to rid himself of the American, whom he considered annoyingly naive; he de-

As a result, the Chinese thought it better to support government by a Vietnamese Communist than by the colonial French—this despite Nationalist Chinese problems with Communists at home. Accordingly, they continually denounced British intrigues on behalf of the French in the south.

Furthermore, Ho acted to alleviate Chinese misgivings about his politics. Recognizing that the Communist label was his chief problem, he expeditiously outlawed the Communist party on November 11. He also ordered elections and opened up about half of the top government posts to non-Communists supported by the Chinese.

On February 28, however, the Chinese signed a treaty with France, agreeing to leave the next month, though they did not do so until summer. The French had made the Chinese an offer they could not resist: In return for the right to replace Chinese occupation forces with their own soldiers, France gave up all concessions claimed in China, renounced its claim to Kwanchouwan, a region taken from China by France in the 1880s during its conquest of Tongking, designated Haiphong a free port for China, granted customs-free status for all goods shipped from China to the port, and sold the Chinese the Yunnan railroad.

The French were eager to return to northern Vietnam. Having successfully reestablished themselves as the dominant governing force in the south, they were now determined to duplicate that victory quickly in the north. But there they would find a more powerful opposition.

Though it obviously had spread itself too thin in the south, Ho's new government had managed to maintain order in the north. It had been issuing popular decrees that its army in the north had the strength to enforce. On September 8, only days after announcing its authority, the Viet Minh established the eight-hour workday, authorized labor unions, ordered educational reforms, eliminated the salt monopoly, barred the sale of opium and alcohol, and confiscated land owned by French citizens and Vietnamese deemed their collaborators.

Four months of fighting guerrillas in the south had already given Leclerc a healthy appreciation for the resolve of the Vietnamese independence movement. He dismissed plans to invade the north and decided to negotiate his way back in. Having bought off the Chinese, the

French began negotiating with the Vietnamese.

Like his French counterpart, Ho had a healthy appreciation for the strength of the adversary. Ho was as eager as Leclerc to avoid war, so that when he and Jean Sainteny sat down at the negotiating table, it took only four hectic days for them to come to terms. In return for Viet Minh promises to end the guerrilla fighting in the south and to allow twenty-five thousand French troops into the north—Tongking and northern Annam—the French recognized the "free state with its own government, parliament, army and finances," and made this "Democratic Republic of Vietnam . . . part of the Indochinese Federation and the French Union." The French also promised a referendum in Cochinchina to decide, in effect, whether the three states of

clared Dewey *persona non grata* and ordered him to leave the country.

That evening, September 24, Dewey filed his last report from Saigon to his OSS superiors: "Cochinchina is burning, the French and British are finished here, and we (the Americans) ought to clear out of Southeast Asia."

That night the Vietnamese took their
(Continued)

The rag-tag Chinese army that occupied northern Vietnam descended like a swarm of locust. Poorly supplied, its troops had to forage along the way, taking from the already impoverished Vietnamese.

violent revenge. Soldiers of the Binh Xuyen went on a rampage through the European district, mutilating and killing white and Eurasian men, women and children.

On September 26 Dewey packed his bags at the Hotel Continental and drove his jeep to Tan Son Nhut airport for departure to Kandy, Ceylon. The flight was delayed twice, so he decided to drive back to OSS headquarters for lunch. A tree had been felled across the road as a partial roadblock, which only required that he slow down while passing it, as he had done earlier in the day. As he did so, Viet Minh soldiers manning a light machine gun opened fire without warning, hitting Dewey in the head, killing him instantly. The Viet Minh then attacked the OSS office. About three hours later British Gurkha soldiers came to the rescue. The Viet Minh fled, taking Dewey's jeep, with him still in it. The body was never recovered.

Dewey's death was apparently a case of mistaken identity. The Viet Minh, it seems, thought he was either French or British, though that explanation does not fully explain the attack on the OSS office. The investigating American officer concluded in his official report: "If the jeep in which he was riding at the time of the incident had been displaying an American flag, I feel positive that the shot would not have been fired. A flag was not being displayed in accordance with verbal instructions issued by General Gracey."

Within hours, word of Dewey's death reached Major Archimedes Patti, the senior OSS officer in Hanoi. Upset, he immediately called on Ho, who, in Patti's words, was "visibly shaken" to learn of the action of his troops. The death of an American at Viet Minh hands while Ho was seeking U.S. support was clearly not in his interest. But for reasons never fully understood the Viet Minh did kill Peter Dewey, who thus became the first American victim of one of Ho's soldiers.

Vietnam would unite under one national government. And the French agreed to withdraw all their troops from Vietnam in stages so that by 1952 French military occupation would end. The agreement was signed March 6, 1946. Two days later the French fleet cruised into Haiphong Harbor and French soldiers started coming ashore.

On February 4, 1945, the day Roosevelt, Stalin and Churchill met at Yalta, Americans' favorable view of the Soviet Union was near its peak. Russians were perceived as "hardworking" and "brave." Secretary of State Cordell Hull had declared its armies had won "the admiration of the liberty-loving peoples of the world." General Douglas MacArthur had lauded their "indomitable stand" against the Germans. "Today the free peoples of the world unite in salute to that great army and great nation which so nobly strives with us for victory, liberty and freedom," he said. Press accounts were equally favorable. Not surprisingly, seven of ten Americans then favored putting Germans to work rebuilding Russia after the war.

Unfortunately, this spirit of goodwill and cooperation between the U.S. and the Soviet Union ended with the war itself. The estrangement began almost immediately after American and Russian troops linked up. In Stalin's view, Germany's surrender eliminated the last reason to cooperate with the Western Allies in Europe.

At Yalta, Roosevelt had negotiated with Stalin and Churchill a deliberately vague declaration that Roosevelt hoped would void the historic pattern of spheres of influence by great powers and instead encourage great-power cooperation. According to the agreement's language, the three nations would collectively effect "the processes which will enable the liberated peoples to destroy the last vestiges of nazism and fascism and to create democratic institutions of their own choice." The U.S., Great Britain and the Soviet Union would "jointly assist" in conducting elections. Their focus was Europe.

Stalin's postwar actions quickly abrogated this agreement, however. He made Roosevelt, after his death, to look the fool, giving rise to accusations that still persist that the American president gave away Eastern Europe. (Actually, he did not have it to give away. By V-E Day Russian troops already occupied most of that region.) Stalin refused to allow the exiled Polish leaders back into their country. American and

British teams trying to monitor elections in Austria were kept out for months. These "control missions," as they were called, were also impeded by Russian forces in Hungary, Bulgaria and Rumania. An outraged Churchill complained that an "iron fence" quite literally had gone up around the British mission in Bucharest. With almost overnight suddenness, it struck Americans that Russia intended to control all the nations along its western border.

Eastern Europe was not the only sign of Russian perfidy. Stalin doubled earlier reparation demands. He now wanted $20 billion from Germany. He demanded internationalization of the Bosporus, which would have meant the end of Turkey as a nation. And to that end, he began supplying Communist guerrillas fighting there as well as in Greece. He refused to withdraw Russian troops from northern Iran. He ordered entire factories in Germany, Eastern Europe and Manchuria dismantled and carted off to Russia. A Manchurian plant manager who complained during an interview with American journalists was murdered the next day. And, as though these actions were insufficient confirmation of ill will, he disavowed the wartime alliance in a speech before the Communist Party Congress on February 9, 1946. He classified the U.S. as a greater threat than Nazi Germany had been and predicted war before the mid-1950s, by which time he expected the U.S. to be in an economic depression. Supreme Court Justice William O. Douglas called Stalin's speech "the Declaration of World War III."

American's warm feelings for Russians dropped as fast as temperatures behind a cold front. By

A French bribe to warm American interest...

French intelligence officer Major Jean Sainteny served as the principal agent in Hanoi of Charles de Gaulle's provisional government during the first weeks after the war. Sainteny was well connected, being the son-in-law of Albert Sarraut, a former governor general of Indochina and almost permanent member of French cabinets from 1920 to 1940.

In August 1945 it was obvious that American help would greatly ease France's path toward reestablishing colonial control of Vietnam. On August 26, 1945, in a room at the governor general's palace in Hanoi, Sainteny told Major Archimedes Patti, in a highly confidential, almost conspiratorial tone, "The French government is prepared to extend a credit of five billion French francs to Americans only, to invest in Indochina, and I would like to know the right person to contact on this matter and to start negotiations."

Patti reacted almost violently, taking the offer as a personal insult, but dutifully conveyed it to OSS superiors in China. Within hours he received instructions "to stay clear of any deals to suborn American officials."

At Yalta, Churchill, Roosevelt and Stalin agreed that their nations would "jointly assist" in conducting elections in Europe after the war. The Cold War and recriminations of betrayal followed Soviet actions to block free elections in Eastern Europe.

FBI director J. Edgar Hoover warned of a great enemy within composed of Communist agents. The Red Scare shaped U.S. policy and led to the country's involvement in Vietnam.

1948 seventy percent of all Americans had an unfavorable opinion of the Soviet Union. Six in ten thought Soviet behavior reflected a disposition to rule the world. A "Red Scare" characterized the mood of the day. Americans were so startled by the turn of events that they turned on themselves. Though there was due cause for concern, the nation's worry became paranoia. In a speech before the American Legion, FBI director J. Edgar Hoover described a vast enemy within—a hundred thousand Communist agents— that was actively undermining the country in "newspapers, magazincs, books, radio, the screen . . . some churches, schools, colleges and even fraternal orders."

Reflecting the public sentiment, the elections of 1946 and 1948 were dominated by the question of which candidates would "get tough with the Russians." Other factors fueled the hysteria— the dramatic defection of a Russian spy in Canada, the Alger Hiss trial and conviction, the Loyalty Review Boards, and the House Un-American Activities Committee hearings.

By 1948 the party of Roosevelt had regrouped sufficiently to have stolen the Cold War issue away from the Republicans, who had introduced it in the congressional elections two years before. Truman had reacted decisively. In response to Great Britain's announcement on February 24, 1947, that it could no longer provide military and economic aid to the Greek and Turkish governments fighting Communist guerrillas, Truman announced plans to fill the breach to a join session of Congress on March 12, asking for $400 million in aid.

"I believe that it must be the policy of the United States to support free peoples who are resisting attempted subjugation by armed minorities or by outside pressures," he said. "We cannot allow changes in the status quo in violation of the Charter of the United Nations by such methods as coercion, or by such subterfuges as political infiltration."

The theme was containment. By implication we acknowledged the impossibility of pushing the Communists back from present positions. But now we intended to hold the line to stop the spread of Communism.

Two other developments quickly followed, the Economic Recovery Plan and the formation of the North Atlantic Treaty Organization (NATO). Marshall announced the former at Harvard commencement ceremonies on June 5, 1947. Though primarily targeted for Europe, Congress's original Marshall Plan appropriation allotted $1.5 billion to Chiang Kai-shek's Nationalists fighting Communists in China, thus setting an early precedent for the diversion of U.S. foreign aid funds to anti-Communist activities outside Europe. Frenchmen fighting Communist nationalists in Vietnam would also benefit. Fighting there had resumed on December 19, 1946, when General Morlière, secure in his knowledge of French military superiority in northern Vietnam, abrogated earlier agreements and demanded that Ho turn over to the French all policing duties in Hanoi. This was, in essence, a demand for Ho to surrender, and he refused.

By that time U.S. policy regarding European colonies had already undergone an almost complete reversal of Roosevelt's intentions. The years to come would see the Berlin blockade, Soviet development of the atomic bomb, the Communist victory in China, and the Korean war, events which of course hardened the U.S. in its new attitude. By 1953, according to the *Pentagon Papers,* this country was paying seventy-eight percent of the costs France incurred to reestablish colonial control over Vietnam. In just a few years, Roosevelt's wartime worries about European colonialism had become as historically remote as Queen Victoria to U.S. policymakers.

Emerging Enemies

The Internal Vietnamese Struggle

Both Ho and French emissary Jean Sainteny probably knew that their agreement of March 6, 1946, would not bring peace. Though it formally recognized Ho's Democratic Republic of Vietnam and made this "free state" part of the French Union, it is likely both men understood that because of powerful French political and business interests, the agreement would only serve to buy time.

Indeed, both parties put the time to good use—the French to post thousands more troops to Vietnam; Ho to consolidate his weak power base. As Joseph Buttinger points out, the military, political and moral position of Ho's government was infinitely weaker in March than it would be in December, when renewed fighting erupted.

Ho had two primary goals to achieve during this time—to train and organize his troops and to wipe out opposition within the Vietnamese nationalist movement. Ho was determined that all Vietnamese look solely to his leadership for independence. Many non-Communist rivals were executed. Viet Minh murder victims included Pham Quynh, a brilliant conservative writer and former adviser to Bao Dai, and Ngo Dinh Khoi, a mandarin and older brother of Diem.

In spite of the wanton political killings being committed by the Communists, French officials managed to strengthen Ho's moral position in the world community and within Vietnam itself by voicing an imperious disdain for their own agreement. The French decided they did not like the agreement even though it let them back into Vietnam without firing a shot. Officials such as Admiral Thierry d'Argenlieu, the ranking French official in Vietnam immediately after the Second World War, also thought France should have its former political powers there restored. Consequently, d'Argenlieu and others set about undermining the agreement, even though it had been negotiated in good faith by Sainteny and approved by General Leclerc, who was, in the absence of d'Argenlieu (away in France on business at the time of the agreement), the ranking official in Vietnam.

Upon his return to Vietnam from Paris, d'Argenlieu, an arch-

Vo Nguyen Giap and Ho Chi Minh in September 1945; above, their rival Ngo Dinh Diem.

The Adversaries—
⁶In their own words⁹

⁶If these dirty peasants want a fight, they shall have it.⁹—Brigadier General Jean Valluy, shortly before the French regained control of Hanoi by force; on December 17, 1946.

⁶Thank God, it's ours!⁹—Lieutenant Colonel Pierre Charles Langlais, commander of the paratroopers at Dien Bien Phu, upon being informed that an aircraft that had just bombed the French garrison had French markings; an indication of the desperate plight of the French forces there; on April 12, 1954.

⁶We have a clean base there [Vietnam], without the taint of colonialism. Dien Bien Phu was a blessing in disguise.⁹—Secretary of State John Foster Dulles to Emmet John Hughes after the Viet Minh had overrun the French garrison; in 1954.

Ho moved quickly to establish a formal government-in-place for the French to deal with while trying to reassert control. The National Assembly of the Democratic Republic of Vietnam first met in a Hanoi auditorium in January 1946.

conservative Carmelite monk as well as an admiral, expressed his "amazement that France had such a fine expeditionary corps in Indochina and yet its leaders prefer to negotiate rather than to fight." He said that it was "the sacred duty of France to reestablish order" in Vietnam. He assured his troops that "France has come, guided not by material or financial interests, but by humanitarian goals." Elevating their mission to an even higher plane, he assured them they would be "fighting for the reestablishment of French greatness."

D'Argenlieu's reaction was the product of the same business and political forces that had controlled Indochina for decades. He owed his appointment to the newly created position of high commissioner of France to Vietnam to the new Catholic political party in France, the MRP, to which colonial interests had rallied. "In regard to Indochina, this party spoke for administrators afraid of losing their posts, for military men in positions of almost unlimited authority, for the many small planters eager to preserve their modest gains, but above all for the relatively few whose handsome profits were derived from the traffic in rice and rubber, and from the even more lucrative transactions of the Bank of Indochina."

De Gaulle also enhanced the prestige of these groups. "United with the overseas territories which she opened to civilization, France is a great power. Without these territories she would be in danger of no longer being one," he said in August when the agreement was being debated.

But the weakening of the agreement had begun long before August. Within six days of the signing of the agreement, special-interest groups forced its partial abrogation. Jean Cédile, the commissioner of Cochinchina, declared there would be no referendum there, as promised, to decide whether residents wanted to join a uni-

fied Vietnam under the authority of Ho's Democratic Republic. This open breach was quickly and officially sanctioned by Marius Moutet, the French Socialist minister for overseas territories.

Furthermore, within five weeks of the agreement, French military commanders were already exploring ways to overthrow Ho's government by force. On April 10 General Etienne Valluy, who had replaced Leclerc as the commander in chief of French military forces in Vietnam, ordered subordinate commanders to undertake "the study of measures which would have the effect of progressively modifying and transforming the plan of action, which is that of a purely military operation, into a plan of action for a coup d'état."

In June Ho traveled to Paris to negotiate with

Leclerc, with Gracey behind him on his right and Jean Cédile on his left, participates in ceremonies held by the French population following his arrival in Saigon. Like Sainteny, Cédile was a Gaullist French agent.

☀ "…there is no greater irony today," writes historian Theodore H. White in *In Search of History,* "than that the French, who debased, defiled and degraded the Vietnamese people, should act on the world stage as public friends of Vietnam, and we, Americans, should be accused as the ravagers of a civilization we tried to save."

The wily Jean Sainteny played key roles in dealing with Ho and the Communists, first as a French intelligence officer, then as commissioner of Tongking; later, as an intermediary for President Nixon.

Moutet the implementation of the March 6 agreement. By then the French military presence in northern Vietnam had increased substantially and included all varieties of heavy armament. As a consequence, Ho acquiesced to all French demands. In essence he agreed to throw out the agreement's key elements. The implementation agreement, or *modus vivendi,* signed September 14, did not provide for the referendum in Cochinchina, did not endorse independence for the DRV, and did not confirm recognition of Vietnam as a free state.

Still, the very fact that the French negotiated with Ho helped to legitimize him as the principal leader of the independence movement. French anti-Communist propaganda also focused favorable Vietnamese attention on Ho, the opposite of its intended effect.

By the time Ho arrived back in Hanoi in October, the intentions of both sides were so clear that a renewal of hostilities awaited the slightest pretext. The French were obviously preparing to recolonize Vietnam. And Ho was obviously agreeing to anything that would buy him time to build a fighting force and establish his primacy within the independence movement.

The pretext came on November 20, 1946. A French patrol boat crew operating in Haiphong Harbor boarded a Chinese junk, looking for contraband. The Viet Minh militia, which deemed itself the only authorized law-enforcement authority in northern Vietnam, then arrested the three Frenchmen and jailed them in the Vietnamese section of the city. Elements of the French army went to the rescue and fighting broke out.

A cease-fire was arranged after a day of conflict. Ho and General Morlière, commander of French forces in northern Vietnam, wanted to negotiate. But Valluy, the latter's superior, did not. Nor did d'Argenlieu, who was back in Paris once more, this time trying to convince the government to sanction Ho's overthrow. The fighting in Haiphong won his case. Premier Georges Bidault, about to leave office after a brief term, okayed a French attack. "Can we go so far as to use cannons?" d'Argenlieu asked. "Even that," answered Bidault.

To avoid listening to Morlière's voice of caution and reconciliation, Valluy took the extraordinary step of breaking the chain of command. He issued orders directly to the junior officer in charge of the French garrison in Haiphong,

✳ In August 1945, when Ho Chi Minh became, for most Vietnamese, the symbol of national independence, he was not particularly associated in their minds with Communism. Thousands of recruits were attracted to his army under the command of Vo Nguyen Giap. The small Armed Propaganda Brigade for the Liberation of Vietnam, founded in December 1944, mushroomed in numbers to thirty thousand by June 1946, by then renamed the Vietnam People's Army. Five months later this regular army numbered sixty thousand. By January 1947, the total reached one hundred thousand.

During negotiations in Paris in September 1946, the French practically abrogated their earlier agreement to recognize Ho's "free state." The large French welcoming delegation, the formal dinners (Ho next to Sainteny) and the demonstrative support of the Vietnamese community in Paris, all went for naught.

Fighting between the Viet Minh and the
French broke out in November 1946 at
Haiphong. Shellfire from the *Suffren*
covered attacking French forces. In
Hanoi, the Vietnamese began building
street fortifications, but soon were driven
out and into the jungles; the First
Indochina War then began. A deliriously
happy French population welcomed the
return of their troops.

Colonel Dèbes. "Use all the means at your
disposal to make yourself complete master of
Haiphong and so bring the Vietnamese Army
around to a better understanding of the situation,"
he told the man.

At 7 A.M. on November 23, 1946, Dèbes gave
the Viet Minh militia two hours to leave town.
At 9:45, when there was still no reply, he
ordered his units to attack. French troops advanced behind a rain of fire from tanks, air-
planes and the cruiser *Suffren,* at anchor in the
harbor. By November 28, Haiphong was once
again under French control. Casualties were
heavy on the Vietnamese side, though French
Admiral Battet downplayed the numbers: "No
more than 6,000 killed, in so far as naval bombardment of fleeing civilians was concerned," he
later told Paul Mus, a writer and former political
adviser to Leclerc. The First Indochina War had
begun; it only awaited official confirmation.

That confirmation was not long in coming. In
response to a Viet Minh attack on an army truck
in which three French soldiers were killed, Valluy
ordered on December 17 a retaliatory strike on a
Viet Minh militia post in Hanoi. Fifteen Vietnamese soldiers were killed and a number of
surrounding houses were burned. A day later a
French parachutist was killed in the Vietnamese
section during a search for the body of a French
soldier. Vietnamese started barricading city
streets. Valluy immediately ordered the barri-
cades torn down. Troops and tanks advanced
behind bulldozers. On December 18 the Minis-
tries of Finance and Communications of Ho's
government were occupied. On December 19 the
French ordered the Viet Minh militia to disarm
and relinquish all law-enforcement duties to the
French. That evening at 8 Vietnamese saboteurs
counterattacked, disabling the electrical works.
They also attacked various French posts and
the French residential district. At 9:30 Giap
issued the order for a general uprising against
the French. The French mark this date as the
start of the Indochina war, ignoring the fact
that fighting with nationalists in the southern
countryside had been raging since Leclerc arrived over a year earlier in October 1945.

Thirty-seven French and Eurasian civilians
were killed the night of December 19 and two
hundred taken prisoner, according to Mus. The
next day French troops resumed the offensive.
Ho's residence was occupied that afternoon, but
he and all his top aides escaped. The French

quickly regained control of Hanoi. By March they again controlled all major cities in the north.

Ho and his troops withdrew to the jungles and mountains. Almost eight long years would pass before they could return. But Ho's life had prepared him well for the challenges that lay ahead.

Most of Ho's biographers agree that he was born in 1890, though some say 1894. He died in 1969.

There is some confusion about his birth name, primarily because he was a revolutionary most of his adult life, assuming many aliases. The late Bernard Fall, a prolific writer about Vietnam, thought Nguyen Van Thanh the most likely. A pamphlet history of the Vietnamese Workers' Party calls Ho Nguyen That Than, which translates as "Nguyen Who Will Be Victorious." Western Communist sources frequently refer to him as Nguyen Ai-Quoc or "Nguyen the Patriot." He did not begin using the name Ho Chi Minh, "He Who Enlightens," until 1944.

Ho's place of birth was the village of Hoang Tru in Annam. He was raised in the village Kim Lien in the province of Nghe An, a part of northern Vietnam known for its revolutionaries. That area was the last region of Vietnam the French brought under their control. Doumer was governor general at the time; Ho was a young boy.

Ho no doubt inherited most of his nationalist and revolutionary tendencies from his father, who was a minor mandarin in the old imperial government until he was forced to resign because of his "implacable animosity toward the French." He had achieved his position by passing the mandarinal examinations following grueling and determined study. But he had the bad luck of doing so at about the time the French were attacking Hue and Hanoi. He then turned to Oriental medicine, using healing techniques based on Vietnamese and Chinese precepts. He did well, being described as part of the "village aristocracy," though he was only slightly better off than the average village peasant. Of a hardy constitution, which, like his politics, he seems to have passed on to his son, he was seen walking briskly through the countryside, prescribing various potions to clients, as late as the 1930s.

Ho spoke fondly of his mother to Archimedes Patti in 1945. He also mentioned two brothers

Ho's American commander...

Some of the Viet Minh soldiers who battled French forces in the streets of Hanoi beginning in December 1946 were trained in the skills of modern weaponry and tactics by American OSS Major Allison K. Thomas and had, in fact, been armed by the United States. Thomas's association with the Viet Minh began in June 1945 when Ho Chi Minh offered OSS Major Archimedes Patti the use of a thousand "well-trained" guerrilla fighters for espionage work against the Japanese in Vietnam. The offer coincided with problems the OSS was having with various French agents operating out of southern China; the French had initially agreed to muster an espoinage team to join Thomas and his group of agents, but at the last instant presented various political and financial objections.

Patti pressed his superiors to approve Ho's offer, acceptance of which presented a variety of advantages over French participation: The Viet Minh enjoyed the support of the local Vietnamese population—the French did not; furthermore, the Viet Minh were already in place and very familiar with the area of operation. Approval was granted and Ho, who was then operating out of his jungle headquarters in Vietnam, was immediately notified. A rendezvous was planned, and during the late afternoon hours of July 16, 1945, Thomas and his small party of two American enlisted men, a French lieutenant, and two Vietnamese sergeants in the French army, parachuted into the jungles near the village of Kim Lung. Three of them, including Thomas, got hung up in the triple-canopy tree covering and had to be helped down by some of Ho's troops, described by Thomas as "a very impressive reception committee"—two hundred Viet Minh armed with "French rifles, a few Brens, a few tommies, a few carbines and a few Sten." Together they rendered Thomas a snappy salute, obviously having been briefed on the significance of an American officer in their midst.

Thomas's first report evidenced this continuing hospitality. "I was then escorted to Mr. Hoe [sic], one of the big leaders of the VML (Viet Minh League) Party. He speaks excellent English but is very weak physically as he recently walked from Tsingsi (Ch'ing-Hsi). He received us most cordially. We then were shown our quarters. They had built for us a special bamboo shelter, consisting of a bamboo floor a few feet off the ground and a roof of palm leaves. We then had supper consisting of beer (recently captured), rice, bamboo sprouts and barbecued steak. They freshly slaughtered a cow in our honor."

Thomas also reported that Ho would not tolerate the presence of the French officer and the two Vietnamese sergeants. They were taken to a nearby village where a group of Europeans, mostly French, were hiding; they had been freed from a Japanese detention camp by the Viet Minh. The French lieutenant led part of this group, on foot, all the way back to China.

Thomas and his highly skilled OSS specialists stayed. Without delay, they began training a handpicked group of two hundred Viet Minh soldiers. For four weeks, the Americans put them through an advanced boot camp of sorts, using American weapons parachuted in. They then set out on their mission, which was to disrupt "the Chen Nam Kuan–Hanoi lines of communication" of the Japanese.

The war was about over, of course, but these men were hardly aware of that. The atomic bomb was unknown to them. When on August 15, 1945, Emperor Hirohito ordered his soldiers to lay down their arms, Thomas was with his newly trained contingent and other Viet Minh troops, along with Vo Nguyen Giap himself, fighting Japanese forces about forty miles from Hanoi. This contest kept up for some time after the called-for surrender, their

and a sister.

Ho attended a village school as a boy and was tutored by his father, possessor of a minor doctoral degree in Chinese ideography. He later was a student at the Quoc Hoc college in Hue, founded by none other than the father of Diem, Ngo Dinh Kha, a high official of the Imperial Court, who shared Ho's father's dislike for the French. The school focused on Western knowledge but tried to eliminate French colonial influences.

Ho left Quoc Hoc in 1910 without receiving a diploma, but managed to parlay his education into a teaching position in the town of Phan-Thiet, a fishing village in southern Annam. Ten years later, ironically, Diem was to distinguish himself in this same Phan-Thiet as the young and able Vietnamese administrator of the province.

In 1911 Ho traveled to Saigon where he attended a trade school for three months. At that point, he decided to see the world, and signed on with the ship *Latouche-Treville* as a kitchen boy, using the alias "Ba," so as not to denigrate the family name by such lowly employ. He traveled for three years, visiting parts of Africa, North America and Europe. According to Fall, "His contacts with the white colonizers on their home grounds shattered any of his illusions as to their 'superiority,' and his association with sailors from Brittany, Cornwall and the Frisian Islands—as illiterate and superstitious as the most backward Vietnamese rice farmer—did the rest." On the other hand, exposure to Western culture bolstered his sense of self-worth. He was no longer treated as a subject native addressed with a deprecating *"tu."*

In 1914, about the time of the outbreak of the First World War, he settled in London where by day he worked at a London school doing odd jobs and by night worked as a kitchen helper under the renowned chef Escoffier at the Carlton Hotel. Escoffier liked Ho's work and promoted him to the pastry division.

While in London Ho joined the secret Overseas Workers Association, led by various Chinese and composed in part of Vietnamese agitating for independence. Among other stands it took, the organization endorsed independence for Ireland, a hot political issue of the day. According to Ho's biographer Ho Van Tao, "Without doubt, it was during that period that Ho Chi Minh's evolution began toward revolutionary socialism and Communism."

By 1918 Ho was in France, where he earned his income working as a photo retoucher. To solicit business, he ran the following ad in the Socialist newspaper *La Vie Ouvrière:*

"You who wish a living remembrance of your parents, have your photos retouched at Nguyen Ai-Quoc's. Handsome portraits and handsome frames for 45 francs. 9, Impasse Compoint, Paris XVIIth District."

Ho continued his political involvement, of course. When the leaders of the world's great powers met at Versailles, he and other young Vietnamese decided the time was propitious to act. They drew up an eight-point petition called "List of Claims for the Vietnamese People" —which was more of a statement than a request for independence—dressed Ho up in a rented black suit and bowler hat, and sent him off to the gilded palace. He was twenty-eight, assuming the 1890 birthday. Not surprisingly, he did not get to see Georges Clemenceau, David Lloyd George or Woodrow Wilson.

Ho became a voracious reader of Socialist and Communist literature while in Paris. He also developed his language skills. Sainteny says he spoke Vietnamese, French, English, Russian and Mandarinal Chinese fluently, as well as several Indochinese dialects.

He also worked on his writing skills. He contributed articles to *L'Humanité* and wrote one political satire, "The Bamboo Dragon." The latter earned him an invitation to the French Socialist Party Congress at Tours in 1920. There he met Moutet, about twenty-five years later to become, as a Socialist, the minister for overseas territories with whom Ho would negotiate the

adversaries not getting the word.

In the meantime, Ho's network of supporters living in Hanoi, principally the Hanoi City Committee and elements of the Armed Propaganda Brigade, took control of the local government from the Japanese without firing a shot. This was accomplished on August 19. However, because of the continuing Japanese resistance, Thomas, the American NCOs and their Viet Minh cohorts were delayed in reaching Hanoi until September 9. Giap had left them so as to arrive there alone sooner. Perhaps because of information provided by Giap, Thomas was somewhat of a local hero by the time he marched into Hanoi with his Viet Minh guerrilla group. He was mentioned by name in a Vietnamese newspaper in an article headlined, "Viet Minh Fighting with U.S. Troops in Tongking Will Soon Be Here to Oust the French Oppressors Who Last Year Starved 2 Million People."

According to Patti, the Viet Minh soldiers whom Thomas trained and briefly led became top leaders in the armies of Generals Giap and Chu Van Tan. "Some of us may have suspected that in the future the weapons and training might be used against the French," he says, "but no one dreamed that they would ever be used against Americans."

In 1920, at age thirty, Ho, then known as Nguyen Ai-Quoc, attended the French Socialist Party Conference. There he walked out with a group of socialists that formed the Communist Party of France.

Ho: Moscow's puppet?...

On the evening of September 30, 1945, Ho invited Major Archimedes Patti to his residence for dinner. Patti was to leave Hanoi the next day, his duties completed, the war finished; within two weeks he would be on his way back to the United States. Other Vietnamese were in attendance, including Vo Nguyen Giap, but later in the evening, one by one, they politely excused themselves, leaving Ho and Patti alone.

Their conversation lasted far into the night, Ho doing most of the talking. Twice, as a courtesy, Patti rose to his feet to leave; both times Ho asked him to stay. Ho talked about world politics, about Indochina, about the French. Finally, he talked about himself. He traced his lifelong wanderings, both political and otherwise. He described his early days, his being naive in every respect—from being afraid to go beyond the port areas he visited as a seaman, to his failure to understand the numbing political discussions of French Socialist and Communist intellectuals in Paris. Their ramblings were too philosophical, their applications too theoretical to make sense to Ho. Then one day someone handed him a copy of

implementation of the famous March 6, 1946, agreement. Ironically, the colonial question caused Ho to vote at Tours with a splinter group, which became the Communist Party of France. Thus, on December 30, 1920, Ho became a founding member of the French Communist Party and the first Vietnamese Communist. According to Ruth Fischer, an ex-German Communist who knew him during those days, it was Ho's "nationalism which impressed us European Communists born and bred in a rather gray kind of abstract internationalism."

The Communist movement harnessed all of Ho's energies. Before that time he had been an ambitious young man whose life was without direction. The Russian Revolution of 1917 not only encouraged him toward his lifelong goal of Vietnamese independence; it also caused the creation of an organized international Communist movement, or Comintern, which trained and directly supported him as a potential revolutionary leader.

Ho responded with alacrity to the opportunities presented. He became an ambitious student and disciple of Communism. Soon his writings became doctrinaire, indicative of his desire to be recognized and to be moved up accordingly. His play, "The Bamboo Dragon," had only earned him acceptance in socialist circles and the occasional press review (One critic had said it was "animated by an Aristophanic verve.") But party writings like the following earned him positions of authority and a trip to Moscow as a delegate to the Fourth Comintern Congress where he met Nikolai Lenin:

After the First World War, Ho (back row, third from left) became a Moscow-trained Communist agent. In this unusual photo, some of the agents, mostly from colonial regions, hide their identity.

"Colonialism is a leech with two suckers, one of which sucks the metropolitan proletariat and the other that of the colonies. If we want to kill this monster, we must cut off both suckers at the same time. If only one is cut off, the other will continue to suck the blood of the proletariat, the animal will continue to live, and the cut-off sucker will grow again."

Under the sponsorship of the French Communist Party, he was appointed editor of the newspaper *Le Paria,* whose staff included Senegalese, Algerian and West Indian Communists. He also began speaking to large groups of Vietnamese brought to France during the First World War to work in factories and to fight, and who were awaiting repatriation. While at the Fourth Comintern he became a member of the new Southeast Asia Bureau of the Comintern. In 1923 he was sent to Moscow again, this time to organize the Peasant International and serve on its ten-man executive committee. During this trip he met Leon Trotsky. He was a delegate to the Fifth Comintern Congress in 1924, at which he argued, "The native peasants are ready to revolt. . . . It is the duty of the Internationale . . . to provide them with leaders, to show them the way to revolution." During this time, he also managed to distinguish himself as an expert on colonial peasantry problems and attended various Communist training schools in Russia.

In December of 1924 he was assigned to accompany the Russian Michael Borodin to Canton, China, as part of a political and military mission during the days the Kuomintang was accepting support from Communist countries. Ho remained three years, acting as an interpreter for Borodin and organizing the disparate groups of Vietnamese agitators that found refuge in southern China. He operated an accelerated training course that graduated twenty to thirty of these revolutionaries every two weeks. By 1927 when the Kuomintang kicked out all Communists, including Ho, he had organized two hundred cadres of four or five people each who returned to Indochina. Ho tried to winnow all but committed Communists from his graduates by indirectly revealing the names of the others to the French secret police, who would then arrest them when they returned to Indochina.

When Ho and his mission were outlawed by the Kuomintang, he fled China by way of a tortuous route through the Gobi Desert on his way to the Soviet Union, an extraordinary jour-

Nikolai Lenin's *Thesis on the National and Colonial Questions.* He told Patti that that was the turning point for him. Finally he had found someone who addressed colonialism and independence with understanding and clarity. Not long thereafter, in 1920, at a conference in Tours, he joined the French Communist Party after splitting with the Socialists. Many years of Communist Party work, worldwide, began.

Then Ho reflected aloud about how wrong he had been to give the European Communists—French, British and Russian—such loyalty. To them, Vietnam was too parochial an issue to be worthy of their time. "In all the years that followed, not one of the so-called liberal elements have come to the aid of colonials [subject people like the Vietnamese]," said Ho. Then came this surprising observation from the famous Vietnamese Communist: "I place more reliance on the United States [than the U.S.S.R.] to support Vietnam's independence."

Ho told Patti that he was aware that in the U.S. he was being called a "Moscow puppet" and an "international Communist" because he had trained in Moscow and spent so many years working for Moscow outside Vietnam. But Ho denied this, according to Patti, saying that "he was not a Communist in the American sense; he owed only his training to Moscow and, for that, he had repaid Moscow with fifteen years of party work. He had no other commitment. He considered himself a free agent. The Americans had given him more material and spiritual support than the USSR. Why should he feel indebted to Moscow?"

Finally, in the wee hours of the morning, Ho said he wanted Patti to convey a special message of "friendship and admiration" to the American people. The United States would always be remembered as a friend and ally, he said; the Vietnamese people would always be grateful for the material support given his men during the war; and he himself would never forget the inspiration of America's history as he struggled for his own country's independence.

When Patti finally reached the front door to depart, Ho put his hands on the American's shoulders, looked him squarely in the eyes, and said with emotion, "Bon voyage, please come back soon. You are always welcome."

Patti never saw him again. In October 1945 all OSS offices in Vietnam and China were closed down. Their staffs were reassigned elsewhere, Patti to a relatively minor bureaucratic responsibility in Washington, D.C. As a result, those Americans with probably the closest personal understanding of the situation in Vietnam were out of the picture. Without their input, the only perspective from which Ho's nationalist movement was evaluated was its Communist context.

Patti has no doubt Ho was being honest with him that evening. Patti's own unswerving conclusion is that Ho was a nationalist first and a Communist second. He believes that in 1945 Ho much preferred an association with the United States to help from the Soviets and the Chinese. He also believes Ho was gradually forced into close cooperation with the Soviet Union because Communist countries eventually became his only source of support, at a time when the U.S. was moving toward direct opposition to Ho because of its commitment to France and its Cold War politics.

ney that must have required weeks of walking and singular determination. In 1928 he attended the Communist Conference Against Imperialism, in Brussels. Later that year he was reported to be in Thailand, where at times he donned the saffron robes of a Buddhist monk while organizing more cadres of exiled Vietnamese. He stayed away from China and Indochina, fearful of being apprehended. "I am a professional revolutionary," he once told a Communist friend. "I am always on strict orders. My itinerary is always carefully prescribed."

On January 6, 1930, he was in Hong Kong where he secretly held the first organizational meeting of the Vietnamese Communist Party in the bleachers of a stadium during a soccer game. The action was later deemed premature because it raised Vietnamese revolutionaries' expectations too soon and unnecessarily exposed the membership to arrest. But the executive committee of the Third International had pushed him to act. "The hesitation of certain groups (Ho, in particular) concerning the immediate creation of a Communist Party are an error. . . . The most important and most urgent task for all Indochinese Communists consists in founding a revolutionary party of the proletariat."

No doubt as a result of this initiative, Ho was sentenced to death in absentia by French authorities in his home province of Nghe An. In April 1931 he was arrested by British police in Hong Kong, his whereabouts betrayed by a captured Comintern member. He received a six-month sentence for subversive activities. Luckily—and inexplicably—the British refused to extradite him to French Indochina.

Little is known about his activities during the next seven years or so. Some suggest that he married and had a daughter, who later served in the Vietnamese People's Army. If so, neither wife nor daughter remained a part of his life for long. Ho did attend a number of training schools in Moscow during this time, including a sort of graduate school for senior Communist leaders. He somehow avoided falling victim to Stalin's purge trials, a plight that befell a number of his Comintern colleagues, including foreign Communists such as himself.

In early 1938 he returned to China during the Kuomintang–Communist rapprochement period brought about by the Japanese invasion. In 1940 he was in southern China not far from Tongking, acting as the political commissar for a unit of guerrillas being trained by "Mao's most capable guerrilla expert, General Yeh Chien-ying."

In December 1940 Ho briefly returned to Vietnam for the first time in thirty years. The Japanese had knocked out some French garrisons near the town of Pac Bo in September, making it safe for Ho to meet for ten days with Vietnamese party members. The meeting was the first of a series that also included Giap and led to the formation of the Vietnam Independence League, or Viet Minh front, on May 19, 1941. Ho became its secretary general.

The purpose of the front was to endow the Communist group with the appearance of a broad-based coalition of nationalists, which would be more attractive to non-Communists. The creation of the front was perfectly timed. One month later, on June 22, 1941, to the surprise of the world, Germany invaded the Soviet Union. Within a few months the great Western nations would ally themselves with Communist Russia and, of course, China to fight Japan and the Fascist powers of Europe.

In this world context, Ho's proposed alliance of Communist and non-Communist Vietnamese nationalists—the Viet Minh front—made perfect sense. The situation also allowed Ho to ingratiate himself with the United States in particular. By the time he entered Hanoi under the Viet Minh banner in August 1945, many Vietnamese would think that his forces also represented the Western Allies. As previously noted, Bao Dai was so deceived that he abdicated in Ho's favor. It is not surprising, therefore, that by early 1942 the Viet Minh front was starting to undermine non-Communist nationalist movements by attracting their followers, even Catholics.

The Chinese were still troubled by Ho, however. In August 1942 they arrested him for reasons not entirely clear. One likely Chinese motivation for the arrest was that Ho was a known Communist. Another basic reason was that the Chinese were trying to sponsor their own Vietnamese leadership group that had Ho as its chief rival. Chinese leaders were very interested in postwar Indochina.

While Ho was incarcerated, the Chinese called a conference in Liuchou of the ten rival Vietnamese nationalist groups operating in southern China, including the Viet Minh. Under Chinese sponsorship, the Vietnam Revolutionary League, known as the Dong Minh Hoi, was formed. The

Ho Chi Minh with his chief lieutenants in fall 1945. Pham Van Dong (left), then thirty-seven, would become prime minister; Vo Nguyen Giap (right), age thirty-three, would head the army.

﹡ Some of the weapons used by Ho Chi Minh's Viet Minh were directly supplied by U.S. officials. In early March 1945, Colonel Richard Helliwell, the chief of OSS Intelligence Division in China, authorized the delivery of "six new Colt .45 automatic pistols and several thousand rounds of ammunition" for Viet Minh self-protection while rescuing American pilots downed by the Japanese. In mid-July 1945, two hundred select Viet Minh troops in training under American OSS Major Allison Thomas were issued "the latest American weapons." Other U.S. weapons were supplied indirectly. In September 1945, after the Nationalist Chinese occupation force had moved in, Ho's government used gold and silver donated by the Vietnamese population to purchase American weapons. Later, the Viet Minh were supplied American weapons and equipment captured by the Communist Chinese during the Korean war.

* Both sides were cruel during the First Indochina War. One French soldier made this horrifying account after a mission in 1952: "Along the route of retreat of the paratroops, the Viets had planted on bamboo pikes the heads of the soldiers they had killed, like so many milestones. Some of the men went berserk from it, others cried hysterically when they recognized the head of somebody they had known; others just swore softly that they'd kill every Vietnamese they'd find as soon as they got to a village." And, of course, they frequently did. One French practice in use for years was to cut off the arm of known revolutionaries. Beheading was another common French practice. As early as the turn of the century, the French dealt with villages on the basis of what was termed "collective responsibility." Regardless of the degree of involvement, the entire village population was held responsible if individual revolutionaries were given refuge. "Consequently, the chief of the village and two or three principal inhabitants are beheaded and the village itself is set on fire and razed to the ground."

Chinese wanted the Vietnamese to organize so as to create a source of intelligence about Japanese goings-on in Indochina. The Viet Minh, who had the only established intelligence network there, were not disposed to cooperate, however. Ho was released to encourage them to do so. The Viet Minh began receiving NC$100,000 per month for their work; the intelligence began to flow. At almost the same time, Ho and the Viet Minh started wooing American officers in China, sharing intelligence information with them and rescuing their pilots.

During this period Ho changed his name from Nguyen Ai-Quoc to Ho Chi Minh to complicate attempts to learn his past, thus obscuring the fact of Communist control of the Viet Minh. For a number of years, Ho would not admit his dual identities to any Westerner.

By the time the second Dong Minh Hoi conference convened in Liuchou on March 25, 1944, the Viet Minh had clearly emerged as the most capable and organized of the nationalist rivals operating out of China. There were much larger groups in Vietnam itself, but they did not seem as organized or as ready to act during the critical months ahead; nor were they as lucky.

The Chinese affirmed Viet Minh preeminence among the Dong Minh Hoi group by granting Ho the portfolio of what was "pompously christened the 'Provisional Republican Government of Viet-Nam,'" in part because Ho was the only one of the leaders willing to accept the risks of re-entering Vietnam to organize a network to fight the Japanese. Apparently because of Chiang's conversations with Roosevelt, the Chinese knew they would be occupying Vietnam after the war and would, if necessary, be in a position to dispose easily of Ho and his Viet Minh.

In December 1944 Ho moved his headquarters from China into a border province in northern Vietnam. On December 22 he and Giap formed the "Armed Propaganda Brigade for the Liberation of Vietnam" composed of thirty-four men, the forerunner of the Vietnamese People's Army. A few days later, on Christmas Eve, the Viet Minh staged their first organized attack against the French, massacring the soldiers of two small garrisons.

Ho finally had a small power base in Vietnam, which in spite of — perhaps because of — setbacks at the conference table, would allow him to gain widespread popular support and eventually overwhelm the French.

Contrary to what Admiral d'Argenlieu told his troops, Vietnam was not a good place to reestablish French greatness. Initial victories augured well, but these successes were the product of overwhelming French force, not wise administration. Unlike the British, the French led themselves to believe they could re-create the past.

British colonial policy changed dramatically when the British Labour Party defeated the Conservatives. Attlee replaced Churchill as prime minister. Even before the war, Attlee argued for independence for India, the greatest of all English colonies.

Like their American counterparts, most English voters in 1945 were more interested in problems at home than international imbroglios. In *Farewell the Trumpets,* James Morris writes, "The people wanted only to live quietly and comfortably, and disillusioned as they had been by the torments of slum and unemployment in the 1930s, they saw in the aftermath of war the chance to make a fresh start—not in the distant fields of Empire, but in their own familiar island. They would not be gulled again by illusions of splendour."

French voters might have forced the same philosophical turn, but their country lacked the political continuity and stability to allow such expression to emerge and become dominant. The Vichy French government of the war years was dissolved because of German collaboration. France struggled to restore internal political stability. There were fifteen different French administrations between 1945 and 1954. Only a few lasted more than a year. In such an environment, the raw political power of various business interests, as represented by officials like d'Argenlieu, dominated colonial policy.

Great Britain quit India suddenly. In June 1947 Mountbatten, the newly appointed viceroy of India, announced that British sovereignty would end on August 15. After staying two hundred and fifty years, the British gave seventy-three days' notice that they would leave. Independence for other British colonies would follow shortly. Displaying remarkable political prescience, British leaders avoided the terrible problems the French would endure in Indochina.

Thus, Communist revolutionaries in former British colonies were denied the high ground, the moral imperative the French handed Ho by their own duplicitous behavior. Furthermore, because the British had always relied heavily on

Ho and Giap's close call...

On October 7, 1947, Ho Chi Minh and Vo Nguyen Giap were almost captured by French paratroopers. Intelligence reports had given the French the exact locations of Ho's headquarters; 1,137 paratroopers were dropped in directly over the site. The exercise was part of "Operation Lea," a deliberate attempt to locate and capture top Viet Minh leaders. The daring raid was executed with such speed and surprise that Ho's letters were left on his working table in the jungle, awaiting his signature. Though one Viet Minh minister was captured, Ho and Giap escaped.

After the 1954 Geneva armistice, Ho and Giap told their version of this war story to General de Beaufort, then president of the French delegation to the International Control Commission and later Charles de Gaulle's special chief of staff. The two Vietnamese leaders said they jumped into a small preplanned hiding hole and covered it with branches. And there they remained, catatonic, their backs pressed together, while the French troops passed back and forth on the jungle floor, tapping the ground, searching for their hiding place. Given their training, commitment, leadership qualities and standing within the revolutionary movement, Ho and Giap were probably irreplaceable at that time. How history might have been changed if the French had been persistent and lucky enough to discover them is interesting to speculate.

A helicopter carrying Bao Dai flies over a broad Saigon boulevard, bringing him back to Vietnam after two and one-half years of self-imposed exile.

At ceremonies befitting a great occasion, the French installed Bao Dai as head of the new State of Vietnam. But the notion that it was a Vietnamese-run government was a fiction.

local populations to administer their colonies, a solid infrastructure was in place in each when they pulled out. For the most part, self-government was achieved by evolution not revolution. Though not painless, with the local infrastruture in place it basically involved putting in new leaders at the top in positions previously held by British viceroys and governors. Former British colonial subjects were inclined to emulate British democratic traditions in filling these positions.

An entirely different set of circumstances faced Vietnamese who yearned for independence but rejected Communism. Even after the Second World War, the French incorporated them into government only in a superficial way. "The Vietnamese were given offices but no authority, titles but no power, and a government allowed to govern only in the narrow spheres where its actions did not conflict with established colonial interest and did not clash with the continued exercise of French control."

The French merely manipulated non-Communists such as Bao Dai to create the impression that their recolonizing efforts were an anti-Communist crusade. The tragedy is that the French succeeded in creating this impression, at least in the United States. Had Communism been their chief concern, the French would have promised independence to the Vietnamese and groomed non-Communist Vietnamese leaders as their own replacements. Had they done so, Ho's Communist movement would have been drawn away from Ho. During the late forties, non-Communists composed the vast majority of Viet Minh membership, though Communists did control its leadership.

Bao Dai became the unwitting instrument of the French anti-Communist ruse after rejecting French entreaties for his return from self-imposed exile for two and a half years. Reflecting the popular mood, he held out for assurances of independence. But he finally relented without receiving them, no doubt hopeful that American pressure might eventually force France to reverse itself, and indeed the United States might have been in a position to do so because of its heavy aid to France (largely through the Marshall Plan) at the time. Bao Dai might also have been counting on U.S. support of a government headed by himself. Former American ambassador to France William C. Bullitt had hinted at such support in a *Life* magazine article in

December 1947.

So, in April 1949 Bao Dai returned to Vietnam from Hong Kong to head what came to be called the State of Vietnam, composed of Cochinchina, Annam and Tongking. But few Vietnamese were fooled into thinking that independence was forthcoming. Diem, for example, refused an offer by Bao Dai to be his first prime minister. Those who continued to have faith in the good intentions of France were finally disabused of their optimism in June 1952 when the French forced the appointment of Nguyen Van Tan as prime minister. He was "the only prominent Vietnamese who was known as being 'entirely devoted to the French.'"

Ho was so emboldened by the weak alternative to his movement that had evolved during the postwar years that in February 1951 he dissolved the Viet Minh front. He saw no reason for prolonging pretenses. He openly established the Communist Party as the Workers Party, or Lao Dong, and began purging non-Communists from leadership positions. Though Westerners in particular continued to use the Viet Minh name to describe Ho's organization, it no longer existed.

What happened is clear. By 1951 the distinction between Communist and non-Communist nationalists had ceased to be of significance to disillusioned Vietnamese. Only one consideration mattered: Who was willing to fight the French? The Communists seemed the only independence leaders eager to do so; certainly they were the most able to do so. Consequently, the Communists attracted soldiers by the thousands and sympathizers by the millions. The French only enlarged the ranks of their adversary each time they killed a Viet Minh or Communist soldier.

By promoting Bao Dai as a leader, France hoped to buttress up a Vietnamese rival to Ho Chi Minh.

To popularize the idea that Bao Dai's government was independent, the French made much of training Vietnamese for government positions.

In the early days of the Viet Minh front, Ho assigned Vo Nguyen Giap the task of building an army. Giap, a former history professor, had been a founding member of the Vietnamese Communist Party in 1930. His wife died in a French prison in 1943—of maltreatment, he alleged; of sickness, said the French. Giap had a reputation for being even more doctrinaire and uncompromising than Ho. He was also ruthlessly pragmatic. Giap organized the death squads that wiped out hundreds of nationalist rivals in 1945-1946. In Cochinchina his agents sometimes tied them together in bundles and threw them into the Mekong River, where one by one they drowned, pulling the others to the bottom. They called this horrifying murder technique "crab fishing."

Giap could be as impetuous as he was ruthless. The first attack he commanded against the French, the surprise massacre of two small French garrisons on Christmas Eve, 1944, went far beyond Ho's guidelines. Ho intended that the group's mission be one of "political action" rather than "military force, because it is an instrument of political propaganda." Though Giap's fiery temperament would in later years nearly cost him his command as well as the lives of thousands of his troops, no one could ever accuse him of being reluctant to fight the French.

Giap was a brilliant as well as a determined commander, capable of learning from his mistakes. He was a gifted organizer too. Operating out of the mountainous jungle sanctuaries of northern Vietnam, he transformed his army into battalions, then regiments, and finally into ten-thousand-man divisions.

He allowed his commanders great flexibility. His standard operating technique was to assign them an objective and allow them to use their own imagination to carry it out. But they lived or died by their wits; they could not expect help.

This independence from any centralized command became the basic strength of the Viet Minh because it was ideally suited to the physical conditions of the country and the slow-reacting nature of the Western adversary; its early success and subsequent development was due in part to Giap's initial lack of heavy equipment and armor. There were no large units of artillery, tanks and aircraft whose positioning in battle required coordination with units of infantry. For years Giap essentially had only infantry at his disposal.

In 1944 Vo Nguyen Giap, a former history teacher, personally organized the first small contingent of soldiers that grew into a formidable multidivision army.

After Mao Tse-tung's Communist forces defeated those of Chiang in 1949, Giap was assisted by Chinese advisers. How many is not clear. But prior to that time, the Viet Minh army was apparently the creation solely of this history professor's readings, and his education by trial and error.

Perhaps the most obvious lesson Giap learned from the Chinese was inspired by Mao's long years of struggle. His description of his grand strategy as elaborated before the political commissars of his 316th Infantry Division in late 1950 reads like a chapter from Mao and was remarkably prophetic:

"The enemy will pass slowly from the offensive to the defensive. The blitzkrieg will transform itself into a war of long duration. Thus, the enemy will be caught in a dilemma: he has to drag out the war in order to win it and does not possess, on the other hand, the psychological and political means to fight a long drawn-out war."

He stated further:

"Our strategy early in the course of the third stage is that of a general counter-offensive. We shall attack without cease until final victory,

✳ As the utter futility of the First Indochina War became increasingly apparent, the French citizenry grew as disenchanted with it as the American public would in the following decade. Particularly aggressive in its opposition was the French Communist Party, for obvious reasons. Its members' reaction was so violent, in fact, that one French government assemblyman found it necessary to complain about "hospital trains with wounded from the Indochina war being stoned by French Communists as they stopped in the stations to unload men in their home towns."

Giap's army first supplied itself by capturing French equipment, such as these artillery pieces that Communist soldiers are firing at French positions.

until we have swept the enemy forces from Indochina. During the first and second stage, we have gnawed away at the enemy forces; now we must destroy them. . . .

"We shall go on to the general counter-offensive when the following conditions will have been fulfilled: (1) superiority of our forces over those of the enemy; (2) the international situation is in our favor; (3) the military situation is in our favor. We will have to receive aid from abroad in order to be able to carry out the counter-offensive."

Though, at first, Giap had grossly inferior firepower and no airpower at his disposal, he had four significant advantages over French commanders: (1) the political commitment of his troops, bordering at times on fanaticism; (2) sanctuary in the jungles and mountains of Vietnam and, after 1949, in China; (3) mobility — the heavy, mechanized equipment around which the French army was built actually slowed its units down; and (4) intelligence — the local population reported the movements of even small French units.

To enhance his army's mobility and reduce the effectiveness of French airpower, Giap ordered

While fighting the French, Vietnamese Communists perfected ambush tactics.

The Communists' greatest and most plentiful resource was people, who, working as porters by the thousands, obviated the usual need for trucks to supply troops.

the use of sophisticated though simple camouflage techniques. Each regular Viet Minh soldier usually wore a large wire-mesh disk over his helmet and another on this back while on the march. As units passed through the countryside, a soldier was responsible for filling the wire mesh of the person in front of him with foliage matching the terrain through which they were passing. Thus, the Viet Minh were effectively concealed whether the vegetation was that of dark green forests, light green grasslands or marshy brown rice fields ready for harvest.

"'I just know the little bastards are somewhere around here,' was the standard complaint of the French reconnaissance pilots, 'But go and find them in that mess.'"

The French were unable to cut Viet Minh supply lines for such reasons. For the most part, Giap supplied his army with antlike chains of porters using narrow paths. Though in the final years of the First Indochina War Giap did have a large number of trucks at his disposal, early on he had but a handful captured from the French and Japanese and converted to run on coal or rice alcohol.

In November 1952, however, a French unit

✳ Successive French and American administrations did such an effective job presenting the First Indochina War as part of a worldwide, anti-Communist crusade led by the United States, many French soldiers forgot that their government's principal war aim was reasserting colonial control. They were convinced their fight was purely an anti-Communist effort. In 1953 one French colonel observed, "We're getting to the point of Rumania under Bismarck, when Bismarck said: 'To be Rumanian is not a nationality. It is a profession.'"

The French made valiant efforts to train Vietnamese loyal to them into an effective fighting force.

(Top) The first black soldiers to fight and die in Vietnam were not American, but those from French colonies. (Center) French soldiers holding a defensive position. (Bottom) A French adviser instructing, just as his American counterparts who followed would do.

operating deep in Viet Minh territory discovered the existence of Russian trucks supplied to Giap's forces. Two heavy-duty, 2½-ton Molotovas were found concealed about five hundred yards off a small road. Nearby was a stockpile of Russian-made rifles, machine guns, light mortars, medium mortars and heavy 120mm mortars, bazookas and recoilless cannons. The find was evidence that the Soviet Union was now backing Ho in a major way. By the end of the First Indochina War in mid-1954, the Russians had supplied eight hundred Molotovas.

The Korean war cease-fire on July 17, 1953, was a boon for the Vietnamese Communists. In a three-party deal, the Russians agreed to pay the Chinese to supply the Vietnamese with American equipment captured during that war. The Chinese as well as the Russians also supplied equipment of their own manufacture. In addition, the Chinese provided anti-aircraft specialists as advisers to the Vietnamese.

Predictably, Giap incorporated the tactics of his allies. The first human wave attack by Viet Minh soldiers occurred on January 16, 1951, during the first of three major battles that Giap thought would lead to the recapture of Hanoi. Human wave assaults in which the enemy tries to overwhelm defenders by sheer numbers without regard to its own casualties characterized North Korean and Chinese tactics during the Korean war.

The French emerged victorious in all three of these battles and confidence in Giap as commander was temporarily shaken. Some wanted him removed. However, at Dien Bien Phu, Giap's boldness would end the war.

French strategy developed in two stages, the second evolving because of the failure of the first. During the first stage, French commanders ordered the construction of hundreds of forts and pillboxes throughout northern Vietnam in the zones of greatest Viet Minh influence. During the second, the French attempted to match Viet Minh mobility with paratroop and armor units. The French used helicopters only for rescue operations.

The first stage was reminscent of pre–Second World War French military planning. In northern France their engineers built the Maginot Line. In northern Vietnam they built the de Lattre Line. As evidence of French authority, real or symbolic, the de Lattre Line was ineffective.

Its real impact was to tie down eighty thousand French troops and huge stockpiles of equipment. The Viet Minh maneuvered around these fortifications like water through rocks.

Before it was halted, the de Lattre Line grew to include nine hundred forts and twenty-two hundred pillboxes. Enormous effort was involved in their construction. Fifty-one million cubic yards of concrete were poured into these twenty-two hundred small encapsulated bunkers which customarily housed nine men and a sergeant. The job of the occupants was to peer through machine-gun slots, waiting to be attacked. The thinking, apparently, was that the Viet Minh, then without heavy weaponry, could not long endure the suicide assaults necessary to knock them out. The French were attempting to

Hundreds of pillboxes such as this one comprised the de Lattre Line, as ineffective in stopping the enemy as the Maginot Line in France was.

break Viet Minh resolve; French commanders throught they could win a war of attrition.

In defense of French military planners, any hope they might have had of developing an enlightened military strategy was dimmed by fatuous political thinking. Political leaders failed to create conditions in which they could win. Winning a war against adequately armed indigenous forces with broad-based popular support and the advantage of sanctuary may be impossible for a foreign army. The problem had never been faced before. During the 1800s, the French armies overwhelmed the Vietnamese because they had the advantage of Western technology and weaponry. Now the French faced a foe with weapons of equal sophistication.

The example of the U.S. in Korea could be of

The Communists fought the French on fairly equal terms because of military supplies from China and the Soviet Union. A staple weapon was the land mine. With little training, anyone who could plant rice could mine roads and trails, tying down thousands of highly trained French soldiers for clearing duties.

little help to the French. Korea covered only 85,000 square miles; Vietnam, 285,000. Korea has vast treeless regions, ideal for the armored units and air forces so characteristic of Western armies. By contrast, eighty-six percent of Vietnam is covered by dense ground vegetation; forty-seven percent of the country is covered with jungle. Most importantly, the non-Communist South Koreans had their own respected leader in Syngman Rhee, their own government, their own future. They had reason and means to fight the Communists.

Another factor that complicated French efforts was the huge number of villages in Vietnam. There were seven thousand in the Red River Delta alone. The French became preoccupied with guarding all the villages and the roads

Patrolling was difficult, even in farming areas, because much of the land was flooded during parts of the year. Dikes dictated the line of march, making soldiers more vulnerable. The French had hardly any helicopters to facilitate troop movement.

throughout the country. General Henri Navarre, one of the French force commanders in chief during the war, estimated that 100,000 of the 190,000 soldiers of the Expeditionary Corps were tied down in static defense duties. Historians Jean Lacouture and Philippe Devillers say the same was true of the Vietnamese conscripted to fight for the French—"of the 500,000 soldiers of which the French disposed after the build-up of the Vietnamese National Army in 1953, no less than 350,000 were engaged in 'static duties.'" As a result, Giap had a larger actual fighting force than that of France in late 1953.

The French might have won even so had they earlier undermined the popular support for Ho. But this would only have been possible had they granted Vietnam true independence and given

(Below) Many Vietnamese fought for the French—a total of 18,714 of them died. (Opposite top) A French army chaplain. (Opposite bottom) France fought their Indochina war without a draft, relying on their professional soldiers and colonial troops; 75,867 French Union force soldiers were killed during the period 1946 through 1954.

the country a non-Communist government that was legitimate. Consequently, it made little difference how many Vietnamese they conscripted to fight for them. Numbers were no substitute for social reform long past due. Of the many errors the French made during the First Indochina War, the most basic was not giving the Vietnamese any reason to support them.

On November 20, 1953, 1,827 French paratroopers began dropping into a remote mountain valley two hundred and twenty miles behind enemy lines, near the village of Dien Bien Phu, only about fifteen miles from Laos. Though eleven French soldiers were killed that first day, the French quickly gained control of the valley. They then established a defense perimeter and began sending patrols into the surrounding mountains. Within a couple of months the French force size increased to about fifteen thousand, almost all brought in by aircraft to two restored landing strips in the seventy-five-square-mile valley. The location had been a small French base before the Second World War.

The mission of these soldiers slowly evolved. Initially Dien Bien Phu was to be a "mooring

✳ The eminent historian William Manchester, a specialist on twentieth-century U.S. history, makes this appraisal of the significance of the battle of Dien Bien Phu: He described it as "a classic engagement which would alter world history and affect the United States more profoundly than Shiloh or the Argonne."

point" for troops intercepting enemy supply lines. Part of Giap's army had invaded Laos, adding to French worries by destabilizing that part of Indochina. Dien Bien Phu was along the supply route to those Communist troops. It was also an opium-producing and tax-collection region that produced revenues for the Communists.

The original goal of the French at Dien Bien

(Top) The siege of Dien Bien Phu lasted fifty-six days, during which time about 5,000 French force troops died. (Right) Giap's army slowly tightened the noose around the French strongpoints, preventing patrols after the first few weeks.

Phu was foreclosed. Patrols increasingly had difficulty getting beyond the perimeter of the valley. Giap had reacted to the French incursion by sending more troops into the surrounding mountains.

Navarre perceived an opportunity in this deteriorating situation. He dramatically increased the force size in the valley, hoping to lure Giap into a major battle. The Communists invariably avoided set-piece battles. Navarre thought Dien Bien Phu might become a meat-grinder for Giap's army.

The idea to lure Giap into battle at Dien Bien Phu was General Henri Navarre's.

The fifteen-thousand-man French force was a motley group of many nations, most belonging to the French Union, an affiliation of French-

controlled territories around the world. The force included Frenchmen, Vietnamese, Laotians, Senegalese, Moroccans, Algerians, Tunisians, Tai mountaineer tribesmen, Meo tribesmen, and large units of the Foreign Legion composed mostly of Germans but also Italians, Spaniards, Poles, Yugoslavs and other Eastern Europeans. Some of the Asians had their families with them. Only about thirty percent of the force was French, though almost all the officers were.

In a sense, the assumptions that governed French efforts to fight the Vietnamese Communists were the same as those which dominated Doumer's thinking while building roads and bridges—what was good for France was good for its colonial subjects. It seems not to have occurred to the French that Algerian and Moroccan soldiers, for example, might not want to squelch the Vietnamese independence move-

The French force at Dien Bien Phu included soldiers of more than fifteen nationalities (who composed colonial or Foreign Legion units) and of ethnic groups of the region, such as these Tai mountaineer tribesmen on their way to reinforce the besieged garrison.

Americans at Dien Bien Phu...

A small group of Americans was directly involved in the battle of Dien Bien Phu. One of them was Major Vaughn of the U.S. Army, who, on the basis of American experience in Korea, advised the French to use "Quad-50" machine guns to counter the "human wave" assaults of the Communists. Quad-50s were four .50-caliber machine guns mounted together, and they were devastating.

The Americans most notably involved were the pilots of the Taiwan-based Civil Air Transport Company. Virtually all were civilians, paid about $2,000 per month, though historian Bernard Fall says a few were American military personnel on active duty flying "to familiarize themselves with the area in case of American air intervention on behalf of the French."

This American contingent piloted twenty-four of the twenty-nine C-119 Flying Boxcars that kept the garrison alive when artillery fire closed its runways. Not anticipating the adversity they would face, the French had not contracted with the Civil Air Transport Company to fly in combat conditions. Nevertheless, the crews kept flying during all the weeks of the siege, except for one brief period when the missions had become so dangerous and so many aircraft were being shot down that both the American civilians and the French military crews refused to fly. Within about a day the Americans were back in the air, however, because of pleas from the garrison commander; the French pilots followed suit, but later stopped again. The Americans kept flying to the bitter end, their missions becoming ever more dangerous as they were forced lower and lower, to try to hit the ever-shrinking parachute drop zones. Fall, himself a former French soldier and, if anything, prone to laud the valor of his former

ment when, at the same time, independence movements were developing in their own countries. Many of these colonial troops would, in fact, later fight the French on their home ground. Ironically, a C-46 transport that brought some of the Moroccans into Dien Bien Phu had earlier been used to deport the sultan of Morocco because of his nationalist activities.

The Dien Bien Phu contingent also included two units from the Medical Field Battalion, an antiseptic name for an interesting outfit composed of prostitutes. Some were Vietnamese but most were from Qulad-Nail tribe of Algeria. Though directly sponsored and organized by the French military, they were paid by the soldiers themselves. They worked throughout the war zone. The dangers of Dien Bien Phu presented no reason for exception. Some of their number had had more dangerous duty. The morale officer of one French unit led two Qulad-Nail volunteers on a thirty-mile trek through enemy lines to Tsinh-Ho so as to lift the spirits of that besieged outpost. The Medical Field Battalion stayed in operation until the last day of Dien Bien Phu.

The commander of the diverse group stationed at the base at Dien Bien Phu was Colonel Christian Marie Ferdinand de la Croix de Castris, a French aristocrat of long and distinguished lineage whose family had fought for France since the Crusades. His forebears included four royal lieutenant governors, a field marshal, an admiral and nine generals, one of whom served under Lafayette in America.

De Castris, whom Fall described as having the profile of a Roman emperor, was reportedly irresistible to women. The word around Dien Bien Phu was that he had named most of the base's strongpoints for his mistresses—Claudine, Marcelle, Huguette, Françoise, Ann-Marie, Gabrielle, Dominique, Béatrice, Eliane and Isabelle. At Dien Bien Phu, at least, each was a self-contained defense perimeter, ringed with artillery and wire. Each was laid out so as to fight the enemy independently, but the safety of the overall base depended on the viability of all and their ability to coordinate their activities. There were five primary strongpoints.

Before the fighting began, the camp was described by many as looking like the site of a Boy Scout jamboree, with pup tents everywhere, washed clothing hung out to dry and, at night, hundreds of friendly little fires warming the food as well as the confident spirits of the troops. Evidence in the flesh of the high morale was Lieutenant Colonel Pierre Langlais, commander of the paratroopers in the valley, who made his rounds astride a snow-white pony.

The base became a point of great interest to all kinds of VIPs who generally had nothing but good things to say about preparations there. Navarre later wrote that "not a single civilian or military authoritative person, including French or foreign ministers, French service chiefs, or American generals . . . ever, to my knowledge, admitted any doubts before the attack or [sic] the ability of Dien Bien Phu to resist."

Visitors had good things to say about de Castris too, who had inherited from his family a highly refined sense of hospitality on the battlefield as well as a ready disposition for the martial arts. VIPs were met at the landing strip by a crack honor guard of Moroccan riflemen whose white rifle webbing matched their imposing turbans. De Castris then personally jeeped them out to one of the outlying strongpoints, usually that of the Legionnaires, who took special pride in camp appearance to the point of painting artillery emplacements. A lunch in de Castris's command mess followed, served of course on a gleaming table service impeccably arranged. Following a four-star meal of French cuisine, the visitors settled down to a briefing called "Dien Bien Phu at War."

Navarre himself did have reservations, though it was he who had ordered the men into the valley in the first place. One concern was whether the base could maintain superior firepower if the Communists chose to fight. The French had forfeited the commanding heights of the surrounding mountains to the enemy. His other concern was about whether the landing strips could be kept open. The base population had reached that of a small city.

Regarding the first concern, the artillery commander, Colonel Charles Piroth, a one-armed extrovert famous for his good humor, had a stock answer:

"Firstly, the Viet Minh won't succeed in getting their artillery through to here. Secondly, if they do get here, we'll smash them."

There the issue always died. The twenty 105mm howitzers, eight 75mm recoilless rifles and company of heavy mortars were indeed impressive. Furthermore, the artillery corps had been the proudest unit of the French army since

compatriots, says the American civilians consistently took greater risks than did the French crews supplying their own troops.

Some of the American contract pilots were killed, of course. Undoubtably the most colorful was James McGovern, a monster of a man in size nicknamed "Earthquake" after a character in *Li'l Abner*. His C-119 pilot's seat was modified so he could fit into it. He had achieved fame among the pilots in the China Theater during the Second World War while flying as an army air corps captain. The day before the garrison fell, McGovern flew in over Dien Bien Phu with a load of ammunition. Antiaircraft fire hit his plane. McGovern reacted calmly, as if the event were part of a day's work. He likely could have gotten out, suggests Bernard Fall, but remained at the controls to avoid French positions. "I'm riding her in," he was heard to say. The Boxcar exploded with a roar into the mountains on top of the Viet Minh. It was his forty-fifth mission.

The French commander at Dien Bien Phu was Colonel Christian de Castris.

Atomic Bombs and Dien Bien Phu...

Using A-bombs at Dien Bien Phu!!? They'd "be about as useful as cross-bows" there, wrote Richard Rovere in his "Letter from Washington" column of April 8, 1954. And about as devastating to French forces as to Giap's army, one would think. But historian Bernard Fall insisted, despite all claims to the contrary and the disbelief of his colleagues, that A-bomb use had been an active option of American military planners. Since Fall's sources were primarily French leaders in power during the Dien Bien Phu disaster, people whose credibility was nil, he was ignored. But in 1978, a brief statement by Richard Nixon in his *Memoirs* supported Fall's contention. Nixon said the U.S. considered using several tactical nuclear weapons. However, not until thirty years after the fact was it revealed how seriously A-bomb use had been advanced by various military agencies. U.S. documents declassified in early 1984 had discussed this option in detail.

On March 25, 1954, army and air force planners decided that nuclear weapons could effectively relieve pressure on the French garrison. They visualized several good drop zones: rear staging areas, the mountains in which Giap's troops were massed, and an area the French might deliberately evacuate to lure the unsuspecting Communists.

On April 8 the Plans section of Army Operations, whose brainstorm this primarily was, even proposed a delivery plan. Aircraft from navy carriers operating in the Gulf of Tonkin would drop them during daylight hours. One to six thirty-one-kiloton weapons would be used, each about three times the power of that used on Hiroshima. The group had no doubt their plan was technically and militarily feasible. Furthermore, they foresaw profound political advantages: "If the act occurred before

the time of Napoleon. Airpower also figured into the equation, though the French had only about one hundred planes in all Indochina. Navarre had not included air force commanders in the Dien Bien Phu preplanning.

As for any debate about keeping the landing strips open, the presumed supremecy of firepower carried the argument. One point overlooked, however, was that in selecting Dien Bien Phu as the site to draw the enemy out for a major battle, the French had extended their supply lines two hundred miles beyond that of any of their previous operations. It was also at the end of the range of their combat aircraft.

Giap accepted the French challenge to fight at Dien Bien Phu. Indeed, he saw the opportunity to duplicate on a huge scale the tactics his smaller units found so successful against French pillboxes and forts. He would concentrate his forces to achieve overwhelming superiority, and only then attack.

First he deployed soldiers to the surrounding mountains to prevent the French from taking any high ground. By mid-December he had blocked off all land routes by which the French force might escape. But even more significant was the huge road construction project Giap directed. Regarding that effort, he later wrote that "hundreds of thousands of dan cong [civilian coolies], women as well as men, surmounted perils and difficulties and spent more than three million work days in the service of the front, in an indescribable enthusiasm." A narrow meandering mountain road that stretched five hundred miles from the Chinese border to the mountains overlooking the valley was transformed. Dozens of bridges were buttressed to support the Molotovas and curves were widened to accommodate artillery pieces. The last fifty miles were so overgrown, the road had to be hacked out of the jungle.

Within three months the entire job was done. Night and day the eight hundred Soviet-supplied trucks carried their loads. And along the sides thousands of porters carried supplies, ranging from ammunition to food. Some had bicycles modified to be pushed and to carry large loads. "Everything for the Front, Everything for Victory," was their slogan. Everywhere in Communist territory it appeared on signs extolling their efforts and urging them on.

This extraordinary effort was no secret to the

French. They tried to stop it with airpower. But they grossly overestimated their capabilities. They only had seventy-five fighters, fighter-bombers and bombers ready for action at any one time along the road. And to make their bombing runs more difficult, Giap's soldiers tied treetops together along many stretches, creating a natural camouflage canopy.

The Museum of the Revolution in Hanoi presents a film to visitors about the battle of Dien Bien Phu. One sequence shot by an unknown photographer is taken from Communist positions directly overlooking Claudine and Huguette. Outlined by green fields, the huge dusty base is as obvious as a cutout on construction paper. Artillery pieces sparkle in the sun.

Suddenly, the cameraman zooms in on a jeep traveling between the two camps. The time is 5 P.M. on March 13, 1954. The earth around the jeep and all over the two camps violently errupts, exploding torrents of dirt, smoke and debris skyward. Giap had gotten his artillery into the mountains surrounding the valley. He had also marshaled fifty thousand troops. The battle had begun.

Historian Bernard Fall in *Hell in a Very Small Place,* his account of the battle, writes that Giap had, in fact, managed to bring in forty-eight 105mm howitzers, forty-eight 75mm pack howitzers, forty-eight heavy 120mm mortars, about fifty 75mm recoilless rifles and at least thirty-six heavy flak guns. "In all," he concludes, "the Communists possessed at least 200 guns above the 57mm caliber. On the French side, the maximum number of such guns ever available amounted to sixty and dropped to an average of less than forty within a week after the battle began."

In other words, the firepower equation was the opposite of what Piroth had complacently anticipated. The Communists had a four-to-one superiority in heavy weapons and about the same superiority in men. And while Piroth's artillery pieces were clearly visible and virtually unprotected, those of the Communists were dug into the sides of the mountains and further concealed by jungle forests. Since only a direct hit would knock them out and they were extremely difficult to spot, French aircraft were rendered virtually useless against the enemy weapons.

French planning based on the presumed supe-

the Geneva Conference, that conference might never be held." The French would not be forced to negotiate, in other words. These planners imagined the A-bombs "turning the entire course of events in Indochina to the advantage of the U.S. and the free world."

The only problem they envisioned was that this dramatic U.S. action might provoke Chinese and Russian intervention. They allayed these fears by proposing that French markings be painted on the U.S. delivery planes.

The chief of Operations Planning approved his officers' proposal and began circulating it through other Army Operations divisions. But almost everyone else deemed the idea preposterous. Intelligence said it wouldn't work because Giap's men were too dispersed and because the mountains and jungle afforded too much protection. Psychological Warfare attacked it from a broader perspective: It would weaken existing security agreements because the allies had not been consulted, and it would alienate other Asian nations such as India and Burma. Air Force Intelligence also got in on the critical reaction: It "may involve the serious risk of initiating allout war," its analysts concluded.

General Matthew Ridgway, the army chief of staff, and Major General James Gavin, his operations chief, concurred with the objections. They squelched the idea. In fact, they opposed American involvement of any kind.

The A-bomb idea may have remained an active option in the mind of Secretary of State John Foster Dulles for a short time longer. Fall implies that Dulles thought the U.S. could avoid direct intervention by giving the atomic bombs to France to drop themselves. He supposedly broached the idea on April 14 to French Foreign Minister Georges Bidault, whose reaction was immediate and negative: Bidault feared the weapons would wipe out the French garrison along with the Viet Minh, says Fall.

riority of French firepower was doomed. The French had not supplied themselves with timber to fortify their artillery emplacements or even to protect individual soldiers. Though some wood bracing was flown in, only enough was available for de Castris's command post and the field hospital.

On March 13, the very first day of fighting, the runways were forced to close. The Communists did allow ambulance planes and helicopters to land, until the French were seen transporting healthy, downed pilots.

On March 14, Béatrice was overrun. On March 15, Colonel Piroth, who had been roaming around the camp apologizing to soldier and officer alike, lay down on his bunk, pulled the pin from a grenade with his teeth and, with his only hand,

Monsoon rains filled the French trenches during the siege; sometimes wounded had to be propped up to keep them from drowning.

placed it on his chest, thus killing himself. "I am completely dishonored," he had told Lieutenant Colonel Transcart, commander of the northern sector. "I have guaranteed de Castris that the enemy artillery couldn't touch us—but now we are going to lose the battle. I'm leaving."

On March 15, Gabrielle fell. On March 17, Legionnaires began deserting Huguette for the relative safety of the banks of a small stream inside the base. By the end of the battle there were "at least 3,000 to 4,000" such deserters, nicknamed the "Rats of Nam Yum." Soldiers still fighting sometimes had to beg them for supplies.

On about March 20, Lieutenant Colonel Keller, de Castris's chief of staff, had a nervous breakdown. A few days later he was evacuated on an ambulance plane. On March 24, Langlais actually forced de Castris to relinquish control. The senior officer thus became Langlais's subordinate who, in Langlais's words, "transmitted our messages," nothing more.

Thousands fought bravely for the French cause, however. They held out until May 7, 1954, fighting against enormous odds in wretched conditions. Giap had amassed 47,500 combat solders and 31,500 logistical support personnel in the mountains—forty percent of his entire army. The French had about 7,000 combat troops, the rest being support personnel who for some inexplicable reason were never made part of the fight in spite of the dire circumstances; altogether this force constituted only five percent of the total French army in Vietnam. At first Giap ordered suicide assaults against them. Finally, he settled in for siege warfare, digging trenches in ever-tightening circles around the last French strongholds. His troops even dug a deep tunnel under one, planted tons of explosives, and blew up its last handful of courageous defenders.

The monsoon rains began March 29. Trenches on both sides began filling up. Wounded soldiers had to be propped up to keep them from drowning. The dead simply sank to the bottom. Rotting corpses were strewn all over the battlefield. About 5,000 French troops would eventually die in the fighting; the enemy suffered an estimated 23,000 casualties, an unknown number of whom were killed, says Bernard Fall. The French managed to bury most of their own while under fire. So many were interred that the graveyard eventually encroached upon

Artillery commander Charles Piroth committed suicide.

Lieutenant Colonel Pierre Langlais led a putsch against de Castris.

Major Marcel Biegeard survived the battle and his captivity to become a member of the Chamber of Deputies.

The French used Communist soldiers captured during the siege to retrieve misdropped supplies that fell into the no-man's-land.

the underground hospital. Huge maggots began appearing in the wounds of horrified patients.

Resupply was a nightmare of a different kind. French commanders anticipated a siege of only about four days; it lasted fifty-six. During the first assault, which occurred on March 13 and 14, the French consumed one-fourth of their entire stockpile of 105mm artillery shells. Replenishments arrived by parachute drop, most from planes piloted by American contract pilots, but from the second day on the French were forced to economize on their ammunition. A large portion of the drops fell into enemy hands because monsoon weather and heavy anti-aircraft fire—as intense as over Germany during the war, some said—made it difficult to position the drops accurately. Two B-26s were shot down from ten thousand feet, so accurate the flak became. The flak guns were radar-controlled and the Vietnamese gunners were assisted by Chinese specialists.

Thousands of tons—mostly food supplies and ammunition—were parachuted in, which, of course, posed an extraordinary logistical problem involving retrieval under fire, sorting and distribution. Captured Communist soldiers were

frequently ordered to pick up pallets dropped in especially dangerous forward areas.

Additional supply problems resulted from the multinational composition of the French force. For example, the Moslems would not eat the standard pork and beans fare. The diet of the French soldiers also reflected special demands. The drops included 49,720 gallons of wine, 7,062

Genevieve de Galard-Terraube, a twenty-nine-year-old French air force nurse, tends a wounded soldier at Dien Bien Phu. She was the only woman to stay in the valley throughout the battle. She became known as the "Angel of Dien Bien Phu."

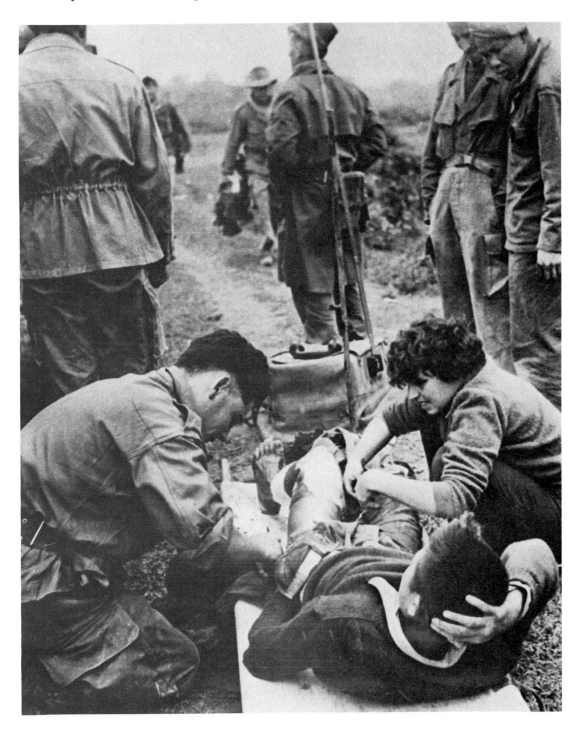

gallons of wine concentrate, and 60 kilograms of mustard.

By May 6 the French bastion was "reduced to a size no larger than a baseball field." The eventual outcome was obvious. There was no avenue of escape, no opportunity of rescue from the outside. De Castris obtained permission for a cease-fire to commence at 5:30 P.M., May 7. There would be no surrender. "This must not end by a white flag," ordered General René Cogney, commander of French forces in northern Vietnam."What you have done is too fine for that."

By 5:40 the red flag of Ho's Communist troops flew over de Castris's bunker. Special stitching had been sewn into it before the battle. "To Fight and to Win," it read, a phrase attributed to Ho himself, and written especially for this battle.

Dien Bien Phu fell the day before the Indochina issue was scheduled for discussion at a Geneva Conference attended by France, Great Britain, the Soviet Union and China. British and Russian initiatives had led to the conference. Contributing to the mood that an agreement could

Giap's army ordered French troops captured at Dien Bien Phu on a forced march reminiscent of the Bataan Death March. Thousands died.

be reached was Ho's stated willingness to negotiate. On November 29, 1953, the Swedish newspaper *Expressen* had published Ho's responses to written questions submitted through a Swedish embassy intermediary in Peking. The news caused a sensation in Paris and put pressure on the French government to negotiate, though the colonial lobby, hoping for a military victory, still held sway. By late 1953 their adamance was bolstered by American military and economic aid. But on March 9, 1954, by a narrow margin, the French Assembly voted to attend the Geneva talks. The ostensible purpose of the meeting, which lasted eighty-seven days, from April 26 to July 21, 1954, was to resolve continuing disputes in Korea in the wake of the armistice, but the primary and not too secret

The French garrison did not surrender. "What you have done is too fine for that," said de Castris's superior. Below, French prisoners after their capitulation.

Veterans of the long fight against the French were greeted by emotional throngs when reentering Hanoi.

agenda was to solve the Indochina problem.

The Geneva Conference very much affected Communist battle plans at Dien Bien Phu. Ho wanted the French defeated before the conference began so that a settlement favorable to him might be forced on France. It was no coincidence that Dien Bien Phu fell May 7 and that the subject of Vietnam was on the May 8 agenda. Giap's battle plan was a function of political timing.

For the first five weeks the talks went nowhere. The issue of Vietnamese representation was one knotty problem. Should Ho's representatives be invited to the conference? Or Bao Dai's? Or both? Finally, both were invited.

French public pressure to leave Indochina was mounting, however. American insistence that France prevent the creation of another Asian Communist government was not persuasive—especially since the Eisenhower administration had denied pleas to save Dien Bien Phu with American bombers.

French recalcitrance at Geneva after May 7 was only superficial. French diplomacy changed to reflect the military realities after the enormous loss at Dien Bien Phu—realities clearly manifested by orders to Navarre on May 18 to evacuate Hanoi. On June 3, after negotiations that were not part of the Geneva conclave, France signed a treaty with Bao Dai, recognizing the State of Vietnam as "a fully independent and sovereign state." France thus committed itself to leave Vietnam eventually, regardless of what transpired at Geneva during the next seven weeks. The treaty

Diem refused to return to Vietnam to join Bao Dai in governing until after the French officially declared the State of Vietnam "a sovereign state."

Ngo Dinh Diem was a devout Catholic, more of the Spanish kind than the Gallacian kind, he once said.

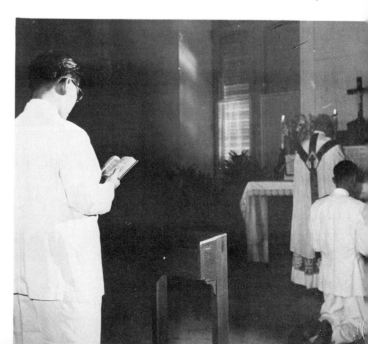

was the last feeble attempt by France to keep Ho's Communists from taking control of Vietnam.

Though it came too late to allow a real alternative to Ho, the signing of the treaty with Bao Dai was to affect events in Vietnam for another decade: it removed the last obstacle to the return of Diem. Bao Dai had repeatedly invited Diem back to form a government but Diem always refused to join a puppet government. On June 16 Bao Dai extended the invitation once more. This time Diem accepted. On July 7 he became prime minister. The only anti-Communist Vietnamese leader resolute and capable enough to challenge Ho for supremacy was now in place. Ironically, it was the Communist victory at Dien Bien Phu that made possible Diem's return.

Diem's life, like Ho's, was dominated by the ambition to free Vietnam from France. There the two parted company, however. Diem envisioned that the class structure within the country would stay about the same after independence. Ho envisioned a social revolution. Diem would have been content to pursue a political career in an independent Vietnam headed by a monarch.

Diem's attitude toward the French, like Ho's, was largely the product of family influences. Diem's father, Ngo Dinh Kha, was a high-ranking mandarin who served as the minister of rites and grand chamberlain in the court of Emperor Thanh Thai. When the French deposed Thanh Thai for allegedly plotting against them, they made implacable enemies of the Ngo family. Kha immediately retired from court service and closely though discreetly allied himself with the nascent independence movement.

Kha had six sons and three daughters. Diem, born in Hue on January 3, 1901, was the third oldest boy of this strict Catholic household. The Ngo family had, in fact, been among the first Vietnamese converts to Catholicism. They were converted in the seventeenth century, probably by Portuguese missionaries, long before the French colonial presence. The family suffered religious persecution because of their faith. In about 1870, when Kha was a young man, the Ngo family was almost wiped out by an anti-Catholic mob that attacked their home, but Diem's father was not among the many killed because he was attending school outside the country.

Diem's first government job was as a village administrator in the Hue area for the French. In 1925, while working in that capacity, he first encountered Communists' organizing activities.

After French colonization, conversion to Catholicism carried an ever greater stigma. Catholics were deemed French collaborators—a conclusion reinforced by the fact that Vietnamese Catholics, relatively speaking, did prosper under the French.

Even as a boy, Diem displayed a disciplined, uncompromising view of life. He was six when his father left the imperial court for the private life of his modest country estate. Diem remained in Hue, living in the home of the premier of the court. His father wanted him to receive the superior education offered by a French Catholic grammar school there.

Even then, young Diem was up by five each morning to pray and study. He was an excellent student. During his teens he transferred to the school founded by his father, Quoc Hoc, the same one attended earlier by Ho. At age fifteen, following the example of his older brother Thuc, he decided to study for the priesthood, and entered a monastery. Though he changed his mind, he never married and is believed to have taken a vow of lifelong chastity. To a French writer who was trying to emphasize Diem's bonds with France due to a common faith, he answered, "You know, I consider myself rather as a 'Spanish Catholic'; in other words, the spiritual son of a fiercely aggressive and militant faith rather than of the easygoing and tolerant approach of Gallacian Catholicism."

Diem did so well on a high-school equivalency examination that the French offered him a scholarship in Paris. He declined, using the excuse that his father was ill, but in reality he just did not want to go to France. Instead he went to Hanoi where he studied in the French-run School for Law and Administration. In 1921 he was graduated at the head of his class.

He easily won appointment to the Royal Library staff in Hue, but his family soon urged him to abandon this sheltered refuge for more active public service. He became the Vietnamese administrator for seventy villages near Hue. Several years later he moved up the mandarinal ladder by being appointed the administrator of a grouping of three hundred villages.

While at this post in 1925, he first encountered Communists. In fact, he was "one of the first Vietnamese officials to learn of Communists' designs on the country. . . . He came across evidence of underground activity on the part of Ho Chi Minh." Diem arrested some of their

By mid-1955, the U.S. was solidly behind Diem, believing him to be the most able leader in the south. On May 14, 1956, Secretary of State John Foster Dulles visited him at the Independence Palace in Saigon while en route to a SEATO Conference in Karachi, Pakistan.

leaders after his agents infiltrated some of their cells. He sent French authorities a report urging action. The French failed to react, however, just as they failed to respond to any of his recommendations for village improvement.

Though his warnings went unheeded, Diem was promoted. That same year he became the Vietnamese governor of Phan-Thiet Province where Ho had taught school ten years before. He established a reputation as a capable and honest official—so much so, in fact, that in 1932 he was appointed to head an investigation of corruption among Vietnamese officials. Whether the French or Bao Dai, then the young and newly crowned emperor, initiated the action is unknown.

In May 1933 Bao Dai, flush with enthusiasm for the possibility of improvement under the French, appointed Diem his minister of the interior for Annam. Both young men thought the French would allow them latitude for greater responsibility, but both were disappointed. Within a few months, the uncompromising Diem was either forced out or quit (the record is unclear). Upon leaving public life, he lived with his mother and brother Can in Hue for the next ten years. During this period he maintained an active correspondence with various non-Communist independence-movement leaders exiled in China and Japan.

Like Ho, Diem saw that the Second World War presented special opportunities for Vietnamese independence. Not fully appreciating the closeness of the collaboration between the Japanese and French in Indochina, he approached the former about independence for Vietnam. As a result, the entire Ngo family was put under surveillance by French agents. In fact, his brother Khoi lost his job as the governor of Quang Nam Province. Finally, in 1944, the French ordered Diem arrested for subversive activities. He hastily departed Hue for Saigon, where he was hidden by Japanese friends.

In March 1945, after the Japanese aborted the planned attack and took control of the administration of Vietnam, the Japanese first asked Diem to be the prime minister under Bao Dai in an "independent" Vietnam. However, at the last instant, before the formal offer was extended by telegram, the Japanese had second thoughts. They decided Diem would be too difficult to control.

Five months later, when Ho entered Hanoi and declared the Democratic Republic of Vietnam

Diem's American friends of Vietnam...

Francis Cardinal Spellman was one of Ngo Dinh Diem's first American supporters. Spellman and Diem were introduced by Diem's brother, Bishop Thuc, while the two Vietnamese traveled through the United States en route to Holy Year celebrations at the Vatican in 1950. It was, of course, their shared religious faith that initially drew Spellman and Thuc together. In fact, Diem's Catholic faith was his most positive political attribute in this country, for it was the only thing about him that did not seem irredeemably foreign to America's parochial leaders. In that context, Spellman's connections with Catholic leaders were especially important for Diem.

These leaders were powerful; some would rise to the highest positions in various branches of American government. John Kennedy and Mike Mansfield were the most notable among them. Both were introduced to Diem by Spellman while they were in the House of Representatives. When Kennedy became president and Mansfield became the Democratic Senate majority leader, together they would formulate the policy that led to the introduction of American combat troops in Vietnam. Another American leader of the early 1950s whose Catholic faith undoubtably predisposed him in Diem's favor was a Republican senator from Wisconsin— Joseph McCarthy.

But it was Mansfield whose support was probably the most important during the early 1950s. Because Mansfield had been a professor of political science and Asian history at Montana State University prior to his election to Congress, his views on Vietnam were accorded greater weight. In the summer of 1954, for example, he traveled to Vietnam on a fact-finding tour for the Senate Foreign Relations Committee. Though he reported that the situation was "grim and discouraging," he defended Diem for his "intense nationalism and equally intense incorruptability, traits which have been sorely needed in the government of Vietnam." He saw no alternative to Diem's leadership, except that of the Communists and the weak Bao Dai, both unacceptable. Mansfield concluded: "In the event that the Diem government falls, therefore, I believe that the U.S. should consider an immediate suspension of all aid to Vietnam and the French Union Forces there."

After Mansfield's report President Eisenhower wrote Diem on October 23, 1954, that the U.S. would proceed with its aid program. Though the promised aid was qualified (because of internal political problems in Vietnam), Diem was informed that the American ambassador had been instructed to work with him in formulating an "intelligent program of American aid given directly"—aid to Vietnam through the French would be terminated. Officials in the Kennedy and especially the Johnson administrations later cited this letter "to relate the origin and continuity of U.S. policy in support of Diem to the

under the auspices of the Viet Minh, ostensibly with American support, Diem tried to return to Hue to warn Bao Dai of Ho's Communist connections. He was captured en route by Viet Minh agents who took him to a hideout in the mountains of Tongking near the Chinese border. He remained in captivity for five months, almost dying from sickness, but was restored to health by the care of some Tho tribesmen.

In February 1946 Ho ordered him brought to Hanoi. Attempting to extend the popular base of his support, Ho invited Diem to become his minister of the interior. Their meeting was short. According to Diem, the following exchange took place:

"Why did you kill my brother?" asked Diem.

"It was a mistake," replied Ho. "The country was all confused. It could not be helped."

"Am I free to go?" said Diem.

Ho said that he was, but warned that the countryside would be hostile to him.

"I am not a child, and will take the risks," Diem said. He then angrily turned and walked out.

In 1947, with the French back in control, Diem unsuccessfully tried to form a political party. In 1949 he secretly took part in negotiations that brought Bao Dai back as head of state from Hong Kong, though, ever aloof and uncompromising, he refused an offer by Bao Dai to be his prime minister. His excuse, says Fall, was "the Viet-Minh might vent its displeasure upon the hundreds of thousands of Catholics residing in its zone," but his real reason was that "he thought the concessions made by France were not far-reaching enough for him to commit himself to their implementation."

In 1950 the Viet Minh added him to their death list. He sought French protection and was denied it, whereupon he fled the country for Rome with his brother Thuc, now a Catholic bishop, by way of Japan and the United States. He told everyone his principal reason for leaving was to attend Holy Year celebrations at the Vatican, because he did not want somehow to provoke either the Viet Minh or the French into taking action against him. He thought they might if they knew he was leaving for an extended period.

During the stop in Tokyo, various Americans advised him on contacts he should make in Washington. He stayed in the United States during September and October 1950. His presen-

Senator John F.   Senator Mike
Kennedy   Mansfield

tation to the small circle of people he met informally while in this country was that the Communist Viet Minh could be easily defeated if France would grant independence so that alternative leadership could develop. During these days, Thuc introduced him to Cardinal Spellman, later also prominent as a close adviser of the Kennedy family. According to Buttinger, Spellman "was probably the first American to look toward a Vietnamese government headed by Diem." What other Americans Diem met in Tokyo and Washington is uncertain.

When he finally did get to Rome, Diem had an audience with Pope Pius XII. He then traveled to Belgium, Switzerland and France, visiting Vietnamese exiles. In early 1951 he returned to the United States and took up residence at the Maryknoll seminaries in Lakewood, New Jersey, and Ossining, New York.

He kept fairly active by lecturing on Vietnam at various universities in the East and Midwest. He also made a number of trips to Washington, cultivating newly made friendships there. "Among the people who favored both his cause and his personal aspirations were Senators Mike Mansfield and John F. Kennedy, Representative Walter Judd and Justice William O. Douglas." During this period he received two more offers from Bao Dai to return as prime minister. He rejected both.

In May 1953 he departed the U.S. for France and later Belgium, where he took up residence at the Benedictine monastery of St. André Les Bruges. Bao Dai submitted him another offer, this one promising "full political power," which he rejected because French officials would not agree to Vietnamese control of the war against Ho's Communist forces.

But Dien Bien Phu ended the First Indochina War, for all practical purposes. It also brought about the independence treaty of June 3. And this time when Bao Dai issued yet another offer to Diem—to assume the prime minister's responsibilities with "all civilian and military powers" —Diem finally agreed.

He stepped onto the runway of Saigon airport on June 26, 1954, greeted by a small crowd of about five hundred made up mostly of mandarins, Catholic dignitaries and government officials. The Geneva Agreement to partition his State of Vietnam was one month away. The period of French colonial Vietnam was ending. The era of American involvement was about to begin.

Francis Cardinal Spellman

Justice William O. Douglas

earliest years of the Eisenhower administration."

Partially because of these early Diem associations, Kennedy and Mansfield, along with such Washington figures as Representative Walter Judd of Minnesota and Justice Wiliam O. Douglas, became charter members of an organization called the American Friends of Vietnam founded by Joseph Buttinger, who would later become known for his writings on Vietnam. He had first become interested in Vietnam when he was sent there in the fall of 1954 by the International Rescue Committee of New York to organize the resettlement of thousands of refugees fleeing the north for the south. The Friends group, founded in 1955, became quite effective for a while because its members, in Buttinger's words, "were in a better position then any Vietnamese agent to convince the American public and government that Diem's achievements were real, that under him the South would become prosperous and eventually democratic, and that Diem's critics made the mistake of regarding the minor flaws of his regime as omens of failure."

When by 1961 Diem's flaws were recognized as fatal rather than minor, American Friends of Vietnam faded away.

Poles Apart

The Red Scare

Vietnam was far from President Harry Truman's mind on February 24, 1947, when Great Britain announced it could no longer support the struggle against Communist insurgents in Greece and Turkey. His attention was focused on Europe. But the British statement led directly to the American decision some eighteen years later to order its soldiers into battle against the Vietnamese Communists, a fateful step resulting from a series of incremental actions, first by Truman, then by Presidents Dwight Eisenhower and John Kennedy, and finally by President Lyndon Johnson.

Truman made the first move within three weeks of the British announcement. On March 12 he asked a Joint Session of Congress for $400 million in aid for Greece and Turkey and authority to send American advisers there. Congress moved quickly to approve his proposals because of the urgency of the situation, but not without debate, the best informed of which began the next day in secret Senate Foreign Relations Committee hearings, where Undersecretary of State Dean Acheson argued the administration's case. Transcripts from those hearings were declassified in 1973, ironically the same year President Richard Nixon pulled the last American soldiers out of Vietnam combat.

"The people of America are mightily concerned about whether this is the opening wedge to our taking over the job that Britain had done so well in the last 150 years around the globe," Senator Alexander Wiley of Wisconsin told Acheson. "They are concerned . . . as to our ability . . . and as to what it will do to our own economy if we charge our own economy with that strategic load."

Claude Pepper, then senator from Florida, agreed. "My America is stepping out into a new field, reaching out and, yes, without mincing words, assuming the function of the British Empire."

The idea of sending American military advisers especially worried some senators. It "scares me to death," said Senator Arthur Vandenberg of Michigan.

Senator H. Alexander Smith of New Jersey saw no end to such a precedent. Pointing to "Communist infiltration of South America," he asked, "Are we going to be called on to finance resistance to

Soviet Premier Joseph Stalin at Yalta; above, Senator Joseph McCarthy.

Following President Truman's March 12, 1947, speech, Congress approved military aid for Greece and Turkey and granted him authority to send military advisers to both countries. Its actions established precedent for later sending aid and advisers to Vietnam.

Dean Acheson was a key figure in formulating and executing the Truman Doctrine.

Communism in other countries like that? . . . I want to see what the implications are throughout the world."

All the senators worried about the reaction of the Soviet Union and especially the American public. To Vandenberg, the language of the administration's proposals was "quite provocative." It seemed to him "close to a blank check that comes pretty close to a potential act of war."

With an initiative by Acheson, they set about rewriting the bill, couching it in arcane legislative language that would seem less a direct challenge to the Soviet Union and less alarming to the American public. Acheson offered the following alternative wording to the committee:

"The provisions of the Act of May 19, 1926, as amended, are hereby extended and made applicable to Turkey and Greece."

Acheson had come prepared. The twenty-one-year-old law provided a clever obfuscation that would not attract press attention. The Soviet Union would not be forced to react in kind, and the American people would be kept complacently quiet. Vandenberg, the committee chairman, was mollified. The cited act permitted the president to send military advisers into the nations of Central and South America; as amended to include Greece and Turkey, the act, as well as a financial package in support of it, was approved by Congress. For the first time, an American president could send military advisers into nations outside this hemisphere. There was now a precedent for sending military advisers or support personnel to Vietnam, and this was done two and a half years later.

This initial piece of Cold War legislation, as well as that dealing with the Marshall Plan and U.S. participation in NATO, both enacted within about a year, became the foundation of what came to be called the Truman Doctrine, the policy of Communist containment. It presumed that Communist revolutionary movements everywhere were controlled from Moscow. Its effect on the fighting in Indochina was to gradually transform a local colonial revolution into another theater of the worldwide ideological struggle.

Truman, Acheson and the congressmen thought they were being pragmatic when in fact they had selected a most difficult course of action. They chose sides not on the basis of the likely winner or even who should win, but rather on the basis of "what kind of society would grow out of the theoretically welcome revolution." They wanted that society to conform to that of our own self-image. Time and again their policy would position the U.S. behind an ally in great need of internal reform but unwilling to address it. But at the time, the U.S. was more worried about the larger threat of Communism than our ability to effect the required internal changes of those countries and their regimes which we supported.

The new activist policy forced American policymakers into a collision between our stated ideals and the contradictory realities. Given our traditionally anticolonial sentiments, the situa-

Poles Apart—
❝*In their own words*❞

❝*The thing to do is hammer away at them!*❞—Senator Joseph McCarthy, reacting to a suggestion by Father Edmund Walsh, vice-president of Georgetown University, that he run for reelection using an anti-Communist theme; on January 7, 1950.

❝*You have a row of dominoes set up, and you knock over the first one, and what will happen to the last one is the certainty that it will go over very quickly. So you have a beginning of a disintegration that would have the most profound influences.*❞—President Dwight D. Eisenhower, when the possibility of direct American military intervention to save the French in Vietnam was being actively considered by his administration; on April 1, 1954.

❝*The Virgin Mary is moving south.*❞—propaganda on leaflets dropped from U.S. planes to encourage North Vietnamese Catholics to flee Ho Chi Minh's Communist government; in late 1954.

Secretary of State George C. Marshall first presented the Truman administration's idea to revive postwar Europe and China with massive amounts of aid. The Marshall Plan, as it came to be called, and NATO were the key elements of the containment policy. With Marshall, General Dwight D. Eisenhower (the first NATO commander) and Mamie.

✴ On August 6, 1945, Ho Chi Minh learned from OSS Major Allison K. Thomas, who was in radio contact with his superiors, that the U.S. had dropped the atomic bomb on Hiroshima. The two were together in the village of Tan Trao, Vietnam, where Thomas was training some of Ho's men to fight the Japanese. Ho immediately called a conference of independence movement leaders. By August 13, they began arriving from Tongking, Annam and Cochinchina, as well as from outside the country in a few cases. Some disputed Ho's primacy within the revolutionary movement; they held such ambitions themselves. Decisive factors were the presence of the American officer in Ho's camp, the two-hundred-man contingent of Ho's soldiers armed with new American weapons of like make and caliber, and the autographed photo of General Claire Chennault hanging next to that of Lenin and Mao in Ho's quarters. Together they strongly suggested that Ho had secret Allied–American backing, a most significant reason to follow Ho's leadership. The delegates thus responded to Ho's initiatives. On the night of August 13, the group formed the National Insurrection Committee, a sort of executive committee, and recommended Military Order 1, which ordered that the general insurrection begin. On August 16, the first People's National Congress was convened. Under Ho's leadership, this larger group of sixty delegates approved the call to arms.

tion in Indochina would prove particularly problematic. We had previously avoided trying to reconcile the irreconcilable by remaining neutral in the fight between the French colonialists and Ho's Viet Minh after the Second World War, but our neutrality would prove short-lived.

Secretary of State George C. Marshall frankly stated the U.S. dilemma in a cablegram sent to the American embassy in Paris in 1947, which read:

"We have fully recognized France's sovereign position and we do not wish to have it appear that we are in any way endeavoring to undermine that position.

"At the same time we cannot shut our eyes to facts, there are two sides this problem and that our reports indicated both a lack of French understanding other side and continued existence dangerously outmoded colonial outlook and methods in areas.

"On other hand we do not lose sight fact that Ho Chi Minh has direct Communist connections and it should be obvious that we are not interested in seeing colonial empire administration supplanted by philosophy and political organization directed from and controlled by Kremlin.

"Frankly we have no solution of problem to suggest."

The Truman administration did start urging the French to establish a non-Communist Vietnamese government that would give Vietnamese wanting independence an alternative to Ho. The U.S. was particularly concerned about this during 1947–1949, in view of the European situation and Chiang Kai-shek's fight with Mao Tse-tung's Communists in China. The administration increasingly worried about Ho's Communist affiliation, though a survey done in the fall of 1948 by the State Department's Office of Intelligence and Research did not find evidence Ho was controlled from Moscow. "If there is a Moscow-directed conspiracy in Southeast Asia, Indochina is an anomaly so far," the report concluded.

In March 1949 France finally managed to prop up an alternative to Ho. Bao Dai was persuaded to return to Vietnam, where he was installed as head of a Vietnamese government for Cochinchina, Annam and Tongking called the Associated States. During the years since his first installation in 1932—especially after his abdication in 1945—he had lost most of his zeal and squandered most of his political goodwill living the widely reported degenerate life of a playboy. Consequently, the State Department as well as millions of Vietnamese suspected a French ruse. Bao Dai had little if any remaining popular support. A State Department cablegram to its Paris embassy voiced this concern:

"We cannot at this time irretrievably commit the U.S. to support of a native government which by failing to develop appeal among Vietnamese might become virtually a puppet government separated from the people and existing only by the presence of French military forces."

Such caution ended abruptly in late 1949, though, when the Communists won control of China. Within days Truman approved a National Security Council study, which recommended that "U.S. policy . . . block further Communist expansion in Asia."

"The United States on its own initiative," the study proposed, "should now scrutinize closely the development of threats from Communist aggression, direct or indirect, and be prepared to help within our means to meet such threats by providing political, economic and military assistance and advice where clearly needed to supplement the resistance of other governments in and out of the area which are more directly involved"— Vietnam and France, in other words. The study recommended that "particular attention should be given to the problems of French Indochina."

The basic policy for future U.S. moves was thus approved and in place when in January 1950 Moscow and Peking recognized Ho as the leader of Vietnam, an action Acheson said "should remove any illusions as to the 'nationalist' nature of Ho Chi Minh's aims and reveals Ho in his true colors as the mortal enemy of native independence in Indochina." Reacting quickly, Great Britain and the U.S. recognized the government of Bao Dai on February 7, Acheson emphasizing America's "fundamental policy of giving support to the peaceful and democratic evolution of dependent peoples toward self-government and independence." Our Asian allies were not persuaded by such thinking, and did not follow by recognizing Bao Dai as Acheson had hoped.

Some State Department officials also dissented, worrying that the U.S. was risking too much prestige, given the complicated situation. Years later Acheson recalled the objections of colleague John Olney, who warned that this country was moving into a position in which "our

John Olney warned Dean Acheson that the extensive U.S. aid given the French for Indochina was gradually making the fighting there an American effort.

General Douglas MacArthur, commander of U.N. forces, and, directly behind him, Lieutenant General Matthew Ridgway, his successor, visit American soldiers at the Korean front on March 7, 1951. Both saw the situation in Indochina as different from that in Korea. Some contend MacArthur warned against involvement there; General William Westmoreland says MacArthur only opposed intervention in Laos. Ridgway strongly advised against committing U.S. troops anywhere in Indochina.

responsibilities tend to supplant rather than complement those of the French." Prophetically, Olney warned, "These situations have a way of snowballing." But Acheson had decided, as he later admitted in his memoirs, "that having put our hand to the plow, we could not look back."

To his credit, Acheson several times warned in public about the danger of becoming "obsessed with military considerations. Important as they are, there are other problems that press, and these other problems are not capable of solution through military means." He even had private doubts about our fundamental premise, that being that Communist activity in Indochina was primarily the result of Moscow's orders. Behind the resistance, there was also "revulsion [by Vietnamese] against the acceptance of misery as the normal condition of life," he said.

But the initial decision to help out developed a momentum of its own, as Olney had warned. Nine days after U.S. recognition of Bao Dai, the French government asked for military aid for Indochina, and Acheson recommended a favorable reply. In a memo to the president, he wrote, "The choice confronting the U.S. is to support the legal governments in Indochina or to face the extension of Communism over the remainder of the continental area of Southeast Asia and possibly westward."

Truman approved Acheson's recommendation and on May 8, 1950, the administration announced that the U.S. would give military and economic aid to the French in Indochina, starting with a $10 million grant.

A short time later, on June 27, two days after Communist North Korean forces invaded South Korea, Truman announced that the U.S. would accelerate this flow of aid "to the forces of France and the Associated States of Indochina," and would dispatch a military mission "to provide close working relations with these forces." The earlier crises in Greece and Turkey served as precedent. At French insistence, the aid went directly to France, not the Associated States, a clear indication of how subordinate Bao Dai's government was to the colonial administration. Colonialism was far from dead in Vietnam, though the French were making a mighty effort to convince the American public it was. General de Lattre visited the United States in September 1951, trying to persuade anyone who would listen that France was now defending a country that was no longer hers. The Truman administration managed to suppress its skepticism, and de Lattre was politely though unenthusiastically received here.

His trip was part of a concerted French effort to raise America's stake in Indochina. The French now wanted more than American financial and military goods and a few support personnel; they wanted American combat troops. But the requests for troops were always denied by the Truman administration. At one point in May 1952, the French contrived a scheme they thought might be successful. Acheson had traveled to Paris to witness the signing of treaties that were supposed to bind the armies of France and West Germany into one. While there, Acheson was invited to a meeting of the French cabinet convened especially for him.

Later that day an amused Acheson described the session to Theodore White and a small group of reporters. "First they played the theme on the oboe, then they played it on the fife; then they let the strings pick it up and they did it all in harmony."

The theme that Acheson described with such amusement was the proposition that "the French Assembly would not accept the Germans as

The U.S. provided France all sorts of fighting vehicles for use in Indochina, including this tank and the rovers named after rivers in Vietnam.

As if acting out a parody, a French officer introduces Major Honaker of the U.S. Military Aid and Advisory Group to a Vietnamese soldier in 1952.

During his first State of the Union address on February 3, 1953, President Eisenhower linked the fighting in Indochina to that in Korea.

During an informal radio broadcast, Secretary of State John Foster Dulles chats with President Eisenhower about discussions with the French concerning Indochina and other matters.

partners in Europe unless the American government accepted partnership with France in the Vietnam War."

The French misled themselves into believing that the U.S. government very much wanted the German-French arrangement. It did not—or not enough to send American combat troops into Vietnam in 1952.

Still, by the time of Dwight Eisenhower's inaugural on January 20, 1953, the United States was paying for a third of the French effort in Indochina, directly supplying France with arms and material, and providing two hundred U.S. Air Force support technicians.

Eisenhower wasted no time reaffirming the importance of Vietnam to his administration. In his first State of the Union address on February 3, 1953, he linked the fighting in Indochina with that in Korea. Both are "part of the same calculated assault that the aggressor is simultaneously pressing in Indochina and Malaya."

About the same time, his secretary of state, John Foster Dulles, warned a national radio audience, "If they [the Soviets] could get this peninsula of Indochina, Siam, Burma, Malaya, they would have what is called the rice bowl of Asia. . . . And you can see that if the Soviet Union had control of the rice bowl of Asia that would be another weapon which would tend to expand their control into Japan and into India."

Eisenhower's position on Indochina only hardened after the months of frustrating negotiations at Panmunjon, which culminated in the signing of the Korean armistice on July 27,

1953. Conservatives considered the settlement there inconclusive. They wanted a clear-cut victory over the Communists. Senator Joseph McCarthy, close to the zenith of his influence during those days, called it an appeasement that fell far short of victory. Such attitudes fostered an intractable fight-to-the-finish mentality. Having been clubbed with the issue since 1946, the Democrats now added their voices to the anti-Communist clamor. Thurston Morton, Eisenhower's undersecretary of state for congressional relations, remembers overhearing Franklin D. Roosevelt, Jr., tell a Democratic colleague, "These damn Republicans blamed us for losing China and now we can blame them for losing Southeast Asia."

Predictably, Eisenhower administration officials raised their estimates of Indochina's strategic importance to match its rising political importance at home. In August 1953, for example, the National Security Council decided that "under present conditions any negotiated settlement would mean the eventual loss to Communism not only of Indochina but of the whole of Southeast Asia. The loss of Indochina would be critical to the security of the U.S. " Later, in the spring of 1954, the NSC even urged Eisenhower "to inform Paris that French acquiescence in a Communist take-over of Indochina would bear on its status as one of the Big Three" and that "U.S. aid to France would automatically cease."

The U.S. essentially closed the door to a political settlement and, as a result, began emphasizing the military solution. Dulles specifically identified U.S. goals in Indochina with those of the Navarre Plan, named for the French commander who took control of the French Indochina forces in May 1953. The Navarre Plan, Dulles optimistically predicted, would defeat "the organized body of Communist aggression by the end of the 1955 fighting season," leaving only mopping up operations, "which could in 1956 be met for the most part" by Vietnamese troops. To boost these efforts, the U.S. dramatically increased financial support and the flow of military supplies to France. A total of $119 million had been given by the end of fiscal year 1951. During fiscal year 1954 alone, the grant was $815 million.

During the fateful year of 1954 several crucial decisions affecting the future of Vietnam and the United States would be made. The unfolding

McCarthyism and America's lost perspective...

Senator Joseph McCarthy's irrational Communist crusade dominated the domestic political scene during the early 1950s, the "ultimate impact" of which, says Theodore White, "came many years later, in Vietnam." All varieties of individuals, great and small, lived in fear of the point of his lance. His targets even included formidable institutions such as the Department of the Army and the Department of State. Capitalizing on the paranoia of the period, he charged that both were rife with Communists working to undermine the nation.

The attack on the army led to his undoing. The establishment closed ranks to protect General Matthew Ridgway and the men in uniform. The State Department was not so fortunate, nor, in fact, were lower-ranking people throughout government, victimized by the fear that remained after McCarthy's passing.

One victim was Major Archimedes Patti, who as an OSS officer had come to know Ho Chi Minh and other top Vietnamese Communists after the Second World War. In the early fifties, Patti, still in uniform, had requested permission to write a book about these experiences. His narrative would have been a valuable contribution, coming at a time when American policymakers were groping with the problem of Indochina and weighing various alternatives there. "Sensitive to adverse criticism of American foreign policy by members of the military establishment," Patti says, "the Department of the Army decreed that any public disclosure of information or opinion by me on the question of American involvement in Vietnam would be regarded with official displeasure and I would be subject to disciplinary action."

But Patti's sacrifice was minor compared to that of various State Department Far Eastern specialists who were blamed for the fall of China to the Communists and were thus purged by John Foster Dulles to please the Republican Right. According to White, these "gallant China Service diplomats . . . had predicted too accurately and too eloquently the ultimate victory of the Communists." These men had been trained in the language and culture of that country. They included John Paton Davies and John Stewart Service. When, after China, Korea and Indochina arose as this country's principal problems in the region, these trained hands were long gone, driven from diplomatic duties. Service, who reportedly knew and understood the Chinese Communist leadership best, was forced to earn a living working for a plumbing manufacturer in New York at $9,000 per year (where "he invented a new and improved steam trap for radiators"). He and others like him, so familiar with the culture of the region, would have been invaluable. In their absence, the American ambassadors who served in Vietnam during the fifties, sixties and seventies were drawn from the ranks of men trained for European duties. Unfortunately, even these men had been adversely effected by McCarthy politics. According to White, these were "diplomats who knew their future career was pawn to political passion at home; who knew that prediction of a Communist victory would be equated with hope for a Communist victory; and who learned to temper their dispatches of observation in the field with what their political superiors in Washington or in Congress wished to hear."

The confrontation of Alger Hiss (left) and Whittaker Chambers (right) before the House Un-American Activities Committee in August 1948 and Hiss's subsequent trials were important events that inflamed the paranoia about the Communist threat.

drama of Dien Bien Phu in the first four months of the year brought the subject of Vietnam to the front page of American newspapers. The debate about whether the U.S. should intervene intensified, involving future presidents Kennedy, Johnson and Nixon—among many other politicians. Pressures on Eisenhower mounted to the point where another president, lacking his stature and experience as a former military leader, might well have been persuaded to order American aircraft, or even combat troops into Indochina to save the French. Eisenhower came close to doing so, as it was.

A couple of important factors influenced his handling of the Indochina crisis. First, he had won election as a peace candidate. He had promised to end the fighting in Korea and was not eager to take up arms elsewhere. Second, he was influenced by what he deemed Truman's bad example. His predecessor had ordered American troops in Korean combat without a congressional act of war, a decision that particularly embittered Senator Robert Taft, very influential with the Republican Right; they were sent in under the auspices of the United Nations. Eisenhower was determined to proceed with congressional sanction in Indochina and not offend powerful elements of his own party in Congress. In early January 1954 he even prepared his State of the Union message in close collaboration with some congressional leaders. The speech included a reference to continued military aid to France, causing a Republican senator to ask whether that included sending American soldiers to Vietnam. The question

startled Eisenhower. "No!" he responded. "I can even write 'material assistance' in." And he did.

But the question came up again during his weekly press conference on February 10, 1954. It had been announced that Lieutenant General John O'Daniel would be sent to Vietnam as chief of the new U.S. Military Advisory Group. Forty B-26 fighter-bombers were to be given the French and two hundred U.S. Air Force technicians would be dispatched to service the aircraft. Worldwide press coverage of the imminent battle at Dien Bien Phu and worries that the French were already trapped heightened public concern. Marvin Arrowsmith of Associated Press immediately asked Eisenhower about the situation in Indochina.

"No one could be more bitterly opposed to ever getting the United States involved in a hot war in that region than I am," he said. "Consequently, every move that I authorize is calculated, so far as humans can do it, to make certain that that does not happen."

"Mr. President," asked Daniel Schorr of CBS Radio, "should your remarks be construed as meaning that you are determined not to become involved or, perhaps, more deeply involved in the war in Indochina regardless of how that war may go?"

Eisenhower responded that he could not anticipate the future, but added, "I say that I cannot conceive of a greater tragedy for America than to get heavily involved now in an all-out war in any of those regions, particularly with large units."

Within days extraordinary pressure was brought to bear on Eisenhower to do just that. On March 13, behind an incredible artillery barrage, in the first of fifty-six days of assaults, Giap's forces swarmed down out of the mountains and onto the French dug into the valley at Dien Bien Phu. By March 22 General Paul Ely, the French chief of staff, had already flown to Washington to plead for American airstrikes to relieve the garrison, so desperate was their plight even then. Eisenhower knew the stakes involved. The French battle commander at Dien Bien Phu, Colonel Christian de Castris, was not exaggerating when on March 16 he told his men, "We are undertaking at Dien Bien Phu a battle in which the whole fate of the Indochina War will be decided." But French planning had not reflected the importance of the battle. Only American airpower or troops or both could save

The bad news bearers...

The tendency of policymakers in Washington to believe the assessment of its traveling VIPs over that of its specialists in the field and to believe the good news over the bad began during the First Indochina War.

In early 1953 the French government invited the Eisenhower administration to send a military mission on a brief tour of Vietnam to appraise the material needs of its forces. The U.S. had agreed to supply the necessary equipment. Lieutenant General John "Iron Mike" O'Daniel, a tough veteran of three wars, was chosen to head up the fact-finding mission. His selection was logical only in an institutional sense—he was commander of the U.S. Army in the Pacific. Though a capable combat commander, he did not possess the political sensitivity to evaluate properly the subtleties of Vietnam. (Once while assigned as a military attaché to the U.S. embasssy in the Soviet Union, he caused an uproar by describing Moscow as "a vast slum" to the press.) Nor did O'Daniel possess the language skills necessary to communicate with either the French or the Vietnamese. But because of the special nature of his mission, he became the eyes of the administration, charged with an accurate evaluation of French prospects for success. The normal chain of command and thus the standard evaluation process was short-circuited.

O'Daniel's reports read like a glossary of phrases later VIPs would use to evaluate the American war effort there. He observed that the French were making "real progress" in Vietnam and had "wrested the initiative from the enemy." He said that General Henri Navarre had "brought a new aggressive psychology to the war." The Viet Minh, said O'Daniel, had "been blocked in all their moves by General Navarre and do not have the strength for a sustained effort." The military situation is "well in hand and will improve rapidly."

As for Dien Bien Phu specifically, he decided the French were in no serious danger. They could "withstand any kind of attack the Viet Minh are capable of launching." His summary conclusion about Dien Bien Phu was that "the French are in no danger of suffering a major military reverse. On the contrary, they are gaining strength and confidence in their ability to fight the war to a successful conclusion."

The reports of the attachés and other experts permanently assigned to Vietnam were exactly the opposite. Brigadier General Thomas Trapnell, the chief of the U.S. Military Advisory Group in Vietnam, and the other three military service attachés there, all noted that the French were not even implementing their own plans—neither the overall Navarre Plan nor operational orders more narrow in scope. Another officer warned that after dark the French held only Hanoi and Haiphong in northern Vietnam. As for Dien Bien Phu, Trapnell concluded that the French were "operating from an inferior defensive position, facing an enemy battle corps stronger by at least one division," and were depending on "overtaxed air facilities" for resupply. He gave the garrison only a 50–50 survival rating.

Few except the Americans in the field and General Matthew Ridgway,

them, and the burden of responding quickly was Eisenhower's.

Characteristically, he brought the State Department, the Pentagon and Congress into the decision-making process. Both publicly and privately, Dulles expressed his support for going to the rescue with aircraft bombing missions. In a speech approved in advance by Eisenhower and delivered to the Overseas Press Club on March 29, he said, "Under the conditions of today, the imposition on Southeast Asia of the political system of Communist Russia and its Chinese Communist ally, by whatever means, would be a grave threat to the whole free community. The United States feels that the possibility should not be passively accepted, but should be met by united action. This might have serious risks, but these risks are far less than would face us a few years from now if we dare not be resolute today."

Sometime during this period the aircraft carriers U.S.S. *Boxer* and *Essex,* with two hundred jet aircraft and nuclear weapons on board, were deployed into the Gulf of Tonkin, within striking distance of Dien Bien Phu. Almost a hundred long-range B-29 heavy-duty bombers stationed in Okinawa and the Philippines were placed on alert. The commander of the U.S. Far Eastern Air Force, Lieutenant General Earle E. Partridge, and the ranking officer of his bomber command, Brigadier General Joseph D. Caldara, flew to Saigon to make tentative plans for the bombing run. They stipulated, according to Bernard Fall, that the three bomber wings "would rendevous east of the Laotian capital of Vientiane,

During the siege of Dien Bien Phu, Eisenhower ordered the carriers *Boxer* and *Essex* to stations off the Vietnam coast and within range of the battle while American military intervention was deliberated.

head for their target; and exit from Indochina via the Gulf of Tonkin. Strict orders were given that any disabled Superfort would do its utmost to crash in the open sea, rather than on the ground, where Communist discovery of B-29s, and, worse, of live American air crews, could have appalling political repercussions." On the night of April 4 Caldara personally piloted a B-17 over Dien Bien Phu to gain a firsthand perspective on the route and the surrounding terrain.

Five days after his Overseas Press Club speech, Dulles met secretly at the State Department with eight congressional leaders. The bipartisan group included Senators Lyndon Johnson (then Senate minority leader), Richard Russell, Earl Clements, William Knowland and Eugene Millikin; and Representatives John McCormack, J. Piercy Priest and Joseph Martin. The meeting was called for the all-purpose reason of briefing the group on the latest developments. But Dulles's real motive for calling them together was to get their support for a congressional resolution authorizing the president to order an airstrike at Dien Bien Phu. Later one of the group said that the secretary of state had conveyed the impression that he had "grave doubts whether the United States could survive the establishment of Communist power in Indochina." Dulles had the chairman of the Joint Chiefs of Staff, Admiral Arthur Radford, on hand to describe the military situation at Dien Bien Phu and recommend the attack.

Knowland, a conservative Republican known for ending meetings of the China Lobby with

the army chief of staff, appreciated that O'Daniel's VIP mission would get only sanitized presentations during their brief visits and that much of what they saw would be contrived for their benefit. During O'Daniel's first visit beginning June 20, 1953 (the first of three inspection tours), the local U.S. military attachés and various CIA officers there persistently warned him about the overly optimistic French presentations. "You may ask why we didn't convince him," said one of the army attachés later. "Naturally a three-star general is more inclined to believe a friendly nation's four-star [sic] general who is in the midst of fighting a war." General Ridgway was not, however, and he persistently sought to tone down O'Daniel's optimistic reports before they were forwarded to higher civilian authorities. Once when O'Daniel reported the "prospects for victory are increasingly encouraging," Ridgway urged the Joint Strategic Plans Committee to qualify the appraisal as "overly optimistic." The best Ridgway could urge upon the group, however, was to describe progress as "limited," a bureaucratically safe word that hedged bets on almost any eventuality.

Worries about Dien Bien Phu finally forced the top civilian officials of the Eisenhower administration to ask for explanations about the differing re-

Senator William Knowland, a Republican from California, Vice-President Richard Nixon and Senator Lyndon Johnson played key roles in the policy debate about saving the French at the time of Dien Bien Phu.

ports they were receiving. Admiral Arthur Radford, the chairman of the Joint Chiefs, being more inclined to please than Ridgway, dismissed their concern with the following explanation: "Our attachés tend to become frustrated as a result of continuously being on the scene. They tend to look at the situation from strictly a service point of view." In testimony before congressional committees on February 16 and 18, Radford, appearing with Undersecretary of State Walter Bedell Smith, discounted "alarmist interpretations of recent military operations" in Vietnam.

Until the Viet Minh overran Dien Bien Phu, optimistic reporting of the French effort was associated with a "can-do" determination. Those who rendered pessimistic appraisals based on the facts jeopardized their careers; truth was not a redeeming virtue. The case of Lieutenant Colonel Robert Tabor, the acting U.S. Army attaché in early 1954, is an example. After visiting Dien Bien Phu in February, Tabor informed Ridgway that the French were no longer even patrolling outside their garrison perimeter. A short time later Tabor was called on the carpet by Donald Heath, the American ambassador to Vietnam, who warned him to stop his negative reporting.

As for the pessimistic General Trapnell, he was replaced as the chief of the U.S. Military Advisory Group by the optimistic General O'Daniel on March 31, 1954.

By the end of the First Indochina War, Giap's army was no doubt the best in Asia, man for man, and continued to improve during the next twenty years.

proclamations of "Back to the Mainland," quickly announced his support. But the Democrats in attendance were much more skeptical, and the two-hour meeting became stormy. The Democrats were suspicious of political maneuvering: They sensed they were being set up for blame. In doubt about whether Eisenhower really wanted to go in, they worried that he was positioning himself to blame the Democrats for blocking decisive action and thus bringing about the loss of Indochina. They thought that if Eisenhower actually wanted to order the airstrike, he would have hosted the meeting himself, rather than depending on Dulles, a man known for his fierce partisanship and a cleverness too highly cultivated to engender trust. Dulles prided himself on his ability to conceal his true motives, and was fond of telling friends "that he had not been the highest paid corporation counsel in New York for nothing; he knew how and when to deal."

Of the Democrats, Russell had the deepest and probably best-informed concern. The Georgian was without peer in the Senate as an expert on defense matters, and because of his seniority and paternal manner, was known to be something of a guiding light for Johnson. Russell's opposition to our escalating involvement in Indochina was well known to the Eisenhower administration. Two months earlier he had opposed giving the French forty B-26s and temporarily assigning two hundred ground support technicians to Indochina to service the planes. When informed of the decision by Thurston Morton, Russell warned that it would not stop at two hundred; that it would go to twenty thousand and eventually two hundred thousand. "I think this is the greatest mistake this country has ever made," he said at the time. "I could not

be more against it." But when Morton told him that Eisenhower and Dulles were determined to do it, he said, "I know, he mentioned he might do it. Tell him, then, that I think it is a terrible mistake but that if he does it, I will never raise my voice." Russell, a lifelong bachelor who spent almost all his free time reading and researching history, had an almost religious reverence for the presidency. He preferred to work behind the scenes, not through the press, being careful not to embarrass a president in foreign policy. His opposition was based on the fear that the U.S. was greatly overextending itself throughout the world, especially in Asia, where he thought we were unwelcome. The combination of Russell's perspective and their shared political concerns dictated the Democrats' response to the recommended airstrikes.

Clements of Kentucky asked Admiral Radford whether the Joint Chiefs unanamously agreed with him. No, answered the admiral.

"How many of them agree with you?"

"None," he replied.

"How do you account for that?"

"I have spent more time in the Far East than any of them and I understand the situation better." This was not true; Army Chief of Staff General Matthew Ridgway had been commander of American forces in Korea; all the Joint Chiefs had Asian experience.

What if the attack failed? he was asked. Would there be other missions? Would ground forces be sent in? Radford was unsure.

Johnson took the lead for the Democrats at this point, probably by prearrangement. Had any allies been consulted? Who among them would be willing to help? How much could they contribute? But the allies had not been consulted.

Johnson told Dulles that in the wake of

Senator Richard Russell, a powerful Georgia Democrat, warned the Eisenhower administration that sending U.S. troops to help the French in Indochina would be "the greatest mistake this country has ever made."

The Joint Chiefs that weighed intervention in Vietnam at the time of Dien Bien Phu: Air Force General Nathan Twining; Admiral Arthur Radford, chairman; Army General Matthew Ridgway; Marine General Lemuel Shepherd; and Admiral Robert Carney. Radford favored intervention; Ridgway did not, and won the argument.

Foreign aid for both Vietnams...

Foreign aid helped both Vietnams get started. On July 7, 1954, China announced that it would give Ho Chi Minh's government $200 million in aid; on July 18, 1954, the Soviet Union announced it would grant $100 million. The Chinese had earlier agreed to supply repair equipment for roads, railways, waterworks, and post and telegraph services, along with construction technicians. Early on, the Russians supplied new coal-mining equipment. Other Communist or "fraternal countries," as they called themselves, helped out. Czechoslovakia supplied some crop-dusting aircraft; East Germany, an ocean-fishing fleet; and Mongolia, a hundred thousand head of breeding cattle, along with experts.

The United States, wrote English observer David Hotham in 1958, "financed many excellent and well-received programs in Vietnam: the resettlement of refugees, the anti-malaria and anti-trachoma work, the agricultural improvements, the supplying of thousands of buffaloes, the restocking of fish ponds, the reclaiming of wastelands, the research on the high plateau of the interior, the invaluable long-term work on statistics, taxation, and other fields, and the training in administration and the introduction of American ideas [in administration] carried out by Michigan State University." Joseph Buttinger enlarges this list to include reorganizing the monetary system, budgetary affairs, and central banking, and noted the "dramatic increase in the number of hospitals, dispensaries, maternity clinics and other health facilities," and schools.

Korea—a war in which this country bore ninety percent of the costs in manpower and money—Americans were war-weary. A consensus quickly developed. Support from congressional leadership would be contingent on three factors:

"(1) United States intervention must be part of a coalition to include the other free nations of Southeast Asia, the Philippines, and the British Commonwealth.

"(2) The French must agree to accelerate their independence program for the Indochina States so that the United States assistance would not appear as supporting colonialism.

"(3) The French must agree to stay in the war."

The following day, a Sunday, Eisenhower met with Dulles and Radford at the White House. The president tentatively decided not to go in alone. He would seek allied support. The next day, April 5, he wrote Churchill, prime minister once again, though eighty years old. Eisenhower suggested that they form a united front to help the French. His long letter read, in part:

"The important thing is that the coalition must be strong and it must be willing to join the fight if necessary. I do not envisage the need of any appreciable ground forces on your or our part....

"If I may refer again to history, we failed to halt Hirohito, Mussolini and Hitler by not acting in unity and in time. That marked the beginning of many years of stark tragedy and desperate peril. May it not be that our nations have learned something from that lesson?"

Churchill and Foreign Minister Anthony Eden received the missive with great consternation. It was they, together with the Russians, who had skillfully engineered plans for the Geneva Conference, scheduled to convene in three weeks, on April 26, at which time the Indochina question would be taken up. While the British wrestled with this diplomatic predicament, Eisenhower, having received a second desperate appeal from the French, continued reviewing the risks of an air attack. On the day Eisenhower wrote Churchill, the American ambassador to France, Douglas Dillon, cabled Dulles about an emergency request from Premier Joseph Laniel and Foreign Minister Georges Bidault:

"URGENT. . . . They said that immediate armed intervention of U.S. carrier aircraft at Dien Bien Phu is now necessary to save the situation. . . .

"[French General] Ely brought back report from Washington that Radford gave him his personal (repeat personal) assurance that if situation at Dien Bien Phu required U.S. naval air support he would do his best to obtain such help from U.S. Government. . . .

"Bidault closed by saying that for good or evil the fate of Southeast Asia now rested on Dien Bien Phu. He said that Geneva would be won or lost depending on outcome at Dien Bien Phu. This was reason for French request for this very serious action on our part. . . ." The cable also included references to Bidault's charge of extensive Chinese involvement in the battle area — fourteen technical advisers and Chinese Communist General Ly Chen-hou stationed at Giap's headquarters, telephone lines installed and operated by them, radar-controlled anti-aircraft guns manned by Chinese, and a thousand supply trucks, "all driven by Chinese army personnel."

That same day, April 5, the National Security Council issued a special action paper recommending that:

"(1) It be U.S. policy to accept nothing short of a military victory in Indo-China.

A stream of French officials desperately sought greater American involvement. Secretary of State John Foster Dulles, here with the French ambassador to the U.S. Henri Bonnet and former Premier Antoine Pinay, was supportive of their requests.

In 1954 Vice-President Richard Nixon told the American Society of Newspaper Editors that the U.S. should take up the fight against the Vietnamese Communists if the French failed. That same year, not long after that failure occurred, he visited Saigon, where, among other activities, he awarded a fellowship to a journalist.

"(2) It be the U.S. position to obtain French support of this position; and that failing this, the U.S. actively oppose any negotiated settlement in Indo-China at Geneva.

"(3) It be the U.S. position in event of failure of (2) above to initiate immediate steps with the governments of the Associated States aimed toward the continuation of the war in Indo-China to include active U.S. participation and without French support should that be necessary."

The State Department and the CIA were to "ensure that there be initiated no cease-fire in Indo-China prior to victory whether that be by successful military action or clear concession of defeat by the Communists."

The NSC concluded, "On balance, it appears that the U.S. should now reach a decision whether or not to intervene with combat forces if that is necessary to save Indochina from Communist control...."

In the heat of the crises, the NSC had raised the stakes. Sending in ground troops was now an active option.

On April 8, Churchill and Eden managed to formulate a reply to Eisenhower's letter, which was, quite simply, that they would personally take up the matter with Dulles in London on April 12. At that time, they informed Dulles that Great Britain would follow the diplomatic route through Geneva, hopeful of resolving the Indochina crisis before considering military options.

The Eisenhower administration was, however, in Dulles's words, "doing everything possible... to prepare public, Congressional and Constitutional basis for united action in Indochina." Administration-inspired news reports and columns began appearing about Chinese Communist involvement at Dien Bien Phu, for example. A dramatic speech by Vice-President Richard Nixon to the annual convention of the American Society of Newspaper Editors in Washington was part of this consensus-building process.

Nixon was asked what the U.S. should do if the French were forced to withdraw from Indochina. He said American soldiers must take their place; that the free world was in a desperate fight and to back down was unthinkable; that "under these circumstances, if in order to avoid further Communist expansion in Asia and particularly in Indochina—if in order to avoid it we must take the risk now by putting American boys in, I believe that the Executive Branch has to take the politically unpopular position of facing up to it and doing it, and I personally would support such a decision." It was the first public admission by a high public official that the U.S. was considering ordering in ground troops. Nixon's remarks were made off the record, but were too sensational to be kept out of print. They broke like a thunderclap. Editorials across the country called on Eisenhower to repudiate Nixon's remarks. Three days later, Dulles returned to Washington after consulting with Eisenhower, who was golfing at Augusta, Georgia. American intervention was "unlikely," he announced.

There were, however, a couple more political efforts to save de Castris and his men, both directed at the British, who because of Johnson's maneuver replaced the Democrats on the hotseat. (Johnson had realized that the British would not likely agree to go into Indochina. Therefore, he had set up the British for blame by the U.S. public instead of the Democrats, if the region fell to the Communists.) On April 24, Radford, while at a NATO Council meeting, tried unsuccessfully to convince Eden "of the necessity of at least providing the United States with a symbolic declaration of support."

Three days later Laniel ordered his ambassador to Great Britain, René Massigli, to visit Churchill and plead for British cooperation so that the American rescue plan could start moving through Congress. Churchill told him that the garrison was probably already lost and that the need to settle larger questions with Communists at Geneva was of overriding importance. "I have known many reverses myself," Churchill told him. "I have held out against them. I have not given in. I have suffered Singapore, Hong Kong, Tobruk; the French will have Dien Bien Phu."

On May 7, they did.

That same day Dulles met with Eisenhower at the White House. The administration had not resigned itself to accepting the Communist victory. According to a memorandum written by the president's executive assistant, Robert Cutler, the two men discussed how "the U.S. should (as a last act to save Indochina) propose to France if the following 5 conditions are met, the U.S. will go to Congress for authority to intervene with combat forces:

"a. grant of genuine freedom for Associated States

The year 1954 was one of intense diplomatic activity for Dulles, before and after the French garrison fell. In October 1954, Eisenhower met Dulles at National Airport, the courtesy a sign of the president's high regard for his secretary of state.

"b. U.S. take major responsibility for training indigenous forces

"c. U.S. share responsibility for military planning

"d. French forces to stay in the fight and no requirement of replacement of U.S. forces

"(e. Action under UN auspices?)."

The words in parenthesis appeared in the memo. British participation had been dropped as a requirement.

Cutler also reported in his memo that he told Eisenhower and Dulles that some members of the National Security Council Planning Board felt that "it had never been made clear to the French that the U.S. was willing to ask for Congressional authority" to come to their aid. It so happened Dulles had scheduled a meeting with French Ambassador Henri Bonnet that afternoon, so the two decided that Dulles should take the opportunity to make "a more broad hint than heretofore" that the U.S. was willing to move on the matter. According to Cutler, Dulles "would not circulate any formal paper to Bonnet, or to anyone else." The administration wanted no evidence that it had actually initiated another French request for American intervention.

The French got the hint. Three days later, on May 10, Laniel again asked Dillon for American intervention to save Indochina. That evening Eisenhower convened another meeting with Dulles and Radford. He ordered Dulles to begin contingency military planning and Dulles to write a joint resolution that Eisenhower would ask Congress to approve. It would authorize the sending of American combat troops into Indochina.

At this point, General Matthew Ridgway, the army chief of staff, entered the picture. The former combat commander was a formidable man, strong enough in stature and disposition to step squarely in the path of Dulles and Radford, who seemed determined to get the U.S. involved. Ridgway had a brilliant combat record. The tall, lean West Point graduate was formerly of the elite paratrooper corps. He had, in fact, organized the first American airborne division, the 82nd, had led the first airborne troops into Sicily during the Second World War, and had jumped into Normandy during the D-Day invasion. Before the dropping of the A-bombs, when an invasion of Japan appeared inevitable, he had been named to command all airborne troops for the invasion. And most recently, Truman had made him commander of American

* A diplomatic incident at the Geneva Conference of 1954 was to rule out the possibility of Communist China intervening as an intermediary in Vietnam. Prior to it, China had forced a somewhat conciliatory approach upon Ho Chi Minh's delegates there, even in the wake of Dien Bien Phu. But then Secretary of State John Foster Dulles publicly humiliated Chou En-lai, Communist China's foreign minister, by refusing to shake his proffered hand. "It was probably the most expensive display of rudeness of any diplomat anywhere, ever," says historian Theodore H. White, noting that Chou thereafter became a dedicated enemy of the U.S. for many years, until Chou decided to engineer a resumption of contact during the administration of Richard Nixon.

forces in Korea (after he fired General Douglas MacArthur), where Ridgway promptly rallied his disorganized forces.

Besides being a brilliant strategist, Ridgway possessed that essential quality of all great military leaders—empathy for soldiers in the field. His was not a maudlin sense of compassion, but rather a sense of what they could be led to do. This subtle understanding manifested itself in many ways. While commander of the Eighth Army in Korea, he always wore his paratrooper's jump harness, a clear sign to the GI that he was an elite troop. And from the harness he always hung two hand grenades, which when resting against his chest were a melodramatic though effective communication to the lowly soldier that their commander was never far from the front lines. Ridgway was tough and hard-nosed. Upon assuming command in Korea, for example, he noticed that soldiers were driving around in canvas-covered jeeps to keep themselves warm. To their consternation, Ridgway ordered the coverings off, exposing them to the bitter cold. He knew that the warmth would give them a false sense of security and get them killed.

It might be said that in a similar manner, Ridgway ripped away the reassuring covering of Dulles's and Radford's plans, exposing Eisenhower to the cold realities of what they wanted him to do. Earlier in the year, while the crisis was escalating, Ridgway ordered a team of army experts to Vietnam to survey conditions and evaluate requirements for the U.S. to win the war there. Their report did not particularly surprise Ridgway, but it staggered those with an inflated sense of American power. The team estimated that between half a million and a million men would be needed. Draft calls would total one hundred thousand per month to sustain the effort. Roads, bridges and harbors would have to be built. The fighting conditions, because of the jungles and the monsoon season, would be much more difficult than in Korea. Worse yet, unlike the situation in Korea, the U.S. could not expect the support of most of the local population; nor were indigenous forces in Vietnam as committed and as capably led as those in Korea.

On May 11 Ridgway briefed the secretary of the army and the secretary of defense on his team's report. Not long thereafter he briefed Eisenhower, who, as the man who led the D-Day

General Matthew Ridgway's frank appraisal of the problems of fighting in Vietnam turned Eisenhower away from a combat troop commitment. Ridgway warned that as many as a million men would be needed to win there.

Tom Dooley and the "Passage to Freedom"...

For millions of Americans Dr. Tom Dooley embodied the ideals of U.S. involvement in Vietnam in the early years. The accounts of his humanitarian works beginning in the summer of 1954 presented such an obvious, one-dimensional picture of American good versus Communist evil that one almost wonders, in retrospect, whether Colonel Edward Lansdale had a hand in propagating and embellishing the story. Dooley's book, entitled *Deliver Us from Evil,* about the exodus of Vietnamese from the Communist north to the south —"Passage to Freedom," as the operation was called—was condensed in the April 1956 issue of *Reader's Digest.* Because of the magazine's huge circulation—more than 20 million in 1956—the condensation was more important than the book itself. Appearing just three months before the date specified for reunification elections by the Geneva Agreement, it no doubt bolstered the case of American leaders who thought that elections should not be held. Ho Chi Minh was perceived as the probable winner; all Vietnam would be forced to go Communist. One of Dooley's themes, in fact, was that the Communists had already broken the agreement by preventing thousands from moving south and that the agreement was, in Dooley's words, "a shameful treaty," anyway.

Dooley was a remarkable and idealistic young man from St. Louis. He had served as a navy enlisted man during the Second World War. He later was graduated from Notre Dame and St. Louis University Medical School, whereupon he resumed active duty in the navy. Apparently by chance, the handsome twenty-eight-year-old Irish Catholic was aboard the U.S.S. *Montague* in July 1954 when it became the first American ship to cruise into Haiphong Harbor to transport Vietnamese refu-

invasion of Europe at Normandy, was able to arrive at some rapid conclusions about the feasibility of the military goals Dulles and Radford intended to pursue in Indochina. Invasion plans quickly lost their momentum. Though a draft of the congressional resolution authorizing combat troops was prepared and circulated through the State, Justice and Defense departments, and the State Department went so far as to prepare a hypothetical timetable for required diplomatic moves if the U.S. went in, the administration—especially the military—began backing off. On May 20 the Joint Chiefs submitted a memo to Secretary of Defense Charles Wilson recommending that U.S. intervention be limited to "air and naval support directed from outside Indochina." They also observed, "From the point of view of the United States, Indochina is devoid of decisive military objectives and the allocation of more than token U.S. armed forces to that area would be a serious diversion of limited U.S. capabilities."

Eisenhower let matters run their course. Dien Bien Phu caused French frustration with the war to boil over. The French public wanted out—and fast. Laniel's government fell. Pierre Mendès-France became premier with a mandate to end the fighting. By June 15 even Dulles decided that the time for American intervention in behalf of the French has passed and he so informed French Ambassador Bonnet.

In the early morning hours of July 21, 1954, the delegates in Geneva finally reached an agreement to stop the fighting in Indochina. They also formulated, in general terms, the transfer of power from France to an elected Vietnamese official who would lead all of Vietnam. The delegates produced two documents to effect these plans, one a cease-fire agreement, the other a statement of general understanding called the "Final Declaration." Only the cease-fire agreement was signed; and the only delegates who signed it were those representing France and Ho.

The cease-fire agreement established the seventeenth parallel as a military demarcation line, on either side of which the two forces would regroup their troops and equipment; the Communists to the north, the French to the south. Vietnamese who wanted to move permanently from one zone to the other would be allowed to do so without interference before May 18, 1955.

An International Control Commission composed of officials from Canada, India and Poland would supervise the execution of the cease-fire.

The Final Declaration consisted of thirteen points, the most significant of which emphasized "that the military demarcation line [along the seventeenth parallel] is provisional and should in no way be interpreting [sic] a political or territorial boundary"; that foreign troop levels would be frozen at those existing on August 11 (the U.S. freeze level would be 342); and that "general elections" would be conducted in the summer of 1956.

Success in implementing the Geneva Accords was complicated by the fact that France had granted independence to the "State of Vietnam" under the leadership of Bao Dai two months earlier. This last-ditch French effort to foil Communist efforts to take control had been agreed to on June 3, less than a month after the fall of Dien Bien Phu. It took no account of the Communists; it was as if Bao Dai had defeated the French at Dien Bien Phu, when, of course, the victory belonged to Ho. Bao Dai had appointed Ngo

gees south. Dooley could speak French and was therefore put ashore to organize the medical processing for the 610,000 who departed through Haiphong. According to the story, Dooley and a handful of enlisted men did the entire job by themselves during a ten-month period, which was "to delouse, vaccinate and inoculate and to screen out those who had communicable diseases."

The plight of these refugees was indeed desperate. Many still suffered from the effects of recent famine. Most also suffered from a wide variety of illnesses ranging from smallpox to typhoid, cholera, trachoma, worm infestations and fungus. Their general debilitation was due mostly to about one hundred years of French indifference to their health and medical needs. The condition of some was the result of the war itself and the cruelty of the Communists toward these predominantly Catholic refugees. Dooley described treating the victims of various atrocities: young men with ears clipped off, children with chopsticks jammed through their inner ears, a priest with nails driven into his skull as a mock crown of thorns. Together they presented a graphic picture of people yearning to worship freely and being persecuted by godless Communists.

Dooley did not discuss the historic association of Catholicism with French rule, nor of the Catholic population's active support of the French during the First Indochina War. Rather, there were references to the darkness descending behind "The Bamboo Curtain"—the re-education camps, religious persecution and collectivization causing famine. And though Dooley's writing con-

President Eisenhower reports to the American public on the Geneva Conference.

demned colonialism, it presented individual Frenchmen and wealthy Vietnamese who had benefited from French rule in a favorable light. There was "Captain Cauvin, the gallant Frenchman who had the courage and determination to toss the Big Lie back into Communist teeth," and Madame Ngai, a Vietnamese lady formerly "of great wealth" who now ran an orphanage, and of whom Dooley wrote, "With women such as you to keep the flame alive, no nation can die; surely there will be a new birth of freedom!" Finally, Dooley described his confrontation with Communist soldiers, whose persistent efforts to lecture him on "dialectical materialism" he denounced. Dooley never once mentioned that the Communist takeover was the result of the Vietnamese independence movement. To read his account was to believe that the Communists had one day appeared on the horizon like a conquering horde in the Dark Ages.

Dooley's account ended on a high note. He described being awarded the Legion of Merit by the U.S. Navy and the medal of *Officier de l'Ordre National de Viet Nam* by Ngo Dinh Diem at the palace in Saigon. He told about lecturing an American ensign who thought that "all this love and altruism and better understanding among people" was not the navy's job, that it was one "for preachers and old women," until finally the ensign choked back tears after recognizing the error of his ways. He related a chance encounter only a few weeks after his departure from Vietnam at the Hickam Air Force Base, Hawaii, terminal lounge with the same Vietnamese boys who had had their ears clipped off by the Communists—and were now on their way to the United States to be trained as mechanics in the new South Vietnamese air force. He lamented the insensitivity of their American escort officer who during their four-day layover had never taken them to the mess hall. He described how he got the Vietnamese on the plane with him and during the

Dinh Diem to be his premier and form a government, a process that began July 7 when Diem took office, two weeks before the Geneva Agreement.

Geneva delegates of the French-created State of Vietnam decried the temporary partition as "catastrophic and immoral." Their unrealistic hope was that Vietnam would remain united under Bao Dai's control; partition amounted to recognition of Ho as dominant in at least part of Vietnam. Bao Dai's delegates asked that their government's reservations be included in the Final Declaration, but the conference chairman, Britain's Anthony Eden, and France's Mendès-France dismissed their request. The two Europeans were simply recognizing the obvious—that Ho commanded the popular support of the vast majority of Vietnamese as well as almost all the military power in Vietnam, north and south. They knew Bao Dai and Diem were lucky that general elections were not scheduled two months hence, as Ho wanted. The two-year interregnum imposed on Ho by Russian Foreign Minister Vyacheslav Molotov, while in a conciliatory mood with the West, at least offered Bao Dai and Diem additional time to win voters' favor. Neither was given much chance, however; Ho had become a national hero for defeating the French.

The Eisenhower administration's public statements masked its true appraisal of the Geneva Accords. A summary of meetings of the National Security Council held August 8 and 12 show that council members deemed the accords a "disaster" that "completed a major forward stride of Communism which may lead to the loss of Southeast Asia." Explaining the loss, the group blamed French lack of will more than they recognized Ho's resolve. In their view, earlier fears of "a Far Eastern Munich" had been realized (the reference being to British Prime Minister Neville Chamberlain's appeasement agreement with Hitler prior to the Second World War).

Not all U.S. leaders were inclined to shore up the faltering two-month-old State of Vietnam, however. On August 3, the National Intelligence Board warned: "Although it is possible that the French and Vietnamese, even with firm support from the U.S. and other powers, may be able to establish a strong regime in South Vietnam, we believe that the chances for this development are poor and moreover, that situation is more likely to continue to deteriorate progressively over the next year."

The following day the Joint Chiefs voiced the same concern in a memorandum to the secretary of defense. "It is absolutely essential," they warned, "that there be a reasonably strong, stable civil government in control. It is hopeless to expect a U.S. military training mission to achieve success unless the nation concerned is able effectively to perform those government functions essential to the successful raising and maintenance of armed forces." Few, it seemed, were impressed with the survivability of Bao Dai and Diem.

Such worries were quickly cast aside, however, or reformulated as warnings about the difficulties that lay ahead rather than conclusions about the inadvisability of our attempting to fill the vacuum left by the French. Dulles felt the U.S had no choice. There was enormous political pressure to confront Communists everywhere on any terms—even on their terms. Because of Senator Joseph McCarthy in particular, leaders who warned against involvement in Vietnam because of unfavorable conditions we would face there did so at risk of being called Communists themselves.

Vietnam was considered a fall-back region in Asia since China had gone Communist five years before. Vietnam was the first of many dominoes that in the administration's eyes stood poised to topple from there to Thailand to Singapore to the Philippines to Hawaii to the West Coast of the United States. Though the administration was not prepared to send large numbers of troops to Vietnam, it was prepared to assume limited risks in bolstering Diem and Bao Dai; aid would be sent them, we would train their army, we would advise Diem—we would violate the Geneva Accords, if necessary. And, of course, it was. The course of action we would follow for the remainder of the 1950s was summarized in an August 20, 1954, NSC paper approved by Eisenhower entitled "Review of U.S. Policy in the Far East."

Sergeant Major Ben Salem Abderrahmann, an Algerian who fought with the French at Dien Bien Phu, will never forget the night he was captured and escorted back behind enemy lines through a mine field. He and a trail of prisoners were ordered to use the bodies of dead Communist soldiers as stepping stones. Just as

flight to San Francisco stood up and lectured all the enlisted men on board, translating the individual stories of his Vietnamese friends, and how all the passengers eventually broke out in song together—the Vietnamese leading their local favorites, the Americans singing "Shake, Rattle and Roll." Finally, he talked about speaking to a San Diego assembly of high-school students, dressed in "faded blue jeans and leather jackets, some of the gals in full-blown sweaters and many of the boys with those long duck-butt haircuts," a "tough" group. He told about their cat-calls when they saw him in his uniform but how he won them over with the "whole sordid story of the refugee camps, the Communist atrocities, the 'Passage to Freedom,' and the perilous future of southern Vietnam." A contrite thirteen-year-old girl, at first embarrassed, eventually rose to ask, "Dr. Dooley, what can we boys and girls *really* do to help improve the situation in Southeast Asia?"

Dooley's presentation sounds all too good to be true. His stories are too pat, the chance encounters too improbable, the images of good and evil too clearly drawn, the theme too obviously directed at Americans' puritanical sense of guilt. Representatives of large groups of American society—the ensign and the escort officer, the enlisted men on the plane to San Francisco, the high-school assembly—were portrayed as doubting the value of American interest in Vietnam prior to the intercession of Dooley himself. Dooley's writing was a simple, emotional argument for an American commitment to Vietnam. Addressing that prospect directly, Dooley told *Reader's Digest* readers, "I have no magic formula to offer. I know nothing about 'foreign aid' in billion-dollar packages. But I do know that American aid, used wisely and generously by individual hands on a people-to-people basis, can create bonds of friendship that will be hard to sever." Dooley himself suggested that if one person can have the effect he had, think what millions of Americans could do.

Dooley was named one of *Look* magazine's ten outstanding young men for 1956. That same year, as a civilian, he returned to Indochina, this time Laos, where he administered medical aid and set up small medical facilities. In 1957 he helped set up a nonprofit agency called Medico, which supported hospitals in Cambodia, Vietnam, Laos and Africa. In May 1958 *Reader's Digest* published another book condensation by Dooley, *The Edge of Tomorrow,* about his work in Laos. In late 1959 he delivered forty-nine lectures in forty-one days in thirty-seven cities to raise funds for Medico, though at the time he was terminally ill. A short time earlier he had been diagnosed as having cancer and given a 50–50 chance of living another year. In 1960 he was one of America's ten most admired individuals, according to the Gallup Poll. The day he died in January 1961 at age thirty-four, he was visited by Cardinal Spellman, who afterward told the press, "I tried to assure him that in his thirty-four years he had done what very few have done in the allotted scriptural life span." His long obituary began on the front page of the *New York Times.*

Ho's resumption of power in the north was commemorated on January 1, 1955, by a parade with 100,000 participants, including these dam workers who pushed along a model of a recently completed project.

Abderrahmann, in the lead, was about to jump onto one lifeless corpse, its head raised up. The soldier was alive, his chest ripped open, his eyes wild with terror.

Abderrahmann halted, whereupon a Communist officer worked his way forward. Giap's two soldiers looked at one another. Without hesitation, the officer ordered Abderrahmann and the others onto the wounded man. "You can step on him," he said. "He has done his duty for the People's Army."

Abderrahmann's story is emblematic of Ho's approach to nation-building in North Vietnam beginning in the fall of 1954. Without regard to individual rights or suffering, he set about implementing all the doctrinaire Communist theory he, Giap and the others had talked about for many years. He was determined to create a textbook Marxist state instantly. His achievements were great in many ways, but the cost in human terms would have been considered prohibitive by all but the most totalitarian governments.

Ho's absolute power was a function of his military strength, of course, but also the fact that his most implacable foes left the north. The last French soldier to leave Hanoi was Colonel d'Argence, who requested the dubious honor of being at the tail end of a long line of French colonial soldiers following in the footsteps of compatriots who for decades had departed for home across the Doumer Bridge. That was on October 9, 1954. Thousands of Ho's Vietnamese opponents departed too. Of these, the Catholics would have caused him the biggest problem. Entire provinces of the southern part of the Red River Delta were dominated by the Catholic population. These regions had mustered militias to fight the Viet Minh. Given the opportunity to escape Communist rule and immigrate south, most abandoned all but what they could carry and left for resettlement camps in South Vietnam. They were joined by professors, journalists, artists, businesspeople and, of course, French collaborators. The Catholics feared Ho's agnostic regime and the possibility of future retribution against them fueled both by their past opposition to his forces as well as the traditional Vietnamese distrust and disapproval of Catholic converts. By contrast, they were attracted to the south because its premier, Ngo Dinh Diem, was Catholic, his brother a bishop. Approximately nine hundred thousand, about sixty percent of whom were Catholic, left North Vietnam for the south before the May 18, 1955, deadline.

During the first years of Ho's rule the peasants might well have wondered if Paul Doumer were back, with the likes of Bazin as his conscription agents. Thousands of "volunteers" were put to work rebuilding the north, which had been more badly damaged than the south. Hundreds of bridges and dams and thousands of miles of roads and railways had been destroyed. The speed with which the reconstruction was accomplished was extraordinary. For example, eighty thousand peasants rebuilt the railroad from Hanoi to the Chinese border in less than six months, on short rations and no medical care. According to Joseph Buttinger, "The conditions under which this so-called 'voluntary' work force was made to labor were in may respects as bad as had been those of the 'coolies' of the colonial regime."

Concurrent with these rebuilding efforts were moves to eradicate all traces of the free enterprise economy and those classes of people who might oppose such efforts. The property of the French was, of course, confiscated without compensation, except in two cases. The coal

✳ France hoped to continue doing business in North Vietnam after the Communist takeover. Jean Sainteny, who had negotiated the agreement of March 6, 1946, with Ho Chi Minh, was sent to negotiate. He was politely received initially, but negotiations gradually trailed away.

Like any good politician, Ho made trips to the countryside to build contact with his people, most of whom saw him as a legendary figure. Here he takes part in an anti-drought campaign in Hadeng village.

mines and the public transportation system of Hanoi were deemed so essential that Ho's government agreed to buy out the French owners gradually if they would not disrupt operations. Vietnamese technicians were trained to take charge of these functions. The Russians and especially the Chinese also dispatched technicians to assist in these and many other operations. The confiscations were not as catastrophic for French business interests as might have been the case, because the Geneva Accords provided that whole factories could be dismantled and shipped out. During the early 1950s many French businesses had reduced operations there anyway because of the fighting. Only about one hundred fifty were operating at the time of Dien Bien Phu. French landowners in the north did lose everything, however.

Ho's government also went after middle-class Vietnamese who owned any sort of manufacturing enterprise. Those known to have opposed the Communist takeover were almost immediately imprisoned, sent to labor camps or killed. However, even those who had managed to remain apolitical gradually lost their businesses due to constraints imposed on the marketplace by the government: no imports were available to them (the government reserved these for state-owned businesses) and all credit and sources of raw materials were controlled by the state. Surviving Vietnamese businesses were gradually sold out to the state. Their property was not confiscated, though; Ho needed their managerial and technical skills and did not want them alienated. A process called "peaceful socialization" evolved to ease their transition into the socialist economy. The government became part owners of their firms and later bought them out. In time they became employees of the state. These business people ceased to exist as a class.

Another class of business people the government tried to eliminate was composed of small traders and artisans. They had for years operated individually, in both creating and selling their wares. They were classified as "toilers." Ho's government set about collectivizing these individuals. It limited their ability to buy, sell, and produce what they wanted. But the group proved almost impossible to eradicate. They maintained a "spontaneous tendency to capitalism."

Agrarian reform was also a fundamental part of Ho's program. Peasant farmers who owned two to three acres or more suffered the brunt of

---

✳ The first official visitor to North Vietnam was Indian Prime Minister Jawaharlal Nehru on October 17, 1954, who stopped briefly by in Hanoi on his way to Peking, China.

Indian Prime Minister Jawaharlal Nehru chats with Ho.

✳ Many American VIPs visited Vietnam during the mid-1950s. They included Vice-President Richard Nixon, Secretary of State John Foster Dulles, Senators Mike Mansfield, Everett Dirksen and John Kennedy, and presidential envoy Harold Stassen.

Mao Tse-tung welcomed Ho and his delegation to Peking in July 1955.

Two years later Ho traveled to Moscow to meet Premier Nikita Khrushchev.

these changes. People's Agricultural Reform Tribunals were established to try these people. The charges against them were for nebulous crimes against the people. Those found guilty were deemed traitors. Except for a very small number who truly were landlords and had in fact exploited fellow Vietnamese, as did their French counterparts, their only offense was owning a small piece of property. Many had actively supported the Viet Minh; some had served in Ho's army. But such distinctions were secondary to Ho and his advisers. What was important was the political necessity of solidifying the allegiance of the poorest members of Vietnamese society. So the entire group of middle-class farmers was eliminated to facilitate this result. The land of these people and that formerly owned by the Catholics and the French was redistributed to landless peasants. The party secretary in charge of the confiscation campaign against the "traitors," Truong Chinh, proudly admitted in December 1955 that it was executed "with utmost ferocity." Quotas for guilty verdicts were imposed. In some regions there were so few of these so-called rich peasants that individuals with as little as one acre were put on trial. The government ran a hate campaign at the same time to urge the trials along. The encouragement was hardly necessary. The landless who passed judgment knew that a conviction released more land for redistribution.

An estimated ten to fifteen thousand were executed on orders by the tribunals. Another fifty to one hundred thousand were imprisoned or deported from their villages. By the summer of 1956, public reaction against the executions threatened to undermine Ho's authority—the

✳ Both sides directed propaganda at Vietnamese in the north inclined to emigrate south. U.S. leaflets predicted religious persecution and even worse economic hardships under the new Communist system. Those of the Communists played on Vietnamese fears of Westerners. One had a drawing of American soldiers sitting around a campfire roasting a Vietnamese baby. Another showed American officers at the foot of a gangplank, giving young Vietnamese women the option of going to Saigon brothels. A third depicted an American military ship dumping its load of Vietnamese passengers, supposedly bound for the south, into the ocean. A fourth had U.S. doctors inoculating Vietnamese with germs.

About forty percent of the Catholic population of the north chose to remain there. Less than a month after the deadline for free movement, the feast of Corpus Christi was celebrated with Mass at the Hanoi cathedral and a large procession afterward.

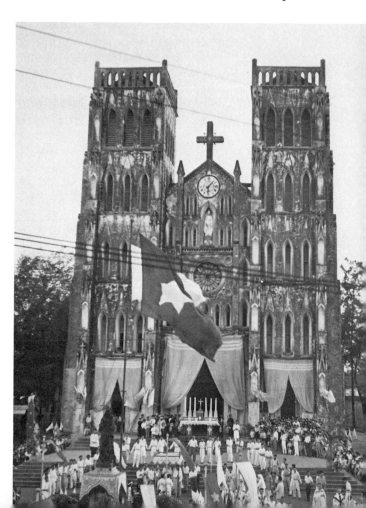

only consideration that could have motivated the Communists to bring the program to a halt. On August 17, 1956, Ho addressed a public letter to his "Compatriots in the country," admitting "errors" in the land reform program. "Corrections" were promised, and Troung Chinh was fired. Ho had reacted too late to avoid rebellion against his rule, however; that broke out in the fall in the province of Nghe An, Ho's childhood home, which had strongly supported the Viet Minh revolutionary movement. Spontaneous revolt spread to adjoining provinces, but the peasants were no match for Ho's seasoned army. He ordered the 325th Infantry Division into the region, where they reportedly killed a thousand and arrested several thousand. The action ended active opposition to Ho.

Unlike Ho, Ngo Dinh Diem did not have a firm base of support when he came to power in mid-1954. He was generally known only among Catholics and various religious leaders of other faiths, wealthy and influential families, those actively involved in politics, various sectarian leaders and the French; many who knew him opposed him. In the countryside, he was not known at all. But that was a longer-range problem. Though Diem's political survival would eventually depend on the support of the vast peasant population, his short-term political survival was dependent upon establishing primacy among those who knew him. This relative handful of individuals controlled all the political power in South Vietnam in the months immediately following independence.

It was Diem's good fortune to be the only South Vietnamese known to American leaders. His earlier trips here, facilitated by his Catholic contacts, served his ambitions well. Though Diem had won appointment as premier without American support, he could not have survived without it, especially during the very difficult early months of his administration.

American support was initially restrained. Though convinced that it must somehow save Vietnam from the Communists, the Eisenhower administration was uncertain that Diem was the Vietnamese leader who would make this possible. Diem would have to prove himself. Colonel Edward Lansdale, a counterinsurgency expert, was assigned to work closely with him. In the meantime, the U.S. began laying the groundwork for a broad commitment to the country,

The ugly American?...

During the mid-1950s, Colonel Edward Lansdale was a principal player in implementing the Eisenhower administration's Vietnam policy decision "to gamble with very limited resources because the potential gains seemed well worth a limited risk," using the words of a writer of the once-secret *Pentagon Papers*.

Lansdale, a former advertising executive, cut a dashing figure in Saigon in the mid-fifties while working as a CIA operative, so much so in fact that his persona was the chief character in two popular novels of the period—William Lederer and Eugene Burdick's *The Ugly American* and Graham Greene's *The Quiet American*. Prior to his Vietnam assignment, Lansdale had established himself as the country's top counterinsurgency expert, having played a key role in Philippine President Ramon Magsaysay's suppression of Communist-led Hukbalahap revolutionaries during the late 1940s. Lansdale was a sort of antiestablishment figure who thrived on day-to-day improvisation and worked best given only broad policy guidelines.

His general assignment in Vietnam was to harass Ho's government as it set about establishing administrative control in the north and to advise Ngo Dinh Diem on how to consolidate power in the south. Lansdale was to become Diem's closest and most loyal American adviser, his advocate within the U.S. government during Diem's early, uncer-

Intensified activity in Asia: Nixon with Philippine leader Ramon Magsaysay.

Diem with Lansdale (second from left).

tain days. It was he who prodded Diem to make sound strategic decisions that reduced the power of politically and militarily fractious elements in the south; who urged Diem's bold and decisive attack on the Binh Xuyen; and it was probably he who could be said to have saved Diem's life by his early recognition of Diem's need for a corps of loyal and well-trained bodyguards. Because of the bizarre political circumstances prevailing in South Vietnam in 1954, Diem's bodyguards had initially been appointed by one of his chief rivals in the south. One day when Lansdale paid a visit to Diem, who was blithely attending to administrative details in his study, he discovered not a single guard on duty. After that, Lansdale brought in Philippine experts to train a cadre of bodyguards for Diem.

Lansdale was a vertable encyclopedia of tricks. He managed to turn some of the mistresses of Diem's rivals into his agents, including the mistress of General Nguyen Van Hinh, who was chief of the South Vietnamese army in 1954. To facilitate their passing information directly to him, Lansdale formed a small English class for the ladies. And to make the South Vietnamese feel better about Diem's leadership, Lansdale paid a number of astrologers to prepare almanacs predicting good things for Diem and bad things for Ho. Many Vietnamese put great faith in astrological forecasts.

But it was in fulfilling his mission to destabilize Ho's government that Lansdale most fully exploited his ingenuity.

while it surveyed Diem's chances.

On September 8, 1954, the Southeast Asia Treaty Organization (SEATO) was created as the result of Dulles's initiative. The signatories included the U.S., the United Kingdom, France, Australia, New Zealand, Thailand, the Philippines and Pakistan. SEATO was modeled after NATO, its counterpart in Europe. Its purpose was to form an alliance to stop further Communist advances in the region and to shape a political context into which our incipient commitment to Vietnam would fit.

Concurrently, the Eisenhower administration began applying pressure on France to leave South Vietnam, where the French had hoped to maintain a strong political and economic presence. Though they had been forced to retreat there as an embarrassed, defeated force, they could point to a number of circumstances that supported the feasibility of their staying. In early September 1954, they still directly controlled the South Vietnamese army; a French general actually issued its orders. All the top Vietnamese officers had been appointed by Frenchmen; Nguyen Van Hinh, the ranking South Vietnamese general, was more French than Vietnamese—his father had long collaborated with the French, Hinh himself was educated in France, his wife was French. Within the South Vietnamese government, the French could also point to powerful support. The Saigon bureaucracy that Diem inherited controlled the administration of Cochinchina, long the French power base in Indochina. All the Vietnamese in that government, most notably Bao Dai, owed their appointments at least indirectly to France. Where Bao Dai stood on the question of a continuing French presence was indicated very clearly by his dwelling place. Though officially the chief of state of South Vietnam under whom Diem served as premier, Bao Dai chose to reside in Cannes, France, surrounded by a covey of concubines. As a final point in their favor, the French could note their continuing dominance of the economy of South Vietnam as represented by the Bank of Indochina, still doing business as usual. Understandably, the French worked against Diem because they knew he wanted to end such influences. And the Americans worked against the French because it was decided that if their colonial presence was not ended soon, the Communists would take over South Vietnam as surely as they had the north.

The battle for the political control of South Vietnam began in earnest in September 1954. There was talk of a coup each day. Hinh, openly disdainful of Diem's authority, boasted that he could remove Diem by merely picking up the phone. Finally, when Diem ordered him out of the country within twenty-four hours for a "study vacation," Hinh ordered army troops supported by tanks to encircle Independence Palace, Diem's Saigon residence. To strengthen his position, Hinh had arranged an alliance with the leaders of the Cao Dai and Hoa Hao sects and the Binh Xuyen. The sects were quasi-religious remnants of feudal Vietnam that controlled large areas south and west of Saigon. Each one had its own army, which served its own self-interests. The Binh Xuyen was actually an outlaw gang that controlled a variety of vice activities ranging from prostitution to gambling. So well established was the Binh Xuyen gang that Bao Dai had even contracted out the country's secret service duties to it before appointing Diem premier. It was a measure of Diem's desperate plight that it was this band of brigands that was charged with guard duty responsibilities at the palace, even though their opposition to Diem was so open that during September they had broken up a pro-Diem rally in Saigon (composed mostly of Catholic refugees from the north).

That Diem survived this particular episode was tribute both to his uncanny ability to play one group against another—and to the persuasive power of American money. Nine of Diem's fifteen cabinet members resigned, thinking that he would certainly fall. However, during the several days that Hinh's troops and their allies loitered around the palace awaiting orders to attack or for Diem to step down, Diem managed to buy the loyalty of the leaders of the Hoa Hao and Cao Dai. It reportedly cost the U.S. several million piasters to underwrite these payoffs, perhaps considerably more. The coup was thus aborted forty-eight hours before it was to have taken place. Diem and Hinh were stalemated for the next six weeks, when finally, as the result of American diplomatic moves, Hinh's position became untenable. At this point, Bao Dai would have preferred to support Hinh against Diem. Though the former emperor had for years tried to attract Diem into his government, now that the French were no longer in a position to keep the ambitious Diem subservient to him, he feared Diem. Thus, Bao Dai, acting from Cannes

The triviality of many of the Lansdale-inspired antics suggests how little he understood about the deep political and historical currents then running with Ho's independence movement and against Western intrusion of any kind. He seems to have believed that if the U.S. could disrupt something as trivial as the Hanoi city bus schedule long enough, the Vietnamese in the north would in frustration get rid of Ho. In fact, Lansdale's CIA team did try to disrupt the Hanoi transportation system. Before the October 9, 1954, deadline for the withdrawal of the French from Hanoi, his agents poured contaminant into the fuel tanks of the city's buses to gradually destroy the engines. They also contaminated some large fuel storage tanks in Hanoi, almost expiring from the fumes as they worked inside one. They tried to destroy the presses of a large printing company, but failed. They did succeed in disseminating thousands of copies of a document his team had expertly and falsely attributed to Ho's administration, in which the Communist government appeared to announce—to devastating effect—its future policy regarding private property and currency. The day after distribution, the number of people registering to move to South Vietnam tripled; within two days, the value of the piaster was half what it had been before the leaflet's distribution.

Lansdale also organized and trained two teams of Vietnamese agents, one operating in the north, the other in the south. To this day, their activities remain classified. What is known is that the Civil Air Transport Company, which was managed and partially owned by General Claire Chennault and which supplied the Dien Bien Phu garrison, won the exclusive contract for the air transport of refugees to the south by agreeing to smuggle arms into Haiphong for Lansdale's Vietnamese agents there.

A painting of Ngo Dinh Diem hung from the Saigon city hall in 1955.

While political struggles raged among the upper strata in the south in 1955, life changed little for the bottom class.

on French General Ely's advice that he not offend the Americans by supporting Hinh, ordered the general to France where, upon arrival, he was relieved of his command.

In September Diem was also a big winner at the conference table, due to American diplomatic initiatives designed to bolster the true independence of South Vietnam. From September 27 to 29, Dulles hosted a Franco-American conference in Washington. The results of the meeting indicate how politically powerful the U.S. was relative to its European ally in the fall of 1954: The liberation of France was still a fresh memory, Marshall Plan funds had helped revive the French economy, and the U.S. had paid for almost all the French war effort in Indochina during the final months of its war, all of which factors put the U.S. very much in the ascendance. By contrast, France's sense of inferiority (caused by its quick defeat during the Second World War) had been reinforced by its more recent loss at Dien Bien Phu and the political instability at home. Of necessity, the French thus agreed to the eventual transfer of control of the South Vietnamese army to the Vietnamese themselves. Over time the U.S. would assume responsibility

Much of Saigon (left) and Hanoi resemble Paris street scenes.

(Top) Troops of the Binh Xuyen, a sort of outlaw organization that opposed Diem, parade in Saigon. (Bottom) Leaders of mountain tribesmen swear fealty to Diem.

for training Vietnam's soldiers, and France would withdraw its entire expeditionary corps when the Vietnamese leadership so requested. The Vietnamese government would be granted control of its own commerce, economy and finances. One rapid result of these agreements was that Diem looked very much the hero when, a couple of months later, his government took charge of Saigon Harbor, issued its own currency, and set up the National Bank of Indochina, through which American financial assistance began to flow directly to the South Vietnamese. The last two actions, by American design, caused the liquidation of the Bank of Indochina, a principal symbol of the French colonial presence.

Diem's power base was still soft, however. The powerful sects and the Binh Xuyen were only temporarily placated by payoffs. By early 1955 they were gradually coming to the realization that a strong central government under Diem would work against their freewheeling behavior. Diem could no longer buy their support.

The French were also having second thoughts. Mendès-France's government was accused of selling out French interests to American demands. In fact, Edgar Faure replaced Mendès-France as premier in February 1955 and immediately expressed his disdain for Diem. As a consequence, the French began reasserting themselves in Vietnam. They much preferred the docile Bao Dai to the stubborn Diem. The French began actively encouraging insurrection by the sects, the Binh Xuyen and various army generals against Diem. The peripatetic Ely, now back in Vietnam, worked to influence the American

Troops loyal to Diem parade in Saigon. The U.S. was about to seek an alternative to Diem when these soldiers established Diem's primacy among rivals in the south.

ambassador against Diem, and apparently succeeded.

By the latter part of April 1955, Ambassador Collins was so convinced Diem had to go that he flew back to Washington to urge Dulles to take action. His judgment was not entirely subjective. He brought ample evidence that Diem's government was disintegrating. The Binh Xuyen, supported by most of the Cao Dai and Hoa Hao sects, had taken control of many strategic positions in Saigon and its Cholon suburb. Several Vietnamese army generals held a press conference, calling for Diem's resignation. Some influential members of Diem's cabinet had resigned, all to be replaced by Diem's relatives. Bao Dai, emboldened by French support, had ordered Diem to fly to France for consultations with him, and Diem was ignoring him. Furthermore, virtually all press accounts in the U.S. and France were predicting Diem's imminent ouster.

On April 27, Dulles reluctantly agreed to Collins's recommendation and cabled the American embassy in Saigon to find a suitable alternative to Diem to support. Word of the policy shift leaked out to the South Vietnamese embassy in Washington, which informed Diem, who immediately took action. He called in Lansdale, his most trusted American adviser, who throughout the April crisis had been meeting for long hours with him on a daily basis. That afternoon Diem ordered five loyal battalions composed mostly of Tongking émigrés (one armor and four paratroop units) to attack the Binh Xuyen positions. To the surprise of almost all observers, the Binh Xuyen fought poorly and Diem's troops fought well. Diem's forces won a major victory after nine hours of fighting in the streets of Saigon and Cholon.

The victory also won for Diem this country's unqualified support. His bold move finally convinced Dulles that the U.S. had indeed found the strong leader that South Vietnam needed. He cabled the Saigon embassy to burn his earlier cable. On May 6, U.S. support of Diem was publicly affirmed by an administration spokesman, and a chorus of American leaders joined in. In the coming months and years, Eisenhower repeatedly used American prestige to enhance Diem's stature. Dulles visited Vietnam in 1955; Nixon in 1956; Diem spoke before a joint session of Congress in 1957.

Thus, Diem's victory of April 27 marked a watershed. Thereafter, this country's support of

After conferring with Lansdale, Diem ordered loyal units to attack Binh Xuyen positions in Saigon.

Diem's victory over the Binh Xuyen cemented U.S. support. In June 1955, Diem, Lieutenant General John O'Daniel, and Senators Earle Clements and Everett Dirksen viewed a South Vietnamese battalion being trained by U.S. advisers.

The U.S. Catholic cardinals with Eisenhower: (l-r) Francis Spellman, Archbishop of New York; Edward Mooney, Archbishop of Detroit, and James McIntyre, Archbishop of Los Angeles. Spellman especially was influential in shaping U.S. support for Diem.

The aloof Diem tries to campaign for votes after calling for an October 23, 1955, election between himself and Bao Dai.

Diem and South Vietnam were one and the same. The Eisenhower administration made Diem a symbol of American success against the Communists in Asia, and everything possible—short of sending in American combat troops—was done to bolster Diem's image throughout the world and his strength at home. But after Communist guerrillas became increasingly active during the latter 1950s, 350 military personnel would be sent to Vietnam in May 1956 on the pretext of assisting the Vietnamese recover and repair French military equipment.

During the week of May 7–12, 1955, the U.S. convened a second Franco-American conference in Paris, this time to consolidate Diem's recent victory. France agreed to recall all officials in Vietnam who had worked against Diem, and promised an early withdrawal of their troops if Diem so requested—which he did. The French were embarrassed by evidence Dulles presented of their complicity in the attempted overthrow

of Diem. During the fighting, Diem's troops captured French advisers working among the Binh Xuyen, discovered the Binh Xuyen radio transmitter operating out of a French army camp, and intercepted a French ambulance filled with weapons destined for the Binh Xuyen.

On May 20, the French withdrew all their troops from the Saigon area. By July, French troop strength would drop from about 175,000 to 30,000 men. The last French soldier would leave South Vietnam less than a year later, on April 28, 1956.

Bao Dai's fortunes followed those of the French, who were his sponsors. In May during the Franco-American conference, Dulles refused to see Bao Dai; and Ambassador Collins, who had been reassigned to European duties, omitted Bao Dai during toasting ceremonies at his farewell dinner. Such an act is tantamount to diplomatic nonrecognition and would only have been done with Dulles's approval. Diem announced in June that a vote would be taken on October 23, 1955, to decide between himself and Bao Dai. The winner would be president. Diem won with 98.2 percent of the votes. He needlessly rigged the election, an act that should have served as a warning to the U.S. about Diem's methods. Diem wanted absolute power, his inherent insecurity and past close calls firing this drive.

In June Diem refused to talk to representatives of Communist North Vietnam about the referendum on reunification, which, according to the Geneva Accords, was scheduled for the following summer. Diem's position was that the South Vietnamese government was not a Geneva signator; nor was the U.S., of course. This action on Diem's part was apparently taken on his own initiative. The *Pentagon Papers,* probably the most candid account of official U.S. policymakers' thinking during those days, says that the "United States did not—as it is often alleged—connive with Diem to ignore the elections. U.S. State Department records indicate that Diem's refusal to be bound by the Geneva accords and his opposition to pre-election consultations were at his initiative."

Be that as it may, many American leaders were certainly active in supporting Diem's decision not to hold the referendum. Senator John Kennedy was one. His contention was that free elections could not be held in the Communist north. In June 1956 he urged that "the United States never give its approval to the only nation-

✳ In June 1956 Senator John F Kennedy supported Ngo Dinh Diem's decision not to hold the elections called for by the Geneva Agreement. His contention was that free elections could not be held in the Communist north. He urged that "the United States never give its approval to the only nationwide elections called for by the Geneva Agreement of 1954 ... neither the United States nor Free Vietnam is ever going to be a party to an election obviously stacked and subverted in advance."

Eisenhower turns to a Vietnamese girl in a crowd of foreign exchange students at the White House in 1955. The American public's vague awareness of their country's commitment to far-off Vietnam slowly emerged.

✳ Ngo Dinh Diem's election contest with former Emperor Bao Dai on October 23, 1955, did not bode well for democracy in the south. It exposed Diem's determination to exercise unchallenged leadership there. Because he was in direct control of the administration of the South Vietnamese government at the time, Diem was able to contrive conditions favorable to himself. The ballot itself was a travesty of the free electoral process. Below a photo of Diem surrounded by contemporary-looking young people was a box containing the words: "I depose Bao Dai and recognize Ngo Dinh Diem as Head of State, charged with the commission of setting up a democratic regime." Alternately, Bao Dai was shown in imperial robes, which he never wore, above the words, "I do not depose Bao Dai and do not regard Ngo Dinh Diem as the Head of State charged with the commission of setting up a democratic regime." The Diem photo was printed on a red background, the color of good luck to Vietnamese. Bao Dai's photo was printed on a green background, the color of bad luck.

Voting procedures were also an abomination. In some cases there were more votes cast than the number of registered voters. In Saigon 605,000 votes were cast, but only 450,000 were registered. Diem got 98.2 percent of the votes nationwide, "a margin of victory which . . . recalls elections in Communist states," wrote Robert Scigliano in 1960.

wide elections called for by the Geneva Agreement of 1954 . . . neither the United States nor Free Vietnam is ever going to be a party to an election obviously stacked and subverted in advance." The same could have been said for Diem's rigged contest with Bao Dai, and in later years the results of the 1961 national election in South Vietnam could be adduced as further conclusive proof of Diem's dictatorial and corrupt tendencies: Opposition candidates received only seven of the 102,031 votes cast in Pleiku Province.

Despite the evidence, U.S. military and financial aid to Diem increased constantly during the late 1950s. It totaled $1.8 billion from the time of the Geneva Conference in 1954 to mid-1959. How it was used was another foreboding sign: Eight of ten American aid dollars went for internal security, not to fight Communist guerrillas or implement reforms such as land redistribution. Diem was more worried about coups than Communists. Ironically, this country granted him unfettered use of these funds because it was reluctant to play the role of the colonial power dictating his every move, according to Chester Cooper, a State Department official during that period, who had been part of the U.S. delegation at Geneva.

As a consequence of his increasingly repressive internal measures, popular discontent with Diem gradually intensified, despite his attempts to squelch it at every opportunity. The millions of peasants in the countryside became estranged from him. While vast numbers of them remained landless, they observed huge plantations continuing operations. Diem guaranteed all large French and Vietnamese landholders that their properties would not be broken up, even though as late as 1960, fifteen percent of the people owned seventy-five percent of the land, and most of that was owned by two thousand people.

Not surprisingly, Communist activity intensified as discontent increased. And Diem's repressive measures increased accordingly. Thousands were put in jail. Though South Vietnam appeared to be an extraordinary example of stability in the late 1950s compared to other emerging nations, this tranquility was achieved by short-sighted, repressive policies that merely delayed political turmoil. By 1960, the only difference between the governments of Ngo Dinh Diem and Ho Chi Minh was their flags.

As a precondition for Khrushchev's 1957 visit, Eisenhower made the Soviet leader drop demands that NATO troops be removed from Berlin. Khrushchev raised the issue again during Kennedy's administration, whose reaction indirectly led to a greater U.S. commitment to South Vietnam.

(Above) Leaders of the elder generation—Eisenhower, Dulles and former Prime Minister Winston Churchill—gather at Dulles's Walter Reed Hospital room in May 1959, shortly before his death. In the U.S., the image of these aging men created the attraction for vigorous, young leadership. (Left) Saigon in 1960: In many aspects, leadership in the south under Diem was as repressive as that in the north under Ho.

Sharing the Sampan

The American Commitment

The evening of July 15, 1960, was a great one for Joseph P. Kennedy. The torch was about to be passed to a new generation of Americans, and the torch-bearer was his son. Like millions of others, Joe Kennedy sat before a television that night watching John F. Kennedy accept the Democratic Party's nomination for president of the United States. What was especially pleasing and important to the Kennedy patriarch on this particular evening was that his son's politics—at least in terms of foreign affairs—were about the same as his own. Around the world, John Kennedy and his generation would distinguish themselves from Joe's more in terms of age and style than substance. When son John later said that his generation would pay any price and bear any burden for the freedom of mankind, he meant it. And this promise was not so different from that which Joe's generation thought they had fulfilled. Both generations would prove themselves to be stridently anti-Communist. And this was very important for Joe Kennedy on this particular night, because the TV set he was watching belonged to Henry Luce.

The two men had long been good friends. In fact, Luce had given John Kennedy's career an early boost by writing the introduction to his book *Why England Slept*. Joe, while chairman of the Securities and Exchange Commission, had reciprocated by appointing Luce's son Hank his special assistant. However, on this night, the two had not gotten together to talk old times. Joe Kennedy's purpose was to convince Luce, the powerful publisher of *Time* and *Life* and an ardent promoter of John Foster Dulles's career and policies, that his son would be as tough on Communists as his Republican opponent, Richard Nixon.

Luce's approach to the conversation was to separate domestic and international politics. He said he understood that John Kennedy would have to be somewhat liberal on various domestic issues to carry the large states of the Northeast and industrial Midwest, but he warned that the liberal approach must end at the nation's borders. If during the campaign John Kennedy showed signs of being soft on Communism, Luce promised to turn his publications against him. Old Joe was somewhat insulted, so confident was he of

Vice-President Lyndon Johnson in Saigon in May 1961; above, John Kennedy accepts the Democratic Party's nomination.

Sharing the Sampan— *In their own words*

The question which concerns me most about this new administration is whether it lacks a genuine sense of conviction about what is right and what is wrong. . . . The Cuban fiasco demonstrates how far astray a man as brilliant and well intentioned as Kennedy can go who lacks a basic moral reference point.—Undersecretary of State Chester Bowles, writing in his diary shortly after the Bay of Pigs; May 1961.

In South Vietnam the U.S. has stumbled into a bog. It will be mired there for a long time.—Nikita Khrushchev to American ambassador to Moscow Llewellyn Thompson; in late summer of 1962.

We are launched on a course from which there is no turning back: the overthrow of the Diem government.—Ambassador Henry Cabot Lodge in a cable to Secretary of State Dean Rusk; on August 29, 1963.

Joseph P. Kennedy, Sr.   Henry Luce

 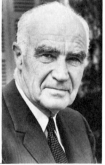

John Kennedy's politics. No son of his would be a damn liberal, especially when it came to dealing with Communists.

The campaign confirmed his conviction. Not long before the election, when editors of *Life* were preparing to run an editorial commending the foreign policy proposals of candidate Nixon, Luce told them to delay it another week because Nixon had not demonstrated that he was any more ardently anti-Communist than Kennedy. Although it did run later, the closeness of the election gave the strongly Republican Luce some second thoughts about the evenhandedness of his treatment of Kennedy. Not so much so, however, that he felt uncomfortable about joining the next president in his private box on the night of the inaugural ball.

Henry Luce had every reason to feel comfortable in such company. In a political sense, Kennedy and his generation were products of the politics and attitudes Luce had helped to mold. While a senator, Kennedy had generally supported the foreign policy of Eisenhower and Dulles. In fact, Kennedy's first two official announcements were reappointments of key figures in the Eisenhower administration: J. Edgar Hoover as director of the FBI, and Allen Dulles, brother of the late John Foster Dulles, as director of the CIA. Henry Luce must have been very pleased about both choices. Dulles and Hoover were perhaps the most vocal anti-Communists of the previous administration. Kennedy also added Douglas Dillion to the list of top-level holdovers, moving him up from undersecretary of state to secretary of the treasury. At the time of Dien Bien Phu he had been ambassador to France.

Luce should have been pleased, too, with selections from the young president's own generation. Dean Rusk, his secretary of state, had been an almost rabid anti-Communist during the latter years of the Truman administration. After his appointment as Dean Acheson's undersecretary of state for Far Eastern affairs in 1950, Rusk had delivered one remarkable speech, which, in the words of David Halberstam, "was a horror," portraying "the blood virtually dripping off the teeth of the Chinese-Russian aggressor." In fact, Rusk's conservative credentials were so sound that John Foster Dulles himself had gotten Rusk the job—as director of the Rockefeller Foundation—which he resigned to accept the Kennedy appointment. Then there

On January 20, 1961, the legend of Camelot was born when forty-three-year-old John Kennedy was sworn in as president. The nation was in love with itself and its elegant young leader. (Clockwise from left) Kennedy delivers his inaugural speech; Jackie and JFK in the inaugural parade down Pennsylvania Avenue; Kennedy and Johnson on the parade reviewing stand; the view from the president's box at the inaugural ball.

Kennedy's first two appointments allayed conservatives' concern that he would be soft on Communists: He reappointed J. Edgar Hoover as FBI director and Allen Dulles as head of the CIA.

McGeorge Bundy   Robert McNamara

At his parents' winter home in Palm Beach, Florida, President-elect Kennedy introduces to the press his secretary of state-designate, Dean Rusk.

was McGeorge Bundy, Kennedy's Special Assistant for National Security Affairs, an elitist with old-line establishment family connections, an archetype of what Halberstam later called the best and the brightest of the whole generation, and a sort of embodiment of Kennedy's famous quip—he was a Harvard educator with a Yale degree. His mother was descended from Percival Lowle who came to America in 1639. The family had controlled so much of the New England textile industry that young girls who came off the farms to work in the mills during the nineteenth century were referred to generically as Lowell (sic) Mill girls. The Lowells of Boston looked upon Harvard as their own private school. Bundy's great-great-grandfather, John Amory Lowell, was credited with personally appointing no fewer than six Harvard presidents. Bundy's father had been the law clerk to Oliver Wendell Holmes after graduating first in his Harvard law class. Later he had served as an aide to Herbert Hoover's secretary of state, Henry Stimson.

McGeorge Bundy's older brother William also became a high-level Kennedy administration official. He was appointed assistant secretary of defense. William, the family's Democrat, was married to Acheson's daughter. In 1965, after Kennedy's death, William exchanged his position at Defense for a similar one in the State Department, a move he made with alacrity. "In our house," he once said, "the State Department and the Pentagon were interchangeable."

Nor did Henry Luce have cause to worry about Kennedy's secretary of defense, Robert

Two of the generation "tempered by war, disciplined by a hard and bitter peace": Lieutenant (j.g.) John Kennedy with his PT 109 crew in the Pacific and Colonel Dean Rusk (below) in China during the Second World War.

McNamara. How politically unpredictable could a president of Henry Ford's motor company be?

If anything, these New Frontiersmen would be more activist in their anti-Communist crusade than their predecessors in the Eisenhower administration. They were, after all, the generation that had fought the last big war, as they were generally fond of saying—which was not really true of most of them, individually. Though many of their generation had indeed been in the trenches, the handful who played top-level roles in early Vietnam policymaking were not among them. Rusk had been a staff colonel, McGeorge Bundy had been an aide to an admiral who was a friend of the family, and Walt Rostow, Bundy's deputy and the top White House adviser on Southeast Asian affairs, had selected targets for others to fly while McNamara was back in some Washington cubicle masterminding the whole thing. (During that pre-computer era, McNamara had coordinated the entire B-29 long-range bomber plan in the Pacific, becoming a repository of all information relative to the new plane's operational capabilities, the crew schedules and the target requirements.) Of the key civilian policymakers, only Kennedy himself had been in combat.

Yet in their public pronouncements and private pursuits they chose to project an image of men "tempered by war [and] disciplined by a hard and bitter peace." They climbed mountains. Rode the rapids. Wrote books. (And, so it was said, could read them in minutes.) Not surprisingly, this group, especially the young, dynamic president, immediately won the hearts of the next generation—the generation that would in fact pay the price and bear the burden this time around, the generation that would be ordered to fight the Vietnam war.

They wanted to emulate this Kennedy group.

All the Kennedy family and top officials of the new administration promoted a fitness craze, setting examples themselves by sailing, swimming, riding rapids, climbing mountains and playing touch football.

(Top) Kennedy was a skilled speaker whose talents allowed him to become the first Catholic elected president.

(Above) Chief Justice Earl Warren administers the oath of office to Kennedy's cabinet. (Right) Charismatic Kennedy campaigns.

In little towns across the country, they eagerly signed up for the president's youth fitness program and enrolled in rapid-reading courses. Not understanding the uniquely fortuitous combination of birth, wealth, education and connections that had caused the Kennedy group to rise so quickly to top leadership positions, they seemed to feel that they could achieve the same degree of success with hard work and determination. Remarkably, the son of a Massachusetts multi-millionaire and power broker came to represent the American dream to the high-school and college-age population more forcefully than any previous president had been able to do. Eisenhower had been far more representative of their background and the route they would need to follow to the top, but somehow Kennedy embodied their future ambitions.

Just as this generation was moving toward adulthood, Kennedy had sounded a clarion call to get the country moving again. It was heavy stuff, to be a young American during those days. When their president told them to ask not what their country could do for them but what they could do for their country, they took him at his word and lined up for the Peace Corps, joined the military services, and developed a precocious interest in the affairs of Washington. Youngsters several thousand miles and light-years away from the bright new galaxy of stars gathering in Washington could name all the members of Kennedy's cabinet. Kennedy would light a fire in their hearts that would continue to burn long after this group of leaders would disappoint their dreams. The same idealism that would cause them to swell with pride for having such leadership during the early sixties would cause them to turn against it later in the decade. In 1961, they would have agreed with one Kennedy adviser, who, upon observing the man-

Ties that bind...

• Truman's Secretary of State Dean Acheson actively used John Foster Dulles as a part-time adviser on Far Eastern affairs during the Truman administration.
• Acheson appointed Dean Rusk asistant secretary of state for Far Eastern affairs.
• Dulles succeeded Acheson as secretary of state during the Eisenhower administration.
• Dulles got Rusk appointed director of the Rockefeller Foundation.
• Rusk became secretary of state for the Kennedy and Johnson administrations.
• William Rogers, a member of Dulles's old New York law firm, succeeded Rusk as secretary of state during the Nixon administration.
• Henry Kissinger succeeded Rogers as secretary of state while retaining his position as President Nixon's special assistant for National Security Affairs in Nixon's White House. He remained secretary of state during the Ford administration.
• McGeorge Bundy had held this same National Security Affairs position at the White House under Presidents Kennedy and Johnson.
• McGeorge Bundy's brother William, who was married to Dean Acheson's daughter, served as assistant secretary of state for Far Eastern affairs during the Johnson administration.
• McGeorge Bundy had resigned from his position as a dean and a government professor at Harvard, where he taught the course "Government 180: The U.S. in World Affairs," in order to take the White House post.
• Kissinger succeeded Bundy at Harvard as the instructor of "Government 180." While teaching at Harvard, Kissinger served as an occasional consultant to Bundy concerning European affairs.

To Serve Is To Rule...

John Kennedy attracted a remarkable group of talented people to government, many of them from Massachusetts or with educational backgrounds there. It is customary, of course, for a president to appoint a disproportionate number of individuals from his home state to positions in his administration. What was unique about Kennedy's adminis- tration in this regard is that so many of them had the credentials to support their appointment to high-level policy- making positions. This was due to the extraordinary concentration of top universities in the state. As a conse- quence, Vietnam policy was, in a sense, a provincial product. Most who played key Vietnam policymaking roles were either from Massachusetts or were the product of its educational institutions.

John and Robert Kennedy were Harvard graduates. McGeorge Bundy, Kennedy's special assistant for National Security Affairs, and Robert McNamara, the secretary of defense, were former Harvard professors. Walt Rostow, Bundy's deputy and the top White House official working on Southeast Asia, taught at M.I.T. William Bundy, McGeorge's older brother who initially served as assistant secretary of defense for international security affairs and was later appointed the assistant secre- tary of state for Far Eastern affairs, was a Harvard graduate like the Ken- nedys. Many who played important secondary roles pertaining to Vietnam policy also had Harvard affiliations, among them Adam Yarmolinsky, a top personal aide to McNamara, and John McNaughton, the assistant secretary of defense for National Security Affairs, both former Harvard Law School profes- sors, and Carl Kayson of McGeorge Bundy's staff, also a former Harvard professor.

The only key Vietnam policymakers without obvious Massachusetts connec- tions were Secretary of State Dean

euvers of a well-trained young group of counter- insurgency soldiers, asked what the country was saving them for—the senior prom? They were ready to serve, and, as strange as it sounds in restrospect, many came to look upon Vietnam as their burden, their test—perhaps even their op- portunity—just as the Second World War had seemed to be for Kennedy's generation.

In 1961 Kenendy was convinced that the United States was entering the most dangerous period in its history. And so it seemed. The so-called missile gap, which had loomed so large since the launching of Sputnik in 1957, had been a major issue in the campaign. Kennedy had promised to close it. Millions of Americans were convinced that the Russians were passing us on all fronts. This sense of decline heightened concern about power struggles in many new nations through- out the world. The geopolitical transformation that Roosevelt anticipated and encouraged had occurred. Dozens of former colonies had gained independence. In 1946 the United Nations roster listed fifty-five member nations. By the time of Kennedy's inauguration, the number had in- creased to one hundred and four. Few of these new nations were politically stable. And though

the internal struggle for power in each was usually complex—sometimes involving centuries-old religious and sectarian rivalries—both the U.S. and the Soviet Union, because of their own ideological rivalry, were eager to involve themselves in the domestic politics of these emerging nations. The leadership of each country was expected to choose camps, which, of course, increased internal tensions as well as tension between the U.S. and the USSR. Dulles once charged that neutralism was immoral.

The United States and the Soviet Union competed on a broad scale to impress and woo the national leadership and, failing that, to develop an opposition party within each society. The Peace Corps, preferential economic treatment, education scholarships, technical advice, administrative expertise and, of course, military training and hardware were all part of the U.S. package. The Soviet Union had its counterpart for each. Successive American administrations also believed—with justification—that the Communists were prone to use subversive tactics to win the loyalty of these colonies. Khrushchev had publicly promised as much: On January 4, 1961, he pledged the Soviet Union to support wars of national liberation.

Rusk; General Maxwell Taylor, initially the senior White House military adviser and later chairman of the Joint Chiefs; and Averell Harriman, his initial administration appointment in October 1961 being undersecretary of state for Far Eastern affairs. Rusk, however, was never fully accepted by Kennedy or his Massachusetts coterie, and he labored under the additional disadvantage that the president preferred being his own secretary of state. As for Taylor, a West Point graduate, Kennedy brought him out of retirement precisely because, despite his background, he fit in so well with his other top staff appointees. ("...if Harvard produced generals," observed David Halberstam, "it would have produced Max Taylor.") The worldly Harriman was not identified with Massachusetts or its institutions and had long since established an identity disassociated from his educational origins, which were Groton prep school and Yale. Significantly, Harriman was one of the few administration officials who early on had reservations about the direction of U.S. policy in Vietnam.

The homogeneity of Kennedy's group did not go unnoticed. In fact, some were worried about it, including David Riesman, a distinguished sociologist at Harvard who knew, better than most of his colleagues, that Harvard was not for all of America the cynosure it was for them. In *The Best and the Brightest*, Halberstam (Harvard '55) tells about a luncheon Riesman had in 1961 with two Harvard colleagues who had joined the administration and were enthralled by the possibilities of their own ideas. While the two talked on and on excitedly, it occurred to Riesman, who possessed a subtle understanding of

(Opposite) The launch of Liberty Bell 7 on July 21, 1961, with Virgil Grissom aboard. For Kennedy, the space program represented not only scientific achievement but also world leadership. (Left) Consciously disassociating himself from his older predecessor, he normally eschewed hats, golf and cigars.

the delicate fabric that held this country together, that these appointed officials had no sense of accountability to the public and virtually no understanding of it. Unable to take it any longer, he interjected. "Have either of you ever been to Utah?" he asked.

"Utah! Why Utah!?" No, they hadn't; but why did he ask?

Riesman's point was that his two former colleagues and too many of their administration peers were provincials—brilliant, but provincial nonetheless.

"You all think . . . you're dealing with an elite society which is just waiting for your leadership. It's not that way at all," he said. "It's not an elite society run for Harvard and the Council on Foreign Relations."

House Speaker Sam Rayburn (East Texas Normal College, '03) had independently come to similar conclusions and reservations about Kennedy's appointees. One day early in the Kennedy administration, Vice-President Lyndon Johnson (Southwest Texas State Teachers College, '30) stopped by his old friend's office. He had just come from Kennedy's first cabinet meeting. Johnson was such an outsider that Kennedy's staff had forgotten to invite him until the others were arriving. Frantic calls had gone out until he was located. Still, Johnson was mightily impressed with Kennedy's team—almost overwhelmed, in fact, by their confidence, brilliance and style. McNamara—in Johnson's words, "the fellow from Ford with the Stacomb in his hair"—especially struck him. Rayburn's reaction was as perceptive as Riesman's, though he drew upon personal experience rather than scholarly research. "Well, Lyndon, you may be right and they may be every bit as intelligent as you say," said the Speaker, "but I'd feel a whole lot better about them if just one of them had run for sheriff once."

The U.S.--Soviet rivalry in Third World nations further fueled the direct U.S.--Soviet arms rivalry, on the theory that if both superpowers offered basically the same aid package to former colonies, new nations would be attracted to that superpower which seemed to be in the ascendance. Thus Sputnik, the missile gap, the race to the moon, and other indicators of technological superiority took on symbolic as well as substantive significance. In the resulting arms race, both the U.S. and the Soviet Union constructed nuclear weapons and delivery systems far in excess of actual need for self-protection.

The emphasis on military power in 1962 was not new thinking within the Democratic Party—such militance was a lineal descendant of the Cold War policies of Harry Truman and Dean Acheson—but it was a departure from the policy of the previous decade. The Democrats had presented in those intervening years a more moderate position with Adlai Stevenson, the philosophical descendant of Roosevelt, running as their presidential candidate against Eisenhower in both 1952 and 1956. By comparison with Eisenhower's ideologues, Nixon and Dulles, Stevenson seemed "soft" on Communism.

Kennedy's election represented the ascendance of the Acheson wing over the Stevenson wing. When making foreign policy, Kennedy invariably moved to strengthen his base within the conservative-moderate wing, which formed his center of support. Liberals were left with a choice between Kennedy and a Republican like Richard Nixon. In foreign affairs, Kennedy man-

JFK and U.N. Ambassador Adlai Stevenson.

aged to give the appearance of liberalism, because his relaxed, confident manner reminded liberal Democrats of their cherished Stevenson. To a remarkable degree, Kennedy managed to combine the politics of Acheson and the style of Stevenson to win the election. He was to the followers of each what they wanted to see: a "Stevenson with balls," as Joseph Alsop described him to a friend. Kennedy would have loved the description. He and key members of his administration relished their macho image. "We've got twenty Vietnams a day to handle," Attorney General Robert Kennedy told Far Eastern reporter Stanley Karnow in early 1961 while dismissing signs of trouble there as anything extraordinary.

Kennedy's administration did not start well, though on the surface it seemed to. Initially, there had been a tremendous burst of energy, the president doing an extraordinary job of duplicating the interest generated by Roosevelt during his first hundred days. His live press conferences became public happenings. Over a third of the population watched the third one. Public opinion polls showed a large majority of Americans smitten by the dashing young chief executive and his beautiful wife. But there were problems.

One pertained to the missile gap. There was none. It had been a good campaign issue, and voters were easily swayed into believing that the Eisenhower administration had been composed of tired old men whose vigor was strained by a Sunday game of golf—but it was a false

Robert Kennedy confers with his top staff members in 1963: Burke Marshall, Deputy Attorney General Nicholas Katzenbach, Harold Reis and Harold Green. Katzenbach later provided Lyndon Johnson key legal advice on the Gulf of Tonkin Resolution.

Kennedy with his wife Jacqueline and their daughter Caroline: He was the first president since Theodore Roosevelt to have a family of young children living in the White House.

Kennedy's handsome, good-humored traits and his beautiful young wife captivated the country that he promised to "get moving again." Rear (l-r), his brother Robert, his parents and his brother-in-law Sargent Shriver.

issue. McNamara himself was said to be surprised to learn, once taking charge at Defense, that there was no gap, that the Russians were not ahead of us in the missile race. It was awkward to explain away. But this was a minor problem compared to the series of crises that were soon to push all else into the background: first Laos, then the Bay of Pigs, and shortly thereafter, the Berlin Wall. The Eisenhower commitment to Vietnam, described as a "limited risk gamble" in the *Pentagon Papers,* would be enlarged into a "broad commitment" as a direct result of the rapid succession of events that began in February 1961.

During a briefing the day before JFK assumed office, Eisenhower startled him by suggesting that the U.S. might soon have to go to war to save Laos.

During a briefing the day before the young president took office, Eisenhower had startled Kennedy by rather passionately suggesting that the U.S. might have to go to war in the near future to save Laos. Clark Clifford accompanied Kennedy and took notes: "Laos was the key to the entire area of Southeast Asia . . . if we permitted Laos to fall, then we would have to write off all the area," Clifford remembers Eisenhower saying.

The Laotian problem had been in large part a U.S. creation. "I struggled for sixteen months to prevent a coalition [government]," Graham Parsons testified before a congressional committee. Parsons had been the U.S. ambassador to Laos during the last years of Eisenhower's administration. A neutralist government was unacceptable to U.S. policymakers, so this country supported a right-wing general named Phoumi Nosavan, who since 1958 "had lived well off the Cold War" and revenues generated from participation in the opium trade. But his lascivious nature was the least of Kennedy's concerns in January 1961. Phoumi was weak and ineffective. "If that's our strong man, we're in trouble,"

A White House gathering of government leaders, new and old, on January 19, 1961.

Kennedy remarked after meeting him. His troops were no better. Averell Harriman remembers being briefed about the major improvements in Phoumi's army: "Only a few months ago, the Laotians used to retreat without their weapons; now they take their weapons with them when they run away," a U.S. officer fresh from the scene related.

American worries about Laos reached crisis proportions in February 1961. The armies of neutralist leader Prince Souvanna Phouma and Communist Pathet Lao leader Prince Soupanuvong joined forces to capture the strategic Plain of Jars in central Laos. Kennedy and his advisers considered sending in aircraft and troops. "We have the Seventh Fleet and we have the planes to wipe Tchepone off the face of the earth," observed Admiral Harry Felt, commander of all U.S. forces in the Pacific. "I look upon our Asian policy as having two pillars, South Vietnam and Thailand," said the ambassador to Vietnam, Frederick Nolting, Jr. "Laos is the keystone to support them. If the keystone falls, the pillars will collapse."

Keystone or not, Laos presented too many problems for her would-be savior: American

Kennedy meets with the press outside the Oval Office after his meeting with Eisenhower.

✳ During the Second World War, one
interesting question discussed in political circles was what impact the returning veterans would have on the political
scene. Most thought they would make a
big grab for special benefits. Some of
the veterans themselves eschewed this
attitude, however. Some thought "that
what was good for the nation was good
for the veteran," said Charles Bolte.
Thus, Bolte and fellow veteran Gilbert
Harrison founded the American Veterans Committee, an alternative to the
American Legion and the special-
interest lobbying it represented. The
idealistic AVCers wanted benefits for
all, without preference for veterans.
They supported national medical health
care and low-cost housing for everyone.
Bolte and Harrison had consulted Walter Lippmann for ideas before setting
up their organization. "Go ahead, but
keep it small," he advised. "Try to get
men who are going to govern the country in twenty-five years, and don't let
the big numbers join."

"Well, we beat Lippmann's goal by
five years," said Bolte. Five members of
John Kennedy's cabinet were former
AVC members: Dean Rusk, Orville
Freeman, Stewart Udall, Arthur
Goldberg and Abraham Ribicoff. (The
AVC still keeps a small office on Con-
necticut Avenue off Dupont Circle in
Washington, D.C.)

troops could not be resupplied by ship, and
fighter planes from the Seventh Fleet would
have to overfly North Vietnam. Furthermore,
Phoumi and his troops were too unreliable to
hold power even if it were handed them.

Kennedy decided to negotiate. On March 23,
he announced during a televised news conference that the U.S. would support "a neutral and
independent Laos." This was later achieved by
the able efforts of Harriman during a fourteen-
nation Laotian conference in Geneva and by
pressure put on Soupanuvong by the Russians,
their man reportedly being as incompetent as
Phoumi. On April 1 a cease-fire was agreed to
even before the conference began. Surprisingly,
it held. Later, a neutral government was installed.
The crisis slowly began to fade following the
cease-fire. In a sense, it was a victory for the
U.S. because it had had no real leverage to effect
this relatively favorable result.

Still, many American leaders looked upon the
settlement with displeasure, their intractability
typical of America's posture during the fifties
and early sixties. Lyndon Johnson's reaction
was representative: Michael Forrestal, a White
House specialist on Southeast Asian affairs,
was sent to brief him in detail on the Laotian
accord; Johnson was already aware of its main
points. Upon arriving for a scheduled appointment,
Forrestal found the vice-president stretched out
on a tabletop for the ministrations of his masseur.
Throughout the briefing, Forrestal had to jockey
for position with the masseur, who was constantly shifting positions and smacking away at
the nude vice-president. Forrestal took the rude
reception as indicative of Johnson's disdain for
the Laos settlement. The attitude that the only
acceptable conclusion of a struggle with Communists was their unconditional surrender would
persist throughout most of the years of struggle
in Vietnam. In 1962 when Undersecretary of
State Chester Bowles suggested to Rusk that
the time was propitious for a negotiated settlement and the neutralization of Vietnam, the
secretary of state turned to him coldly and said,
"You realize, of course, you're spouting the
Communist line." Sensitive to such attitudes,
Kennedy told the American people in his March
23 televised news conference, "The security of
all Southeast Asia will be endangered if Laos
loses its neutral independence. Its own safety
runs with the safety of us all."

The Bay of Pigs crisis came next. The idea of

an American-sponsored invasion of Cuba designed to overthrow Fidel Castro had been
developed by the CIA during the Eisenhower
administration. Kennedy learned of the plan on
November 29, 1960, shortly after his election.
He had time to stop it, but did not. He was
persuaded to grant approval by CIA director
Allen Dulles and the Joint Chiefs headed by
General Lyman Lemnitzer. They agreed unani-
mously that the plan would work. But, because
of the almost incredible stupidity and sloppiness
of both plan and execution, it did not. For
example, the landing area was supposedly in a
deserted, remote part of the island; what the
CIA did not know, but could easily have learned,
was that in the years since Castro's takeover, an
amusement park had been built there.

The fourteen-hundred-man invasion force landed
on April 17, 1961. Within seventy-two hours a
large percentage of them had been killed and the
rest were captured, later to be put on trial in
Havana's Sports Palace. For the U.S., the Bay
of Pigs was an international public relations
disaster, a gross foreign policy failure acutely
embarrassing to Kennedy. The *Frankfurter Neue
Presse* declared that Kennedy was "to be regarded as politically and morally defeated." "In
one day," said the *Cordiere della Sera* of Milan,
"American prestige collapsed lower than in
eight years of Eisenhower timidity and lack of
determination." The Englishman who so ad-

Kennedy faced a series of crises during
his first year: over Laos in March; the
Bay of Pigs in Cuba in April; and Berlin
in late summer. (Top) Kennedy during
a televised news conference about Laos.
(Above) His adversaries, Fidel Castro
and Khrushchev. (Left) He confers with
Eisenhower at Camp David after the
Bay of Pigs debacle.

mired the performance of Lord Hailey at Mont Tremblont in 1942 must surely have been convinced that all his worst fears about the "management of great affairs" being taken over by amateurish American professors had been realized.

Kennedy's formal reaction to the Bay of Pigs was a speech delivered to a convention of the American Society of Newspaper Editors a few days after the invasion force was overwhelmed. He came on strong, warning Communists from Havana to Moscow. The U.S. was prepared to act "alone, if necessary," to "safeguard its security." He had shown restraint this time, he said, but he warned that "should the time ever come, we do not intend to be lectured on intervention by those whose character was stamped for all time on the bloody streets of Budapest." The danger, he told his audience, was that "our security may be lost, piece by piece, country by country, without the firing of a single missile or the crossing of a single border. . . . Let me then make clear as the President of the United States that I am determined upon our system's survival and success, regardless of the cost and regardless of the peril."

After the Bay of Pigs came Berlin, which had been a cause of U.S.–Soviet friction for fifteen years. The presence of NATO troops in West Berlin, deep inside East Germany, bothered Stalin so much that he had closed off all western land access to the city in 1948. The massive Berlin airlift finally broke the siege.

In 1957, after Sputnik raised Russian prestige, Khrushchev was emboldened to make Berlin an issue once again. He demanded of Eisenhower that Berlin be made a demilitarized "free city." But the president deftly pushed the issue into the background. Knowing that Khrushchev very much wanted to make a state visit to the United States, Eisenhower made the Russian leader drop the Berlin problem as a precondition for the desired invitation.

However, Kennedy's handling of the Bay of Pigs emboldened Khrushchev once more. He began calling the status of West Berlin "a bone stuck in the throat," "a sort of cancerous tumor requiring a surgical operation," and a "Sarajevo," likely to lead to another world war.

Early in Kennedy's administration, a summit conference with Khrushchev had been tentatively scheduled for June. In May Kennedy reconfirmed the scheduled meeting upon inquiry from

Though Robert Kennedy was his brother's attorney general (so that Bobby could get some legal experience, JFK joked), he also acted as a foreign emissary, visiting Southeast Asia, including Vietnam.

Khrushchev. Kennedy was reluctant to attend a summit conference so soon after the Bay of Pigs, but decided that postponement would be a sign of weakness.

On June 3, 1961, they met at the American embassy in Vienna, Austria, for the first of two days of meetings—Kennedy and Khrushchev alone with an interpreter. A brief stopover in Paris beforehand had seemed to portend good things. The French were enthralled with the handsome president and especially his bilingual, sophisticated young wife. "I do not think it altogether improper for me to introduce myself," Kennedy told those gathered at a huge press conference. "I am the man who accompanied Jacqueline Kennedy to Paris." In Vienna, however, the gay mood turned somber.

The dashing first couple was greeted enthusiastically during state visits. This was especially so in France; Jacqueline Kennedy spoke French fluently, having attended school at the Sorbonne.

✳ When John Kennedy began his run for the presidency in 1960, he was conscious of the fact that he was not identified with a strong defense program. Other senators who were potential Democratic presidential nominees had established such images by becoming the patrons of various weapons systems. Henry Jackson had the Polaris submarine, Stuart Symington had the B-52 and Lyndon Johnson had Space. Kennedy staffer Deirdre Henderson called an unknown Defense Department intellectual for suggestions about what Kennedy could patronize. "How about the infantryman?" he said. Good idea, decided Kennedy; so his specialty became the infantryman, and from that evolved his interest in counterinsurgency and Green Beret–type soldiering. The Green Berets, of course, would be the first large contingent he would order to Vietnam. The Defense intellectual who gave Kennedy the infantryman idea and started him along this line of thinking was, ironically, Daniel Ellsberg, who years later, out of disgust with the Vietnam war, released the classified *Pentagon Papers* to the *New York Times*.

Kennedy's planned approach was to discuss openly and frankly the options the two leaders faced on the Berlin question, on the basis of which some sort of understanding could be arrived at. This typified the rational approach Kennedy hoped would characterize his term in office, and for the purpose of which he had gathered the brilliant professors and Rhodes Scholars who composed much of his administration. Kennedy always liked to say, "You can't beat brains." But he had not met Khrushchev; nor had he or any of his close advisers adequately contended with the deep emotions and differing perspectives that separate cultures— reason not always bridging such gaps. The wise old Harriman, the administration's own as yet unrecognized Lord Hailey, had taken Kennedy aside during the Paris stopover to advise him not to get his hopes up, in fact to expect some bullying from the Russian leader. His recommendation was to shrug off such behavior, to deflect it but not belittle it, even to have some fun if possible. Harriman had had considerable experience in dealing with the Russians, dating back to Franklin Roosevelt's administration when he served as the American ambassador to Moscow. His prediction and advice proved to be on target, but Kennedy was still not prepared for the abuse he received.

As it happened, Kennedy had agreed to an interview with *New York Times* Washington bureau chief James Reston immediately after the last meeting. The rest of the press corps was kept unaware of the appointment, while Reston slipped into the embassy and was secretly escorted into the ambassador's office where he pulled the blinds, lest someone see him inside. For four hours he waited in the darkness. Finally, the door opened and Kennedy walked in. He slumped heavily on the couch where Reston was seated, pulled the brim of the hat he was wearing down over his eyes, and sighed deeply.

"Pretty rough?" asked Reston.

"The toughest thing in my life," said Kennedy.

On the basis of their conversation, Reston, about a year after Kennedy's death, wrote:

"Khrushchev had studied the events of the Bay of Pigs; he would have understood if Kennedy had left Castro alone or destroyed him; but when Kennedy was rash enough to strike at Cuba but not bold enough to finish the job, Khrushchev decided he was dealing with an inexperienced young leader who could be intimi-

dated and blackmailed."

The Russian had been savage, seemingly uncontrolled during most of the meetings. At times, he seemed about to lunge at him, Kennedy said. Khrushchev had given him an ultimatum on Berlin: By the end of December the U.S. must sign a treaty agreeing to remove Western troops from Berlin. Khrushchev refused to reason with Kennedy. "I want peace," the Russian premier told him, "but if you want war that is your problem."

Kennedy was shaken by the confrontation. Khrushchev's method was so primitive; war now seemed so close. "So I've got a terrible problem," Kennedy told Reston. "If he thinks I'm inexperienced and have no guts, until we remove those ideas we won't get anywhere with him. So we have to act."

And he did; in fact, both men did—matching each other move for move. Khrushchev announced a large military budget increase immediately upon his return and began delivering a series of wildly chauvinistic speeches. Kennedy countered by asking Congress for an increase in military spending, calling up the reserves, tripling the draft calls, raising the ceiling level for

Kennedy called his face-off with Khrushchev in Vienna "the toughest thing in my life." The Soviet leader tried to bully him. Shortly thereafter Khrushchev tested Kennedy's mettle over the status of Berlin.

Kennedy preferred acting almost as his own secretary of state. In contrast to Rusk's low profile in the administration, McNamara became a dominant figure, supposedly an embodiment of Kennedy's "rational approach" to problem-solving. Above, the president views the Berlin wall.

combat troops and ordering the reconditioning of aircraft and ships in mothballs. "If war breaks out," he told the American people on June 25, "it will have been started in Moscow and not in Berlin. . . . Only the Soviet government can use the Berlin frontier as a pretext for war." Acheson and Johnson even urged him to declare a national emergency, but Kennedy held off, thinking that overreaction would end all possibility of a peaceful settlement.

Refugees began streaming into West Berlin from the Communist-controlled half of Germany. During July, 30,444 arrived; during the first ten days of August, 16,500; on August 12 alone, another 4,000. Most were highly skilled and educated. The flow was more than embarrassing to Khrushchev; the "brain drain" was undermining his Five-Year Program. So he reacted. Shortly after midnight on August 13, sirens could be heard in the streets of East Berlin. Police cars, army trucks and tanks rumbled up to the dividing line. Before the eyes of startled American, French and British border guards, Russian troops piled out of the vehicles with sawhorses, concertina wire and construction equipment. Within hours, a rudimentary form of the Berlin wall was in place. Protests by Kennedy and the governments of Great Britain and France were ignored.

Then, on September 1, Khrushchev raised the stakes again. The Soviets resumed atmospheric tests of nuclear weapons. In all, they detonated thirty such devices in about thirty days. After the first few, Kennedy responded with resumption of underground nuclear testing for the U.S.

On September 8, Khrushchev demanded that flights into Berlin be limited, a demand Kennedy immediately rejected. Several days later, United Nations Secretary General Dag Hammarskjöld was killed in a mysterious plane crash in the Congo. Khrushchev had long despised Hammarskjöld, accusing him of acting as a pawn of the colonial powers. When the plane crash could not be explained, suspicions about its cause increased tensions between the U.S. and the Soviet Union.

Then, almost as unpredictably as he had created the crisis, the mercurial Khrushchev began to back off. In early October he told Belgian diplomat Paul-Henri Spaak during a Moscow visit, "I realize that contrary to what I had hoped the western powers will not sign the . . . treaty. . . . I'm not trying to put you in an impossible situation. . . . Berlin is not such a big problem for me. What are two million people among a billion Communists!" The biggest world crisis since 1945 quickly began to ease.

Kennedy had stood the test. He had matched Khrushchev move for move; the Russian leader had backed down from his demands. The conclusion within the administration was that Kennedy had won newfound respect in the eyes of Khrushchev, who would now be wary of direct confrontation with the U.S.

Very quickly a consensus developed among foreign policy formulators within the administration: Khrushchev and the Communists must be taught the same lesson about indirect threats to the "free world."

At the time, "[South] Vietnam was the only place in the world where the administration faced a well developed Communist effort to topple a pro-Western government with an externally-aided pro-Communist" force, a writer of the *Pentagon Papers* noted. It was easy, under the circumstances, and given Khrushchev's promise to support wars of national liberation, for administration members to believe that the Russians were behind all the trouble there. And so Kennedy and his advisers decided that if the

The death of U.N. Secretary General Dag Hammarskjöld in Africa during the Berlin crisis heightened tensions. Khrushchev had accused him of favoring U.S. policies, which led to suspicions about Hammarskjöld's plane crash.

50¢ for your hearts and minds...

Enormous amounts of direct American aid were given to the South Vietnamese government. One flaw in its apportionment, says Joseph Buttinger, was that far too much was military rather than economic aid. Congress never seriously questioned this policy. Rather it focused on whether it was being wasted and to what degree the overall amounts were affecting the Vietnamese people. This pattern began even in 1954 and persisted through the early sixties. By that time, of course, the political conditions were such that military aid composed an even greater portion of the direct American commitment. (This misapportionment was not the primary reason for the deteriorating situation, however. Diem's rule and other historical factors were much more profound causes.)

From 1954 through 1961, about seventy-eight percent of all U.S. money given Vietnam was spent on military programs. The remaining twenty-two percent, called "project money," was apportioned as follows: forty percent of the project money went for rebuilding roads, seventeen percent for agricultural projects, seventeen percent for administration (a large portion of which flowed into police and secret service agencies), seven percent for water and sanitation, seven percent for education, and three percent for community development (social welfare and housing). The remaining percentage went for miscellaneous categories.

What is surprising is the very small percentage devoted to community development. The publicity accorded it suggested a much larger percentage. It amounted to only 0.6 percent of the total direct U.S. expenditures. Putting this into perspective, a twenty-mile road between Bien Hoa and Saigon paid for by this country "cost more money than the United States provided

U.S. stood firm in Vietnam with the same resolve as they had at Berlin, the Russians would again back off and the fighting would subside—not only there but anywhere else in the world where Khrushchev had ideas of fomenting revolution. ". . . now we have a problem in trying to make our power credible," Kennedy told Reston in another interview, "and Vietnam looks like the place."

The day after the collapse of the Bay of Pigs invasion, Kennedy had ordered a quick review of the situation in Vietnam. According to McNamara, the president's instructions were to "appraise . . . the Communist drive to dominate South Vietnam" and "recommend a series of actions (military, political and/or economic, overt and/or covert) which, in your opinion, will prevent Communist domination of that country." Deputy Secretary of Defense Roswell Gilpatrick headed the study group. On April 27 they submitted their initial set of recommendations, which included "a 100-man increase in the American military advisory mission in Saigon, more American arms and aid for the Vietnamese regional forces known as the Civil Guard, the release of funds for a previously approved expansion of the South Vietnamese army and the dropping of . . . conditions that President Diem undertake political and social reforms in return." These actions should be characterized by a sense of urgency, the group suggested. The U.S., the report read, must create the impression that "come what may, the U.S. intends to *win* this battle." Emphasis on the word *win* appeared in their recommendations.

While this report was being written, the fate of Laos still hung in the balance. No one was certain the cease-fire of April 1 would hold. Consequently, when the CIA-sponsored invasion force was overrun on the beaches of the Bay of Pigs on April 20, the alert status of American forces in Southeast Asia was raised, lest Communists embarrass the U.S. there, too. On the night of April 26, the Joint Chiefs ordered Admiral Harry Felt, the commander of American Pacific forces, "to be prepared to undertake air strikes against North Vietnam, and possibly Southern China," according to the *Pentagon Papers*. The problems in Laos were being indirectly attributed to North Vietnam. Thus the Gilpatrick group's recommendations were quickly changed to reflect increased concern about Vietnam. The study group now proposed a forty-thousand-man increase in the South Vietnamese army and a major deployment there of American troops for training purposes.

In the midst of all these April developments, Kennedy agreed to the hundred-man increase in the U.S. military mission in South Vietnam, the significance of which, according to one of the anonymous writers of the *Pentagon Papers*, was that it signaled American willingness to go beyond the limit imposed by the Geneva agreements—the first, this writer observed, not taking into account Colonel Lansdale's sabotage team's activities, and American government support of Diem's decision not to hold the plebiscite in the summer of 1956.

Though a small step, once Kennedy made the initial decision to exceed the troop limit, he acceded to future violations much more readily. In fact, on May 11 he added four hundred Special Forces troops to the hundred advisers already on their way, ordered a covert campaign against North Vietnam, and agreed to the National Security Council's ambitious new goal: "to prevent Communist domination of Vietnam." That implied the possibility of Americans getting directly involved in the fighting if necessary; this was much different from a disposition "to assist Vietnam to obtain its independence," the former goal.

While Kennedy was making these decisions, he decided to send Johnson to South Vietnam and other SEATO nations in Asia to project Kennedy's personal prestige and concern. Eisenhower had done the same with Nixon during Diem's shaky early months.

Johnson was somewhat a caricature of himself during those days, off-balance by being out of the mainstream of high-level decision-making for the first time in years. He was uncharacteristically reluctant to make the stop in Vietnam, but Kennedy talked—or joked—him into it. "Don't worry, Lyndon," he said. "If anything happens to you, Sam Rayburn and I will give you the biggest funeral Austin, Texas, ever saw."

Once under way, Johnson displayed his usual exuberance, campaigning Texas-style. In Pakistan he pressed the flesh with a leper, rode in oxen carts, and became friends with a camel driver whom he invited to the United States. While in Vietnam he called Diem the "Winston Churchill of Southeast Asia." When later questioned whether he really believed that, he replied,

for all labor, community development, social welfare, housing, health and education projects in Vietnam combined during the entire period 1954-61." In monetary terms, expenditures for these social-sector projects totaled fifty cents per Vietnamese per year.

Kennedy sent Johnson to South Vietnam in 1961 to affirm the president's personal commitment to that country.

Master Sergeant John Stover, one of the Special Forces soldiers ordered to Vietnam by Kennedy, working with a militia unit near Ban Me Thout in March 1962.

Kennedy reviews soldiers of the 82nd Airborne Division at Fort Bragg. The visit dramatized his determination to be prepared for Communist-inspired "wars of national liberation." He also watched the Green Berets in action while there.

White House adviser Walt Rostow

"Shit, Diem's the only boy we got out there."

But in fact Diem genuinely impressed Johnson, and Johnson's appraisal of the situation in Vietnam undoubtedly encouraged lower-ranking U.S. officials in their tendency to see the Vietnam problem in black-and-white terms: "We must decide whether to help these countries to the best of our ability," he reported to Kennedy upon his return, "or throw in the towel in the area and pull back our defenses to San Francisco."

Diem had been coy with Johnson about the need for American help. No, he was not particularly interested in a bilateral defense treaty. No, American troops were not necessary at this time. He did not ask Johnson for much of anything.

However, a letter from Diem to Kennedy arrived not long after Johnson submitted his report. His June 9, 1961, missive asked the U.S. to finance a 170,000- to 270,000-man increase in the South Vietnamese army and to agree to a "considerable" buildup of "selected elements of the American armed forces" to "counter the ominous threat" of Communist domination. Johnson had perhaps hinted that he should ask for such aid. Dulles had employed just such a technique in dealing with French Ambassador Henri Bonnet during the Dien Bien Phu crisis in 1954. In terms of domestic politics, it was much safer for the request for aid to come from the intended recipient.

But a number of administration officials were, in fact, ahead of Diem in proposing aid for Vietnam. Rostow, whom Kennedy described as "the biggest Cold Warrior I've got," had been churning out memos since January urging action there. During one June 5 White House meeting (before Diem's letter was written), for example, Rostow passed the following note to McNamara:

"Bob:

"We must think of the kind of forces and missions for Thailand now, Vietnam later.

"We need a guerrilla *deterrence* in Thailand's northeast.

"We shall need forces to support a counter-guerrilla war in Vietnam:

"aircraft

"helicopters

"communications men

"special forces

"militia teachers

"etc.

                                    "WWR"

Rostow was like so many of Kennedy's professors, men who acted as if they had finally been allowed into the laboratory of life.

The Joint Chiefs were caught up in the same spirit. Gone was the restraining presence of General Ridgway. They thought Diem too timid in requesting help: If only the South Vietnamese leader could be convinced to invite American troops in, the Communists could be defeated, they confidently believed. A military analyst wrote in the *Pentagon Papers:* The Joint Chiefs' real interest was "in getting U.S. combat units into Vietnam, with the training mission a possible device for getting this accepted by Diem." The rhetoric coming out of the State Department was almost as hawkish, but, to his credit, Rusk was urging that internal reform be forced upon Diem as "a precondition to increased support."

Just as the Laotian and Bay of Pigs crises had become the backdrop for Kennedy's decision to have his administration violate the Geneva Accords for the first time by sending in one hundred American advisers, the Berlin crisis became the backdrop for a dramatic increase in U.S. troop levels in Vietnam. Though the Berlin crisis allowed Kennedy to do no more than conduct delaying actions in Vietnam, during September he did approve a thirty-thousand-man U.S.-financed increase in the size of the South Vietnamese army in response to Diem's letter. Once Berlin pressures eased, he cleared the tables for Vietnam agenda discussions. All the key foreign affairs policymakers participated.

The favorable end to the Berlin crisis restored

Some of Kennedy's cabinet complained that he compartmentalized their talents, not drawing upon their experience in international affairs, and relying too much on the advice of his specialists.

The president with his secretaries of state and defense: Under Kennedy, McNamara was dominant; under Johnson, Rusk eventually eclipsed MaNamara in influence with the president they served.

In the "disservice" of his country...

The first person on record to propose at a high-level policy meeting that the United States pull out of Vietnam was thirty-nine-year-old Paul Kattenburg, who at the time headed the Vietnam Interdepartmental Working Group. The occasion was an August 31, 1963, National Security Council meeting with all the major policymakers present except President Kennedy himself, according to the *Pentagon Papers.* In Vietnam, protests against Ngo Dinh Diem's harsh rule were mounting daily behind Buddhist leadership. A coup led by disgruntled Vietnamese army generals had been anticipated the week before. Kennedy had decided to give American approval for it, though top administration officials were split on the question and Kennedy himself shared their reservations. Now, as the August 31 meeting convened, U.S. officials were resigning themselves to continued alliance with Diem. The South Vietnamese generals had so far failed to act against him and were not now expected to do so. "Where do we go from here?" was the question that faced those at the meeting.

Kattenburg had extensive Vietnam experience. During most of the fifties he had worked in Vietnam for the State Department. He had been part of a faction that urged that the U.S. withdraw support for the French and resolve the Vietnam problem with some form of independent Vietnamese nationalism. Significantly, Dean Rusk had been a member of an opposing faction that favored continued support of the French.

Kattenburg sat quietly as the meeting opened, listening to the other more senior participants slowly drift toward the old consensus, the idea that some sort of working relationship with Diem should be restored. Just the week before, they had given Ambassador Henry

the group's confidence and reinforced their aggressive nature. Their attitude was that the Bay of Pigs and Laos were the fault of Eisenhower people, past and present. (Allen Dulles and Lemnitzer were eventually eased out of their positions, as a result.) Berlin is the way *we* do things, they thought.

They attacked the Vietnam issue with a renewed sense of urgency—partly because that was the administration's style and partly because the estimated seventeen-thousand-man Viet Cong force had tripled its terrorist attack rate during September (450 during the month), capping it with a spectacular attack on the provincial capital Phuoc Thanh, only fifty-five miles from Saigon. They held the city most of the day, and beheaded the province chief before government troops arrived.

By October Kennedy had a pile of memos giving the "go" recommendation for Vietnam. Deputy Undersecretary of State U. Alexis Johnson urged Kennedy to accept "as our real and ultimate objective the defeat of the Vietcong." As for the number of American troops needed to do the job, Johnson said "three divisions would be my guess." The Joint Chiefs recommended that an allied force seize some Laotian border towns to protect South Vietnam and Thailand. Rostow too saw the border problem as key, but he thought that a twenty-five-thousand-man SEATO force ought to be inserted for deployment inside Vietnam along the Laotian border. William Bundy, the assistant secretary of defense, wrote: "It is really now or never if we are to arrest the gains made by the Vietcong." He went on to say, "An early and hard-hitting operation has a good chance (70 percent would be my guess) of arresting things and giving Diem a chance to do better and clean up. . . . On a 70–30 basis, I would myself favor going in. But if we let, say, a month go by before we move, the odds will slide . . . down to 60–40, 50–50 and so on."

On what basis such precise formulations were made is unknown—certainly not on the basis of the pessimistic, and, as it turned out, realistic data supplied by the U.S. intelligence community. The key element of an October special national intelligence estimate was "that 80–90 percent of the estimated 17,000 VC had been locally recruited, and that there was little evidence that the VC relied on external supplies." Thus, the Maginot Line concept of the Joint Chiefs and Rostow was nonsense, just as the de Lattre Line of the

French had been in Vietnam during the fifties.

Troubled by these intelligence reports, Kennedy sent Walt Rostow and General Maxwell Taylor, his senior White House military adviser, to Vietnam for a quick fact-finding tour. The trip was a pivotal event in the history of American involvement in Vietnam. The resulting cables and final report led to the first large-scale commitment of U.S. troops, and introduced some of the sweeping assumptions that would come back to haunt the U.S. in later years: that there was no danger of sliding into a land war through a gradually increasing commitment of ground troops, that the example of American fighting troops would make the South Vietnamese fight better, that American airstrikes against North Vietnam, or perhaps merely the threat of them, could save the situation if conditions did deteriorate.

Taylor, Rostow and their party landed at Tan Son Nhut Air Base in Saigon on October 18, 1961, prompting the wily Diem to an immediate declaration of national emergency. Adrenaline had already been flowing through the group as well as among those back at the White House; now everybody's heart pumped faster. Cable messages bounced back and forth between Washington and Saigon, as well as between Washington and Tokyo, where Rusk was attending a conference.

Cabot Lodge authority to work against Diem by supporting a coup. Now they saw no alternative but to follow the old course.

Kattenburg perceived another choice. He proposed disengagement. He thought that the U.S. would be "thrown out of the country in six months" if it continued supporting Diem. His appraisal was that the population "will gradually go to the other side and we will be forced to leave." In truth, he already believed the war was lost, but given the earlier agreement between Rusk and McNamara that State Department officials not comment on the military situation, he remained silent on that point.

Even so, Kattenburg's appraisal of Vietnam's internal politics was immediately challenged: first by Maxwell Taylor, then by Rusk, McNamara and Johnson. Kattenburg found a measure of support from Roger Hilsman, the assistant secretary of state for Far Eastern affairs, who worried about the impact on the U.S. image elsewhere if it allowed itself to be dictated to by "a strong Nhu-dominated government." Rusk, however, said that it was "unrealistic" to insist that Nhu, Diem's brother, "must go." Rusk reminded the group that American Vietnam policy had two basic tenets: "that we will not pull out of Vietnam until the war is won, and that we will not run a coup," the latter the very opposite of the instructions Lodge was operating under in Saigon. McNamara supported Rusk, as did Johnson: ". . . we should stop playing cops and robbers and get back to talking straight to the [Saigon government] . . . and once again go about winning the war." Kattenburg's caution was quickly dismissed and he became a marked man within

General Maxwell Taylor greets General Duong Van ("Big") Minh in October 1961. Kennedy had sent Taylor and Rostow on a fact-finding trip that led to a substantially changed U.S. commitment to South Vietnam.

the administration for his negative, no-win attitude.

During the next five weeks, the administration drifted without a policy in Vietnam, says the *Pentagon Papers*. At another National Security Council meeting on September 6, Attorney General Robert Kennedy picked up on Kattenburg's earlier warnings. He said that if the war were unwinnable under any foreseeable South Vietnamese regime, perhaps the time had come to pull out. No one followed up on that point, including the president, and the meeting ended inconclusively.

After Diem's death, Kattenburg traveled to South Vietnam on an inspection trip and was shocked by the progress of the enemy and the political decay that had set in under Diem. He foresaw that the U.S. could avoid imminent disaster only by sending in American troops. He personally had observed what happened to the French there and wanted no part of it. In his last meeting on the Vietnam committee, he got into a heated argument with William Bundy, then assistant secretary of defense for international security. Bundy charged that his pessimism was a "disservice." Kattenburg resigned his position to take another of lower rank in the State Department. In his final report as chair-

Paul Kattenburg in 1984.

Taylor had two meetings with Diem. During the first Diem asked for a bilateral defense treaty and the helicopters, combat support items and personnel Rostow had already suggested to McNamara in his handwritten memo. Kennedy seems to have approved all these requests, save the treaty, before Taylor and Rostow had even departed Washington. The treaty idea, however, was shelved. In the second meeting, the idea of using a devastating Mekong River Delta flood as pretext for sending in a large number of American troops came up. Taylor thought it was a great suggestion that had propaganda value in Vietnam and around the world because of its humanitarian overtones. It also offered flexibility. "As the task is a specific one," Taylor cabled Washington, "we can extricate our troops when it is done if we so desire. Alternatively, we can phase them into other activities if we wish to remain longer." He was talking about six thousand to eight thousand soldiers.

Picking up on the cable traffic, Rusk, from Tokyo, urged that such heavy commitments not be made without assurances from Diem that he reform his government. Why commit so much American prestige for the sake of "a losing horse"? he asked. State Department officials in Saigon undercut him, however. On October 31, the U.S. embassy there cabled Washington about the Vietnamese people's "virtually unanimous desire" for American troops.

By early November, the Taylor-Rostow group had completed their meetings and inspections in Vietnam and had traveled to Baguio Air Force Base in the Philippines, a resort facility in the mountains, where they prepared their final report and cabled it back. For the first time, high-level American officials recommended a commitment of U.S. ground troops. Additionally, they observed that "The risks of backing into a major Asian War by way of SVN are present but not impressive. NVN is extremely vulnerable to conventional bombing, a weakness which should be exploited in convincing Hanoi to lay off SVN." They followed through with their earlier reference to a six-thousand- to eight-thousand-man ground troop commitment, but discarded the flood pretext idea. On November 8, McNamara forwarded it to Kennedy with an accompanying memo that stated he and the Joint Chiefs were "inclined to recommend" it. McNamara also noted that "the struggle may be prolonged and Hanoi and Peiping may intervene overtly." Even so, he surmised that "the maximum U.S. forces required on the ground in Southeast Asia will not exceed six divisions, or about 205,000 men."

Kennedy rejected the proposal, but its effect was profound. According to the *Pentagon Papers*, it misdirected the focus of the entire sequence of White House deliberations. The ground-troops issue so dominated everyone's interest that Kennedy agreed to a gradual though rapid increase in the number of advisers and combat support troops "without a careful examination" of what result they were expected to produce and how they were to go about it. The administration was set on taking some kind of action, and doing so quickly.

The commitment was also fatally flawed because it did not, as Rusk had recommended, hold fast to demands that Diem reform his government. On November 14, Ambassador Nolting was told by cable to demand a "concrete demonstration by Diem that he is now prepared to work in an orderly way [with] his subordinates and broaden the political base of his regime." And for the first time the U.S. was motivated to ask for a role in managing the war itself: "We would expect to share in the decision-making process in the political, economic and military fields as they affect the security situation."

Diem did not react well to these proposals. Two days after Nolting presented them, Diem was reportedly "upset and brooding."

Astonishingly, the administration immediately backed off. It was as if American officials were worried that Diem would not let the U.S. get involved. On December 7, 1961, the embassy received new instructions. A "close partnership" would be an agreeable compromise. As long as the South Vietnamese government frequently conferred with American officials, that would be fine. The effect was to give the military aspect of the problem in South Vietnam top priority; political problems became secondary concerns.

"To continue to support Diem without reform," a *Pentagon Papers* analyst concluded, "meant quite simply that he, not we, would determine the course of the counterinsurgent effort and that the steps he took to assure his continuance in power would continue to take priority over all else."

The unfortunate result was that the escalation in U.S. manpower coincided with South Vietnamese citizens' growing disaffection from Diem. By the end of November 1961, 948 U.S.

man of the Interdepartmental Working Group, he said that the war was already lost and predicted that if the U.S. dispatched troops there, half a million would be sent in, the fight would last five to ten years and cost five thousand casualties per year—very close to what later transpired.

In his new State Department job, Kattenburg devoted his time to long-term planning, working out possible scenarios (one involving the use of Charles de Gaulle as intermediary) for extricating the country from Vietnam. He seemed content in his new job until some time in 1964, when he got a new boss: William Bundy.

Kattenburg was then transferred to the Policy Planning Council, where he worked for two years. He managed to get back into the State Department proper by promising to stay away from Vietnam-related discussions. He finished his career at the Foreign Service Institute, briefing new foreign service officers on the joys of the long careers ahead of them. As for himself, he retired prematurely at the age of fifty in 1972.

Diem steps out of his Mercedes-Benz shortly before National Day ceremonies on October 26, 1962, the anniversary of his election victory over Bao Dai.

advisers and combat support personnel were in South Vietnam; by January 9, 1962, 2,646; by June 30, 5,576; by the end of 1962, about 11,000; and by October 1963, when Vietnamese as well as American frustration with Diem was about to boil over, 16,732.

In 1956, while a senator, John Kennedy stated succinctly what Ngo Dinh Diem and the United States needed to do to defeat the Communists in South Vietnam: "What we must offer [the Vietnamese people] is a revolution—a political, economic and social revolution far more peaceful, far more democratic, and far more locally controlled." What Diem proceeded to do and what we proceeded to support were moves in the opposite direction. Diem instituted no fundamental changes for the average Vietnamese— there was little land reform or progress toward industrialization as in the north. Better living conditions, where found, were mostly the product of massive infusions of American money;

and any stability was the result of American military hardware, loyal army units and the huge security force that Diem built up. In time, they proved insufficient to keep the country pacified. Kennedy as president failed to try to implement the ideas he proposed as a senator.

As a result, by 1963 Diem presented Kennedy and his policymakers with a dilemma that was impossible to solve—the American effort to keep South Vietnam from going Communist could not succeed with him, nor, in all probability, could it succeed without him. Because his government had been so repressive, no rivals had emerged, which meant that Diem was unquestionably the most able of South Vietnam's possible leaders. But ironically, the very character traits that had enabled Diem to rise to power and then consolidate his position during the first two years of tenuous control evolved, over time, into the liabilities that led to his undoing. Diem's highly principled nature, which had been a source of strength, now fostered a tendency to be intractable and unforgiving. His singular determination caused him to be obdurate and narrow. His strong religious faith led to intolerance and arrogance. It was as though he believed that the purity of his personal behavior gave him the right to do what he wanted with the country. Likewise, his strong family ties, initially a source of strength, became a negative influence.

Diem developed a disposition to rule, not lead. His political moves had been to centralize his control, not broaden his support base. He eventually wielded more power than Paul Doumer or any emperor had. He eliminated all local government. Since the fifteenth century villages and towns had governed themselves through locally elected councils. Diem outlawed them, appointing in their place government functionar-

✳ One great problem for the South Vietnamese government was high-level officials who secretly worked for the Communists. In 1961 an American expert developed an elaborate scheme to solve it by using lie detectors. Everyone was convinced his plan would work, but at the last instant, the CIA quashed it. They were afraid that Diem and Nhu would use the lie detectors to discover who in their government was spying for the CIA. Nhu himself was rumored to be on the CIA payroll. Without question, his Special Forces, whose ostensible mission was covert warfare against the Communists but which in practice directed its efforts at all dissidents, were completely financed by the CIA.

Resettlement hamlets such as Ben Thong, in which these women lived, were unpopular because people disliked being uprooted from their traditional homes.

ies out of Saigon who were loyal to him. These officials usually held the villagers in contempt, and many were corrupt. "It is said that when a man puts on a white collar in Vietnam," reported Malcolm Browne of Associated Press, "he has the right to step all over his neighbors and take whatever he can get. Careers in the civil service too often are merely platforms for a lifetime of extortion." Thus, killing these officials became one means by which the Communists won popular support. "If bad local government was the source of [the people's] unhappiness, the Viet Cong would execute the offending village official while the peasants watched," David Halberstam observed.

At the national level, Diem dominated all the affairs of state. The National Assembly was subordinate to his powers. The constitution, which had been written with his guidance (and American assistance), had "few safeguards against one-party rule and dictatorship." It gave Diem the right to rule by decree when the assembly was not in session and the right to suspend any law any time. And on the pretext of preserving the public order it read: "The President of the Republic may decree a temporary suspension of

Captain Ronald Shackleton, a Green Beret, interrogates a Viet Cong defector on March 14, 1962. (Opposite) A young Montagnard woman weeps for the loss of her entire family after an attack on the village Dak Son. The VC went house to house with flamethrowers, killing those hiding inside; 114 civilians died.

One critical mistake Diem made was to centralize control of local government. For centuries, Vietnamese village leaders had been elected locally. But under Diem, leaders of the villages of Ban Don, like those throughout the south, were appointed by the government in Saigon.

the rights of freedom of circulation and residence, of speech and the press, of assembly and association, and of the formation of labor unions and strikes, to meet the legitimate demands of public security and order and national defense."

Diem threw thousands of people in detention camps, frequently without a warrant or a trial, using public order as an excuse. The exact number is uncertain. Writer P.J. Honey, whose anti-Communist credentials were well known, reported that "the majority of the detainees are neither Communist nor pro-Communist." Some were tortured. Diem's paranoia even caused him to turn against those who had supported his rise to power. He had an almost Stalin-like worry about possible rivals. None of the individuals who had been in his first cabinet were still with him by 1963. They had been either exiled or sent off to serve in meaningless diplomatic posts. Officials whom he and his family distrusted were frequently assigned to administer provinces under Communist control, where they were likely to be murdered. (In 1960, "1400 local government officials and civilians were assassinated and more than 700 persons kidnapped.")

Diem turned to his family to fill the void in the upper levels. His brother Luyen was ambassador to Great Britain. His sister-in-law's father, Tran Van Chuong, was ambassador to the United States. Chuong's two brothers were cabinet ministers, as were two other of Nhu's in-laws. Eventually Diem came to distrust even these people. His brothers Can, Kha and Nhu and his sister-in-law Madame Nhu emerged as the most influential in affairs of state.

Can wielded unfettered power in central South Vietnam. All public officials there were appointed only with his approval. He built up a huge network of agents in his area. Many of these were, in turn, appointed to official positions in government to keep an eye on possible dissenters. These intelligence activities were paid for with public funds and money exacted from business people. It was impossible to get a government contract in central South Vietnam without paying a percentage to his organization, the National Revolutionary Movement. And like the colonials, Can monopolized the sale of cinnamon, controlled local trade, and made huge profits on government-owned rice, which he resold. John Mecklin, a former American official in Saigon, says that Can "controlled a virtual monopoly of Central Vietnam's economy."

However, like his brother Diem, Can lived a rather austere life. What he did with this graft is not clear; the most likely answer is that it supported efforts to keep his brother and the family in power.

Bishop Thuc was not officially involved in government. Nevertheless, as the archbishop of Hue and dean of the Catholic episcopacy of Vietnam, he used his brother's position to benefit the Church while acting as an unofficial adviser to Diem. His critics charged that Thuc used the relationship to force government officials to use public funds on Church projects and to position the Church to participate in lucrative business transactions. The Church's estimated 370,000 acres of land were exempt from redistribution to the peasants. And on a related

The aircraft ferry *Core* arrives at Saigon Harbor in 1962 with a shipment of fixed-wing aircraft. Not long after the Taylor-Rostow trip, the *Core* was kept busy. It carried the first major shipment of helicopters—thirty-three, and their four hundred pilots and support crews—which arrived on December 11, 1961.

Ngo Dinh Diem with his two brothers and influential sister-in-law: (l-r) Diem, Ngo Dinh Nhu, Madame Nhu (center) and Archbishop Thuc.

South Vietnamese from surrounding villages gather where a U.S. Special Forces soldier is headquartered. When the war was a low-intensity conflict, advisers focused on teaching villagers self-defense.

Roger Hilsman

matter, the only chaplains who served in the army were Catholic, though most of the troops were Buddhist. At the time of Kennedy's death, Lew Sarris, a deputy director of intelligence and research at the State Department, was investigating charges that virtually all South Vietnamese army officers were Catholic, while Buddhists were confined to the enlisted ranks. (Sarris was also working on a broader assessment of the war, which turned out to be very negative. His reporting and career were greatly undermined by Kennedy's death because Roger Hilsman, his chief, had been a Kennedy favorite. So when Sarris submitted his findings, which dealt primarily with the decline of the military effort, McNamara moved against him. With no one to support them from the top, Hilsman and Sarris could be and were silenced. A memo written by McNamara to Rusk, now framed and hanging in the living room of one of the dissenters of the period, reveals how McNamara, a bureaucratically wise in-fighter, achieved this end. It reads: "Dean: If you promise me that the Department of State will not issue any more military appraisals without getting the approval of the Joint Chiefs, we will let this matter die. Bob.")

The worst of Diem's family confidants were his brother Nhu and the latter's wife, known as Madame Nhu. Nhu, who deemed himself a brilliant intellectual, was fascinated with Communist methods, and imitated many of them successfully. One of his ideas was the strategic hamlet program, in which peasants were uprooted from their native villages and made to live in compounds. The aim was not only to protect the

villagers but also to make if difficult for the Communists to receive support from those inclined to provide it. The program received American backing because it duplicated certain tactics used successfully by the British in Malaysia to fight Communist insurgents. However, the Vietnamese had far deeper roots in traditional village life than the Malaysians had. These resettlement camps only succeeded in alienating a large percentage of the population, many of whom compromised the security of the hamlets by opening up the compound gates when under attack by the Viet Cong. Nhu formed the Personalist Labor Party, which employed Communist as well as fascist techniques, such as "self-criticism" sessions, mass rallies, and the use of storm troopers called Special Forces, who

Resettlement villages such as this one, Boun Enao, were built ostensibly to provide better protection from the Viet Cong. But Ngo Dinh Nhu, Diem's Rasputin-like brother, recognized their value as population control centers.

Sanctimonious Madame Nhu was beyond even Diem's control. She could apparently get him to agree to anything. Responsible for the detested "morality" laws, she had her own all-female quasi-army for enforcement.

became Nhu's private army. Nhu also headed all the national secret service agencies. According to David Halberstam, there were no fewer than thirteen, each one probably keeping an eye on the others as well as on the general population. The large number of these organizations was an accurate indicator of the size of the national government: More people were employed in government work than in any other activity except agriculture.

Madame Nhu served as Diem's official hostess, since he was not married. But her actual role in the government was much more substantive. She even had her own army, the Women's Solidarity Movement. She considered herself a feminist who embodied all the virtues of the modern Vietnamese woman. "With the stroke of a pen," wrote Malcolm Browne, "Mme. Nhu outlawed divorce, dancing, beauty contests, gambling, fortune-telling, cockfighting, prostitution, and a hundred other things dear to the heart of Vietnamese men. Neither her husband nor his brother, the President, dared interfere with these amazing legislative decrees." Her morality laws exacted harsh penalties against those using contraceptives or committing adultery, "which included being seen in public with a person of another sex." Her zeal knew no bounds: Dancing in one's own home became a crime—this decree having been put into effect to "promote the war effort." In April 1963 she banned what she called "sentimental songs."

Not surprisingly, it was problems with the Buddhist population that finally set in motion the series of events and decisions that led to the end of the Diem regime. Buddhists comprised between seventy and eighty percent of the South Vietnamese population; the Catholic population, of which Diem was the most notable member, only ten—yet they controlled the whole government.

On May 8, 1963, thousands of Buddhists paraded in Hue to protest an edict forbidding the display of religious banners. The law had been enacted to disrupt the forthcoming celebration of the 2587th anniversary of Buddha's birth. What particularly angered the crowd was that a few days before, Catholics with religious banners had marched in Hue to celebrate the twenty-fifth anniversary of Thuc's elevation to bishop; Thuc, of course, was Diem's brother. As the Buddhists marched, government troops in armored personnel carriers opened fire, killing nine and wounding fourteen.

Diem blamed Communist provocateurs, but no one was fooled. Buddhist leaders demanded that the troops be punished and that the government pay reparations to the families of those killed and injured. Diem refused, and tension between Buddhists and the government began escalating. On June 11, Thich Quang Duc, an elderly Buddhist monk, had himself set afire to dramatize disaffection with Diem. From that time to November, six more monks and one Buddhist nun followed Thich Quang Duc's

One June 11, 1963, Thich Quang Duc became the first Buddhist monk to burn himself to death. That and subsequent immolations focused worldwide attention on discontent with Diem.

Ambassador Frederick Nolting

Ambassador Henry Cabot Lodge

example. Antigovernment demonstrations grew larger and larger. Government troops continued forcibly breaking up the crowds. Madam Nhu also exacerbated the situation by scornfully describing the self-immolations as "barbecues" to the press. Concurring with his wife, Nhu said that "if the Buddhists want to have another barbecue, I will be glad to supply the gasoline." Other disaffected elements of Vietnamese society began joining the Buddhist protest movement. For the first time, the general population's pent-up hatred for Diem and the Nhus coalesced, gathering force behind the Buddhist leadership.

Ambassador Nolting and especially his deputy, William Truehart, urged Diem to reconcile his differences with the Buddhist leadership, but he refused even to meet with them. Truehart warned that the U.S. might be forced to disavow him if he did not.

In August Kennedy decided to replace Nolting. The decision reflected the president's personal displeasure with the ambassador—who, during the crisis, had taken an extended vacation, making himself incommunicado on a yacht in the Aegean Sea—and his determination to be tougher with Diem. Nolting had been very protective of Diem. "Your ambassador," Nhu once said of Nolting to a reporter, "is the first one who has ever understood us."

Nolting's replacement was Henry Cabot Lodge, a self-confident Boston Brahmin whom Kennedy had twice defeated in political contests. (He had wrestled Lodge's Senate seat from him in 1952, and beat him again in 1960 when Lodge, running as vice-president, headed the Republican ticket with Nixon.) The appointment was another example of Kennedy's tendency to appoint conservative Republicans to top foreign policy-making positions. (Not long before he had replaced Dulles at CIA with John McCone, an extremely conservative multimillionaire California Republican.) With primary elections only six months away, Kennedy had additional motivation to appoint Lodge, whose ambassadorship would make American involvement in Vietnam a distinctly bipartisan affair. Furthermore, Lodge represented to Kennedy that patrician element of Boston society his parents had for a lifetime aspired to join. (In 1939 Rose Kennedy had startled a college classmate of John's, the son of one of Boston's aristocratic families, by asking, "Tell me, when are the good people of Boston going to accept us Irish?") Though John Kennedy did not inherit his family's sense of inferiority, he undoubtably did inherit a healthy respect for what Lodge and the Brahmin caste in general represented. The effect, as it pertained to Vietnam policy, was that Kennedy consistently deferred to Lodge's judgment.

Lodge proved himself to be a sly, decisive operator, a ghostwriter of sorts of Diem's final chapter. Though Vietnamese generals would stage the coup and their soldiers would kill Diem and Nhu, they acted with Lodge's explicit approval. For nine years the U.S. had helped keep Diem in power by threatening to cut off aid if he were deposed. Withdrawal of support, therefore, represented a dramatic departure from existing policy. The result would be a substantial escalation of U.S. involvement in Vietnam.

After the coup that dislodged Diem, Kennedy policymakers, having encouraged this course of action, felt a personal obligation to support the generals. They also felt obligated to increase the American war effort against the Communists because so much of the army's energy would be diverted to filling the power vacuum. Coup after coup was to follow Diem's overthrow before the South Vietnamese government would stabilize.

Nolting, Diem's special American friend, departed Vietnam on August 15, 1963. As a final goodwill gesture, Diem promised him he would work to reconcile his differences with the Buddhists, as Nolting had asked him to do. Nevertheless, six days later, Vietnamese Special Forces staged dramatic midnight raids on Buddhist pagodas throughout the country. The attacks were brutal. Though no one was killed, many Buddhists were beaten and fourteen hundred, mostly monks, were arrested. Diem and Nhu at first succeeded in blaming the army. Believing this line, the Voice of America in Saigon broadcast this erroneous information. The two brothers wanted the generals blamed, not themselves. But everyone knew that Nhu personally controlled the Special Forces, and though some of the Special Forces had donned paratrooper uniforms as disguise during the raids, the truth could not be covered up indefinitely. Still, Nhu tried to further confuse matters for the U.S. by ordering the embassy's telephone lines cut.

Lodge arrived in Saigon on August 22 and within forty-eight hours cabled an urgent message back to Washington, informing the State

✳ One of the great internal debates of successive administrations during the Vietnam war was whether the reports by the military were overly optimistic. President Kennedy was initially pleased with the reports because they supported the conclusion that his policies in Vietnam were succeeding. Consequently, he was not bothered by the constant stream of military brass traveling to Vietnam, issuing pronouncements to the press that the war was being won. However, once Kennedy suspected that something was awry, he became annoyed with their trips. Not least among his concerns were the travels of Robert McNamara, who always took a planeload of reporters with him, at a time when few correspondents were premanently assigned to Vietnam. Though Kennedy decided he could not tell his secretary of defense to stay home, he decided he could tell the generals to do so. So, in mid-1963 he ordered Roger Hilsman, his assistant secretary of state for Far Eastern affairs, who was highly critical of the optimistic reporting, to write a National Security memo forbidding travel to Vietnam by all general officers without prior written approval from the assistant secretary of state for Far Eastern affairs—Hilsman himself.

McNamara, escorted by two unidentified South Vietnamese officers, visits a model village on May 9, 1962.

Taylor and McNamara consult with
Kennedy on September 28, 1963, before
an important "fact-finding" trip to South
Vietnam. Their mission report was on
Kennedy's desk the day he died in
Dallas.

Department that various American officials were
receiving feelers from Vietnamese generals about
the U.S. attitude concerning a possible coup.
Lodge wanted guidelines.

His message rolled out of a Washington teletype on a Saturday morning, not the best of
times to conduct business there, especially in
late August. McNamara and McCone were on
vacation. Rusk was in New York, Kennedy was
in Hyannis Port. Nevertheless, all involved
thought Lodge's cable required an immediate
reply. Acting Secretary of State George Ball,
Roger Hilsman, White House Vietnam specialist Michael Forrestal and Averell Harriman
were the primary authors. Kennedy and Rusk
suggested revisions by telephone and then approved it. Acting Secretary of Defense Roswell
Gilpatrick signed off on it for the civilian side of
Defense. General Taylor, located at a Washington
restaurant, did the same for the military after
being told that the president had approved it.
Within hours, the return message, a dramatic
departure from long-standing U.S. policy, was
clattering out on the embassy teletype in Saigon.
The key passage read:

"We wish give Diem reasonable opportunity
to remove Nhus, but if he remains obdurate,
then we are prepared to accept the obvious
implication that we can no longer support Diem.
You may also tell appropriate military commanders we will give them direct support in any
interim period of breakdown central government
mechanism."

Lodge promptly called a Sunday meeting
with General Harkins, the ranking U.S. officer
in Vietnam, and John Richardson, the CIA
station chief. Quickly they reached a consensus
and cabled Washington once more: "Believe
that chances of Diem's meeting our demands nil.
At the same time, by making them we give Nhu
chance to forestall or block action by military.
Risk, we believe, is not worth taking, with Nhu
in control combat forces Saigon.

"Therefore, propose we go straight to generals
with our demands, without informing Diem.
Would tell them we prepared have Diem without
Nhus but it is in effect up to them whether we
keep him. Would insist generals take steps to
release Buddhist leaders. . . . Request modification instruction."

According to the *New York Times,* Ball and
Hilsman immediately replied. It remains unclear
whether Kennedy approved their response to

Lodge's second cable. Perhaps the two thought that the requested modification fell within the parameters of the new guidelines established the day before. "Agree to modification proposed," they quickly informed Lodge. Kennedy did later affirm their instructions, however. Lodge acted immediately. He called another meeting of top U.S. officials in Saigon for Monday morning. They decided to avoid any appearance of official American involvement in the coup. Encouragement and support of the coup would pass through lower-ranking CIA officers. As it evolved, CIA agent Lieutenant Colonel Lucien Conein became a principal player. He had long-standing friendships with some of the Vietnamese generals, dating back to Second World War days when he served in the OSS. He immediately began informing various key generals of the new U.S. position, and became actively and directly involved in their planning. For example, he provided them with detailed plans of one of Nhu's secret Special Forces bases, including its armament inventory, and worked in the plotters' command post from time to time.

Back in Washington, the sobering effect of reporting back to work on Monday morning gave a number of key officials second thoughts about what they had approved. Taylor especially was disturbed. Thus Kennedy called an emergency Monday meeting of the National Security Council. The State Department continued to support the change of policy. Taylor, McNamara, McCone, and particularly Johnson, opposed it. Another NSC meeting was called for Tuesday. Though the administration would remain badly split until Diem and Nhu's demise in the early morning hours of November 2, Kennedy never withdrew support for the coup and, as Hedrick Smith of the *New York Times* later wrote, "the President understood how firm and explicit he had to be to overrule the Ambassador." In fact, on October 2, the president gave unequivocal notice of the break with Diem and Nhu when "he specifically authorized suspension of economic subsidies for South Vietnam's commercial imports, a freeze on loans to enable Saigon to build a waterworks and an electric-power plant for the capital region, and, significantly, a cut-off of financial support for the Vietnamese Special Forces—controlled by Nhu—unless they were put under the Joint General Staff, headed by the plotting generals."

At 1:30 P.M. on November 1, 1963, All Souls'

Diem's authority first faded in the countryside, where Viet Cong soldiers executed classic guerrilla doctrine—attacking only when success was almost certain, and withdrawing otherwise. Above, some of Diem's troops pass through a village in which only women and children remain. All the men, probably VC, have temporarily fled.

What if JFK had lived?...

Many believe that had John Kennedy lived he would have withdrawn American troops from Vietnam rather than have relentlessly followed the path down which Lyndon Johnson led the country. This belief derives in large part from a *Life* magazine article written by Kenneth O'Donnell, a longtime Kennedy friend and White House associate. According to O'Donnell, Kennedy told him in early 1963 that he planned to withdraw U.S. forces following the 1964 elections. Senator Mike Mansfield remembers a similar conversation in early 1963. To further support this conclusion, Kennedy admirers point to the fact that a thousand soldiers were withdrawn from Vietnam in December 1963. Rober McNamara and Maxwell Taylor had recommended this troop reduction on October 2, 1963, following a fact-finding trip to Vietnam. In the same report the two optimistically predicted that "the bulk of U.S. personnel" could be withdrawn by the end of 1965.

A number of high-ranking officials of the Kennedy administration discount the O'Donnell and Mansfield suggestions. Dean Rusk says that "Kennedy never said anything like that to me, and we discussed Vietnam—oh, I'd say hundreds of times. He never said it, never suggested it." Rusk also observed that if Kennedy "had decided in 1962 or 1963 that he would take the troops out after the election of 1964 sometime during 1965, then that would have been a suggestion that he would leave Americans in uniform in a combat situation for domestic political purposes, and no president can do that."

Undersecretary of State George Ball, who thought that the Vietnam involvement was a mistake from the start, supports Rusk's conclusion. "By the time Kennedy was killed we had 16,500 men in Vietnam and there were two or three thousand more prepared to move. I think you can safely say that escala-

Day for Catholics, the generals set in motion their plan. Diem and Nhu succeeded in fleeing the palace via a tunnel and took refuge in a secret hiding place in Cholon, the Chinese section of the city. Before doing so, Diem had contacted Lodge by telephone: "Some units have made a rebellion, and I want to know what is the attitude of the U.S.," he inquired.

Feigning ignorance of the operation, Lodge replied, "I do not feel well enough informed to be able to tell you." He told Diem to call back if he could do anything for his personal safety.

The two brothers finally agreed to surrender at 6:20 A.M. the next day. The generals guaranteed them safe passage out of the country, but Diem would not reveal their whereabouts. However, a short time later they were discovered by troops commanded by a longtime foe. Diem and Nhu were ordered into the back of an armored personnel carrier; there they were shot to death. Nhu's lifeless body was stabbed repeatedly. Fortunately for Madame Nhu, she was out of the country. While her husband and brother-in-law were being shot, she was asleep in her room at the Beverly-Wilshire Hotel in Los Angeles.

Twenty days after Diem's death, President Kennedy was himself assassinated in Dallas. A period of mourning and transition began. The country joined in support of the new president, as did Kennedy's old staff. "I need you more than he did," Johnson told them. And so all the brilliant professors, Rhodes Scholars and Harvard graduates rallied around the overachiever from Southwest Texas State Teachers College, whose remarkably forceful character had propelled him from the depths of poverty to the outer limits of power. The result, observed David Halberstam in *The Best and the Brightest*, was that "the brilliant, activist can-do Kennedy team, a team somewhat tempered in the past by Kennedy's own skepticism . . . now found itself harnessed to the classic can-do President."

Understandably, Vietnam-related decisions were pushed into the background for a time. Johnson's primary concern was to restore domestic confidence, which better suited his disposition and talents anyway. Johnson possessed an intuitive mastery of domestic politics; he knew what could be done and how to do it. His command of international politics was another matter. His reactions were more visceral, his understanding not so subtle. When asked by *New York Times* reporter Russell Baker several weeks after Kennedy's assassination what ran through his mind when the shots rang out above Commerce Street, Johnson replied, "That the Communists had done it."

Though Johnson spent the first months of his administration shaping Great Society legislation and laying the groundwork for the general elections in the fall, Vietnam was very much on his mind. In fact, a report from McNamara about a recent Vietnam tour of inspection was waiting on Kennedy's desk when Johnson returned from Dallas; Kennedy had never had the chance to read it. And on that very same day, Ambassador Lodge was on the last leg of a journey from Saigon to Washington to confer with Kennedy. Johnson had told him to continue in spite of the circumstances. Upon arrival, Lodge gave him the news, which was all bad. With Diem gone, Vietnamese officials throughout the country had begun reporting the truth for the first time in years; they had been afraid to before. What dozens of them said was that the Communists, not the government, controlled their provinces—though they, Diem and, down

Diem and his brother Nhu were shot to death in the back of an armored personnel carrier. The Kennedy administration had assured the plotting generals continued U.S. support beforehand.

tion was proceeding rapidly before Johnson took office."

The *Pentagon Papers* buttresses Ball's point that the thousand-man reduction in troop strength was an aberration. It was "essentially an accounting exercise," the report says. Furthermore, the McNamara-Taylor report proved to be wildly optimistic. Data that surfaced after Diem's and Kennedy's deaths revealed a very dismal state of affairs that did not in any way support the conclusion that most American forces could be replaced in late 1965 by South Vietnamese.

However, no two men handle the same situation in identical fashion. Kennedy would have reacted differently to the exigencies faced by Johnson. How and to what degree is the question, and the continuity of staff between the two administrations need not necessarily suggest that the Kennedy policies, once set, were carved in stone. At Johnson's insistence, Rusk, McNamara, the Bundys, Taylor and the rest had all stayed on. But Johnson was probably more inclined to listen to their advice than Kennedy was at that point in his administration. There is evidence that Johnson wanted to prove to Kennedy's staff that he was up to the task and that he would hold true to the policies of the late president. As Max Frankel of the *New York Times* observed, "[Johnson] was trying to live up to something. The fact that Kennedy had set a certain course and made certain commitments and, more important, that the Kennedy men around, whom he respected, would give him this kind of advice made it much harder for Johnson to disregard than otherwise." Clark Clifford, a close adviser to both Kennedy and Johnson, also points out that "When Johnson inherited [Kennedy's staff], these senior advisers to President Kennedy all felt that we were headed correctly in Vietnam."

Clifford's observation brings up a key point. Johnson was prone to listen only to the advice of senior advisers. He associated good judgment with rank and age, forgetting that such men's views in government are frequently the product of bureaucratic loyalties. Thus, under Johnson, Rusk had much greater influence than previously, and McNamara, always powerful, even more. Kennedy, by contrast, was delighted by the unconventional approach, and was pleased when younger staff members had the audacity to prick the egos of more senior persons. This was especially true after the Cuban missile crisis, which restored to Kennedy all the confidence and prestige lost during the Bay of Pigs.

Consistent with his support of the unconventional idea, Kennedy supported the promotion of Averell Harriman and Roger Hilsman in the State Department, the later in turn fostering the reporting of Lewis Sarris. Michael Forrestal of the White House national security staff, like the others, had a more realistic understanding of the problems in Vietnam. And like the others, he saw his career suffer under Johnson. Harriman, Hilsman, Sarris and Forrestal believed that the military's reporting of the war was grossly optimistic and they supported an altered Vietnam policy. They lost their shield of protection when Kennedy died. One by one, they found their participation in Vietnam policy discussions minimized or foreclosed completely. Though Harriman's role remained substantial, some think that had Kennedy lived, Harriman would have eventually replaced Rusk as secretary of state. During the first months of Kennedy's presidency, Harriman was without portfolio, but had rapidly moved himself up through the ranks of ambassador, assistant secretary and finally undersecretary of state.

Another key difference between the

the line, U.S. officials had been reporting otherwise. American reporting had been largely a function of Vietnamese-supplied data. The plight of South Vietnam was, therefore, more desperate than anyone had previously imagined. Kennedy had bequeathed Johnson a much more serious situation than he had realized at the time of his death.

Though still unsure of himself that November of 1963, Johnson had assured Lodge, "I am not going to lose Vietnam. I am not going to be the President who saw Southeast Asia go the way China went." Several days later he made the same point, though in different language, to a large gathering of State Department professionals. After attempting to restore their morale and build up their confidence in him, he ended his speech with this statement: "And before you go to bed at night I want you to do one thing for me: ask yourself one question—What have I done for Vietnam today?" His message was clear. There would be no reevaluation of Kennedy's "broad commitment"; he, in fact, would deepen and widen it. He wanted them to do everything they could to defeat the Communists in Vietnam. And as they would learn in the coming months,

Johnson visits Kennedy's grave after church services on December 1, 1963. The late president had bequeathed his successor a leaderless South Vietnam on the verge of collapse.

he would demand the same commitment of himself.

One striking instance of the greater candor of South Vietnamese officials in the wake of Diem's overthrow was observed by David Halberstam, then covering the war for the *New York Times.* Two weeks after the coup he was traveling with General Pham Van Dong, the new commander of the 7th Division (operating just south of Saigon), who was interviewing local officials about the war effort.

"How many villages are in your province?" the general asked the province chief.

"Twenty-four," he answered.

"And how many do you control?" asked Dong.

"Eight," he said.

"And how many," said Dong with a grin, "did you tell Saigon you controlled?"

"Twenty-four," said the official, somewhat embarrassed.

Such dismal revised statistics caused senior American commanders to conclude mistakenly that there had been a radical deterioration of the war effort since Diem's fall, according to Halberstam. Still, it was true that the Communists were now moving to take advantage of the political turmoil in the south by markedly increasing their activities.

Three months after overthrowing Diem, the military junta was itself overthrown. The bad news in the south shifted American leaders' attention to the north. That was where the trouble was coming from, they thought. Therefore, American officials began planning ways to punish North Vietnam for its involvement. The result was Operation Plan 34A, approved by Johnson on March 17, 1964, which the *Pentagon Papers* described as "an elaborate program of covert military operations against the state of North Vietnam," directly controlled by American military commanders using Vietnamese and Thai soldiers and pilots. It was not a CIA operation; it belonged to the Defense Department from the start. McNamara recommended it. Johnson ordered it. And Harkins controlled it; until, June 20, 1964, that is — when General William Westmoreland, as the new senior commander, took over.

The goal of Plan 34A was to apply enough "progressively escalating pressure" to force Hanoi to order the Communists in South Vietnam and Laos to stop fighting. Laos was also reemerging

Vietnam policymaking approach of Presidents Kennedy and Johnson was the contribution of Robert Kennedy. Johnson distrusted him, primarily because of political rivalry. Robert Kennedy had begun as the administration tough guy—tough on Teamsters, tough on Communists. We have to give as good as we get—that was the gist of his thinking. Regarding Vietnam, his view began to change following a brief stopover in Saigon in 1962. After a speech at Tan Son Nhut airport in which he promised that the U.S. would stay until it won the war, Kennedy was briefed there by members of the American mission. Afterwards, he asked, "Do you have any problems?" No problems, they said. "No problems?" he said. "You've really got no problems? Does anyone here want to speak to me in private about his problems?"

Only then did they come forward. One by one they privately discussed lots of problems. It was said that after that point, Robert Kennedy learned the valuable lesson that there is a great difference between what people will say for the official record and what they will admit privately. Thereafter, he developed a reputation within the administration as the top man most receptive to unconventional ideas. Thus, the genesis of Robert Kennedy's decision to run against Lyndon Johnson in 1968 was in 1962. How much sooner his protest might have burst forth had his brother lived is perhaps the key variable in assessing whether John Kennedy might have acted differently than Lyndon Johnson did regarding Vietnam.

The father of eight-year-old Pham Thi Hai grieves over her body. She was killed on the way home from school by VC shooting at government troops.

In 1964 a tribesman stands lookout duty at the village Ban Don, which had U.S.-built homes, school, hospital and clinic.

as a problem. "Through 1964, the 34A operations ranged from flights over North Vietnam by U-2 spy planes and kidnapping of North Vietnamese citizens for intelligence information, to parachuting sabotage and psychological warfare teams into the North, commando raids from the sea to blow up rail and highway bridges and the bombardment of North Vietnamese coastal installations by PT boats." According to the *Pentagon Pagers,* the targets were those "identified with North Vietnam's economic and industrial well-being."

After a slow start, these activities were being executed at a brisk pace by mid-1964. As a consequence, North Vietnam was reacting aggressively, both on the scene and in the world press. On June 6 and 7, two American reconnaissance jets were shot down while on a Plan 34A mission over Laos. Thereafter, these flights were accompanied by armed fighter escorts that began bombing and strafing Pathet Lao gun positions and command posts. The American public was informed of these, the rationale for the attacks presented as self-defense. But the Johnson administration denied knowledge of almost all the other Plan 34A activities even to

Congress. For example, lawmakers were kept unaware of airstrikes against two North Vietnamese villages, flown by Thai-piloted T-28s. These attacks were part of Plan 34A. Although they might have been inadvertent violations of North Vietnamese territory—both villages were close to the Laotian border—Marshall Green, the assistant secretary of state for Far Eastern affairs, observed in a secret memo to William Bundy that North Vietnamese "charges [about bombing there] are probably accurate." Congress was also unaware that Westermoreland had ordered raids by South Vietnamese commandos on the islands of Hon Me and Hon Nieu in the Gulf of Tonkin on the night of July 30, as indeed the captain of the destroyer U.S.S. *Maddox* may have been. The record is not clear on that point.

What is known is that the night of the commando raids the *Maddox* entered the gulf at a point about one hundred thirty miles away from there to begin an intelligence-gathering mission that would take it as close as eight miles from the North Vietnamese mainland and four miles from Hon Me and Hon Nieu. Three days later, three North Vietnamese PT boats and a flotilla of junks were still looking for the commandos who had attacked the islands. By then, the *Maddox* captain had completed the last of his northernmost runs in the gulf and had turned the *Maddox* southward, heading for open sea.

Johnson with the Joint Chiefs of the early days of his presidency: (l-r) Marine General David Shoup, Air Force General Curtis LeMay, General Earle Wheeler, Navy Admiral David McDonald and Army General Maxwell Taylor, chairman.

The *Maddox* was twenty-three miles from the North Vietnamese coast and ten miles from the three North Vietnamese PT boats when they began their high-speed run at her. "Apparently these boats . . . had mistaken *Maddox* for a South Vietnamese escort vessel," reports the *Pentagon Papers*. Planes from the carrier U.S.S. *Ticonderoga* were immediately launched, and during the ensuing engagement, the planes damaged two of the attacking craft while the five-inch guns of the *Maddox* scored a direct hit on the third, knocking it dead in the water.

The following night, August 3, a second destroyer, the U.S.S. *C. Turner Joy*, was personally ordered by Johnson to join the *Maddox* on another run into the Gulf of Tonkin. At the same time another Plan 34A attack was under way in the area. South Vietnamese torpedo boats attacked targets at the Rhon River estuary and a radar installation at Vinhson. The

American destroyer commanders were definitely aware of these raids, Westmoreland and the admiral of the 7th Fleet having exchange numerous messages concerning them.

The *Maddox* and the *C. Turner Joy* were still in the gulf the next evening. That day, August 4, was to be a turning point in the history of the Vietnam war. At about eleven that night the destroyer commanders flashed the message that they were under attack. Though word would reach the Pentagon five hours later that the destroyer commanders were in fact uncertain whether they really had been attacked, the initial message set in motion a secret contingency plan drawn up in April that would be executed rapidly and with clockwork precision. Within ten minutes of the initial flash message (about 11 A.M. Washington time and 11 P.M. Vietnamese time), McNamara convened a meeting of the Joint Chiefs, with McGeorge Bundy and Dean Rusk present, to discuss retaliation. Within thirty-five minutes of the flash, McNamara, Rusk and Bundy were off to the White House for a prescheduled National Security Council meeting, leaving target selection to the Joint Chiefs. Within two and a half hours of the flash, the Joint Chiefs informed McNamara, who was having lunch with Johnson, Rusk, McCone and Bundy at the White House, that the Chiefs had agreed on the targets, which would be four torpedo bases, at Hongay, Lochau, Phucloi and Quangkhe, and an oil storage depot near Vinh that held ten percent of North Vietnam's storage capacity. Six hours after the flash, the formal order for the reprisals was transmitted from the Pentagon to the commander of U.S. forces in the Pacific, Admiral Ulysses Grant Sharp, Jr. Less than seven hours after the flash, Johnson met with sixteen congressional leaders at the White House, informing them of developments. He told them that he was ordering the reprisal raids because of the second "unprovoked" attack on U.S. destroyers. According to the *Pentagon Papers,* there is no evidence that he informed the lawmakers about the Plan 34A raids. Less than twelve hours after the flash, jet fighters laden with bombs were launched from the decks of the *Ticonderoga*; about two hours later they would be over the targets, when at the same time the U.S.S. *Constellation* would be launching its aircraft. About twelve and a half hours after the flash, Johnson was on television and radio talking to

✳ The chief Senate sponsor of the Gulf of Tonkin Resolution was the chairman of the Senate Foreign Relations Committee, J. William Fulbright, who later became one of the principal opponents of Lyndon Johnson's escalation of the war. Only two members of Congress voted against it, Senator Ernest Gruening of Alaska and Senator Wayne Morse of Oregon, both Democrats. Later, when matters in Vietnam began to sour, many congressmen said they had been deceived; they accused Johnson of using the resolution as the means to unlimited commitment to Vietnam. Most said they had no idea ground troops would be sent in, but Johnson's vice-president, Hubert Humphrey, disagreed. Humphrey was a member of the Senate when the resolution was voted on. "I asked at the time whether the resolution meant that we could end up with American men on the field of battle, whether it committed us to American armed intervention," said Humphrey. "Senator Fulbright, who handled the resolution on the floor, said, 'Yes.' There was no ambiguity, no question about what we were voting on."

The Senate Foreign Relations Committee, chaired by William Fulbright (seventh from left), discusses events in Vietnam.

the American people. These retaliatory actions were "limited and fitting," he said. "We still seek no wider war."

The next morning McNamara announced that redeployed F-102 Delta Dagger aircraft were already arriving in Saigon and that an array of air force units had been ordered redeployed: an attack carrier squadron from the Pacific U.S. coast to Vietnam waters, interceptor and fighter-bomber squadrons to Vietnam, fighter-bomber aircraft to Thailand, interceptor and fighter-bomber squadrons from the United States to advance bases in the Pacific. An antisubmarine force was also ordered to Vietnam, and army and marine units were put on alert and readied for movement. The air war that Walt Rostow— "Air Marshal Rostow" as some White House aides jokingly referred to him—had long maintained would bring the North Vietnamese to their senses and save the situation in the south was about to begin. All that Johnson needed was broader authority—and August 7 he would have it. On that day, by a vote of 88 to 2 in the Senate and 416 to 0 in the House of Representatives, Congress approved the Gulf of Tonkin Resolution, which read, in part: "Consonant with the Constitution of the United States and the Charter of the United Nations and in accordance with its obligations under the Southeast Asia Collective Defense Treaty, the United States is, therefore, prepared, as the President determines, to take all necessary steps, including the use of armed force, to assist any member or protocol state of the Southeast Asia Collective Defense Treaty requesting assistance in defense of its freedom."

Though it was hard to envision at the time, the United States was about to begin many long hard years of all-out war. And the place where it began in earnest was in the skies over North Vietnam.

(Left) One of the three North Vietnamese PT boats that attacked the *Maddox* (right) in the Tonkin Gulf on August 2, 1964.

Johnson relied heavily on McNamara's judgment as he escalated U.S. involvement in Vietnam. While vice president, he had been more impressed with McNamara than with any other Kennedy cabinet member.

Down We Dive

The Air War

General Curtis LeMay was upset. His Blue Team, which included Assistant Secretary of Defense John McNaughton, and McGeorge Bundy playing the role of the president, was having difficulty making headway against the Red Team of General Earle Wheeler, the chairman of the Joint Chiefs, and Marshall Green of the State Department. The two groups were locked in a war game at the Pentagon. The high rank of the participants suggested the obvious: this was not just another of the war games military planners routinely wage to test plans and plot contingencies for future wars. This game, the cause of LeMay's frustration, was a dry run for the real thing—an air war directed at North Vietnam. The Blue Team played America's leaders, the Red Team Hanoi's. It was the fall of 1964, and although few below the top levels of American government were aware of it at the time, most of the National Security Council had already decided, according to the *Pentagon Papers*, that a prolonged air war against North Vietnam was inevitable. One important holdout was the president, however. Lyndon Johnson had not yet resigned himself to it.

Staff members had spent two weeks programming this computer war game. It involved exceedingly complex calculations that attempted to quantify the real situation—the variables and constants of North and South Vietnam's armies, allies, economies and politics: everything that could have a bearing on the outcome. The question in everyone's mind was whether air attacks directed at North Vietnam would aid the South Vietnamese war effort against the Communists. The answer suggested by the results of this game was no. The Red Team rather easily countered every Blue Team move. When LeMay and Bundy's Blue Team increased the tempo of their air attacks, Wheeler and Green would disperse their forces and resources so that the Red Team's own armies and its Communist guerrilla allies in the south were not much affected. When LeMay and Bundy mined Haiphong Harbor in North Vietnam, Wheeler and Green applied counterpressure by attacking American air bases in South Vietnam, thus forcing the Blue Team to wage a ground war in the south, deploying troops to protect the airfields there.

Johnson at the ranch planning the air war with LeMay and Wheeler; above, Lieutenant James Shively being captured.

Down We Dive—
In their own words

This is a political war and it calls for discrimination in killing. The best weapon for killing would be a knife.... The worst is an airplane.... Barring a knife, the best is a rifle—you know who you're killing.— Colonel John Paul Vann, an American army adviser to the South Vietnamese, to *New York Times* reporter David Halberstam; about 1963.

Don't I need more authority for what I'm doing?—President Lyndon Johnson questioning Attorney General Nicholas Katzenbach about whether the Gulf of Tonkin Resolution allowed him to order the rapidly escalating air war over North Vietnam and the American combat troop commitment in the south. *No* was Katzenbach's answer; in 1965.

I finally understand the difference between Walt and me. I was the navigator who was shot down and spent two years in a German prison camp, and Walt was the guy who was picking my targets.—Undersecretary of State Nicholas Katzenbach to a friend after a heated exchange with Walt Rostow, the special assistant to the president for national security affairs, who had unwavering confidence in the air war on North Vietnam; in 1967.

Wheeler and Green would then easily slip more troops into the south to keep up the pressure on the bases, which would make it harder for the Blue Team to supply its army and airfields.

The ease with which the Red Team countered every Blue Team move at a disproportionately low cost surprised and troubled the participants. Given the geography of the region, North Vietnam's proximity to the primary field of operation in the south and other military and political considerations, North Vietnam was a much more formidable foe than any of them had previously anticipated. It seemed such an inconsequential foe, such a small country, until one was forced to do battle with its 250,000 troops and its allies on their own terms.

LeMay blamed the constraints placed on his Blue Team. They could bomb only military and industrial targets; population centers and other targets like dikes, whose destruction would be much more disruptive to the agricultural economy of North Vietnam than would industries, were excluded because of their human cost and the concomitant political repercussions worldwide for the U.S. LeMay was also critical of the limited goal assigned the Blue Team—more political in nature than military—which was to apply just enough force to convince the Red Team that its fight in South Vietnam was futile.

During an intermission, LeMay confronted Bundy and the two began a running dialogue. LeMay sensed that the rules of this game were unlike those of any war he had fought, and he objected to them. Even the Korean conflict, with its limited objectives and the U.S. government's self-imposed constraints on its military forces there (vehemently opposed by Douglas MacArthur), had been different. And the Second World War was in another realm altogether. In LeMay's view, there was only one way to fight a war, and that was all-out. If the U.S. went to war in Vietnam, Lemay wanted the reserves called up so that the whole country would be involved, and he wanted saturation bombing of every conceivable target in North Vietnam. The notion of restricting targets made no sense to him. "We should bomb them into the Stone Age," he told Bundy. The only alternative he could see was completely unsatisfactory: a few pilots and soldiers bearing the brunt of the fighting in a war with an uncertain conclusion.

LeMay was perhaps the best known and most

capable air force general of the late fifties and early sixties. Though the air force is a branch of the service in which hardware often overwhelms the identities of individual commanders and makes them seem nothing more than working parts of a vast machine, LeMay managed to apply his personal stamp to it. He was not just another anonymous "businessman in blue." LeMay had demonstrated that one person could make a difference, even in an air force dominated by weapons systems. During the fifties, when the threat of a nuclear attack against the United States first became a possibility, LeMay, by the force of his own character, had forged Strategic Air Command into a powerful deterrent to surprise attack by the Soviet Union. As SAC's commander, he had taken many disjointed units composed of many varieties of aircraft—bombers and tankers, some long range, some short range (a combination that defied coordination)—added missiles, and made the parts function with the remarkably intricate precision of the innards of a fine Swiss watch.

LeMay's advocacy of unrestricted bombing of North Vietnam would, as the Vietnam war progressed, cause critics to describe him as the Genghis Khan of the air. But LeMay was no madman. Though his proposed tactics were brutal and his manner crude, he was very much the classic American general in the tradition of the country's most famous and honored commanders—Ulysses S. Grant, William Tecumseh Sherman, John J. Pershing and Dwight D. Eisenhower.

They were all managers of sorts, men who distinguished themselves by an eagerness to engage the enemy and slug it out at all costs, toe-to-toe, unit-to-unit, force-to-force, until the U.S. military machine finally overwhelmed its foe with more men and weaponry than the adversary could ever dream of marshaling on or over the battlefield. Theirs was not particularly imaginative warfare. Tactical daring and surprise played little part in their plans. Theirs were largely wars of attrition that no opponent to date had been willing or able to match.

LeMay's disagreement with Bundy therefore represented a fundamental dispute, a basic difference of opinion that was to split civilian leadership from the military (particularly the air force) throughout the Vietnam war. And it would leave in its wake questions that are still unresolved—that is, would the outcome in

General Curtis LeMay, who had been a bomber commander and pilot during the Second World War when American air forces bombed virtually every target, vigorously opposed the tight restrictions on the air war over North Vietnam.

✳ At the time of the 1968 Tet offensive, ten U.S. air force generals were assigned to Vietnam. All of them were headquartered at Tan Son Nhut Air Base near Saigon. Their living quarters were modular units resembling mobile homes, surrounded by a high cyclone fence directly across a street from the officers' club.

Tan Son Nhut was a principal target of Viet Cong forces during the offensive that began in the early morning hours of January 31, 1968. Some VC overran a strongpoint on the Tan Son Nhut perimeter and reached the heart of the base. Shortly after the initial attack, the base command post had sounded a siren normally used to warn of incoming rockets. The generals had gotten out of their beds and raced into a covered bunker inside their small compound. Captain Chris Delaporte, the aide to Bridgadier General Burl McLaughlin, the commander of the 834th Air Division, was with them. Only Delaporte had a weapon, a .38-caliber pistol.

One of the Viet Cong soldiers reached the generals' compound and climbed a telephone pole next to the fence. Fortunately, he had no idea where he was. Instead of jumping into the compound and running no more than fifty feet to the bunker with all the generals huddled inside, he focused his attention and his automatic rifle on late-night revelers trying to flee out the front door of the officers' club (which was open about twenty hours daily to accommodate the hours of pilots flying missions around the clock). Communist advances during Tet, albeit temporary, were shock enough to the American public. The added impact of their possibly also having killed all the American air force generals in Vietnam at the same time is hard to imagine. Delaporte with his .38 would have been no match for the Communist soldier with the automatic rifle who was eventually killed.

Vietnam have been different had Johnson decided to unleash the full force of American aircraft on North Vietnam and had he developed the political consensus at home to do so? Those on both sides of the issue have little doubt about the correct conclusion. "Despite its failure in Vietnam," writes James Fallows, a respected analyst of American military affairs, in his book *National Defense,* "attrition remains embedded in current American military philosophy . . . The Air Force and Navy pursue the ultimate in attrition warfare — 'interdiction' bombing far behind enemy lines," which is strategic bombing. He observes that "it is hard to make a serious argument that deep interdiction bombing, far from the battlefield, has ever had a significant military effect — except possibly to harden the will of the bombed civilian population to persevere." General William Momyer, the commander of U.S. Air Force units in South Vietnam from July 1966 to August 1968, disagrees with Fallows's observation that strategic bombing campaigns are not fundamentally sound. He believes that the sustained bombing campaign on the north that started in 1965 and ended in early 1968 would have worked had civilian officials in the Johnson administration not severely restricted its execution. Citing the success of the eleven-day Linebacker II plan ordered by Nixon in 1972 — the first unrestricted bombing campaign of the war against the north (one that very nearly conformed to LeMay's recommendations to Bundy back in 1964) — Momyer concluded in retrospect, in 1977, that "our air strategy persuaded a determined adversary with a remarkably elaborate air defense system that overt aggression could not be sustained in the presence of unrestricted U.S. airpower." He believes that Linebacker II forced the North Vietnamese back to the bargaining table and brought the American POWs home.

The disagreements between LeMay and Bundy and Fallows and Momyer are part of a dispute about the proper use of airpower and its impact that has been going on in this country since the Second World War. During that worldwide struggle, aircraft bombed every conceivable target, including population centers. By war's end, none of the adversaries — Germany, Japan, Great Britain and the United States — had any compunction about reducing to rubble any city their planes could reach. The bombing was generally indiscriminate, though some cities were deliberately kept off the U.S. target lists. The potential of Paris and Rome as military targets was thought to be less than their political and historic value. For every Paris and Rome, however, there was a Hamburg and Tokyo, where American bombers whipped up firestorms that kindled cities like matchboxes. People jumped into canals and waterways to save themselves, but from such infernos there were few avenues of escape. Hundreds of thousands died in the two cities.

After the last bomb was dropped and the final shot was fired, civilian officials in this country resolved to learn whether all this bombing carnage had made a meaningful difference in the outcome of the war. The product of the investigation was the *U.S. Bombing Survey,* which, says Fallows, "found virtually no correlation between how heavily different regions of Germany had been bombed and how much their morale or productivity had declined." The survey "proved conclusively," says David Halberstam, "that the strategic bombing had not worked; on the contrary, it had intensified the will of the German population to resist (as it would [later do] in North Vietnam, binding the population to the Hanoi regime)." Two members of the survey evaluation team were John Kenneth Galbraith and George Ball, both of whom would later argue against the bombing of the north. In November 1964, Ball, as undersecretary of state, first presented his case officially, expressing strong doubts at the same time about the "domino theory."

Almost all air force leaders disagreed with the

Like LeMay, General William Momyer, commander of American air forces in Vietnam from 1966 to 1968, had come up through the ranks as a bomber pilot.

Throughout the fifties and sixties, U.S. deterrence depended largely upon massive retaliation with virtually no restrictions, consistent with policies of the Second World War.

✳ During the early sixties, American air force instructor pilots were assigned to Vietnam to train pilots of our fledgling ally. Some of the training missions were in actual combat, though at the time the war was a low-intensity conflict. The T-28 was the type of aircraft used; it was a propeller-driven two-seater converted into a light fighter-bomber.

Many of the Vietnamese trainees were reluctant to fly the combat missions, however. When emergency calls came in, they wouldn't show up. The mission then had to be canceled because U.S. policy required that a Vietnamese be on board with the American instructor. For American pilots to have flown solo would have changed the nature of the U.S. commitment from a secondary training role to a primary combat role. The T-28s even had South Vietnamese markings.

But the American pilots were determined to respond to the calls for close air support. U.S. soldiers acting as advisers were usually with the South Vietnamese ground units that needed help. The problem, thus, was how to respond quickly while abiding by policy constraints.

One subterfuge was tried to solve it. An arrangement was worked out with Nguyen Cao Ky, the head of the South Vietnamese Air Force. At the request of the Americans, he ordered a small group of Vietnamese enlisted men to sit around the ready room like so many spare parts. When an emergency call for air support came in, a U.S. Air

negative interpretations of the *U.S. Bombing Survey,* however. They believed that the bombings signaled the loss of the war to our enemies' populations and forced their governments to divert resources and men from the front. Momyer writes in *Air Power in Three Wars,* speaking of our strategy in the Second World War, Korea and Vietnam: "In each case, planners first perceived airpower as a subordinate part of a joint strategy that would employ an extensive ground campaign to end the war on favorable terms. On the other hand, airmen came increasingly to believe that airpower, in its own right, could produce decisive results. The validity of such a view was suggested by results of the Allies' combined bomber offensive in Europe and by the surrender of Japan in the 1940s. Additional evidence came from the skies over Hanoi in December 1972."

Influential civilians shared Momyer's reading of pre-Vietnam air history. One was McNamara, who during the Second World War had masterminded the B-29 bombing campaign. Another was Walt Rostow, who had been a target selector assigned to Europe during the Second World War. Others included McNaughton at Defense, William Bundy at State and McGeorge Bundy at the White House, all of whom agreed that selective targeting would force Ho Chi Minh to see the futility of his effort and quit supporting the Communist insurrection in the south.

These civilians did not quarrel with LeMay about the effectiveness of airpower. In fact, all these top civilian advisers believed that a moderate, restricted bombing campaign would end it all. But air force generals believed that restricted bombing made no sense. Their contention was that the enemy would use the restrictions to render the whole air campaign ineffective. Yet in the end it was the air strategy proposed by the civilians that prevailed. As a result, the U.S. bombing campaign that began in early 1965 and ended in early 1968 was good for no one: certainly not for the North Vietnamese whose buildings, roads and bridges were bombed and whose people were killed; nor for the U.S., which projected an image of being both morally bankrupt and militarily inept; nor for the young pilots and their commanders, whose missions were made more dangerous by the limitations imposed on them.

When Emmet John Hughes, an adviser to Eisenhower, confided to McGeorge Bundy his

The slow-moving old A-1Es were ideal for finding and bombing targets in the jungle, but were difficult to maintain and more vulnerable than jets.

worries that the bombing would lead to escalation by both sides, Bundy had replied, "We're just not as pessimistic as you are. We just don't think that's going to happen," implying that Ho would yield to the pressure. Bundy, McNamara and the rest had a peculiarly bloodless, cerebral perception of how the air war would be waged. They imagined American pilots diving down into North Vietnam to destroy depots, bridges, fuel tanks and arsenals with surgical precision, leaving Communist soldiers standing around without weapons or transportation. With this neat scenario in mind, they paid little attention to planning for the possibility that Ho would not back down; strategy for a land war was rarely discussed. When Johnson finally decided on his civilian advisers' proposed source of action, he too got caught up in the unreality of their thinking. "If they [the air force] hit people, I'll bust their ass," he said.

Besides believing in the effectiveness of an air campaign based on carefully controlled targeting and gradual escalation, McNamara, McNaughton and the rest also believed it to be a more rational way to wage war against a foe as small and unworthy as North Vietnam. Only formidable enemies such as Germany and Japan (in the past) or the Soviet Union (possibly in the future) merited unrestricted bombing. Such a campaign had the additional virtue, in their minds, of being the type of war they could manage from Washington. Their approach eventually became adminstration policy, but as LeMay forecast, the restrictions and the gradual escalation rendered the bombing campaign ineffectual, compromising the shock value and allowing North Vietnamese leadership to prepare itself and its population psychologically and militarily for each incremental move by the U.S. Although the first phase of the air war on the north, which

Force pilot would requisition one to sit in the back seat. These enlisted men were not trainees; they were nothing more than bodies that filled a back seat and fulfilled a policy requirement. As a result, they frequently got sick during the dives, twists, turns and rolls that a combat mission required. Vomit would flow down to the front under the Americans' feet, sometimes even fouling the canopy. The U.S. pilots tolerated all this until one mission in which a Vietnamese got so sick he passed out during a dive and his body pushed heavily against the back seat control stick. The T-28 almost crashed; the American in the front seat barely pulled it out of the dive. The practice was terminated.

was called Rolling Thunder, lasted more than three years, it was obvious within a few months of its being launched that it would fail in its initial purpose: It would not intimidate Ho into ending North Vietnamese support of the Communist insurrection in the south. The objective that quickly evolved was a weak substitute— to force Ho to the bargaining table, a mission that Ho, Giap and other Communist leaders themselves viewed with scorn: "Wars aren't fought to have a cease-fire, but a victory," said one North Vietnamese emissary.

One influential American who in 1964 shared that sentiment and who also agreed with LeMay was a general in the U.S. Air Force Reserves named Barry Goldwater, a U.S. senator from Arizona who was the Republican nominee for president. Johnson could not have had a better opponent to make him appear reasonable, restrained and wise in the conduct of foreign affairs. Goldwater seemed determined to strike out at Communists everywhere. In one campaign speech, he "mentioned nuclear weapons, war and devastation twenty-six times," according to reporters covering him, who made a game of keeping count. Goldwater seemed too quick on the trigger, too willing to wage nuclear war, too eager to get us into trouble in Vietnam. He said we ought to use nuclear weapons to "defoliate" the Ho Chi Minh Trail, the Communist supply route through Laos.

Barry Goldwater campaigns on October 3, 1964, in Rock Island, Illinois. The senator, who was also a general in the Air Force Reserve, was the perfect foil for Lyndon Johnson during the presidential campaign.

Johnson, of course, deftly exploited Goldwater's trigger-happy image. "I have been advised to load our planes with bombs," the president told supporters gathered for a belated birthday barbecue near his ranch on the evening of August 29, 1964, "and to drop them on certain areas that I think would enlarge the war and escalate the war, and result in our committing a good many American boys to fighting a war that I think ought to be fought by the boys of Asia to help protect their own land." He went on to emphasize that up to that point the country had "lost less than 200 men in the last several years," and that "it is better to lose 200 than to lose 200,000. For that reason we have tried very carefully to restrain ourselves and not to enlarge the war." It was a theme he would repeat again and again during the campaign. To reinforce the warmonger image of Goldwater, Johnson television commercials were run showing an atomic bomb blast, suggesting this would be the result of Goldwater's being elected. And so, on November 3, 1964, American voters, wanting no part of any war or any candidate who might lead them into one, elected "peace candidate" Lyndon Johnson by the largest popular majority in American history to that date—sixty-one percent. Johnson got 43 million votes to Goldwater's 27 million, and carried into office with him thirty-seven new Democratic House members, at the same time that he strengthened the Democratic majority in the Senate to an overwhelming sixty-eight members.

Johnson's campaign speeches were deceptive, however. They implied that only Goldwater and the military were urging him to bomb the north, and that only good old Lyndon Johnson stood between voters and the men of Apocalypse. The reality was very different. Almost all of Johnson's civilian advisers were at that time pressing him to bomb North Vietnam, and he would very shortly succumb to their urgings.

But it was true enough that, for better or for worse, the war under Johnson would be conducted from offices in Washington by civilians who fancied themselves military strategists, not by military commanders. And Johnson did indeed ignore the Joint Chiefs, who were recommending a much stronger bombing campaign. He never admitted the Joint Chiefs to his inner circle of advisers, never really trusted the military, associating them with the right-wing politicians who blamed Roosevelt for Communist expansionism after the Second World War and caused Truman problems during the Korean war. He remembered how they encouraged MacArthur's actions at Truman's expense. He also recognized that increased military spending threatened his Great Society plans, which he dreamed would put him in the history books as the greatest president of this century when it came to domestic affairs.

Johnson increasingly used the Joint Chiefs to deflect criticism about his administration's growing militancy toward Vietnam. When the bombing did finally commence and liberal groups like the Americans for Democratic Action, which had long been a base constituency within the Democratic Party and thus had direct access to him, visited the Oval Office, he would press upon them the notion that his actions were really very moderate: You should hear what the military is telling me to do, he would say.

Most of Johnson's civilian advisers had even

Under huge portraits of himself and Mayor Richard Daley, Johnson speaks to Chicago Democrats a few days before the 1964 election. While Johnson presented himself as the peace candidate and Goldwater as the man who would lead the country into a major war in Indochina, his aides were laying the groundwork for the air war on North Vietnam.

John McNaughton, one of McNamara's top advisers, had no altruistic delusions about American involvement. "Our stakes in South Vietnam are," he wrote, "a) Buffer real estate near Thailand and Malaysia and b) Our reputation."

stronger negative feelings about the military services. McGeorge Bundy, McNamara and McNaughton sometimes openly exhibited contempt for them. There were a number of reasons for this attitude. In Bundy's case, it was a function of class differences. No one, especially those in the military, measured up to his self-image and blue-blood status. (Lyndon Johnson didn't either, but Johnson had the power to fulfill Bundy's ambition to become secretary of state.) McNamara and others like him who had served in the military looked upon the generals as men who had stayed in uniform after the Second World War because they couldn't make it in the civilian world—a world in which McNamara himself had risen to the top, as president of one of the largest corporations. McNaughton typified those who, having graduated from Harvard (or other Ivy League schools), felt superior to the generals, whose education was generally the product of military academies and state universities. John Kennedy had encouraged this attitude, perhaps inadvertently, his sense of humor causing him to enjoy those instances when a bright young civilian staff member twitted a general's ego during a staff meeting. The generals' rigid demeanor did not suit them for the give and take that characterized the Kennedy style.

Consequently, the Joint Chiefs hardly participated in the high-level decision-making that led directly to the air war on North Vietnam. During the several months that immediately preceded the decision to bomb, they met with Johnson only twice. They had wanted to meet with him to make the point that only an all-out campaign would work. And they were in total agreement with one another on this point, LeMay and General Wallace Greene, the Marine Corps commandant, being especially adamant about it. But they were blocked from meeting with Johnson by the civilian advisers, who deemed them adversaries. Once when they pressed McNamara about a meeting with the president, the defense secretary replied, "It's your constitutional right, but if I were you I wouldn't do it. He doesn't like you to come over and I can do it better for you"—which they knew to be true, if only McNamara would represent their view fairly, which he did not. Photographs of them with Johnson clearly show their unease in his presence. Even with four stars on their shoulders, the Joint Chiefs look like academy cadets in the commandant's office. And so they failed to press on, unwilling to incur the abuse of Johnson, who was especially good at dishing it out. Furthermore, they were reluctant to put their careers on the line by making their views public, although this would have been the correct and courageous course of action, given the depth of their convictions and the enormous implications of the issue at hand.

By design and default, Johnson's top civilian advisers dominated the discussions that lead to the bombing campaign. The *Pentagon Papers* clearly show that the principal civilian players had direct input to the president, while the Joint Chiefs were left to protest on the periphery, like baying dogs locked out of the house.

A pilot and support crews of the U.S.S. *Kitty Hawk* line up an A-4 Skyhawk on a steam catapult prior to takeoff. Navy, marine and air force pilots shared the duty of the air war on North Vietnam.

Proposals for the air campaign were flowing through the upper-level bureaucracy and onto Johnson's desk even before Johnson set the tone for the peace theme of his election campaign while speaking to supporters at his birthday barbecue. Ambassador Taylor, who had replaced Lodge after he resigned (reportedly under pressure from Republican establishment figures), had cabled Johnson from Saigon that "something must be added in the coming months" to reverse the deteriorating situation in the south. The political scene there was still chaotic following Diem's assassination. The *Pentagon Papers* described it as having an "Alice-in-Wonderland atmosphere." The government of General Nguyen Khanh was so shaky that some Vietnamese army generals kept their troops out of combat with the Communists to use them instead for political leverage. Taylor proposed "a carefully orchestrated bombing attack on NVN, directed primarily at infiltration and other military targets," with "Jan. 1, 1965, as a target D-Day." He envisioned two ways to proceed, one being to use the promise of a bombing campaign on the north as a carrot to get South Vietnamese leaders to reform and stablize their government. In the other, he saw the U.S. proceeding with a bombing campaign regardless of developments in Saigon, with the hope that this dramatic initiative would prevent "a collapse of national morale" in South Vietnam.

The latter objective presupposed that what pleased the government of South Vietnam pleased the country's general population, which was far from true. Partially because of the chaos, the government was as remote from the people as it

✸ Interservice rivalry marred some of the American military efforts in Vietnam during the early sixties. The antagonists were the army and the air force; their points of contention were control over the small fixed-wing transport called the C-7 Caribou constructed by de Havilland Aircraft of Canada; and the close air support capability provided by helicopters. The air force was worried that the army was building another air force within the army.

The army argued that the Caribous, which were capable of carrying about a 2½-ton load while flying in and out of short, dirt strips, should be under the direct control of army field commanders, not under the centralized control of air force airlift commanders. The army won the argument about the Caribous. However, by 1966 army leadership was ready to get rid of them because the air force had a much more institutionalized management system for fixed-wing aircraft. The air force took control of all the Caribous in Vietnam on January 1, 1967.

In 1959 the air force agreed that the army should have control of the rotary-wing force, which is what helicopters are called. But when the army began installing machine guns into helicopters in Vietnam, many air force leaders became upset. Air Force Chief of Staff Curtis LeMay felt that the army was trying to reduce the close tactical air support role of the air force provided by its fighter aircraft. Westmoreland says that LeMay "upbraided" him in late 1964 about how he was using the air force in Vietnam and that several weeks later LeMay administered a "tongue-lashing" to Lieutenant General Joseph Moore, the top air force officer in Vietnam, for not upholding air force doctrine. The army won the right to continue arming its helicopters without, it seems, taking any work away from air force fighter pilots.

had been under Diem. On the subject of bombing the north, the people of South Vietnam apparently held just the opposite view of the generals who led them. A survey conducted in South Vietnam by American, Vietnamese-speaking CIA agents after the Gulf of Tonkin airstrikes revealed that only one person in two dozen South Vietnamese interviewed approved, that individual being an American-trained airborne sergeant.

On September 3, McNaughton developed Taylor's ideas more fully. In a memo to McNamara he outlined several ways North Vietnam might be provoked into taking actions that would allow the U.S. to order a sustained air war. The problem he was addressing was a fundamental worry. How was the U.S. going to justify the bombing to the American people and the world at large? Chester Cooper, a former intelligence officer working on McGeorge Bundy's staff, was trying to put together a report that would persuasively show that North Vietnam was sponsoring massive infiltration into the south. McNaughton thought that the right provocation, resulting in a North Vietnamese reprisal that would outrage the American people, would serve the same purpose. His suggestions included American airstrikes in Laos that "would slowly 'march' up the trails and eventually across the North Vietnamese border"; resumption of the DeSoto patrols by American destroyers; and resumption of the Plan 34A covert raids that had preceded the Gulf of Tonkin incident.

Taylor's and McNaughton's suggestions were taken up by all the principals during meetings chaired by Johnson at the White House on September 7 and 10; Taylor had even flown in from Saigon. Worries about the shaky condition of the Saigon government dominated the thinking; the forthcoming general elections in the U.S. were also a major factor to be taken into account. The consensus opinion was that the U.S. should

be wary of provoking too strong a counterresponse from the Communists during the next "2 or 3 months" in order not to further destabilize the government of South Vietnam. However, McNaughton's ideas were all essentially approved, if scaled back considerably as a precaution. For example, the DeSoto patrols would initially stay far from the North Vietnamese coast and the airstrikes would be confined to Laos and be executed by South Vietnamese aircraft and pilots. However, the U.S. "should be prepared to launch tit-for-tat" reprisal strikes like those following the Gulf of Tonkin incident, the group decided.

And pressure for a sustained air war was building. Figures like McNamara, McNaughton, McGeorge Bundy, Walt Rostow, Taylor and William Bundy slowly built their cases for the bombing campaign and worked to isolate dissenters, notably George Ball. In early fall, for example, Ball had written what apparently was the first of a number of important memos stating his case against the air war. He sent the memo to McNamara, Rusk and McGeorge Bundy, expecting Bundy to forward it to the president. He did not; Johnson never saw it. Being wise about such power plays within government bureaucracy, Ball searched out a receptive ear for his position within the White House and found a bright young aide whose association with Johnson was quite personal and dated back to the president's days in the Senate. His name was Bill Moyers. Moyers volunteered to deliver personally to the president Ball's next memo. Thereafter Ball had direct access to the president via additional memos (and sometimes in person) despite the opposition of those persistently working to get the bombing campaign under way.

Events in Vietnam worked against Ball, however. On November 1, Communist terrorists attacked Bien Hoa Air Base near Saigon, killing four Americans and destroying five U.S. aircraft. Though his ambassador to Vietnam recommended "bombing attacks on selected DRV targets," Johnson decided not to retaliate. However, he did take one move that eventually was of great significance. He appointed William Bundy to head an interdepartmental working group with the "mandate to re-examine the entire American policy toward Vietnam." This group was not composed of individuals representing a broad range of views; this was a group inclined to take aggressive action. According to the *Pentagon*

Bill Moyers, described by some as a surrogate son to Johnson, kept George Ball's line of communication to the president open as he attempted to dissuade him from involving the country in a war in Vietnam.

Key advisers share a light moment: (l-r)
CIA Director John McCone, adviser
McGeorge Bundy, Undersecretary of
State George Ball, Secretary of State
Dean Rusk, and adviser Walt Rostow.

Papers, the necessity of "an independent non-Communist South Vietnam did not seem open to question" to them.

The Bundy Working Group, as it was known unofficially, held its first meeting on November 3, 1964, election day, and within several weeks had formulated its proposals, all of which were recommendations to bomb the north. Reflecting their bureaucratic ways, they recommended three options, one light air action, one heavy air action and one moderate air action. The light action, Option A, involved reprisal strikes and intensified overt action. The heavy, Option B, involved bombing the north "at a fairly rapid pace and without interruption" until all U.S. demands were met. Option C was the graduated air campaign that, in passing, mentioned the possible deployment of ground troops.

The bureaucracy was now locked onto the bombing track. On November 24, when a select committee of the NSC composed of Rusk, McNamara, McCone, Wheeler, McGeorge Bundy and Ball met, their discussions were confined to the options submitted to them by the Bundy Working Group. Predictably, only Ball favored the light action, Option A; only Wheeler favored the heavy action, Option B; and the rest gravitated toward the "moderate" action of Option C. But the group adjourned without making a decision, awaiting the arrival of Taylor from Saigon. They reconvened on November 27. Taylor presented a modified Option C that made it appear even more reasonable. He proposed a two-phase bombing campaign. The first phase would last thirty days, during which time Plan 34A coastal raids would be intensified, American jets would fly interdiction missions against infiltration routes, and the U.S. would respond with a couple of reprisal strikes for Communist guerrilla activities in the south such as the Bien Hoa raid. During this thirty-day period, Taylor envisioned that he could force the South Vietnamese generals to agree to reforms. Phase Two would last two to six months, during which time Ho Chi Minh and his government presumably would acquiesce. Phase Two would consist of sustained, but not unrestricted, air war on the north. Many targets and areas would be excluded. It would be tightly controlled from the White House, would gradually escalate and slowly enlarge in scope.

The risk of failure was not much discussed; these men were not accustomed to it personally.

What they were concerned about, oddly enough, was that our European allies would have less faith in the U.S. if it did not intervene to keep South Vietnam anti-Communist—this at a time when Great Britain was actively working with the Soviet Union to reconvene talks on Vietnam in Geneva, and Charles de Gaulle had spoken out against American military intervention and bluntly announced that France would have nothing to do with such efforts. George Ball came back from Paris with that message when in December the administration ordered him, of all people, to explain the U.S. government's tentative decision to bomb North Vietnam. Ball dutifully presented the argument that if the U.S. did not act against North Vietnam, the shaky South Vietnamese government would collapse. De Gaulle observed that he could speak about Vietnam with some authority. It was a rotten place to fight, he said. The U.S. could not win by applying force; negotiation was the only route. And should the U.S. choose to fight, she would do so alone, he said.

On December 1, the NSC select committee, which had decided on Taylor's modified Option C plan, met with the president to submit it formally. Though there were dissenters, all agreed to present a "united front" to the president and push the idea that "the threat implicit in minimum but increasing amounts of force ["slow squeeze," in McNaughton's words] would . . . ultimately bring Hanoi to the table on terms favorable to the U.S."

The dissenters numbered among them the Joint Chiefs and all the major intelligence agencies (the CIA, the Defense Intelligence Agency and the State Department's Bureau of Intelligence and Research). According to the *Pentagon Papers,* "The J.C.S. differed from this view on the grounds that if we were really interested in affecting Hanoi's will, we would have to hit hard at its capabilities"; the intelligence agencies' appraisal gave the plan no chance of success under any circumstances—they "did not concede very strong chances for breaking the will of Hanoi."

The view of intelligence was the product of a working group with representatives from each of the agencies. They pointed out with prescience the following: "We have many indications that the Hanoi leadership is acutely and nervously aware of the extent to which North Vietnam's transportation system and industrial plant is

Charles de Gaulle warned the Johnson administration that the U.S. could not win its way in Vietnam by force.

(Above) Kham Duc was a remote Special Forces camp overrun by Communist troops on May 12, 1968. During the evacuation of allied forces by air, a three-man U.S. combat control team was inadvertently left behind. Lieutenant Colonel Joe Jackson decided to make a rescue attempt. Jackson's plane on the ground at Kam Duc that fateful day is shown in the upper part of the photo, between the two runways. At this instant, the combat control team is about thirty feet in front of the nose, running to get inside. Two enemy gun positions are located between the lower wing and tail of the C-130 on the left runway and near the 0-2 directly across on the right runway. Both aircraft made crash landings, as did a helicopter engulfed in black smoke in the center of the runway shown at the bottom of the photo. One of these gun units fired a 122mm rocket at Jackson's C-123 as it taxied. Horrified, the crew watched it streak at them and then bounce and roll to a stop in front of their plane; fortunately, it was a dud. Taxiing around it, Jackson took off safely with the combat control team. Though under fire the entire time, the aircraft was not hit once. Jackson was awarded the Congressional Medal of Honor. (Opposite) Ten MK-36 bombs fall on North Vietnam from an F-4D fighter-bomber of the 555th Tactical Fighter Squadron.

vulnerable to attack. On the other hand, North Vietnam's economy is overwhelmingly agricultural and to a large extent, decentralized in a myriad of more or less economically self-sufficient villages. Interdiction of imports and extensive destruction of transportation facilities and industrial plants would cripple D.R.V. industry. These actions would also seriously restrict D.R.V. military capabilities and would degrade, though to a lesser extent, Hanoi's capabilities to support guerrilla warfare in South Vietnam and Laos. We do not believe that such actions would have a crucial effect on the daily lives of the overwhelming majority of the North Vietnam population."

Johnson's reaction to the two-phase bombing proposal presented on December 1 is not altogether clear, because there exists no National Security Council memorandum recording it. One of the *Pentagon Papers* writers said that Johnson "made a tentative decision" to bomb, to implement Phases One and Two, in other words. A second writer of the *Papers* says that though Johnson approved the bombing proposal "in general outline at least . . . it is also clear that he gave his approval to implement only the first phase of the concept."

Whatever the case, Johnson was no doubt still agonizing over the idea of a sustained bombing campaign. He was the one who, more than any of his appointees, would have to live with the political consequences of the decision. During this period, Ball continued to have remarkably open access to the president. Johnson continually sounded him out on the question of the bombing. And Ball would repeat his arguments, one of which was that "once on the tiger's back we cannot be sure of picking the place to dismount." His arguments were chiefly political. He knew that how the U.S. handled itself in Vietnam would have worldwide ramifications. McNamara, so sure of himself during this period, would counter, sounding reasonable and reassuring. "George, here," he said, "is exaggerating the dangers. It is not a final act." It could be cut off at any time; it was a sort of production problem. A management decision. As easily done as shutting down an assembly line.

Why McNamara took such a personal interest in fostering the campaign is difficult to understand. The Joint Chiefs were not pressing him to follow the "moderate and reasonable" bombing campaign that he and Johnson's top civilian

advisers were urging on Johnson like New York
lawyers. Perhaps excessive self-confidence and a
desire to win a bureaucratic battle are explanations. Whatever the case, while Ball kept meeting with Johnson, McNamara coordinated closely
with McGeorge Bundy, the two working in
tandem to enhance their influence.

As the pressures to act mounted on Johnson—
those favoring the bombing saying South Vietnam
could not survive for long otherwise—Johnson
became more and more upset. "This bombing
bullshit," he kept calling their proposals.
McNaughton found it amusing, reporting to
friends Johnson's agitated movement as he was
slowly pushed along by all the carefully crafted
memos and warnings.

And behind all their actions loomed the spec-
ter of the past, another Democratic president
being blamed for a country lost to the Communists. "If I don't go in now and later they
show I should have gone," said Johnson, "they'll
be all over me in Congress. They won't be
talking about my civil rights bill, or education
or beautification. No sir, they'll push Vietnam
up my ass every time. Vietnam. Vietnam.
Vietnam. Right up my ass." But he figured they
had him coming or going: "If we do get into this
war, I know what's going to happen. Those
damn conservatives are going to sit in Congress
and they're going to use this war as a way of
opposing my Great Society legislation. People
like [Senator John] Stennis and [Congressman
H. R.] Gross. They hate this stuff, they don't
want to help the poor and the Negroes but
they're afraid to be against it at a time like this
when there's been all this prosperity. But the
war, oh, they'll like the war. They'll take the war
as their weapon. They'll be against my programs
because of the war. I know what they'll say,
they'll say they're not against it, not against the
poor, but we have this job to do, beating the
Communists. We beat the Communists first,
then we can look around and maybe give something to the poor."

The irony is that had he taken the advice of
those on either end of the spectrum—the liberals'
view as espoused by Ball or the conservatives'
view as espoused by the Joint Chiefs—he might
have decided not to bomb. The advice of the
Chiefs was, in effect, that nothing short of an
all-out, unrestricted air campaign would work.
If Johnson had agreed with them but at the
same time decided he could not develop the

About three months before the Gulf of Tonkin incident, William Bundy drew up plans that involved using U.S. destroyers to provoke a North Vietnamese attack.

William Bundy believed that American airpower would intimidate Ho Chi Minh.

political consensus for it, his logical choice would have been to follow Ball's option not to bomb at all. (Ball's reservations were not worries about establishing a consensus, however; he had other reasons, previously elucidated, for opposing the bombing.) But, of course, worries about being blamed for the consequences of *not* acting eventually dominated his thinking. Firsthand, Johnson had seen what damage a man like Joe McCarthy could do with such material. And so, the graduated, controlled air campaign sounded more and more like a good way out. If McNamara were right, it wouldn't be a final act. He could keep things in control. Not let matters get out of hand. Stay on top of the generals.

Before December had passed, he apparently had it all pretty well worked out in his mind. He even managed to apply his own personal experience to the issue at hand. The North Vietnamese were kind of like Mexicans, he thought. And Mexicans he knew something about: "If you didn't watch they'll come right into your yard and take it over if you let them," he explained to friends. "And the next day they'll be right there on your porch, barefoot and weighing one hundred and thirty pounds, and they'll take that too. But if you say to 'em right at the start, 'Hold on, just wait a minute,' they'll know they're dealing with someone who'll stand up. And after that you can get along fine." So "I guess we have to touch up those North Vietnamese a little," he said almost in passing, while in a relaxed mood, to a State Department official attending a holiday party at the White House in late 1964.

By then, all he needed was a little shove and the air war would be on. And the Bundy brothers stepped boldly to center stage to provide it.

At the time, William Bundy, now the assistant secretary of state for Far Eastern affairs, was near the peak of his influence in the administration. He had been the author of the scenario that governed U.S. actions during the Gulf of Tonkin incident. About three months before the *Maddox* and *C. Turner Joy* were attacked, he had formulated an operations plan that began with DeSoto destroyer patrols provoking a North Vietnamese attack, included reprisal strikes, and culminated with a resolution that Johnson would take to Congress; he had even written a sample resolution. The whole scenario had been a masterpiece of bureaucratic mechanics and planning. His plan, which was followed almost to the letter, made Johnson appear protective of American servicemen but restrained in his response. Thus Johnson simultaneously won the admiration of both conservative and liberal voters during an election year. It was a major reason Goldwater's campaign never got off the ground. During an informal conversation Johnson had with a journalist about the Gulf of Tonkin response, he seemed to revel in the success of Bundy's technique: "I didn't just screw Ho Chi Minh," Johnson said, "I cut his pecker off."

In a memo to Rusk dated January 6, 1965, William Bundy said, "I think we must accept that Saigon morale in all quarters is now very shaky indeed and that this relates directly to a widespread feeling that the U.S. is not ready for

(Top) Three carriers with escorts cruise in the Gulf of Tonkin off the coast of North Vietnam. (Bottom) Enemy gunners in the DMZ, surprised by a reconnaissance jet, race to their positions. Many such installations were in place before the air war began.

stronger action and indeed is possibly looking for a way out."

And as was his wont in previous memos, Bundy confidently (and preposterously) presented his perception of U.S. prestige in measurements as precise as barometer readings: "As . . . key parts of Asia see us, we looked strong in May and early June, weaker in late June and July, and then appeared to be taking a quite firm line in August with the Gulf of Tonkin. Since then we must have seemed to be gradually weakening—and . . . insisting on perfectionism in the Saigon Government before we moved."

Bundy proposed that in the "near future" the U.S. engage in reprisal strikes against North Vietnam, initiate low-level reconnaissance there, order all American dependents in South Vietnam home so that "we can clear the decks in this way" and consider assigning "limited U.S. ground

Nguyen Cao Ky, the head of the Vietnamese air force, emerged as a political leader in Vietnam in early 1965 as leader of the Military Revolutionary Committee.

forces into the northern area of South Vietnam." His conclusion was that this last action "would have a real stiffening effect in Saigon and a strong signal effect to Hanoi"; his only reservation was that American soldiers would thereby become "attrition targets."

"The impact of [Bundy's]...views can be seen in the policy guidance emanating from Washington in mid and late January 1965," says the *Pentagon Papers*. On January 11, Rusk cabled Taylor "to avoid actions that would further commit the United States to any particular form of political solution" to the power struggle within the South Vietnamese government. (The ruling faction had changed again, this time to a combination of Khanh, a civilian cabinet and a Military Revolutionary Committee composed of generals headed by Nguyen Cao Ky, the chief of staff of the South Vietnamese Air Force.) Once again, the U.S. backed away from making demands for reforms in the South Vietnamese government. "...we might well have to swallow our pride and work with it," Rusk told Taylor. A memo from McNaughton to McNamara on January 27 clarified our priorities even further: Our objective in South Vietnam was "not to 'help friend' but to contain China." McNamara agreed, and "both favored initiating strikes against North Vietnam," says the *Pentagon Papers*. When Taylor suggested an imminent evacuation of American dependents, it was clear that the day for the airstrikes was at hand.

Then McGeorge Bundy stepped forward. Along with McNamara he had concluded it was time for the president to act. They decided that a fact-finding trip by Bundy to Vietnam could be the decisive factor. He would go as the president's personal representative and be his eyes and ears. His recommendations upon returning would carry great weight. They proposed their idea by joint memo on January 27, the day after Johnson's inauguration; "the time has come for harder choices," they wrote. Johnson quickly approved. On February 2 he announced that Bundy, accompanied by McNaughton, was going to Vietnam.

Many at the State Department opposed the trip. They were aware of its critical timing, of how closely McNamara and Bundy were working together, and of how impossible it was to form an accurate picture from all the plastic briefings that the military and all the other agencies there would deliver. (During the 1968 presidential primary campaign, Republican candidate George Romney would charge that he was "brainwashed" by them, so smooth and impenetrable they were.) Many at State held out hope that Ball would carry the day.

There was another reason some State Department officials opposed Bundy's trip. Analysts at the Bureau of Intelligence and Research predicted that the Communists would stage an attack as a result. They surmised that the Communists understood its implications and knew that the trip was of great import—Bundy traveled to Vietnam on Air Force One, a clear sign that the administration was considering a dramatic step, most likely the bombing of the north. They further predicted that the Communists would seek to show the U.S. and the Soviet Union that they did not fear such attacks and would not be pushed around. By chance, Soviet Premier Aleksei Kosygin would be in Hanoi when Bundy was in Saigon; so the Vietnamese Communists could deliver this message simultaneously and personally to both superpowers, at a critical time in Soviet-Vietnamese relations. The two Communist countries had never been that close, the Soviet Union

McGeorge Bundy with Lyndon Johnson. Bundy's emotional memo to Johnson, written after a disturbing trip to South Vietnam, was a key influence on Johnson, who subsequently decided to order reprisal airstrikes against North Vietnam for any Viet Cong act of violence in South Vietnam.

A sign that the air war was about to begin was the order that U.S. military dependents living in Vietnam return home—thus clearing the decks, as William Bundy phrased it.

Too late to help, a U.S. reconnaissance jet zooms in low to photograph an ARVN truck on fire after being ambushed in 1964 in central South Vietnam by the Viet Cong. Such constant harassment was virtually impossible to prevent and drained morale and resources.

having waited three years before recognizing Ho's government. But now the Communist giant was off-balance from its public humiliation during the Cuban missile crisis; analysts thought it best not to precipitate any actions that might cause Soviet leaders to get personally involved, especially since the Soviets were a potential restraining influence on their North Vietnamese allies.

Johnson seems to have appreciated the balancing factors in the Russians' state of mind and the possibility of exploiting them for some peaceful resolution of the differences between the two superpowers. Two days after Bundy departed for Saigon, the president announced that he hoped to have an exchange of visits with Soviet leaders during the next year. "I believe such visits would reassure an anxious world that our two nations are striving toward the goal of peace." Given these considerations, one wonders, in retrospect, what the U.S. might have been able to achieve through the British-Russian initiatives to reconvene in Geneva. But the administration was so obsessed with the thought of the North Vietnamese acting as a proxy for Chinese leadership bent on expansionism that it would have none of it.

Admittedly, the choice facing the U.S. was not easy. Without U.S. intervention, the North Vietnamese Communists were likely to take over the south. De Gaulle had acknowledged this when Ball visited him in December. But de Gaulle had refuted Ball's suggestion that China at the time was like Russia in 1917. He said that Peking's leadership would need years to consolidate its power and that it was without the industrial base that Russia possessed even in 1917. Besides, the Communism that the north would impose on the south would be "a messy kind of Communism," as he described it in 1968 to Arthur Goldberg, nothing to worry about in the world scheme of things, and certainly not a government that the Communist superpowers could control. In fact, four years after the fall of Saigon in 1975, the Vietnamese and Chinese Communists were fighting one another in bloody battles on their contiguous borders. But there was no one in the U.S. government to argue this point effectively in 1964–65, the China experts having been purged at State during the fifties, when they were blamed for the loss of China to Mao and his Communists.

The analysts not only predicted that Bundy's

visit would precipitate an attack, but also that the attack would be against one of three bases—Tan Son Nhut, Bien Hoa or Pleiku—because of the heavy concentration of American personnel at each. Pleiku, as it turned out, was the one. On the night of February 7, Communist guerrillas attacked a U.S. military advisers compound there and an army helicopter base four miles away.

As word of the attack spread through the American hierarchy in Saigon, the MACV (Military Assistance Command, Vietnam) operations room there began filling up with brass. Taylor, Westmoreland, McNaughton, Deputy Ambassador Alexis Johnson and finally Bundy himself, the president's own man, the guy who was normally on the other end of the phone. So many packed in for the show, there was little for anyone to do. Alexis Johnson ended up writing the news release, greatly offending the embassy press officer. Taylor kept busy examining a 1:50,000-scale map of the Pleiku area with a magnifying glass. Everyone was quite impressive. Especially Bundy, who before long was on the line to the White House. All eyes on him. Crisp and confident. Pleiku. Nine Americans killed. Seventy-six wounded. Reprisal in order.

Within fourteen hours, forty-nine navy jets from the carriers U.S.S. *Coral Sea* and *Hancock* dived down through the monsoon clouds to drop their bombs on the barracks of a guerrilla training base at Donghoi, North Vietnam, about forty miles from the border with the south. The operation was called Flaming Dart. It was a one-shot action consistent with the tit-for-tat policy that had slowly evolved.

On the flight back to Washington, Bundy, working with McNaughton, sat down to compose his report to the president. It exuded emotion, no doubt the product of a quick trip to Pleiku to visit the wounded. William Manchester says Bundy "could not stand the sight of blood," which may have been part of the reason for his reaction. Those who knew him had never seen him so moved, as if, for the first time, Bundy associated the suffering with decisions in Washington. In his case, it fostered a disposition to get even. "Well, they made a believer out of you, didn't they?" Johnson later said to him. "A little fire will do that." In his memo Bundy urged that Johnson order a policy of "sustained reprisal" on North Vietnam "against *any* VC act of violence to person or property." The italics

A sailor on the U.S.S. *Constellation* pushes two Snakeye five-hundred-pound bombs across the flight deck. During the Vietnam war, American aircraft dropped more than three times the tonnage of bombs dropped by U.S. forces during the Second World War.

The U.S. embassy in Saigon, after it was bombed by terrorists in 1965. The Johnson administration then commissioned a new building with more formidable defenses.

Navy pilot Robert Shumaker, who was shot down during Flaming Dart II, was the second American taken captive in the north. He had been a preliminary selectee for astronaut training.

were Bundy's.

Three days after Pleiku, Communist guerrillas blew up the Viet Cuong Hotel, a barracks for American soldiers in Quinhon, killing twenty-three and injuring twenty-one. Infuriated, Johnson ordered Flaming Dart II, a second, heavier raid against military depots, which lasted three hours on February 11.

While Bundy was still in Saigon, McNamara had continued building a case for the sustained bombing campaign. The possibility that Communists were torturing American captives came to mind. It was a known fact that they were torturing South Vietnames soldiers, so he ordered two staff members to look into it. Americans had indeed been tortured, they discovered. Only recently a captain and a sergeant had been tortured unmercifully in unspeakable fashion. McNamara wanted every detail. On the night of the Quinhon attack, his two staffers were on the phone to Saigon getting it all down. McNamara personally delivered the disturbing information to the president. Word later came down that it had had a profound impact on Johnson.

On the day of Flaming Dart II, guerrillas once again attacked Quinhon. At that point, Johnson's reservations about an air war went by the board; he was emotionally committed. No Vietnamese was going to push Lyndon Johnson around and torture and kill American boys without being punished. Furthermore, as Tom Wicker observed, "He would look around him and see in Bob McNamara that it was technologically feasible, in McGeorge Bundy that it was intellectually respectable, and in Dean Rusk that it was historically necessary." On February 13, 1965, he ordered Rolling Thunder, the sustained air war against North Vietnam, to begin. The first strike was conducted March 2.

Rolling Thunder was executed in stages and completely controlled from Washington by the men at the White House and the Pentagon, whom Admiral Ulysses S. Grant Sharp, the commander of U.S. forces in the Pacific at the time, sarcastically calls "experts." McNamara and even Johnson spent long hours poring over maps of North Vietnam, planning raids and searching for just the right pressure points to bring Ho to his knees. Control from Washington was so complete, writes Sharp in his book *Strategy for Defeat,* that officials there dictated not only strategy but also tactics, including

A camera mounted on the under-fuselage of a navy aircraft photographs A-4 Skyhawks piloted by crews from the U.S.S. *Oriskany* attacking the Phuong Dinh railroad bypass bridge in North Vietnam. One plane can be seen at lower right as it approaches the target. Another, slightly to the left of the large smoke flume, is pulling up after dropping its bombs.

A North Vietnamese woman weeps over the ruins of her home. As a matter of policy, U.S. planes did not bomb residential areas. But attacks aimed at military and industrial installations were not always on target.

Lieutenant General Joseph Moore, a high-school classmate of Westmoreland, was the senior air force officer in Vietnam from 1964 through early 1966, a time of intense interservice rivalry. LeMay accused Moore of relinquishing some close air support responsibilities to the army.

types and numbers of bombs to be dropped, flight patterns, formation size, attack approaches and time of attack.

During the first stage of Rolling Thunder, only the southernmost regions of North Vietnam were hit. Within a month, the campaign rolled north, encompassing various targets south of the twentieth parallel, including the important Thanh Hoa Bridge on Highway One about seventy miles south of Hanoi. By mid-1966—more than a year later—the approved list was enlarged to include oil and fuel storage targets in the Hanoi–Haiphong region. By the end of that year, navy fighter-bombers operating from Yankee Station in the Gulf of Tonkin, air force fighter-bombers based in South Vietnam and Thailand, and the huge B-52s based in Guam and Thailand were flying more than twelve thousand sorties per month over the north. (A sortie is one mission by a single aircraft.) The B-52s worked only the southern regions of North Vietnam during Rolling Thunder, never approaching Hanoi. However, by August 1967, the fighter-bombers were going "downtown," as pilots called missions over Hanoi itself. Washington officials approved six targets within a ten-mile radius of the center of Hanoi, one of them being the famous Paul Doumer Bridge over which all the rail traffic from China to Hanoi passed.

Initially the objective of Rolling Thunder was to intimidate Ho into ordering a halt to the Communist insurrection in the south, the presumption being that he controlled the South Vietnamese Communists, at least to the degree that withdrawal of North Vietnamese supplies and manpower would cause the insurrection to wither away. However, when this goal was revealed as impossible, following the initial failures of Rolling Thunder in early 1965, the objectives rather than the strategy were reevaluated. The air war became an interdiction effort far behind enemy lines, its revised objectives to undermine the Communist fighting effort in the south and to induce Ho to send delegates to the bargaining table. To encourage the latter, Johnson ordered a number of bombing pauses during the three and a half years of the campaign, during which time the administration feverishly worked to get talks with Ho under way. Each time they were disappointed.

Throughout the years of Rolling Thunder, most missions were directed at lines of communications, such as roads, bridges and railroads.

Nonmilitary targets were generally excluded, save power plants and other installations that indirectly affected North Vietnam's ability to support the war. Nevertheless, this extended bombing campaign caused considerable damage to civilian structures and loss of life to many noncombatants, in part because of the proximity of military targets to such structures, in part because pilots flying through intense anti-aircraft fire could not always deliver their bomb loads with precision. Furthermore, many pilots were more accustomed to practicing nuclear weapon delivery than conventional bombing; the techniques were entirely different. However, accuracy improved as the campaign progressed. Practice, better bombsites and the development by 1967 of so-called smart bombs all helped. Some of the smart bombs had TV cameras in their noses that a weapons officer in the back seat of a fighter-bomber would guide to the target using a display screen. Another kind employed special high-resolution lenses that kept the bombs locked on a target. The best, of course, were the later generation smart bombs incorporating laser technology that had been developed by the time Nixon resumed the bombing of the north in 1972.

What especially embittered many American pilots was that for many months MiG aircraft (Russian-supplied jets flown by Vietnamese) bases and numerous anti-aircraft installations were excluded from the approved target list. Enemy fighters would swoop down from their proscribed bases, attack American aircraft laden with bombs (especially vulnerable while carry-

Anti-aircraft weaponry and control systems were the most sophisticated that the Soviet Union could provide.

Russian pilots assigned to bases in the north trained Vietnamese to fly MiG fighters. Such bases were kept off U.S. target lists for months.

(Top) An air force RF-4C, with officers
Ed Atterberry and Tom Parrott aboard,
goes out of control after being hit by a
Russian-made surface-to-air missile.
Both Atterberry and Parrott managed
to eject safely, though they became
POWs; Atterberry died in captivity.
During the war, the air force lost 2,257
planes due to combat or operational
losses. Crew member casualties totaled
2,218 killed and 3,460 wounded.
(Bottom) An SA-2 missile used against
U.S. planes.

ing the extra weight), and then fly back north into airspace restricted to U.S. pilots. At one time U.S. pilots were even forbidden to bomb surface-to-air missile (SAM) sites. In 1965 Westmoreland and Lieutenant General Joseph Moore, the air force commander in Vietnam at the time, complained to John McNaughton about this policy. McNaughton ridiculed Moore for his concern: "You don't think the North Vietnamese are going to use them!" he said. "Putting them in is just a political ploy by the Russians to appease Hanoi." Later when SAMs began shooting down U.S. planes and these missiles were finally added as targets, those near dikes were still excluded unless missiles were being fired from them. LeMay's homely metaphor for the action, as he expressed it to Bundy during the war game, was "we're swatting flies when we should be going after the manure piles."

Effective strategies were developed to protect the American bombers from MiG fighters, however. F-4 and F-100 fighters would fly what were called MiG CAP missions above the attacking American planes, ever watchful of enemy aircraft. During Rolling Thunder, 55 U.S. planes were shot down by MiGs; but American pilots shot down 116 enemy aircraft. Most of the kills were accomplished by F-4s with both a pilot and a weapons officer on board, using radar-guided or heat-seeking missiles.

Techniques for evading SAMs also evolved. Most of these missiles looked like telephone poles rising up from the ground; if a pilot could spot them in time, he dived away from the missiles and toward the ground. The SAMs could not turn sharply enough to stay with the evading aircraft.

What American pilots feared most was fire from radar-controlled anti-aircraft artillery; it could reach as high as fifteen thousand feet. They sometimes had to dive into it to avoid the SAMs, and they almost always had to dive into it to hit their targets, some of which were more heavily defended than Hitler's bunker. The concentration of anti-aircraft fire was generally the most intense in the history of air warfare.

Two of the most fiercely defended targets were the Thanh Hoa and Paul Doumer bridges. The Thanh Hoa, about seventy miles south of Hanoi, was on the administration's approved target list for three years—from April 3, 1965, to March 31, 1968. The Doumer Bridge was on the list only seven months—from August 11,

1967, to March 31, 1968. Both bridges were of great military and symbolic importance to each side. And the struggles to destroy them are representative of the tactics, deficiencies and strengths of the overall American air war in the north during the sixties. The fact that two bridges towered in significance over all other areas and structures approved as targets shows how limited the air campaign was and why it failed to intimidate the North Vietnamese. As David Halberstam observed, there was "no absence of danger but a real absence of targets."

The Thanh Hoa Bridge, which carried rail and road traffic along Highway One across the Song Ma River, had been built by the North Vietnamese themselves, replacing one of French construction that the Viet Minh had destroyed in 1945. Most of the bridges in North Vietnam were French-built. The Thanh Hoa Bridge took seven years to complete and was grossly overbuilt. Unsure of themselves, Vietnamese engineers had compensated with ever-greater quantities of concrete and steel during construction. Ho himself dedicated it in 1964. The bridge became a symbol of achievement to the citizens of North Vietnam, a young Communist country obsessed with its public works projects. Soon after the air war commenced, it became a symbol of defiance.

Air Force Lieutenant Colonel Robinson Risner led the first American attack on the bridge on April 3, 1965. Few pilots in the American air force were as skilled and well known as this veteran of two wars. During the Korean conflict, he had become an ace, shooting down eight enemy aircraft.

The gun camera of the F-105 flown by Major Ralph Kuster and Captain Larry Wiggins records the destruction of a MiG-17.

In an effort reminiscent of missions flown in the Second World War and Korea, a huge attack force of seventy-nine planes was assembled for Risner to lead. Two types of aircraft composed the force. F-100 fighters armed with rockets were to attack the anti-aircraft artillery that surrounded the bridge; the larger F-105 fighter-bombers targeted the bridge itself. Some of the F-105s carried two of the 250-pound guided missiles called "Bullpups," others carried 750-pound bombs.

The plan called for the F-100s to strike first. Then, after the anti-aircraft guns had, it was hoped, been knocked out, the F-105s would dive in at the bridge one at a time. Given the symbolic considerations and the initial objective of the American air campaign, the day of the

The most rudimentary and the most sophisticated equipment combined to make anti-aircraft defenses over North Vietnam the most dangerous in the history of air warfare. (Top) Militiamen with rifles line up to spray bullets in a U.S. plane's flight path. (Bottom) An anti-aircraft crew mans a remote-control position.

Navy Lieutenants Randall Cunningham (left) and William Driscoll shortly after being pulled from the sea. A SAM shot them down on the mission that made them the first U.S. aces of the war.

first Thanh Hoa Bridge strike was perhaps the most important of the long Rolling Thunder campaign. If the U.S. was going to impress Ho and other North Vietnamese with its overwhelming airpower, April 3, 1965, was the day to do it.

But the strike was an almost total failure, though not for lack of courage or determination. Most of the problem lay with the weapons employed. The F-100s failed to knock out a single anti-aircraft gun, and two jets—an F-100 and a reconnaissance plane—were shot down. A few others, including Risner's F-105, were severely damaged. He made an emergency landing at Danang in South Vietnam, his fuel line leaking and his cockpit filled with smoke.

The F-105s carrying the Bullpups had gone in ahead of the ones carrying the heavier bombs. The technique was to release them one at a time from an altitude of twelve thousand feet. The Bullpups left an orange smoke trail; each pilot personally guided the Bullpups released from his plane, using remote controls in his cockpit. He did this visually, the smoke trail helping him keep track of the position of the missile while he circled above. Thus, each pilot laboriously dived and circled twice to release and target both Bullpups. The procedure kept American planes over the heavily defended target for what seemed an eternity. It might have worked had the Bullpups been effective. But according to Risner, the Bullpups "bounced off [the bridge] like popcorn."

The planes carrying the 750-pound bombs did not do much better and had trouble hitting the narrow target as thousands of rounds of anti-aircraft shells whizzed by. Thirty-two missiles and ten dozen bombs were directed at the bridge that day—and afterward it still stood with only superficial damage.

Undaunted, Risner and a smaller strike force of forty-eight F-105s returned to the bridge the next day. This time no flak-suppression missions were flown, so ineffective had been the weaponry employed the day before. A few F-100s came along for MiG CAP, however. No Bullpups were used this time. The strike planes carried only the 750-pound bombs. Risner was ordered not to bomb this time, so he swung around in circles above the bridge at about fifteen thousand feet, cheering the others on and ordering target adjustments, Communist gunners shooting at him all the while. They had a worry-free day, with no aircraft directed against them.

The first plane to attack the bridge, piloted by Captain Carlyle Harris, was shot down. Harris ejected and became a prisoner of war. Without hesitation, the rest of the strike force roared in one after the other. Just as the last flight of Thunderchiefs was preparing to go in, four North Vietnamese MiGs dived down on them from out of the overcast with their 20-millimeter cannons blazing. Both American pilots were caught completely off guard and had no time to react. Their planes were shot down and they were killed. The North Vietnamese had scored the first air-to-air victories of the war. The MiG pilots immediately accelerated into the safety of airspace north of the twentieth parallel.

On this second day, about three hundred forty 750-pound bombs, by Risner's count, struck the bridge, some breaking truss beams and severely damaging the access roadways. But the bridge still stood and was repaired within a month.

The ironic truth of these Thanh Hoa raids is that they had the opposite of the effect intended. Though the attacks during that period dropped twenty-six other bridges (all those on the approved list *except* the Thanh Hoa Bridge), the fact that the most important bridge still stood encouraged the enemy. The bridge was to remain a source of inspiration to the North Vietnamese, and frustration to the U.S., throughout Rolling Thunder. The air force pitched its best pilots, planes and weapons (except nuclear) against the bridge and its defenses, to no avail. The navy did no better. In November 1965, North Vietnam was divided up into bombing regions by the air force and navy. The area assigned the navy included the Thanh Hoa Bridge. Intermittently throughout Rolling Thunder they attacked it, but never put it more than temporarily out of commission. Whenever weather conditions postponed bombing raids, and always at night, North Vietnamese workmen swarmed over the bridge, repairing whatever damage had occurred. Dozens of American planes were lost trying to destroy the bridge permanently and cripple its defenses. One of the casualties was Risner, shot down and taken prisoner on September 16, 1965, while trying to destroy a SAM site near the bridge. A short time beforehand, his portrait had appeared on the cover of *Time* for an article about Americans in battle in Vietnam.

Significantly, supplies kept moving across the Song Ma on a pontoon bridge, though at a

Though not impressive visually, the Thanh Hoa Bridge was the most formidable target in North Vietnam. First struck in 1965, it stood until 1972. The bridge was surrounded by anti-aircraft defenses that were able to shoot down dozens of planes.

Air force ace Captain Steve Ritchie. The North Vietnamese lost one hundred and ninety-three planes in air-to-air combat; the U.S., ninety-two.

Lieutenant Jack Terhune ejects from his F-8E over the South China Sea. The plane was too damaged to reach its carrier. Terhune was rescued within minutes.

Women members of a North Vietnamese coast guard unit walk past the grave of an American pilot shot down during a mission against a target near the nineteenth parallel.

slower rate, even when the Thanh Hoa Bridge was temporarily out of commission. For some time this was unknown to the U.S. Navy Lieutenant Commander Howard Rutledge personally observed this clever subterfuge after he was shot down during a Thanh Hoa strike in November 1965. After nightfall on the day he was captured, Rutledge was blindfolded and placed in the back of a truck for a trip to Hanoi. Shortly after his journey began, the driver halted the truck and his guards removed the blindfold. Rutledge was amazed to find the truck in the middle of the Song Ma, its wheels partially submerged in the water. Towering above him and a short distance away was the Thanh Hoa Bridge. The North Vietnamese had constructed an underwater pontoon bridge of which he and the other pilots were totally unaware. Mockingly, his captors pointed both to the permanent bridge, still standing, and the pontoon bridge on which they were traveling.

When an encrypted message was received by commanders of the Thailand-based 388th and 8th USAF Fighter Wings on August 11, 1967, immediately authorizing strikes on the Doumer Bridge, their F-105s were already loaded with 750-pound bombs destined for other targets. But eager ground crews quickly reconfigured the Thunderchiefs with 3,000-pound bombs; they swarmed over the jets, removing the smaller bombs, installing the larger ones, changing the fuel tank configuration and refueling the tanks. This simultaneous process violated air force safety procedures. But by ignoring safety regulations, the crews reconfigured each aircraft in eighteen minutes instead of the usual thirty. Four hours after the go-ahead message had been received, thirty-six F-105s were roaring off the end of the runways at fifteen-second intervals.

The mission incorporated some of the lessons learned from the missions against the Thanh Hoa Bridge, the most obvious being bomb size. When Rolling Thunder began, there were no 2,000- or 3,000-pound bombs in all Southeast Asia. The first shipments had arrived in late summer of 1965. Also new were "Wild Weasel" aircraft, whose weapons could lock on to any SAM site, anti-aircraft artillery or MiG that was using radar.

The first Doumer Bridge mission also reflected an evolution in American tactics. The Wild Weasel aircraft traveled in front of the

bomber force, scanning for the enemy's radar-controlled weapons, and behind them, in formations of four each, came the bomb-laden Thunderchiefs. The route took them over northern Laos, where they were refueled in midair, and then on to Hanoi from the northwest. Ninety-five miles out, as the attack force crossed the Red River, speed was increased to almost

F-105s head for targets in North Vietnam.

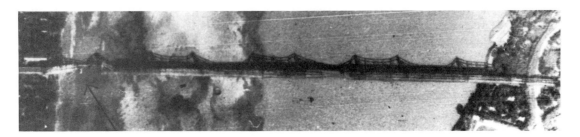

the speed of sound. Altitude was about ten thousand feet. As the planes approached Hanoi, they hugged a prominent limestone karst outcropping that ran northwest from Hanoi. American pilots called it "Thud Ridge," after the F-105s it shielded from ground defenses. (The F-105 was a very heavy aircraft that landed with a thud; hence its nickname.) About four miles out, the force reached the southeast end of the ridge and turned toward the Doumer Bridge, now clearly visible, its mile-long length highlighted against the wide Red River. Quickly, the planes now climbed to thirteen thousand feet to evade most of the flak. This maneuver was called the "pop-up." At the apex, the planes began their dive along a forty-five-degree glide slope, picking up speed, still in tight clusters of

Paul Doumer's bridge, a landmark of the French colonial period, was attacked and closed by U.S. pilots. It has since been rebuilt and is in use.

To the rescue...

Everything possible was done to rescue a downed pilot. That knowledge fortified the resolve of pilots and crews during dangerous missions. The story of Lieutenant Colonel Iceal Hambleton is an extreme example. His was the largest rescue effort of the war involving a single person.

On April 2, 1972, an EB-66 in which Hambleton was flying as navigator was shot down by an SA-2 missile while escorting a cell of three B-52s near the DMZ. The plane, filled with electronics equipment that jammed enemy anti-aircraft weapons, exploded. Only Hambleton got out alive.

The area of South Vietnam into which Hambleton descended was swarming with Communist troops. The south was being invaded as part of the largest North Vietnamese operation of the war. Two forward air controllers monitored Hambleton's descent, talking to him via his emergency radio.

By lucky coincidence for him, a search-and-rescue team, consisting of an HH-53 "Super Jolly Green" rescue helicopter and four supporting A-1E propeller-driven attack aircraft, was operating nearby. The area around Hambleton was too hot for the large Jolly Green, but two of the Sandys, as

A Super Jolly Green with Sandys.

the A-1s were called, were diverted to help Hambleton. Flying on the deck, they began bombing and shooting Communist troops trying to reach him. They kept this up for two hours.

In the meantime, one of the FACs

four in two echelons of two, the plane on the right of each echelon flying by reference to the wingtip of the plane on his left. At seven thousand feet, they released their bombs. Speed brakes then went out and the formation began pulling up while making a hard-left turn over the Hanoi Hilton, where other American pilots were being held prisoner, and then down the Red River to the east.

All the while the North Vietnamese were firing thousands of rounds of anti-aircraft shells, clearly visible to the pilots as they streaked past their cockpits and exploded in puffs all about the sky. SAMs were also fired, and, just as the formation was turning the corner at Thud Ridge, MiGs were taking off from Phuc Yen Airfield only a few miles from the strike force flight path. But the Americans streaked right through their midst and were down on their targets and gone before the MiGs could turn around.

Unlike the first mission over the Thanh Hoa Bridge, the first attack on the Doumer Bridge was successful. The Wild Weasels destroyed one 85-millimeter anti-aircraft site with seven guns on the southeast side of the bridge, and the big bombs dropped one railway span and two highway spans into the river without the loss of any aircraft, and with damage to only two. But the bridge was repaired by October 3. During the interim, a barge a few miles from the Doumer Bridge ferried railroad cars across. (A pontoon bridge was under construction when the bombing in the Hanoi area was ended in 1968.) New strikes thereafter were ordered when weather permitted once repairs had made the bridge operational again. There were a total of four before Johnson removed the Doumer Bridge and the entire northern region of North Vietnam from the target list, beginning on March 31, 1968.

Why Johnson and his advisers imagined that such a bombing campaign would produce decisive results is hard to imagine. Roads, bridges, trucks, petroleum and weapons destroyed and missiles expended were too easily repaired by thousands of workers or replenished by ship after ship arriving in Haiphong Harbor, mostly from the Soviet Union. The North Vietnamese were also adept in minimizing the effectiveness of air attacks. For example, when the U.S. began attacking oil storage areas, Hanoi leaders began ordering fuel shipments in fifty-gallon drums instead of in bulk. The drums were then dispersed throughout the countryside, presenting American pilots with a myriad of small targets that were virtually impossible to find and destroy.

Furthermore, Rostow's estimate of the depth of Ho's concern about the destruction of factories constructed since independence proved inaccurate. In fact, North Vietnam's industrial base was so minuscule that its gross national product actually increased during most of the bombing — not because of increased production but because its allies easily supplied much more than it lost. The U.S. never moved to close off its ports during Rolling Thunder. A study ordered by McNamara showed that North Vietnam's allies supplied it with $1.6 billion in economic and military aid during Rolling Thunder, four times the losses it incurred in the bombing. The report by McNamara's systems analysis division read: "If economic criteria were the only consideration, NVN would show a substantial net gain from the bombing, primarily in military equipment." The U.S. dollar loss, by contrast, because of the sophisticated weaponry, was much greater than North Vietnamese losses. The McNamara-ordered study, conducted in 1967, projected that the 230 aircraft losses anticipated because of increased air activity that year would have a monetary value of $1.1 billion.

These data are evidence that Rolling Thunder, primarily because of the restrictions placed upon it, was not worth the cost. That is the conclusion of the former chief of the air force's Southeast Asia Historical Branch, Colonel Ray Bowers, who in 1978 told an Air Force Academy symposium, "Measured by its unsatisfactory outcome and by the more than 900 American planes lost in North Vietnam, the controlled application of air power that was Rolling Thunder stands as a sad failure." The exact number of U.S. losses were 918 aircraft destroyed and 818 airmen killed.

A number of explanations have been offered to account for what one *Pentagon Papers* analyst called the "gap" between the drastic concession expected from Hanoi and the relatively modest bombing campaign being conducted against it. First, Johnson administration officials underestimated the enemy. Trapped by a false sense of cultural superiority over North Vietnam, they attributed the French defeat in Indochina to French military unpreparedness

had flown south for more help. He returned with a small force of army helicopters—two UH-1B Cobra gunships and two UH-1H passenger-carrying "slicks" with machine guns mounted on the sides. The enemy filled the sky with anti-aircraft and small arms fire. One slick crashed, killing all four crew members. A gunship was also struck but managed to make it to the ocean and crash-land on a beach. Both crew members were rescued. The other two helicopters escaped, though without Hambleton, who was now hiding in a thick clump of bushes in the middle of a large field.

With darkness at hand, the rescue attempt was called off until morning, though an OV-10 pilot remained overhead in contact with Hambleton. The weather had been bad that day, a low overcast covering the movement of thousands of Communist troops through the area. More heavy, low overcast was expected. Air operations are extremely difficult in such conditions.

Because of the weather, two OV-10s with special navigation equipment that could be used to plot the coordinates of Hambleton's position were flown in from Thailand by their two-men crews. One crew went on station during the night. After some quick, careful figuring, they radioed the downed pilot's position to a special air command post in Thailand. Working with recent aerial reconnaissance photos of the area, the staff there pinpointed the bushes in which Hambleton was hiding and then plotted the coordinates of various attack points all around him. These were transmitted to a unit of all-weather jet fighter-bombers equipped to drop bombs on a target without the benefit of visual sighting. Within several hours of the Thailand FACs' arrival, these fighter-bombers were on the scene, saturating the zone around Hambleton.

After a couple more changes of guard overhead by the FACs, an OV-10 with Captains Bill Henderson and Mark Clark on board was hit by a surface-to-air missile. The small craft burst into flames, but, miraculously, two chutes popped open almost immediately. Both men had survived. Henderson was chased into a bamboo patch by about a dozen Vietnamese, who initially could not find him. However, that night, when they returned to chop down the bamboo for camouflage, they happened upon Henderson hiding among the shoots. He was taken north to Hanoi and, as it turned out, was released with other POWs in early 1973. Clark found a good hiding place within a small lot surrounded by barbed wire about three miles from Hambleton. He was not discovered. Now there were two pilots to rescue.

Another day passed. More all-weather fighter-bombers were ordered in to drop bombs on coordinates all around the two. Because both had gone down right behind the advancing front of the enemy's forces, bombing runs to save them complemented the general interdiction effort. In fact, while keeping watch over Hambleton and Clark, a FAC spotted a long column of North Vietnamese tanks moving down Highway One nearby. Six B-52s were immediately diverted from another mission. Thirty minutes later they came in and "rippled the road." According to the FAC, "they got thirty-five tanks and we found out later the command bunker of a NVA division in that area."

That day the cloud coverage finally broke up, and so fighter-bombers began working over the area visually. These operations went on for about three days, Hambleton and Clark sustaining themselves with water and food from their survival kits.

Afterward, all appeared quiet. Another rescue team composed of a Jolly Green and four Sandys decided to make a rescue run. The big helicopter had gotten well into the area, when intense ground fire opened up. Parts began flying off the craft. It nosed up, turned on its side, and slammed to earth. Fire quickly consumed the wreckage. All four crew members died.

A meeting was held at Danang Air

and political instability rather than to the strength of the Vietnamese. It was assumed that Ho and his peasant citizenry would be awed by the power and sophistication of U.S. weaponry. "If the Viet Cong could see this, they'd give up," a reporter aboard the U.S.S. *Constellation* was overheard saying as the mammoth aircraft carrier cruised in the Gulf of Tonkin in early 1965.

Administration officials were equally beguiled. They thought that what they themselves would fear and respect would similarly affect the North Vietnamese, and anyone who had witnessed one of LeMay's SAC alerts or a sky blackened with B-52s taking off could be excused for thinking so. However, the sophistication of our weaponry and the costliness of our planes and carriers did not translate directly into the desired results.

Another reason for the gap is that the Bundy brothers, Rostow, McNaughton, McNamara and others — the theoreticians who held sway within the administration — were more articulate and more persuasive than the men of practical experience forced to deal with the realities — LeMay, the Joint Chiefs and the intelligence community. Johnson did not know the former group well, since they were Kennedy's men, but his own humble origins caused him to accord them too much respect. Many had achieved their powerful positions by brilliant careers in academia, not government. William Fulbright, upon whose foreign affairs advice Johnson had depended heavily when he was Senate majority leader, was "somewhat bitter about this point," according to David Halberstam, telling his friends that "all those flashy Harvard people had excited Johnson, he thought they were so smart, and Fulbright, why, Fulbright was simply an Arkansas hillbilly from the Senate. . . . [Johnson] was in awe of his new advisers, but not his old one."

Another factor contributing to the gap between expectations and reality was the sheer momentum of ideas that had long been in the air. Since the early days of the Kennedy administration, for example, Rostow had been pushing his thesis that North Vietnamese leaders would do almost anything to avoid destruction of the factories that they had constructed at great sacrifice since 1954. As early as October 27, 1961, Sterling Cottrell, the head of the interagency Vietnam task force, recommended in a memo to Taylor that the U.S. move "to the 'Rostow Plan' of applying graduated punitive measures on the D.R.V. with weapons of our choosing" if the combined American and South Vietnamese effort did not stop Communist insurgency in the south. Thus, as conditions worsened there, bombing of the north became more attractive to policymakers.

Finally, the Gulf of Tonkin incident led administration officials to underestimate the domestic political costs of an air war on North Vietnam. The American public had reacted positively to the reprisal strikes, helping Johnson to his landslide victory over Goldwater, and contributing to the administration's overconfidence; officials developed too high a regard for their own clever nature. Vietnam was a war they could manage from Washington, they thought: They would apply just the right amount of force, hit just the right targets, wait just the right amount of time for Hanoi's reaction.

Their thinking, their proposals, were anointed once a week at a Tuesday afternoon luncheon at the White House reserved for this purpose. CBS correspondent Dan Rather described one such session during a radio broadcast on October 17, 1967, the transcript of which was reproduced in the *Pentagon Papers:* "After a bit of chatter over drinks in the sitting room, the President signals the move to the dining room. It is semi-oval, with a huge chandelier, a mural around the wall: brightly colored scenes of Cornwallis surrendering his sword at Yorktown. The President sits at the head, of course—sits in a high-back stiletto chair. Rusk is at his right, McNamara on his left, Rostow is at the other end, and the extras, if any, in between. Lunch begins, so does the serious conversation. There's an occasional pause, punctuated by the whirl of Mr. Johnson's battery-powered pepper grinder. He likes pepper and he likes the gadget."

Such was the way the air war was run—the president and top administration officials making an operations room out of a handsomely appointed White House dining room. Maybe they thought they could be more reasonable and less emotional in such an environment than their commanders could in the field. Perhaps this was what Rusk was getting at when he remarked, "At those Tuesday luncheon sessions, there were times when we'd require our fliers to go in to the more heavily defended areas to deliver their bombs on military targets rather than easier areas because of the possible threat to civilian neighborhoods." But, after a time, this procedure, these decisions, the risks incurred,

Base to decide what to do next. Most thought it too risky to send in another chopper. During discussions, a Marine Corps colonel "built like a fire hydrant" walked in. "I understand you have people you want taken out," he said. "Well, I have a full carrier of guys that would love to do that."

He was given the position of Hambleton and Clark and authority to proceed. Quickly he rounded up a volunteer marine ground team and some Vietnamese rangers. His plan was to proceed up a river between the positions of the two pilots. Via radio, Hambleton and Clark were instructed to make their way to the river and proceed as far downstream as possible.

The trek was especially difficult for Hambleton, who had to pass through a mile-wide mine field. Both reached the river, however. After a rest, Hambleton found a log and used it to float with and hide behind. His radio still worked, so FACs above monitored his progress from a discreet distance.

After three days of traveling on the river by night and resting by day, he came upon the sampan. Using a prearranged signal, he yelled out his rank and favorite color. The marines acknowledged, pulled him aboard, and covered him with underbrush. Clark had made it earlier. Thus ended the story of Hambleton's rescue. It had taken twelve days and cost three helicopters, one plane, one pilot taken prisoner and eight American lives.

General John McConnell

A U.S. pilot killed in North Vietnam.

the losses endured and the negligible results began to weigh heavily on Air Force Chief of Staff John McConnell, who though headquartered in Washington and only one step closer in the chain of command to the pilots, was much closer to them emotionally. About the time of Rather's report, after a Pentagon briefing about another exasperating day in the air war, McConnell sat there motionless, his head drooped forward, his face in his hands. "I can't tell you how I feel," he said, speaking to no one in particular. "I'm so sick of it. . . . I have never been so goddamn frustrated by it all. . . . I'm so sick of it."

Johnson became sick of it too. Finally, after about three years of awaiting Ho's reaction, he brought the bombing in the northern regions of North Vietnam to a halt. During his dramatic speech delivered to a national television audience on the evening of March 31, 1968, he announced, "I shall not seek and I will not accept the nomination of my party for another term as your president," and he unconditionally halted all bombing north of the twentieth parallel. Shortly thereafter, even more of North Vietnam was unconditionally excluded; no American planes would cross the nineteenth parallel. Finally, on

October 31, he unconditionally ended all bombing of North Vietnam, except for a small strip along the demilitarized zone. He timed the announcement to benefit the candidacy of the Democratic nominee for president, Hubert Humphrey. But Richard Nixon won anyway in the election that was held six days later.

American fighter-bombers were flying two missions a day against targets in the Hanoi area when Johnson ordered them to stop on March 31. American pilots held prisoner there had been able to hear the missions, says Risner. Initially, the POWs perceived the silence following the halt as a sign of cheer. "The President didn't stop the bombing without concessions," Air Force Major Jack Bomar boldly told one Communist interrogator. "There is no doubt in my mind about that. And I'm the concession. I don't know what the other concessions are, but the release of the POWs is primary. We'll be out of here within ninety days." Bomar was wrong, of course. The bombing was stopped unconditionally and the POWs were forced to suffer the silence of their hopeless condition for almost five more years.

Because of their courage in enduring the hardships of long years of imprisonment and torture, pilots held prisoner in North Vietnam were perhaps the only U.S. servicemen of the entire Vietnam war to emerge in 1973 as noble figures in the eyes of the American public. Their superhuman courage was almost universally recognized, though Jane Fonda called them "hypocrites and liars" when the POWs shocked the nation in 1973 with their accounts of years of torture at the hands of the North Vietnamese.

If the nation was stunned, it was because it again ignored historical precedent. During the First Indochina War, less than a third of the 36,979 French force soldiers who were taken prisoner were ever seen again. Those captured after the fall of Dien Bien Phu received the worst treatment. About ten thousand died during a forced march or the short three-month imprisonment that preceded their repatriation. No special provisions were made for the seriously wounded. Lieutenant Jean-Louis Rondy, the doctor of the First Foreign Legion Parachute Battalion at Dien Bien Phu, never forgot the pitiful sight of a soldier whose legs had been amputated to the thighs, dragging himself along on his hands and the stumps, forced to make the

The principal result of the air war on North Vietnam was to unite the population in hatred of the U.S. and in a commitment even stronger than before to the ground war in the south.

Jane Fonda visited Hanoi to show support for the North Vietnamese. She posed for photographers looking through the sights of anti-aircraft guns used to shoot down American pilots.

✷ American prisoners of war quickly recognized the need for a system to communicate with one another. During the early years especially, they were kept in separate cells. Some remained in solitary confinement for years. Talking brought reprisals, usually beatings and torture. Luckily, Captain Carlyle ("Smitty") Harris of Preston, Maryland, remembered a communications system used by American POWs during the Korean war. An instructor at the air force survival school at Stead Air Force Base, Nevada, had taught it to him. It was easier to use and memorize than Morse code. It used a twenty-five-letter alphabet, the letter *C* doubling as a *K*. The basis of the code was the arrangement of the twenty-five letters into rows and columns as follows:

A	B	C	D	E
F	G	H	I	J
L	M	N	O	P
Q	R	S	T	U
V	W	X	Y	Z

The first tap by a prisoner would indicate the row number of the desired letter, the second its column number. To communicate the letter *P*, the prisoner would tap three times for row three and five times for column five. In a system created by Navy Commander Jeremiah Denton, certain voice sounds were substituted for taps. A cough was one tap; two coughs and a spit, four; clearing the throat and spitting, five. Frequently a cellblock sounded like a consumption ward. Prisoners risked their lives to explain the code to new prisoners, and it became the key element in their survival during the early years, establishing group cohesiveness and a chain of command as well as bolstering spirits during the years that sometimes passed before prisoners had the chance to talk to their fellow captives. One early message tapped out in code followed a North Vietnamese attempt to demoralize the small number held captive in June 1965. An antiwar

march on his own or not at all.

The Communist Viet Minh had harbored special enmity for the French pilots. The commander of the Air Base Detachment at Dien Bien Phu, Captain Charnod, was forced to exhume the bodies of victims of a French air attack buried in a mass grave, look at each one individually as it rotted in the sun, and then rebury them. The Viet Minh considered Charnod and other French pilots criminals, not soldiers, no doubt partially because they themselves did not have fighters and bombers at their disposal. This categorization continued during the Second Indochina War. "You are not a prisoner of war," a Communist officer told Howard Rutledge in his initial interrogation after shoot-down on November 28, 1965. "Your government has not declared war upon the Vietnamese people. You must answer my questions. You are protected by no international law."

The standard of behavior to which captured Americans were ordered to adhere by their own government was called the "Fighting Man's Code of Conduct," which was written on Eisenhower's orders following the Korean war. Communist North Koreans had subjected American POWs to brainwashing and worked to turn them against one another. Some had collaborated with the enemy and a few decided to remain in North Korea following repatriation. The code was written to combat the unusual treatment that Communist captors seemed especially inclined to administer.

There are six parts to the Code of Conduct. Particularly relevant to the Vietnam POWs was Article I: "I am an American fighting man. I serve in the forces which guard my country and our way of life. I am prepared to give my life in their defense." Article IV states: "If I become a prisoner of war, I will keep faith with my fellow prisoners. I will give no information nor take part in any action which might be harmful to my comrades. If I am senior, I will take command. If not, I will obey the lawful orders of those appointed over me and will back them up in every way." Article V: "When questioned, should I become a prisoner of war, I am bound to give only name, rank, service number, and date of birth. I will evade answering further questions to the utmost of my ability. I will make no oral or written statements disloyal to my country and its allies or harmful to their cause." Article VI: "I will never forget that I am an American fighting man, responsible for my actions and dedicated to the principles which made my country free. I will trust in my God and in the United States of America."

Virtually all the prisoners made valiant efforts to follow the code, to keep faith with one another, to impart no information and to trust in their God and their country. But as the years passed with no decisive movement in the war and as the protests in the U.S. grew (news of which the prisoners' captors relished presenting them in print and film), most developed a much greater faith in God than in their country—a deep religious conviction that seems not to have waned during the years since.

The pilots who were shot down during Rolling Thunder and during the reprisal strikes that preceded it were among the best ever to wear the American military uniform. They were highly educated and trained, all were volunteers, most were career servicemen, and virtually all were officers. (Pilots in the air force and navy are all officers.) They believed in their cause, trusted and supported their president, and, it is fair to say, were prepared to pay any price or bear any burden to keep the Communists from taking control of South Vietnam. Furthermore, they intended to return home with their heads held high.

The first captured was Navy Lieutenant Junior Grade Everett Alvarez, Jr., twenty-six, of San Jose, California (now deputy administrator of the Veterans Administration), whose A-4 Skyhawk was downed during an attack on torpedo boat bases at Hon Gay on August 5, 1964, the day Johnson asked Congress to approve the Gulf of Tonkin Resolution.

The second pilot captured was Navy Lieutenant Commander Robert Shumaker, a Naval Academy graduate shot down during Flaming Dart II on February 11, 1965. Had luck been with Shumaker, he might have achieved fame in more agreeable circumstances. He had been an astronaut, but a very minor physical aberration disqualified him. Eventually the collection of pilots held prisoner read like a who's who of American military aviation. Air Force Major Samuel Johnson had once flown with the Thunderbirds, the air force precision flying team. Navy Commander James Stockdale had led the Gulf of Tonkin reprisal raids. Air Force Major James Kasler was a Korean war ace who led the

song popular in the U.S. was broadcast on the camp speaker system. Tapped out with a broomstick by someone sweeping a hallway, the response evoked laughter from all the separate cells. "JOAN BAEZ SUCCS," it read. Years later, Air Force Captain Jon Reynolds fondly remembered that: "It brightened my whole day."

Everett Alvarez, Jr., here with a guard in 1964, was the first American pilot captured and the longest held. He was twenty-six years old when shot down; thirty-six when released.

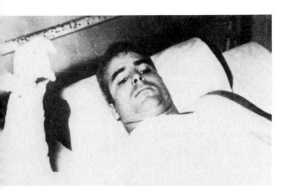

Navy pilot John McCain III, shown shortly after his capture, injured his arm during ejection. His father, an admiral, was commander of all American forces in the Pacific, including Vietnam, during most of young McCain's incarceration. The latter is now a congressman from Arizona.

first strike on the oil depots near Hanoi. Robinson Risner was also a Korean war ace. Navy Lieutenant Commander John McCain III was the son of the then commander of U.S. forces in Europe, and later of U.S. forces in the Pacific, including Vietnam. (The young McCain, now a congressman from Arizona, became a subject of great fascination to the North Vietnamese, who called him the "crown prince." Many high-ranking Communist officials dropped by to look at him, including General Giap, who while alone stared at him silently for a few minutes and then departed.) More ended up in North Vietnamese prisons when President Nixon resumed the bombing campaign over the north in 1972, those efforts called Linebacker I and Linebacker II. Four hundred and ninety-five pilots survived to be repatriated after the cease-fire agreement of January 27, 1973. Some, however, such as Captain Ron Storz and Major Ed Atterberry, both air force officers, were tortured to death.

North Vietnamese interrogators initially sought information about U.S. aircraft and tactics. But the primary aim of their interrogations and torture throughout the years was to force admissions of atrocities that never occurred and statements that would abet the antiwar movement that was building against the Johnson administration in the U.S., Europe, Japan and elsewhere. Armed only with their Code of Conduct, these Americans did the best they could.

Torture was ordered for a variety of reasons. Being caught trying to communicate with other prisoners by voice or a tap code was one. Escape attempts were another, in which case just about everyone was tortured in retaliation. However, most torture was initiated when a POW refused to answer any question beyond his name, rank, service number and date of birth.

During the early years especially, POWs refused to answer even the most inane question, thinking that they would shame themselves and eventually compromise the others. Those kept at the Hanoi Hilton would then be taken to a place called the Knobby Room, named for some rudimentary soundproofing that helped muffle a man's screams. A common and fairly complicated torture began with the victim seated on the floor with his ankles shackled together. A pipe and ropes would then be applied across the shins to lock the ankles in place. His hands, as a matter of course, would already be tied behind him. Slowly, the guards and the interrogator would then begin tying both arms together, from the wrists all the way up past the elbows, methodically cinching the ropes tighter and tighter until a man's elbows would meet behind his back, forcing his head down between his legs at the same time, to get enough leverage, while standing on his back, to tighten the ropes to the point that the victim's upper arms would be brought together behind his back. His arms, of course, would pop out of his shoulder sockets and the ropes would cut to the bone, but there was no bleeding because the circulation was cut off. The pain was overwhelming, but for some reason no one seemed able to pass out. Navy Commander Jeremiah Denton tried banging his head against the wall to knock himself out, to no avail. The process went on for hours, the victim screaming until he had no voice. Howard Rutledge held out all night in this position, in stretches of about three hours each time, during which he was beaten with a bamboo stick or struck in the face with fists until finally he answered the question, "What is your service?"

In time the pilots discovered they could usually get away with preposterous answers. And so, by practical necessity, the code was modified informally by the POWs to reflect this life-giving pragmatism. Navy Lieutenants Charles Tanner and Ross Terry used these new guidelines after being tortured off and on for two weeks. They decided it was the only way to save their lives; they were tortured so severely that Tanner's arms were rendered useless for months afterward, Terry having to attend to his every need. Collaborating on their stories, the two navy officers told their interrogators that two squadron mates, Lieutenant Clark Kent and Lieutenant Commander Ben Casey, had been court-martialed and sent home for refusing to bomb North Vietnam. This bit of information greatly pleased their torturers, who rewarded them by leaving them alone. Through Japanese Communist journalists, this news was relayed to the world, making fools out of their interrogators, who needless to say were unfamiliar with American television heroes. Tanner and Terry were tortured again after a letter from U.S. Communist Party officials exposed the young officers' subterfuge.

There were other forms of torture. Pilots were beaten with strips of rubber taken from tires; strapped in ankle-locks in their darkened cells,

Picking up the pieces...

Phyllis Rutledge had just returned from church and the grocery store with her four children. As she unloaded her car, two friends pulled into her driveway. At first she didn't notice the navy chaplain in their back seat. When she did, her knees buckled and she began crying uncontrollably. "No, no, no," she said over and over. She thought that her husband, Howard, a pilot in Vietnam, had been killed. But no one knew; there was a chance he was still alive. Five years passed before she knew for certain. In October 1970, the North Vietnamese finally permitted him to

write her a six-line letter. "Keep faith," he said. "We will have our reunion whether in this world or the next."

The case of Phyllis and Howard Rutledge is a classic example of how the Vietnam war disrupted and forever affected the lives of many who fought there and their families, but the situation for long-term POW families was particularly dramatic. For years POW status froze relationships in time at the point of separation. And yet, each marriage partner changed while living in wildly different environments and while forced to deal with completely different problems. They shared only memories. Of this limbo, Phyllis Rutledge later wrote, "I was not a wife. I was not a widow. I was nothing."

In many ways POW status was generally less troubling for men who were single. Though having a family at home was no doubt a source of strength for married POWs, this was offset to some degree by worries about how the families were doing.

Bachelors could pick up where life left them after their imprisonment— make new friends, marry someone who had never known them before. The POW and his wife who chose to remain together, like the Rutledges, were forced to retrace the lost years, reconcile what had occurred, and reconstruct a base on which to rebuild their lives together. Furthermore, many POWs had to reacquaint themselves with children now much older.

Respect for the way the other had handled terrible problems was the first building block for the Rutledges. Though the horrors of Howard's ordeal were obvious, Phyllis, too, had endured much. While Howard was prisoner, their son John had a swimming accident that left him paralyzed from the neck down. Phyllis had to contend with that tragedy and its complications alone. Because of their respect and love for each other, aided by reawakened religious convictions, the Rutledges were fortunate enough to reestablish a strong marriage.

Then they faced Howard's career readjustment problems, common to all POWs, married or not. What work could offer a meaningful outlet for a released POW? An unusually high percentage of the men became involved in politics, the motivation for many being to pass on a special message about Communism to Americans grown jaded about their own society during the post-Vietnam years.

After several responsible post-captivity military assignments, a masters degree (his thesis being a study of POWs in post-imprisonment years), and retirement from the service, Rutledge, too, entered politics. In 1980 he ran for Congress in his native Oklahoma on the Republican ticket. He did well, losing by only about five thousand votes,

thus kept immobile for days at a time, managing their bodily functions as best they could; and put in solitary confinement. Rutledge spent fifty-eight months in solitary for his continued resistance. He spent six years in windowless cells.

Enduring even without these punishments would have been difficult enough. Sanitary conditions were atrocious, the prisoners contending with all varieties of vermin, including large rats. Boils and other infections were a constant problem. Meals usually consisted of a pumpkin soup and a little rice. Each POW had a bucket for waste, which was kept in his cell. The North Vietnamese worked quite effectively to create an entirely different impression of treatment. Using POWs who had been rewarded for their cooperation, they orchestrated propaganda sessions with the press. Photos from one appeared in the October 20, 1967, issue of *Life*.

The Communists frequently underestimated their captives, however. Following prolonged torture and mistreatment, the North Vietnamese convinced themselves that Denton, Stockdale and Navy Lieutenant Commander Richard Stratton were sufficiently intimidated to behave at a press conference. When his time came, Stratton thought the best way to thwart his captors was to keep bowing, his eyes always affixed blankly over the heads of the audience. Though Stratton had in fact retained his sanity, television viewing audiences thought him either brainwashed or crazy, and thus deduced that his treatment was irregular. Before another scheduled press conference, Stockdale was given a razor with which to shave. When the guards stepped out of the room, he began slashing away at his head, creating a sort of inverse Mohawk and scraping away chunks of flesh. When the guards returned to take him before the cameras, his face and shoulders were covered with blood. Horrified but undaunted, they raced off to get a hat to hide his wounds, because of their consternation inadvertently leaving him unattended again. This time Stockdale, knowing that he bruised easily, began hitting himself in the face with a stone. When the North Vietnamese arrived with the hat, Stockdale's eyes were swelling shut. The press conference was cancelled. Denton took a different tack when forced before the cameras. Convinced that the U.S. government needed to know that the pilots were being tortured, he spelled out the word torture in

Morse code by blinking his eyes. Viewers thought that he too had gone crazy, but navy intelligence eventually picked up his signal.

Actually the Johnson administration had already confirmed that the North Vietnamese were torturing the American pilots, but chose not to release the information on the dubious grounds that disclosure might spark a paroxysm of torture. Later the Nixon administration reversed this policy and began publicly demanding better treatment. The American public's response was overwhelming; thousands of letters were mailed to Hanoi in protest. This initiative and apparently the death of Ho Chi Minh in September 1969 caused a change in treatment that evolved rather dramatically that fall. Perhaps Ho was sullen and bitter during his final years because of the long war, knowing he would die before the two Vietnams would be unified, and, as a result, took out his frustration on the pilots. There is no evidence that he personally ordered the torture, but he was surely aware of it, given his recognition that the POWs were valuable bargaining pawns.

The summer of 1969 had been a terrible period of torture, the darkness before the dawn. In the fall, some POW camp commanders were changed; some interrogators were never seen again; some who remained were apparently forced to apolo-

though he was initially unknown, had decided to run only at the last instant, and had no campaign organization. Nor did his uncompromisingly strong convictions make his campaign any easier. In 1982 he ran again for the same office, but lost rather handily to the same opponent.

In spite of these disappointments, Howard and Phyllis Rutledge had reason to feel good about themselves and their lives. And they did. They were comfortably retired; their children were well adjusted. Then Rutledge began having stomach problems. At first doctors diagnosed it as a previously dormant parasite he had picked up during his incarceration. Instead it was a terminal case of cancer. But Rutledge met his death with the same courage he lived his life. He bravely endured the treatment—chemotherapy in huge doses—until the end. He and Phyllis never complained, never felt victimized. In June 1984 he died, once again leaving Phyllis alone. But this time, because of the past, she was not unprepared.

The Hao Lo Prison, called the Hanoi Hilton by American prisoners, was where most were initially taken for interrogation and torture.

(L-r, foreground) The mother of Lieutenant Markham Gartley leads her son and Lieutenant Norris Charles aboard a Soviet airliner in Hanoi on September 27, 1972. The two navy officers and air force Major Edward Elias, all former pilots who had become POWs, were released to an antiwar delegation that in addition to Mrs. Gartley included the Reverend William Sloane Coffin, Jr., of Yale, Professor Richard Falk of Princeton, David Dellinger and Cora Weiss. The three officers were ostracized by fellow POWs for allowing themselves to be used for propaganda purposes and for going home early. Each had pledged to go home together or not at all. When Gartley later ran for statewide office in Maine, former POWs' active opposition was instrumental in causing his defeat.

gize to some of the Americans. Denton was shocked by the admission of one that for a thousand years the treatment afforded prisoners by his country was humane and lenient, "but that in the case of the Americans, he and a number of other officers and guards had misinterpreted and misapplied this policy. (The man obviously had a selective memory of Vietnamese history; French POWs were horribly mistreated during the fifties.) He said that he and the others had been required to criticize themselves and to confess their mistakes." Thereafter the torture ended almost completely.

Also contributory to better living conditions was the U.S. Special Forces raid on Son Tay led by Colonel Arthur "Bull" Simon. This POW rescue attempt failed in its primary mission because the Americans held prisoner there had been moved to another camp four months earlier. However, according to the POWs, the November 21, 1970, incident so frightened the North Vietnamese that they closed the outlying camps and concentrated their prisoners in the Hanoi area, where the men now shared rooms because of space problems. Having company after years of loneliness was a great improvement.

The POWs finally began coming home during February and March of 1973, those longest held and the injured returning on the first planes. The first contingent departed on February 12. Three gleaming C-141 Starlifter jet transports glided down onto the runway at Gia Lam Airport near Hanoi to pick them up. Almost in disbelief that their ordeal was over, they stepped forward, one by one saluting the air force colonel who waited to greet them. One of the first was a young man held prisoner for more than seven years and the first to be tortured. "Sir, Knutson, Rodney Allen; lieutenant junior grade, United States Navy," he said while rendering a snappy salute. "Reporting my honorable return as a prisoner of war to the United States."

The LeMay-Bundy war games turned out to have been an all too accurate predictor. Just as in the game sequence, the airstrikes on North Vietnam caused the Johnson administration, like the Blue Team, to order American combat troops into South Vietnam to protect the air bases. The most exposed and important of these at the time was Danang Air Base, not far from the border dividing the two Vietnams. On March 8, 1965, less than a month after the sustained air

(Top) The first POWs to be released included sick or wounded and those who had been held captive longest. Everett Alvarez, Jr., at the front of a column of POWs, was one of the first to board a C-141 jet transport that had landed at Gia Lam International Airport near Hanoi. (Center) Robinson Risner, followed by James Stockdale, waves to the crowd greeting them at Clark Air Force Base, the Philippines, the first stop en route home after long years of captivity. (Bottom) Jeremiah Denton, Jr., hugs his wife Jane upon arriving at Norfolk Naval Air Station.

The one-man air force...

Captain Hilliard Wilbanks was a forward air controller who flew a Cessna Bird Dog, a plane very much like a Piper Cub—small, slow, vulnerable. Not an aircraft one would choose to go to war in. But during Vietnam fighting, such planes were indispensable for allied forces. From them, pilots like Wilbanks could more easily spot the enemy lying in ambush and direct the swift American fighter-bombers down upon them.

Wilbanks, a few other FACs and some American army advisers were assigned to a South Vietnamese Ranger unit whose area of operation was about one hundred miles northeast of Saigon. His airport was a small dirt strip outside the South Vietnamese defense compound that at night belonged as much to the enemy as to the South Vietnamese. Still, Wilbanks and other FACs went out on night missions. Before his return landing, a couple of U.S. enlisted men who were his mechanics would race through the darkness in a jeep, laying down portable runway lights. Once on the ground, Wilbanks would gun his Bird Dog up to the edge of the compound, pile out quickly, hop into the jeep, and race down the runway with his men, retrieving the runway lights, one man hanging off the side as they went down and back. It was an inglorious and dangerous way to fight a war.

On February 24, 1967, at dusk, Wilbanks was spotting for some Vietnamese Rangers in search of Viet Cong units known to be in the vicinity. During his ten months in the war zone, Wilbanks had flown 488 combat missions. In just two more months, he would be back home in Cornelia, Georgia, with his wife and children.

Wilbanks was intimately familiar with the region—its ridges, jungle areas, roads, many of the paths, the tea plantations, some still owned by Frenchmen.

war was ordered and only six days after it actually began, 3,500 marines waded ashore at Nam O Beach, three miles from Danang. They were the first U.S. combat troops assigned to South Vietnam.

The marines' mission was, for a short time, passive defense. The day before they arrived, Rusk said during a television interview that their mission was to assure base security, "not to kill the Viet Cong." However, by April 1, when the realization that Hanoi would not yield to the bombing campaign had started to set in and the administration began worrying about expanding the air war too rapidly lest China intervene, Johnson decided during a White House strategy meeting to upgrade the marines' mission from defensive to offensive operations. McGeorge Bundy had proposed the change, and he in fact signed National Security Action Memorandum 328 for the president to put into effect. Thus, in 1965 American troops began going out on combat patrols for the first time in Vietnam. They would soon be joined by tens of thousands more. The arrival of the marines on March 8 had increased the number of American servicemen there to about 30,000. By May 12 the total was 46,500. By June 16, it was 74,500. By October 23, it had climbed to 148,300. By December 29, the total reached 184,000. The land war in South Vietnam was on in earnest.

The air force had begun preparing for the possibility of a ground war in late 1961, when a detachment of transport planes and Second World War–vintage propeller-driven combat aircraft was deployed to South Vietnam, using a training role as their cover. But the real mission of these pilots and unit commanders was to develop tactics and techniques that could later be employed if U.S. ground troops became involved in the fighting. The operation was called Jungle Jim and had LeMay's personal attention.

Unfortunately, the detachment's combat aircraft were too old to be kept properly maintained. Accidents and enemy ground fire caused "depressing losses." As a result, "in the years of low-intensity conflict before 1965, the most effective expression of air power in Vietnam was the transport plane," says Ray Bowers. Ngo Dinh Diem, recognizing that air transportation could help centralize the South Vietnamese economy and administration, ordered small landing strips built throughout the country. Using American

C-123 cargo planes, "civilian passengers, government development teams, troops and their equipment and cargo ranging from livestock to large munitions" were brought into the far-flung network of villages and cities. Later in the war, the large C-130 Hercules and the small C-7 Caribou, capable of landing and taking off on an eight-hundred-foot dirt strip, were incorporated into the supply system that had as its key junctures the airfields at Tan Son Nhut, Cam Ranh Bay and Danang. Cargo was brought to these huge shipping centers usually by either the large jet-powered C-141s, the C-130s, or sea transport.

One very significant development of the Jungle Jim testing was the reintroduction of the Forward Air Controller, or FAC. These were pilots who flew small observation aircraft, initially the O-1 Bird Dog, a military version of a single-engine Cessna, and later the OV-10, a much more sophisticated twin-engine aircraft that was armed. Airborne FACs were used extensively during the Korean war, but, until the testing in Vietnam, they were thought too small and slow to survive over the modern battlefield. But the FACs became an indispensable adjunct to the use of airpower in South Vietnam, where targets in the jungle were almost impossible to locate by the fast-moving jet aircraft. The FAC would fire a smoke rocket near the target and then vector in the jet fighter-bombers, using the smoke flume rising from the ground as a reference point.

After the ground troop buildup in 1965, the dominant role of airpower in South Vietnam was its use essentially "as a complement to or a substitute for ground artillery," says Bowers.

Often he could see them sunbathing around their pools while opposing forces fought in the area. These wealthy landowners paid taxes to both sides, the Viet Cong and the South Vietnamese, and were normally left alone.

The night before, the Viet Cong had laid a trap. They had pressed some Vietnamese tea plantation workers into their service, forcing them to dig foxholes along the slope of a hill that overlooked an outlying section of the plantation. They then completely concealed their positions in the foxholes with bushes.

Wilbanks spotted the Viet Cong as the Rangers and their American advisers walked among the small tea bushes toward the trap. As he radioed Captain J. R. Wooten, who was with the South Vietnamese, the Viet Cong opened fire with mortars, rifles and machine guns, realizing Wilbanks had probably seen them. The battle was on, the South Vietnamese Rangers greatly outnumbered.

Wilbanks dived his plane toward the enemy, firing a smoke rocket that he aimed by aligning a nose aerial with a Magic Marker circle on his windshield. (The FAC's equipment was rudimentary in those days.) The white plume of smoke from the burning phosphorus marked the center of the enemy's position. Three helicopter gunships, soon on the scene, swooped low firing. One was hit by a fifty-caliber shell and was

Two O-1 Bird Dogs fly in formation. Such planes' pilots had dangerous jobs.

in danger of crashing. Knowing that two fighter-bombers were on their way, Wilbanks advised the pilots of the undamaged helicopters to escort the other to safety. Shortly thereafter, the Viet Cong force emerged from their foxholes with knives and bayonets affixed to do hand-to-hand combat with the outnumbered Rangers and Americans.

With the helicopter gunships gone and the fighter-bombers not yet on the scene, Wilbanks decided that only he could save the allied forces, though his only armament consisted of three smoke rockets, an M-16 automatic rifle and a pistol. He again began diving down on the enemy, flying as low as a hundred feet each time. The smoke rockets were harmless unless they struck someone, but his antics confused and distracted the enemy, most of whom stopped to fire at Wilbanks as he jerked his plane back and forth, up and down. Wooten could hear bullets hitting the small craft.

After three such passes, Wilbanks was out of rockets, so he grabbed his M-16 and banked again. The Bird Dog had no plexiglass in the side windows, so Wilbanks struck the barrel out an opening and began firing during yet another pass. After leveling off very low, he actually let the plane fly itself as he fired. Though it was already riddled with bullet holes, he banked it once more and made another run after reloading.

By now the Rangers and the Americans had pulled back and consolidated somewhat. Wilbanks had given them a few precious life-saving minutes to do so. During his fifth pass, his plane did not pull up. Unconscious from wounds, he crashed his plane between the opposing forces. An American adviser, Captain Gary Vote, raced forward to save him.

Wilbanks was flown to a field hospital, but died en route. He was posthumously awarded the Congressional Medal of Honor.

Though the U.S. and its Vietnamese allies eventually had most of South Vietnam within the range of fire of ground artillery, aircraft fighter-bombers afforded several advantages. One was that aircraft could quickly marshal an enormous concentration of firepower over a battle area such as a besieged outpost. Another advantage was the variety of air-delivered weapons. Planes could carry bombs such as the typical 500- or 750-pounders, which had much more explosive power than an artillery shell; they also carried specialized weapons such as the controversial napalm bombs and cluster bombs. Napalm, approved for use on March 9, 1965, by Johnson, was a jelly-like substance that blanketed an area and ignited a veritable inferno. Cluster bombs included dozens of baseball-like units that exploded on contact into thousands of devastating pellets. Both napalm and cluster bombs were antipersonnel bombs, intended for enemy troops or anti-aircraft gunners, for example; the 750-pounders were designed primarily for tanks, structures, gun implacements or dug-in troops.

The B-52 was America's most feared bomber. Though LeMay had made these huge aircraft the backbone of his SAC nuclear bomber fleet, their sustained use in South Vietnam had not been foreseen by air force planners. For use there they were modified to carry thirty tons of 500- and 750-pound bombs—five times what the largest jet fighter-bomber could carry. They operated from bases in Guam and Thailand and were vectored over their targets by ground control centers. They bombed from very high altitudes, day and night.

Because of airpower, one of the tactics of U.S. forces was to draw large Communist units into an engagement so that the full brunt of American aircraft could be brought to bear on them. Communist commanders developed counterstrategies, of course. They learned to disengage quickly and usually attacked at night to minimize the effectiveness of aircraft used against them. U.S. forces, in turn, attempted to counter these tactics with the use of transport planes modified with machine guns mounted on one side. Pilots of these planes could aim much more precisely than those flying jets with bombs, and their machine gun bullets did not spray shrapnel in every direction as exploding bombs did; their planes' weaponry was thus much less likely to injure friendly troops. The first such gunship was an AC-47, or "Spooky"; the most common were AC-130s with 7.62- and 20-millimeter machine guns capable of firing thousands of rounds per minute. Later in the war some AC-130s were even equipped with 150-millimeter howitzer cannons that could destroy tanks. The gunships were nicknamed Puffs by many, a reference to the gunfire they spewed and Peter, Paul and Mary's "Puff the Magic Dragon." When an outpost was attacked at night, a gunship would be dispatched immediately. Crew members would throw specially developed flares that would fall slowly to earth, illuminating the entire battle area. The pilot would then point one wing directly toward the ground and loiter in small circles while the guns mounted on the side of the craft sprayed down a withering barrage. This firing technique became very accurate, especially with the advent of special sights and laser mechanisms that the pilot himself controlled. He could fire effectively up to the edge of the outpost perimeter. By the time of the Communist offensive of 1972, the gunships had become so accurate that South Vietnamese troops fighting in An Loc called them in to assist in house-to-house fighting.

The rules of engagement for American airpower

(Below) A time exposure photo of an AC-47 gunship firing on enemy troops attacking an American combat base. The plane fired up to eighteen thousand rounds per minute from three side-mounted 7.62mm mini-guns. (Bottom) The pilot of an OV-10 observation plane launches a smoke rocket at a target in the Mekong Delta to mark it for fast-moving jet fighter-bombers.

A rocket fired from a navy F-8 Crusader streaks toward Viet Cong positions in South Vietnam.

in South Vietnam were roughly defined by McNamara early in the war when he directed General Momyer not to "take a chance on killing innocent people in order to kill a few Viet Cong." But, of course, bombs are not precision instruments of death; shrapnel from them flies in all directions. The bombing was not, however, as indiscriminate as is generally believed. Attempts were made to avoid killing or injuring innocent civilians. As a general rule, targets had to be approved by the South Vietnamese government. "American pilots routinely refused to bomb in seemingly compelling circumstances if the necessary clearance was unavailable. Infantry requests for preparatory strikes on village targets were denied, with the stipulation that strikes would be approved if the troops were fired upon."

Nevertheless, aerial bombardment killed many noncombatants in South Vietnam as it did in the north. In fact, Ray Bowers reports that "a significant minority of U.S. Army generals (29 percent of those polled) responded that, considering the nature of the war, air power and artillery had been overused" in South Vietnam. Their appraisal underscores the difficulty of waging war against a portion of an ally's own population.

One of the most controversial aspects of the air war in the south, especially in subsequent years, was the chemical defoliation missions flown by American aircraft, beginning in 1961. The Kennedy administration did not stumble into the program inadvertently, but ordered it only after considerable discussion at the highest levels — not that there was any concern about possible side effects on human beings; no one was aware of any. The government had in fact used herbicides as early as March 1946 to spray weeds on the mall in front of the nation's capitol. But the administration was concerned about the possibility of propaganda generated by the Vietnamese Communists in response to the spraying.

Movement toward herbicide use in Vietnam had started within days after Kennedy took office. Walt Rostow sent him a memo on April 12, 1961, calling for a high-level meeting in the near future to consider "gearing up" American activities in Vietnam. The memo recommended that a military research and development team go to work developing "techniques and gadgets" that could be used to combat the Communist insurgency. Aerial defoliation aimed at hiding places for the Communist forces and at their

food crops became one of these techniques, although it was not mentioned specifically in Rostow's memo.

Rusk told Kennedy, "The use of defoliant does not violate any rule of international law concerning the conduct of chemical warfare and is an accepted tactic of war." He cited as precedent a similar operation by the British in Malaysia against Communist insurgents during the early fifties. In the Defense Department, however, military leaders in uniform voiced more concern than their civilian superiors. In a memo to McNamara on November 3, the Joint Chiefs said that "care must be taken to assure that the United States does not become the target of charges of employing chemical or biological warfare." Furthermore, General Lyman Lemnitzer, the chairman of the Joint Chiefs, expressed doubts both about whether the British operation in Malaysia had been very successful and about whether similar operations—especially those involving destruction of enemy crops—had any application value in Vietnam. McNamara was ambivalent, voicing some of the same reservations expressed by the Joint Chiefs. But Deputy Secretary of Defense Roswell Gilpatrick and William Bundy, assistant secretary of defense at the time, generally supported the idea, with Rusk endorsing their view. And on November 30, 1961, Kennedy accepted their recommendation. According to National Security Action Memo 115, Kennedy approved a "selective and carefully controlled joint program of defoliant operations in Viet Nam starting with the clearance of key routes and proceeding thereafter to food denial only if the most careful basis of resettlement and alternative food supply has been created."

McNamara, always the careful manager, had about a month earlier ordered the air force to organize a defoliation unit, which he immediately put on standby. As a result, six C-123 defoliant aircraft with thirty-six crew members (some backup) took off for Vietnam from the U.S. on the very day Kennedy approved defoliation missions.

Though Operation Ranch Hand, as the defoliation program was called, had the strong backing of Diem, the U.S. ambassador to Vietnam, Frederick Nolting, insisted that the aircraft involved carry civilian markings and the crews wear only civilian clothes. However, Secretary of the Air Force Eugene Zuckert worried about

✳ An air force unit famous for its esprit was the squadron composed of C-123 defoliation planes whose operations were code-named Ranch Hand. Their arrival very early in the war was not universally welcomed, even among Americans. During a reception that Ambassador Frederick Nolting hosted for the first small Ranch Hand contingent upon their arrival in Saigon, an American naval officer asked one of them how they could sleep at night knowing that they were such "violent men." Some associated defoliation with chemical warfare. Defoliation units were generally popular with soldiers and commanders in the field, however—at least until health problems were associated with defoliants—because their work exposed enemy hiding places. Their courage was universally recognized. The planes were slow and usually had to make several low passes over their target area during missions. Small arms fire frequently riddled their planes. To protect themselves, crew members sat on special shields and wore flak panties and vests. The informal motto of the Ranch Handers was "Only you can prevent forests," a tongue-in-cheek expression somewhat indicative of their raucous spirit. Their parties, at which they all wore purple flight suits, were some of the wildest in Vietnam. One of the better-known members of the squadron was Airman Patrick Nugent, the son-in-law of President Johnson. He was an enlisted man who served as a loadmaster and flew Ranch Hand missions during 1968–1969. His assignment to that unit is one indication that Johnson, at least, had no knowledge of the health problems the chemicals cause; Nugent handled them on an almost daily basis.

Air Force Secretary Eugene Zuckert

During 1968, Lyndon Johnson's son-in-law, Patrick Nugent, served as a loadmaster on defoliation planes such as these.

what would happen to the crew members so disguised if they were shot down and captured. Zuckert received support from William Bundy, and on December 14 it was decided that "the identity of United States crews and aircraft participating in the spraying operations of the defoliation program will not be disguised."

The first defoliant supplies arrived on January 8, 1962, in the hold of a ship called the S.S. *Sooner State*, its long journey to Vietnam having commenced, on McNamara's orders, before Kennedy's approval. The first target for the planes, personally selected by McNamara and Kennedy, was foliage along sixteen miles of road in southern South Vietnam.

On January 3, Rusk had cabled the embassy in Saigon to "make no advance announcement other than local warnings, in low key, to population which will witness process." However, contrary to Rusk's wishes, the South Vietnamese government issued a press release on January 10 announcing the defoliant operation. "The purpose of this operation," it read, "is to improve the country's economy by permitting free communications along these routes. . . . If the results of this initial operation are satisfactory, extensive operations will be conducted to clear roads and railroad links in key cities of Vietnam." The release also offered assurances that the defoliants will not "harm wild life, domestic animals, human beings, or the soil."

Results of early missions were not all that impressive. The forests still provided refuge because the triple-canopy forests were so thick; stronger chemicals gradually came into use. Later, B-52s, bombing with incendiaries, were incorporated into the Ranch Hand clearing operations to burn the trees away. Defoliation missions deemed most effective were those around canals, because smaller underbrush was the target. American riverboats equipped with flame-throwers would then come along to burn the defoliated brush away.

Controversy about the possible effects on humans of Agent Orange, one of the herbicides used, began to surface in 1969. On June 26, 1969, a report appeared in a South Vietnamese newspaper "alleging that herbicide organisms had caused human birth defects in that country." That fall the National Institutes of Health in the U.S. published a report written by K. Diane Courtney and others presenting evidence that chemical 2,4,5-T, a component of Agent Orange, caused malformed babies and stillborns in mice when large doses were administered. As a consequence, Deputy Secretary of Defense David Packard ordered that from that point forward Agent Orange could be spread only in remote areas.

In December 1969, the American Association for the Advancement of Science funded a study group headed by Harvard University professor Matthew Meselson to travel to South Vietnam the next summer to investigate the effects of spraying. His study group contributed to the discontinuation of the Ranch Hand missions, though their work was inconclusive—partially because the Joint Chiefs would not release operational data that was classified. Meselson's group did find disturbing signs that the forests were not regenerating as anticipated. For example, bamboo was taking over some forest areas, preventing sprayed trees from growing back.

On April 15, 1970, the Defense Department announced the suspension of the use of Agent Orange. It was being sprayed at a rate of 150,000 to 200,000 gallons per month in Vietnam at the time. The day of the DOD suspension, the secretaries of health, education and welfare, interior, and agriculture announced in a joint statement that the use of defoliants containing 2,4,5-T was suspended in the United States, too, "except for carefully controlled and registered applications on non-crop land such as range and pastures."

The last Ranch Hand mission of the war, using other forms of herbicides, was flown on January 7, 1971.

When Johnson ordered the air war over North Vietnam in early 1965, he also ordered an intense, concurrent air war over Laos. The objective of this effort, called Commando Hunt, was to cut off the flow of supplies being shipped down the Ho Chi Minh Trail. This supply route through the remote, sparsely populated, heavily forested mountain region of eastern Laos was indispensable to Communist units operating in South Vietnam. Most of their weapons and ammunition came down the trail, though large quantities were also shipped in by sampans and other boats. Daily necessities were usually locally obtained.

As the war in the south intensified, so did the traffic on the Ho Chi Minh Trail. By one account Giap deployed fifty thousand workers to operate and defend it. From porters to engineers,

An armada of spray planes lines up for takeoff for a mission over the Boi Loi forest on March 31, 1965.

On the beam with lasers...

Technology improved throughout the long war, enhancing the ability of aircraft to support ground troops. The use of lasers to guide bombs onto a target was one such development. In one application, the pilot of a small, specially equipped OV-10 propeller aircraft would fly over the target and direct a laser beam down onto it, at which time an F-4 fighter-bomber carrying the laser-guided bomb would swoop down to drop it into the laser envelope—an area in the sky close enough to the laser beam so that the bomb can lock onto it. The bomb would then follow the laser beam to the target. The advantages were pinpoint accuracy and the fact that both aircraft could execute the operation at higher altitudes than they could with conventional bombs, making them less vulnerable to ground fire.

The technology was called Pave Nail and American Special Forces soldiers who were in the central highlands during the 1972 North Vietnamese invasion will attest to its effectiveness. In early May of that year, one of their camps was about to be overrun. A tank had broken through the defense perimeter. A desperate call went up to a FAC.

"I've got a tank trying to crush the command bunker!" a soldier screamed into his radio.

The FAC immediately called in a Pave Nail team that was in the battle area.

"What's a Pave Nail?" asked the soldier, listening in on the conversation, but unaware of the new development.

"Stand by and we'll show you," said the FAC.

The OV-10 locked the laser beam onto

bulldozer drivers to anti-aircraft crews, they worked at maintaining the passability of the trail. "By 1970, the North Vietnamese had more than 2,500 trucks in Laos, with even larger numbers stockpiled in North Vietnam." Each driver drove only a short segment of the trail so that he could become intimately familiar with every turn and aware of those stretches of road on which his vehicle was most vulnerable to air attack. The thick forests generally provided a natural canopy and, where they did not, treetops were tied together to further camouflage the road. The trail included dispersal points along the way, where each morning before dawn trucks would be unloaded and cargoes would be concealed. Troops, trucks and other equipment such as tanks usually moved at night to minimize the effectiveness of American airstrikes. Anti-aircraft installations were interspersed along the way at key junctures. This supply system eventually became so sophisticated that it included a petroleum pipeline.

The same American aircraft assigned missions over North Vietnam were assigned missions over the Ho Chi Minh Trail. Fighter-bombers from carriers in the Gulf of Tonkin, air force bombers (including B-52s) operating out of Thailand, South Vietnam and Guam—all flew both target regions and, because weather conditions in the two areas differed substantially (because of the mountain chain separating North Vietnam from the trail), pilots frequently found themselves diverted from one region to the other depending on the weather.

However, there were specialized air force units assigned exclusively to interdiction along the trail. These included transports whose job was to illuminate various target areas at night with flares, and a unit of C-123 transports that dropped cluster bombs and carried special sensor devices to locate traffic along the roads below. Another unit of C-123s sprayed Agent Orange to help expose the roads. In addition to the jet fighter-bombers and the B-52s, strike aircraft included propeller-driven, Korean war-vintage A-26s that sometimes operated more effectively than the jets, because their slower speed made them more manageable in the mountainous terrain; also AC-119 and AC-130 gunships. The efforts of all these planes were coordinated from command and control C-130s orbiting overhead. (So many planes were in the air that there were occasional midair collisions.) In some cases, the strike aircraft hit preplanned targets; in other instances, they were assigned to fly along looking for targets of opportunity. The AC-130 gunships, which were acknowledged as "the war's most effective truck-killers," were best suited for the latter mission.

In 1966 a Harvard Law School professor proposed that sensor devices be dropped along the trail to enable pilots to pinpoint targets in the darkness. A special scientific advisory group was convened by the Defense Department to analyze the idea, and by late 1967 the professor's plan was put into effect. Long projectiles containing acoustic and seismic sensors were dropped along the trail from transport planes. Each was designed to embed itself, leaving crudely shaped antennas that resembled the underbrush protruding above the ground. EC-121 aircraft circled above, loaded with equipment to pick up signals from these devices and relay the data to the Infiltration Surveillance Center at a base in Thailand. Commanders at the center would then order airstrikes on areas where signals were being picked up. This elaborate system worked better in theory than in practice. Ray Bowers describes it as "relatively inefficient."

The overall success of Commando Hunt was difficult to measure. Pilots would report destroying trucks at night, but reconnaissance photos taken later would not confirm the report. Nothing could be found. Pilots joked about there being a giant dragon that ate burned-out trucks. The discrepancy was later deemed to be the result of two factors: the speed with which the trucks were removed and repaired by the North Vietnamese, and the exaggerated numbers contained in the reports. Such inaccurate reporting was a product of the consuming interest of Washington officials to have some measurement of the success of the war effort. Progress could not be measured in terms of territory taken from the enemy, given the nature of the war in the south; progress was quantified in terms of trucks destroyed or enemy soldiers killed. It was a one-dimensional war of attrition, with body counts and truck destruction numbers rather than news of advances along a front being standard daily news fare for home-U.S.A. consumption.

Military officials reported twenty thousand trucks destroyed in Commando Hunt 5 during one stage of the war; ten thousand in Commando Hunts 3 and 7. The number designation referred to a different phase of the campaign,

the tank and the F-4 released a 2,000-pound laser-guided bomb, which glided in perfectly, detonating next to the tank. The explosion blew the tank off the command post and back through the perimeter wire.

There followed a long silence on the radio.

Finally the soldier got back on his radio.

"What did you call that?" he asked.

"Pave Nail."

"I need about two more," he said.

A North Vietnamese examines an air-dropped sensor that picked up vehicle movement.

Lieutenant (j.g.) Norman Lessard (right) tends to Lieutenant (j.g.) Dieter Dengler aboard the U.S.S. *Ranger* on July 21, 1966. The emaciated Dengler had just been rescued after escaping captivity and evading the enemy for twenty-two days.

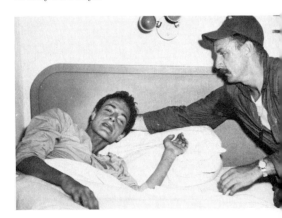

usually the winter dry season. Other estimates included the percentage of equipment that the enemy managed to get all the way down the trail—one-ninth of sixty-one thousand tons was the estimate for Commando Hunt 5; one-sixth for Commando Hunt 7.

Ray Bowers estimates that the success of the Commando Hunt operations was less than what was thought at the time. However, his appraisal is that they generally prevented Communists in the south from marshaling large-scale, sustained ground operations. His overall assessment is that the "Commando Hunt campaigns were conducted while harming relatively few civilians, without risk of great power retaliation, with relatively little outcry from the world community and with far fewer losses in men and planes than Rolling Thunder."

The year 1972 was the most decisive for American air forces during the Vietnam war. The reason was twofold: because Giap, emboldened by the departure of 450,000 American servicemen since 1969, mostly ground troops, adopted conventional, large-unit tactics which American air forces are highly trained to counter; and because when Nixon decided to resume the air war on North Vietnam that Johnson had halted in 1968, he gradually lifted most of the restrictions that had inhibited Rolling Thunder, and ordered bombings day and night until a settlement was agreed to.

A GI from the First Infantry Division walks by a crater created by one of the bombs dropped from B-52s into the Iron Triangle.

By early 1972 the Nixon Doctrine was the controlling U.S. policy in Vietnam: "America would aid its Asian allies with materials, technical advice, and, if necessary, with air and naval power. Beyond this, the nation remained determined to avoid further new commitments of U.S. ground forces." In March 1972, only 95,000 American servicemen remained on duty in Vietnam, down from the peak commitment several years earlier of more than one-half million. American air strength had dramatically shrunk also. Only seventy-six fighter-bombers were assigned to South Vietnam, down from the peak number of three hundred fifty in 1969. SAC's commitment of B-52s in Guam and Thailand, the commitment of air force fighter-bombers in Thailand, and the commitment of various marine and naval air units were reduced commensurately, though two carriers, the *Hancock* and the *Coral Sea,* remained offshore. Large numbers of support and transport aircraft such as the C-130s had returned home too.

South Vietnamese were being trained and equipped to fight the war by themselves. The Nixon administration called this transition process the "Vietnamization" of the war, a term coined by Secretary of Defense Melvin Laird. The U.S., for example, had built up the South Vietnamese Air Force to the point that it was the fourth largest in the world. But as the coming several years would prove, there were extraordinary differences between the fourth largest and the largest (that of the U.S.). The most significant difference was the greater skill and commitment of the American pilots.

Convinced that for political and practical reasons this country could not redeploy significant numbers of forces to South Vietnam, North Vietnamese leaders (a collective leadership by then) ordered a full-scale invasion of the south in 1972. Preparations were so massive and obvious that only the timing and attack points were subject to doubt. Aerial reconnaissance photos showed seven thousand to eight thousand loaded trucks in North Vietnamese supply depots, their drivers ready to move south when the dry season began.

Most American intelligence officers picked mid-February as the probable invasion date because of the concurrence of two events—Nixon's historic trip to China, and Tet, the Vietnamese Lunar New Year celebration and the anniversary of so many other Vietnamese Communist attacks. The invasion came on a Christian religious holiday, however—Easter weekend. On Good Friday, March 30, Giap's forces launched across the DMZ the first of a three-pronged offensive. Three divisions of about forty thousand combat troops supported by hundreds of tanks, mobile anti-aircraft guns, surface-to-air missiles (some large, some hand-held, the latter a new development), trucks, artillery (including 130-millimeter weapons capable of firing up to seventeen miles), other heavy equipment and thousands of logistics personnel began pushing back South Vietnamese forward combat units numbering only nine thousand troops. The main South Vietnamese force was being held in reserve, pending a clearer picture of Communist plans. Within days two other strong Communist drives had pierced South Vietnam's borders, one from Laos in the central highlands, another farther south from Laos and Cambodia at a point only about one hundred miles north-northwest of Saigon. An

Ordnancemen aboard the U.S.S. *Constellation* in the Tonkin Gulf strain to hoist a bomb to the rack of an A-5 Intruder.

Honeycomb revetments made of steel and concrete, such as these housing two A-37s (left) and two F-100s (right) at Bien Hoa Air Base, were built to protect aircraft from Viet Cong mortar attacks.

The F-100 Supersabre was a mainstay of the air force's mission of close air support for ground troops. Here a pilot drops a bomb on enemy positions.

estimated twenty thousand combat troops were involved in the central highlands invasion; an unknown number in the other. These units were also supported by tanks, artillery and heavy equipment. As the three Communist forces pushed inward, they linked up with Communist units within the country.

By 1972 political leadership in the south had stabilized under President Nguyen Van Thieu, a former army general, who exhorted his nation to "the final battle to decide the survival of the people." But it was really the American air forces that would save his nation on this occasion, a fact that became painfully obvious in 1975 when the North Vietnamese launched a second such offensive, this time overrunning the country—largely because of the absence of

American air forces. In 1972 Nixon acted decisively. In 1975 Gerald Ford could not.

The 1972 U.S. response was awesome in both size and speed and consisted almost entirely of air attacks—by the air force, the marines and the navy—which began on March 30. Initial deployments consisted of B-52 bombers ordered in February from stateside bases for standby duty in Asia. Other stateside B-52 crews were flying combat missions over Vietnam within seventy-two hours of receiving deployment orders. In all, Strategic Air Command deployed one hundred sixty-one B-52s to bases in Guam and Thailand.

These huge bombers were complemented by an armada of fighter-bombers, some in the air and on their way to South Vietnam within hours

of the invasion. From stateside air force bases in North Carolina, Florida and New Mexico came one hundred forty-four F-4 Phantoms; from a Kansas base came twelve F-105 Thunderchiefs; from South Carolina, eight EB-66s. From American air bases in the Pacific came eighteen air force F-4s from Korea, thirty-six marine corps F-4s and thirty-six A-4 Sky Hawks from Japan, and eighteen Marine Corps F-4s from Hawaii. The total was one hundred ninety-two fighter-bombers and eight electronic warfare planes. Deployed along with this huge force was a larger number of support aircraft—sixty-four C-130s from bases in Arkansas, Virginia and Taiwan and one hundred sixty-eight KC-135 tankers that refueled the fighter-bombers in flight over the Pacific Ocean. The tankers remained in the

(Top) The tail of a B-52G, with its four 50-caliber machine guns, resembled that of a strange insect. During the first night of Linebacker II, Staff Sergeant Sam Turner became the first B-52 tailgunner to shoot down an enemy aircraft in combat. (Above) A B-52's bombs detonate on suspected enemy positions in South Vietnam. These huge aircraft were usually never spotted visually from the ground because they approached their targets from such high altitudes.

President Richard Nixon

B-52s and smaller fighter-bombers turned this section of the DMZ into a moonscape.

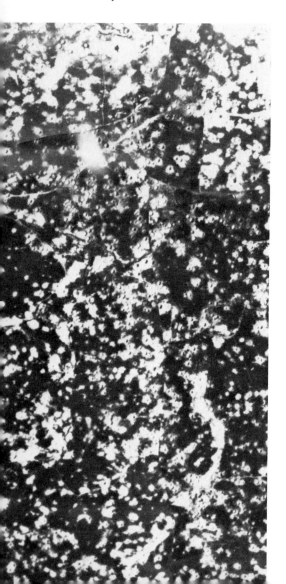

Western Pacific at Andersen Air Force Base, Guam, and refueled in midair the B-52s from Andersen during their long bombing missions over North and South Vietnam.

The navy's air redeployment was just as impressive. The *Saratoga* from the Atlantic fleet and the *Kitty Hawk*, the *Constellation* and the *Midway* from elsewhere in the Pacific fleet were ordered to join the two carriers on duty at Yankee Station. Each carrier had about ninety fighter-bombers on board. Within days, the total navy fighter-bomber strength had been tripled to about five hundred and forty aircraft.

Nixon's quick reaction to the crisis and the U.S. military's ability to marshal forces dispersed throughout the U.S. and the Pacific made the outcome in the south a foregone conclusion, though twelve weeks of bitter fighting ensued. During all the years of the American commitment to South Vietnam, pilots had never witnessed so many targets of the elusive enemy. Convoys a hundred trucks long were caught driving in the open during daylight. "My God," screamed a young American OV-10 pilot upon breaking through the clouds over the DMZ, "you should see the people down here—all over the place—People, Tanks, Trucks, the whole nine yards—and everybody is shooting."

Captured North Vietnamese soldiers said they had been told not to worry about fighter-bomber and B-52 strikes. But the American air forces of more than a thousand combat aircraft, supplemented by those of the Vietnamese Air Force, obliterated the artillery and unit cohesiveness of the Communist forces, and prevented their resupply. What did prove difficult to accomplish by air was the dislodging of invading forces from towns that had been captured. In this effort, AC-119 and AC-130 gunships were instrumental.

By the end of June, all three Communist drives had been turned back. Giap was forced to order a withdrawal. The battle was temporarily won in the south. According to one senior American artilleryman, the victories in the three regions were "monuments to airpower." These monuments had a price, however. The U.S. Air Force lost seventy-seven aircraft from March through June 1972—nineteen of them the small planes piloted by forward air controllers. About half the overall losses occurred in South Vietnam; the other half over the Communist supply network in Cambodia, Laos and North Vietnam. Most of these planes' pilots and crew members were killed.

The North Vietnamese invasion caused Nixon to order resumption of the air war over the north, waged concurrently with the counterinvasion struggle in the south. Most of the attacks there were by fighter-bombers hitting the southern region of North Vietnam known as the panhandle; these began on April 6. However, later that month B-52s staged four major strikes north, including one on rail and petroleum targets near Haiphong. The huge bombers had never attacked that far north before, so the strikes were a test of their survivability. A wide array of aircraft accompanied them—some fighter-bombers patrolling the skies for MiGs; the new F-111s, a sort of superjet, attacking MiG bases; F-4s specially equipped with the Wild Weasel; EB-66s sending out signals to confuse enemy radar; and more F-4s dropping chaf, a sort of aluminum foil that also confuses radar. The combination worked. Thirty-five SAMs were fired that night, but all the B-52s returned to their bases safely.

In May the air war on the north intensified, partly because of another Nixon summit trip, this time to Moscow. Nixon was scheduled to meet with Leonid Brezhnev on May 22. The timing bothered Nixon greatly. He would be in Moscow toasting Russian leaders while Americans and the Vietnamese allies were fighting for the survival of South Vietnam against invading Communists supplied with Russian arms. Nixon was unwilling to cancel the meeting, however; two years of preparations were invested in the project. So he decided to put his Russian hosts on the defensive; he ordered an unprecedented air campaign (known as Linebacker) against the north. On May 8, speaking to a national television audience, he declared that "Hanoi must be denied the weapons and supplies it needs." At that moment, he said, American aircraft were mining Haiphong Harbor, trapping Russian ships already there and keeping others out. That was only part of the campaign. Linebacker included heavy B-52 strikes around Hanoi and Haiphong and fighter-bomber strikes throughout the country. Some of the latter used newly developed 2,000- and 3,000-pound guided bombs with television- or laser-guided systems. One air force fighter-bomber wing operating out of Thailand destroyed more than one hundred

(Top) B-52s taking off from Andersen Air Force Base, Guam—"The Rock," as it was called—blackened the sky during the Linebacker II campaign. So many were launched each day that the operation took hours. (Bottom) Crew members listen to pre-mission Linebacker II briefings. Each bomber had a crew of either six or seven, depending on the model. "Gentlemen, your target for tonight is Hanoi," was the attention-getting opening line of the first briefing.

Secretary of Defense Melvin Laird talks
with General George Brown, the 7th Air
Force commander, and Ambassador
Ellsworth Bunker at Tan Son Nhut
during February 1970.

The one hundred and fifty-two B-52s
ordered to Andersen for Linebacker II
composed the largest concentration of
those bombers in the history of SAC.
Five miles of ramp space was needed to
park them. About half appear in this
aerial view.

bridges in North Vietnam during May. On May
11 spans of the Paul Doumer Bridge near Hanoi
were dropped into the Red River. On May 13,
the infamous Thanh Hoa Bridge suffered the
same fate.

The Russians did not cancel the summit. "It
was one of those terribly curious stories of
relationships of super-powers," writes journalist
Tad Szulc. "It was one of the great poker games
in history." Nixon had played his hand with his
air forces and the Russians had not walked away
from the table. He got his much-sought summit
trip during an election year without appearing
weak to the American voters. He had outflanked
the North Vietnamese on all fronts—earlier, in
Peking, by making a triumphant visit, the first
by a U.S. president since the Communists had
taken control; in Moscow, by laying the groundwork for detente; in the U.S., by winning the
confidence of the majority of American voters;
and in South Vietnam, by beating back the
invasion with American air forces.

As a result, North Vietnamese leaders requested a meeting in Paris on October 8 between
Le Duc Tho, their chief negotiator, and Henry
Kissinger, Nixon's special assistant for national
security affairs. At the meeting the North
Vietnamese emissary proposed a military settlement: a cease-fire, the return of five hundred
and fifty-six imprisoned Americans, mostly pilots,
and the withdrawal of all American forces. Previous North Vietnamese demands for a coalition
government and Thieu's resignation were dropped.
Nixon persevered with the Linebacker bombing
raids, however, judging from Johnson's experiences that bombing pauses were counterproduc-
tive. Kissinger believed "we've got a deal,"
pending Thieu's approval. The signing was set
for October 31. But Thieu would not go along. A
personal visit to Saigon by Kissinger and his
assistant, Alexander Haig, did not convince
him. Thieu refused to announce his support for
an agreement that allowed the 150,000 North
Vietnamese troops in his country to remain. On
October 25, Nixon cabled Hanoi, explaining
Thieu's objections and requesting a delay in the
signing.

The North Vietnamese apparently thought
they had been set up by Nixon to benefit his
reelection campaign. Consequently, the next
day, without notifying Nixon first, they broke
the secrecy of the negotiations via an announcement on Hanoi radio, explaining the terms of

the agreement that had been rejected. Their intent, no doubt, was to damage Nixon's reelection chances, but in that effort they failed miserably. Nixon defeated Democratic Senator George McGovern on November 7 with a 60.7 percent plurality.

On November 20 Kissinger was back in Paris for more secret meetings with Le Duc Tho. Slowly, the two sides began to drift farther apart. "Specifically in December," writes Winston Lord, a Kissinger assistant, "it was clear that the North Vietnamese were sliding away from an agreement. Every time we would get close they would slide in new conditions. It was clear that they were playing on public opinion, undercutting us at home and stonewalling us in Paris, and there was no choice but to break off the negotiations." On December 13, the talks collapsed. Five days later, the final American air action of the war began.

Frustrated by the impasse and determined to end American involvement without humiliation, Nixon ordered Linebacker II. By one account, Kissinger had signaled that this might occur about six weeks earlier while returning with Haig from their disappointing meeting with Thieu in Saigon. According to Tad Szulc's account, Kissinger "said to one of his associates something to the effect—You know, this war simply cannot go for another four years. We have to end it even if it takes a very brutal—this is a verbatim word—a very brutal way of doing away with this war." Later, on Nixon's orders, Kissinger had warned Le Duc Tho that a breakdown of talks would cause massive retaliation.

On December 18, Nixon began making good the threat. He ordered Linebacker II to begin. Fighter-bombers struck by day and the giant B-52s by night. Targets for the B-52s were "rail yards, dock areas, power plants, munitions stores and . . . [petroleum] storage areas" in and around Hanoi and Haiphong. The fighter-bombers' primary targets were counterweaponry, such as SAM sites.

The first night three waves totaling one hundred twenty-one B-52s came gliding in over the two cities from the northwest at thirty thousand feet. The size of such a force is difficult to visualize. "I never fully realized just how many of us there were up there or how close together we all were," remembers Major Bill Stocker, a B-52 pilot, "until we headed north over the Gulf [of Tonkin]. It looked like a highway at night—

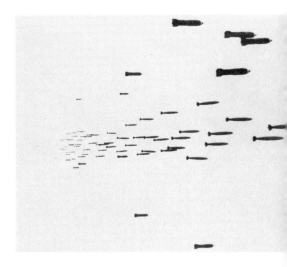

(Top) An undercast slightly obscures a B-52's load of one hundred and eight 500- and 750-pound bombs falling on the target. Precision electronic equipment allowed bomb runs night or day. (Bottom) The huge size of the plane is evidenced by this photo of a maintenance technician working on a B-52's vertical stabilizer from a "cherry picker."

Bomb damage caused by Linebacker II: (Top) Haiphong residents examine bomb damage. All targets were military-related, but some residential damage occurred. (Bottom) The total destruction of the Ai Mo warehouse complex near Hanoi.

nothing but a stream of upper rotating beacons as far as I could see."

The pace was maintained night and day, day after day, except for Christmas. The earth shook for long intervals during eleven days and ten nights. The skies were filled with planes and missiles and anti-aircraft bursts and smoke. The first night the North Vietnamese fired two hundred surface-to-air missiles, the second night one hundred eighty. Three B-52s were downed that first night, one the second night; six the third night; eleven, total, the first four nights. Forty-three American pilots and crewmen had been either killed or captured by that time.

According to Nixon, he personally intervened to order less predictable tactics. Undaunted by the American casualties, he ordered the operation to proceed. After the fifth night, the enemy fired only about twenty missiles per night. Most SAM sites had been destroyed by the fighters — and the North Vietnamese were running out of missiles. On the final two nights, December 28 and 29, no B-52s were damaged. According to historian Ray Bowers, "the enemy's defense had apparently been broken." They had fired more than a thousand missiles and shot down twenty-six American aircraft, killing thirty-three crewmen and capturing thirty-three. American air forces had dropped one hundred thousand bombs. North Vietnam reported fifteen hundred deaths, according to Bowers (the same number killed by the Germans on a single night during the bombing of Coventry, England, in the Second World War).

For his decision to bomb, Nixon was vilified around the world. "Genocide," a Buenos Aires newspaper called his actions; "a crime against humanity," said another in West Germany; "beyond all reason," said the *Los Angeles Times*. "Civilized man will be horrified," said the *New York Times*. It was, however, what was needed to force a final settlement.

"Unpleasant as it is," reflects Winston Lord, "one has to, in the agony of those years and in the agony of diplomacy in conflict, weigh the unpleasantness of having to resort to force against the fact that it did achieve the breakthrough. And there's no other explanation for Hanoi changing its attitude."

British military analyst Sir Robert Thompson believes that the U.S. "had the war won" — that if Linebacker II had continued, North Vietnamese leaders would have been forced to order home their troops in South Vietnam. But as Bowers observes, the "Paris cease-fire correctly reflected the wishes of the American people."

On January 23, twenty-five days after the last bomb was dropped, the final settlement was initialed. American airmen and other prisoners held captive in North Vietnam were released in intervals starting on February 12. For navy pilot Everett Alvarez, Jr., who was shot down on the day it all began—the day of the first Gulf of Tonkin reprisal strike—the twelfth was the end of eight years, six months and six days in prison. When the C-141 jet transport carrying him and the first POW contingent to be released landed at Clark Air Force Base in the Philippines where they were initially taken for medical examinations and a brief rehabilitation, Jeremiah Denton, the senior ranking officer on board, stepped forward to speak for Alvarez and the rest. Addressing the crowd that greeted them and a live television audience in the United States, he said, "We are honored to have had the opportunity to serve our country under difficult circumstances. We are profoundly grateful to our Commander-in-Chief and to our Nation for this day. God bless America."

The air war was over.

(Top) Jeremiah Denton waves to well-wishers at Hickam Air Force Base, Hawaii, during the final leg of his trip home. (Bottom) Exultant former POWs celebrate as an air force C-141 lifts them off the end of the runway at Gia Lam International Airport, North Vietnam, on March 28, 1973.

7

War Without End, Amen

The Land War: Part 1

During the early days of the Kennedy administration, the commandant of the Marine Corps, General David Shoup, delivered a memorable military briefing to administration policymakers about Cuba. At the time, the American-sponsored invasion of that country on the beaches of the Bay of Pigs was being actively planned. Shoup recognized that policy planners had no sense of the difficulty of the military operation they were supporting. He was convinced that they were so motivated by their wish to get rid of Castro and his Communists that they were ignoring all the obstacles.

The point of Shoup's briefing was summed up by a couple of overlays that he pulled down one by one onto a map of the United States. The first was a map of Cuba. Everyone was surprised that Cuba was so large. It was not just another Long Island, but a large body of land that on the overlay stretched from New York to Chicago — about eight hundred miles. Once the import of this sunk in, Shoup silenced the group with a second overlay. This one had only a small black dot on its surface.

"What's that?" someone asked.

"That, gentlemen, represents the size of the island of Tarawa," said Shoup, who had won the Congressional Medal of Honor there, "and it took us three days and eighteen thousand Marines to take it." Despite his warning, the ill-conceived Bay of Pigs invasion went ahead — with disastrous results, of course.

To a striking degree, the deliberations that preceded Kennedy's decision to commit American prestige to the war in South Vietnam were typified by the same overconfidence and lack of careful analysis that preceded the Bay of Pigs invasion. Because preventing a Communist takeover there seemed such a desirable objective, worries about the difficulty of doing so were pushed aside. Manifest destiny — a sense of the inevitability of victory, which in writer Denis Brogan's estimation only Americans have — undoubtedly influenced policymakers' attitudes. This trait was especially characteristic of Kennedy's generation, young men for whom war had, in truth, been a very positive influence on their lives and careers.

A chaplain leads GIs in prayer; above, General William Westmoreland.

War without End, Amen— ❝In their own words❞

❝*George, you're crazier than hell!*❞— President Kennedy's reaction to George Ball's warning that if Kennedy were not careful, he would have three hundred thousand American troops fighting in South Vietnam before long; in 1961.

❝*I think forever.*❞—Secretary of Defense Robert McNamara's answer to a question posed during a Senate committee hearing about how long the U.S. could afford the Vietnam war without adverse effect on other government programs and the overall economy; in 1967.

❝*What's going on up there?*❞ ❝*I wish the hell I knew.*❞ —An exchange between a reporter and an army captain whose unit was engaged in a fight with Communist soldiers along Highway 13; in late 1967.

Consequently, the decision to make Vietnam the place to teach Communists a lesson about wars of national liberation had an arbitrariness about it which in hindsight seems appalling. Kennedy and his advisers did not choose South Vietnam because conditions there favored the U.S.; in fact, almost all the conditions favored our adversary. But the Kennedy team chose Vietnam as the battleground on which to make American intentions clear simply because it was there that the most significant struggle for national liberation was taking place. They ignored the fact that it was the Communists under Ho Chi Minh who had defeated the hated French, forcing them out of Vietnam, which provided reason enough for most Vietnamese to support Ho. Diem and his successors could never compete with Ho's achievements in the eyes of the Vietnamese. And the painful irony of the decision to send American troops into battle to win the war for the south was that it only added credence to Communist charges that Saigon's leaders were mere puppets of yet another Western imperialist nation. Thus, from the outset, this country violated a principle basic to all rules of military combat, which is that, given the choice, you should select a battleground favorable to your side.

Since the United States was the most powerful nation in the world, both economically and militarily, Kennedy and his advisers and later Johnson and the same group of advisers thought that our soldiers, sailors and airmen could handle such an inconsequential foe under any circumstances—could, in fact, win despite self-imposed constraints and in the absence of domestic support for the conflict. It may have been such overconfidence that the Duke of Wellington had in mind when he told the House of Lords, "A great country cannot wage a little war."

The spring of 1962 was especially memorable for that year's senior class at West Point. Graduation day alone would have been enough to make it special, but visits by two very important people made it even more so. One was a distinguished alumnus, General Douglas MacArthur; the other was the president of the United States, John F. Kennedy.

It was to be MacArthur's last official visit to West Point. He came to receive the Sylvanus Thayer Award, given by the school's alumni association to that American who best personifies the school's motto, "Duty, Honor, Country." However, his visit would be memorable not for that ceremony, but for a speech he delivered to the Class of '62 and the underclassmen during lunchtime at the cadet dining hall. The last few lines reflect the style, beauty and emotion with which it was written and delivered.

"The shadows are lengthening for me. The twilight is here. . . . I listen vainly for the bewitching melody of faint bugles blowing reveille, of far drums beating the long roll. In my dreams, I hear again the crash of guns, the rattle of musketry, the strange mournful mutter of the battlefield." In retrospect, that speech, which became known as MacArthur's "Duty, Honor, Country" speech, parts of which are now memorized by West Point plebes, may be viewed as a natural segue to the one the graduating class would hear shortly from the president.

Only days after MacArthur's speech, John Kennedy delivered the West Point commencement address in words remarkable for their prescience. Kennedy seemed to know exactly the kind of war he was committing the country to; had he lived, perhaps he could have prepared its citizens for it, as he was attempting in that speech to prepare its army.

Kennedy warned the Class of '62 that during the sixties, their responsibilities as officers would "require a versatility and an adaptability never before required in either war or peace." He spoke of "another type of war, new in its intensity, ancient in its origins—war by guerrillas, subversives, insurgents, assassins, war by ambush instead of by combat, by infiltration instead of aggression, seeking victory by eroding and exhausting the enemy instead of engaging him.

"Where there is a visible enemy to fight in open combat," he said, "the answer is not so difficult. Many serve, all applaud, and the tide of patriotism runs high. But when there is a long, slow struggle, with no immediately visible foe, your choice will seem hard indeed." This was surely a kind of farewell to MacArthur's bewitching melody of bugles, a farewell to an era of American military history.

One man who listened intently with the Class of '62 to what both MacArthur and Kennedy had to say was the superintendent of West Point at the time, a major general then unknown outside military circles named William Westmoreland. Not long after Kennedy became

(Top) General David Shoup and Attorney General Robert Kennedy talk to a young marine. Shoup was a favorite of the Kennedys. (Middle) Douglas MacArthur delivers his famous "Duty, Honor, Country" speech.
(Bottom) President Kennedy at West Point in 1962.

president, Westmoreland sensed that one day soon he would serve in Vietnam. As a result, he began preparing himself as best he could by reading all he could find on counterinsurgency warfare. Unforunately, the army had done very little research on the subject. In fact, one of the first official army documents written about counterinsurgency during the early sixties candidly admitted, "The tactical doctrine for the employment of regular forces against insurgent guerrilla forces has not been adequately developed, and the Army does not have a clear concept of the proper scale and type of equipment necessary for these operations."

The primary reason for the dearth of information was that during the fifties the army had been busy responding to a different mandate from civilian leadership: The army was preparing for battles in which nuclear weapons would be used. According to Maxwell Taylor, who was commander of the Eighth Army in Korea in 1953, the only reason they were not used there was that the U.S. nuclear inventory was too low at that time to warrant wasting any of it in the mountainous terrain of Korea. Also, the U.S. worried that if the nuclear weapons were not as effective on the battlefield as anticipated, their deterrent effect elsewhere would be reduced. However, with the buildup of the U.S. nuclear inventory during the Eisenhower–Dulles years, such worries were on the way to being eliminated. The "New Force" concept emphasized not only the strategic but also the tactical use of nuclear weapons—the latter meaning that American soldiers locked in combat would use small nuclear weapons on the battlefield, firing them at enemy positions just as they would artillery shells. In 1954 General Charles Bolte, the army vice chief of staff, made this point in a speech to the Infantry School at Fort Benning, Georgia. He predicted that the use of nuclear weapons might be as "commonplace on future battlefields as heavy artillery is today."

There were many who disagreed privately. The emphasis on the nuclear had come "despite a clear consensus among Army leaders that this was the least likely type of war," according to a study of the fifties undertaken in 1979 by the army's Combat Studies Institute, a division of the army's Command and General Staff College at Fort Leavenworth, Kansas. (The institute's mission is to research and interpret military history so that the lessons learned can be ap-

The U.S. Military Assistance Advisory Group headquarters in Saigon during the fifties.

plied to the development of future U.S. Army doctrine.) Consequently, the army wasted the better part of a decade planning for a type of war that few of its leaders envisioned for the foreseeable future.

The ever alert and courageous General Matthew Ridgway had vigorously protested the ideas of nuclear military strategists. When he retired from the army in 1955, stepping down of his own accord after only one frustrating two-year term as army chief of staff, he wrote a farewell statement that harshly criticized the inflexibility of Eisenhower administration policy and its dependence on nuclear weapons—which document Secretary of Defense Charles Wilson immediately classified so as to prevent Ridgway's dissent from reaching the public.

Ridgway's replacement was Maxwell Taylor, who shared his doubts. With contemporary strategists having predicted that the army might not be needed in the next conflict, the air force in those days was winning all the bureaucratic and appropriations battles. At the time, there was a group of bright young officers—all colonels, all seemingly destined for stars, all but one West Point graduates—working in a think-tank-type unit attached to the office of the army chief. They were alarmed at what Eisenhower, of all people, was doing to the army, how he and his administration were opting for the bigger-bang-for-the-buck approach of the air force, and cutting back the size and mission of the army. The idea of a conflict without ground troops or one in which only nuclear weapons would be used was absurd to them. They approached Taylor, who was sympathetic and seemed to encourage their plan to make the problem public and possibly an issue in the presidential elections of 1956. One of them, Donovan Yeuell, was the brother-in-law of the news editor for the *New York Times*'s Washington bureau, Wallace Carroll. After *Times* editors had been discreetly introduced to various Pentagon army generals disturbed by the country's new defense policy, and thus had assured themselves that the colonels were not zealous mavericks acting on their own, Carroll asked for some of the young colonels' staff work attacking the New Force concept and the army's diminished role. The information became the basis for a series of articles in the *Times* by reporter Anthony Leviero in May 1956.

Secretary of Defense Charles Wilson exploded. The colonels were traced as the source and were

Secretary of Defense Charles Wilson relegated the army to a secondary role to that of the air force. The next war, it was thought, would be short, and both sides would use nuclear weapons on the battlefield.

ordered not to return to their offices. Yeuell's files were confiscated and burned. He was subsequently investigated three times; finally he chose to leave the army. The other colonels were quickly reassigned to meaningless slots outside the Pentagon. Taylor did not defend them and technically was able to say that he had had nothing to do with the colonels' activities. Westmoreland, then a brigadier general serving as secretary of the general staff, a position that gave him considerable control over appointments and scheduling for the chief, seems to have used his job to do what he could for Taylor. According to David Halberstam, "Within the Army command the colonels were told that Westmoreland, who was halfway in and halfway out of the cabal, had assured Taylor that he would take care of the colonels for him and clean it all out." So the ruckus did not even break the stride of the smooth Taylor (West Point Class of '22) nor the calculating, ambitious Westmoreland (West Point Class of '36)—of whom Associated Press correspondent Peter Arnett would later say, "He wants to be CINC World."

Westmoreland continued his rise through the ranks while Taylor served two successive two-year terms as army chief of staff. No longer looking to turn the tide of events, Taylor now sponsored changes in the army that he had earlier opposed, even incorporating what he himself had described as "Madison Avenue adjectives" (such as that used to describe his newly reorganized units—the "Pentomic" divisions) to glamorize the army's role in modern warfare. Testing revealed that on the nuclear battlefield army units would have to operate at considerable distances from each other, the danger of total annihilation of any one being so great that no one unit could depend on another for support. Therefore, each army division was reorganized into five separate battle groups (thus the name Pentomic) that could operate autonomously. Infantry divisions had traditionally been composed of three regiments; after modification to conform with the Pentomic concept, the battle group replaced the regiment. Each battle group, which was slightly smaller than the old regiment, was composed of five rifle companies, a combat support company that included a mortar battery, and a headquarters and service company. The Pentomic infantry division also included an armored battalion of five tank companies, a cavalry squadron of three

Westmoreland during his days as West Point's superintendent. The assignment was confirmation that he was destined for one of the army's top commands. Maxwell Taylor had helped sponsor his progress. President Kennedy was another Westmoreland booster.

troops, five direct support artillery battalions and one general support artillery battalion. Total manning of the Pentomic infantry division, ten thousand, was about three thousand men fewer than the former traditional infantry division. Other basic army units such as armored divisions were also reordered to conform to the Pentomic concept, but the infantry division was the type most affected. Of course, army doctrine had to be completely rewritten during the Taylor years to accommodate the reorganization. And these fundamental changes amounted to what the Combat Studies Institute in 1979 called probably the most "radical change in peacetime in [army] thought, doctrine and organizations."

However, by the time Kennedy became president, Taylor had come out publicly against the changes that he had presided over while chief of staff. His book *The Uncertain Trumpet* enjoyed a timely publication date that allowed its message to catch the attention of the Democrats' nominee for president. The book warned that the army, not surprisingly, was unprepared for conventional war. That idea (and probably the urbane Taylor's position as president of the Lincoln Center for the Performing Arts in New York) won him appointment as the president's top adviser for military affairs at the White House. His title, chosen by Kennedy himself, was Special Military Representative.

Thus, the military man with the ear of the president in 1961 was not some visionary whose time had come ("He is a very handsome man, and a very impressive one," said Averell Harriman in 1967, "and he is always wrong"), but a man who had earlier compromised his own best judgment and the careers of some promising officers who might have made a difference—hardly the man to temper the naïveté of Kennedy's civilian specialists or counsel the president in a difficult situation. As a result, Kennedy committed his country to win a war in Vietnam at a time when no one had a clear picture of how to proceed or, even more basically, whether to proceed. None of his advisers could properly evaluate the winnability of the war there. The fears of the young colonels had been realized. The army was "unprepared," said the Combat Studies Institute in 1979; "confusion reigned."

Many ideas were quickly advanced, however. One was to expand the training of the Special Forces at Fort Bragg, North Carolina. The purpose of the training there, says David

General Maxwell Taylor during an early inspection trip to Vietnam. Taylor's book on the army caused President Kennedy to bring the former army chief out of retirement.

Accompanied by General Lyman Lemnitzer, chairman of the Joint Chiefs, McNamara takes notes during a 1962 briefing in Vietnam.

Halberstam, not altogether tongue-in-cheek, was to turn out "uncommon men, extraordinary physical specimens and intellectual Ph.Ds swinging from trees, speaking Russian and Chinese, eating snake meat and other fauna at night, [and] springing counterambushes on unwary Asian ambushers who had read Mao and Giap."

To emphasize the importance of this program, Kennedy in October 1961 traveled to Fort Bragg. The administration thought it was on to something, an easy way to win a war against these "scavengers of revolution," as Walt Rostow called Ho and Giap. Kennedy's visit turned into "a real whiz-bang day," with ambushes and counterambushes being staged and, in one event, a soldier flying over a pond with a Buck Rogers jet pack on his back. The crowning touch, of

On Christmas Day, 1962, Francis Cardinal Spellman walks in a procession to the cathedral at My Tho. For a decade Spellman had been keenly interested personally in the fate of South Vietnam. The archbishop of New York also served as military vicar to the Roman Catholic chaplains, a position that gave him official cause for traveling to South Vietnam.

course, and the clearest signal that we had no earthly idea what we were up to or against, was the spectacle of all the Special Forces troops lined up in the new French berets that Kennedy himself had ordered them to wear. Unfortunately, the president and his staff had no understanding of the negative implications for the Vietnamese of any association with the colonial French.

Tom Wicker of the *New York Times* was there that day. As he was departing with the press corps that had accompanied Kennedy, Francis Lara, an *Agence France-Presse* correspondent who had covered the First Indochina War, said to him, "All this looks very impressive, doesn't it?" Wicker agreed that it did. "Funny," Lara said, "none of it worked for us when we tried it in 1951."

Walt Rostow contributed a number of ideas, of course. Simultaneously awed and exasperated, Kennedy once remarked, "Walt can write faster than I can read." One of Rostow's ideas, says Halberstam, was to get the South Vietnamese hooked up to television reception. He thought that would be a good way to bring the government closer to its people and at the same time demonstrate to the peasants the technological marvels of the West. But Rostow's ideas were not confined to life-style improvements. He fancied himself a tactician too, presumably drawing upon counterinsurgency experience in Boston. As such, he was invited to West Point in late 1963 to keynote a symposium on counterinsurgency. Apparently there were no experts on the subject in the army itself at the time (though many were no doubt well versed on Pentomic force structure). You must keep on the offensive against insurgents, Rostow told a gathering of career officers, one of whom was Westmoreland. "If you wait passively," he said, "you will be cut to ribbons."

Obviously, there was an incredible dearth of professional counsel for Westmoreland to draw upon when, in January 1964, his premonition was realized and he found himself on his way to Vietnam to become deputy commander of American forces there. And part of the fault was his own—dating back to the time when he and Taylor had failed to stand behind the young colonels. Westmoreland's appointment had come after Johnson became president, but his progress during the Kennedy years had assured him a rapid ascent. He was awarded his third star upon leaving the post of superintendent of West Point, one of the most prized assignments in the army, on his way to his new position as commander of the XVIII Airborne Corps, which put him in charge of the 82nd and the 101st Airborne Divisions.

Two whose counsel Westmoreland did draw upon before leaving for Saigon were the Chinese military philosopher Sun Tzu and the venerable Douglas MacArthur. Westmoreland discussed their influence on his thinking in his book *A Soldier Reports*. He describes Sun Tzu, who lived centuries ago, as the "Clausewitz of the Orient." Undoubtedly the best advice that Westmoreland could have gotten from Sun Tzu was the following, which the American general cited himself: "There has never been a protracted war from which a country has benefited."

Robin Tennes, a dancer-harpist, high-kicks during a USO show in May 1962 at Tan Son Nhut Air Base. As the war got bigger, more prominent celebrities began booking performances in Vietnam.

MacArthur's advice was more particular in nature and was received during a meeting of the two at the old general's Waldorf apartment. On how to work with Vietnamese officers: "Treat them as you did your cadets: be understanding, basic in your advice, patient, work with them to develop their sense of responsibility and their ability to make decisions." On how to conduct the war: Have plenty of artillery available. The Oriental "greatly fears artillery." And keep in mind that you might have to resort to a scorched-earth policy to win.

Contrary to what is widely thought, MacArthur, by Westmoreland's account, did not advise against committing American troops on the Asian mainland; he only advised against committing them in landlocked Laos.

When Westmoreland arrived in Vietnam in January 1964, there were already signs that the United States was committing itself to the most bizarre war its soldiers had ever fought and, quite possibly, a losing cause. Some of these signs pointed to an issue of paramount importance—the fact that a large segment of the South Vietnamese population did not welcome the presence of American troops in their country.

American airmen fishing along the coast disappeared one day. Later their bloated bodies were found floating in the ocean. They had been weighted down with rocks and thrown into the water to drown. On another occasion a terrorist bomb was planted under the bleachers of a baseball park in Saigon used by American soldiers. The resulting explosion killed two Americans

Viet Cong soldiers advance along a small irrigation waterway in South Vietnam. Such intimate familiarity with the terrain in which they fought made the insurgents especially effective.

and injured twenty-five, including American wives and children. As disturbing as the casualties themselves was the fact that on the day they occurred, no Vietnamese attended the game; normally many did. Word of the planned attack had clearly gotten around the Vietnamese community, but no one felt obliged to warn their allies.

With good reason, Americans began wondering who their friends were. U.S. soldiers were obviously having trouble shaking the association with the French. This was a problem even in dealing with the South Vietnamese Army, which was totally dependent on American money and arms. During those days, says Westmoreland, a quick way to ruin the career of a promising Vietnamese officer was for an American to patronize him. The French colonial experience was too fresh a memory—as indicated by the very address of the villa in which General Harkins and later Westmoreland, as U.S. forces commanders, lived—No. 60 Tran Quy Cap. Tran Quy Cap was a Vietnamese patriot whom the French beheaded.

There were also signs that the instability of the South Vietnamese government would render

In May 1962, South Vietnamese troops disembark into the central highlands from a helicopter with an American pilot at the controls. Efforts to turn ARVN troops into an effective fighting force were slow in achieving results.

"The Handbook for U.S. Forces in Vietnam" was given to each soldier assigned there. Small enough to fit in a fatigue pocket, it was filled with drawings explaining enemy tactics and how its soldiers used all sorts of booby traps and mines to kill Americans. The following are some of the drawings from the Handbook:

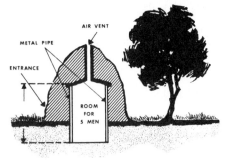

Haystack used for hiding and meeting place . . .

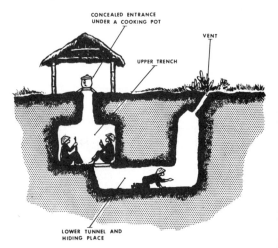

Hiding places under local homes . . .

any amount of American support ineffectual. A succession of coups had followed Diem's assassination. Ruling generals were so insecure about their positions within the government that they had, for the most part, withdrawn from the fight against the Communists those units most loyal to them personally. One of them, General Nguyen Khanh, who had taken over in a coup two days after Westmoreland arrived in Saigon, was so paranoid that he selected as his residence a home on the Saigon River from which he could more easily escape if he were overthrown. His contingency plan was to flee by motorboat down the river to the coast, where he maintained a second residence in the city of Vung Tau, from which he would fly to France. Just how nervous Khanh was, and thus how shaky his government, was revealed by an episode that occurred not long after he took over. A shipload of American tanks had arrived at the Saigon port for use by the South Vietnamese. To avoid disruption of traffic, American advisers decided to offload and move the tanks out of the city during the night. When Khanh heard them rumbling through the city, he thought a coup was under way. He immediately jumped into his boat and raced down the river to Vung Tau. He was so shaken (and later embarrassed) that Westmoreland had to fly down to Vung Tau to convince him to return.

The enemy that Khanh and other Vietnamese leaders were neglecting because of their internal intriguing had been slowly building strength since 1954. They were called Viet Cong. Though the literal translation of the words means Vietnamese Communists, the term took on a derogatory connotation—so much so that the enemy reportedly would shoot on the spot any prisoner who referred to his captors by that name. The Viet Cong organization had evolved from those thousands of local Communists who remained in South Vietnam after Ho's victory and the partition in 1954. Some traced their Communist affiliation to Ho and Giap's personal organizing efforts before and during the Second World War. Unlike Catholics who fled the Communist north for fear of persecution, the Viet Cong had no compelling reason to emigrate. The south was their home. Furthermore, they had good cause to believe that the plebiscite scheduled for 1956 would vote Ho in as leader of a unified Vietnam. But when the vote was cancelled,

the Viet Cong began laying the groundwork for military operations against Diem's government. These guerrilla activities were directly supported by Hanoi. Some support was organizational, some material—the most tangible being the Russian and Chinese weaponry supplied by the north.

But Diem's government may have been at least as helpful to the VC as Hanoi was. The more centralized and repressive his regime became, the easier it was for the Viet Cong to convert peasants to the Communist cause. In Bernard Fall's estimation, "the countryside largely went Communist in 1958–60." This was reflected in late 1960 by the creation of the political wing of the Viet Cong called the National Liberation Front, designed to attract a wide cross-section of dissidents. Their recruitment was so successful, says Robert Scigliano, an author and expert on Vietnam, that by 1963 "the Communists had in fact extended their influence, in varying degrees, to about 80 per cent of the Vietnamese countryside."

The military wing of the Viet Cong consisted of several groups—local, provincial and main force units. The local Viet Cong were part-time soldiers, mostly male but some female, who on occasion fought at night and blended back into the population by day. They fought in units the size of a squad, platoon or company, the last composed of about eighty-five soldiers. The men

A Viet Cong support unit in Quang Ngai Province builds foot traps using iron nails.

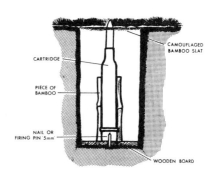

Cartridge booby trap . . .

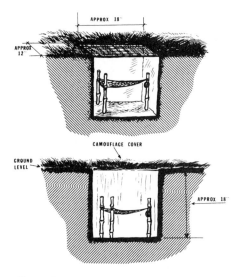

Grenade trap . . .

Punji beartrap . . .

Command-detonated overhead mine .

and women in the provincial units for the most part were recruited from the villages in the province in which they operated. Full-time soldiers, they were organized into battalions of about three hundred fifty guerrillas. Main force Viet Cong units were also composed of full-time soldiers organized into battalions, regiments, and even divisions that fought anywhere in South Vietnam and on any scale, sometimes breaking down into very small units, sometimes fighting at full strength, depending on the mission. These large Viet Cong units operated out of sanctuaries in the jungles and forests that were surprisingly close to major population centers. One not far from Saigon in Tay Ninh Province included a hospital, kitchens and printing plant facilities in its underground complex. Some dated back to the First Indochina War.

In 1964 North Vietnamese troops began supplementing the troop strength of the Viet Cong. Initially they arrived as individual replacements for Viet Cong soldiers, beginning in October 1964, according to Westmoreland, who also says that in December 1964 the Hanoi government started infiltrating entire units into South Vietnam, the first such unit being a regiment.

What made Viet Cong units so effective— more so than the North Vietnamese—was their intimate knowledge of the terrain. Their intelligence was also fast and accurate, given the number of Communist agents and sympathizers; the Viet Cong and North Vietnamese shared this information, of course. South Vietnamese government forces and, later, those of the U.S. could hardly move without the Viet Cong being forewarned.

Viet Cong units operated by the tested guerrilla maxim: When the enemy advances, withdraw; when he defends, harass; when he is tired, attack; when he withdraws, pursue. And by all accounts, the individual Viet Cong soldier was committed enough to his cause to persist over the years in this patient process. One American officer described the Viet Cong as "a fanatically dedicated opponent who would take on tanks, if necessary, armed only with a bow and arrow."

Government forces did not display the same zeal for combat. Part of the problem was that their organization and training followed the U.S. pattern. And since the United States was not ready to deal with insurgency operations in Vietnam, government forces were not either. The South Vietnamese had been prepared for the possibility of an invasion from the north, such as had occurred in Korea.

But the most deficient aspect of government forces was leadership. The early careers of many South Vietnamese officers had been advanced primarily because of their close French ties, and thus they were compromised in the eyes of their subordinates. One notable example was General Nguyen Cao Ky, the head of the South Vietnamese Air Force, whose first wife—whom he later divorced to marry a Vietnamese woman—was French. But Ky, unlike others of his background, earned a reputation for being skilled and daring in combat and he would eventually share the leadership of his country with General Nguyen Van Thieu.

Many officers had a reputation for being

North Vietnamese troops on the march in August 1965. They enjoyed virtually universal support from their population for the war in the south, chiefly because of U.S. airstrikes on the north.

corrupt, their salaries obviously not sufficient to support the huge villas in which they resided. Some were ineffective because of their attitudes: They sought promotion to gain the privilege of not having to fight in the field. Military leadership was also compromised by politics. Diem promoted his higher-ranking officers on the basis of political loyalty, not competence. Furthermore, for domestic political reasons, Diem had a tendency to judge a general's performance on the basis of how low his unit's casualties were. Government troops were, therefore, timid taking to the field—a disposition Westmoreland called a "caserne mentality." They were even reluctant to close on the enemy when it was surrounded—so much so that Westmoreland could only believe that the South Vietnamese commanders, like himself, had also read Sun Tzu, paying particular attention to his dictum: "To a surrounded enemy you must leave a way of escape" (lest he turn on you like a cornered tiger).

The most dramatic early example of the lack of leadership within the South Vietnamese Army was the battle of Ap Bac, which occurred on January 2, 1963. An "army force of 2,500 men, equipped with huge quantities of automatic weapons and armored amphibious personnel carriers, and supported by bombers and helicopters, failed to overrun, destroy, or capture a group of 200 guerrillas, who after inflicting heavy casualties on the army and shooting down five helicopters, succeeded in escaping almost unharmed." American advisers on the scene could not get the South Vietnamese commander to close in on the enemy. The unhappy truth is that the Vietnamese government's army was never led as well and never fought as well as their Viet Cong adversaries. This relative lack of commitment was also reflected in national policy, most notably the South Vietnamese government's refusal to lower the draft age from twenty to eighteen, though Americans that age would be ordered to fight and die there. The reason for this unconscionable inequity was that, according to Vietnamese tradition, a boy does not become a man until the age of twenty. The Communists, however, did not allow this tradition to interfere with their conscription policy, although they understood the consequences of conscription only too well: In the north, some villages even conducted quasi-funerals for enlistees before they departed. "Born in the north to

Ten U.S. Army H-21 helicopters pick up three hundred South Vietnamese rangers and civil guards after a mission in the Mekong Delta. Use of helicopters initially knocked Viet Cong units off balance, but they quickly adjusted their tactics.

die in the south" was a tattoo found on many
dead North Vietnamese soldiers.

Westmoreland looks back with some bitterness
at another South Vietnamese government policy,
that which allowed the children of their leaders
"who should have been fighting . . . [to sit] out
the war in European schools." He says that
without success he prodded the Vietnamese to
end this practice, pointing out that family members of prominent Americans were fighting in
Vietnam. The son of Maxwell Taylor and both
sons-in-law of Lyndon Johnson—Charles Robb
(now governor of Virginia) and Patrick Nugent—
served there.

By late 1964 the South Vietnamese Army
included 230,000 serving in the regular army
and another 270,000 serving in the Regional and
Popular Forces. The Viet Cong army they faced
numbered 170,000 and was growing rapidly. A
sign of how poorly the war was going was that
more young South Vietnamese were deserting
each month then were voluntarily enlisting—5,000
to 7,000 of the former compared to 3,000 of the
latter. Though a percentage of these were on
"French leave" to return home to help the family
with harvesting, the figures did not augur well
for the future.

Despite all these ominous signs, General
Harkins was irrepressibly optimistic about a
short-term victory. In May 1964, when McNamara
visited Saigon, he asked Harkins, "How long will
it take to pacify the country?" Harkins replied,
"Mr. Secretary, I believe we can do it in six
months. If I am given command of the Vietnamese, we can reverse this thing immediately."

Westmoreland's estimate of the situation, as
he remembers it, was entirely different. By his
account, he told McNamara that the war would
be long, hard and frustrating, with no end in
sight; he described the commitment there as a
"bottomless pit." Nonetheless, he was confident
that the war could eventually be won, and this
assessment was apparently more in line with
what McNamara wanted to hear: Not long after
McNamara's May 1964 trip to Saigon, Westmoreland replaced Harkins as commander of the
Military Assistance Command, Vietnam (MACV).
Six months after that, when, according to
Harkins's estimate, South Vietnam was to have
been "pacified," it was instead on the verge of
collapse.

The time was December 1964, and the introduction of American units into combat was only

MACV commander General Paul Harkins

(Top) The Brink Hotel, a BOQ, after the terrorist bomb blast of December 24, 1964. (Above) Bob Hope and actress Jill St. John perform for U.S. airmen and soldiers two days later at Bien Hoa Air Base. Hope's troupe was due for arrival in the Brink lobby at the time of the explosion.

months away. The Viet Cong held the initiative and were staging attacks throughout the country. The most dramatic one occurred on Christmas Eve at the Brink Hotel in Saigon, used as a billet for American officers. (The hotel was named after Brigadier General Francis Brink, the first American commander in Vietnam, who had committed suicide while on a visit to Washington during his Vietnam assignment.) A terrorist bomb exploded about the time a USO troupe headed by Bob Hope was scheduled to arrive in the lobby. Two embassy personnel were killed and more than a hundred wounded. Documents later captured from the Viet Cong confirmed that Hope and his party had indeed been the primary targets. By luck, they had been delayed at Tan Son Nhut Air Base while large boxes of cue cards were unloaded. Hope was later able to joke about it during performances there: "When I landed at Tan Son Nhut, I saw a hotel go by," he quipped during one performance. At another he remarked, "When I landed at Tan Son Nhut, I got a nineteen-gun salute. One of them was ours."

In February 1965, after President Johnson ordered Rolling Thunder, the sustained, graduated air war on North Vietnam (which was to continue for more than three and a half years), Westmoreland requested that U.S. Marines be brought in to protect American aircraft at the base at Danang. The war games had anticipated that this would happen, of course. On February 26, Johnson approved the request. On March 8, they came ashore. They were the first units of American combat soldiers to be ordered into South Vietnam. (Those Americans who preceded them during the early sixties did not compose cohesive combat units, but were mostly advisers and trainers who generally operated independently of one another while working directly with the South Vietnamese.)

This initial deployment involved about sixteen hundred men, who, on orders from Admiral Ulysses Grant Sharp, the American Pacific forces commander, stormed Nam O Beach a few miles from Danang in full battle gear aboard LSTs, as though they were coming ashore at Iwo Jima. But in Danang they were not met by the enemy. The welcoming party consisted of ten pretty Vietnamese girls with flower leis in hand and a four-man U.S. Army district advisory team consisting of a captain, lieutenant and two

sergeants. Poking fun at their service rivals for
the melodrama, the four army men stood there
grinning while holding a sheet painted with the
message, "Welcome to the gallant Marines."

This two-battalion marine force, which became
the umbrella unit for all marines in Vietnam,
was called the "Marine Expeditionary Force"—at
least until someone at the embassy thought the
Vietnamese might associate them with the French
Expeditionary Corps. Quickly their unit designation was changed to the "III Marine Amphibious Force." Their arrival precipitated one other
brouhaha, the cause being the eight-inch howitzers they brought ashore that were capable of
firing nuclear shells. Deputy Ambassador Alexis
Johnson, fearful that the press and the enemy
might accuse the marines of planning to use
atomic weapons, wanted the howitzers shipped
out of the country. But officials in Washington
overruled him, and the marines were allowed to
use the howitzers with conventional shells.

Meanwhile, back in Washington, Lyndon Johnson was agitated while awaiting the North
Vietnamese response to the bombing; he was
worried about where his decision to bomb the
north was going to lead. In early March he
ordered General Harold Johnson (the army chief)
to the White House for a meeting in which he
would vent his anguish. Belatedly the president
was developing the feeling that the bombing
was going to lead to a land war in Asia.

"Bomb, bomb, bomb. That's all you know,"
the president screamed. "Well, I want to know
why there's nothing else. You generals have all
been educated at the taxpayers' expense and
you're not giving me any ideas and any solutions for this damn little piss-ant country. Now,
I don't need ten generals to come in here ten
times and tell me to bomb. I want some solutions.
I want some answers." And then for effect, the
president pushed his index finger against the
general's chest and leaned into his face like a
cadet first classman talking to a plebe. "You get
things bubbling, General," he warned him.

It was not the sort of performance from a
president that invites disagreement or discussion,
especially in this case, since the general's humiliation had occurred in front of his personal staff.
Had Johnson invited his army chief's opinion instead of dressing him down, the general might
well have told him that he was, in fact, against
the whole enterprise. The general had a strong
sense of what Vietnam was going to be like. It

(Top) The first U.S. combat units, two
battalions of marines, enter South
Vietnam on March 8, 1965. (Middle) A
marine tank roars ashore at Nam O
Beach, the landing point. (Bottom) U.S.
Army advisers in the area hung signs to
tease the marines.

(Above) Army chief of staff General Harold Johnson in South Vietnam. (Below) Private Charles Lopez accidentally fell into a "spider hole" with two North Vietnamese soldiers hiding inside. He killed one and captured the other.

was going to be Korea all over again, maybe worse. As he foresaw it, there would be the same restrictions, the same frustrations, and the same no-win policy. He wanted no part of it for himself or his soldiers. During meetings of the Joint Chiefs the preceding fall he had voiced these opinions. And the irony of it all, in view of his treatment by the president, was that he was really the only senior general who opposed the bombing campaign. But Lyndon Johnson did not know this, his civilian advisers having dominated the bombing-campaign decision-making.

Nevertheless, properly chastened, General Johnson, traditional soldier that he was, raced off to Vietnam without complaint to get some ideas for getting things bubbling. There, both Maxwell Taylor as ambassador (as of June 1964) and Westmoreland (as commander of U.S. forces) were most preoccupied with the question of what to do with the marines peering out of bunkers around Danang perimeter defenses. Because of his military background, Taylor had some strongly held ideas, and because of his past three successive government assignments— army chief of staff from 1955 to 1959, Special Military Representative to President Kennedy from 1961 to 1962, and chairman of the Joint Chiefs of Staff from 1962 to 1964—he was actually in a stronger position to press his case than was Westmoreland. Taylor thought the marines and other American soldiers to follow should initially be confined to enclaves along the coast from which they could go out on patrol, but only for the purpose of protecting the bases. The lower the profile—politically and militarily— the better, he thought. Casualties could be kept down this way.

Westmoreland saw things differently. He wanted the flexibility to send troops anywhere in the country. His staff's evaluation of the enclave strategy was that it was "an inglorious static use of U.S. forces in overpopulated areas with little chance of direct or immediate impact on the outcome of events." The evaluation had merit. The South Vietnamese Army was falling apart at the time. The enemy had moved into the third stage of revolutionary warfare, forming large units from its hundreds of smaller ones, to deliver the final knockout blow. The situation was so bad that the idea of forming another South Vietnamese Army division had to be scrapped, even though the U.S. had agreed to finance it, because Communist forces were killing and wounding South Vietnamese soldiers more quickly than the South Vietnamese could train replacements for existing units. Thus, the bases for Westmoreland's recommendation were his assessment that the South Vietnamese would soon fall without American combat troops and his skepticism regarding the bombing campaign on the north. How could it break the will of the Communists when they were doing so well in the south? he wondered—quite rightly.

Another more general factor was at work in shaping Westmoreland's policies. He and his staff were aggressive, young men; they didn't like to see American soldiers being used in an "inglorious" way. When Colonel John Paul Vann, a highly regarded army adviser with long experience in Vietnam, tried to give Brigadier General William DePuy, Westmoreland's deputy for operations, some historical perspective on the fighting in Vietnam, DePuy refused to listen. To him, it was all part of a flawed past that was irrelevant to a triumphant U.S. future.

Westmoreland's rise and that of those around him was largely the result of a conscious policy by John F. Kennedy to reach down into the ranks and put young generals in charge. The older generals reminded Kennedy of the tired blood of the Eisenhower administration. He thought they had lost touch with the modern world, perhaps even lost their nerve. This attitude became a conviction for Kennedy after the Bay of Pigs fiasco. He wanted to dip way down into the seniority roster to make Westmoreland, a very junior major general at the time, the army chief of staff. Though Kennedy's advisers eventually changed his mind, warning him that such a move was entirely too unorthodox, Kennedy's patronage of Westmoreland had already propelled him far when, by the summer of 1964, President Johnson and McNamara began thinking about replacing Harkins. The youth movement within the army had caused Westmoreland to get his third star in a very short time, get the deputy MACV slot, and thus be in an ideal position to move to the four-star slot as top military man in Vietnam. There were three other candidates—Harold Johnson, then serving as deputy chief of staff for military operations; Creighton Abrams, a tank commander who had been a favorite of General George S. Patton, Jr.; and Bruce Palmer, the youngest of the four and considered probably the brightest general in the army.

A young marine in South Vietnam in August 1965. Of the U.S. soldiers killed during the war, 3,104 were eighteen years old or younger.

Brigadier General William DePuy: his career rose with that of Westmoreland.

The lessons of Nui Ba Dinh...

In early 1965, before American combat units were sent to Vietnam, a young Green Beret officer learned a couple of lessons about South Vietnam that could have served as examples for the thousands of American soldiers who would follow. The officer was Captain James ("Bo") Gritz, who years later would become well known as the leader of the force that attempted to rescue the American hostages in Iran.

Gritz was a district and Special Forces camp adviser assigned to the village Sui Da, not far from Tay Ninh City in southern South Vietnam. A 3200-foot mountain called Nui Ba Dinh literally and figuratively cast its shadow on the village. Controlled by the Viet Cong, it was the only hill or mountain of any kind in the surrounding flat plains, making it one of the most prominent and bizarre natural formations in all Vietnam. The mountain actually had three distinct highpoints—the center formation with the peak, and a smaller one on each side.

Being the aggressive young soldier that he was, Gritz decided to drive the Communists off the mountain. What he quickly learned was that in South Vietnam, almost any military action could have political and cultural ramifications that outweighed purely strategic concerns. For historical and religious reasons, Nui Ba Dinh was of almost mystical importance for Vietnamese in the area. During the Second World War, soldiers of the Cao Dai religious sect had held it against the Japanese; during the long fight with the French, the Viet Minh had held it; since the partition in 1954, the Viet Cong had held it. Understandably, Vietnamese believed that those who held these heights were vested with some sort of indomitable spirit. The Buddhist pagoda located

Westmoreland had much going for him: Having attended Harvard Business School's advanced management program, he impressed McNamara, who spoke the same language. And President Johnson, who had first met Westmoreland on a visit to West Point (the year before Kennedy's visit) to deliver the commencement address, liked him personally. Westmoreland's being from South Carolina had helped, too, since Johnson was a Southerner who felt himself to be surrounded by intimidating advisers from the Northeast. Finally tipping the scale for Westmoreland was Maxwell Taylor, who thought that his protégé's having been a parachute commander would stand him in good stead in Vietnam. (Taylor did not know at the time that there would be only one parachute drop during all the years of fighting in Vietnam.)

General Johnson, who lost out to Westmoreland on the Vietnam assignment, was soon afterward appointed army chief of staff. Though he was only two years older than Westmoreland, Johnson was a man more tempered by experience than emboldened by youth, and thus very different from Westmoreland. He understood that even the most confident of men cannot always control events—thus his worry that even well-trained, well-led American troops could not do the job in Vietnam, given all the political problems. In their differing assessments, Johnson and Westmoreland reflected their entirely different career experiences. At the same time that Westmoreland had been streaking up through the ranks while fighting in Europe during the Second World War, Johnson had been counting the days and struggling for survival in a Japanese POW camp. He had been captured on Corrigidor shortly after Pearl Harbor, endured the Bataan death march, and spent the rest of the war incarcerated. Years passed before Johnson caught up with his contemporaries.

Westmoreland, by contrast, had never suffered such humiliation or the feeling of failure at any point in his life. The title of his biography by Ernest Furgurson says it all—*Westmoreland: The Inevitable General*. Eagle scout, cadet commander of the Corps at West Point, and a general at the age of thirty-eight, Westmoreland was not the sort of man to have doubts about anything he was asked to do. Not surprisingly, he was convinced that given sufficient time, he could turn things around in Vietnam, in spite of all the restrictions that President Johnson and his civilian advisers might impose.

There is nothing evil about confidence, of course. Generals and soldiers charged with winning wars must have it. However, the time was March 1965 and the U.S. had not yet committed itself to a land war. Johnson's civilian advisers, so sure of their optimistic forecasts about the air war, had not really given serious thought to a land war. Therefore, the recommendations of Westmoreland and his staff were especially significant at this stage. Their confidence in themselves and their recommendations about tactics—how best to use the marines—moved the administration closer to committing itself to a land war. Johnson and his top civilian and military advisers began focusing on tactics instead of fundamental questions such as what we could hope to achieve in Vietnam and whether it was worth American troops' lives. The effect of the administration's decisions on tactics was a deepening U.S. commitment. And because of the focus on tactics, Westmoreland gradually became the dominant influence on U.S. policy in Vietnam. The president began deferring to his commander in the field, which at this stage of the decision-making process was inappropriate.

General Johnson stayed in Vietnam one week. Upon his return the Joint Chiefs adopted Westmoreland's recommendations that the U.S. commitment be raised to two divisions, about twenty thousand combat troops. Implicit was that they be authorized to participate in offensive combat operations. On April 1 and 2, the National Security Council met to weigh Westmoreland's proposal, as submitted by the Joint Chiefs, and Ambassador Taylor's enclave idea, which he came back from Vietnam to present in person. Although they opted for the enclave plan for the time being, they in large measure incorporated Westmoreland's thinking. They ordered two more battalions to Vietnam and okayed offensive operations up to fifty miles from the coastal bases to which these soldiers were assigned. The latter decision was kept secret, though reporters in Vietnam could see the marines and later army units going out on combat operations. Many days passed before the broadened role of American soldiers was confirmed by Pentagon press officials.

On April 20, less than three weeks after the important National Security Council meeting, Westmoreland met with McNamara, the Bundy

halfway up the center peak, and tolerated by the Viet Cong, contributed to the villagers' feelings of reverence for the mountain. The pagoda was the objective of religious pilgrims, who climbed ninety-nine steps to reach it; monks and nuns resided there. Being ignorant of Vietnamese culture, as virtually all Americans were, Gritz believed that the mountain's historic and religious significance made it all the more important as a military objective: If he and his South Vietnamese charges could take it, he thought, all the people in the area would be mightily impressed.

One evening, just as darkness came, Gritz had himself and twenty-five Vietnamese deployed by helicopters to the base of Nui Ba Dinh. Not until they reached that assembly point did he tell them his plan. Initially they balked, but eventually he talked them into the assault, with the help of his top Vietnamese assistant (who was himself tentative about the idea). They then began scaling the heights. Their objective was a spot about 1500 feet above, on a slope shaped like a saddle connecting two of the highpoints. The position offered the best vantage point for observing the approaches to Tay Ninh City and War Zone C, which was why some of the Viet Cong on the mountain were dug in there.

The enemy did not expect an attack. Although the South Vietnamese Army had attempted to scale the heights once, after quickly suffering a hundred casualties they had withdrawn, never to return. So an understanding about the mountain had evolved. Everyone knew who the Viet Cong commander of the mountain was, and over a period of time, Major Mung had worked out a tacit live-and-let-live understanding with not only the villagers, but even with the Americans. Mung allowed Buddhists to visit the pagoda unmolested, and had permitted the U.S. to establish a radio relay station on the highest point of Nui Ba Dinh. It was useless to him as an observation point because the peak was too often shrouded in clouds.

After scaling the heights to their objective, slowly pulling themselves up over the boulder-strewn, moonlike terrain, Gritz's men attacked and quickly drove the Viet Cong off the observation point, whose defensive positions had been configured to repel an attack from the opposite direction, which had a more obvious and accessible approach.

Gritz and his men held on for ten days without too much difficulty. Then Gritz's superior ordered Gritz to come back down because keeping the unit resupplied was tying up too many of the relatively few helicopters then available in South Vietnam. You have proved your point that the mountain is not invincible, he told Gritz.

Major Mung was not at all pleased by Gritz's initiative, and was not placated when the American and his soldiers abandoned their position on Nui Ba Dinh. He announced that Gritz had turned the mountain into a war zone and that henceforth Buddhists could not visit the mountain.

Monks demanded that Gritz secure the pagoda, which he found that he could do. But, with so few men available, he could not secure the path up to it. The result was a net loss for the allied cause. Gritz might have impressed the local population that he could take and hold a position on the mountain, but his venture had alienated the Buddhists.

For the remainder of the war, Nui Ba Dinh remained the exclusive province of Mung and his men. It was off-limits for American troops, except for those assigned to the radio relay station on the peak. But it never lost its attraction to ambitious young soldiers: Gritz himself, who served four years in Vietnam, was occasionally called upon by senior American commanders to dissuade junior officers from attacking Nui Ba Dinh.

brothers, John McNaughton and General Wheeler in Honolulu. The Washington officials quickly adopted the idea of sending six more U.S. Army battalions, three more U.S. Marine battalions, one from Australia and three from South Korea — thirteen more altogether. In other words, within three weeks of denying Westmoreland's request for a total of seventeen battalions, they had acceded to this exact request. Added to the four already in-country, the new ones, when they arrived, would bring the total commitment to seventeen battalions — 82,000 U.S. troops and 7,250 from Australia and South Korea. Taylor's coastal enclave strategy was still in place, however.

South Vietnam continued to deteriorate as these troops began arriving. The government was still unstable and its units were still being routed in the field. On June 7 Westmoreland cabled the Joint Chiefs that the South Vietnamese could not match the rapidly increasing force size of the Communists. He predicted that the North Vietnamese would commit the number of troops necessary to "tip the balance" and cause the South Vietnamese effort to collapse. More reinforcements from outside Vietnam would be necessary, he said. He now asked that the American, Australian and South Korean troop commitment be raised to a total of forty-four battalions to stave off disaster. The United States had to make an "active commitment" to help South Vietnam survive, he wrote. Furthermore, these forces must be allowed to "maneuver freely." The U.S., he said, must have "a substantial and hard-hitting offensive capability on the ground to convince the VC that they cannot win." He also again argued for termination of the coastal enclave idea.

Lyndon Johnson, still hanging on to the hope that Ho and the Communists, north and south, would give up, asked the Joint Chiefs to ask Westmoreland if the forty-four battalions (175,000 troops) would be enough to effect that goal. "The direct answer to your question," cabled Westmoreland, "is 'No.'" He also said that "instinctively, we believe that there may be substantial additional U.S. force requirements."

While the administration grappled with this troop request, the president made an interim decision that, for all practical purposes, amounted to the last critical step leading to U.S. participation in a land war in South Vietnam. He granted Westmoreland authority to commit American combat troops "in any situation . . . when in

COMUSMACV's [Westmoreland's] judgment, their use is necessary to strengthen the relative position" of South Vietnamese forces. It was clear, at this point, that free maneuver anywhere outside the enclaves was limited more by the number of troops Westmoreland had under his command than any policy constraints. On July 17 Westmoreland was informed that the forty-four-battalion proposal had been approved. The enclave strategy faded away. On July 28 Johnson informed the American people of his decision via a press conference, and he added that "additional forces will be needed later, and they will be sent as requested."

Strategic objectives in wars are those which when achieved will end the fighting. Thus during the Second World War the ultimate strategic objective in Europe was the capture of Berlin. The achievement of that goal was seen as the obvious way to end the fighting.

There was no such strategic objective for American forces during the Vietnam war. There was no physical goal that, when achieved, would result in an end to the fighting. The capture of Hanoi was excluded as a goal—though that would certainly have ended the fighting, even in the south—because of the Johnson administration's self-imposed policy constraints. The result was a very nebulous objective (which General Matthew Ridgway felt was not really an objective): to convince Vietnamese Communist leaders that they could not win the war. This, of course, was the initial goal of the air war in the north. However, by July the president realized that bombing alone would not achieve this purpose. Therefore, American soldiers in the south inherited this primary mission, while the air campaign was relegated to secondary roles—in the north, interdicting enemy units and supplies far from the war zone; in the south, providing close air support.

The U.S. strategic objective in Vietnam committed the country to an open-ended war. Westmoreland recognized this. In July—even before Johnson had approved the forty-four battalions—when McNamara asked him how many troops it would take to convince the Communists they could not win, Westmoreland admitted that he had no idea. "It was virtually impossible to provide the Secretary with a meaningful figure," he later wrote in *A Soldier Reports*. "In the end I told him only that I thought twenty-four more

(Above) McNamara visits with a GI at Quinhon on July 19, 1965, two days after the first big troop increase was authorized. (Below) Australian troops arrive on August 10, 1965. Allied support was minimal.

Guns and butter: the economics of Vietnam fighting

The advisers of Presidents Kennedy and Johnson had reached political maturity during years in which economic considerations were almost irrelevant to foreign policy decisions. During those years, the country held a lion's share of the world's monetary reserves, and expected to continue in that enviable position. American products were the most sought after in the world, which seemed to guarantee a favorable balance of payments.

But the Vietnam war dramatically changed the situation and altered the assumptions. Though a number of other factors were involved, Godfrey Hodgson points out in *America in Our Time*, "What is clear, without attempting to resolve technical and theoretical arguments, is that the sharp rise in military spending in late 1965, not balanced by any deflationary countermeasures [increased taxes or reduced domestic spending, for example] did set the inflationary snowball moving." And inflation unhinged Johnson's Great Society programs, increased labor costs, reduced productivity, encouraged American multinational corporations to relocate manufacturing operations in foreign countries, and made foreign goods much more competitive in the American marketplace—reversing the balance of payments and depleting the U.S. reserves.

The seeds of the problem were planted during the Kennedy years. To stimulate the economy, his administration had sponsored an investment tax credit in 1962, and then in 1963 proposed a tax cut that was enacted after Kennedy's death. The economy responded and boomed.

Another result of these tax decreases, which primarily benefited the high-income taxpayer, was that the

battalions in addition to the forty-four more battalions under consideration, plus more combat support and logistical troops, would put us in a position to *begin* the 'win phase' of our strategy. That meant about 170,000 American troops to start, followed by about 100,000. Yet I warned that VC and North Vietnamese actions well might alter the figures. Which they did. Any number of times." In other words, the U.S. was committing itself to matching every North Vietnamese troop increase, yet doing nothing, because of the restrictions, to take away the Communists' war-making capacity. The result, as John McNaughton described it two years later, was an "escalating stalemate." And, it should be added, a grisly competition for casualties. Unfortunately, the North Vietnamese were willing to accept almost any casualty figure as long as their forces could stay in the field. Giap has admitted the loss of five hundred thousand North Vietnamese soldiers between 1965 and 1968. The U.S. lost about fifty-eight thousand during the entire war.

General Matthew Ridgway had all along recognized the difficulty of Westmoreland's assigned task, his lack of a strategic objective. Unfortunately, Ridgway was not in a position to make the point during the sixties as he had been during the fifties. He understood that even Korea, as difficult and different as that assignment had been, was not like Vietnam. There Ridgway was ordered to drive invading North Korean and Chinese back across the thirty-eighth parallel and to hold the line. That achievement, it was thought, would eventually end the war—and it did. In Vietnam, such a physical objective was impossible for Westmoreland because his forces would also be fighting a large percentage of the South Vietnamese population he supposedly was protecting. Furthermore, South Korea was a peninsula; there were no contiguous borders with other countries, unlike the case of Vietnam, through which the enemy could move troops and supplies. Only in February 1968, just days before the Vietnam war was to force Lyndon Johnson to decide to leave office, did Ridgway have the chance to make his point to the president. Johnson had called him to the White House to discuss the war. Vice-President Hubert Humphrey was present during the Oval Office meeting. The phone rang as the three talked. While the president was handling the call, Ridgway turned to Humphrey and remarked that something still puzzled him about the Vietnam issue.

"What's that?" Humphrey asked.

"I have never known what the mission for General Westmoreland was," Ridgway said.

"That's a good question," said Humphrey. "Ask the president."

Unfortunately, when Johnson got off the phone, he launched into a long monologue and Ridgway missed his chance. But by then it was too late, anyway.

In July 1965, Westmoreland presented to McNamara not only his projected troop requirements but also his plan for winning the war. He envisioned three phases:

"*Phase I:* the commitment of U.S./F.W.M.A. [United States/Free World Military Assistance] forces necessary to halt the losing trend by the end of 1965.

"*Phase II:* The resumption of the offensive by U.S./F.W.M.A. forces during the first half of 1966 in high-priority areas necessary to destroy enemy forces, and reinstitution of rural-construction activities.

"*Phase III:* If the enemy persisted, a period of a year to a year and a half following Phase II would be required for the defeat and destruction of the remaining enemy forces and base areas.

"Withdrawal of U.S./F.W.M.A. forces would commence following Phase III as the GVN [government of Vietnam] became able to establish and maintain internal order and to defend its borders."

The important aspect of the three phases was the length of time Westmoreland thought each would require. For Phases I and III he was specific; for Phase II, which really constituted the major effort, he allowed himself an indeterminate amount of time. The *Pentagon Papers* writers misinterpreted this timing. Taking into account only the time for Phase III, they concluded, using the end of Phase I (December 1965) as their starting point, that "General Westmoreland expected to take the offensive and, with appropriate additional reinforcements to have defeated the enemy by the end of 1967." Understandably, Westmoreland bitterly contested their mistake at the time of the publication of the *Pentagon Papers* and later in *A Soldier Reports.* There is no evidence that Johnson's decisions were affected by the same misinterpretation.

government was less able to bear the burden of the cost of fighting a war when the decision to do so was made in 1965. And even though domestic spending began escalating concurrently, the Johnson administration failed to come to grips with the problem and tell the American people that increased tax revenues were required to pay for both. Johnson was averse to leveling with the public because he felt certain that Congress would cut Great Society programs before raising taxes, a prospect he wanted to avoid.

So, despite concern within the administration, administration officials' pronouncements accentuated the positive. In December 1965, for example, the Council of Economic Advisers' annual report to Congress read: ". . . our vigorous economy is in a strong position to carry the new burden imposed by expanded national defense requirements." But in December 1966, Johnson reluctantly admitted that there had been a "$10 billion error" in forecasting the cost of the war. (Still, he continued to back away from any significant tax increase to make up the shortfall.) Tom Wicker of the *New York Times* questioned McNamara about this erroneous forecasting. The defense secretary casually dismissed the matter, and his answer shocked Wicker: "Do you really think that if I had estimated the cost of the war correctly, Congress would have given any more for schools and housing?" McNamara responded.

The effect of the administration's guns and butter policy is evidenced by the movement of the consumer price index. During the years 1963 through 1965, the index had risen only two percent each year. But in 1966, when the war began in earnest, it rose by almost three percent. In 1967, it went up by more than three percent. In 1968, by more than four percent. In 1969, by more than six percent.

Of course, this inflation made American goods less competitive and foreign

Congressman Wilbur Mills

goods more so. These by-products—
"buoyant imports, lagging exports,
sluggish investment leading to medio-
cre productivity," as Hodgson lists
—"could be traced to one grand
cause: inflation. And inflation was
caused by the Vietnam War." In
fact, economists generally agree that
the effect of the inflation that the
war caused was more debilitating
than the direct cost of the war itself.

Not until late 1967 was the administration forced to begin confronting
the problem. And, just as he'd predicted, part of the price Johnson paid
for the House Ways and Means Committee's support (i.e., chairman Wilbur
Mills's support) for a tax hike was the
cutting back of his cherished Great
Society programs. On June 28, Congress okayed a ten percent tax sur-
charge in return for Johnson's cutting
$6 billion from his domestic budget.
These actions, of course, took place
"almost three years after the decision
that made it inevitable," says Hodgson
the decision to fight in Vietnam.

One measure of the impact was the
depletion of the country's gold reserves. In 1949 the value of U.S. gold
reserves stood at $24.5 billion. No
other country had even $3 billion.
The gold at Fort Knox and the Federal Reserve Bank in New York was
"well over half the entire world's monetary gold." By 1971, the value of the
U.S. gold reserves had slipped to less
than a third of what it had been in
1949.

By the time the marines landed in Danang,
Westmoreland and his staff had worked out
what tactics they would use against the enemy.
They envisioned three basic types of combat
operations. The first was search-and-destroy; the
second, clearing; and the third, securing. Each
was different in what it required of the soldier,
and ideally, one followed the other sequentially.

Search-and-destroy operations came first. During these, American commanders were ordered
to "find, fix in place, fight and destroy enemy
forces." Westmoreland says "destroy" referred
to the actual enemy force and their base areas
and supply caches, but for soldiers in the field,
the reality was that in certain regions American
soldiers destroyed anything believed to be of use
to the enemy, including villages. ". . . if they
weren't pro-Vietcong before we got there, they
sure as hell were by the time we left," says
former marine William Ehrhart, as quoted by
Stanley Karnow in *Vietnam: A History.*

In some remote areas the South Vietnamese
government ordered emigration to deprive the
Communists the support of the local population
and facilitate search-and-destroy operations. The
evacuated regions became "free fire zones." Anyone found there after the ordered evacuation
was deemed the enemy and could be shot without warning. Senator Richard Russell, wise old
politician that he was, readily perceived the
long-term social drawbacks of free fire zones,
however tactically desirable they may have been
in the short term. "I don't know those Asian
people," he warned Johnson and his White House
staff, "but they tell me they worship their
ancestors and so I wouldn't play with their land
if I were you. You know whenever the Corps of
Engineers has some dam to dedicate in Georgia,
I make a point of being out of state, because
those people don't seem to like the economic
improvements as much as they dislike being
moved off their ancestral land."

American forces tried to overcome the adverse impact of such operations by building new
villages and sending military doctors and den-
tists out into the field to tend to villagers' health
care. But winning the "hearts and minds" of
displaced Vietnamese was not easy. Nevertheless,
American soldiers were ordered to be forever
mindful of the impression they left behind. Most
were, at their peril, especially during the years
before 1968, when American attitudes about the
war (even those of men in uniform) began to

sour.

Having learned some lessons the hard way about projecting the right image while waging the war, Westmoreland later decided that "search and destroy" was a poor choice of words for this type of operation. "Many people, to my surprise, came to associate it with aimless searches in the jungle and the random destroying of villages and property." In 1968, at the recommendation of John Charles Daley, the head of the Voice of America, Westmoreland changed the name of this type of American tactic to "sweeping operations" and "reconnaissance in force." "You are your own worst enemy to perpetuate a term that has been so distorted," Daley told Westmoreland. But despite Westmoreland's efforts to change it, the original terminology stuck.

Clearing operations, the second in the sequence of Westmoreland's tactical operations, focused on driving enemy units, once found and broken up, out of a region so that pacification could begin. "While search and destroy operations chased the enemy from an area or destroyed him," says the Combat Studies Institute, "clearing operations kept him off balance and allowed the South Vietnamese government to extend its influence into the area." Generally speaking, the pacification program was "a specific strategy or program to bring security and political and economic stability to the countryside of Vietnam," writes military historian Thomas Scoville in *Reorganizing for Pacification Support.*

(Above) McNamara and Westmoreland talk to a South Vietnamese general near Danang in August 1965. (Below) An army medic tends to a Vietnamese child during a civic action project at Pleiku in 1966.

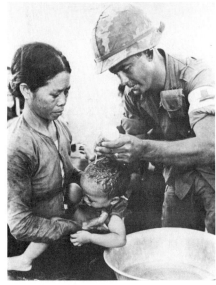

Marines of the 1st Battalion, 3rd Marine Division await orders to commence a search-and-destroy operation fifteen miles west of Danang Air Base on August 3, 1965.

(Top) The crew of a disabled tank watches another with flamethrowers clear brush in the distance. (Middle) A Viet Cong woman shot dead while chasing a marine. (Bottom) A GI closely surveys the jungle while looking for a sniper during operations in the jungle north of Con Thien.

Unfortunately, he notes, "there was never agreement among Americans in Vietnam on just what pacification was and how it might be achieved. Some saw it as controlling the population; others as winning the people's allegiance. Some viewed it as a long-term process of bringing, in addition to security, economic, political, and social development to the people."

The third step in Westmoreland's tactical sequence, securing operations, was an effort to ferret out individual guerrilla fighters still in an area and uproot their political infrastructure. As an area was secured, government officials would move in to issue everyone in the region identification cards and establish government services such as police protection and social services. The objective was to make life under the South Vietnamese government more attractive than that which the Communists could offer.

As logical as Westmoreland's prescribed sequence of operations sounds, it masks the difficulty of winning a war being fought against approximately half of the population of the so-called ally country. The sequence suggests that the enemy was set apart from the local population, when in fact many of them were part of that population, and indistinguishable from it. Who in a village was an active Communist or sympathizer was almost impossible to determine with certainty. Inevitably, many Vietnamese became innocent victims, caught between the crossfire of the adversaries. An estimated 587,000 Vietnamese civilians were killed during the war; about 1.2 million were made homeless during the period 1968-1969, at the height of the war. Most of the latter immigrated to the cities, where they lived in the squalor of burgeoning, fetid suburbs. Unless the allies were able to end the fighting in a region, support for the enemy usually increased along with the intensity of the American and South Vietnamese effort. The enemy won as long as it was able to continue to fight because villagers tended to blame Americans for the great disruption to their lives. This dilemma was well understood by individual American GIs. "We had to kill them to win," says Frederick Downs, a former army lieutenant who served in combat in Vietnam and later wrote the book *The Killing Zone.* "For them to win, all they had to do was stay alive."

Critics of Westmoreland's aggressive sequential strategy offered alternatives. One alternative, of course, was the enclave strategy, which Taylor initially proposed, but which, according to Westmoreland, even Taylor envisioned as only a temporary tactic. General James Gavin, however, saw it as a permanent, basic strategy. In February 1966, a long letter written by Gavin, then retired, appeared in *Harper's*, explaining why he advocated the enclave plan. His opinion was that many more American troops than were committed at the time and a greatly intensified air war on North Vietnam would be necessary to win a military victory. To avoid these escalations (the former he thought was politically impractical, the latter he thought might bring China into the war), he proposed that American forces be concentrated in various strategic enclaves in certain areas along the coast of South Vietnam. He thought his plan would demonstrate American resolve while keeping casualties down and encouraging the Communists to bargain.

Westmoreland dismissed Gavin's plan, later citing Hanoi's intransigence in negotiations as confirmation that the enclave plan would not have worked. However militarily unfeasible Gavin's plan may have been, it seems to have been based on a more politically accurate assessment of the American public's tolerance for the war.

The Marine Corps also offered an alternative plan formulated by its top officer in Vietnam, Lieutenant General Lewis Walt. He called it the "inkblot strategy." The idea was to spread dominance over a region slowly, by patrolling day and night with small units operating out of gradually enlarging, secured areas, initially the coastal enclave at Danang. Walt saw the Viet Cong political and military infrastructure in the countryside as the chief threat, not the large North Vietnamese units in the mountains. "General Walt stressed that the objective of the war was to win the loyalty of the populace to the government, and the only way to obtain this objective was to eradicate the Viet Cong in the villages and hamlets," says Jack Shulimson writing in the official history of the Marine Corps' early years in Vietnam fighting.

Walt's view was supported by all his marine superiors—Lieutenant General Victor Krulak, the top marine in the Pacific, headquartered in Hawaii with Admiral Sharp; and General Wallace Greene, the commandant of the Marine Corps. Krulak wrote in 1978 that he tried to persuade

GIs take cover behind an altar.

Marines slowly and carefully proceed through the village Dai Dang in August 1966 during Operation Colorado, a clearing maneuver.

Marine Lieutenant General Victor Krulak strongly opposed Westmoreland's strategy. The latter prevailed.

GIs search a village near the DMZ for Viet Cong suspects on October 27, 1966.

The tale of the little black box ...

In December 1965, a U-2 reconnaissance plane returning from a mission over North Vietnam exploded at twenty-six thousand feet. The wreckage plummeted to earth into dense jungle in an area of Cambodia controlled by the Viet Cong. Luckily, the pilot had ejected and was rescued. But General William Momyer, the air force commander in Vietnam, was worried that the enemy would find the wreckage. Inside was a top-secret black box. The air force was fairly certain that its self-destruct mechanism had not worked. If enemy technicians got hold of the box, they could determine the performance capabilities of the U-2, which was used worldwide to gather intelligence.

The job of finding and retrieving the box was assigned to Bo Gritz. He was shown a photo of it and given a map of the 450-square-mile area where air force experts had determined the crash had occurred. Bringing the black box out would require luck as well as courage. Undaunted, Gritz took eleven other Green Berets and a 150-man Cambodian guerrilla force with him into Cambodia to find it.

Helicopters transported them in.

Sharp "that there was no virtue at all in seeking out the NVA in the mountains and jungle; that so long as they stayed there they were a threat to nobody, that our efforts should be addressed to the rich, populous lowlands." In 1967, at a symposium for general officers on the subject of "Pacific Operations," Krulak argued: "It is our conviction that if we can destroy the guerrilla fabric among the people, we will automatically deny the larger units the food and the intelligence and the taxes, and the other support they need. At the same time, if the big units want to sortie out of the mountains and come down where they can be cut up by our supporting arms [airpower, for example], the Marines are glad to take them on, but the real war is among the people and not among these mountains." This concept of operation, Krulak said in 1978, differed with Westmoreland's "not in a limited but in a profound way. Our effort belonged where the people were, not where they weren't. I shared these thoughts with Westmoreland frequently, but made no progress in persuading him."

Greene's sentiment was the same. "From the very beginning the prime error had been the failure to make the population secure—to stamp out the VC hidden in town and hamlet," he said in 1978. Greene says he pushed Walt's concept "in a presentation to the Joint Chiefs and to General Westmoreland. The Chiefs were interested but Westmoreland wasn't and being CG MACV [commanding general in Vietnam] his views of the 'big picture,' the 'broad arrow,' prevailed."

Westmoreland thought that the war should be fought in the mountains, jungles and other remote regions as much as possible precisely because there were so few people there. He argued that combat in these thinly populated areas minimized disruption to the population centers and the pacification program. Furthermore, he thought that the introduction of large North Vietnamese units changed the threat to South Vietnam in a fundamental way and that the marines, as well as the army, must go after them in force strength of commensurate size. He saw this as necessary to break them up and keep them off balance so that they could not attack the population centers.

Westmoreland's plan was difficult for the American public to understand, of course, for the reason, as Westmoreland himself points out, that "a specific hill or other piece of terrain had no intrinsic value except that the enemy was there or that he was using it as a stepping-stone to some objective among the population." Over time, Americans became intolerant of these costly and apparently aimless exercises—which, in fairness to Westmoreland, could arguably be said to have been dictated by the self-imposed restrictions of the U.S. and the weak internal political conditions of South Vietnam. American GIs would storm some remote hillside—for example, Apbia Mountain, in May 1969, which became only too accurately known as Hamburger Hill—and then withdraw as soon as it was taken, though its heights had been gained at a heavy cost in casualties. But Westmoreland says he could not keep men in place in these outposts

Immediately, Gritz's force was attacked and began taking casualties. When Gritz's force finally managed to break contact with the enemy, they began the arduous search, hacking through thick underbrush, climbing up and down rugged terrain. Miraculously, they stumbled onto the U-2's wreckage at the end of the third day of searching. But the portion of the aircraft containing the black box was missing. Noting signs of previous activity around the site, Gritz surmised that enemy soldiers had recognized its possible significance and carted it off. Thinking that news of so unusual a discovery would have circulated among enemy troops throughout the area, Gritz decided to take a prisoner, who might know where the prize was being kept.

That evening Gritz and ten of his men hid along a trail that showed signs of recent use. Before long, six enemy soldiers came walking along, and on Gritz's signal the Cambodians opened fire. But two escaped and the other four were killed.

The next night Gritz prepared for a second ambush in the same area, believing that the enemy would return for their dead. This time Gritz was more explicit about his orders. The Cambodians would kill all but the first two VC in the column—whom Gritz and another Green Beret would take on in hand-to-hand combat.

No sooner had they set up, than ten VC came down the trail. After claymore mines went off, and while gunfire was still blazing, the two Americans, wielding CIA-supplied telescope billy clubs, jumped the first two enemy soldiers. When the fight-

During Operation Hastings, marines charge up a hill, two miles south of the DMZ, that was held by North Vietnamese regulars. An artillery and mortar barrage almost cleared the slope of vegetation beforehand.

ing ended, nine VC lay dead; Gritz had accidentally killed his victim, but the other American had captured his. The lone enemy survivor was seriously injured, but Gritz turned that condition to his advantage. Speaking rudimentary Vietnamese he had learned, Gritz convinced the injured VC, about sixteen years old, that he was going to die without medical care and that he would not get it unless he cooperated—which he did.

Luck was still with Gritz. The black box was in the soldier's base camp several miles away. The injured man had seen it himself. And he told Gritz how best to attack the camp, which was on alert because of the previous night's ambush.

Gritz scheduled his attack at dusk, giving his unit just enough time to attack and find the box before nightfall. The assault went exactly as planned. Caught by surprise, the enemy soldiers dove for cover in tunnels and holes. The black box was quickly found, and Gritz and his men disappeared into the darkness. After putting distance between themselves and the enemy, Gritz's force was evacuated by helicopters.

One footnote concerns the fate of the prisoner. Gritz had him brought back to South Vietnam, where he was admitted to the army hospital at Bien Hoa. But several days later, when Gritz went to check on the youngster, he was gone; no one had told the doctors that he was an enemy soldier. After treating him, they released him. "They gave him a uniform and a carbine, patted him on the ass, and told him to go back to his unit," says Gritz.

because U.S. and allied forces did not "have anywhere near enough troops even to consider holding all the commanding terrain. Once we had accomplished our goal of bringing the enemy to battle and inflicting heavy losses, in the process thwarting his objective and driving him back across the frontiers, what point in continuing to hold the high ground?"

In retrospect, it seems that Westmoreland's plan played to the enemy's tactical and strategic strength—they were on the high ground and they had, for all practical purposes, unlimited manpower. In fact, he may have accommodated Giap's battle plan, that being to keep inflicting as many American casualties as possible until the American public's intolerance for the fighting boiled over.

The marine plan, on the other hand, by placing greater emphasis on territorial control, might have made the U.S. effort there easier for the American public to understand and support. Public support, of course, turned out to be crucial. Also in their favor, small-unit tactics resulted in loss ratios more favorable to the U.S., as reported by the Combat Studies Institute in 1979.

The question then becomes how great the threat of the large enemy units hiding in the jungles really was. This is the crux of the disagreement between the army and the marines over tactics. The army itself now seems not so certain of the answer to that question. In 1979 the Combat Studies Institute said that "viable alternatives to the actual *tactical* methods used in South Vietnam are no more apparent today than they were from 1965 to 1972."

Before American soldiers entered the fight, Maxwell Taylor, a paratrooper in the Second World War himself, thought that parachute units would be especially effective in Vietnam fighting. But paratroop operations turned out to be of no use at all. Vietnam fighting quickly taught such lessons, normally without suggesting better alternatives. However, for better or worse, certain features of Westmoreland's battle plan gradually evolved and came to typify the American war effort.

One was the use of helicopters. The problem with paratroop operations was that even though planes could speed soldiers to a point over the battle zone, the soldiers found it extremely difficult to reassemble quickly after landing in the jungles and mountains below. Helicopters were different. The U.S. eventually had thousands of helicopters in Vietnam that could quickly transport units of almost any size. The army had experimented with such tactics during the fifties, but not with the demands of guerrilla warfare in mind. After a period in which helicopters were used merely as trucks that flew, tactics began evolving to incorporate their offensive potential. Colonel Jay Vanderpool, the man who directed most of this early conceptual development, used horse cavalry tactics of bygone days as his basic approach to the problem. In fact, Vanderpool, by his own admission, "plagiarized the last field manual written for horse cavalrymen in 1936." The techniques involving their use became so sophisticated that entire divisions—about twelve thousand men—could be inserted into battle within a very short time. However, most helicopter assaults in Vietnam, especially after 1967, involved smaller units, either brigades, battalions or companies.

Because of their speed, ease of traveling over the rugged terrain and ability to land or hover almost anywhere, helicopters were used for numerous other duties: transporting food, mail, ammunition and other supplies. Large ones, called flying cranes, could hoist artillery through the air as well as aircraft that had been downed. Evacuation of the dead and wounded, aerial observation, command and control, and close air fire support were other assigned tasks. So extensive was its use, the helicopter has become an almost iconographic representation of the Vietnam war in years since—in movies, on book jackets and magazine covers, and in the popular imagination.

Another characteristic feature of the deployment of American forces in support of Westmoreland's battle plan was the extensive use of fire support bases. Eventually, interdependent fire support bases dotted the countryside; from them soldiers went out on search-and-destroy missions, all the while attempting to stay within range of the artillery pieces manned at the bases. Platoon leaders were charged with constantly plotting the coordinates of their unit, so that if attacked, they could call in artillery support. The practice was overused by small-unit field commanders, says Westmoreland, who regrets that it led to what he termed a "fire base psychosis," a fear of moving beyond the range of artillery support. Field commanders had other

(Top) Marines rush from CH-46 Sea Knight helicopters during a search-and-destroy operation twenty miles north of Chu Lai. (Bottom) Sergeant Leroy Lavois of Kankakee, Illinois, fires a 105mm howitzer at enemy positions.

✳ Tunnel rats were small American soldiers whose specialty was crawling through the labyrinths the Viet Cong seemed capable of digging through almost any subsurface. The enemy hid themselves and their supplies in them. The job of the tunnel rats was to ferret them out. In doing so, they encountered not only enemy soldiers and their booby traps but natural obstacles as well, such as snakes and huge jungle ants.

All the tunnel rats were volunteers; their job was exceedingly dangerous But more was required than courage. They had to possess a strange mentality that challenged them to discover what lurked in the darkness of the confining spaces below.

One day reporter Michael Herr of *Esquire* decided to draw upon a tunnel rat's different perspective on the war. At the time, says Herr, Westmoreland was talking about seeing the light at the end of the tunnel in Vietnam. What did the tunnel rat think about that? asked Herr. The soldier smiled slightly and answered, "What does that asshole know about tunnels?"

Smoke pumped underground by GIs rolls out the rear exit of a bunker in an operation designed to gauge the extent of a tunnel system. Soldiers called tunnel rats then crawled inside looking for enemy soldiers, supplies and intelligence. A type of tear gas was also eventually approved for use.

types of firepower support, of course; helicopter gunships, fighter-bombers and (in coastal operations), navy ships could all be called upon for firepower. But the most readily available support was that from fire base artillery.

Fire support bases were, generally speaking, constantly being moved. As contact with the enemy gradually faded away while the enemy withdrew from the area, a unit would pack up and redeploy to another region where intelligence information indicated the enemy might be. This process was repeated over and over throughout the Vietnam war, especially in the northern regions and central highlands where the terrain was more rugged and the enemy stronger. Finding the enemy soldiers in those regions was more difficult, even though they were there in greater numbers, because the area was so vast and the jungles, forests and mountains afforded so much better sanctuary then the flat Delta area.

The Mekong Delta region in the south presented a completely different problen for search-and-destroy and clearing operations. Rivers, streams, marshes, waterways and flooded rice paddies greatly hindered movement, but were of course intimately familiar to the Viet Cong, who constituted the bulk of the enemy force (as opposed to North Vietnamese regulars) in this region. Helicopters were useful, but soldiers still had to contend with the obstacles presented by the terrain once on the ground. The Mobile Riverine Force, an idea of Navy Captain David Welch, was formed to address the problem.

The Riverine Force was an imposing if not bizarre outfit whose basic equipment consisted of various types of floating craft. One component was troop barges that served as base camps. From these barges soldiers would go out to assault their objective in navy troop carrier boats. Providing firepower support were helicopters, boats armed with machine guns, 40-millimeter guns and 81-millimeter mortars, and barges carrying army artillery. Minesweepers and armored boats called Monitors preceded these forces during operations. Ambushes were common, of course. To protect the boats from enemy rockets, each was surrounded by iron grillwork that caused projectiles to detonate before hitting the body of the craft. Soldiers on Riverine operations had to be rotated out every two or three days to keep them from getting what was called "immersion foot," caused by constantly slogging through the water for long periods.

Initially, Westmoreland and other American commanders thought that tanks and various types of mechanized equipment such as armored personnel carriers would not fit into the scheme of American combat operations. The jungles, mountains and flooded terrain of the south seemed too formidable to be tackled by such equipment. Furthermore, they feared that tanks would destroy the rice fields and dikes of farmers, causing hostility. But the role of armor gradually increased in importance in spite of these obstacles and reservations.

Tanks and armored personnel carriers afforded several basic advantages. They could patrol many more miles of terrain during search operations than foot soldiers could. They had great firepower. They were useful in some defensive roles, too, such as the protection of bridges, roads and bases. And they offered significant protection for the soldiers; Communist units did not normally carry antitank weapons, probably because they weighed so much and the presence of tanks continued to be more the exception than the rule. Tanks also afforded an overwhelming psychological advantage in the engagements they precipitated.

With the increasing use of tanks, tactics were developed to maximize their effectiveness. They were used for "jungle busting," in which they would roar through elephant grass, underbrush and over small trees ahead of infantry; and they were deployed on what were known as "thunder runs," which occurred late at night, when they would drive down unsecured roads at full speed, trying to catch Viet Cong in the act of planting mines on the roads.

The enemy developed countertactics, of course. Communists forces waited until American soldiers on search-and-destroy missions were within a few steps of them, sometimes among them. Then they opened up with automatic weapons and rifles. These were called "hugging tactics." With both sides so closely engaged, American commanders were reluctant to call in artillery fire because it might hit their own troops. Communist units tried to inflict as many casualties as possible during the first few minutes of contact and then withdraw.

"Sometimes Communist units would stay and fight, however. In some cases, this decision was part of a trap for American units coming to

An American soldier makes his way across an open dike in a rice paddy. The Viet Cong sometimes rigged grenades below the water line at such crossing points.

✷ In the January 1968 issue of *Times Talk* (a *New York Times* internal publication for its employees), reporter Bernard Weintraub related the story of an army brigadier general who appeared at the "Five O'Clock Follies"—as the daily press briefing in Saigon was known. With a smile on his face, the general delivered himself of his good news:

"Well, I'm happy to say that the Army's casualties finally caught up with the Marines' last week," he said.

The audience gasped. A civilian U.S. mission officer turned to the general and said incredulously: "You don't mean you're *happy*."

The general was adamant. "Well, the Army should be doing their job, too," he said.

Communist militia troops rig a likely helicopter LZ with elevated wire to keep the craft from landing, and with punji sticks to cripple the soldiers forced to jump.

✳ Enemy troop estimates formulated by Westmoreland's staff in Vietnam did not include those who supported the Communist cause by serving as members of "self-defense units." Such loosely knit squads were usually composed of women, old men and children. The central point of CBS News's "60 Minutes" documentary called "The Uncounted Enemy: A Vietnam Deception" was that the U.S. military command deliberately excluded these people from enemy troop strength estimates so as to make it appear that progress was being made by American forces in Vietnam. By excluding enemy self-defense units, the U.S. military was implicitly suggesting that they were not a threat to allied soldiers. However, the testimony of Colonel Edward Caton during Westmoreland's libel suit trial against CBS, Inc., suggested otherwise. Though called as a witness for Westmoreland, Caton, who was chief of joint intelligence under Westmoreland in 1966 and 1967, admitted under cross-examination that some enemy self-defense units used "passive devices" such as claymore mines, booby traps and explosives to kill and injure allied soldiers.

the rescue. Another enemy unit would be waiting silently in ambush." Large enemy units determined to hold ground prepared for possible American assault by digging revetments, bunkers and tunnels in the jungles and mountains. But "the enemy rarely accepted battle in unfavorable situations and only accepted decisive contact under exceptional circumstances." The primary enemy objective was not to hold ground but to cause American casualties. Confident that their staying power exceeded that of the U.S. government (because of their past successful experience in fighting the forces of France, another Western democracy), Ho and other Communist leaders were convinced that their forces could win if they could merely avoid destruction and stay in the field, thus ensuring that American casualties continued to mount over the months and years. North Vietnamese Prime Minister Pham Van Dong was frank about this strategy during a visit to Hanoi by Harrison Salisbury of the *New York Times* in December 1966: "And how long do you Americans want to fight, Mr. Salisbury . . . one year? Two years? Three years? Five years? Ten years? Twenty years? We will be glad to accommodate you."

Communists soldiers caused widespread American casualties with the extensive use of explosives, mines and booby traps. These insidious devices were as emblematic of the Communist effort in Vietnam as helicopters were of the American. They were planted everywhere: in cities, in cars and buses; in the countryside, on roads and under bridges; in the mountains, in marshes and jungles, along trails and under water. Some mines exploded under foot; others, called "Bouncing Bettys," sprang into the air to explode about chest high, the above-ground detonation spreading shrapnel and killing or wounding more people than subsurface detonations would. In the flooded lowlands, grenades, activated by trip wires, would be hidden under water.

The booby traps included such contrivances as spears, smeared with feces, that would spring into a soldier's midsection if he tripped over a vine that activated the crude mechanism, and ten-foot-deep pits filled with punji sticks. Likely helicopter landing zones were sometimes covered with such sharpened sticks (some made of metal and manufactured in volume in small jungle factories where workers used molds). American GIs making a helicopter assault while initiating search-and-destroy operations in a region might find the landing zone mined and covered with punji sticks, presenting them with the choice of charging enemy machine guns along the tree line or hitting the ground to be punctured. If a man punctured a foot with a feces-covered punji, he was taken out of action to a field hospital as soon as possible; otherwise his leg ballooned with infection within several days.

The wide variety of programs and operations instituted to support Westmoreland's overall battle plan was complemented by a typically American disposition for innovation. Many high-technology solutions were brought to bear on the special problems of Vietnam fighting.

The most notable program was the construction of the huge logistical network that sustained the American and allied combat effort. It eventually made the infrastructure of South Vietnam one of the most advanced among the developing countries. Foremost among these construction projects were the sea- and airports through which an endless stream of transport ships and planes carrying supplies and equipment flowed. In 1965, there was only one antiquated deep-draft seaport in all South Vietnam; U.S. engineers and contractors eventually built seven. Initially there were only three airports capable of handling jet aircraft; eventually there were eight. (By 1967, when most were completed, these airports handled more than a million tons per month.) Eighty-four other smaller landing strips were constructed that could handle all varieties of propeller aircraft. Literally hundreds of helicopter landing pads were built.

These sea- and airports required backup storage facilities such as warehouses. Eleven million square feet of covered storage was built, as well as about 45 million square feet of open storage, and 2.5 million cubic feet of refrigerated storage. To move these supplies out of the warehouses, roads were improved or new ones constructed; some miles were even paved. Bridges were built and, this being a war zone, were rebuilt when the enemy destroyed them.

The U.S. built a state of the art communications system in South Vietnam. A complex grid of telephone and radio facilities eventually blanketed the whole country. And to facilitate communications with the U.S. and in turn the rest of the world, a cable was laid on the ocean floor from Saigon to Hawaii.

(Top) This ox is being transported by the air force, which supplied villages as well as soldiers. (Middle) A huge air logistics network regularly supplied allied positions, even this one with a dirt landing strip. (Bottom) The C-130 Hercules, the mainstay of the air transport fleet, occasionally delivered supplies by various extraction means during low-altitude passes. Hooks or parachutes were used to pull the loads out. These methods were used only on an emergency basis.

(Above) Cam Ranh Bay, a combined sea- and airport, became one of the largest in all of Asia during the war. (Below) Gunships open up on enemy sappers trying to attack the logistics base at Danang.

✳ A news announcement broadcast over American Forces Vietnam Network, picked up by U.S. troops on their radios during the first week of December 1967: "The Pentagon announced today that, compared to Korea, the Vietnam War will be an economy [sic] war, provided that it does not exceed the Korean War in length, which means that it will have to end sometime in 1968."

South Vietnam experienced a construction boom during the war, with new buildings ranging from sophisticated aircraft control centers to austere offices and barracks. Virtually all air force bases and army and marine division base camps housed men in wooden structures, tents being of little use because of the duration of the war and the tropical weather conditions. In some cases, preexisting facilities were used for a time. For example, until 1968 most officers assigned to Tan Son Nhut Air Base were quartered in Saigon in homes and former hotels rented by the U.S. military, where a dorm-type arrangement could be set up. (Some of these structures were guarded by mercenary soldiers who manned machine-gun implacements nearby around the clock.) However, when many pilots were temporarily cut off from the base during the Tet offensive and could not fly missions, this practice ended. Dozens more barracks at Tan Son Nhut and on other bases went up.

Base exchanges, dining halls, clubs and various recreation facilities were also constructed throughout the country. The BXs or PXs, as these military department-store operations are called, were stocked with everything from souvenirs of Vietnam to cameras and small refrigerators, the idea being that these outlets would encourage American servicemen to spend their money at the bases rather than within the local Vietnamese economy, which was already gorged with the dollars spent by the U.S. government. Inflation was rampant. And the local economy was so unstable that the exchange rate for American dollars on the black market was more than twice the official rate. In fact, from dollars to dope, there was almost nothing you couldn't buy on the black market. Thousands of displaced South Vietnamese earned their living selling items pilfered from the docks and the bases. Their rudimentary department stores operated openly—in Saigon, only a few blocks from the U.S. embassy.

All the various American service branches took part in the massive construction program in South Vietnam, their engineering units either supervising or doing the work. But the air- and seaport projects were mostly the work of a partnership of four huge civilian construction companies—initially Raymond International and Morrison-Knudson, known as RMK, later joined by Brown and Root and J. A. Jones, at which time it became known as RMK-BRJ. A civilian named Bert Perkins was the man who headed this gigantic partnership. During the peak of construction activity, the companies employed fifty-one thousand people of about a half-dozen nationalities, mostly American, Korean, Filipino and Vietnamese. In addition, the Vietnamese were employed by the American service branches, not only in construction, but also in the PXs, clubs, and so forth. Thousands of other unskilled Vietnamese worked directly for individual American servicemen, laundering uniforms by hand in shower stalls and cleaning living quarters.

Much of the technology that advanced the American war effort involved support equipment and supplies, not weaponry. But the different branches of the military were also well served by such sophisticated weapons systems developments as the air force's smart bombs, OV-10 observation craft, and AC-130 gunships, and the army's Huey Cobra gunships with fuselage-mounted machine guns and rocket mounts.

Many of the newly developed support pieces were aimed at helping American troops locate enemy units hiding in the jungles and forests. For example, the "people sniffer," a device resembling a microphone, was lowered by hovering helicopters through the triple-canopy jungles. It was activated by trace elements in sweat and urine. However, since the people sniffer was not a remote device and remained attached to the helicopter using it, confirmation of the enemy's presence was frequently ground fire, not the device itself. The Starlight Scope was another

(Top) John Wayne visits with soldiers at Chu Lai on June 20, 1966. (Bottom) Bob Hope's annual pilgrimage drew fifteen thousand servicemen and women, who sat on a hillside to watch the show of Christmas Eve, 1968.

(Above) Men from a reconnaissance
platoon of the 1st Air Cavalry Division
conduct a search-and-destroy mission
in Quang Ngai Province on April 24,
1967. (Below) Navy Lieutenant Joseph
Lang, an adviser to a Vietnamese
coastal unit, helps examine a boat
during Operation Market Time; his
weapon is an M-14.

innovation. It enhanced the light of the stars,
enabling a soldier on lookout to see images in
the night. The Rome Plow acted against concealed
enemy troops by destroying their jungle refuge.
With huge blades and spikes, these enormous
bulldozers could plow over the tallest trees. The
machine was manufactured in Rome, Georgia,
and one thousand of them were delivered to
Vietnam. In early 1967, as part of Operation
Cedar Falls, a fleet of them plowed under a
thick, sixty-square-mile forest near Saigon called
the Iron Triangle, from which the enemy had
been launching attacks on the city.

The most grandiose plan to implement American technology and gadgetry, aside from the
sensor system the air force used to patrol the Ho
Chi Minh Trail, was what came to be called the
McNamara Line, an electronic barrier that was
to extend the entire length of the border dividing the Vietnams, from the coast to Laos. The
idea was to clear a no-man's-land with bulldozers and then implant mines, wire and electronic
sensing devices to detect enemy infiltration. But
McNamara announced news of the project prematurely at a press conference, and by the time
all the equipment and material were marshaled
for the deployment, the North Vietnamese had
moved 152-millimeter artillery within range. As
a result, Westmoreland canceled the project,
fearful of heavy casualties during the construction process. (Later, similar defensive lines would
be built in stretches near established allied
strongpoints.) He had opposed it anyway on the
grounds that such a barrier was superfluous
without troops to back it up—and this he considered impossible, given the thousands of troops
that would be required.

Key operations in support of Westmoreland's
battle plan were Market Time and Game Warden,
code names for efforts to interdict Communist
supply deliveries along South Vietnam's ocean
coastline and on its many miles of inland waterways throughout the Mekong Delta region.
Westmoreland ordered Market Time, the coastal
operation, in February 1965, after South Vietnamese aircraft spotted two large trawlers
unloading weapons and supplies inside the territorial limits off the southern coastline. By late
1966, Market Time was at peak intensity. About
one hundred aluminum-hulled, high-speed boats,
thirty-one 82-foot U.S. Coast Guard cutters, and
fifteen navy patrol aircraft roamed the waters

close to shore. Aided by South Vietnamese junks, this force checked about four thousand vessels per day for arms and supplies destined for Communist forces. Navy destroyers and minesweepers formed a second belt farther out at sea. Aircraft and naval gunfire provided cover for the overall operation. Estimates are that Communist forces received approximately seventy percent of their supplies by sea until Market Time; by late 1966, only ten percent.

Game Warden vessels performed similar duties on internal waterways. One hundred twenty U.S. Navy patrol boats powered by twin water-jet engines (instead of propellers) skimmed over the shallow marshlands with ease, and checked about two thousand junks and sampans daily. Another prime objective of these vessels was to keep open the forty-mile river route from the coast to Saigon that handled the dozens of oceangoing supply ships arriving from the states. Helicopter gunships (initially manned by army crews and later by those of the navy), navy commandos known as Seals (an acronym for sea, air, land) and a battalion of the First Infantry Division complemented the patrol boat operations. Fighting conditions for these soldiers were almost unimaginable. The mangrove swamps where they patrolled and fought experienced a six-foot tidal variation. For this reason, GIs on Game Warden slept on air mattresses, sometimes awakening at night to find themselves floating if the tide was particularly high. Soldiers frequently patrolled for hours in waist-high water. Landing pads for the helicopters that supported their missions were wooden platforms built on stilts. For obvious reasons, troops were periodically rotated out of such combat duty.

The year 1965 was the time of the American crash program to "save" Vietnam, "the fire brigade" period, as Westmoreland termed it. Early that year, Johnson administration officials were predicting that the air attacks on the north would end the war; when this did not happen, the U.S. began moving inexorably toward the land war quagmire.

Fighter-bombers on the first Rolling Thunder missions took to the air on March 2. On March 8, the marines came ashore to protect Danang. On April 2, American combat troops were authorized to operate up to fifty miles from their coastal enclave bases. Concurrently, Operation

(Above) After a Game Warden operation on the Song Cau Lon River, South Vietnamese troops try wading through mud to reach a U.S. boat. (Below) Monsoon rains pelt two weary soldiers searching for the enemy in the Bantangan Peninsula.

✳ In 1964, British freelance journalist Brian Moynaham interviewed Nguyen Cao Ky, then a rather obscure Vietnamese air force officer. The interview covered many subjects, among them Ky's political views. One of Ky's comments, for obvious reasons, startled Moynaham. "People ask me who my heroes are," Moynaham quoted Ky as saying. "I have only one hero—Hitler. . . . We need four or five Hitlers in Vietnam." The comment was irrelevant to the story Moynaham was working on at the time, but he took careful note of it. The following year, when Ky became premier, Moynaham resurrected the quote from his notes and sold the story to the London *Sunday Mirror.* The U.S. embassy's reaction was to deny that Ky had made the statement, but on the day the denial was published in U.S. papers, Ky repeated his admiration for Hitler to Reuters and BBC correspondents in Saigon.

Market Time was begun. In May, at the beginning of the monsoon season, Communist forces started their first large-unit offensive in South Vietnam, one of the large units being a North Vietnamese division that reached the central highlands that month; additional North Vietnamese units were on the way. Several district headquarters towns in the central highlands had to be abandoned by government forces. One whole battalion was virtually wiped out by Viet Cong units.

Things were problematic on the civilian front, too. Another coup in Saigon was attempted that May. It failed, but in June the government's leader, Premier Phan Huy Quat, resigned. A ten-man military committee then took complete control. Two relatively strong leaders eventually emerged from that committee—Nguyen Van Thieu and Nguyen Cao Ky. During the following year, the two would prove themselves to be formidable figures, weathering domestic conflicts with Buddhists, dissident students and minority factions such as the Montagnards.

In June, President Johnson authorized the first B-52 strikes on known enemy troop concentrations in the south, and he approved fire support from U.S. Navy destroyers and cruisers in the south. That same month Westmoreland was granted approval for joint planning with South Vietnamese military leaders, which meant that the U.S. could now begin preparing for major combat operations. On June 27, under Johnson's authority to commence any operation that would "strengthen the relative position" of allied forces, Westmoreland ordered the first sizable foray involving American troops—three U.S. battalions conducted a cautious three-day search-and-destroy mission with one Australian and two South Vietnamese battalions.

By mid-July, Westmoreland had, for all practical purposes, all the authority he needed to fight anywhere and on any scale in South Vietnam. His general battle plan was approved. His tactics were worked out. Large numbers of American GIs were on their way. The land war was on.

The appointment of a new American ambassador in July—Lodge, back again, replacing Taylor, who had completed the one-year term he had agreed to before accepting the appointment— seemed to mark the beginning of this new phase in American involvement in Vietnam. Construction of the huge logistic and communications support infrastructure was off to a feverish start. And command and control areas of responsibility had been worked out. In addition to his own men, Westmoreland would directly control Australian, New Zealand and Thai troops. South Vietnamese troops, as well as those of South Korea and the Philippines, would be under independent command, and it was Westmoreland's job to coordinate the combat objectives of all the allied troops. (Third-country participation was the result of Johnson's effort, beginning in early 1964, to seek "more flags" to help the U.S. in South Vietnam. At the time, he was concerned more with politics than with troop strength, hoping to create a United Nations–type framework for U.S. participation—something that would help him to sell Vietnam involvement to the American public. Eventually fifteen other nations would provide South Vietnam with technical assistance. Australia, New Zealand, Thailand and South Korea sent combat troops; the Philippines sent a civic action group. The Nationalist Chinese government wanted to send combat troops, but the U.S. declined the offer because of worries about the Communist Chinese government's reaction.) In general, the division of responsibility called for U.S. soldiers to take on the big enemy units, South Vietnamese troops to secure populated regions and conduct small-unit operations. The marines, under General Walt, controlled the northernmost I ("Eye") Corps region abutting the demilitarized zone, though Walt was under Westmoreland's ultimate operational command authority. The army would dominate operations in the rest of the country—the II, III and IV Corps regions.

During the spring and summer months of 1965 Westmoreland worried about what would happen to American troops in their first major battle with the Vietnamese Communists. But his worries were cut short by events. He had thought that the first big fight would occur once U.S. units were deployed to the central highlands. Instead it came in the north. In August 1965, a Viet Cong regiment was discovered massing on the Bantangan Peninsula, from which it would be able to attack the marines' new base called Chu Lai (which Victor Krulak had named for himself, Chu Lai being the Mandarin characters for his own name). General Walt reacted quickly.

Elements of a marine division were coming ashore at the time. Walt redeployed one of its battalions by helicopter to block the enemy's

(Above) Marines of E Company, 2nd Battalion, 9th Marines get a final briefing before Operation Harvest Moon in December 1965. (Below) A large Communist force moves down a trail in South Vietnam.

"Theirs but to do and die: Into the valley of Death"

ABC-TV correspondent Jack Smith brought home the cruel nature of combat to the readers of *Saturday Evening Post* in an article published January 28, 1967. In November 1965, Smith had been an enlisted man in the relief force that fought its way through the jungles of the Ia Drang Valley to rescue the 1st Air Cavalry soldiers surrounded by a much larger North Vietnamese force (referred to by Smith as PAVN—People's Army of Vietnam—and Viet Cong soldiers). On the way to the rescue, Smith's company was also cut off and surrounded.

"Men all around me were screaming. The fire was now a continuous roar. We were even being fired at by our own guys. No one knew where the fire was coming from, and so the men were shooting everywhere. Some were in shock and were blazing away at everything they saw or imagined they saw. The XO [executive officer] let out a low moan, and his head sank. I felt a flash of panic. I had been assuming that he would get us out of this. Enlisted men may scoff at officers back in the billets, but when the fighting begins, the men automatically become very dependent upon them. Now I felt terribly alone. . . .

"A rifleman named Wilson and I removed his gear as best we could, and I bandaged his wound. It was not bleeding much on the outside, but he was very close to passing out. Just then Wilson let out a 'huh!' A bullet had creased his upper arm and entered his side. He was bleeding in spurts. I ripped away his shirt with a knife and did him up. Then the XO screamed: A bullet had gone through his boot, taking all his toes with it. He

escape from the peninsula. Then he reembarked another battalion in the landing craft in which they had just come ashore, positioning them at the end of the peninsula. The two marine units then slowly worked their way together, squeezing the Viet Cong between them. A navy cruiser fired its six-inch guns at the VC caught in the trap.

The enemy was badly mauled; about seven hundred were killed. It was a good start for American forces. According to Westmoreland, "from this beginning until American withdrawal some seven and a half years later no American unit in South Vietnam other than a few companies on the offensive or an occasional small outpost ever incurred what could fairly be called a setback."

Colonel Harry Summers, Jr., a respected military strategist and the author of *On Strategy: A Critical Analysis of the Vietnam War,* made the same observation to a North Vietnamese colonel in early 1975 when Summers was part of the negotiating mission sent to Hanoi. "You know you never defeated us on the battlefield," Summers told the North Vietnamese. "That may be so," the Communist replied, "but it is also irrelevant." The North Vietnamese colonel's point, with which Summers agrees, is that the objective of the Communist forces was the gradual wearing down of the American forces, not the winning of individual battles. Summers feels that U.S. leaders were fundamentally shortsighted, having overlooked the applicable lessons of military history, as laid out by Clausewitz one hundred and fifty years before: "If we do not learn to

Lance Corporal T. J. Gledhill races to resupply ammunition during an attack on Fire Support Base Russell.

regard a war, and the separate campaigns of which it is composed, as a chain of linked engagements each leading to the next . . . we are liable to regard them as windfall profits. In so doing, and in ignoring the fact that they were links in a continuous chain of events, we also ignore the possibility that [a successful battle] may later lead to definite disadvantages. This mistake is illustrated again and again in military history . . . an isolated advantage gained in war cannot be assessed separately from the general results [for] in war the advantages and disadvantages of a single action could only be determined by the final balance." And so it was that at the end of the Vietnam war it was the Communists who controlled the south.

By late August 1965 Westmoreland was ready to establish his first large inland base for operations. He chose a spot at An Khe astride Highway 19 in the critical highlands. His basic intent was to thwart the possible enemy drive, through the highlands to the sea, that he worried about—with good reason—throughout his command years: In 1975, during the invasion that led to South Vietnam's collapse, the major North Vietnamese thrust followed this route and quickly led to victory. (Admittedly, conditions by then were much different because of the absence of American airpower, most notably the B-52s.)

The unit Westmoreland chose to be the first deployed to the central highlands was the newly constituted 1st Air Cavalry Division, which, after its arrival by ship in late summer, was immediately shuttled to its inland base by about four hundred helicopters. The 1st Air Cavalry moved all its troops, support equipment and artillery by air. Because the air mobile concept had never before been tested in battle with American troops, Westmoreland hoped that the North Vietnamese in the region would not force a battle until the 1st had had time to develop confidence in its equipment and slowly test its helicopter tactics. But the fight came quickly. On October 19 a North Vietnamese unit of about twenty-two hundred soldiers began a siege of a remote camp manned by some South Vietnamese tribesmen and a few American Special Forces troops. The action did not immediately threaten the 1st Air Cavalry, but Westmoreland felt compelled to save the camp. He ordered Operation Silver Bayonet.

was in agony and crying. Wallace was swearing and in shock. I was crying and holding on to the XO's hand to keep from going crazy.

"The grass in front of Wallace's head began to fall as if a lawnmower were passing. It was a machine gun, and I could see the vague outline of the Cong's head behind the foot or so of elephant grass. The noise of firing from all directions was so great that I couldn't even hear a machine gun being fired three feet in front of me and one foot above my head. As if in a dream, I picked up my rifle, put it on automatic, pushed the barrel into the Cong's face and pulled the trigger. I saw his face disappear. I guess I blew his head off, but I never saw his body and did not look for it. . . .

"Then our artillery and air strikes started coming in. Just before they started, I could hear North Vietnamese voices on our right. The PAVN battalion was moving in on us, into the woods. The Skyraiders were dropping napalm bombs a hundred feet in front of me on a PAVN machine-gun complex. I felt the hot blast and saw the elephant grass curling ahead of me. The victims were screaming. . . .

"No matter what you did, you got hit. The snipers in the trees just waited for someone to move, then shot him. . . .

"I don't know why, but when a man is hit in the belly, he screams an unearthly scream. Something you cannot imagine; you actually have to hear it. When a man is hit in the chest or the belly, he keeps on screaming, sometimes until he dies. I just lay there, numb, listening to the bullets whining over me and the 15 or 20 men close to me screaming and screaming and screaming. They didn't even stop for breath. They kept on until they were hoarse, then they would bleed through their mouths and pass out. They would wake up and start screaming again. Then they would die. I started crying. . . .

"All afternoon there was smoke,

artillery, screaming, moaning, fear, bullets, blood, and little yellow men running around screeching with glee when they found one of us alive, or screaming and moaning with fear when they ran into a grenade or a bullet. I suppose that all massacres in wars are a bloody mess, but this one seemed bloodier to me because I was caught in it.

"At dusk the North Vietnamese started to mortar us. . . . Suddenly the ground behind me lifted up, and there was a tremendous noise. I knew that something big had gone off right behind me. At the same time I felt something white-hot go into my right thigh. I started screaming and screaming. The pain was terrible. Then I said, 'My legs, God, my legs,' over and over.

"Still screaming, I ripped the bandage off my face and tied it around my thigh. It didn't fit, so I held it as tight as I could with my fingers. I could feel the blood pouring out of the hole. I cried and moaned. It was hurting unbelievably. The realization came to me now, for the first time, that I was not going to live. . . .

"All night long the Cong had been moving around killing the wounded. Every few minutes I heard some guy start screaming, 'no no no please,' and then a burst of bullets. When they found a guy who was wounded, they'd make an awful racket.

"They'd yell for their buddies and babble awhile, then turn the poor devil over and listen to him while they stuck a barrel in his face and squeezed. About an hour before dawn the artillery stopped, except for an occasional shell. . . .

"We were all sprawled out in various stages of unconsciousness. My wounds started bleeding again, and ants were getting to my legs. . . .

"I heard the guys coming. They were shooting as they walked along. I screamed into the radio, 'Don't shoot, don't shoot,' but they called back and said they were just shooting PAVN. Then I saw them: The 1st sergeant,

The North Vietnamese commander had anticipated a rescue attempt and had deployed another twenty-two hundred soldiers along Highway 19, waiting in ambush, but he had not taken into account the air mobility that characterized the 1st Air Cavalry. An entire brigade and its supporting artillery flew over his troops. The siege was broken and the attacking enemy forces were mauled by troops from the 1st, supported by airstrikes, artillery and South Vietnamese troops that had made it up Highway 19 when the North Vietnamese ambush force fled into the mountains. The army believed that only seven hundred of the original twenty-two hundred enemy soldiers attacking the outpost survived.

Nevertheless, the North Vietnamese commander was not one to forgo his objective, which was to overrun the Special Forces camp. In preparation for a late November attack against the camp, he redeployed his troops to the valley of the Ia Drang River at the very edge of a low mountain range and brought in two thousand more troops as reinforcements from a staging area in Cambodia. In the meantime, Major General Harry Kinnard, the 1st's commander, unaware that the enemy unit had been reinforced and was even larger now than before the battle, had some of his units out looking for the North Vietnamese who had survived the initial engagement. On November 14, twenty of his officers and four hundred twenty-two of his men found the enemy. Their helicopters put them down on what seemed at first sight to be a nice clearing near the Ia Drang, which turned out to be a field of five-foot-high elephant grass dotted with bizarre anthills eight feet high. Worse still, without knowing it the American had landed virtually on top of the enemy. Most had already disembarked when the enemy opened up with machine guns, mortars and rockets. The fire was so intense that Lieutenant Colonel Harold Moore, the assault force commander, waved off other helicopters trying to land.

For two days the vastly outnumbered Americans held on, taking heavy casualties and frequently engaging in hand-to-hand combat. Reinforcements could not land. Their plight was so desperate that the first B-52 strikes of the war in direct tactical support were authorized. A relief force was unable to land any closer than two and a half miles from the action.

Duplicating his earlier tactic, the North Vietnamese commander had deployed part of his force to await in ambush. This time it worked. As a result, another desperate fight erupted along the relief line. One small unit of the rescue force was cut off from the rest and almost wiped out. Army Specialist Jack Smith, the son of Howard K. Smith and now an ABC Television correspondent himself, described how he came to be one of the few survivors. The North Vietnamese had calmly walked among the wounded Americans of Smith's unit, executing them one by one. Smith survived because they thought he was already dead; he had been wounded several times.

The rescue force got through after two days, and before long the North Vietnamese broke off contact and withdrew into the mountains. About three hundred Americans were killed and, according to Westmoreland, about thirteen hundred North Vietnamese.

At the end of 1965, there were 184,314 U.S. troops in Vietnam; the total of Americans killed in Vietnam had reached 1,636.

The beginning of 1966 marked the successful end of the fire brigade period. The arrival of American troops had averted the collapse of South Vietnam. After the battle of the Ia Drang Valley, most of the North Vietnamese withdrew from the central highlands for a time; the country was saved from any immediate threat to cut it in half. No major city in the central highlands had fallen. Furthermore, the immediate danger of big bases such as Danang being overrun had passed. With these military successes behind him, President Johnson decided to order a temporary bombing halt of the north, which lasted thirty-seven days. In January the bombing resumed, however; the Communists had not responded to the peace initiative. But Phase I of Westmoreland's battle plan had been achieved; the losing trend had been halted, though the countryside still generally belonged to the Communists. To begin taking it back, Westmoreland ordered American units to the offensive in high-priority areas. Phase II of his battle plan began.

Huge multidivision operations characterized the action during 1966, in conjunction with hundreds of small units on search-and-destroy missions throughout the country. These small-unit tactics were especially characteristic of the Marine Corps effort in I Corps. But the huge operations understandably captured most of the public's attention; the press began calling the

our captain and the two radio operators. The captain came up to me and asked me how I was. . . .

"The medics at the L.Z. cut off my boots and put bandages on me. My wounds were in pretty bad shape. . . . I was put in a MedEvac chopper and flown to Pleiku, where . . . I learned that Stern and Deschamps, close friends, had been found dead together, shot in the backs of their heads, executed by the Cong. . . . Like most of the men in our battalion, I had lost all my Army friends. . . ."

• Excerpted from "Death in the Ia Drang Valley" by Jack Smith, *Saturday Evening Post*, January 28, 1968.

A two-man Viet Cong mortar crew feverishly pumps mortar rounds into allied positions in the A Shau Valley.

(Top) Soldiers watch as artillery fire preps enemy positions before an advance. (Above) First Air Cavalry troops fire at a Viet Cong bunker during Operation Masher. (Below) Viet Cong soldiers advance under fire against allied positions.

fighting "Westmoreland's big-unit war." These fights, it should be noted, were near population centers, though Westmoreland's earlier defense of aggressive, large-unit operations had been based on their distance from populous areas. He had envisioned such operations taking place in mountains and jungles and other remote regions, and now was disappointed to learn that it did not always work out that way.

The first large campaign of the year was initially called Operation Masher by the commander of the 1st Air Cavalry, but DOD officials asked him to change its name because that sounded too heavy-handed. Operation White Wing, formerly Masher, involved the whole 1st Air Cavalry Division and part of the 101st Airborne Division. Its ultimate objective was to break up Viet Cong dominance of the rich coastal plains east of the central highlands. A regiment-sized VC unit was operating in the plain and a North Vietnamese regiment was dug into the rugged mountain fringes that overlooked it. Operation White Wing, which lasted well into the year, was successful in breaking up both units; the region became more secure. Small-unit operations followed.

Another major campaign that year involved large North Vietnamese units that had returned from Cambodia to the western central highlands in June. Elements of the 25th Infantry Division and the 101st Airborne Division were sent in to find them. Throughout the summer American troops assigned to these units hopped from one hilltop to another, building fire support bases and then going out on patrol into the trackless jungles below.

At the same time, the 1st Infantry Division had begun an effort to open Route 13, an important road that traveled directly north from Saigon into Binh Long Province, about fifty miles away. Because Binh Long contained a

large concentration of rubber plantations, Route 13 was of economic importance to the country as a whole. Though there were other such road clearing efforts during the year, the Route 13 campaign was the most important. It lasted about six weeks and involved extensive use of mechanized equipment for the first time. In part because of the success of armor during this phase of the fighting, the 11th Armored Regiment was shipped to Vietnam in September. The 11th was the first in Vietnam equipped with the huge Patton tanks. (One of the unit's commanders during the war was, in fact, Colonel George Patton, the son of the famous general of the Second World War for whom the tanks were named.)

Meanwhile, in July the marines were temporarily forced out of their small-unit mode of operation. A marine battalion met a large North Vietnamese force that had infiltrated south. The North Vietnamese held their ground and the largest battle of the war up to that time broke out near Dong Ha along Highway One, not far from the DMZ. General Walt ordered five more marine battalions into the fray; the campaign was called Operation Hastings.

In response to such infiltration, McNamara announced Project Jason later in the year, which was the soon-to-be-abandoned plan to construct an electronic barrier across the DMZ. In its place, Westmoreland ordered a string of strongpoints constructed along the DMZ. (Two of them, Con Thien and Khe Sanh, later became famous.) The purpose of these was not to stop infiltration but rather to detect it and channel it into certain areas where American bombers could be used most effectively against the enemy. The ferocity of the North Vietnamese attacks on these strongholds is a testimonial to their effectiveness.

By October of 1966 Communist forces, composed of one VC division and a North Vietnamese regiment, had returned in force to the rubber plantation region north of Saigon that the 1st Infantry Division had partially cleared in June and July. (Clearing an area of Communist soldiers was as endless a job as cleaning streets — no sooner had an area been cleared than the process had to begin again.) The two Communist units began their campaign to retake lost territory by overrunning a small outpost along the Cambodian border manned by tribesmen and a few American Special Forces soldiers. Thus alerted to their presence, the commander of the region, Lieuten-

✳ Central to measuring progress in fighting the Communists in South Vietnam were estimates of enemy troop strength. Because of the nature of the war, captured territory was not one of the indices. After the first year of fighting, the Joint Chiefs became optimistic about progress; they assured President Johnson that enemy troop strength had topped out and was moving down. However, in early 1967, General William Westmoreland reported to General Earle Wheeler, chairman of the Joint Chiefs, that the opposite was true. The bad news shocked Wheeler, who ordered Westmoreland to reexamine his data while keeping the new estimates secret; he warned that they "would literally blow the lid off Washington" if made public. In a cable sent Westmoreland on March 9, 1967, Wheeler told him to "do whatever is necessary to insure these figures are not, repeat not, released to news media or otherwise exposed to public knowledge." After being declassified, the March 9 cable and a followup sent two days later were made public for the first time on October 18, 1984, during testimony involving Westmoreland's libel case against CBS, Inc. In the second cable, Wheeler warned Westmoreland against any efforts to "load the dice" in intelligence data during the reevaluation — meaning, presumably, that he did not want Westmoreland's staff to contrive enemy troop estimates more favorable to the U.S. position. However, at the same time, Wheeler reminded Westmoreland what was at stake. The new data had "major and serious" implications, he said — the chief one being that the war was not being won. "I cannot go to the President and tell him that — contrary to my reports and those of other Chiefs as to progress of the war in which we have laid great stress upon the thesis [that] you have seized the initiative — we are not sure who has the initiative in South Vietnam."

Rudimentary factories hidden in the jungle helped keep Viet Cong troops supplied. The manufacturing process was slow and tedious, but the number of available workers was large. (Top) Workers make hand grenades. (Bottom) A man and a woman sew uniforms just outside their tunnel.

ant General Jonathan Seaman, ordered Operation Attleboro, involving twenty-two thousand South Vietnamese soldiers and American GIs from the 1st, 4th and 25th Infantry Divisions. Attleboro became the largest operation of the war up to that time. The fighting lasted well into November and involved B-52s in tactical air support. Eventually the enemy withdrew back into Cambodia.

By the end of 1966 there were 389,000 American servicemen and -women in Vietnam; 6,644 had been killed—increases of 203,700 and 5,008 respectively since the end of 1965.

During 1966, while the struggle intensified in the field, fighting of a different kind broke out among top U.S. decision-makers who had been drawn into disagreements between the army (notably Westmoreland) and the Marine Corps on subjects ranging from military strategy to Cambodia, the pacification program and, finally, the basic U.S. commitment to Vietnam.

As discussed, Westmoreland won the battle over tactics. And partly to compel obedience from the marines, he assigned marine units to operations in the north being conducted by the army. Large numbers of army soldiers were also assigned to I Corps, thus reducing the Marine Corps' influence over the region.

But Westmoreland would not prevail in administration policy toward Cambodia. The enemy's use of Cambodia bothered all military men, no matter what their service branch or rank. By 1966 there were seven VC or North Vietnamese staging areas in Cambodia, one only thirty miles from Saigon. Furthermore, the coastal interdiction achieved by Operation Market Time had forced the Communists to extend the Ho Chi Minh Trail from Laos down into Cambodia as an alternate route to southern South Vietnam.

War supplies and armaments for Communist troops were also being shipped across Cambodia from China. More than twenty-one thousand metric tons passed over this route between 1966 and 1969, according to Westmoreland's top intelligence officer, Major General George McChristian, including six hundred tons of Russian rockets. Westmoreland contends that the total tonnage transshipped was enough to meet the enemy's requirements for eight years at the level the war was then being waged. McChristian also estimated that Communist forces purchased fifty-five thousand tons of rice annually from

Cambodian farmers. This support obviously had the personal approval of Prince Norodom Sihanouk, the Cambodian head of state, who in May 1965 had cast his lot with the Communists. That month he broke diplomatic relations with the U.S., visited Peking, and began praising the Vietnamese Communists publicly.

Sihanouk was in a difficult position, of course. His army was small and weak, his control of his kingdom somewhat tenuous. He had made his move to support the Communists in part because at the time the prospect of Vietnam's falling to them seemed certain and imminent.

The Johnson administration remained hopeful that Sihanouk would change his mind, however. Understandably, they did not want to widen the war into Cambodia, nor did they want, by doing so, to admit to the American public that the war was going to be more difficult than was generally supposed. For these reasons, Westmoreland was denied permission in April 1966 to attack a North Vietnamese unit that American forces had chased into Cambodia. The Communist troops had set up camp several miles beyond the border on the opposite side of a mountain ridge. It was Westmoreland's first such request, and in the future he would make more without success. In fact, the administration refused him permission even to make public the Communists' use of Cambodia, for that too would have contributed to the public's perception of the difficulty of waging war in Vietnam. Sihanouk always denied any accusations that surfaced in the press, and the administration also remained silent on the subject. Not until late 1967 would the Johnson administration admit the use of Cambodia by Communist forces. And that admission came only after George MacArthur and Horst Faas of Associated Press found a VC camp a mere one thousand yards beyond the border, and filed their story. Shortly thereafter, in January 1968, Johnson sent Chester Bowles, who was serving as U.S. ambassador to India, to talk to Sihanouk about the sanctuaries. The Cambodian leader obviously did not think he could drive the Vietnamese Communists out of his country nor did he particularly want the U.S. to try to do so. But he did tell Bowles that U.S. forces could cross into Cambodia if they were in "hot pursuit" of their adversary, the implication being that such forays would be of short duration and limited range. He also agreed to some bombing in unpopulated areas. "We Cambodians do

(Top) An air force F-100 swoops in low to napalm enemy positions several hundred yards in front of these GIs. (Bottom) A patrol fights back after being ambushed in a ravine southwest of Phu Bai.

Father Bohula, a navy chaplain, presents money collected from his former parish in Chicago, Illinois, to the nuns of Phu Thung orphanage near Danang in 1966.

not like any Vietnamese—red, white or blue," Sihanouk said. But the Johnson administration never used the bombing prerogative, probably because of tactical reassessments following the Communist Tet offensive, which occurred within the month.

The internal fights over pacification and the basic U.S. commitment were interrelated. By 1966 many in the administration had decided that military progress was almost imperceptible; "escalating military stalemate," as McNaughton described the situation. The assistant secretary of defense was now for finding a way out. In a memo to McNamara on January 18, 1966, he listed several outcomes he thought the U.S. could live with:

"Coalition government including Communists.

"A free decision by the South to succumb to the VC or to the North.

"A neutral (or even anti-U.S.) government in SVN.

"A live-and let-live 'reversion to 1959.'"

The man who was making these pull-back recommendations was, of course, the same John McNaughton who one year earlier had laughed with friends about the president's agitated movement toward the air war (which he, McNamara, McGeorge Bundy and others had been pushing Johnson into); the same dilettante who in another memo to McNamara in early 1965 arrogantly stated that the U.S. objective in Vietnam was not to help a friend, but to avoid a humiliating U.S. defeat to our reputation as a guarantor— as if the prospect of thousands of combat deaths on both sides and the horrible suffering and displacement of the Vietnam people were inconsequential considerations relative to some vague need to prove a point.

McNaughton's new pessimism was based on his feeling that the North Vietnamese would offset every U.S. initiative to get the edge in the south: If the U.S. posted more troops in Vietnam, the North Vietnamese would send more soldiers down the Ho Chi Minh Trail, if the U.S. assigned more aircraft squadrons to Vietnam, the North Vietnamese would send down even more soldiers; and if aggressive U.S. tactics were gaining the advantage in a region, the North Vietnamese would send down still more soldiers. This was what he meant by "escalating stalemate."

In 1964 and early 1965, McNaughton and McNamara, among others, had moved in lock-step toward a military commitment, dragging a reluctant Lyndon Johnson along with them. Johnson, his humble origins having marked him with a permanent sense of inferiority that even the presidency could not cure, trusted all too much in the judgment of his brilliant, highly educated Kennedy men. But once Hanoi's leadership, apparently unintimidated by American air attacks on the north, made the decision to commit combat units in the south, the basis for McNaughton's and McNamara's earlier optimistic forecasts crumbled. The two men very quickly recognized what was going to happen. Their judgment might be bad, but they certainly could analyze figures, and the figures showed that the Communists were far better prepared for a war of attrition than the U.S. To keep up with attrition and U.S. escalation, the North Vietnamese needed to deploy about one hundred thousand fresh troops per year to the south. Because of the unusually high birth rate in the north, twice that number of young men reached eighteen years of age each year in North Vietnam.

A military presence was important. Soldiers such as these increased villagers' confidence in the government.

McNamara's pessimism about the situation in South Vietnam was not based solely on the actions of the Communists. The inability of South Vietnam's leaders to reconcile differences among the major factions of their population was a great concern, especially when the Buddhists, who constituted the majority, were involved. McNamara was reminded of the problem firsthand during a visit to South Vietnam in late 1965. Angry Buddhist demonstrations were commonplace and student activists were strengthening the protest movement. They wanted the military junta to resign in favor of a civilian assembly. In early 1966 their displeasure reached the flash point, particularly in I Corps, where the Buddhist contingent was especially powerful. The U.S. Marines were literally caught in the middle of the feuding South Vietnamese factions.

On March 11, Premier Ky, with the backing of the National Leadership Council (composed mostly of generals), removed the Vietnamese I Corps commander, Lieutenant General Nguyen Chanh Thi, who was openly critical of the government. A South Vietnamese government spokesman announced that Thi was taking sick leave because of "sinus trouble," but no one was fooled. Thi, who had grown up in the area and was the son of peasant parents, was unusually popular; his rebellious nature made him even more so. Dissident leaders called for a general strike in I

Private John Rose reads the February 14, 1966, issue of *Stars and Stripes,* the newspaper for servicemen overseas. The front-page headline notes that LBJ will not call up the reserves.

Corps to protest his firing. On March 13, ninety percent of the South Vietnamese workers employed at Danang Air Base failed to show up for work. The Danang seaport was virtually shut down, and shops everywhere closed. Soon U.S. Marine operations in the field were brought to a halt because supplies slowed to a trickle. Rather quickly the protests developed an increasingly anti-American tone, with radio stations occupied by protesting students in Hue broadcasting accusations of U.S. interference in internal South Vietnamese politics.

Just how confused young American soldiers were by these events is exemplified by the plight of a marine who on March 26 tore down an anti-American banner from a wall near his unit's position in Hue, no doubt thinking that the protests were Communist inspired. The leader of the student protesters, Buu Ton, made the hapless marine's action a cause célèbre. He threatened to have the U.S. Information Service building in Hue destroyed if he did not receive an apology within two hours—a demand that was quickly granted by a marine colonel; but Buu Ton wanted more. He wanted to confront the marine personally and to have American authorities order the marine to replace the banner "in public view" and apologize over the Hue radio station.

The U.S. embassy in Saigon quickly got involved in the mini-crisis, as did other high-ranking marine officers. Eventually Buu Ton was placated, though American officials adamantly refused to make the marine apologize publicly. Buu Ton was given a letter signed by Colonel Geoffrey Boston, the U.S. Army senior adviser to the 1st ARVN Division and the subarea coordinator, that assured Buu Ton and his followers "that he would do what he could to prevent such actions in the future." American officials also promised to punish the poor marine—who by then must have believed that the sands of Iwo Jima were on another planet—"within the framework of U.S. military justice."

The crisis in I Corps erupted at intervals during the next two months. At one point President Thieu announced that general elections would be held within three to five months. That cooled tempers down. Even Thich Tri Quang, the Buddhist monk who had led the protest movements that caused Diem's downfall, called for a moratorium on strikes and demonstrations. But General Thi, whose firing had precipitated the crisis in the first place, called for the resignation of Thieu, Ky and the entire General Ruling Council. The mayor of Danang, Dr. Nguyen Van Man, publicly seconded the motion, while the rebel-controlled radio stations in Hue and Danang began denouncing Ky. Buddhist antagonism flared anew. Radical Buddhist leaders announced that sixty monks and nuns were ready to begin another self-immolation campaign.

On May 15, 1966, in the middle of the night, Ky moved to put down the revolt. He airlifted two government marine battalions and two airborne battalions into Danang Air Base. Quickly they took control of most of the city and arrested Mayor Man. There was little bloodshed, because of the element of surprise, but rebel groups still controlled pockets in the area. And the fact that the rebels included in their number various units of disgruntled government troops made for great danger—even for the Americans, once again caught in the middle. Marine Lieutenant General Lewis Walt was ordered by Deputy Ambassador William Porter to "use [his] good offices to prevent bloodshed." On May 18, he had occasion to do so.

Rebel soldiers had dug themselves into positions at the east end of the Danang River Bridge, which connected the city to the Tiensha Peninsula. Government forces had advanced to positions on the opposite side and attempted to cross until stopped by gunfire from the rebels, whose leader sent word that he had ordered the bridge rigged with explosives. He threatened to blow it up if loyal troops tried to advance.

Johnson reviews army troops in the rain at Fort Campbell, Kentucky, while seeing them off to Vietnam in July 1966.

A patrol passes by the only remaining facade of a heavily damaged Catholic church in Quang Tri Province.

The bridge was an important supply link for the U.S. Marines, and they acted quickly. Colonel John Chaisson, an articulate and persuasive officer who had successfully negotiated with the rebels before, helicoptered to the east shore and began talking to the rebel leaders. At the same time, the government troops on the west shore withdrew at the marines' request to ease the tension. Americans took up their positions.

Unable to convince the rebels to withdraw too, Chaisson ordered a company of U.S. Marines led by Captain William Lee to walk down among the rebels and take a seat. While the young soldiers of both sides sat side by side, Chaisson took off for Walt's headquarters. Within minutes he was back at the bridge, arriving with none other than Walt himself in the general's staff car. The two Americans strode briskly across the bridge that was still rigged with explosives. At some point on the bridge, they were met by the rebel commander, a Vietnamese warrant officer. Walt, a large, husky man, decided that the time for subtle negotiation had passed. He "really gave ... [the Vietnamese] hell and was trying to intimidate him," remembers Chaisson. But the Vietnamese stood his ground, so Walt called for a platoon of marines.

The Vietnamese then raised his hand above his head, as if preparing to signal for the bridge to be blown up. It was now Walt's turn to stand his ground. He "stood right in there," says Chaisson, who, of course, was obliged to do the same. After a few (very long) seconds, the Vietnamese said, in a firm voice, "General, we will die together," then immediately brought his hand down sharply to his side.

General Lewis Walt (left) and Nguyen Chanh Thi, key players in the political crisis in the north of South Vietnam during May 1966.

Fortunately, the explosives did not detonate. The only thing that fell was the look on the rebel leader's face. He had fully expected that all three of them would die. "I shall never forget the expression on his face," says Walt.

The confrontation ended the threat to the Danang River Bridge and that particular group of rebels' enthusiasm for their cause. Five days later the whole rebel movement collapsed when loyal government troops attacked the Tinh Hoi pagodas in Danang; thirty-three rebels were killed and another three hundred twenty-five surrendered. Thirteen hundred weapons were found inside. Having survived this serious crisis, Thieu and Ky became more confident; their position had been substantially strengthened. Soon thereafter they ordered national elections, which were conducted on September 11. Eighty-one percent of registered South Vietnamese voted and thereby helped to legitimize Thieu and Ky's leadership. But despite this favorable and dramatic turn of events, Walt and the marines who were caught up in our allies' infighting had every reason to believe that the U.S. had too many other bridges to cross to win this war.

Walt's confrontation with a rebellious South Vietnamese army officer on this bridge over the Danang River was a pivotal turning point in ending the threat to Saigon's authority in the area.

Paying the Price, Bearing the Burden

The Land War: Part 2

On the surface, events in South Vietnam during the fall of 1966 might have seemed to bode well not just militarily, but politically. When national elections were held that September, the *New York Times* reported that "foreign observers who roamed freely on election day generally agreed there were few irregularities." As the government appeared to stabilize, violent Buddhist dissent died down, and Westmoreland said, "I felt for the first time a genuine optimism over political developments." But just weeks after Westmoreland's optimistic remarks, Robert McNamara, perhaps like General Walt, had come to feel that there were too many bridges still to be crossed in Vietnam to warrant a deepening commitment. As he testified during a court-ordered deposition taken in 1984 for Westmoreland's libel suit against CBS, Inc., regarding a "60 Minutes" story, by October 1966, "I did not believe [the war] could be won militarily." On October 14, 1966, McNamara wrote in a memo to Johnson that the Vietnamese Communist leaders "continue to believe that the war will be a long one, that time is their ally and that their own staying power is superior to ours.

"It follows, therefore," he continued, "that the odds are about even that, even with the recommended deployments, we will be faced in early 1967 with a military standoff at a much higher level, with pacification still stalled, and with any prospect of military success marred by the chances of an active Chinese intervention and with the requirement for a deployment of still more U.S. forces."

And on the basis of a personal visit he had concluded only days before, he observed that "Pacification has if anything gone backward." Therefore, McNamara proposed that Johnson "Limit the increase in U.S. forces"; "Stabilize the Rolling Thunder program against the North"; "Pursue a vigorous pacification program"; and "Take steps to increase the credibility of our peace gestures in the minds of the enemy." One of the steps he thought "we should consider" in order to get negotiations under way was to "stop bombing all of North Vietnam."

The week before McNamara's memo landed on Johnson's desk,

GIs carry the body of a comrade away from the fighting. Above, General Creighton Abrams.

the Joint Chiefs had suggested an entirely different course of action. They proposed what the *Pentagon Papers* writers called a "full-blown" mobilization of 688,500 army, navy, air force and marine reservists to be sent to Vietnam as well as to American defense posts around the world, to bolster units whose troop strength had been depleted by call-ups for service in Vietnam.

Prime Minister Nguyen Cao Ky and President Nguyen Van Thieu listen intently to President Johnson at the Manila Conference on October 24, 1966.

The Chiefs' reaction to McNamara's October 14 memo was "predictably rapid—and violent," says the *Pentagon Papers*. By then the military was emotionally caught up in the war and wanted to win. They had taken on the war as their own, even though prior to the summer of 1965 it had been more Harvard's than West Point's. Now, the military was responsible for virtually all Vietnam initiatives.

During this period, Johnson's thinking was closer to that of the Joint Chiefs than to McNamara's. Though political considerations (such as the cost of the war and resultant budget problems, and also the anticipated public reaction to too rapid an escalation) tempered what he wanted to do more than it did the judgment of the Joint Chiefs, he certainly was with them emotionally. His flying all the way to Vietnam for a visit with American troops at Cam Ranh Bay after the Manila Conference of allied leaders showed his sense of personal involvement. In his mind, the soldiers were his boys, the pilots flying the planes, his fliers. So even though he did not give the Chiefs the reserve call-up they wanted, he granted moderate increases in troops level and in the pace of the air war over the north. And his estrangement from his secretary of defense began. "You've never seen such a lot of shit," Johnson said as he turned over to an aide McNamara's proposals for a bombing cutback. On another occasion, Johnson interrupted himself in midstream as he started automatically to suggest to a senator that he talk to McNamara about a war-related matter: "No, don't go see Bob—he's gone dovish on me."

The American effort continued to intensify during the last months of 1967. Nevertheless, the year was a period of transition because leaders on both sides were becoming frustrated—Johnson by allied inability to pacify the countryside, his Vietnamese Communist counterparts by the clear albeit slow trend in favor of the U.S. and its allies in military operations. The result was that both sides independently altered their tactics. The Communist change first manifested itself in early 1968. The U.S. change began during 1967. The last American multidivision offensive operation of the war would be conducted during that year, after which the emphasis began to be on pacification and Vietnamization. Pacification was in fact one of the key topics addressed at the Guam Conference convened on March 20, 1967. Thieu and Ky were the top-ranking South Vietnamese attending. The president himself led the U.S. delegation, which included McNamara, Westmoreland, McNaughton and, among others, three major new players—Ellsworth Bunker, William Leonhart and Robert Komer. Several days prior to the meeting, Johnson had announced that Bunker would replace Lodge (who had asked to retire) as ambassador to South Vietnam; that Leonhart, who was an old friend then serving as ambassador to Pakistan, would become deputy ambassador; and that Komer, a civilian White House staffer, would become Westmoreland's deputy responsible for pacification. The appointment of a civilian to serve within the military chain of command was highly unusual, if not without precedent. Previously the ambassador had been directly responsible for pacification. Westmoreland says McNamara had led him to believe that that activity would be added to his military duties, putting him in a position similar to MacArthur's in post-Second World War Japan. But, chiefly because of Rusk's reservations about the militarization of the war, Robert Komer was appointed to head pacifica-

Paying the Price
In their own words

It's the old story. Five days of fighting like hell and on the sixth day they give it to you for nothing.—a U.S. officer of the 196th Light Infantry Brigade after his men captured a remote spot called Hill 102; in August 1969.

I sent them a good boy and they made him a murderer.—the mother of Paul Meadlo, a former Americal Division soldier who participated in the My Lai slaughter, blaming the army for her son's acts; on CBS Television in December 1969.

We had to destroy it in order to save it.—an American artillery officer to an Associated Press reporter after shelling wiped out half the village of Ben Tre in the Mekong Delta; in early 1968.

(Top) American soldiers trudge up a dusty road in the DMZ after two days of hard fighting with North Vietnamese units. (Bottom) These hootches, almost invisible from the air, housed North Vietnamese soldiers until GIs drove them off during a search-and-destroy mission.

tion. How much was riding on that effort was made obvious by Westmoreland's briefing to the group. He said that unless the Viet Cong infrastructure was broken up, a prospect he saw as unlikely given the present pacification program progress, and unless infiltration was stopped, he thought the war could go on indefinitely.

The elevation of another figure who was to become a major player in the Vietnam war was first broached at this meeting, when McNamara discussed with Westmoreland his and Earle Wheeler's plan to appoint a four-star military deputy to serve in Vietnam and eventually to replace Westmoreland (although the latter has said that he wanted to see the war to its end). The two agreed that Creighton Abrams, who was then serving as vice chief of staff of the army, and heading a study group evaluating U.S. strategy in Vietnam, would be the ideal person for the job: Abram's primary assignment while serving as Westmoreland's deputy would be the development of the South Vietnamese army toward "self sufficiency."

The first big offensive of 1967 was Operation Cedar Falls. Troops from four large American units were involved. The attack area was the Iron Triangle, which had been a base area for the Communists since the fighting against the French. The objective was to drive the Viet Cong out of this heavily forested refuge, kill as many as possible, and make Saigon, only twenty-five miles away, more secure. In the wake of the fighting, a huge underground complex was discovered, complete with command headquarters, dining halls, hospital rooms, munitions factories and living quarters. It was here that papers were found confirming that Bob Hope had been the object of the attack on the Brink Hotel back in December 1964. After the VC were driven out, the forest, which had been home to seven thousand villagers as well as the VC, was leveled by Rome Plows. The villagers were forced to resettle.

The next major operation was the largest of the war for the U.S., and would, in fact, be its last big-unit offensive in South Vietnam. (The last big-unit operation of the war for the U.S. would be the "incursion" into Cambodia in 1970.) Junction City was launched in February in a region called War Zone C, which lay beyond the Iron Triangle. The area is contiguous to Cambodia and had for years been an almost exclusively

Communist reserve. The U.S. military staff was convinced that the Communist command center in South Vietnam, known as COSVN, was somewhere in War Zone C; they hoped to find it and capture its staff. Twenty-two American battalions (about thirty thousand troops) and four South Vietnamese battalions were involved.

The plan was to form a huge horseshoe around most of the region, which, it was hoped, would trap the enemy, while tanks and troops in mechanized vehicles charged north through the gap in the horseshoe. This was the only operation of the war in which airborne troops were parachuted from planes, one entire battalion being dropped deep into the jungle. But COSVN was not found and the enemy gradually retreated into Cambodia, choosing to stand and fight in only two instances. Though later intelligence sources indicated that the Communists had been sufficiently alarmed to transfer their training facilities to Cambodia, the fighting units gradually began returning after allied forces withdrew. Westmoreland says he did not have enough soldiers to keep the enemy out, but a belt of Special Forces camps manned mostly by South Vietnamese was quickly built and left behind in the wake of the allied force's departure, their purpose being to detect future infiltration.

Another major offensive during 1967 was Operation Fairfax, which had as its goal the improved security of Saigon. Though many soldiers were involved, Fairfax was very different from Junction City and Cedar Falls. Fairfax did not involve the mass deployment of big units working in coordination with one another. Rather it involved hundreds of small units going out on patrol, day and night, in the countryside surrounding Saigon. The soldiers searched villages, checked for weapons, looked for anything suspicious. Their pervasive presence made the area more secure by making the enemy more reluctant to attack, except at nighttime, when most of the actual fighting occurred. From rooftops high above Saigon (such as that at the Caravelle Hotel) people could watch as tracer bullets, exploding shells and flares lit up the night and created spectacular displays.

This type of operation, known as small-unit saturation patrolling, characterized the American campaign for the duration of the war. The only major deviation from this mode of operation during the years to come was the operation into Cambodia. (Tet and Khe Sanh were also big

Finding the enemy was one of the toughest assignments of fighting the war. Year after year, units like this platoon operating near An Hoa combed some of the most difficult terrain in the world looking for them. Under Abrams, smaller unit operations characterized the effort.

The Tet offensive brought the war to every major city in South Vietnam. In Hue the urban fighting lasted longest. A soldier wounded during that battle is lowered from a rooftop.

operations, of course, but they were defensive reactions to Communist forces on the offensive.)

Though small-unit patrolling had occurred since the beginning of the American combat commitment, it had not been the dominant mode, in part because Westmoreland opposed it. Westmoreland would later argue that it was his big-unit operations that had permitted this change of tactics and that, in fact, all was progressing according to his battle plan. Others, especially the Marine Corps, would argue that small-unit operations should have characterized American offensive tactics all along. And in 1979 the army's Combat Studies Institute did document the fact that small-unit tactics caused more enemy casualties per American casualty.

By the end of 1967, American troop strength in Vietnam had risen to 465,000. That year, 9,378 Americans were killed in the fighting.

About seven months before the start of the 1968 celebration of Tet, the Vietnamese lunar New Year, North Vietnamese diplomats in key posts throughout the world began returning to Hanoi. Joined by the top Vietnamese Communist military leaders, they formulated a dramatic change in strategy, resulting in preparations for a huge Communist offensive that would be launched during the middle of Tet. By most accounts, the Communists thought that the time had come for the final offensive. Their soldiers were told that Vietnamese in the south, even government soldiers, stirred by the example of the attacking force, would rally to the Communist cause. But the Communists had underestimated the strength of the allies, and overestimated the forbearance of the South Vietnamese in the face of a violent interruption of their most sacred holiday. It has been argued that there was historic precedent for a Tet attack — the 1789 offensive launched by a Vietnamese leader against Chinese forces occupying Hue. But to suggest that South Vietnamese would hearken back to such a remote historic event as justification for a truce violation strains credibility.

The Tet offensive was a horrible military and psychological loss for the Communists. ". . . we suffered large losses in material and manpower, especially cadres at various echelons, which clearly weakened us," wrote former Communist General Tan Van Tra in 1982 (who had served in the south during Tet). Consequently, "we were not only unable to retain the gains we had made

but had to overcome a myriad of difficulties in 1969 and 1970." In fact, the Viet Cong, who bore the brunt of most of the attacks, suffered losses so severe that they never fully recovered. Later their strength was sapped even more by increased numbers of defectors, demoralized by reversion to protracted war tactics, which were perceived as a step backward.

But Tet was probably even more psychologically debilitating to the U.S. Until then, the Johnson administration had made the war at least tolerable to the American public. Liberal draft deferments, such as those for college students, had kept thousands of vocal middle-class families, the political core of the country, from becoming too upset with the war. For similar reasons Johnson had refused the Joint Chiefs' request the previous October for a general call-up of the reserves, and an even earlier request for a call-up in the summer of 1965 — this one by none other than McNamara. Up to the time of Tet, the only Americans who had served in Vietnam, generally speaking, were professional military men and women, volunteers stirred by feelings of patriotic duty and draftees from mostly lower-class families. The first two groups

(Top) The Joan of Arc Cathedral in Hue was an enemy strongpoint until marines routed them from their positions. (Bottom) A grenadier from the 3rd Platoon, Company H, Fifth Marines carries a Vietnamese woman from the Hue hospital to safety.

From a classroom in the University of Hue, a marine fires his M-16 rifle at an enemy sniper on February 3, 1968.

supported their government's prosecution of the war without question for obvious reasons. For draftees, the war was made reasonably tolerable by the promise that their combat tour would last only one year; after that, Vietnam became someone else's war, even if it went on interminably. Furthermore, up to the time of Tet, the media covered the war much in the mode of the Second World War experience. Thus, those who fought in Vietnam were still received back into their communities with a measure of respect.

Tet ended the complacency of the American public, press and officialdom. The cliché used at the time to describe to the public the status of the war had even appeared on invitations to the U.S. embassy's New Year's party only days before Tet. "Come see the light at the end of the tunnel," read the invitation. That the Communists could launch such a massive offensive ended delusions about the war being on the verge of winding down. The chaos in the early days of the Communist offensive — which created 600,000 South Vietnamese refugees — shocked the American public. Tet revealed to all that the war was going to last a long, long time if the U.S. remained determined to win.

Whether this change in the American public's perception of the war was the primary goal of the Communist offensive is subject to debate. But it is inarguably the case that this *was* the major achievement of Tet for the Communists, their ostensible military goals having failed so miserably. Futhermore, it was easy to see the growing discontent in the United States, and this would not have been the first time that the Communists had played to the domestic opinion of their adversary. (During their fight with the French, domestic discontent in France was a crucial factor.) Surely they knew that there was no better time than January of an election year to convince the American public that a much greater sacrifice than previously anticipated would be required of them to win. But this is all speculation, and the North Vietnamese themselves differ in their analysis of the main goals of the Tet offensive.

Not long after the historic meeting of Vietnamese Communist leaders in Hanoi, American leaders became aware of their plans in broad outline form. Initially there was physical evidence to suggest that something big was in the offing. Enemy prisoners began talking about the coming "final victory." The number of enemy soldiers defecting to the allies—*chieu hois,* they were called—began dropping sharply. A noticeable enemy buildup in the DMZ was observed. Traffic sightings on the Ho Chi Minh Trail increased two hundred percent.

At the height of fighting, 1968-1969...

A statistical picture:

- American troops   543,000
- South Vietnamese troops   819,200
- Total allied troops   1,593,000
- Communist forces   810,000
  - In South Vietnam   250,000
- American ground attacks
  - Battalion or larger   1,000/year
- Communist ground attacks
  - Battalion or larger   126/year
- American air attacks   400,000/year
- Bombs dropped 1.2 million tons/year
- U.S. expenditures
  - for bombing $14 billion/year
- Military defoliation   20,000 acres/year
- Communists killed in
  - action   200,000/year
- Refugees   585,000/year
- Civilian casualties   130,000/month

For fear of destroying the historic city, the allies initially refrained from using heavy firepower and tactical aircraft on Communist soldiers entrenched in Hue. Thieu eventually authorized all weaponry. Even then, the battle lasted twenty-five days.

Documentation was also discovered. In November American troops found papers left behind by fleeing enemy soldiers. One called for "a concentrated offensive effort in coordination with other units in various battle areas throughout South Vietnam." Another stated that "Central Headquarters concludes that the time has come for a direct revolution and that the opportunity for a general offensive and general uprising is within reach."

This information was passed along to Johnson, of course. He subsequently warned the Australian cabinet of "dark days ahead." Word also began getting out through the press. On January 12, 1968, for example, Dan Oberdorfer wrote in the *Miami Herald*, "There is a growing hunch on the part of many [American officials] that the next month or two is likely to bring some critical—perhaps spectacular—moves on the part of the enemy. The next three weeks—from now until Tet, the Vietnamese lunar New Year—are considered particularly important." And on January 22, Westmoreland was even more specific during an interview with Howard Tuckner of NBC Television. "I think his [the enemy's] plans concern a major effort to win a spectacular battlefield success on the eve of the Tet festival next Monday."

Despite the accuracy of their own predictions, the Americans and the South Vietnamese were caught off guard when the Tet offensive began at about three in the morning of January 31. The allies were guilty of two serious miscalculations: for believing that the Communists would attack before or after rather than during Tet, and for underestimating the intensity and range of the offensive.

Eight-four thousand enemy troops, mostly Viet Cong, were involved. They attacked "thirty-six of the forty-four provincial capitals, five of the autonomous cities, sixty-four of the 242 district capitals, and fifty hamlets." They penetrated thirteen of these cities, including Saigon, Danang, and Hue—the three largest—in strength.

In most cities Communist soldiers were quickly driven out within two or three days; in some cases, within hours. But in six cities, including Saigon, the fighting raged for several more days. And in Hue, North Vietnamese units held on for twenty-five days before counterattacks finally overwhelmed them.

In Saigon, a fifteen-man suicide squad opened

✷ After years of fighting, the average GI began to have doubts about all the fancy U.S. government programs that were supposed to pacify the South Vietnamese countryside. They had been told that their civil action projects would help win "the hearts and minds" of villagers while their rifles kept the enemy at bay. The projects included everything from washing babies to filling teeth. But some areas remained as hostile as ever. A one-liner evolved, reflecting the frustration and, at the same time, the belief in a more pragmatic approach. It went something like this: "If you've got 'em by the balls, their hearts and minds will follow." The slogan was carried back to the United States, of course, where it became a favorite of the man who once said he would walk on his own grandmother, if necessary, to ensure Richard Nixon's reelection—Charles Colson, the president's special counsel and designated hatchet-man. Since the words so accurately described his own approach to politics, Colson had them framed for hanging over his bar at home.

the offensive by attacking the U.S. embassy. With explosives, they blew a hole in the wall surrounding the complex and raced through. Two marines and two Viet Cong were killed in the first exchange of fire. The mini-battle within the embassy walls raged for several hours. By the time American reinforcements arrived by helicopter at dawn, the fighting was over. Bodies were strewn all over the embassy lawn. Five marines, four South Vietnamese embassy employees (one of whom might have been a collaborator) and all fifteen of the Viet Cong had been killed. The enemy had not gotten inside the chancery, the main embassy building, where a skeleton staff on duty stayed on an open line to the State Department in Washington throughout the fight.

On February 24, 1968, after the Citadel, the last enemy stronghold, was recaptured, Sergeant P. L. Thompson posed for a photograph of himself sitting on the throne of Emperor Tu Duc.

The body of an allied soldier lies near Bunker 051 at Tan Son Nhut Air Base on January 31, 1968. The opening shot by Viet Cong forces attacking the huge base was fired at this position manned by South Vietnamese soldiers. A rocket scored a direct hit.

But two embassy employees who lived in an old French villa on the embassy grounds had a closer call. Robert Josephson and George Jacobson were sleeping in rooms on the second floor when the Viet Cong breached the wall. They heard one of them enter the ground floor and move from room to room looking for people. Frantically the two began looking for weapons; one found a hand grenade and the other bent a clothes hanger into a poker. Fortunately for them a unit of MPs arrived just about the time the Communist soldier began slowly climbing the stairs, and one MP, alerted to their plight, tossed them a .45 caliber pistol through an upstairs window. Jacobson, a retired colonel, killed the VC.

There were tense moments at Tan Son Nhut in the Saigon suburbs as well. Sappers—commandos with explosives—made it to the flight line. Obviously overwhelmed by the selection of aircraft, they blew up an ancient C-47 prop-transport instead of one of the scores of valuable RF-4 reconnaissance jets lining the airfield. Communist soldiers also attacked a compound adjacent to Tan Son Nhut that contained the villas of senior officers of the Vietnamese Joint General Staff. Vietnamese guards held them off, assisted by American MPs guarding a similar complex across the street for senior American officers. The fighting was intense, with some of the senior officers joining the fray. A truckload of MPs trying to come to the rescue was hit head-on by a VC rocket as they traveled down an alley. The blast and machine-gun fire that raked the wounded killed sixteen of the Americans, but without the reinforcements, the American senior officers' compound might have been overwhelmed by the Viet Cong, says Westmoreland. In any case, the enemy persistently kept to its battle plan of attacking the compound across the street. (Such inflexibility was characteristic of Communist units because of their shortage of communications equipment and the rigidity with which orders were imposed on their commanders.)

Just as at the embassy, the fighting near Tan Son Nhut ended rather quickly, though an estimated three battalions had attacked the base. At dawn, some of the Viet Cong tried to hide in a cotton mill nearby. When they were spotted, American commanders called in fighter-bombers and gunships. One hundred and sixty-two dead Viet Cong were later found in the rubble. The bodies of another three hundred and twenty-five were found on the base. Two of them were men who had cut hair at the officers' barbershop.

The struggle in the Cholon district of Saigon lasted longer because of house-to-house fighting. This type of fighting also typified the action to retake Hue. Sixteen enemy battalions, the equivalent of two divisions, had attacked that city. Driving them out required eleven South Vietnamese and three U.S. Marine battalions, while the 1st Air Cavalry Division flew in to the north of the city to block enemy reinforcements.

Enemy troops had moved into Hue on the night of January 30, mingling with thousands of revelers in the streets. At a prescribed time, they reassembled and attacked, quickly taking control of most of the city (population 140,000)

During Tet, the worst fighting in Saigon was concentrated in the Cholon district. This aerial photo shows the devastation.

Hundreds of Hue residents were murdered while Communist soldiers controlled most of the city. Some of them had been buried alive. Their bodies were exhumed and their mass funeral was made a national day of mourning.

Medic D. R. Howe of Glencoe, Minnesota, tends to the wounds of Private D. A. Crum of New Brighton, Pennsylvania, during the battle of Hue.

and most of the Citadel (the walled complex of the old imperial court, which was surrounded by a moat and which contained a South Vietnamese Army division headquarters), where they raised the North Vietnamese flag at the center of the complex.

American aircraft and artillery were deliberately kept out of the action at first, in order to minimize damage to the many historic structures. But the Communists were too well entrenched and the allies were suffering too many casualties, so President Thieu authorized airstrikes on the city.

During the twenty-five days of fighting in Hue, one hundred and forty-two marines and three hundred and eighty-four South Vietnamese soldiers were killed. About five thousand Communist soldiers were also killed, that disproportionate total the result of airstrikes and artillery. But the most shocking casualty figure concerned the toll on residents of Hue: During their occupation of the city, the North Vietnamese buried alive or executed more than twenty-eight hundred people—priests, city officials and teachers among the victims.

According to Brigadier General John Chaisson, who served on Westmoreland's staff as director of the combat operations center, there were certain moves the enemy could make that would always cause Westmoreland to spring to action, as if an alarm bell had gone off in his deep consciousness. He would "come out of the corner like a, like a, a pug," Chaisson once observed, hesitating to choose just the right words. "And

two of the bells [they could] ring . . . [to] get this
reaction [were] A Shau and the Highlands."

Concern about the central highlands originated with the enemy drive in 1965 to cut South
Vietnam in half by slicing through the region.
The battle of the Ia Drang had thwarted those
plans. Concern about the A Shau Valley had
come after an early and careful study of the
geography of that region. The rugged A Shau in
the far northwest of the country pointed like "a
spear," in Westmoreland's words, at the important cities of Quang Tri and Hue.

Westmoreland had flown north to inspect the
valley shortly after taking command in mid-1964.
What he saw was a strikingly beautiful landscape—jungles, lush mountains, sheer stone
cliffs, waterfalls, trout streams, bucolic coffee
plantations still run by Frenchmen and fasci-
nating small villages of Montagnards. However,
Westmoreland had not traveled there as a tourist,
but as a commander. And so the most vivid
impression he carried back to Saigon was of a
pleateau rising from the valley not far from the
DMZ and the Laotian border. Years ago the
French had had a small base there. The village
of Khe Sanh was nearby, and would lend its
name to the base eventually established by the
Americans.

"The critical importance of the little plateau
was immediately apparent," remembers Westmoreland. "Khe Sanh could serve as a patrol
base for blocking enemy infiltration from Laos
along Route 9; a base for . . . [long-range patrol]
operations in Laos; an airstrip for reconnaissance planes surveying the Ho Chi Minh Trail; a

During the "hill fights" in the A Shau
Valley in May 1967, a marine blasts
away with a recoilless rifle at North
Vietnamese troops on Hill 881 North.

This Brou Montagnard village called
Tum Plang was very close to the Khe
Sanh combat base.

(Top) Seabees work to lay the temporary runway planks at Khe Sanh. The strip easily accommodated the large C-130 transports. (Bottom) A member of a long-range patrol team radios his position while a comrade returns enemy fire. Such small units used Khe Sanh as a stepping-off point for multiday treks deep into Communist-controlled territory while monitoring movements along the Ho Chi Minh Trail.

western anchor for defense south of the DMZ; and an eventual jump-off point for ground operations to cut the Ho Chi Minh Trail."

But the move to seize the opportunities that the plateau presented would come later, after American units had arrived in numbers large enough for Westmoreland to feel confident about being able to reinforce quickly any allied units sent into the A Shau for operations. The enemy was very strong in the valley. In fact, during his 1964 inspection visit to the plateau, Westmoreland himself had had a close call. His aircraft had landed on the short strip the French had constructed there. Before taking off, his party was mortared.

In mid-1966 Americans under his orders came back to stay. A few Special Forces soldiers and a contingent of South Vietnamese soldiers and tribesmen transformed the plateau into an outpost of the "strongpoint obstacle system" that Westmoreland established about the time the McNamara Line was abandoned. From it the Special Forces went out on patrol, checking for enemy infiltration, being especially watchful of increased enemy activity. Khe Sanh base also became a launching point for long-range patrols

into Laos by units formally known as Studies and Observation Groups, or SOGs, an innocuous name suggestive of field trips devoted to the gathering of flora and fauna. But botany was not their interest; the Ho Chi Minh Trail was. They disappeared into Laos for weeks at a time, avoiding contact and spying out bombing targets. They fought only if forced to do so to survive. Word was that these superstealth soldiers were very good at surviving.

During the last half of 1966, the SOG units had begun observing a dramatic increase of traffic along the Ho Chi Minh Trail. And the Special Forces units operating out of Khe Sanh and other strongpoints of the system, such as Con Thien, began detecting a large North Vietnamese buildup south of the DMZ, including the A Shau. Westmoreland became convinced that the enemy intended Khe Sanh to be a major attack point, the Dien Bien Phu of the American involvement in Vietnam, after which they would press the attack down through the valley and on to the coast. Accordingly, in September Westmoreland ordered the Seabees to upgrade the landing strip on the Khe Sanh plateau to accommodate C-130 transports in all-weather conditions. They worked feverishly against time to get the job done—surprisingly without enemy interference; Westmoreland later surmised that the North Vietnamese thought they could eventually use it themselves if they overran Khe Sanh. Then, in coordination with General Walt, Westmoreland ordered the Special Forces contingent at Khe Sanh to build another base down Highway 9, even closer to Laos, near a place called Lang Vei. Marines replaced the Special Forces at Khe Sanh. To support them from a distance, Westmoreland deployed big 175-millimeter guns at Camp Carroll, more secure than Khe Sanh but still within the twenty-mile range of the shells.

Not much happened until April 1967, when a marine patrol ran into an ambush near one of the hills in the valley surrounding the plateau. Another patrol trying to come to the rescue suffered heavy casualties. Dozens of marines were killed during the brief firefight. Beginning with that engagement, Khe Sanh began gaining notoriety back in the United States. Many of the marines had died because their M-16 rifles jammed. Reports of the pitiful scene of nineteen-year-olds found dead slumped over their weapons,

"These rifles are getting a lot of guys killed"...

During the early years, of the war, hundreds of soldiers wrote home complaining about their M-16 rifle, the standard issue weapon of U.S. ground forces. "Our M-16s aren't worth much," one soldier wrote his parents. "If there's dust in them, they will jam." Another wrote a manufacturer of a cleaning compound: "During this fight and previous ones, I lost some of my best buddies. I personally checked their weapons. Close to 70 percent had a round stuck in the chamber, and take my word, it was not their fault." The brother of a soldier wrote the following to a member of the House Armed Services Committee: "He went on to tell me how, in battles there in Vietnam, the only things that were left by the enemy after they had stripped the dead of our side were the rifles, which they considered worthless." And Senator Gaylord Nelson received this protest: "I know of at least two marines who died within 10 feet of the enemy with jammed rifles. No telling how many have been wounded on that account and it is difficult to count the NVA who should be dead but live because the M-16 failed. Of course, the political ramifications of this border on national scandal . . . Yesterday we got in a big one . . . The day found one Marine beating an NVA with his helmet and a hunting knife because his rifle failed— this can't continue—32 of about 80 rifles failed."

By 1967 so many such letters had been written that Congress began investigating the matter. A committee headed by Representative Richard Ichord of Missouri conducted extensive hearings and eventually published a comprehensive six-hundred-page report, which concluded that "the failure on the part of officials with authority in the Army to correct the deficiencies of the [M-16] . . . borders on criminal negligence."

The original version of this controversial weapon was called the AR-15. Eugene Stoner of the Armalite Corporation was its designer. The army took the AR-15, modified it in several basic ways, and called the new model the M-16. All the changes were done against the advice of Stoner, and each one compromised the best characteristics of the original design.

Stoner based his design on the basis of two interesting findings. The first is that a small caliber bullet propelled at high speed is potentially more lethal than a larger caliber bullet because the small bullet has a greater tendency to become unstable and begin a tumbling motion when it hits its target, this causing much more damage than it would if it merely passed straight through the body of the victim; the result is a small entrance hole and a huge exit hole. Stoner specified a .22 caliber shell for use in the AR-15 instead of the .30 caliber ammunition with which the army had traditionally armed its soldiers.

The second finding that Stoner took into account in designing his AR-15 was the discovery by military historian S.L.A. Marshall that four-fifths of combat soldiers during the Second World War never fired their weapons during battle. Those who did usually carried a fully automatic weapon such as the Browning Automatic Rifle (BAR). The reason, it was discovered, was psychological. A soldier with a BAR felt that he was doing damage when he "hosed down" the area from which the enemy was firing; he had hope of killing the enemy even though he and his compatriots could see nothing. By contrast, soldiers carrying the semi-automatic M-1, which required a trigger pull for each bullet to be fired, experienced feelings of futility. Therefore, Stoner designed his AR-15 so that the soldier could put his weapon on automatic and fire about seven hundred rounds per minute. The rifle was remarkably reliable, even at this rapid rate of fire; it seldom jammed. And it weighed less than seven pounds loaded, about four pounds lighter than the M-1, which

with cleaning rods in the barrels, caused great consternation in Congress and around the country. The young soldiers had spent the last minutes of their lives frantically trying to dislodge jammed rounds. The problem was blamed on improper weapon-cleaning habits; the marines had been issued the M-16s only recently, to replace the more durable but heavier M-14, and hadn't been sufficiently instructed in their care and cleaning. Later investigation also pointed to a problem with the powder in the shells. McNamara ordered all M-16 ammunition in Vietnam to be replaced as quickly as possible with rounds containing the new powder.

Following this tragic fight, the marines based at Khe Sanh stormed three of the hills in which North Vietnamese soldiers were entrenched. The struggles for the heights became known as the hill fights and featured some of the most fierce, close-quarters fighting of the war—marines scaling the hills in the face of machine-gun fire, gradually knocking out North Vietnamese gun emplacements, sometimes only after hand-to-hand combat. One hundred and sixty marines were killed and another seven hundred were wounded. Apparently one North Vietnamese

(Above) Exhausted soldiers catch some sleep in a trench during the siege of Con Thien in 1967. (Opposite) Two marines string barbed wire around their base at Khe Sanh. Behind them is the coiled, razor-sharp concertina wire.

regiment was thwarted in attempts to bring artillery in and attack the Khe Sanh combat base. Another of the bases on the strongpoint defense line was brought to siege, however: Con Thien was surrounded by attacking enemy units. The attacks ended only after a massive aerial bombing drove the enemy away. Air Force General William Momyer and his staff developed a precisely coordinated bombing campaign known as SLAM that gave Westmoreland great confidence in his belief that a well-fortified American position could survive almost any assault, even if the defenders were greatly outnumbered. That confidence would affect his thinking in a profound way later in 1967, when he began receiving unmistakable signs of another massive buildup in the north—much bigger than the one the year before—this time the buildup prior to the Communist offensive of Tet 1968.

At about 8:30 on the evening of January 2, 1968, an American marine was walking the perimeter defenses of the main Khe Sanh base on the plateau with his sentry dog. Suddenly the dog stiffened, alerting his handler to movement outside the wire. Immediately a squad led by Second Lieutenant Niles Buffington was sent to investigate. Several minutes later they spotted six men, one of tall stature, dressed in marine green uniforms, standing on the slope of the plateau, surveying from that vantage point the

meant that it went a long way toward solving one of the basic problems of combat—running out of ammunition. The combination of the lighter weapon and the lighter .22 caliber bullets allowed the average soldier to carry more than three times as many rounds as he could with .30 caliber ammunition.

In the late fifties, about the time Stoner perfected the AR-15, the army began replacing the old standard-issue M-1 with a new rifle called the M-14. Like Stoner's rifle, the M-14 was capable of firing as a fully automatic weapon, but in keeping with army tradition, it fired .30 caliber bullets. The result was a weapon that was virtually impossible to control when fired at a rapid rate. A soldier firing from the prone position usually ended up with a bloody nose because he couldn't keep the butt of the gun against his shoulder. So much more powder is required to propel the heavier .30 caliber bullet through the air that the M-14 had an extremely powerful kick even if only a single shot was fired. Stoner's AR-15 presented no such problem because of its smaller caliber .22 bullets.

But the army resisted all attempts to replace the M-14 with the more efficient AR-15. There was institutional bias against it. Ignoring the scientific principal upon which the gun was designed, army ordnance corps officers deemed Stoner's weapon a popgun because of its small caliber. They also had a concept of fighting conditions fundamentally different from what had been revealed by S.L.A. Marshall's research. In their view of warfare, marksmen dueled one another from three hundred yards. And indeed, in a battlefield environment like that, the larger caliber weapon *was* the better of the two because its bullets followed a stable flight for a longer distance.

During the early sixties, both weapons and both theories were put to the test. The clear winner was Stoner's AR-15. The first to order it was the air force. General Curtis LeMay, a gun enthusiast, tried it out personally and immediately had it purchased for airmen guarding bases. Next to use it were Green Berets, who were firing it in combat conditions while working as advisers with South Vietnamese troops. The AR-15 was clearly so much better than the M-14 that they were buying it on the black market with their own money—paying about $600 for it, though it retailed to the military for about $100. Finally, in 1963, President Kennedy and Robert McNamara intervened in behalf of the Green Berets, ordering the army to buy the weapon of choice for them.

With all the glowing reports coming back from Vietnam about the AR-15, Secretary of the Army Cyrus Vance ordered an investigation to determine how the army had managed to ignore such a superior weapon. His findings, according to James Fallows, in his book *National Defense,* showed that tests by the ordnance corps comparing the AR-15 and the M-14 were "blatantly rigged" in favor of the latter.

Almost immediately McNamara ordered the army to begin a careful study of the AR-15—the objective being official confirmation of its superiority so that it could begin replacing the M-14. At the same time, McNamara made the army the Defense Department's central purchasing agent for infantry weapons. This meant that the army would dictate what airmen and marines carried too. It was at this point that the army began modifying Stoner's remarkable weapon, "the most reliable, and the most lethal infantry rifle ever invented," says Fallows. The result was the M-16. Again, institutional bias came into play. And with each modification, the army compromised the effectiveness of the original.

The most significant modifications concerned the type of powder that was used in the .22 cartridges and an increase in the number of turns in the barrel. The army decided it wanted the powder to conform to that used in almost all its other weapons, one supplied almost exclusively by Olin-Mathieson

American positions in the valley. They were talking quietly, occasionally referring to maps.

Buffington was startled. Americans could go down to the village of Khe Sanh to sample the soup at a little restaurant that had opened up since their deployment to Khe Sanh—they called it Howard Johnson's—or to do business with the prostitutes who had moved into the village about the same time as the little restaurant. But nobody stayed out past nightfall. Buffington shouted a challenge, but got no reply. When one of the six appeared to reach for a grenade on his belt, the marines opened fire. Five of the intruders fell to the ground dead; the sixth, though wounded, got away in the darkness. All five killed were North Vietnamese officers. One of them was a regimental commander. Lying beside him were his operations and communications officers.

Why they believed they could be so bold is hard to imagine. Obviously they had underestimated the young Americans, which probably was easy for the North Vietnamese to do. An army of soldiers whose Beatle music blared from their camps all hours of the day, who sometimes carried Frisbees and fishing rods on their packs, and whose trash and garbage was filling up assorted ravines in the coffee plantation of Felix Poilane, must have been incomprehensible to them. But Westmoreland did not similarly underestimate the North Vietnamese. Notified almost immediately after the incident, Westmoreland understood the significance of a regimental commander's presence; it could only mean that his unit of six thousand must also be in the vicinity. Westmoreland also knew that for such a high-ranking officer to take such a huge risk must mean that Giap had big plans for Khe Sanh. The American commander was convinced that the long-awaited attempted replay of Dien Bien Phu by Giap (who had a well-known fixation for associating his military moves with Vietnamese history) was about to begin. And Westmoreland was pleased to invite him to try. For almost three years his generals and soldiers had been chasing Communist units through swamps, jungles and mountains, the elusive enemy almost always getting away. Now, unbelievably, the Communists were about to come to them.

Westmoreland immediately ordered the American intelligence gathering system to focus on Khe Sanh. Specially trained long-range patrols were airlifted into the area to slip through enemy lines; photo reconnaissance analysts began microscopic examination of yards and yards of film. And Momyer began planning an even bigger SLAM bombing campaign than the Con Thien attackers had endured. The code name given it was apt: Niagara.

Within days Giap's big plans for Khe Sanh became clear. Two regiments of the North Vietnamese 325C Division had crossed into South Vietnam from Laos about twenty-five miles northwest of the base. Two regiments of the North Vietnamese 320th Division had come down into South Vietnam through the DMZ, taking up positions twenty miles to the northeast. Sensor devices picked up radio communication from an enemy front headquarters located just inside Laos, coordinating the movements of the 325C and a third division, the 304th. Supporting these units would be two artillery regiments, perhaps also armor. In short, at least twenty thousand North Vietnamese troops were closing in on Khe Sanh, perhaps as many as forty thousand. Photo analysts saw further indication of Dien Bien Phu–type preparations in

Corporation. Unfortunately, the Olin-Mathieson powder was much dirtier; it left a heavy residue in the chamber. The powder which Stoner had selected did not. As for the number of turns, the change made the bullet more stable in flight by making it spin faster as it left the barrel. This, of course, compromised the lethality of the original, but was justified on the grounds that it was needed to make the weapon more useful in arctic warfare! Since the U.S. had never fought a war in the arctic and was, in fact, well on its way to fighting one in steaming jungles, one would have hoped—in vain—that more practical considerations would prevail.

Cumulatively, the changes affected the whole "resonant mechanism" of the gun—how all the parts work together. The result was that it fired about two hundred rounds-per-minute faster than the original, which was not desirable, since the more rapid fire-rate, coupled with the dirty powder, caused the rifle to jam frequently.

The result was a weapon so unreliable that soldiers now struggled to keep their M-14s, the same gun that some of them had tried to replace with black market purchases of Stoner's rifle. Still, the army's ordnance corps labored under the delusion that they were putting into U.S. soldiers' hands an uncompromised Stoner weapon. Instruction leaflets issued with the M-16 read: "This rifle will fire longer without cleaning or oiling than any other known rifle," and "an occassional cleaning will keep the weapon functioning indefinitely." It was only after the public outcry that the problems were minimized. A cleaner powder was ordered for M-16 cartridges (but not what Stoner had originally specified), and after the proper cleaning equipment and instructions were universally supplied, weapon maintenance resumed being the ritual it had always been in the old army.

A GI carefully scans the horizon around Khe Sanh for enemy activity. The strategy was to draw the enemy into battle.

the new roads that had been hacked out of the jungle. One twisted down through the rugged Laotian terrain to a junction with a trail inside South Vietnam only fifteen mile away. Another crossed the border only eight miles from the American combat base.

The American command began pouring supplies into Khe Sanh. One C-130 transport after another disgorged loads of ammunition, food and other supplies. Generals flew in and out. And the press came too—reporters, photographers and television crews. Khe Sanh became a major, worldwide news story before anything happened. Westmoreland started receiving letters from around the globe, most of them from Americans who did not think the marines could hold and therefore urged him to evacuate the base. About the only encouraging letters came from French officers who had fought at Dien Bien Phu; they urged him to stay.

By mid January about six thousand American soldiers were dug into positions around Khe Sanh. They stood ready to defend the main base on the plateau and four of the hills in the valley (named for their height): Hills 558 and 950, the "latter commanding the river valley leading into Khe Sanh from the northwest," and Hills 861 and 881 South. Each position had 105- and 155-millimeter howitzers and 4.2-inch mortars.

At 5:30 on the morning of January 20, Captain Bill Dabney and his entire company of 185 men, called India Company, stepped off the summit of Hill 881 South that was their assignment to hold. Their destination was Hill 881 North, a

(Top) Khe Sanh's air traffic control center, in the background, was put out of action by artillery fire during the siege. The truck in the revetment was used to fight fires. (Bottom) Marines race to board a C-123 on the Khe Sanh strip. Those whose tour of duty ended during the siege were flown out.

mile away, that had been left undefended. Daily, round the clock, marine patrols had been walking up and down ravines and through thickets, elephant grass and jungle, looking for Charlie (a name derivative of the phonetic alphabet for the letters VC, Victor-Charles; thus Charlie), hoping to deprive the enemy of the advantage of surprise that generally accrues to the attacking force. On two recent successive days, marines had come under fire while on Hill 881 North. Two members of a tiny reconnaissance team had been shot to death. The next day a soldier walking point (ahead of his platoon) had exchanged volleys with an enemy soldier before falling into thick, tall elephant grass, unhurt but stunned. He had seen the North Vietnamese for only an instant. But as he lay there in the grass, his senses swirling, he heard whispers and men running over sticks and rocks.

Dabney, a Virginia Military Institute graduate and the son-in-law of Lieutenant General Lewis "Chesty" Puller (an almost legendary marine of Second World War days), was so certain that he and his men would find the enemy this day that he had requested—and been granted—a reconnaissance in force, involving all three platoons of his company. Colonel David Lownds, the field officer in charge of the overall defenses of Khe Sanh, helicoptered another two hundred men in to strengthen Hill 881 South while Dabney and his men were gone.

Dabney had split his force into two groups as they began ascending 881 North on almost parallel ridges—one platoon on one, two on the other. They were careful, but made no effort at concealment. There was no need. The enemy knew that the marines were in the valley. This day it was decided to have artillery fire precede their advance up the hill. The technique was called reconnaissance by fire. Realistically, the purpose of such fire was not to wipe out unseen enemy positions, but rather to frighten enemy soldiers into firing prematurely. But the North Vietnamese soldiers who had slipped into the valley and fortified positions on 881 North were not green soldiers who could be easily frightened. Veterans of the hill fights the year before, they would not fire prematurely.

They waited to open up until the platoon of Second Lieutenant Tom Brindley had come into close range. Then they opened up with all they had—automatic rifles, machine guns and rocket grenades. The point man fell dead immediately.

Colonel David Lownds was commander of the Khe Sanh combat base.

Gunnery Sergeant R. L. DeArmond fought on Hill 881 South.

(Top) One of Captain Bill Dabney's men fires his M-60 machine gun from his position on Hill 881 South. The writing on his helmet reads, "We are no children of America. We are head-hunters." (Bottom) A bunker on Hill 881 South.

Some were wounded. All who could scrambled for shallow ravines and began returning fire.

From the parallel ridge, Dabney ordered Second Lieutenant Harry Fromme's platoon to race across a broad ravine and outflank the enemy's positions. He also ordered Brindley to start calling in coordinates for artillery fire. Fromme's unit had just begun their climb from the bottom of the ravine when a machine gun opened up on them, its shells cutting through the grass and slamming into the lower bodies of twenty of his men, shattering bones and ripping away flesh.

The heretofore peaceful landscape was bedlam. Ninety-five-pound howitzer shells were now screaming in from the base, exploding big chunks of rock, soil and trees into the air, the concussion drowning out the screams and shouts of soldiers on both sides and even the *burrrr* of automatic rifles and the deep coughs of machine guns.

Already a helicopter was coming in to take out the wounded. These teenage Frisbee soldiers were serious about such business. Without being told, American soldiers assumed virtually any risk to retrieve their wounded. A heavy machine gun from another, higher ridge line opened up on the craft as it came in. Flames began streaming from its engine, the pilot lost control, and the helicopter careened sideways over the heads of Brindley's men before slamming to the ground. The crew chief managed to jump from the doomed

Smoke from an airstrike rises from North Vietnamese rocket and mortar positions on Hill 881 North. In the foreground is a bunker on 881 South.

craft, landing hard next to Brindley, breaking his leg. But other rescue helicopters followed successfully.

While the rescue work proceeded, Brindley led an attack to the top of the hill, his men racing ahead a few feet at a time, firing and tossing grenades. They succeeded in pushing a numerically superior force off the top of 881 North, but not without cost: Brindley himself was killed at the summit; others were killed and wounded along the way.

Feverishly the marines dug in, awaiting a counterattack. Dabney was now controlling artillery fire and jet fighter-bombers screeching down to drop their payloads—napalm and explosives. The counterattack never came. The two sides fought one another from a distance. At 5:30 Dabney ordered the men to return to their base on 881 South before nightfall. During the day seven of his men had been killed and thirty-five wounded. Enemy casualties on 881 North were at least that high, and American aircraft and artillery had obviously inflicted many more casualties on surrounding enemy positions, as the absence of a counterattack indicated.

As it turned out, this opening engagement was one of the few times during the next seventy-seven days that opposing soldiers slugged it out within such close quarters. Just as artillery and aircraft had thwarted a counterattack on 881 North, they would prevent the thousands of enemy troops from marshaling for a large sustained attack on any of the American strongpoints in the valley.

Inside his command post at the main Khe Sanh position on the plateau, Colonel Lownds had anxiously monitored India Company's struggle. Adding to his concern was his belief that the enemy would that day launch its first assault on the defended positions. His men were on high alert. About three thousand were on the plateau; another thousand guarded a rock quarry a mile away; a thousand were on top of Hill 558; two hundred replacements for Dabney's company were on Hill 881 South; a company held Hill 861, a platoon held Hill 950. They all stared intently through the concertina wire surrounding their positions, looking for any movement, distracted occasionally by the jets and artillery supporting Dabney's men on 881 North.

An Ontos: the machine could blast attacking units with thousands of darts.

Suddenly a small white flag popped up from the underbrush below the main plateau near the landing strip. A North Vietnamese in a camouflage uniform holding an AK-47 rifle stood up and slowly walked up the slope. Dabney's fight was by then four hours old and the Americans were understandably edgy. It was all they could do to hold their fire. Two Ontos, designed to thwart human-wave assaults, were driven into position and pointed at the lone soldier. Each machine contained tens of thousands of steel darts.

Fortunately, no one fired at the enemy soldier, a lieutenant who wanted to desert and pass along valuable information. He had turned against his side, he said, because someone less qualified than he had been promoted to a position he wanted. He informed the Americans that the first attacks would begin at half-past midnight that very night, with assaults on Hills 881 South and 861. He also detailed the general battle plan as he knew it—which was to overwhelm U.S. defenses at Khe Sanh and roll to the southeast through the A Shau, taking Quang Tri along the way, finally attacking Hue as part of the overall Tet offensive. Because this was the very plan that Westmoreland had anticipated, the lieutenant was deemed credible.

At precisely half-past midnight North Vietnamese attacked marine defenses on 861. Commando-type soldiers led the assault, pushing bangalore charges—long pole-like explosive units—up under the perimeter wire among the claymore mines and trip-flares. The marines opened up from their interlocking machine-gun positions, but the North Vietnamese broke through to the helicopter landing area. The Americans retreated from that sector to a higher point on the hill. Support fire came in from the main base while the marines on Hill 861 mortared their former positions and fired away with rifles and machine guns.

On Hill 881 South, only a thousand yards away, Dabney and his men, exhausted from the firefight they had been through only hours earlier, were nonetheless alert in anticipation of an attack which, as it turned out, never came. Perhaps their foray onto Hill 881 North had thwarted enemy plans. Meanwhile their comrades on 861 launched a 5:00 A.M. counterattack against the enemy. Fighting just feet from one another, both sides lobbed grenades back and forth. By 5:15 the Americans had pushed the enemy off the hill, and the sound of soldiers singing the marine hymn as they loaded their mortars could be heard above the noise of battle. American casualties were surprisingly light. Twelve North Vietnamese were killed in a final counterassault, their bodies left on the hilltop.

Once the siege began, forward spotters constantly surveyed the terrain for muzzle flashes from enemy artillery and mortar units.

(Top) A photographer caught on film one of the blasts caused by the direct hit on the ammunition dump. (Bottom) Removing refuse—including great quantities of discarded artillery casings—became a problem during the siege.

With the night's only attack repelled and daylight fast approaching, there seemed reason to relax. But at 5:30 North Vietnamese from positions on 881 North (where India Company had fought the day before), opened up an intense rocket attack on the main plateau base, resulting in a massive explosion when the ammunition dump sustained a direct hit. The accompanying shock wave flattened tents, turned over helicopters and collapsed the walls of the post office and the small PX. Petroleum and oil tanks were set ablaze. Unexploded hot shells rained down on the trenches of Bravo Company, only fifty yards from the inferno. They could not evacuate the general area because the North Vietnamese deserter had warned that a regiment of the 304th would attack that point. The explosions and fire continued for hours. Sandbags that the soldiers had soaked in oil to help repel rats now smoldered. Some trenches were literally brimming with unexploded shells dislodged from the ammo stacks. One explosion spewed a cache of steel darts, some of which stuck in the arms, faces and flak jackets of Bravo's command group. By nightfall five of these six junior officers were evacuated for "extreme combat fatigue."

An hour after the initial rocket barrage, North Vietnamese attacked the village of Khe Sanh itself, which was lightly defended by South Vietnamese and a few Americans. But the attack was repulsed with the help of artillery support fire from the main base, whose gun crews braved not only their own exploding ammunition dump but also the enemy's 122-millimeter rockets and long-range 130- and 152-millimeter artillery shells coming in from firing positions in Laos. Finding and firing on enemy positions was hampered by a morning fog that blanketed the area. But Major Roger Campbell, a seasoned artillery officer, ran from one shell hole to another, gauging the enemy's position by studying hole depth and shrapnel splash, and ordering counterfire on the basis of those rough findings.

The action continued apace all day, though massive assaults never came. In the afternoon, enemy forces renewed their attack on the village. American supporting fire had to be directed on new enemy positions in the village itself. A pagoda caved in; Howard Johnson's was blown away. Combatants shot at one another on opposite sides of the schoolyard where children had played the day before. Close air support and artillery shells fused to explode in the air a few feet above the North Vietnamese soldiers allowed the village's defenders once again to repel the assault and regain lost ground. But Lownds decided to abandon the village defense line. Helicopters evacuated the Americans while the other soldiers and many villagers began fleeing up the road to seek refuge on the plateau.

The allies had prevailed in all the action of January 21, but because of the direct hit on the ammo dump, the Americans had sustained a very serious blow. By one account, ninety-eight percent of the ammo reserve had been destroyed. Because of anti-aircraft fire and damage to the landing strip, only six C-130s had gotten in that day. Deliveries of one hundred and sixty tons per day were necessary to maintain levels; only

A 105mm howitzer crew at Khe Sanh slams another shell at the enemy. Unlike the French at Dien Bien Phu, the marines at Khe Sanh had numerically superior firepower throughout the siege.

A North Vietnamese mortar round hits in front of a C-123 bringing in supplies and fresh troops. Taxiing at Khe Sanh was more dangerous than flying into the combat base. Enemy gunners had bracketed the runway.

Memorial ceremony for troops of the
3rd Battalion, 26th Marines killed in
action.

The U.S. commitment in Vietnam...

- Americans who served   3,300,000
- Americans killed   57,605
- Americans wounded   303,700
- Americans taken prisoner   766
  - Returned   651
  - Died in captivity   114
  - Still in captivity   1

(Department of Defense officials do not
believe that any American POWs are
still living in Southeast Asia; however,
so as not to foreclose officially the possibility, one POW is listed in the current status report.)

- Americans declared missing
  (1965-1975):
  - Returned   121
  - Later declared dead   4,872
  - Still missing (9/80)   18

twenty-four tons had been delivered. Complicating problems and adding to the confusion were
the village refugees. By nightfall a thousand of
them huddled nervously just outside the plateau
defenses. Lownds kept them outside, fearful of a
Trojan horse situation. During the coming days
they and other refugees were escorted in and
evacuated to Danang by aircraft. According to
Robert Pisor, the author of *The End of the Line*,
an account of the Khe Sanh battle, three thousand tried to make the trek through enemy lines
up Highway 9 to the plateau base; the U.S.
count of those flown out was only 1,432.
Presumably, those not accounted for were casualties of war.

The ammo dump blast caused shock waves in
Washington too. The dramatic incident, a temporary setback, made the state of affairs in the
valley seem even more precarious than it was.
News of the evacuation further startled administration leaders, though U.S. forces had not
committed to holding the village; being on the
valley floor, it was untenable. Even before these
events, Johnson had been almost totally preoccupied with Vietnam and the offensive forecast for
the time of Tet. Back in December, during a
visit with Pope Paul VI, he had voiced worries
about "Kamikaze attacks." Now, because of the
sobering news, he couldn't get enough information about the goings-on at Khe Sanh. If this talk
about another Dien Bien Phu was true, he knew
the whole war and his presidency were on the
line, all because Westmoreland wanted to make
a fight over those remote hilltops.

Johnson demanded photographs, figures of
the number of planes that had landed at Khe
Sanh, tonnage figures, bombing sorties, sightings—the works. He even had a sand model of
the Khe Sanh area constructed in the White
House situation room, just like the one that Westmoreland was having constructed in a hangar
at Tan Son Nhut. Books on Dien Bien Phu
became popular reading among the president's
staff; copies of Bernard Fall's *Hell in a Very
Small Place* and Jules Roy's *The Battle of
Dienbienphu* were in short supply in Washington.
Looking for reassurance, Johnson eventually
asked Maxwell Taylor to visit CIA headquarters to assess the situation. The general came
back concerned. He noted striking similarities
between the marines' predicament and the demise of the French.

Events elsewhere did little to ease the president's tension. On January 23 North Koreans captured the U.S.S. *Pueblo,* the intelligence-gathering ship, and a B-52 armed with nuclear weapons crashed in Greenland. Both were major international incidents. In Korea, allied troops went on full alert, fearful of an invasion replay of June 1950, and the Korean government wanted their troops in South Vietnam sent home immediately. Khe Sanh would be directly affected because Korean units were key to the defense of Danang Air Base, from which support missions for the marines were being flown. Fortunately, the Korean crisis cooled down and the recall request was rescinded.

Perhaps these few days in late January had as much impact on Johnson's subsequent decision not to seek reelection as any other. The generally bad news created a feeling of impending doom. He was becoming an insomniac, rolling around in his bed at night with ghastly visions, one after another, racing through his mind. Describing one fitful night, Johnson later recalled, "I couldn't stand it anymore. I knew that one of my boys must have been killed. . . . I jumped out of bed, put on my robe, took my flashlight, and went into the Situation Room."

He spent many hours there staring at the sand molds. Over and over he would ask the Joint Chiefs whether they thought Khe Sanh could hold. He asked each for an independent written appraisal. Before the end of January he had a letter signed by all of them expressing confidence in Westmoreland's plan. "I don't want any damn Dinbinfoos," he told them repeatedly.

Westmoreland was also upset by events of January 21. Though the massive explosion did not shake his confidence, it reinforced his feeling that the marines were being too casual about the whole operation, that they were underestimating the enemy. This observation on his part was, of course, derivative of the long-standing dispute over tactics—all along he had thought that the marines' small-unit proposals betrayed a cocky, dangerous overconfidence.

His first move was to take control of their air arm. He wanted marine aircraft more closely coordinated in the overall air effort at Khe Sanh. Westmoreland personally began picking the bombing targets around Khe Sanh. Creighton Abrams and Lieutenant General William Rosson,

Johnson with Pope Paul VI in December 1967 during the president's round-the-world trip.

The capture of the U.S.S. *Pueblo* by North Koreans added to LBJ's worries during Tet.

Captain Lloyd Bucher of the *Pueblo*

A CH-53 brings in a 105mm howitzer to the LZ atop Hill 881 South.

A marine races for cover on the helicopter landing zone after being caught out in the open during a Communist rocket attack.

two of the army's best tacticians, were put to work picking likely enemy marshaling and approach points and incorporating into their strategy information given by the North Vietnamese deserter.

The bombs began to fall at a rate never seen before. Though no one was aware of it at the time, it was the beginning of the end of enemy plans to restage Dien Bien Phu. Later, Westmoreland observed, "Khe Sanh will stand in history, I am convinced, as a classic example of how to defeat a numerically superior besieging force by coordinated application of firepower."

The onslaught that followed is difficult to visualize. Numbers alone cannot adequately convey the destructive force of all the bombs that were dropped, though the numbers themselves are awesome. Six B-52s flew over every three hours, around the clock, day after day, dropping a total of seventy-five thousand tons of bombs in the course of 2,602 sorties. The smaller fighter-bombers were also in action. They averaged three hundred sorties per day.

Missions were devised to meet every exigency. When trenchwork was discovered approaching the plateau base camp, the trenches were drenched with fuel jelly and then set afire with phosphorus bombs. When a cave in Laos that was being used as a major command center was discovered—radio signals coming from sophisticated communications equipment made Westmoreland believe it was the command post for the Khe Sanh battle and perhaps for all I Corps—thirty-six B-52s went after it on a single raid. Another nine B-52s bombed the target later in the day after dark. The signals stopped. When enemy harassment fire and trenchwork on the slope of the American-defended high points became a concern, the B-52s started bombing as close as four hundred yards (their previous limit having been two miles). Of the close-in missions, one air force officer observed, "One hiccup, and we would have decimated the base."

Marine Major General Rathvon Tompkins, commander of the 3rd Marine Division, was awestruck by the B-52s, which came in so high they could be neither seen nor heard. "Then suddenly a long strip of earth just erupts, dirt and debris flying five hundred feet into the air," he remembered. "Then a few seconds later another nearby strip erupts the same way. One day I saw eight or ten North Vietnamese staggering out of the dirt of the first eruption,

struggling for their lives, only to be engulfed by the second eruption. It was as if a little part of the world blew up for no apparent reason." Needless to say, such raids caused great psychological strain among enemy troops.

Life was extremely difficult and dangerous for the marines during the siege. Though the bombing and their own artillery fire cut down on the threat of ground attacks and incoming fire, almost every day marines would still be caught in the open by enemy rockets (usually coming in from 881 North) or by artillery fire. Sometimes these shells scored direct hits, as when a rocket came through the front door of the Signal Corps bunker, instantly killing the four soldiers inside. Five times enemy fire destroyed helicopters trying to resupply Hill 881 South. The North Vietnamese had the tiny pad bracketed. Once when a chopper was offloading there, enemy gunners scored a direct hit, killing five marines and wounding fifteen. After that the helicopters usually did not land, but instead came in with their loads dangling from slings. But two-man unloading crews on the ground still had to run out into the open to guide them in and unhook the load. Dabney went through four teams in February, most injured or killed by sniper fire. "We had trouble with psychological breakdowns," admits Dabney. Some marines were known to have painted their toes with peanut butter before sleep in hopes of being bitten by a rat from

(Top) The concentrated power of the B-52 strikes around Khe Sanh, such as this one in support of army troops at Ben Het, awed even seasoned marine officers. (Bottom) A patrol walks past the remnants of a truck destroyed near Khe Sanh by B-52s.

the swarm attracted to the hilltops by the smells; a bite meant medical evacuation.

The smells and filth were major debilitating factors, too. The sleeping bunkers were dank, fetid pits reeking of body odor and urine. Outside, smoke from numerous sources—from outgoing and incoming shellfire, from napalm and B-52 bomb loads, from generator exhausts, from burning garbage, from the burning mixture of diesel fuel and human excrement—was inhaled constantly, leaving a bad-tasting film in the back of the mouth.

Morale seems to have remained generally high throughout the ordeal, however. On Hill 881 South, Dabney's men conducted a flag-raising ceremony each morning, using a radio aerial for a flagpole. While Second Lieutenant Owen Matthews blurted out a rough rendition of "To the Colors," the North Vietnamese always tried to break up the ceremony with incoming fire. But the marines were always prepared, and they routinely gave enemy gunners the finger while waving a pair of red underpants back and forth on the end of a stick—the traditional symbol on the rifle range for a miss.

Even the life-and-death duels with snipers

(Top) The U.S. flag flutters atop Dabney's command post on Hill 881 South. When reporters carried the story of his unit's flag-raising ceremonies, hundreds of Americans mailed him more flags.
(Bottom) A soldier walks through one of the many covered trenches at Khe Sanh.

were sometimes marked with humor of a kind. One North Vietnamese soldier who had fired more than thirty shots without a hit was left alone—better to keep a bad marksman alive than have him replaced by a better shot. The marines ignored him and he never hit anyone, even in the open.

Another North Vietnamese gunner became a pet of sorts. He had lugged a 50-caliber machine gun up near a hill strongpoint, where he posed a serious problem. The marines couldn't kill him—he had a sort of spider hole in which to hide—so fighter-bombers were ordered in. A sheet of napalm boiled right on top of him, burning off vegetation and blackening the earth. Unbelievably, the North Vietnamese popped up and fired one shot after the fire subsided. From that point on, the marines rooted for him. Anyone who survived all that deserved to live, they thought. The Americans nicknamed him Luke the Gook.

After the action on the twenty-first, the Tet holiday came and went without a major attack at Khe Sanh. In fact, after the twenty-first, the only serious enemy ground action was directed at lightly defended positions—Hill 861 Alpha, a new position established between 861 and 881 South after the siege started, and Hill 64, a bump in the terrain near the quarry.

Hill 861 Alpha was attacked during the early hours of February 5, following an intense barrage that killed seven marines. The North Vietnamese advanced behind exploding rocket grenades; after a couple of hours of fighting, they held about a quarter of the hilltop. To slow the enemy advance, Captain Earle Breeding ordered his two hundred men to don their gas masks. Tear gas cannisters were then lobbed into the enemy positions.

Breeding's unit received fire support from every strongpoint around Khe Sanh, from the big 175-millimeter guns at Camp Carroll, and from fighter-bombers. From Hill 881 South alone, India Company's three heavy mortar crews fired eleven hundred rounds. When the overheated mortars began glowing in the dark, the crewmen cooled them down with water initially, then with fruit juice, and finally with urine.

About daylight, Breeding ordered a counterattack. It began with grenades and ended with hand-to-hand fights with knives and fists. "It was like a World War II movie," says Breeding. "We walked all over them."

The marines on Hill 64 were not so lucky

During a visit to the base, Lieutenant General Robert Cushman, the senior marine officer in Vietnam at the time of Khe Sanh, talks with his men assigned there.

These huge 175mm guns at Camp Carroll fired on enemy positions around Khe Sanh from miles away.

A patrol carrying one of its wounded returns to Khe Sanh. Such units ventured forth to find troublesome enemy mortar crews and to get a closer look at North Vietnamese movements.

several nights later. Only fifty-two of them held the hill. Following a barrage of hundreds of shells, North Vietnamese overran the position. By the time a relief force arrived, twenty-one marines lay dead, twenty-six were wounded and four were missing in action. Only one man was uninjured. One marine in shock, catatonic with his eyes locked open but entirely conscious, later remembered an enemy soldier going through his things and walking off with a Christmas photo of his family as a souvenir. One hundred and fifty of the enemy were reported as killed in this engagement.

There were other incidents that snuffed out the lives of large numbers of marines. On February 25, twenty-nine marines set out from the main base to find a mortar unit whose fire was causing trouble. About eight hundred yards out, they spotted three unarmed North Vietnamese soldiers walking along a road in Felix Poilane's coffee plantation. Second Lieutenant Don Jacques led a charge to capture them. The marines ran directly into a long covered enemy bunker. Machine guns protruding from the slits opened fire. The first to fall was a black marine with the self-proclaimed nickname "Motown Doc" writ-

ten on his helmet. A bullet went through his left eye and exited out the side of his head. A medic diagnosed him as dead—until Motown Doc asked for his rifle.

The squad was trapped. When a relief force was blocked from reaching them, Lownds refused to commit more troops to the fight, fearful of merely adding to the casualty list in a futile attempt to save the unit. At least half were already dead by the time he made his decision. Those still alive were ordered to save themselves after aircraft and artillery were brought in all around them. Only three survived. A full-blooded Sioux Indian, Corporal Roland Ball, came out carrying the body of Jacques. And three hours after it all began, Motown Doc crawled out of the underbrush and back to safety. The bodies of twenty-five marines lay sprawled where they fell for more than a month until the siege was broken.

Air crashes brought death even more suddenly. On March 6 a C-123 cargo plane with forty-three marine replacements, four crew members and two newsmen crashed four miles from Khe Sanh, one engine shot out during approach, the other suffering mechanical failure. All on board were

The body of a marine helicopter pilot is removed from a CH-53. While landing at the base, the craft was hit by a mortar round.

killed. That same week a large chopper coming in suddenly plummeted to the earth, apparently shot down. Another twenty-two died in that incident.

After studying aerial reconnaissance photos, Westmoreland decided on March 6 that the enemy was moving its main force units away from Khe Sanh. On March 9 he informed President Johnson that enemy strength had dropped to "between 6,000 and 8,000 men." The next day the North Vietnamese stopped repairing their trench system. On April 1 the American command ended Operation Scotland, which is what the defense of Khe Sanh was called; the base was kept open for the time being, however. On April 8, after light action, elements of the 1st Air Cavalry Division, which on the first had begun opening up Highway 9 from the east, linked up with marines on patrol from Khe Sanh. The operation was called Pegasus. On April 9, for the first time in forty-five days, no enemy shells fell on American positions around Khe Sanh. Westmoreland had been correct; Khe Sanh would not be another Dien Bien Phu. The two battles were alike only in the physical conditions in which they were fought—bad weather (though not monsoon rains at Khe Sanh) and a remote valley surrounded by mountains. The analogy ended at that point.

How many North Vietnamese soliders were killed during the battle of Khe Sanh is uncertain. Laotian refugees, who trekked east into South Vietnam via Highway 9 and eventually up to the gate of the plateau base during the battle, reported seeing bodies of Communist troops stacked like cords of wood along the road in places, according to Westmoreland. His staff estimated that between ten thousand and fifteen thousand North Vietnamese died at Khe Sanh. The official count for Americans killed during Operation Scotland is two hundred and five, which does not include the forty-three marines killed on the C-123 crash.

"Soon after Tet, the [question of the] price America was willing to pay moved to the top of the presidential agenda," as Marvin Kalb and Elie Abel note in their book *Roots of Involvement*. And because of Khe Sanh especially, the American public now had a clearer vision of the nature of the sacrifices. What they saw, they did not like. This was like a turn-of-the-century boxing

(Top) An M-48 tank leads troops of the First Marine Regiment along Highway 9 during Operation Pegasus, which re-established ground contact with Khe Sanh. (Bottom) General Wheeler confers with the president about post-Tet strategy.

match—the kind without a fixed number of rounds; the kind that is finally won when one bloodied, mangled, exhausted contestant drags himself to the center of the ring, still game for another round, and his opponent does not—a pure fight of attrition. The public had not seen the war in these terms before. But Khe Sanh had given them a "microcosm" of the war itself, as Walter Cronkite said.

But while Khe Sanh and Tet may have persuaded the American public the U.S. should leave Vietnam, they momentarily strengthened Lyndon Johnson's resolve. His understandable, reflexive reaction was to support the troops there by sending them reinforcements. During an early February meeting with Rusk, McNamara, Wheeler, Rostow and Clark Clifford (soon to be his secretary of defense), he instructed Wheeler to ask Westmoreland what reinforcements he needed. Clifford was struck by the president's attitude: "It was to find out what Westy needed, not whether he needed more men. In this crucial time, he wanted it clear that his field commander would not be in the posture later on of claiming he did not get what he needed."

Complying with orders, Wheeler on February 3 cabled Westmoreland through secret channels: "The president asks me if there is any reinforcement or help that we can give you." Totally preoccupied with Tet and Khe Sanh (he was sleeping on a cot in the Combat Operations Center at Tan Son Nhut), Westmoreland did not respond. So five days later, Wheeler cabled him again.

"Query: Do you need reinforcements? Our capabilities are limited. We can provide 82nd Airborne Division and about one half a Marine Corps Division, both loaded with Vietnam veterans. However, if you consider reinforcements imperative, you should not be bound by earlier agreements. . . . United States government is not prepared to accept defeat in Vietnam. In summary, if you need more troops, ask for them."

Almost explicit in Johnson's message, as Wheeler conveyed it, was a willingness to exceed the 525,000 troop limit in effect since 1967. Westmoreland immediately accepted the proffered army and Marine Corps units and slated them for an April arrival. At the same time, he and the Joint Chiefs began thinking that the turning point in the war had come—the enemy had finally exposed its forces and the president

Johnson presides over his regular Tuesday luncheon meeting with his top foreign policy advisers. The *Pueblo* had been seized that day. Those in attendance include (l-r) McNamara, Wheeler, Clifford, Rostow and Rusk, next to the president.

Westmoreland and Bunker meet Wheeler upon his arrival at Tan Son Nhut on February 23, 1968. When he returned to Washington, Wheeler immediately went to the White House and proposed a dramatic increase in troop levels.

seemed ready to take dramatic steps to end the war. But there was also a recognition that the war could go either way. As Secretary of the Navy Paul Nitze saw the situation, it was a matter of which side "would pick themselves out of the dust first." And Wheeler, fearful of blowing the big chance, began enticing Westmoreland to make troop requests heavy enough to cause the president to call up the reserves and put the country on a war footing. Given the president's mood, Wheeler and the Joint Chiefs thought that Johnson was more likely to approve such ideas if they originated with Westmoreland, so Wheeler began to draw such proposals from him.

". . . it occurs to me that the deployment of the 82nd Airborne Division and Marine elements might be desirable earlier than April to assist in defense and pursuit operations. . . . Please understand that I am not trying to sell you on the deployment of additional forces which in any event I cannot guarantee. . . . However, my sensing is that the critical phase of the war is upon us, and I do not believe that you should refrain from asking for what you believe is required under the circumstances."

Predictably, on February 12 Westmoreland requested the immediate deployment of "a Marine Regiment package" and "a brigade package of the 82nd Airborne Division."

About two weeks later, Wheeler flew to Saigon to assess personally the situation with Westmoreland. "As Bus Wheeler and I conferred," Westmoreland later wrote, "we did so in the expectation that there was to be a reappraisal of American policy on conducting the war, presumably a new and broadened strategy. A change in strategy almost inevitably would involve a sizable call-up of National Guard and Reserves. In view of Secretary McNamara's coming replacement by a presumably hawkish Clark Clifford that seemed a plausible possibility."

So Westmoreland's staff roughed out a more aggressive program, which essentially was Phase Three of Westmoreland's battle plan, calling for approximately two hundred thousand more troops to implement it—the same number, according to Westmoreland, that "I had proposed in my maximum or optimum force at the White House in 1967."

Westmoreland says, "My intention was not to make a specific request for troop deployment. It was instead a field commander's input to consideration of mobilizing resources to meet any contingency or to pursue an alternative strategy. At the heart of it was the Joint Chiefs' concerns to rebuild the strategic reserve in the United States." Vietnam was not the only worry of the Joint Chiefs. Communist forces in other parts of the world seemed to be testing American military units thinned because of resource transfers to Vietnam. Russian planes had started buzzing West Berlin. Pathet Lao Communists had captured an outpost and virtually wiped out two Lao general reserve battalions. And in Korea, in addition to capturing the *Pueblo,* the North Koreans had infiltrated a suicide squad to murder South Korean President Park Chung Hee. They were killed on the grounds of the Blue House, his official residence in Seoul.

Against this backdrop, Wheeler moved quickly. Within hours after his return from Saigon on February 28, he presented to the president at a White House breakfast meeting the plan he had elicited from Westmoreland. Johnson perceived it as Westmoreland's request. The plan "amounted to increasing the troop commitment in Vietnam by fifteen tactical fighter squadrons and the equivalent of three combat divisions." Johnson listened gloomily, but there seemed little doubt that he was still determined to see Vietnam through. One indication of his militant mood during this period was his reaction to a memo written by his United Nations ambassador, Arthur Goldberg, received on March 15. Goldberg had proposed a bombing halt of the north to get negotiations going. His memo came up during a meeting of Johnson and senior advisers shortly thereafter. The president reacted almost violently. "Let's get one thing clear," he said. "I'm telling you now I'm not going to stop the bombing. Now I don't want to hear any more about it. Goldberg has written to me about the whole thing, and I've heard every argument. I'm not going to stop it. Now is there anybody here who doesn't understand that?"

Many of the president's advisers were stunned by the scope of the so-called Westmoreland plan. They had anticipated some post-Tet restabilizing ideas, not initiatives that entailed large-scale reserve call-ups adding $10 billion to the yearly cost of a war that was already running about $30 billion. One of those most stunned was Clifford, whom the military was counting on to support the Westmoreland plan. Ironically, Clifford, a Washington lawyer with

U.N. Ambassador Arthur Goldberg makes a point with Johnson while Senator Wayne Morse of Oregon listens. The president initially rejected Goldberg's March 15, 1968, proposal for a bombing halt. Morse and Senator Ernest Gruening of Alaska were the only two members of congress to vote against the Gulf of Tonkin Resolution.

Clark Clifford and Abe Fortas (a Johnson appointee to the Supreme Court) were longtime friends of Johnson, and both influenced his views on the war. As McNamara's successor, Clifford caused a basic reevaluation of U.S. policy in Vietnam. Fortas's involvement in foreign policy was not appreciated by seasoned diplomats such as Dean Acheson.

important credentials dating back to the Truman administration, had been chosen as the new defense secretary because Johnson thought he was a hawk—unlike McNamara, the new dove he had politely fired. But within days, Clifford would be instrumental in changing Johnson's thinking about the war, causing the president to put a lid to the American commitment in Vietnam.

That Clifford should have been thought a hawk was understandable. He had long publicly argued the correctness of Johnson's Vietnam policies, and had even opposed the thirty-seven-day bombing halt that began in December 1965. But, significantly, his views were largely a function of optimistic reports saying that progress was being made in Vietnam. The Communist offensives of early 1968 shook the foundation of his support for the war. Nor were Khe Sanh and Tet the first shocks to that foundation.

In the summer of 1967, Johnson had sent Clifford and Maxwell Taylor on a diplomatic mission to allied capitals to ask for more combat troops for Vietnam. Though Clifford was then practicing law, he sometimes took on temporary assignments for his good friend Lyndon Johnson. Clifford and Taylor visited Thailand, the Philippines, South Korea, New Zealand and Australia. The Thai government, whose country was supposedly the next domino, as the theory went, was not inclined to commit more than the twenty-five hundred men they had in Vietnam. President Ferdinand Marcos was so opposed that he asked Johnson not to send the duo to Manila for fear of adverse public reaction to their presence. The governments of Australia and New Zealand also refused to send more troops. The latter had raised seventy thousand soldiers for the Second World War, but had seen fit to send only five hundred to Vietnam.

"I returned home," Clifford wrote, "puzzled, troubled, concerned. Was it possible that our assessment of the danger to the stability of Southeast Asia and the Western Pacific was exaggerated? Was it possible that those nations which were neighbors of Vietnam had a clearer perception of the tides of world events in 1967 than we?"

Consequently, Clifford immediately set out to reexamine the U.S. assumptions about the country's Vietnam involvement when, after Tet had begun, he was named McNamara's replacement. By the time he was sworn in on March 1, his reexamination was well under way. With Johnson's concurrence, Clifford set up a task force to appraise the situation. Members included Nicholas Katzenbach, William Bundy and Philip Habib of the State Department; Paul Nitze, Paul Warnke and Phil Goulding from Defense; Richard Helms of the CIA; Walt Rostow of the White House; Henry Fowler of the Treasury Department; Maxwell Taylor, as a special adviser; and Earle Wheeler, representing the Joint Chiefs. They met every day and evening in a private dining room reserved for the defense secretary at the Pentagon.

Rostow, Taylor and Wheeler saw the Tet offensive "as a heaven-sent opportunity," write Kalb and Abel. The three thought that "the enemy had suddenly exposed himself after years of avoiding battle; this was the moment to reinforce Westmoreland so he could clobber the enemy once and for all time." They perceived Tet as a last-ditch desperation tactic. But Nitze, Warnke and Katzenbach saw no such indication. Though they recognized that the Communist offensive had failed militarily, they thought the scope of it had demonstrated the strength and resiliency of the enemy, not its desperation.

Being the first-rate attorney that he was, Clifford began focusing the task force's attention on fundamental issues and away from peripheral points about tactics. Most of the questions were directed at Wheeler. And the answers that he provided, after discussions with the Joint Chiefs, doomed proposals for further escalation. In a *Foreign Affairs* article published in July 1969, Clifford delineated the questions and the answers:

✳ U.S. military men and women who served in Vietnam were provided vacation time. Each was allotted two one-week periods. One was a standard leave that was charged against his thirty days of annual vacation; the other, called an R-and-R, was not so charged. (Vacation policy for those in the navy was also a function of when their ship put ashore.) Officially, R-and-R stood for rest-and-rehabilitation, but some troops nicknamed it rape-and-run.

There were ten different R-and-R locations: Hong Kong, Bangkok, Sydney, Tokyo, Manila, Singapore, Taipei, Kuala Lumpur, Penang and Honolulu. Those who were married usually chose Honolulu, where they could meet their spouses.

Air transportation was provided by the U.S. government free of charge; U.S. commercial carriers were contracted for the service. The R-and-R program generated substantial revenues for the destination cities, of course. And because the war lasted so long, many cottage industries grew in response to the commercial demands of these American visitors. One product high on the priority list was sex. Bordellos catering to the GI developed in most R-and-R cities. In Bangkok, for example, some houses of prostitution put together catalogues of a sort, complete with photos of their inventory of women and the fees. Those traveling to Manila were inclined to buy all sorts of wood products, such as giant forks and spoons to hang on walls, and figurines.

For many soldiers, especially young ones from small towns, these exotic destinations were no substitute for home. Not surprisingly, it did not take too long before people recognized the business potential of this fact. For example, some former American servicemen established a combination bar-bordello in Sydney called the Texas Tavern. Its motif was all Wild-West.

While policy battles were being fought in Washington, the war raged on in Vietnam. The battleship U.S.S. *New Jersey,* shown here blasting away at Communist positions with its sixteen-inch guns, was recommissioned on April 6, 1968.

"Q. Would 206,000 [more] men do the job?

"*A. There is no assurance that they would.*

"Q. If not, how many more might be needed—and when?

"*A. No one can say.*

"Q. Could the enemy respond with a buildup of his own?

"*A. Yes, he could and probably would.*

"Q. Could bombing end the war?

"*A. Not by itself.*

"Q. Would a step-up in bombing decrease American casualties?

"*A. Very little, if at all. The United States has already dropped a heavier tonnage of bombs on North Vietnam than in all theaters of war during World War II. Yet, during 1967, some 90,000 North Vietnamese made their way to the South and, in the first weeks of 1968, were still coming at three to four times the rate of a year earlier.*

"Q. How long must the United States go on carrying the main burden of combat?

"*A. The South Vietnamese are making great progress, but they are not yet ready to replace American troops in the field.*

"Q. What is the plan for victory?

"*A. There is no plan.*

"Q. Why not?

"*A. Because American forces operate under three major restrictions: The President has forbidden them to invade the North, lest China intervene; he has forbidden the mining of Haiphong harbor, lest a Soviet supply ship be sunk; he has also forbidden pursuing the enemy into Laos and Cambodia because that would widen the war, geographically and politically.*

"Q. Given these circumstances, how can we win?

"*A. The United States is improving its posture all the time, the enemy can not afford the attrition being inflicted on him; at some point he will discover there is no purpose in fighting any more.*

"Q. How long with this take? Six months? One year? Two years?

"*A. There is no agreement on the answer.*

"Q. Does anyone see any evidence that four years of enormous casualties and massive destruction through bombing have diminished the enemy's will to fight?

"*A. No.*"

As a result, Clifford concluded that the war could not be won.

At the same time, Johnson, judging from his

public announcements, was becoming even more hawkish on the war. In a speech delivered on March 17, he called for "a total national effort to win the war, to win the peace, and to complete the job that must be done here at home." He told the gathering, "Make no mistake about it—I don't want a man in here to go back thinking otherwise—we are going to win." And this was a statement he made *after* the shock waves that followed the *New York Times* report on March 10 of Westmoreland's 206,000 troop request; *after* the New Hampshire primary results of March 12, in which Senator Eugene McCarthy stunned everyone by almost defeating Johnson on the single issue of Vietnam; and *after* Robert Kennedy declared his candidacy against Johnson.

So Clifford decided he would need help if Johnson's thinking was to be turned around. He hung his hopes on a group called the Senior Advisory Group on Vietnam, better known as the Wise Men, established earlier in the war, whom Johnson called on occasionally for advice. Clifford had been a member of the group before becoming defense secretary. He asked Johnson to meet with them before making a decision about sending the additional 206,000 troops. The president agreed; March 25 and 26 were set aside for this purpose.

Public pronouncements aside, Lyndon Johnson's position on the troop request was softening—as was perhaps his position on the war itself. Johnson's thinking was usually much more subtle than he bespoke. There were a number of influences that caused Johnson to rethink his position. On February 27, Walter Cronkite of CBS Television told millions of Americans, "To say that we are closer to victory today is to believe, in the face of evidence, the optimists who have been wrong in the past. It seems now more certain than ever that the bloody experience of Vietnam is to end in a stalemate." Johnson is supposed to have said to an aide, "If I've lost Walter, I've lost the support of Mr. Average Citizen."

Another influence was Dean Acheson, who met with the president in late February. Johnson asked him for his assessment of the situation in Vietnam. Acheson replied that, on the basis of the briefings he had received, it was impossible to tell. "With all due respect," said Acheson, "the Joint Chiefs of Staff don't know

Monitors, bizarre in appearance and ironclad, were used on inner waterways for Operation Game Warden. Here one such craft uses its flamethrowers to burn brush that Viet Cong soldiers might use as ambush cover.

(Top) Former Secretary of State Dean Acheson bluntly told Johnson he didn't think the Joint Chiefs knew what they were talking about regarding Vietnam policy. (Bottom) On March 4, 1968, Rusk advised Johnson to halt bombing of North Vietnam down to the nineteenth parallel.

what they're talking about." To Johnson, these remarks were terribly unsettling, since they came from the man who, as Truman's secretary of state, had first implemented the policy of containment.

Dean Rusk also played a role, the secretary of state being the most influential member of the cabinet. On March 4 he suggested to Johnson that the U.S. hold back bombing below the nineteenth parallel in hopes of getting peace talks started. "We were proposing to stop only 5 percent of our sorties, in fact," Rusk later observed. "Most of the sorties at that time of year were in the southern part of North Vietnam. So there was no military disadvantage to our side in cutting back." Without adopting Rusk's proposal outright, the president told him, "Get it ready."

On March 10, McGeorge Bundy, Johnson's former national security adviser and then head of the Ford Foundation, made his position known during a debate sponsored by Harvard University. "I do not myself believe that a persuasive case has yet been made for a significant military increase on our side." As a courtesy and to keep his lines of communication open with the administration, Bundy had informed Johnson beforehand through Walt Rostow that he was going to oppose escalation.

One of the first clear signs that the president was moving away from escalation was his invitation to Goldberg to come to Washington to discuss the memo to which he had initially reacted so adversely. But the most telling sign was Johnson's announcement on March 22 that Westmoreland would become army chief of staff and that Abrams would take command in Vietnam. Westmoreland was greatly disappointed; he had wanted to see the war through. By replacing Westmoreland, Johnson was disassociating himself from escalation proposals.

When the Wise Men convened on March 25, the Joint Chiefs had already correctly surmised that the president would reject their escalation proposals. There would be no reserve call-up, nor, they thought, would there be any change in national policy. Wheeler even notified Westmoreland beforehand to that effect. Westmoreland replied that with the arrival of the 3rd Brigade of the 82nd Airborne Division and the 27th Regimental Landing Team, he could hold his own. By the time the Wise Men sat down to confer, American and South

Vietnamese forces were clearly turning back the Communist offensive and Khe Sanh was very nearly over.

The Wise Men were a remarkable aggregation representing all the phases of American foreign policy since the end of the Second World War. Some had led our greatest armies. Some had first formulated and implemented America's reaction to aggressive Communist actions in Europe and Asia. Others had taken that basic containment policy to its logical Kennedy-esque conclusion: This country "shall pay any price, bear any burden, meet any hardship, support any friend, oppose any foe to assure the survival and the success of liberty."

The Wise Men included Dean Acheson, George

Ball, General Omar Bradley, McGeorge Bundy, Arthur Dean, Douglas Dillon, Supreme Court Justice Abe Fortas, Arthur Goldberg, Henry Cabot Lodge, John McCloy, Robert Murphy, General Matthew Ridgway, General Maxwell Taylor and Cyrus Vance.

They assembled in the afternoon, read background papers, adjourned for dinner at the State Department and afterward listened to a Vietnam status report from Philip Habib of the State Department, George Carver of the CIA, and Major General DePuy, now back from Vietnam and serving on the Joint Staff. Ball remembers the briefing as having been perhaps more honest and candid than any other he had listened to on Vietnam. What came through was how Tet had left the pacification program in ruins. "What

Johnson plays with his grandson Patrick Lyn Nugent while Westmoreland, appearing uncomfortable, observes. The two were meeting to discuss Westmoreland's reassignment from his Vietnam command and his appointment as army chief of staff. The move signaled Johnson's intention to cap off troop levels in Vietnam and find a way out of the war.

shocked my colleagues," Ball later recalled, "was that I don't think they'd had any sense of the demoralization that [Tet] produced. I felt that the loss to the other side of areas that had been more or less under South Vietnamese control came through pretty clearly. It was exactly what I had expected. But the rest of them seemed to have been quite demoralized by this, quite shocked." (The next day when the president met with these men, he was so stunned by their changed thinking that he later accused Habib, Carver and DePuy of some sort of nefarious activity. Calling Carver and DePuy into his office—Habib was out of town—he ordered them to repeat the briefing to him. "You aren't telling me what you told them," he said. "You must have given them a different briefing." Later he told some staff members that the three had been "reached." "Who poisoned the well?" Johnson asked angrily.)

At the morning meeting on the second day of the Wise Men's deliberations, preparatory to the group's first meeting with Johnson, they gathered around the green felt table in the State Department's operations center in order to formulate some recommendations for the president. Ball gave what he describes as "my usual pitch about the goddam futility of it all." He wanted the U.S. to cut its losses and get out. At the opposite pole were Taylor, Murphy and Fortas, who favored intensification of the present effort. Lodge, Dean and Bradley were reluctant to recommend a change of policy in either direction. What was surprising was how general the support had become for the notion that the U.S. had taken on an impossible task in Vietnam. McGeorge Bundy and Acheson especially supported this view. Dillon, Goldberg, Ridgway and Vance wanted the president to start scaling down involvement while trying to negotiate a way out. As Vance put it: "We were weighing not only what was happening in Vietnam but the social and political effects in the United States, the impact on the U.S. economy, the attitude of other nations. The divisiveness in the country was growing with such acuteness that it was threatening to tear the United States apart."

Before the group adjourned for lunch with Johnson, there was general consensus in favor of Clifford's proposal for a 12,500 troop increase in Vietnam—basically more support troops for the number of combat troops already serving. The 206,000 troop increase was out of the question.

Two of the "Wise Men" involved in Vietnam policy reevaluation that began on March 25, 1968: (Top) General Omar Bradley and Arthur Dean.

Then Rusk asked what the men thought about a partial bombing halt, perhaps to the nineteenth parallel. Generally, the group thought the idea was worth exploring.

Johnson had invited a special guest to join him and the Wise Men for lunch—Creighton Abrams, with whom he had already conferred privately at some length. The general was asked to talk about Vietnam. He did so for forty-five minutes, presenting the conclusions he had arrived at as the American officer chiefly responsible for improving the South Vietnamese Army. The group was universally impressed with him. His main point was that the South Vietnamese armed forces should be doing much more to defend their own country. The U.S. should start arming them better and training them better; prepare them to fight their own war. Later, during the administration of Richard Nixon, Secretary of Defense Melvin Laird would present this idea as a new concept and call it "Vietnamization," but the decision to shift the burden from this country to our ally was born of Abrams's trip to Washington in March 1968. Abrams also outlined to the group his plans for new allied tactics in Vietnam: basically the population security idea that the marines had first espoused back in 1965. The U.S. and the allies would back off the major offensive activity that had characterized Westmoreland's years.

Creighton Abrams was called by Johnson to the White House to brief the Wise Men. He left a strong and favorable impression. At left is Vice-President Hubert Humphey.

By Kalb and Abel's account, Bundy was then asked to report on the morning's deliberations. "He reported a broad consensus that the President had set his sights too high. . . . Without applying virtually unlimited resources, the objectives of present policy could not be achieved, . . . and with public support for the war eroding, a changed policy was called for." Bradley, Murphy and Fortas objected that Bundy's appraisal did not reflect their views. Then Acheson interrupted sharply; Bundy had certainly correctly presented *his* views, he said. Then Johnson, already somewhat shaken by the intense divisions, went around the table, asking each man for his personal view. Quickly it was evident that men who had stood with him, had in fact helped formulate his Vietnam policy, now opposed it— Bundy, Vance, Acheson. And in spite of Bradley's earlier statement, the old general also voiced objections: "Well, I've listened to all this," he said, "and I've heard the briefing. I don't think we can do what we set out to do here with the limitations that have been set by the situation. I think, Mr. President, you're going to have to lower your sights."

When Acheson voiced the opinion that the U.S. strategy was still hung up on military victory, General Wheeler, invited with Abrams to attend, took exception. The country was not trying to win a "classic military victory," he said. According to Kalb and Abel, "Acheson called that disingenuous. If the use of half a million men to eradicate the Viet Cong and to drive the North Vietnamese back out of the South was not an effort aimed at a military solution, then words had lost their meaning."

LBJ delivers his famous speech of March 31, 1968, in which he announced a partial bombing halt and his decision not to seek reelection.

How dramatically Johnson's attitude changed during those few days in March was revealed by the stunning speech he delivered on nationwide television on Sunday evening, March 31, 1968. The opening line, which in earlier drafts had read, "My fellow Americans, I want to talk to you about the war in Vietnam," now said: "Good evening, my fellow Americans. Tonight I want to talk to you of peace in Vietnam and Southeast Asia." Johnson went on to announce that he would halt the bombing of North Vietnam, and that, in order to devote the remaining months of his administration to the quest for peace, he would not seek reelection. Unfortunately for himself, the Democratic Party, and most of all for those still fighting in Vietnam, Johnson had not made these initiatives soon enough. As David Halberstam observes, he "had always dreamed of being the greatest domestic President in this century, and he had become, without being able to stop it, a war President, and not a very good one at that." Consequently, another man would have his turn as president, promising to bring American soldiers home. Most American voters were reassured with Richard Nixon's promise to end the fighting and achieve an "honorable peace." What they did not know, significantly, was how long he planned to take.

In early 1969 a group of visiting Asians asked senior national security adviser Henry Kissinger whether the Nixon administration would repeat the mistakes of the Johnson administration on Vietnam.

"No," answered Kissinger, "we will not repeat their mistakes. We will not send 500,000. We will make our own mistakes and they will be completely our own."

Appreciating the joke that it was intended to be, the Asians laughed heartily. The statement was untrue, of course. Though Nixon would make his own mistakes, he would also repeat many made by Johnson, such as:

• elevating the importance of Vietnam to cosmic proportions, in accordance with the advice of people like Sir Robert Thompson, a Briton reputed to be a guerrilla war expert, who told Nixon, "The future of Western civilization is at stake in the way you handle yourselves in Vietnam";

• believing that with a little more effort and time the war could be won;

• believing that better equipment and more training would make the South Vietnamese Army an effective fighting force (although the South Vietnamese government of Thieu and Ky was never able to command the respect and allegiance that Ho and his political heirs could; and thus their soldiers never fought as hard as the Communists did);

• underestimating the extent of the American public's discontent with the war;

• expecting the enemy to give up (Kissinger, for example, described a massive Communist offensive in 1972 as "One last throw of the dice," overlooking the fact that the enemy had been coming back for more in the wake of one major offensive after another dating back to 1965);

• believing that the U.S. could disassociate itself from the French legacy and overcome historical forces that had been building momentum in Vietnam for more than one hundred years;

• trying to wage war with the backing of a bare majority of the American people and their Congress; and

• deceiving Congress and the general population for short-term benefit, as when Nixon ordered the secret bombing of Cambodia.

For repeating these mistakes, Nixon became as isolated a president as his predecessor had been. And his paranoia, born of the Vietnam war, led directly to his becoming the first president in American history forced to resign from office.

When Nixon first assumed office, Congress and the public generally stepped back, giving him time and maneuvering room to figure out how to extricate the country from Vietnam. Nixon's

Johnson's decision not to run again for president was a stunning surprise, as this *Chicago Tribune* headline indicates.

Johnson's decisive act did not bring peace, however. There were more years of fighting before us than behind us. (Above) Army soldiers examine another bunker while searching for the enemy.

Another president comes to South Vietnam. Richard Nixon and his wife, Pat, visited Saigon on July 30, 1969. Walking down the ramp from Air Force One are Bunker, followed by Abrams and foreign affairs advisor Henry Kissinger.

administration shaped its Indochina policy during the first half of 1969. His secretary of defense, Melvin Laird, wanted out of Vietnam. Describing the American people as "fed up with the war," Laird also objected to it on the grounds that the country was compromising far more important national security interests elsewhere in the world by continuing to prosecute the war in Vietnam. He pushed for a timetable for disengagement. As for Kissinger, Nixon's other top adviser on the war, he conformed with Nixon's desire to end the war "honorably"— presumably via military victory. In a statement reminiscent of Johnson, Kissinger told his staff in September 1969, "I can't believe that a fourth-rate power like North Vietnam doesn't have a breaking point." Without Laird's knowledge, he ordered some of them to prepare a plan to deliver North Vietnam a "savage, punishing" blow which would presumably push the enemy beyond the breaking point. After working on the project, three of them—Lawrence Lynn, Anthony Lake and Roger Morris—objected. They had decided in the course of their deliberations that the country should work out some settlement to save American lives and extricate the country. Otherwise "we see the president sinking deeper into the Johnsonian bog," they said. They recommended that a coalition government involving the Communists be negotiated in Vietnam.

But Nixon was not yet ready to admit defeat in Vietnam, though his public pronouncements differed markedly from his behind-the-scenes actions. Only a few top administration officials, a handful of select congressmen and some military leaders were aware that since March, he had had B-52s bombing enemy sanctuaries in Cambodia. Publicly, however, he played the part of peacemaker, announcing on June 8 that the first U.S. troop withdrawals from Vietnam— involving twenty-five thousand men—would be completed by August. The Nixon Doctrine, as it came to be called, would limit U.S. involvement in future Vietnam-type struggles to the providing of economic and military aid—no combat troops. In September he announced a second scheduled withdrawal, this one involving thirty-five thousand men. By this time, Laird had given the name "Vietnamization" to the process of gradually turning the fighting effort over to the South Vietnamese.

But at the same time that they were withdrawing American soldiers, Nixon and his vice-president, Spiro Agnew, began lashing out against those opposing the war, and thus fueled the fires of protest. The vehemence of the Nixon administration's counterattacks gradually established him as a co-author of Johnson's war. Agnew described the older, establishment people who began joining the protest movement as "an effete corps of impudent snobs who characterize themselves as intellectuals." And adding to the public's outrage, Nixon professed indifference to their views. "Under no circumstances will I be affected," he said. During the fall of 1969, in response to hundreds of thousands joining Vietnam "moratorium" demonstrations that were attracting a broad cross section of the country's population and, according to *Time,* giving the protest movement "new respectability and popularity," Nixon, with remarkable insensitivity, had a staff member put out the word that the president was doing "business as usual." Approximately ninety-five hundred American soldiers were killed in Vietnam during Nixon's first year in office.

As the new commander of U.S. forces in Vietnam, Abrams had begun a changeover in American tactics even before Nixon was sworn in. He told reporters, "We [will] work in small patrols because that's how the enemy moves — in groups of four and five. When he fights in squad size, we now fight in squad size. When he cuts to half squad, so do we." The impact was dramatic. During the first half of 1969, the end of the period in which Westmoreland's plan was in place, there were six hundred operations of battalion size or larger involving U.S. troops. In 1970, under Abrams, there were only six hundred and twenty during the whole year. Abrams's basic belief was that in Vietnam, protection of the native population was all-important: Keep the enemy from disrupting villagers' lives, and support for the South Vietnamese government would take root. He believed that control of territory and kill ratios were almost irrelevant — so much so that he granted the request of Marine General Raymond Davis to abandon the strong-point defense line that Westmoreland had ordered.

In implementing his policy, Abrams enjoyed (in direct contrast to his predecessor) the full support of the marines, but labored against stiff resistance from his fellow senior army commanders. "I've got a hundred-odd generals, and

Years of fighting reduced lush growth to wasteland in some areas.

(Top) A Viet Cong soldier surprised by GIs lies dead while the latter direct machine-gun fire into a tunnel entrance where other Viet Cong soldiers fled. (Bottom) General Julian Ewell.

only two of them understand this war!" an exasperated Abrams confided to Lieutenant Colonel Donald Marshall, who worked closely with Abrams in developing the strategy.

The extent of the resistance Abrams faced was typified by Lieutenant General Julian Ewell, the field force commander of II Corps. Abrams had ordered Ewell and his senior commanders and staff to gather for a briefing by Marshall on the new strategy. While Marshall carefully went through the new small-unit tactics point by point, Ewell fidgeted, feverishly chewing on and spitting out a whole pencil, bit by bit. When Marshall finished, Ewell stood up and turned to his staff, saying, "I've made my entire career and reputation by going 180 degrees counter to such orders as this"—after which he walked out.

While Abrams struggled to reshape American strategy in Vietnam, many diehard army commanders continued to fight classic battles of attrition. In April 1969, a macabre benchmark was reached: The number of American combat deaths in Vietnam surpassed the 33,629 killed during all the Korean war. But battles at places like Apbia Mountain (Hamburger Hill)—in May 1969—were still being fought, even as Nixon announced the first troop withdrawals.

One cause of the resistance that Abrams was facing within his own command was the perception of the nation's military leaders that Nixon was going to take a hard line in Vietnam. This perception was no doubt reinforced by Nixon's secret bombing of enemy sanctuaries in Cambodia (knowledge of which surely circulated among generals in Vietnam) and by Nixon's support, even during the withdrawal period, of the invasion of Cambodian border areas by South Vietnamese and American ground units. The Cambodian "incursion," as it came to be called, took place in April 1970, after General Lon Nol deposed Sihanouk while the portly prince was trying to lose weight at a clinic on the Côte d'Azur in France. Though there is no hard evidence that American agents led Lon Nol to expect American support, Nixon thought he should help him, and ordered a supply of captured Communist weapons sent to Lon Nol's troops. Communist weapons would soon be followed by American troops, as Nixon went Abrams one better in plans for a large-scale offensive to wipe out Communist sanctuaries in Cambodia. Abrams, who was actively encouraging a large-unit operation there, presumably had plans to involve only South Vietnamese troops. But Nixon encouraged a much larger operation involving American soldiers, even though he was encountering a lot of opposition to his Cambodian invasion plans—from Laird, who had submitted a compromise plan for a much smaller foray (which Nixon later described as "the most pusillanimous little nitpicker I ever saw"); from some of Kissinger's top assistants, who were threatening to resign; and from members of Congress, who were so worried that Nixon might do just what he was planning to do, that Senators Frank Church and John Sherman Cooper began drafting legislation to block such actions.

But Nixon moved too fast for them. After getting the support of Kissinger, who was initially undecided, Nixon was ready to move and, after yet another viewing of his favorite movie, *Patton,* with his crony Bebe Rebozo, Nixon gave the go—without informing Lon Nol that he was invading his country. (Nixon was infatuated with General George Patton, Jr., whom he saw as a profile in courage, a Churchillian character who had defied popular opinion and been vindicated—as Nixon himself expected to be.) On April 29, forty-eight thousand South Vietnamese troops, accompanied by American advisers and supported by American aircraft and artillery, invaded the Parrot's Beak; on April 30, thirty thousand American soldiers invaded the Fish Hook. Other smaller allied units crossed into Cambodia at other points during the next few days.

Another helicopter supplies another generation of soldiers who served in Vietnam. The character of the war gradually changed for Americans who served there. Initially it was, in a sense, a hopeful endeavor. Later, the positive associations with earlier U.S. conflicts were found not to apply.

The war is over for Corporal Larry Miklos (lower center), artillery forward observer wounded in action being medevacked out of the fighting.

✳ There were three major causes of American combat deaths during the Vietnam war. Fifty-one percent were killed by small-arms fire; thirty-six percent by fragments from artillery fire; and eleven percent by booby traps and mines. The percentage killed by small arms during Vietnam fighting was a substantial increase over that of earlier U.S. wars. During both the Second World War, and the Korean War, only thirty-three percent were killed by small arms. The Vietnam percentage was much greater because of both the fact that ambush was a major tactic of the Vietnamese Communists and the Communists' use of a Russian-supplied rifle, which was high-velocity, rapid-fire, light and extremely effective. American soldiers suffered wounds from four major sources: sixty-five percent from artillery fire; sixteen percent from small-arms fire; fifteen percent from booby traps and mines; and two percent from punji sticks.

Of those soldiers killed in action, thirty-nine percent were hit in the head, nineteen percent in the chest, eighteen percent in the stomach or groin area, seventeen percent in the legs, and one percent in the shoulders or arms; sixteen percent suffered multi-

Nixon went on nationwide television the evening of the thirtieth. It was as if Sir Robert Thompson had written the speech. Listening to it, the public might have imagined a breakthrough as significant as that accomplished by the Battle of the Bulge, though in reality they were charging into vast empty jungles and down dusty roads through abandoned villages. After stiff resistance at the beginning, the enemy went into retreat, leaving allied soldiers poking around for arms caches. Nixon said he would risk the political consequences rather than see "America become a second-rate power." Giving the operation a global dimension, he said, "If, when the chips are down, the world's most powerful nation, the United States of America, acts like a pitiful helpless giant, the forces of totalitarianism and anarchy will threaten free nations and free institutions throughout the world."

COSVN, the Communist command center which had become as legendary as Shangri-La, and as difficult to find, once again escaped detection, though locating it had been a major objective. However, thousands of tons of supplies and ammunition were discovered and soldiers worked feverishly either to transport them back to South Vietnam or to destroy them before withdrawing from Cambodia by late summer. Of the huge caches found, one soldier remarked, "I thought that the North Vietnamese were hurting until I saw these supplies."

The short-term results in the war zone were positive. Enemy activity dropped appreciably in the southern region of South Vietnam. But the long-term impact, because American units were involved, was negative. The U.S. public had thought the war was winding down. Nixon's reservoir of goodwill dwindled. Demonstrations, some violent, erupted across the country. At Kent State University, on May 4, National Guardsmen fired into a crowd of protesters, killing four students. The operation also caused defections in Nixon's administration. Interior Secretary Walter Hickel was forced to resign for objecting; four of Kissinger's top assistants did so voluntarily. And members of Congress moved to restrict Nixon's flexibility. In December they repealed the Gulf of Tonkin Resolution, thus preventing Nixon from sending American advisers to accompany the South Vietnamese units that crossed into Laos on February 8, 1971.

The operation was called Lamson 719, after a

Vietnamese military victory over China centuries earlier. Its specific objective was the city of Tchepone, about twenty miles across the Laotian border, which, because of its strategic location near the Ho Chi Minh Trail, the allied command wanted to capture as part of its plan to halt the delivery of supplies to Communist soldiers in South Vietnam.

All went well until the South Vietnamese reached Tchepone; then Communist units counterattacked, pushing government soldiers back in disarray. "Long accustomed to working with American advisors, subordinate ARVN commanders had difficulty without them in arranging fire support and resupply," according to Westmoreland, who was army chief of staff at the time. "Several senior ARVN commanders folded, prompting President Thieu to intervene and start issuing orders himself as far down as regiments." Lamson 719, which, in Kissinger's words, was "conceived in doubt and . . . proceeded in confusion," did not bode well for the day when all American combat troops would be withdrawn from South Vietnam—then only sixteen months away. The last American combat soldier would depart for the U.S. in June 1972. Scenes from this operation in Laos—like those showing stricken ARVN soldiers fleeing the battle by clinging to helicopter skids—were painful signs that even after the vast expenditures of American lives and money, our ally had not progressed much since Ap Bac back in January 1963.

American soldiers who served in Vietnam during the withdrawal years had no romantic notions about the war they were fighting. By the time they arrived in Vietnam, they were already jaded, both by firsthand accounts they had received from friends and neighbors who had already served, and by scenes they had been watching on their TV screens since junior high. An endless string of battles such as those at Khe Sanh, Hamburger Hill and hundreds more without a name stripped away any remaining illusions they might have had that this war was anything more than a matter of trading the lives of "grunts" for those of "gooks." Hollow shibboleths could no longer stir nor fool those young men ordered to serve. If Vietnam was as important as a succession of presidents said it was, why did their more privileged peers not have to serve, they wondered.

location wounds. The percentage that died due to head wounds is considered high and is attributed to the reluctance of many GIs to wear a helmet because of the heat; quite a large number wore floppy, cloth hats instead.

Americans who survived their wounds were hit in the following locations: thirty-six percent in the legs, eighteen percent in the arms or shoulders, fourteen percent in the head, seven percent in the chest, and five percent in the stomach or groin; twenty percent suffered multilocation wounds.

Many who were wounded during Vietnam fighting survived because of both the helicopter and improvements in medical treatment. In Vietnam, only 2.6 percent of those who survived long enough to reach field hospitals died; during the Second World War, almost twice that many died on hospital tables—4.5 percent.

Lieutenant William Calley

Finally, they were robbed of whatever dignity they might have managed to associate with their service and sacrifice by the images propagated by television and newspaper reports back home—torrents of bombs being dropped on thatch huts, refugees fleeing down country roads, American soldiers burning down villages and killing women and children.

On November 13, 1969, after trying to sell the story to *Life* and *Look,* thirty-two-year-old freelance writer Seymour Hersh filed a story with the tiny Dispatch News Service of Washington, D.C., about the mass murder of a village of civilians by a platoon in the command of a young officer named William Calley. (Dispatch News was owned by Hersh's neighbor, twenty-three-year-old David Obst, who contacted fifty newspapers, offering the article to each for $100. Thirty-six published it, including the *St. Louis Post-Dispatch,* the *San Francisco Chronicle,* the *Boston Globe* and the *Times* of London.) During the early morning hours of March 16, 1968, Calley had led thirty Charlie Company soldiers of the Americal Division into the village of My Lai for an assault timed to take place shortly after the women departed for market. They hoped to snare some of the estimated two hundred and fifty VC operating in an area where the concentration of Communist soldiers and sympathizers was so great that the surrounding cluster of villages was known as Pinkville to GIs. Americans on patrol there were constantly wary of the many booby traps and mines that had been rigged for them. Maiming and death had become daily occurrences. Only two weeks before Calley's men entered My Lai, another unit of C Company had stumbled into a mine field there; six were killed, twelve wounded. (Being wounded by mine explosions usually meant loss of limbs.)

On the day of the massacre, Calley's platoon was operating as part of a company-sized operation commanded by Captain Ernest Medina. Helicopters brought the Americans in; it was to be a classic search-and-destroy mission. But in this case, Calley's unit ran wild. They opened fire as people ran from their hootches, mowing them down indiscriminately. After the initial bursts of fire, the platoon began rounding up survivors. Some were led over to a ditch where they were executed.

The slaughter was finally stopped by Army Warrant Officer Hugh Thompson, who was aboard one of the command helicopters circling the area. He ordered his chopper down once he determined what was happening, and threatened to open fire on Calley and his men unless the bloodbath stopped. He is credited with saving the lives of sixteen children. A GI who kept a diary said he was aware of one hundred and fifty-five deaths; ninety was another number passed around. Officially, Charlie Company reported killing one hundred and seventy-eight VC that day in My Lai and in another village called My Khe. Some estimates are three times the official count. Whatever the number, Calley observed that it was "no big deal."

Though there had been isolated incidents of murder and rape down through the years, there had never been anything in U.S. military experience like My Lai. But in retrospect, so many factors contributed to it that it seems almost inevitable. The frustration and fear of fighting a war in which the enemy was potentially anyone and everyone—including women and children— was a large part of the problem; every soldier carried in the back of his mind stories of comrades in arms who had been picked off by an apparently harmless *mama-san* or other unsuspected foe. But, specifically, the My Lai massacre occurred because of Calley's lack of command leadership. As George Walton observed, "When an army is required to fight a war without the support of society, it is forced to commission its Calleys."

During the first years of the war, the army had had an adequate supply of young officers, but as the war dragged on, these capable men were promoted through the ranks, leaving too many holes for the dwindling supply of service academy and ROTC graduates to fill. West Point, for example, graduated only about six hundred replacements per year, and, because of the unpopularity of the war on civilian college campuses, ROTC programs—a standard source of supply—shrank dramatically. In 1960, ROTC enrollment for all service branches stood at 230,000; in 1969, during the time of greatest need, enrollment was only 123,000. Some colleges kicked ROTC off campus. With ROTC undermined and draft deferments granted to college students, the army was deprived of the talents of the intelligent young men generally most fit to lead. And many college students prolonged their immunity to the draft beyond graduation day, some by extreme actions. For

(Top) Private David Whitman of Knoxville, Tennessee, takes a break on a mountaintop near the Laotian border. (Bottom) Second Lieutenant J. E. Carney of Richmond Heights, Ohio, urges his men forward near Cam Lo. Junior officer slots became hard to fill.

Private Robin Olsen of Staples, Minnesota, opens a C-ration can for a Vietnamese girl. Many individual soldiers and whole units worked hard to win the goodwill of villagers.

example, James Fallows, the prominent military affairs writer, and now an advocate of the draft, has written about having nearly starved himself to lose forty pounds so as to flunk the Selective Service physical he took while at Harvard.

Deprived of its traditional sources of officer leadership, the army was forced to make officers out of draftees and dropouts, who, like Calley, were sent through the six-month Officer Candidate School at Fort Benning, Georgia. Most performed adequately, but the diminished talent pool augured ill. Calley, typical of many, had flunked out of Palm Beach Junior College in Lake Worth, Florida, after getting two C's, one D and four F's during his first year. Even so, without ever having learned to read a map, Calley managed to graduate in the middle of his OCS class, leading one army colonel to observe during the My Lai investigation, "We have at least two or three thousand Calleys in the army just waiting for the next calamity."

The Vietnam war had a seriously compromising effect on the service academies as a source of leadership (for both short and long term). Though it had had little to do with the initial commitment to Vietnam, the military was being blamed for the unpopular war. Consequently, thousands of young men who would otherwise have been applying to West Point, Annapolis or the Air Force Academy, never considered it. Furthermore, many of the young men who did graduate from these institutions later resigned their commissions, military life being so unpopular because of the war and because events such as My Lai were associated with everyone in uniform. For example, the West Point Class of 1965 had almost as many men resign their commissions in five years as the Class of 1961 did in nine. These men felt betrayed — deceived by the promise of the Kennedy years.

On paper, at least, the military academy cadets of the mid-sixties were the most capable ever to attend. They were motivated both by feelings of patriotism inspired by the Cold War atmosphere, and by the example of their vigorous young president, whose military service had made him such a hero. His influence was felt for a time even after his death. Nor did it go unnoticed by young men in high schools pondering their future that many of Kennedy's top men had served in the military during the Second World War. Military service seemed almost a rite of passage. So many academically superior young people were attracted to military service that the Air Force Academy classes that enrolled during the period 1962 through 1967 registered College Entrance Examination Board scores far superior to that of any classes before or since. Yet, a high percentage of these classes dropped out of the academies or later resigned their commissions. Take, for example, the Class of 1967. By the time of the Vietnam cease-fire in 1973, fourteen of the top fifty graduates of the Class of 1967 had resigned their commissions; another seven later decided not to make the air force a career—thus, the attrition rate among these top graduates who survived the war was almost fifty percent. The number-two graduate, Lieutenant Charles Clements, who served in Vietnam for a time as a C-130 transport pilot, decided one day, after a long period of soul searching, that he could no longer serve the war effort in any capacity. Clements, the son of a career air force officer, and a member of the Ethics Committee while at the academy, refused to fly any more missions. Because he was subjecting himself to courtmartial proceedings and compromising what showed every indication of being a brilliant career, Clements's senior officers thought he might have suffered a nervous breakdown. He was sent back to the states for physical evaluation, and finally discharged for medical reasons. Several years later he enrolled at the University of Washington medical school. Then in 1982, moved by events in El Salvador and noting similarities to Vietnam, Clements made his way to remote villages there, where for a year he tended the sick and wounded, all the time staying just ahead of government troops out to kill him for his supposed Communist ties. (His patients lived in rebel-controlled areas, beyond medical treatment.)

Only Clements can know for certain the reasons he subjected himself to such danger. Remuneration is not the answer; he served under the auspices of a Quaker organization and there was none. But it does seem certain that his reasons have their origin halfway around the world in Vietnam. And that his going to El Salvador was perhaps a kind of expiation.

Without question the American military suffered long-term losses because of the resignation of young officers like Clements. And their loss reverberates beyond the present, which is a seldom discussed aspect of the Vietnam tragedy. Losing many of the best of graduates of the

An 81mm mortar crew trades fire with Communist troops.

Two soldiers find a way to beat the stifling heat temporarily.

Americans killed in action by state and territory...

Alabama	1,181
Alaska	55
Arizona	604
Arkansas	579
California	5,448
Colorado	608
Connecticut	589
Delaware	120
District of Columbia	235
Florida	1,897
Georgia	1,548
Hawaii	271
Idaho	207
Illinois	2,876
Indiana	1,510
Iowa	818

service academies deprives the military of its future, for stellar performance at the academies has always been an accurate indicator of potential: witness Generals Robert E. Lee, John J. Pershing and Douglas MacArthur — all of them were commanders of the West Point corps of cadets.

The Vietnam war caused many young men to break generations-old family traditions of military service. For example, a number of sons of generals resigned, including Joseph Kruzel, Jr., the number-eight-ranking graduate in Clements's class, who went on to earn a Ph.D. in political science from Harvard University and become a research associate for the International Strategic Studies Institute at London University. The number-one graduate of Clements's class of 1967, a Rhodes Scholar, also resigned. Daniel Twomey later became the senior staff member for the U.S. Senate Budget Committee.

Vietnam wrought serious institutional damage to the very core of the service academies. In 1969, when news of My Lai surfaced, the superintendent of West Point was Major General Samuel Koster, who had been commander of the Americal Division when Calley's men slaughtered the villagers of My Lai. Consequently, the man who was working out of the office formerly held by Pershing, MacArthur, Taylor and Westmoreland was charged with violations of Article 92 of the Code of Military Justice—failure to obey lawful regulations, and dereliction in the performance of duty—specifically, having participated in the My Lai cover-up. Koster was later reduced in rank, and he retired shortly thereafter. The resulting shock at West Point and throughout the army was profound. Ward Just, who covered the war for *Newsweek* and the *Washington Post,* was sent to West Point to measure the cadets' reaction. There he expected outrage, a feeling that the military in general and the superintendent in particular were being used as scapegoats. He was surprised to discover otherwise. "Instead," he says, "there was only a kind of embarrassed silence. What was there to say? *The superintendent had been charged with dereliction in the performance of duty.*"

Koster's problems reflected an erosion of standards that began during the Vietnam period, when dishonesty became policy, established at the highest levels. Many air force officers, for example, were commanded to participate in the deception over the secret bombing of Cambodia beginning in March 1969. On orders from

Commander-in-Chief Richard Nixon, Strategic Air Command records were falsified to keep the B-52 strikes from public knowledge. In fact, the subterfuge that began with the secret bombing campaign was what led to the pattern of abuses that would later be uncovered during the Watergate hearings, and would ultimately result in Nixon's forced resignation. It all started in May 1969, when *New York Times* correspondent William Beecher filed a report that the administration had okayed some bombing in Cambodia. Though the story went largely overlooked, Nixon and Kissinger were outraged. As a result, the two had phone taps installed on the lines of four journalists and thirteen public officials, some of whom were Kissinger's staff members. According to J. Edgar Hoover, Kissinger said at the time that the Nixon administration "will destroy whoever did this."

Not surprisingly, with deception so institutionalized because of Vietnam, individuals began freelancing their own forms of dishonesty and deception:

• In April 1972, General John Lavelle, the commander of 7th Air Force and as such the top air force officer in Vietnam, was removed from his command for authorizing airstrikes on oil dumps and truck parks in North Vietnam, thus violating the unconditional bombing halt ordered by Johnson. He justified them as "protective reaction" strikes. Seymour Hersh, while reporting for the *New York Times,* was working to prove that the general was acting with the direct approval of Kissinger, but he dropped his investigation of that story in order to cover the unfolding of Watergate. Hersh believed Kissinger was involved, but his suspicion has never been proved.

• Major General Carl Turner, the former provost general of the army, was convicted in federal court of obtaining guns under false pretenses and given a three-year sentence.

• A former chief staff judge advocate for all Vietnam was forced to admit having accepted illegal favors.

• Ellsworth Bunker's personal pilot, an air force colonel, was caught using the ambassador's personal plane to smuggle drugs.

• Sergeant Major of the Army William Woolridge, the senior enlisted man in all the army and a protégé of DePuy, was indicted for "taking illicit profits from the military non-commissioned-officer-club system, for threaten-

Kansas	613
Kentucky	1,037
Louisiana	870
Maine	331
Maryland	992
Massachusetts	1,300
Michigan	2,597
Minnesota	1,043
Mississippi	627
Missouri	1,380
Montana	259
Nebraska	385
Nevada	143
New Hampshire	218
New Jersey	1,435
New Mexico	391
New York	4,033
North Carolina	1,573
North Dakota	192
Ohio	3,021
Oklahoma	973
Oregon	686
Pennsylvania	3,066
Rhode Island	200
South Carolina	883
South Dakota	187
Tennessee	1,274
Texas	3,316
Utah	353
Vermont	100
Virginia	1,268
Washington	1,012
West Virginia	713
Wisconsin	1,131
Wyoming	117
Canal Zone	2
Guam	70
American Samoa	4
Puerto Rico	342
U.S. Virgin Islands	15
Other	120

ing an officer with physical violence, and for using General Creighton Abrams's personal plane to carry crates of whiskey in and out of Vietnam." Four other senior enlisted men were indicted along with Woolridge. One of them, Master Sergeant William Higdon, who was in charge of one of the largest service clubs in Vietnam, was convicted and received a dishonorable discharge and a $25,000 fine. According to a senior army officer who used the pen name Cincinnatus to write a book entitled *Self Destruction* (about "the disintegration and decay of the United States Army during the Vietnam era"): The "'sergeants scandal' revealed widespread bribes, kickbacks, irregularities, extortion and negligence of duty at many levels of rank."

Whatever their other differences of opinion on the war in Vietnam may have been, McGeorge Bundy and William Westmoreland seemed to agree on the effect it had on the military. During the withdrawal years Bundy observed: "Extraction is now the necessary precondition for the renewal of the Army as an institution." Noting the deterioration from his vantage point as army chief of staff, Westmoreland correctly pointed out the danger: "An army without discipline, morale, and pride is a menace to the country that it is sworn to defend."

Corporal D. W. Griffin of Newberry, South Carolina, gives Corporal J. P. O'Neill of Denham Springs, Louisiana, a haircut.

Most generals and admirals — indeed most professional military people — blame the McGeorge Bundys, the John McNaughtons and the Robert McNamaras for the loss in Vietnam and all its attendant problems. They cite "too much civilian interference and restraints"; they say that it was "impossible to fight with imposed constraints"; they argue that the military's performance during those days was undermined by the same forces that disrupted the rest of society. Westmoreland still holds firm to this belief. During an interview in April 1978 with George Esper of Associated Press, he said that "we had the power" but that "in the final analysis" we "didn't have the will."

But those who make such broad generalizations about the reasons for the decline of the military ignore the contribution of the military itself to what occurred. As one military man observed, "The heart of many of our problems of leadership, integrity, and professionalism in Vietnam is quite simply that . . . we lowered our standards and deserved the mess we wound up with."

The lowering of standards began during the early days of the war as a direct result of policy decisions. One such disastrous decision decreed that army officers would serve tours of combat duty in Vietnam which were limited to six months, after which they were guaranteed transfer to staff (non-combat) positions and the war became someone else's worry. The justification given for this officer rotation system was that the psychological stress of Vietnam service was so great that optimum performance on the battlefield was possible only for brief periods. But Cincinnatus dismisses the "burnout" factor as subterfuge, claiming that the real reason for the decision about rotation was to provide twice as many officers with combat command experience on their records at a time when the military didn't take Vietnam seriously. Though the *Pentagon Papers* show Westmoreland warning McNamara and Johnson that the Vietnam conflict would be a long one, Cincinnatus contends that in fact the army did not think it would be much of a war. This was certainly true during the early years of the fighting, when lower- and middle-echelon officers were frequently heard to remark, and only half in jest, "It's not much of a war, but it's the only one we've got." Whatever the truth about the army's expectations, there is considerable cause for skepticism about whether burnout really was a problem. A survey conducted in 1976 at the army's Command and General Staff College supports Cincinnatus: ". . . the majority of respondents [mostly majors who had fought in Vietnam] felt that officers did not 'burn out' after approximately six months in command and that frequent changes [had] an adverse effect on morale and discipline." Sixty-one percent found fault with the concept of burnout; only eight percent agreed with it.

It was the effect that officer rotation had on the morale and commitment of both officers and enlisted men that made it such an unfortunate policy. Because of the constant changeover of personnel, there was a serious discontinuity of effort and a lack of unit cohesiveness. The arrangement also fostered inequities, resentment, and an every-man-for-himself attitude, as officers who saw Vietnam as just another notch on their belts, another step on the career ladder, became overly concerned with earning medals and résumé points while ignoring situations that might stir up trouble and reflect badly on them. Commanders, for example, tended to per-

Servicemen and -women assigned to Vietnam usually served tours of duty of one year. Career military people commonly served a number of one-year tours. To be "short" was to have but a few days of duty left in the war zone.

"My men have refused to go"...

During the withdrawal years, insubordination became a recurring problem for American commanders in Vietnam. Individual soldiers, sometimes whole units, refused to go into combat, in large part because the risk rarely seemed commensurate with the gain—especially since the army had been capturing and then abandoning territory for years. Furthermore, these soldiers had been inducted into combat service from a society that, after Tet 1968, was mostly against the war, and they were inevitably affected by that attitude.

Still, it was hard for Americans to believe that their army was falling apart. Two instances in particular reinforced the point, however. Newsmen happened to be along when American units refused their commanders' orders.

The first occurred in August 1969 in the Song Chang Valley in I Corps. Reporter Peter Arnett and photographer Horst Faas, both of Associated Press, were on the scene when Alpha Company of the 3rd Battalion, 196th Infantry Brigade, Americal Division, refused to attack North Vietnamese dug into a virtually invisible trenchline on Nui Lon Mountain. The company had made five assaults and suffered heavy casualties. Lieutenant Colonel Robert Bacon, with Arnett and Fass standing behind him, had ordered Lieutenant Eugene Schurtz, the Alpha Company commander, to give it another go.

A couple of moments passed and then Schurtz's voice was heard coming in on Bacon's radio. "I am sorry, sir, but my men have refused to go . . . We cannot move out."

"Repeat that, please," said Bacon. "Have you told them what it means to disobey orders under fire?"

"I think they understand," Schurtz replied, "but some of them simply have had enough. They are broken. There

petuate existing problems within their units by failing to report them. Since their predecessors, men like themselves with only a six-month commitment to the war, had not mentioned any problems, they feared that anything they said would only reflect badly on themselves. This probably accidental conspiracy of silence contributed to an atmosphere of evasion and obfuscation, which made it increasingly impossible to arrive at any meaningful evaluation of the competence of officers on combat duty. But there was one measurement that would increasingly be brought to bear.

In a war where the military objectives were so hard to define and standards of performance so difficult to measure, the body count—that grisly statistic which first achieved such prominence during the Vietnam war—became a frequently applied measure of combat performance. Other equally arbitrary numbers games were played, too. General Ewell, for example, who earned the nickname "the Delta Butcher," kept close track of how many combat medals his men were winning, not only for purposes of comparing his 9th Infantry Division with other divisions, but also, according to Cincinnatus, in order "to determine whether his men . . . were braver this month than last."

Many air force commanders played a similar game. Those of the 460th Tactical Reconnaissance Wing headquartered at Tan Son Nhut present one example. This wing was the largest reconnaissance unit in the air force, and its commander was always a senior colonel. Early on in the war a pattern was set that the commander of the 460th was promoted to general after his one-year term. This obviously became a strong inducement for subsequent 460th commanders to outdo those who preceded them. Essentially, the only measure of performance was the number of sorties flown. Consequently, the sortie totals went up and up throughout the war, regardless of the amount of enemy activity. Photo-intelligence analysts could not come close to examining all the film. During some battles more than one aircraft would be over the battle area at the same time; during Khe Sanh, reconnaissance aircraft took photos of one another!

The twelve-month limit on combat service for enlisted men was as damaging to morale and conducive to complacency as the six-month rotation for officers. For both the men and their families, the war was over with as soon as they themselves came marching home, so it took much longer than it probably would have under other circumstances for many GIs to turn against the war. But the continuing sacrifices that were demanded during the years of the withdrawal, when it became increasingly obvious that we had no achievable military objectives in Vietnam, eventually caused great bitterness and disillusionment within the ranks, as did the inequities of a system in which the privileged were exempt from service and the races were so disproportionately represented in combat. The unpopularity of the war back home, the shame of being involved in a war whose atrocities had horrified the world, the no-win strategy, and the utter meaninglessness of the sacrifice these men were asked to make were among the factors that transformed the once-proud American army. As Colonel Robert Heinl, a marine combat veteran and an expert on military strategy and organization, wrote at the time: By "every conceivable indicator, our army that now remains in Vietnam is in a state approaching collapse, with individual units avoiding or having refused combat, murdering their officers and noncommissioned officers, drug-ridden, and dispirited where not near mutinous."

Desertion figures were, of course, the clearest sign of the rising number of combat refusals. In 1967, when the commitment of American personnel in Vietnam totaled 465,400, 27,000 deserted worldwide (mostly in Vietnam, however). In 1970, 65,643 deserted, though the personnel level was a much lower 334,600 at the end of that year. And these figures do not include men who went AWOL (away without leave), or who refused combat. Nor were the combat refusals just individual; whole units began avoiding combat. The joke told by the men themselves was that search-and-destroy operations had become search-and-evade missions. William Broyles, Jr., the former editor in chief of *Newsweek* who served as a marine lieutenant from 1969 to 1970, has talked frankly about his unit faking patrol action "on our radios, talking to each other from a few feet away as if we were crossing rivers, climbing hills, taking up new positions. We weren't about to risk our lives."

Many professional soldiers, if not most, were similarly disposed, once the truth of the situation—that the U.S. was withdrawing from Vietnam no matter what—became clear. As one army lieutenant colonel expressed it, "The most are boys here who have only ninety days left in Vietman."

Bacon sent his executive officer and a senior NCO over to Alpha Company to give them "a pep talk and a kick in the butt." They eventually succeeded in getting them moving by fabricating a story about another of the battalion's companies, which had suffered even heavier casualties but was still in action: "Maybe they got something more than you've got." In response, one soldier, fists clinched, jumped to his feet. "Don't call us cowards," he screamed. "We are not cowards."

CBS Television reporter John Laurence and his camera crew were present during another instance of what the army called "combat refusal." In April 1970, they were accompanying Charlie Company of 2nd Battalion, 7th Cavalry, 1st Air Cavalry Division, on its way to a landing zone and evacuation from the jungles of War Zone C.

The most obvious route to the landing zone was a small road through the jungle. Captain Al Rice, the Charlie Company commander, ordered his men to follow it, but they refused. As standard operating procedure, Communist soldiers usually set up ambush positions along the road.

Thus challenged in front of the newsmen, whose camera was rolling, Rice, no doubt embarrassed, made the matter a test of will. "We're going to move on the road, period," he told Laurence.

But one of Rice's three squad leaders immediately contradicted him: "I'm not going to walk there. Nothing doing. My whole squad ain't walking down that trail . . . [It's] a suicide walk . . . We've had too many companies, too many battalions want to walk the road. They got blown away."

In the end, the soldiers won out. Charlie Company took an alternate route. And neither they nor the soldiers of Alpha Company were disciplined for insubordination. The army had to learn to live with these problems.

important part of my job now is to get as many men as possible back to the U.S. alive."

Those officers and noncommissioned officers who did not get this message were frequently given crude warnings, such as smoke grenades rolled under their beds. Those who still failed to ease the pressure were sometimes killed. Such murders were called "fraggings" after the weapons most frequently used: the fragmentation grenade, which, of course, left no fingerprints.

Reports of a young West Point graduate from Montana being fragged by his men caused Senator Mike Mansfield to order the army to investigate. The resulting study reported 209 fraggings in 1970, double the count from the year before. But that total is not complete: It was virtually impossible to determine how many officers and noncommissioned officers were shot by their own men during firefights with the

Three men from Company E, 2nd Battalion, 3rd Marines throw grenades ahead of their advance up Mutters Ridge near the DMZ, north of Dong Ha. Blacks served in disproportionate numbers in the war, especially in the later years.

enemy. Understandably, most combat leaders did not need a smoke grenade under their bunk to get the message. Stories got around. But men who didn't get the message might find that there was a price on their head. For example, writers for an underground newspaper called *GI Says* offered a $10,000 bounty for anyone who killed Lieutenant Colonel Weldon Honeycutt, who had led the Hamburger Hill assaults. (He returned home safely, however.)

With unit discipline breaking down so drastically, the societal and personal differences normally kept in check for the good of the group began causing violent eruptions. At Camp Evans, black and white soldiers, after facing off and yelling racial epithets at one another, rushed for their weapons. A firefight was averted only by their commander's timely intervention. At Tien Sha, near Danang, a brawl ensued after two white soldiers called black soldiers who had just staged a civil rights rally "black motherfuckers." Twelve blacks "caught them and did a job." Whites then joined the melee. In Saigon, because of strained racial relations, black soldiers had a black-only off-duty zone. "White military policemen refused to enter that area of the city except when accompanied by armed convoys." On the aircraft carriers *Constellation* and *Kitty Hawk,* race riots broke out. During one ten-month period, the 1st Marine Division reported seventy-nine racial incidents, including one in which a grenade was tossed into an enlisted men's club, killing one man and injuring sixty-two others.

Part of the problem was that the fire-hot racial problems in the U.S. during the sixties were exported to Vietnam. But the situation was also particular to the war, since blacks were serving there in such disproportionate numbers. (White men in the same age group enjoyed many avenues of escape from service in Vietnam which were not open to their disadvantaged brothers.) Furthermore, "Although they represented only one-ninth of the U.S. forces in Vietnam, blacks constituted one-fifth of combat troops. Some infantry units were nearly 50 percent black. And blacks accounted for 14 percent of all battle casualties." Discrimination showed up in other ways too. The black soldier's contribution was not fully recognized—as the account of Motown Doc, the black marine shot in the eye at Khe Sanh, indicates. In another war and if of another race, there would have

A boatload of GIs and Vietnamese prepare to cross the Yen River in Quang Nam Province for a village med-cap night. The idea was to win "the hearts and minds" of the Vietnamese people by attending to their medical needs.

The last draftee...

The last of the 1,766,911 draftees inducted into military service during the Vietnam war was Dwight Elliott Stone of Sacramento, California. He was sworn into the army on June 30, 1973.

Stone was initially called to duty in 1969 at the peak of the U.S. manpower commitment to the fighting. But his induction was deferred because of a knee injury sustained in an automobile accident.

Stone's draft board was too diligent to forget his case, however. Members monitored his improving health and eventually ordered him to report for induction. Seeing the war winding down and mindful of his brother's combat experiences in Vietnam, Stone refused to report. He ignored one notice after another. Finally he was charged with draft evasion. The indictment got his attention. As a result of plea bargaining with federal prosecutors, he agreed to report. He was sworn in on the last day of congressional authorization for the draft.

For all practical purposes the draft had ended six months earlier. In January 1973 President Nixon replaced it with the all-volunteer force. But because of Stone's violation of draft laws, he was pressed into service as punishment, though the last American combat soldier had left Vietnam in March.

Stone spent his sixteen months of active duty going to army training schools located in four different states. He was released eight months early because the army decided it wanted only volunteers in its ranks.

been books written and movies made about Motown Doc. But no one even recorded his real name.

It's not surprising that, given all these frustrations and pressures, so many American soldiers in Vietnam turned to drugs. Availability alone would have induced many to try them: Marijuana cigarettes cost only ten cents apiece in Saigon; opium sold for a dollar per injection, morphine for five dollars a vial; a heroin habit could be supported for as little as $2 per day. Street peddlers sold all forms of drugs. As one brigade officer observed: "When a man is in Vietnam, he can be sure that no matter where he is, who he is with, or who he is talking to, there are probably drugs within twenty-five feet of him." Defense Department studies confirmed this appraisal, revealing that drug use was on the upswing beginning in 1968; previously it had been more the exception than the rule. Of the soldiers in Vietnam in 1968, about twenty-five percent used marijuana. But between 1969 and 1970, almost fifty percent "were using marijuana on either a regular or occasional basis." Drugs became an escape-in-place from Vietnam, but there was no escape from the resulting addiction.

Mercifully, it all came to an end for American combat soldiers on March 29, 1973, when the last of them was ordered home. The little war had become the nation's longest; it had lasted eight years and cost the lives of 57,605 Americans. If not the most difficult the United States had ever fought, it was certainly the strangest. Our armies, navies and air forces had not lost a single major battle, but we left in defeat, knowing that our ally could not keep the Communists from eventually overrunning South Vietnam—which happened only two years after the return of the last American combat soldier.

It may have been that Westmoreland, Ewell, DePuy and other American generals who served in Vietnam would have earned positions in the front rank of our history's greatest commanders had the armies they led fought on the plains of Europe—a type of war for which they had been trained and against an enemy they understood. But, in the final analysis, the country's failure in Vietnam was not because of what we did not know about our enemy—considerable as that was. We failed because we knew so little about ourselves.

A Viet Cong soldier reported to have shot down two helicopters and destroyed two American armored personnel carriers poses with the rifles of four GIs.

✳ The money spent by the United States in South Vietnam after the partition in 1954 is roughly equal to the national debt as of January 1985—$24 billion in aid to South Vietnam from 1955 through 1975, plus $165 billion on war expenditures.

The Politics of Peace

The Press, The Protests, The Talks

O n October 22, 1963, Arthur Ochs Sulzberger, the new publisher of the *New York Times,* paid a courtesy call on President John F. Kennedy at the White House. At the time, the administration was riding high. Confidence born of an economy that was beginning to boom and the successful resolution of the Cuban missile crisis the previous fall made the president feel good about his forthcoming reelection campaign. The only problem on the horizon was Vietnam. The South Vietnamese government under Ngo Dinh Diem was losing the war against the Communists—a reality made worse by the fact that until recently the administration's commitment had been as much to Diem personally as it had been to South Vietnam.

A short time before Sulzberger's appointment with Kennedy, the *Times* had published an important story that its correspondent in Saigon, David Halberstam, had written in collaboration with Neil Sheehan of United Press. The two reported that the South Vietnamese Special Forces unit, which had been conducting violent raids on Buddhist pagodas, was funded by the U.S. government through the CIA. Although the U.S. was financing the six-battalion unit to fight the Communists, they wrote, it almost never did; rather, it had become Diem's private security force. The Vietnamese leader was more interested in keeping himself in power than he was in fighting the Communists. Displeased by this and other reports filed by Halberstam, who had become particularly adept at digging up bad news about the American effort in Vietnam, Kennedy decided to talk to Sulzberger about him. He did not want Vietnam to become an issue. With an election year so close at hand, he wanted only good news about Vietnam in the papers, especially in the most influential one in the country.

Almost the first question from Kennedy during his meeting with Sulzberger was "What do you think of your young man in Saigon?" Sulzberger replied that he thought that Halberstam was doing a fine job. Then Kennedy wondered aloud whether Halberstam was getting too close, too involved in the story; it was a not very subtle way of telling Sulzberger that the president of the United States wanted the publisher's twenty-eight-year-old reporter reassigned.

War protester John Khanlian of Columbia University; above, three "young Turks," early Vietnam reporters.

The Politics of Peace
❝In their own words.❞

❝*Hey! Hey! LBJ! How many kids did you kill today?*❞—War protest chant used for the first time by twenty thousand students at a rally in Washington, D.C.; in November 1965.

❝*Every government is run by liars and nothing they say should be believed.*❞—Journalist I. F. Stone, a vigorous opponent of the war; in 1967.

❝*My God, they're killing us!*❞—A young woman at Kent State University whose scream was the first voice heard after national guardsmen shot to death four student protesters; on May 4, 1970.

❝*I think that Vietnam was what we had instead of happy childhoods.*❞—Reporter Michael Herr, writing about what the experience of covering the Vietnam war was like for himself and other young journalists; in 1970.

But the paper refused to cooperate. In fact, its editors postponed an imminent two-week vacation scheduled for Halberstam so as not to appear to have succumbed to presidential pressure.

Kennedy's attempt to have Halberstam removed is an early, typical, example of behavior by a succession of presidents and their top officials in dealing with the press in Vietnam. From the time Kennedy decided that that country was the place to draw the line against Communist-supported wars of national liberation, his administration grappled with reporters covering events there. Initially, the source of Kennedy's problem with the Vietnam press corps was "the long-standing desire of the United States government to see the American involvement minimized, even represented as something less in reality than it is," as Robert Manning, one of Kennedy's own assistant secretaries of state, wrote in a report on the situation after a visit to Vietnam. Later, as the scope of the increased U.S. involvement became generally known, the Kennedy administration strove to create the impression that the U.S. effort in Vietnam was working; the administration then tried to discredit or, in Halberstam's case, remove those who reported otherwise.

So the bitter fruit that grew was first sown on the fertile fields of Camelot. For Kennedy, the activist president who changed the nature of the U.S. commitment in Vietnam, and for Johnson—until the war overwhelmed him—Vietnam seemed too small a problem about which to tell the American public the truth. Both men thought they were smart enough and the country powerful enough to dispose of it easily. As it turned out, each was too clever for the country's good. The U.S. was deeply involved before most Americans knew where Vietnam was. The war there was to become probably the single most divisive issue in American history since the Civil War. And once it had escalated to that stage, Vietnam seemed too *big* a problem for Johnson and Nixon to tell the American public the truth about.

One of the misconceptions that evolved as a result of the government's dishonesty is that it was the press, which was inclined to attempt to tell the truth, that caused the country to lose the war in Vietnam. The press is blamed for the disintegration of public support for the war. The reality is far different, however. Because U.S. leaders had never bothered to build a firm foundation of support, the consensus favoring the military effort in Vietnam was always thin and based mostly on the mistaken belief that the U.S. was proceeding toward a victory there. Tet of 1968 was decisive in ridding the American public of that delusion. Tet was also a turning point in the press's coverage of Vietnam. Up to that time, so-called negative reporting, including Halberstam's, had generally concentrated on disputing the optimistic appraisals of generals and embassy officials in Saigon. It was not until after Tet that the press considered the question of whether we belonged in Vietnam at all—and, as a consequence, turned against the conflict.

In the early years of the American commitment to South Vietnam, the basic tendency of the media was to support whatever U.S. presidents decided to do there. The fact that our adversaries were Communist was reason enough. Consensus was almost universal that the U.S. should breathe life into the government of South Vietnam. Reports were invariably sympathetic and supportive. Of the many Vietnamese who made their way from the north to the south after the partition in 1954, *Look* reported on January 25, 1955: "Battered and shunted by the war, they are too weary to resist the Reds without us." Nobody bothered to point out that our scare-tactic propaganda had helped to create the massive exodus of mainly Catholic refugees. Instead, the usual coverage maintained that South Vietnam "is still free but will fall under Red control if Communists win elections set for July of 1956. . . . Asians are convinced that U.S. prestige and influence in Asia cannot survive another defeat."

When Diem visited the U.S. in May 1957, President Eisenhower sent the *Columbine*, his personal plane, to fetch him from Saigon, and met him at the airport for what was a rare personal greeting. The press took its lead from Ike. *Time*'s Henry Luce presided over a banquet in honor of Diem, and he was hailed as the "miracle man of Vietnam." Concurrently, the *New York Times* editorialized that the form of "democracy" that Diem was espousing for Vietnam was of a type with which "Thomas Jefferson would have no quarrel." *Times* reporters noted that "by establishing democratic forms, President Diem had carved a deep niche in official esteem in Washington." On May 13, 1957, *Life* listed as one of Diem's greatest achievements his refusal to allow "the famous Geneva election"

Ho Chi Minh's efforts to woo American public opinion began during the Second World War. On August 26, 1945, Vo Nguyen Giap (front right) and other Ho lieutenants honored a small American military delegation headed by Major Archimedes Patti (front left) upon its arrival in Hanoi. Together they saluted the U.S. flag during official ceremonies.

Dr. Tom Dooley helped shape America's view of Vietnam as a land of persecution and deprivation under siege by Communists.

The Reverend Billy Graham smiles for the cameraman during one of a number of visits to South Vietnam. Religious leaders were initially a potent force of support for the anti-Communist crusade there.

that would have unified the two Vietnams under one government. The magazine noted that most Vietnamese thought Ho Chi Minh would have won the plebiscite and that, therefore, Diem saved South Vietnam from "national suicide."

Press support for Diem continued for years, despite obvious signs of nepotism, corruption and authoritarian rule. In the December 24, 1959, issue of the now-defunct *Reporter* magazine (a press trade journal), an article on Vietnam maintained that Diem's government was imperfect only in that he was "compelled to ration" democracy because of the Communist threat. The June 29, 1960, issue of *Newsweek* called Diem "one of Asia's ablest leaders." The November 21, 1960, issue of *Time* called him "doughty little Diem."

Such uniformly favorable reporting was not surprising given the Red Scare and the residual pressures of the McCarthy period. What was surprising was the extent of the coverage South Vietnam and Diem received. In retrospect, it is possible to trace how this came about, for it was by no means accidental.

Though editors and readers were not inherently interested in goings-on in Vietnam, a small but powerful group of men, including Francis Cardinal Spellman, set out to arouse public interest. Spellman, known as "the most vocal lobbyist for Diem in the United States," spoke throughout the country on the subject of Vietnam. In August 1954, he told those gathered at an American Legion convention: "If Geneva and what was agreed upon there means anything at all, it means . . . taps for the buried hopes of freedom in Southeast Asia." Spellman mobilized the interest of the Catholic Relief Service and, as a gesture of his strong support, personally delivered that organization's first check to Diem in Saigon. The Friends of Vietnam, a lobbying group and clearinghouse for favorable information, was set up at about the same time. Listed on its letterhead, among others, were historian Arthur Schlesinger, Jr., and columnist Max Lerner. As previously discussed, its membership also included Senators John F. Kennedy, Mike Mansfield and Supreme Court Justice William O. Douglas, and because its members were so prominent, they were often called by reporters writing about Vietnam. "As a result," Robert Scheer observed in his 1965 study entitled *How the United States Got Involved in Vietnam*, "those who were most intimately involved in the American program there generally blossomed as the chief sources of information and opinion. This was natural, but most of them were committed protagonists and their writing soon became propaganda for the cause."

Joseph Buttinger was one of the key members and most prolific writers of the Friends group. (He was an Austrian émigré intellectual who was an ardent anti-Communist. He served as an adviser to Diem until turning against him because of his policies. Later Buttinger wrote a two-volume history of Vietnam.) According to James Aronson, author of *The Press and the Cold War,* it was Buttinger, along with Spellman and Colonel Edward Lansdale of the CIA, who assuaged Joseph Alsop's early reservations about how Diem was running his government. Alsop, a columnist who carried great influence with editorial boards as well as with public and private officials, thereafter remained an unwavering proponent of the American commitment to Vietnam and the war.

The overall effort to create support for South Vietnam and Diem in the press was organized and aggressive. Spellman arranged for the passionate and persuasive Buttinger to make presentations to the editors of the *New York Times,* the editorial board of the *New York Herald-Tribune,* and the chief editors of *Time* and *Life.* Spellman also introduced Buttinger to Joseph P. Kennedy, and together the men formulated plans for a professional publicity program supporting Diem. Eventually, the agency of Newcomb-Oram was signed up to help out and was paid three thousand dollars per month plus expenses.

Before long, support for Diem and South Vietnam was so mainstream that Michigan State University, to its future and everlasting embarrassment, was training Diem's special police — whom American servicemen later disparagingly referred to as the "white mice," because of the white shirts they wore and their cowardice in the face of Communist terrorists. (They were quite adept at beating up the average South Vietnamese, however.) The program was headed by Dr. Wesley Fishel of MSU's criminology school.

Perhaps not coincidentally, coverage by the *New York Times* started changing when Buttinger turned against Diem and actively supported Vietnamese dissidents in the United States. However, there were other signals warning *Times* editors that something was wrong in

The American perception of South Vietnam's troubles was formed in a vacuum without benefit of cultural and historical understanding. During the fifties, insurrection in South Vietnam was perceived as a crime problem. A team of experts headed by Michigan State University's Dr. Wesley Fishel, shown here arriving at Tan Son Nhut airport with his family, was sent to train Ngo Dinh Diem's police.

Vietnam. For example, on November 21, 1960, South Vietnamese paratroopers revolted against Diem. The rebellion was suppressed, but four hundred civilians who joined in the march on the presidential palace were killed. To report on the developments, the *Times* sent one of its more distinguished reporters, Homer Bigart, a two-time Pulitzer Prize winner, to South Vietnam. Until late 1963, Bigart and his successor, David Halberstam, were the only representatives of a U.S. daily newspaper assigned there. These men, along with Neil Sheehan of United Press, Malcolm Browne of Associated Press, François Sully of *Newsweek,* Charles Mohr of *Time,* and a few others comprised a small but unusually capable press corps.

Their mandate was not to question the grounds for a U.S. commitment in Vietnam but rather to observe Diem's government and assess how well his troops, financed by the U.S., were fighting. Their verdict was that neither Diem nor his troops were doing very well and that the American commitment was increasing in inverse proportion to our ally's poor performance. Such negative publicity irked Kennedy no end. Pierre Salinger later wrote in *With Kennedy* that the residual effect of the Bay of Pigs and Berlin crises, the latter necessitating a troop buildup in Europe, was that the president was "not anxious to admit the existence of a real war in Southeast Asia." And so Kennedy made things difficult for the Saigon press corps.

One step taken by the administration was to issue a State Department directive (later known as Cable 1006) to its information service in Saigon. Its purpose was to restrict the movement of news correspondents and their dissemination of certain information on the grounds of compromised national security; but it didn't work and, as Salinger noted, stories began appearing in print and on television "describing heavy involvement of United States forces in Vietnamese operations, and . . . the shooting down of United States helicopters."

After some months of putting up with the administration's obstructions, Malcolm Browne filed an unusually frank and personal story that was picked up from the AP by the *New York Times* and other papers on March 24, 1962. Browne wrote that many correspondents "feel they are losing" in their effort to report what is going on. "The Vietnamese government is against us," he said. "They figure we are all spies or

(L-r) David Halberstam of the *New York Times,* Malcolm Browne of AP and Neil Sheehan of UPI wait to board a helicopter in the Mekong Delta region in November 1963. Their reporting refuted optimistic accounts by American officials and stirred President Kennedy's ire.

Communist propagandists. The United States will not tell us much beyond the broad outlines of their policy and we cannot even be sure of that. After trying for weeks to get a story from unofficial sources, we may end up being blocked by the censors."

What motivated Browne to write the piece was a South Vietnamese government expulsion order issued against Sully and Bigart. Although the order was later withdrawn after the U.S. State Department had its mission explain the potential political ramifications of expelling so distinguished a reporter as Bigart on so powerful a paper as the *Times,* Bigart had had enough, and he bluntly stated his attitude in the April 1962 issue of *Times Talk,* his paper's organ: "I regarded my reprieve with mixed feelings. This has not been a happy assignment. Saigon is a nice place to spend a few days in. The food and wine are good, the city is attractive, most hotels and restaurants are air-conditioned. But to work here is peculiarly depressing. Too often correspondents seem to be regarded by the American mission as tools of our foreign policy. Those who balk are apt to find it a bit lonely, for they are likely to be distrusted and shunned by American and Vietnam officials. I am sick of it. Each morning I take a pen and blot off another day on the Saigon calendar. At this writing I have 83 more days to go."

In May 1962, the administration persuaded John Mecklin, a foreign reporter and San Francisco bureau chief for *Time,* to take a temporary leave from his employer to become the public affairs officer for the U.S. mission in Saigon. But relations with the small press corps did not improve, the root of the problem being "that the U.S. had bet all its chips on Diem," as Mecklin later wrote in *Mission in Torment,* his account of his experiences in Vietnam. "There was no alternative, fall-back policy if Diem failed us," he said. Nor did disappointment with Diem lessen the U.S. government's displeasure with the newsmen. In Washington and Saigon, the administration worked all the harder to undermine the press's credibility. Salinger attacked reports filed from Vietnam as inaccurate and emotional, while other Kennedy assistants accused journalists there of never going out into the field to see what was going on—which was untrue, as anyone could tell by examining the photos they took in the field or the stories they wrote. In fact, some of Halberstam's Saigon peers were

The patriotism of some correspondents was questioned because of their "negative reporting." After *Newsweek*'s François Sully reported that the war was a "losing proposition," fellow reporters demanded that he declare whether he was a Communist or not.

telling him that he was spending too much time in the field; that the principal story at the time was the political saga unfolding in Saigon, not the war being waged in the hinterlands.

Administration officials also began dubbing the Saigon press corps "the young Turks." It was an attempt to convey an image of them as—in Halberstam's words—"punk kids." But Bigart was in his midfifties, and Halberstam, though a young man, had already distinguished himself as a *Times* reporter covering the Congo, another hot-spot during those days. Sully, a Frenchman who had fought in the Resistance as a teenager during the Second World War, had lived in Vietnam for seventeen years, covering for *Newsweek* and other publications the French attempt to reestablish control in Vietnam.

In Saigon, criticism of the press corps was even more personal and harsh; some accused them of being unpatriotic and suffering from personal prejudice. When Admiral Harry Felt, the commander of U.S. forces in the Pacific, was asked a tough question by Browne during a Saigon press conference, the officer paused, taking a couple of seconds to size up the newsman, and then said, "So you're Browne. Why don't you get on the team?" And during a meeting attended by senior American officials in Saigon, when the subject of one of Bigart's "negative stories" came up one man remarked that "Mr. Bigart spells his name wrong"—it should be "bigot."

Sniping like this, especially when it emanated from the White House, helped undercut the credibility of some of the reporters with their home offices, where editors were inclined to believe conventional government sources and support any anti-Communist crusade. To further encourage this second-guessing of the reporters in the field, the Kennedy administration sponsored short visits to Vietnam for some of the influential journalists who, because of their connections to high government officials, had more of an institutional bias—most notably Joseph Alsop, who was treated like a visiting head of state, with planes being placed at his disposal and dinner engagements with the ambassador and all the top generals. The columnist made a number of such trips. After one 1963 visit, he likened the behavior of the "young crusaders," as he called the reporters, to that of unnamed newsmen whom he accused of having contributed to the fall of China and Cuba to the Communists. He

Joseph Alsop receives a briefing from two marine officers, Lieutenant Colonel Barnard and Major General D. J. Robertson. Alsop and other influential journalists who supported U.S. policy in Vietnam received VIP treatment during visits there.

even held them responsible for some of "the Diem government's misguidedness. . . . [W]e actually were winning the war this spring," he wrote in his column, "until the Diem government went right around the bend with considerable help from the highminded crusaders."

Another of the reporters—and there were many—who on the basis of brief trips to Saigon deemed the press coverage there to be biased was the *New York Herald-Tribune*'s Marguerite Higgins, who was married to a general. "Reporters here would like to see us lose the war to prove they are right," she wrote. Halberstam says that a false story about himself and Higgins later made the rounds, which Marine General Victor Krulak delighted in telling. At a meeting with Higgins in a Saigon bar, Halberstam supposedly showed her a photograph of dead bodies, asked her if she had ever seen dead men, and then burst into tears. Halberstam says he does not know whether the story was Krulak's or Higgins's invention. (Years later, Halberstam remarked that he would feel better about himself if the story had indeed been true.)

Such support emboldened Diem, his brother Nhu and Madame Nhu in dealing with the American newsmen, of course. The South Vietnamese press, controlled by Diem, accused Sully of being "a Communist, a French spy, a participant in sex orgies, an opium smuggler, and even a promoter of the bombing attack on the presidential palace in February 1962." Browne, who took the famous photograph of the Buddhist monk Thich Quang Duc's self-immolation (see page 191), was indirectly accused by Diem of paying other monks to murder the man so he could get a good photo. Regrettably, such bizarre accusations were not confined to the Diem government. Halberstam was later told by a friend in the State Department that "It was a damn good thing you never belonged to any left-wing groups or anything like that, because they [officials in the Kennedy administration] were really looking for stuff like that."

Inevitably, reporters' relationships with the U.S. government, the Diem government, their home offices and even their colleagues ruptured. The American mission clamped down on the reporters' sources—mostly middle-level men (like Lieutenant Colonel John Paul Vann) who were responsible for implementing policy and knew how bad things were—and made it much more difficult to get uncensored news out of the coun-

Middle-level officers in the field such as Lieutenant Colonel John Paul Vann (left), shown here with Major Harold Dill and South Vietnamese officers, were the source of the candid, pessimistic progress reports by journalists such as David Halberstam.

NBC's John Sharkey prepares to interview Brigadier General Frederick Karch, the commander of the 9th Marine Expeditionary Brigade, on April 10, 1965, during the early marine landings in South Vietnam. The historic landings caused little stir in the U.S. At this point, the press turned supportive of the war and, for several years, did not question that American commitment.

try. The reporters circumvented those restrictions by smuggling film and stories out via airline pilots and departing soldiers. Because of the crackdown on sources and surveillance by Diem's secret police, reporters from different news organizations were frequently forced to pool their information to develop a story, as Halberstam and Sheehan had done on the Vietnamese Special Forces story that was published shortly before Sulzberger met with Kennedy. The two men felt so much pressure, in fact, that they traveled to the Philippines to write the story, and published it without a byline.

One early dramatic result of these constraints on freedom of the press involved Sully, after his article entitled "Vietnam: The Unpleasant Truth" was published in the August 22, 1962, issue of *Newsweek*. In it he quoted Bernard Fall as saying that the war was a "losing proposition" and that the U.S. did not know how to train the South Vietnamese for the kind of battles they had to fight. Diem promptly ordered him out of the country—this was Sully's second expulsion order—and when reporters met with one another to decide whether they could protect him, another rupture occurred, this one among the reporters themselves. According to Mecklin, "A dozen of them argued until 3 A.M. in a room at the Hotel Caravelle. They were torn between those who wanted to fight back with a strongly worded protest, and those who feared that they too might be expelled if the protest angered the palace. There were numerous epithets, e.g., 'coward.' The dispute reached a McCarthyesque moment when Sully was formally required to say whether he was (1) a French spy or (2) a Communist. He replied no to both questions."

No agreement was reached, but reporters from the *New York Times, Time,* AP, UPI, CBS and NBC mailed letters of protest to Diem and Kennedy. Though Diem called their missives "iniquitous blackmail," Kennedy was at least superficially conciliatory, assuring them that "our officials will continue to assist you in every way feasible to carry out your all-important task." Eager for reassurance, most of the reporters were pleased by Kennedy's response, but Mecklin saw it as a "brush-off," a judgment in which he was confirmed by the U.S. mission's tepid and ineffective support of NBC's James Robinson several weeks later when Diem ordered his expulsion. According to Aronson, Robinson's crime was telling someone "that an interview with [Diem] was a waste of time." Word of the remark got back to Diem, who successfully forced Robinson to leave the country.

Newsweek, which like other publications had been receiving all sorts of complaints from administration officials about their reporting from Vietnam, sent columnist Kenneth Crawford to Saigon for a "new look" after Sully was forced out. In the December 10, 1962, issue of the magazine, Crawford reported that Diem was pursuing "the right strategy," that his government was reforming, and that he enjoyed the peasants' enthusiastic support.

Time went through a similarly sudden metamorphosis in its reporting, though it was less obvious to its readers than *Newsweek*'s because Sully had had less trouble getting his stories past home-office editors intact. Mohr, by contrast, complained constantly about his copy being rewritten by editors who "uniformly" told him "that he was too close to the scene and couldn't see 'the big picture.'" The rupture at *Time* occurred in August 1963 when editors asked Mohr to write a comprehensive story detailing the reasons for the differences between the press and the governments of both South Vietnam and the U.S. No sooner had that assignment been completed than *Time* editors asked Mohr to write, with his assistant Matt Perry, a roundup story on the U.S. presence in Vietnam. For that assignment, the two men produced in three days a twenty-five-page story. Both articles arrived in *Time*'s New York offices at about the same time. The roundup began with the line, "The war in Vietnam is being lost." According to Halberstam, "The roundup left no doubt that the American mission had come to the end of one road, and that our past policy had failed. Unfortunately, this was not what the editors of *Time* wanted to hear; in New York, Mohr's file was put aside, and Greg Dunne, a young contributing editor, was told to write an optimistic piece. Dunne refused and announced that he would write no more stories about Vietnam, but others stepped into the breach. Eventually a story was printed which bore no relation to Mohr and Perry's file; among other things, it said that 'Government troops are fighting better than ever.'"

In the meantime, *Time*'s managing editor, Otto Fuerbringer, had decided, without informing Mohr, to discard his press piece as well and have another written. He called a writer into his

Ed Needham of ABC interviews a young soldier in late 1966. Vietnam was the first war covered extensively by television.

Reporting the Communist side...

Few Western reporters covered the Vietnam war from the North Vietnamese–Viet Cong side of the fighting. One who did was Wilfred Burchett, an Australian journalist whose most notable achievement prior to Vietnam was his being the first to report to the West from the Hiroshima bomb site. In Vietnam he freelanced for the British Communist daily *Morning Star,* the American *National Guardian* and the Japanese *Mainichi* group.

Burchett wore the black-pajama, conical-hat, peasant uniform of the Viet Cong guerrilla. He traveled with the enemy by foot, bicycle and sampan, sometimes within several miles of Saigon in allied-controlled territory. His sympathies were no secret: "The U.S. puppet regime, no matter what new personalities the puppet masters may push to the top in the endless cycle of coup and counter-coup, is doomed," he once reported.

Burchett's presence was no secret, either. He was well known and, so he claims, a target for the Americans. "My size and grey hair probably showed up on reconnaissance photographs," he says.

In 1972 Burchett was in China during Richard Nixon's visit. After a banquet in Hangchow, Chinese leader Chou En-lai motioned Burchett forward and with a twinkle in his eyes introduced him to Nixon. "Ah, yes," said the president. "You're the Australian correspondent. I've heard of you."

New York office, twelve thousand miles away from events in Saigon, and dictated his own perceptions of the press corps to the writer, who then shaped the dictation into a story. Part of Fuerbringer's motivation was to explain why *Time*'s roundup differed so markedly from the reporting in other publications and on the radio and television networks. He blamed pack journalism—the reporters were spending too much time together, he said, pooling "their convictions, information, misinformation and grievances." He offered this conclusion to *Time* readers: "The reporters have tended to reach unanimous agreement on almost everything they have seen. But such agreement is suspect because it is so obviously inbred. The newsmen have themselves become a part of Vietnam's confusion; they have covered a complex situation from only one angle, as if their own conclusions offered all the necessary illumination. Such reporting is prone to distortions. The complicated greys of a complicated country fade into oversimplified blacks and whites. . . . Any other version of the Vietnam story is dismissed as the fancy of a bemused observer."

What Fuerbringer apparently did not know was that the Kennedy administration had by then reached conclusions about Diem identical to those of the reporters in Saigon. U.S. officials under Ambassador Lodge were working with Vietnamese generals to get rid of Diem. Fuerbringer's story appeared in *Time* on September 20, 1963. Forty-three days later, Diem was overthrown and killed. By that time, Mohr and Perry had resigned as a direct result of the discarding of their pieces.

In many respects, the turmoil that the young Turks caused seemed only a tempest in a teapot, but the suspicions they aroused and the divisions they exposed would have a gradual and significant impact for years after the stories they filed. However, for the most part, their only immediate effect was to upset a few men in the boardrooms of government and the media, where all the captains remained convinced that the ship of state was on course. But far below deck, a few people saw some cracks in the hull and, as a consequence, had a much different vision of the future. And though these underlings would be ignored for a long time, they would eventually take over the ship.

The origin of organized opposition to the Vietnam

war can be traced to 1964, when eight hundred mostly white college students recruited from throughout the country participated in a black voter registration drive called the Mississippi Summer Project. The largest contingent of students was from the Berkeley campus of the University of California. The project was the idea of Robert Moses, a young black activist who a couple of years before had set up the Council of Federated Organizations (COFO), an operating coalition that included the Student Non-Violent Coordinating Committee (SNCC), the Congress of Racial Equality (CORE), the Southern Christian Leadership Conference (SCLC), and local chapters of the National Association for the Advancement of Colored People (NAACP).

The work for which these students had volunteered was dangerous, probably much more so than they had realized when they signed up. But Police Chief "Bull" Connor's dogs tearing into a thousand black children on May 2, 1963, in Birmingham, and Alabama state police overwhelming peaceful protest marchers with tear gas and billy clubs on March 7, 1964, at Selma, for example, had aroused the interest and stirred the passion of these young men and women. So too had the dramatic civil rights march on Washington on August 29, 1963, at which Martin Luther King delivered his famous "I have a dream" speech. Though the students were from mainly middle- and upper-class homes and could easily have ignored the whole civil rights movement in the South, they were from an idealistic generation raised to believe in the perfectability of American society, and they continued to believe that all things were possible even after their hero, John Kennedy, lay dead and buried.

And so they set out to rid the country of what Chief Justice Earl Warren called the "forces of hatred and malevolence" that were "eating into the bloodstream of American life." Warren, President Lyndon Johnson and other national leaders had publicly attributed Kennedy's assassination in Dallas to a climate of hatred that the students naïvely believed existed only in the South. This notion was confirmed in their minds by the images of Connor and Alabama Governor George Wallace that they had seen in the news and by the fact that Kennedy had been murdered in a southern city. But the summer of 1964 would alter that perception for them. They would not only come to appreciate for the first time the

Alabama Governor George Wallace and other Southern leaders, by resisting the civil rights movement, fired the passions of many students and indirectly spurred the anti–Vietnam war movement.

Civil rights protests, such as the huge
March on Washington on August 29,
1963, demonstrated the political power
of grass-roots organization and mass
mobilization.

intensity of the hatred that separated the races;
they would come to the conclusion that the
problem was not simply regional but national in
scope. Indeed, even as they were being recruited
to go, Wallace, the very embodiment of racist
views, was racking up impressive vote totals in
Democratic presidential primaries in Wisconsin,
Indiana and Maryland. His success in these
three states would allow him to become a full-
fledged candidate for president four years later.

What would eventually disturb the eight hundred students almost as much as the racism was
that their national government in Washington,
with which they had always associated the
forces of good in both peace and war, seemed to
them either unwilling or unable to correct the
problems they would experience firsthand. The
process of disillusionment began almost as soon
as they gathered on the campus of Western
College for Women in Oxford, Ohio, for a one-
week training course preparatory to driving
down into Mississippi to begin their work. The
training included many briefings, including one
by Burke Marshall and John Doar of the Justice
Department, who explained the difficulty of
protecting someone's civil rights in the South.
"How is it," one of the students asked, "that the
government can protect the Vietnamese from
the Viet Cong, and the same government will
not accept the moral responsibility of protecting
the people of Mississippi?" As part of their
training they also learned passive resistance
techniques that they could use to protect themselves from southern law-enforcement officials
prone to use violence; they were to assume the
fetal position when attacked by police, hands
clasped behind the neck in such a way as to
protect the temples with their elbows, feet crossed
so that the police couldn't swing nightsticks
between their legs—quite a lesson in reality for
middle-class college students!

The eight hundred had been divided into two
groups and were trained separately in successive weeks, with a number of civil rights veterans joining them as participants. On the first
morning of the second course, Moses was lecturing when an associate walked into the meeting
hall and quietly interrupted him, whispering in
his ear. Moses had just finished saying, "The
country is unwilling yet to admit it has the
plague, but it pervades the whole society."

The news that the visitor brought was bad,
and the shock on Moses's face reflected it. Three

trainees who had sat in the very same hall the previous week and had departed for Mississippi only two days before had been reported missing following their arrest by the Neshoba County police.

Reacting quickly, President Johnson ordered sailors from a nearby naval installation to begin a search, and he assigned the investigation not only to J. Edgar Hoover of the FBI but also to Allen Dulles of the CIA. Six weeks of searching turned up not a clue, though the mutilated bodies of two blacks not associated with the summer project were dredged up from nearby rivers. Finally, a tip broke the case open, and the bodies of the missing civil rights workers, two white and one black, were found. All three had been beaten and shot and then buried in a newly constructed earthen dam. The pathologist who examined their bodies said the black man had been beaten with chains and that his injuries were like no other he had seen except for victims of plane crashes.

The local investigation to bring the perpetrators to justice stalled; however, on December 4 that year, the federal government charged the Neshoba County sheriff, a deputy and nineteen others with civil rights violations—namely, killing the three men. But only six days later the charges were dropped because they were based on "incompetent" hearsay evidence developed by the FBI.

The summer project went on without interruption following the disappearances. Both training groups had been warned of the dangers, of course, the latter especially having reason to reevaluate their decision to participate. Only two withdrew.

That fall the students returned to their campuses as battle-tested activists schooled in the techniques of civil disobedience. Almost immediately some of them went to work. At Berkeley they formed an ad hoc committee that organized picketing of the conservative *Oakland Tribune,* whose publisher was none other than former Republican Senator William Knowland, an advocate of American intervention in Vietnam since the time of Dien Bien Phu. But Vietnam was not yet the students' complaint; they accused the paper of racial discrimination and said so on their placards.

To put an end to the picketing, someone at the paper called the University of California--Berkeley administration, protesting the fact that organizing efforts for the picketing were

Martin Luther King, Jr., with his wife Coretta by his side and his lieutenant Andrew Young (arms upraised), moves out from a massing point for a voting rights march on Montgomery, Alabama, on March 25, 1965. King quickly perceived the war in Vietnam as a threat to the civil rights movement; his public opposition to the war followed this realization.

Student demonstrators supporting the Free Speech Movement march through Sather Gate at the University of California at Berkeley on November 20, 1964. By the time the marines landed on the shores of South Vietnam, "A rebellion was already in being and searching for a cause," observes one historian.

being conducted on school property—specifically, a strip of sidewalk outside the main gate on Bancroft Way where all types of organizations and causes (ranging from ad hoc civil rights groups to Youth for Goldwater) recruited volunteers and solicited funds. Tables were usually set up for administrative use, and speakers nearby tried to capture the attention of passersby. The area had become a sort of Hyde Park.

Responding to the phone call from the *Oakland Tribune* executive, the school closed the strip to political organizing ten days after picketing of the paper began. Three days later, on September 17, a coalition of student organizations protested. And on the twenty-first, the first day of classes, the school administration under President Clark Kerr announced what it apparently thought was a compromise policy—the students could have their tables on Bancroft Way, but they couldn't use them for raising funds or membership or any advocacy proceedings, which were the only reasons for having tables. Soon students began ignoring the new school policy, and on September 30 the administration ordered five of them to the office. Sensing trouble, five hundred students showed up with them, led by Mario Savio, a graduate philosophy student. The group said that if the five were punished, all five hundred should be. Ignoring the show of student solidarity, the school suspended eight students. There followed the next day what Godfrey Hodgson in *America in Our Time* calls the "Boston Tea Party of the student revolution."

A young man named Jack Weinberg, a graduate student in mathematics who had temporarily dropped out of school, was manning a table on Bancroft Way for CORE. He was ordered to leave but refused to do so. Campus officials then called the police. By the time one arrived, a crowd had gathered, so he went for reinforcements. In the meantime, Weinberg explained his position, which someone tape-recorded. "This is a knowledge factory," he said. "If you read Clark Kerr's book, those are his words. . . . This is mass production; no deviations from the norm are tolerated. . . . We feel that we, as human beings first and students second, must take our stand on every vital issue of discrimination, of segregation, of poverty, of unemployment."

Like others in the civil rights movement, Weinberg invited arrest to make a point. He stood his ground and soon policemen arrived in a cruiser to take him into custody for trespass.

Weinberg immediately fell limp, employing a passive-resistance technique. And while the policemen struggled to carry him to the car, the crowd, some of whom were also schooled in the techniques of the civil rights movement, sat down all around the cruiser. And there they remained for thirty-two hours, immobilizing the vehicle. As a result, its roof became the first rostrum of the student movement. One speaker after another railed against the school administration. Professors joined the conclave, too, some speaking for, some against the protest.

The next day Kerr warned that the school administration and regents would not be intimidated into changing rules "in the face of mob action." And so nearly a thousand policemen from Oakland, the county and the California Highway Patrol occupied the campus.

The tension quickly subsided after a temporary compromise was worked out. A numbing dialogue ensued over the following weeks, with the activist students now loosely bound by Savio's leadership under the banner of the Free Speech Movement (FSM). By one estimate, only about ten percent of the student body supported the organization at that time, but then Kerr, probably frustrated by the distraction as much as anything else, made the mistake of threatening to expel Savio and another student leader, though both had been guaranteed immunity. The effect was to broaden the base of support for the FSM. On December 2, 1964, six thousand students gathered for a sit-in at the school's administration building. Fifteen hundred actually got inside the structure and eventually eight hundred were arrested. Quickly the school was brought to a halt. Students walked out and classes stopped.

Desperately trying to reestablish control over his campus, Kerr announced that he would speak to all who cared to listen at an outdoor amphitheater. Eight thousand students and faculty members showed up to hear him implore all to opt for "the powers of persuasion against the use of force." When Kerr finished talking, Savio stepped forward to the microphone to announce that a mass meeting (to which Kerr had been invited) would be held to discuss Kerr's remarks and the issues. While Savio was talking, two policemen stepped up behind him, one grabbing his arms and pinning his elbows behind his back, the other wrapping an arm around his neck and twisting, as they removed him from

✳ In one of history's ironic footnotes, the divisiveness of the four years of fighting in Vietnam from 1964 to 1968 becomes brutally clear from a look at the names on Lyndon Johnson's 1964 short list of possible vice-presidential running mates. He seriously considered only two men: Hubert Humphrey, whom he eventually chose; and Eugene McCarthy, by 1968 the leader of the antiwar movement within the Democratic Party.

The making of a sixties radical...

Many of the sixties generation were radicalized by a series of traumatic events—in Dallas, in Mississippi and in Vietnam. "But even more, perhaps," suggests author Godfrey Hodgson, "they were driven into radical rebellion by their personal experience of those whom they expected to be their allies: by what they saw as the liberals' equivocation and manipulation." Tom Hayden, the former Student for Democratic Society (SDS) leader and Chicago Seven defendant who is now a California assemblyman and married to Jane Fonda, is one such person, and his story is told because it is so typical.

Hayden's journey to the left began in the summer of 1960, when as the editor of the University of Michigan student newspaper, he hitchhiked to California to cover the Democratic National Convention and John Kennedy's nomination. On the way he stopped at Berkeley, where he introduced himself to a person handing out leaflets. "I'd never seen anything like this before," he says, "and being political, they took me home and gave me a room to stay in for a few weeks and tried to educate me politically." His political education included trips to the nuclear reactor at Livermore where hydrogen bombs were made and to the fertile farmlands where Chicanos labored and were trying to organize.

Hayden's summer experience with his Berkeley mentors was his first contact with the Left. Questions about the ethics of nuclear war and the need to organize certain disadvantaged elements of American society were new to him. But Hayden, the son of working-class parents from the Detroit suburbs, was not yet ready for disillusionment. "I was in part tied to the Kennedy image also, the appeal of the New Frontier."

The next step in Hayden's radicalization occurred the following summer. In 1961 he and Paul Potter, a Michigan

the stage. Only Kerr's quick intervention kept students from rushing the stage; Savio was released. Outraged by the incident and the invasion of the campus by hundreds of police, the faculty that very afternoon voted 824 to 115 to grant the Free Speech Movement's demands that restrictions on political activities and speech on campus be the same as in the community at large, thereby removing essentially all the objections that had caused the turmoil. But sporadic protests continued during the next several months for no particular reason. As Godfrey Hodgson describes the situation, "A rebellion was already in being and searching for a cause."

Within a couple of months of the faculty vote, Lyndon Johnson, the man who as a candidate had promised the nation peace, ordered American fighter-bombers into the air against North Vietnam. The Flaming Dart I and II raids were executed on February 8 and 11, 1965; and by early March, Rolling Thunder, the sustained air war, had begun and the marines had landed on Nam O Beach.

With a semester's worth of organizing and activism behind them, students at Berkeley reacted immediately with "marches, pickets, rallies and debates on the subject." And even before the marines had landed, about one hundred members of the Free Speech Movement, led by Art Goldberg, a Savio lieutenant, had staged a protest march on the Oakland army terminal. Some faculty members were also stirred to act; about eighty of them signed a protest advertisement that appeared in the *New York Times* on March 1.

The Oakland terminal was twice more the object of protest marches that month. During the second one, on the twenty-third, fifteen were arrested. That same day the son of a Berkeley professor burned his draft card in public.

Students in other parts of the country reacted to the bombing of North Vietnam, too. They followed the lead of their peers at Berkeley, who had both reflected and influenced their political attitudes during the preceding six months. This was a generation whose idealism had been stirred by Kennedy, the first president they had known as adults, and encouraged by affluence: they thought they had the time for political protest, for it was an article of faith of middle-class white students that their economic status in life would almost automatically be greater than that of their parents.

Students at the University of Michigan at Ann Arbor, which had sent a sizable contingent to the Mississippi Summer Project, joined with faculty members to make a unique and important contribution to the anti–Vietnam war movement in response to Flaming Dart I and II. On March 11, 1965, about fifteen Michigan professors gathered at the home of one of them to decide what to do. The group included philosopher Arnold Kaufman, who had been the local chairman of the Johnson-Humphrey campaign three months before, and Dr. William Gamson, a sociologist who, though not a political activist with great experience, made the key contribution to the discussions of the evening. Gamson had been a member of CORE in the Boston area when a school boycott there had been organized. To occupy the time of Boston students not attending normal classes, a "Freedom School" had been organized to teach black history and civil rights. Gamson recounted the details of this experience to his associates, who quickly locked onto it as a constructive and significant form of protest to American policy in Southeast Asia. Other ideas discussed were newspaper ads and a hunger strike.

The group immediately went about recruiting additional support for the idea, and on March 17 the school paper, the *Michigan Daily,* reported that thirty-five faculty members were ready to walk out of classes on March 24 to protest the Johnson administration's Vietnam policy and also to show support for civil rights workers who had staged memorable marches at Selma, Alabama, on March 7 and 9. (A third would be held on March 21.)

On March 19, two days after the story reporting the walk-out idea, the *Daily* reported a change of plans. The Michigan legislature had reacted strongly and adversely to the walkout idea; they too had watched events at Berkeley and did not intend to lose control of one of their campuses. The headline for the second *Daily* story read, "Faculty Group Cuts Off Walkout, Plans Teach-In." It was the first time the term *teach-in* had been used.

On March 24 the faculty sponsors of the teach-in ran the following ad, headlined "An Appeal To Our Students," in the *Daily:*

"We the faculty are deeply worried about the war in Vietnam.

"We think its moral, political and military consequences are very grave, and that we must

friend who would later become a president of SDS, were motivated by the fledgling southern civil rights movement to drive to Mississippi. One day while sitting in their cars watching a peaceful demonstration, they were set upon by a band of whites who pulled them from the vehicle. The local sheriff had put the mob up to it, says Hayden. A high state official subsequently gave them the choice of leaving town or going to jail.

Outraged by what had happened to them, Hayden and Potter caught a flight to Washington, D.C., where they anticipated that their tale would provoke outrage and cause all the forces of government to descend on Mississippi. Instead, John Doar of Robert Kennedy's Justice Department administration told them that there was nothing the federal government could do. "From that time on," says Hayden, "it was clear."

Finally, that fall, they had what was probably their most embittering experience. Hayden and a few other members of the recently founded SDS decided to run for national office in the National Student Association (NSA). What Hayden and other SDS members didn't know then was that the NSA was controlled by the CIA, and that its top leaders were on the CIA payroll. The fact that some outside organization did control the NSA became evident to Hayden and other SDS members quite by accident, as Hayden recalled in a 1971 *Rolling Stone* interview:

". . . one day we were in the office of the president of the NSA just before the congress and found on his desk a chart written in his hand. . . . He was a CIA agent from the University of Wisconsin, and he had a chart of the congress. Me, Haber, and other people, SDS people, were listed as being the Left on this chart, and there was a Right and a Center, in terms of power blocs. And at the top there was a group called the control group. . . .

"Control group!" Hayden repeated. "Capital C, capital G!" The CIA, as it turned out.

That winter Hayden drafted the first SDS manifesto, called the Port Huron statement (named after the place north of Detroit where fifty-nine members from a dozen campuses were to gather in June 1962); in it he explained the origins of their activism:

"When we were kids the United States was the wealthiest and strongest country in the world . . . many of us began maturing in complacency.

"As we grew, however, our comfort was penetrated by events too troubling to dismiss. First the permeating and victimizing fact of human degradation, symbolized by the Southern struggle against racial bigotry, compelled most of us from silence to activism. Second, the enclosing fact of the Cold War, symbolized by the presence of the Bomb, brought awareness that we ourselves, and our friends, and millions of abstract 'others' we knew more directly because of our common peril, might die at any time."

By the following year, when SDS published its next manifesto, called *America and the New Era*, the estrangement from established leadership, even the liberal kind, had been completed:

". . . the capture of liberal rhetoric and the liberal power base by the corporate liberalism of the New Frontiersmen means that the reformers and the democratically oriented liberals are trapped by the limitations of the Democratic Party. . . ." Hayden and the others were disillusioned by what they perceived as the unfulfilled promise of the Kennedy era even before it ended abruptly and tragically that November.

During the summer of 1964, Hayden, Rennie Davis and other SDS members began a grass-roots attempt to organize a mass movement for social change. Supported in part by a grant from the UAW, they began knocking on doors in poor neighborhoods in Chicago and Newark, hoping to build a political coalition whose members were drawn together by "bad housing, meager and degrading welfare, irrelevant schools,

examine them and find new alternatives before irreparable actions occur.

"We are devoting this night, March 24-25, to seminars, lectures, informal discussions and a protest rally to focus attention on the war, its consequences, and ways to stop it."

The teach-in was a huge success, an orderly gathering attended by thousands of students. The idea quickly spread to other campuses, in part because of the aggressive efforts of fifty Michigan faculty members who called associates elsewhere. On the twenty-fifth, a letter of support from ten Stanford professors appeared in the *Daily*; they noted that a teach-in would be conducted at their school. Within two weeks of the University of Michigan events, teach-ins had been conducted on dozens of college campuses. In June a nationally televised teach-in was held.

The first indication that these individual protests were beginning to coalesce into one national movement occurred on April 17, 1965. Fifteen thousand young people took part in a Students for a Democratic Society (SDS)-sponsored protest march in Washington, D.C. The crowd assembled on the mall a short walk from Dean Rusk's office at the State Department. He professed indifference when, on May 11, he called Soviet Ambassador Anatoly Dobrynin to his office to warn that the U.S. would not permanently halt its bombing campaign of North Vietnam until Ho Chi Minh ordered the Viet Cong in the south to stop fighting. Rusk spoke confidently of the administration's firm resolve, which he said would not be undermined by "very small domestic pressure."

Elements of American society that might otherwise have quickly joined the war protest movement at this point refrained from doing so because of Johnson's landslide victory over Barry Goldwater in the fall of 1964. Swept into office on Johnson's coattails, the most liberal Congress in years gave hope to their various liberal constituencies, who were reluctant to oppose the Johnson administration so soon after its representatives had been sworn in. This attitude held true even for traditional antiwar groups of the Left, who, because they were so frightened by the possibility of a Goldwater victory, had stifled any protest other than the rhetorical kind in reaction to the Gulf of Tonkin reprisal strikes in August 1964. "We were outspoken enough about Johnson and the war in 1964, but we did discourage demonstrations," David McReynolds of the War Resisters' League admitted to Godfrey Hodgson during an interview. "We thought it important to elect Johnson." In that context, Rusk's confidence when he spoke to Dobrynin is better understood. But Johnson and his advisers misread the lack of protest to the Tonkin strikes as evidence of near-universal support for their actions. Individual legislators undoubtedly also misread the public response, which partially explains why the Gulf of Tonkin Resolution breezed through Congress.

Black leaders, too, remained silent about Johnson's Vietnam initiatives, because his administration had vowed to sponsor their social reform agenda. On March 15, thirteen days after the first Rolling Thunder raid, the president had traveled up to the Hill to speak to a Joint Session of Congress. During his speech, he made the strongest commitment to racial equality of any American president in history. "It is not just Negroes, but really it is all of us who must overcome the crippling legacy of bigotry and injustice," he said. And then slowly drawing out his words for effect, he said, "And . . . we . . . shall . . . overcome." His speech was emotionally charged. During the month, he had been grappling with Wallace about protecting the protest marchers in Selma. Two days before he spoke, a mob armed with iron bars had beaten a white Unitarian minister to death outside a Selma café while yelling "Nigger lover." Incensed, Johnson had called the Alabama governor, telling him that if his national guard were not called out to protect the protest marchers, he would send in federal troops. Wallace had relented and thereafter, acting under U.S. government direction, the Alabama guard had allowed a peaceful march to take place on March 21.

When Johnson began ramming Great Society legislation through Congress—the Economic Opportunity Act, the Elementary and Secondary Education Act, Medicare, and about a dozen others—there was further incentive for black leaders to take a wait-and-see attitude about the war. But gradually, and in retrospect inevitably, the black population's opposition to the war became almost universal. According to a Gallup poll, by the spring of 1971 eighty-three percent of the black population believed that American involvement in Vietnam was a mistake. The war there was taking a terrible toll on economically vulnerable black America. The cost

[and] inadequate community facilities." Vietnam, at this point, was not yet an SDS cause. The Gulf of Tonkin raids that August got their attention, however. Though some SDS leaders opposed focusing on Vietnam, most of them saw Vietnam as an issue that could be used to build a base for radical reform in the United States. At that point, Hayden and the SDS raced to the front of the antiwar activists who were already on the march. On April 17, 1965, they sponsored the first of the large demonstrations against the war, a gathering of fifteen thousand young people in Washington, D.C.

✷ Draft laws during the Vietnam war were shaped by the Johnson administration's worries about open rebellion by the nation's youth. *New York Times* Washington bureau chief James Reston stated the problem succinctly in a 1967 column: "The estimate here is that if college students were called like any other 19-year-olds, as many as 25 percent of them might refuse to serve." So student deferments were granted to help defuse the situation. This entailed shifting the burden of Vietnam service to the poor and the powerless, a disproportionate number of whom were black.

But one young black called up was not so docile. He happened to be the heavyweight boxing champion of the world—Muhammad Ali. Belying the violence of his chosen profession, he was an introspective man very much shaped by the forces of his time. As a fifteen-year-old living in Louisville, he had been "profoundly influenced" by Arkansas Governor Orville Faubus's decision to use national guard troops to block integration of Little Rock's Central High School. Later he found that even the Olympic Gold Medal that he won in 1960 was no shield against racial attacks; in fact, a white motorcycle gang leader tried to take it away from him. Ali, then known as Cassius Clay, beat up his attacker, but the champ threw it into the Ohio River anyway in disgust. The name change came about not long after he won the professional world heavyweight championship (by knocking out Sonny Liston in the first round). After meeting with Malcolm X, he decided to become a Black Muslim. The next day he announced his new faith and name. Inevitably, perhaps, he became a symbol of early opposition to the war by the black population. He was drafted but refused to serve on the grounds that his religion forbade it. "I ain't got no quarrel with those Vietcong," he said. "They never called me nigger."

For refusing to be drafted, Ali in 1967 was stripped of his heavyweight

of our military commitment on Vietnam began escalating even as Great Society programs were signed into law; and young blacks, who generally were not in a position to take advantage of student deferments, served in disproportionate numbers and suffered casualties at roughly twice the rate of their white counterparts.

But before the cost of the war had become clear, Johnson continued to support policies that only succeeded in swelling the rising tide of black aspirations. On June 4, 1965, Johnson spoke at Howard University in Washington, D.C., espousing "the principle of compensatory policies intended to achieve equality not just as 'a right and theory' but 'as a fact and a result.'" He based his presentation on a study prepared the summer before under the direction of a former Harvard social scientist serving as an assistant secretary of labor—Daniel Patrick Moynihan. Moynihan had written the first draft of the report; Richard Goodwin, the second. Focusing on the breakup of black families in America, the writers attributed it to high unemployment, which was found to correlate closely and directly with the divorce rate in the black community, and to the legacy of slavery, when white masters had deliberately separated black families in order to break their will and make the individual members more manageable. At the end of his Howard University speech, Johnson announced plans to convene a White House conference to determine how, in the president's words, "to fulfill these rights."

But almost immediately Vietnam intervened, stealing away the promise before it could be fulfilled. Accordingly, the signing of the Voting Rights Act, perhaps the greatest achievement of the civil rights movement, marked the beginning of the movement's decline. During the two-month period between his Howard University speech and the signing of the Voting Rights Act into law on August 6, 1965, Rolling Thunder failed and Johnson made his fateful decision to commit the country to a ground war in Vietnam. The conflict quickly began to divert the resources and attention of his administration. As one unnamed high-ranking Johnson administration official put it: "There are less than twenty men in the government who can get something new done, and they really have to work and fight to do it; with Vietnam building up, they just had to drop this other thing."

Martin Luther King, Jr. immediately sensed

what was going to happen and raised the subject of Vietnam with Johnson, even as they participated in the voting act signing ceremonies at the White House. King urged Johnson to focus his and the nation's energies on the urban ghettos. Johnson was reportedly piqued, upset by what he perceived as King's presumptuous intrusion into foreign affairs.

Events quickly confirmed King's assessment of the state of black America. The civil rights leader might know little about foreign affairs, but he knew a great deal about potential troubles in the nation's cities. Five days after the Voting Rights Act was signed into law, the most devastating urban riot in the U.S. in decades erupted in Watts. When a traffic cop stopped a black driver, a crowd gathered and began assaulting white motorists. Firebombing in Watts two miles away started thirty hours later. Thirty-four people were killed. During the next several years, the flames of race riots, fanned in the heat of summer, were to engulf major cities across the country. The worst one occurred in Detroit in July 1967, where much of the inner city was burned down, forty-three people were killed, and elements of two airborne divisions had to be ordered in to reestablish order. The worst single night was April 4, 1968, when blacks, reacting to the assassination of King, rioted in more than a hundred cities. One of the hardest hit that night was the nation's capital, where fires burned only a mile from the White House. Twelve people died in the Washington rioting.

Perhaps foreseeing such troubles, King first went public with his opposition to the U.S. military effort in Vietnam on January 1, 1966. At that point, he opposed it on pacifist grounds. "I believe that war is wrong," he wrote in his column in the *Chicago Defender*. Might does not make right, he argued, a belief that blacks especially could appreciate. Later that month, leaders of SNCC, such as Stokely Carmichael, who spoke for younger, more militant blacks, also came out against the war.

The black population's opposition intensified unabated throughout the long period of the U.S. military involvement in Vietnam, as the cost of war not only halted the development of new government programs, but undermined those already on the books. The administration's realigned priorities are reflected by the budget of the Office of Economic Opportunity (OEO). For

crown and ordered to prison for five years. During the appeal process, the public reaction to Ali ranged from those who threatened to kill him, to others who held him up as a courageous hero. In a letter, British philosopher and peace activist Bertrand Russell offered encouragement: "They will try to break you because you are a symbol of a force they are unable to destroy, namely, the aroused consciousness of a whole people determined no longer to be butchered and debased with fear and oppression. You have my wholehearted support...."

In 1970 the U.S. Supreme Court reversed Ali's conviction. Though the controversy robbed him of his peak fighting years, he subsequently regained his boxing championship.

Muhammad Ali stands outside the federal courthouse in Houston on April 27, 1967, following a hearing on his struggle with the draft board.

the fiscal year 1967 budget that was being worked on in the fall of 1965, OEO had initially planned on having $3.5 billion at its disposal. But the administration finally proposed only $1.75 billion and Congress trimmed even that to $1.625 billion. There were other factors involved in this budget cut, of course, but to the black population it seemed clear that it was Vietnam that had altered the political climate for their domestic programs. Moynihan supports this contention. "The underfunding was at least as much associated with the war in Vietnam as with any political difficulties the War on Poverty might have caused," he says. King expressed the connection in more dramatic terms: "The Great Society was shot down on the battlefields of Vietnam," he said.

And so the civil rights movement merged with the anti-Vietnam war movement. And though civil rights leaders continued to address the goals of their people, their immediate objective was U.S. withdrawal from Vietnam, which they perceived as the route to any advancement of their interests at home.

Johnson greets King after signing the Voting Rights Act on August 6, 1965. King used the occasion to warn the president about Vietnam involvement.

Initially, the general population found it difficult to identify with this burgeoning protest for peace. Their natural inclination was to support a president during wartime. Furthermore, many felt threatened by the increased militancy of blacks. Like the president himself, they felt that civil rights had advanced far enough, fast enough, for the time being. Indeed, some thought that civil rights had gone too far too fast. Many whites also resented a lack of the gratitude they thought blacks owed them.

Nor did the general population find it easy to identify with protesting college students, who seemed to be making the worst of the opportunities handed them. The prevailing image of college students was that of undisciplined, slovenly dressed ingrates with a penchant for loud music and political activism paid for by their parents. For many if not most of the population, these perceptions of the individuals who formed the basic anti-Vietnam constituency never changed; however, as the years passed and fighting continued in Vietnam, various events and influences legitimatized for them the anti-Vietnam feelings of blacks and students.

The assassinations were probably foremost among them: those of John Kennedy, Robert Kennedy, Martin Luther King, Jr., and Malcolm

X, who at the time of his death was emerging as the chief rival to King's leadership in the black community. The assassinations were not directly related to Vietnam, but they were shocking and destabilizing and caused unease across the land. They were perceived as symptoms that something was wrong with the country.

Almost as traumatic was the 1968 Democratic National Convention in Chicago. Images of anger and chaos were forever etched in the minds of those who watched events there. They unsettled many Americans, no matter what their basic political attitudes. The effect was much the same as that of the civil rights protest marches in the South during the early sixties. Many Americans concluded that they had witnessed a "police riot" in Chicago. Daley looked almost like Bull Connor, and his burly policemen looked like those who charged into marchers at Birmingham and Selma. And just as the latter scenes had touched the sympathies and raised the consciousness of a broad cross-section of Americans and encouraged them to support the cause of blacks more actively, so these later scenes did the same for the anti--Vietnam war protestors.

The urban riots, spiraling crime rates, proliferating drug use, and turmoil on campuses also fostered concern among Americans. And many people found the feminist movement—a by-product of the black civil rights movement—no less unsettling. Though concern did not necessarily translate into sympathy—and very often did not—people unable to articulate reasons why all these forces were loose in the land could still judge that they required closer attention than they were receiving. Consequently, Americans began turning inward, sensing the need to focus on the problems at home, whether or not they believed that fighting the Communists in Vietnam was a noble effort. This shift is revealed by a couple of studies, one published in 1964 by the Institute of International Social Research. According to the institute, Americans that year listed in "order of urgency" the following priorities:

"1. Keeping the country out of war

"2. Combating world communism

"3. Keeping our military defense strong

"4. Controlling the use of nuclear weapons

"5. Maintaining respect for the United States in other countries."

Not until the sixth position did a domestic issue, "law and order," emerge as a priority.

On the evening of August 29, 1968, a Chicago policeman squirts mace into a crowd in front of the Hilton, Hubert Humphrey's headquarters during the Democratic National Convention. Hundreds were injured in clashes between police and demonstrators that evening. Many Americans blamed the media for the turmoil; their reaction affected subsequent press coverage in Vietnam.

Only eight years later there was a complete reversal in priorities, as William Watts and Lloyd Free reported in their book *State of the Nation*, published in 1972. The two authors had commissioned the Gallup Organization to analyze Americans' attitudes. Listed ahead of all foreign policy concerns except Vietnam were "rising prices, cost of living, violence in American life, drugs, water and air pollution, health care, misleading advertising, garbage disposal, the problems of the elderly, unemployment, poverty, and education."

Finally, during the late sixties, worldwide condemnation of U.S. Vietnam policies, the sheer numbers of those joining the protest movement at home and abroad, and the fact that many respected politicians began turning against the military commitment legitimatized the views being espoused in the streets and made them subjects of debate in the formal political process.

The hearings before the Senate Foreign Relations Committee under the direction of Senator J. William Fulbright were important in this regard, causing many Americans to be suspicious of the way their leaders had led them into this war. They began to question, for example, whether the *Maddox* and the *C. Turner Joy* had even been attacked on the fateful night of August 4, 1964. Had they been hoodwinked? many Americans wanted to know. They began focusing on the cost of the war too—the monetary cost as discussed in hearings before the House Ways and Means Committee chaired by Representative Wilbur Mills, and the human cost, of which the daily body counts were constant reminders.

Senator J. William Fulbright (left), chairman of the Senate Foreign Relations Committee, conducted public hearings that aroused suspicion about Johnson's actions during the Gulf of Tonkin affair.

When, during the 1968 presidential campaign, candidates began saying that the country had to get out of Vietnam, the effect was not just to further legitimize the views of protesters, but to allow them to channel their energies into the political process by supporting candidates who had stepped into the front ranks of their movement. The first of these men was Senator Eugene McCarthy; then came Senator Robert Kennedy; and, finally, Vice-President Hubert Humphrey. Out of loyalty to Johnson, he had delayed coming out against the war. When, late in the campaign, he did, his campaign surged forward. Most political experts agree that had the campaign lasted a day or two longer, he would have won, the momentum in his favor being so pronounced. But even Richard Nixon, the eventual winner of the 1968 election, recognized that the country wanted out of Vietnam.

What added impact and immediacy to these already extraordinary events was, of course, television. It was no wonder the media became known as the bad news bearers—on TV, at least, there was little room for anything else. From the top of the newscast to the bottom, lead-type stories followed one after the other— stories about soldiers locked in battle, civilians being killed, targets being bombed, planes being shot down, pilots being captured, urban riots, trouble on campuses, protest marches, protest bombings, and, finally, stories about frustrating and futile peace initiatives. In this sort of crowded news environment, stories on drug use and rising divorce rates qualified as soft features.

After problems during the early years with the "young Turks," by 1966 the government had every reason to be pleased with Vietnam press coverage. Diem, the very symbol of the illusory promise of Vietnam to early-day reporters, was gone; they didn't have him to kick around anymore. Furthermore, the South Vietnamese Army, another symbol for U.S. newsmen of the futility of it all, had moved into the background as American soldiers took over most of the fighting. It was, of course, the commitment of U.S. combat units that was basically responsible for the change in reporting. Hundreds of the country's soldiers and airmen were now dying in battle each month. Consequently, Americans rallied around the flag and newsmen joined them. Writer Hanson Baldwin noted the change in the February 24, 1966, issue of *Reporter* magazine. Press organizations were "cleaning house," he said, "putting an end to the distorted, biased and sensational reporting" that they attributed to "younger" offenders.

Baldwin wrote: "Fortunately for the representatives of the press and the good of the country, the quality of reporting in Vietnam has improved. Mature and responsible correspondents head all the major bureaus of press associations, broadcasting companies, and major newspapers, and the worst offenders have departed. A good thing too, for the Vietnamese war is at a crisis, and what we do, how we do it, and how we report the situation will color the history of all our tomorrows. For unless the American public feels the war is worth winning and must be won, we face defeat no matter how many military victories we win."

Senator Eugene McCarthy stares at LBJ during a meeting between the two men. The Minnesota senator's long-shot presidential campaign contributed to Johnson's decision not to seek reelection.

Mr. Salisbury goes to Washington...

The press was not a monolithic institution whose individual members uniformly opposed the war in Vietnam—a false perception that has taken hold in years since. Reaction to Harrison Salisbury's Hanoi reporting in the early stages of the war is evidence of just how supportive of the war the media could be when it felt that U.S. interests were being undermined. Salisbury, the *New York Times* assistant managing editor for international reporting, was the first journalist for a major American newspaper to be granted a visa for a visit to North Vietnam after the air war began. During a two-week period from December 23, 1966, to January 7, 1967, he filed page-one reports from that country, the first of which was published in the *Times* on December 25 without advance publicity. Its focus was damage caused by U.S. aircraft. It read, in part: "Contrary to the impression by United States communiqués, on-the-spot inspection indicates that American bombing has been inflicting considerable civilian casualties in Hanoi and its environs for some time past. . . . It is fair to say that, based on the evidence of their own eyes, Hanoi residents do not find much credibility in United States bombing communiqués."

Two days later from Nam Dinh, Salisbury wrote: "Whatever the explanation, one can see that United States planes are dropping an enormous weight of explosives on purely civilian targets. Whatever else there may be or might have been in Nam Dinh, it is the civilians who have taken punishment.

"The cathedral tower looks out on block after block of utter desolation; the city's population of 90,000 has been reduced to less than 20,000 because of the evacuation; 13 percent of the city's housing, including the homes of 12,464

The military was very candid about being pleased with the change. In its June 10, 1966, issue, *Time* quoted a "relieved" Pentagon official as saying, "Today there is no Halberstam group." And in the same article, the writer observed that "Today Vietnam reporters hardly get along with each other." In fact, the trend among reporters was to criticize colleagues' earlier work. For example, Richard Critchfield of the *Washington Star* wrote, "I don't think Tri Quang [the leader of the Buddhist protest movement that led to Diem's downfall] would have really existed without the American press."

Other newsmen supported the war effort by putting the conflict in a context far beyond the imagination of even President Kennedy, who first sent American combat troops to Vietnam. Paul Dean of the *Arizona Republic,* a rich and influential newspaper in the Southwest, served as a Vietnam combat correspondent for four months, and then addressed the Phoenix press club. "We want Vietnam as the final stepping stone across the Pacific," Dean said, "a chain of defense that right now goes from the United States to Honolulu, to Guam to Manila. Look ahead 10, 15, and 20 years. Sometime in the future, we are going to come eyeball to eyeball with Red China and/or Russia. . . . Showdown time will come one day. And when it does, this country of ours will need Vietnam as a very sturdy springboard from which to raise a fist at whatever aggressor seems anxious to take us on."

Dean's was vintage fifties stuff, of course, a sort of domino theory in reverse. He was one of hundreds of reporters who traveled to Vietnam on temporary assignment while representing local and regional news outlets that never wavered in their support of the U.S. military commitment in Vietnam. Those who blame the loss there on the press invariably overlook how supportive of the effort these news organizations remained to the very end. And papers such as the *Arizona Republic* and the *Daily Oklahoman* are far more influential with the people and politicians of their states than any national news outlet.

This fact was not overlooked by Lyndon Johnson or by the military, which readily coauthored the war as its own. As revealed in testimony before the Senate Foreign Relations Committee on August 31, 1966, by Arthur Sylvester, one of Johnson's assistant secretaries of defense, DOD had paid the travel expenses to

Vietnam for 419 members of the media, some from foreign news outlets.

"It is noteworthy," says James Aronson, author of *The Press and the Cold War,* "that the effort began just before the incident in the Gulf of Tonkin and coincident with the buildup of troops in South Vietnam." From July 17, 1964, to August 1965, eighty-two reporters from newspapers, magazines, radio and television were accommodated. Sylvester described the program as being highly successful in "priming the pump."

Richard West of the *New Statesman* of London wrote about the difficulty of writing objectively when a reporter took such temporary-duty trips. "Even those who came at their newspapers' expense are likely to be overwhelmed by the help and hospitality they receive from the American propaganda machine. . . . [These] journalists are bound to be grateful. Moreover, they feel a natural sympathy for the pleasant and long-suffering GIs. In consequence there is danger of their becoming simply a part of the military propaganda machine. . . . Even liberal U.S. journalists cannot help but feel that their criticism is letting down the soldiers who actually run the risk. They share Kipling's dislike for 'making mock of the uniforms that guard us while we sleep.'"

This thinking dominated the approach of the vast majority of reporters, right up to the time of Tet, 1968. Essentially, coverage was vintage Second World War, with special emphasis on body counts, of course—that ghastly numerical exercise that after a time defined the face of the Vietnam war. And whenever reporters and writers were seen as being too aggressive or critical, the Johnson administration did its best to undermine them, just as the Kennedy administration had before. When I. F. Stone, a revered and iconoclastic journalist whose *Weekly* opposed Vietnam involvement early on, wrote reviews of Halberstam's and Browne's books on the subject for the *New York Review of Books,* editors there received a call from Richard Goodwin, a Johnson White House assistant. Goodwin objected to the points made by Stone in the review. Why not write a letter stating those objectives? he was asked. No, he couldn't do that, Goodwin said. But why not invite someone like Joseph Alsop to do such a review next time? he countered.

Sometimes prominent journalists took it upon themselves to step in. For example, when newsmen began reporting that Johnson was planning to

people, have been destroyed; 89 people have been killed and 405 wounded."

These accounts and others by Salisbury were roundly criticized—scornfully so, in some cases—by many in the media. In a January 1, 1967, column, William Randolph Hearst, Jr., with Salisbury in mind, compared "news and opinion by war critics" to treasonable broadcasts by Lord Haw Haw in Germany and Tokyo Rose in Japan during the Second World War. Crosby Noyes, foreign editor for the *Washington Star,* denounced the Johnson administration for allowing Salisbury to go; it had allowed the "systematic subversion" of its Vietnam commitment, he wrote. In the same article, he also criticized "an important segment of the press" for its "utter lack of identification . . . with what the government defines as the national interest."

Harsh criticism also came from the *Washington Post,* whose reporters were quick to report the official administration view and then support it in opinion pieces. On December 28, Murrey Marder wrote: "Officials are particularly bitter that the attention to civilian casualties in the North has obscured the murder, kidnappings, arson and other acts of terrorism continually directed against civilians in South Vietnam by the Communists." On January 1, George Wilson attacked Salisbury's credibility with a story headlined, "Salisbury's 'Casualties' Tally With Viet Reds." The article's implication was that Salisbury was a Communist dupe, using figures supplied by the North Vietnamese. The paper treated the finding as an important revelation, though it seems it was a given that only the North Vietnamese themselves could have been the source of the casualty information. Wilson's story was followed up by another in the *Post* on January 2 written by Chalmer Roberts under the headline, "Ho Tries A New Propaganda Weapon." It read: "Ho Chi Minh, master of guerrilla warfare and political propaganda, is now embarked on one of his most daring exploits. . . . Now he is using another weapon, one as cleverly conceived as the poison-tipped bamboo spikes his men emplant underfoot for the unwary enemy. At long last, he has opened his country, or part of it, to an American journalist. . . . To force a halt in the American bombing of his country . . . Harrison Salisbury of the *New York Times* is Ho's instrument. . . ."

Such accounts reflected what was by far the majority view of the nation's newsmen toward Salisbury's trip, though some prominent journalists did defend Salisbury. On January 9, 1967, columnist Joseph Kraft called Salisbury's attackers "the handmaidens of official [U.S.] policy on Vietnam," though he damned Salisbury with faint praise, describing his reporting as second-rate. Walter Lippmann defended him from a broader perspective: "Mr. Salisbury's offense, we are told, is that in reporting the war as seen from Hanoi, he has made himself a tool of enemy propaganda. We must remember that in time of war what is said on the enemy's side of the front is always propaganda, and what is said on our side of the front is truth and righteousness, the cause of humanity and a crusade for peace. Is it necessary for us at the height of our power to stoop to such self-deceiving nonsense?"

The anti-Salisbury sentiment reached its climactic expression in the events following his nomination by the *New York Times* for the Pulitzer Prize for International Reporting. Though Salisbury's reporting had been confirmed by Harry Ashmore, former editor of the *Arkansas Gazette,* and William Baggs, editor of the *Miami News,* during a visit to North Vietnam shortly after Salisbury's departure, and even though the Pulitzer Prize jury of editors recommended by a vote of four to one that their advisory board award the prize to Salisbury, the board—in a rare reversal—decided to give it to another journalist for non-Vietnam-related reporting.

escalate the air war by ordering airstrikes on oil refineries and power plants, James Reston of the *New York Times* wrote that Johnson "had some reason to complain . . . this goes beyond the proper bounds of public military information." Reston's point was that the lives of American pilots were being put in jeopardy by such public disclosures. But he ignored the fact that the addition of such targets amounted to another escalation in an undeclared war that was being enlarged inch by inch and target by target. Since Congress had never contemplated an expansion to this degree at the time of the Gulf of Tonkin Resolution, it could be argued that it was not only the right but the duty of the press to make the information available for public debate. In any case, given Johnson's past threats to escalate the air war, the North Vietnamese were undoubtedly already as prepared for attack as they could be at such significant targets as power plants. But whatever one's conclusions, the situation demonstrates the complications that evolved because the war was undeclared: The press was never fully confident of its obligations or the ground rules under which it was supposed to be operating. The administration exploited their uncertainty by claiming the safety of its men in the field as reason enough for not sharing its plans with the country.

However, by the eve of 1968, the administration was aware that it had pushed this argument as far as it could. Antiwar protest was growing rapidly; escalation of the war itself had continued unabated for almost three years. The corner should have been turned by then. And most Americans knew it. Somewhere buried deep in the national psyche was the knowledge that American wars didn't last much longer than four years—the Civil War, three years, nine months; the First World War, one and a half years; the Second World War, four years, eight months; the Korean War, three years, one month. In several months, U.S. soldiers would begin their fourth year of fighting in Vietnam, with no end in sight. Westmoreland's staff would entitle their year-end report to the president "1967— Year of Progress," but many in the administration were not so certain of that, especially since everyone suspected that the Communists were about to launch a massive offensive.

Accordingly, Hubert Humphrey was almost begging when during a visit to Vietnam in November 1967 he met with thirty reporters at

Chu Lai. "When you speak to the American people," the vice-president said, "give the benefit of the doubt to our side. I don't think that it is asking too much. We're in this together."

One veteran correspondent was incredulous, given his awareness of the generally supportive coverage of the past. "Benefit of the doubt?" he asked a colleague. "What does he think we've been doing for the past six years?"

Indeed, it was because of generally positive press coverage and a policy of concealment by the Kennedy and Johnson administrations that Tet arrived with such a shock. It was at that point that the large national press organizations reacted with almost sanctimonious rage, overstating, in fact, the enemy's achievements and immediate threat. Editorial direction from their big offices on the East Coast changed almost overnight. Ironically, by being too supportive, top officials at various news organizations had helped create the condition of ignorance that led to their own surprise during Tet. "What the hell is going on?" roared CBS's venerable Walter Cronkite, as he viewed reports of Tet and read the piles of dispatches coming in. "I thought we were winning the war." However, to his credit, Cronkite packed his bags and hurried off to South Vietnam, where his reporting, given his stature and his network's huge audience, helped set the mood for future press coverage.

After Tet, instead of giving the benefit of the doubt to American commanders, many reporters now assumed the opposite as their starting point. Furthermore, some reporters who felt betrayed by the military's past optimistic projections now quickly presumed to be tacticians themselves, offering amateur analyses of complicated troop deployments. This presumption is a principal reason that many American commanders, to this day, blame the media for the loss in Vietnam. Walter Cronkite, for example, during his special report on the status of the Vietnam war that aired February 27, 1968, said that Khe Sanh, which had been built up "to block enemy infiltration," was now "surrounded and bypassed," that "for reasons of U.S. pride as much as U.S. tactics, Khe Sanh has been built into a major bastion, where 5,500 Marines are isolated, and not far from which 20,000 more reserves are tied down, far from the now unprotected coastal plains. . . . Khe Sanh could well fall, with a terrible loss in American lives, prestige, and morale, and this is a tragedy of our stubbornness there."

Vice-President Hubert Humphrey is interviewed in South Vietnam in November 1967 after presenting Silver Stars to two marines. A good soldier himself, Humphrey loyally supported the Vietnam policies of Johnson until his own presidential campaign forced a shift.

An NBC crew films a report at Khe Sanh. The siege became a long-running suspense play followed nervously by millions of viewers.

Of course, Khe Sanh had never been intended as a block to enemy infiltration and, as it turned out, was never in serious danger of falling, in large part because of the incredible concentration of airpower over the surrounding mountains, which Cronkite never mentioned.

Additional evidence of what the future press-military relationship was going to be like was offered in Cronkite's report. Immediately following a soundcut of Lieutenant General Robert Cushman, Jr., the senior marine commander in Vietnam, saying that he did not think that the enemy could keep up its tempo of fighting for "longer than a matter of months," Cronkite drew just the opposite conclusion: "Whatever the battle for Khe Sanh and the DMZ means, whatever all this means, there is one meaning to the Vietcong's winter-spring offensive that is inescapable. The nature of the Vietnamese war has changed. It no longer is a series of small engagements fought for local areas against small bands of Communists. It no longer is to be fought primarily in the sparsely occupied countryside. It is now more along the classic Western fashion of war, large armies locked in combat, moving toward a decision on the battlefield."

The exact opposite proved to be the case. Cushman's appraisal was the correct one. But the Cronkite report was significant for several reasons, including both his sterling reputation and the size of his audience. Because of Cronkite's fame, this program heralded the beginning of the fourth phase of Vietnam reporting, very similar to coverage from the time of the young Turks. Reporters began tearing apart the projections of government administration and military officials. In his report, Cronkite had both reflected this new attitude and helped make it the norm. He told CBS viewers, "We have been too often disappointed by the optimism of the American leaders, both in Vietnam and Washington, to have faith any longer in the silver linings they find in the darkest clouds." And this observation led him to his conclusion: "To say that we are closer to victory today is to believe, in the face of the evidence, the optimists who have been wrong in the past. To suggest we are on the edge of defeat is to yield to unrealistic pessimism. To say that we are mired in stalemate seems the only realistic, yet unsatisfactory conclusion." This new phase of reporting—another "negative news" phase in which reporters questioned not only government pronouncements but the very validity of the commitment in terms of its cost, i.e., is Vietnam worth it? —lasted for almost two years. Contributing to the more negative tone was greater focus, once again, on the fighting capability of South Vietnamese units.

The breaking of the My Lai story in November 1969 by Seymour Hersh would mark the beginning of the last phase. During that period, questions about the morality of the war in Vietnam would become a staple of mainstream reporting, adding more fuel to the fires of protest. Not coincidentally, this was also the time of the Nixon administration's counterattack on the press, in which it deployed Vice-President Spiro Agnew as point man.

During the long years of fighting, there were hundreds of reporters covering the Vietnam war. Many stayed only a few weeks. A couple, such as Peter Arnett of Associated Press and Joe Fried of the *New York Daily News*, stayed for the duration of U.S. combat involvement— more than eight years. In 1968, at peak press interest in the war, there were about eight hundred reporters in South Vietnam.

To become accredited by U.S. officials to cover the war was quite easy, even if one were not affiliated with a news organization. The process involved first applying for a visa to travel to South Vietnam. Once there, a prospective reporter, photographer and associated staff person presented the required correspondence to the Joint U.S. Public Affairs Office (JUSPAO). If affiliated, a person needed only a letter from his employer. If freelance, the person applying needed letters from two news organizations stating that they were prepared to purchase his work. Even a small hometown paper would suffice; AP would readily supply the other, along with a camera-on-loan and an agreement to purchase a newsworthy photograph for fifteen dollars. Not surprisingly, an incredible range of people became Vietnam war correspondents—men and women, young and old, from college students on summer vacation reporting for their campus newspapers to Pulitzer Prize winners; from quasi-tourists who wanted to mix a little adventure with their travels to network correspondents. Even freelance television reporters showed up, carrying their own cameras and doing interviews with average GIs from a specific area for showing on local TV stations there. Whatever their arrangement or

CBS's Walter Cronkite prepares to interview Professor Mai of the University of Hue on February 20, 1968. The influential anchorman traveled to South Vietnam on his own fact-finding trip following enemy attacks during the Tet holiday. He predicted stalemate in the war.

Peter Arnett and "The Agony and Death of Supply Column 21"...

Peter Arnett, who covered the Vietnam war for Associated Press, was awarded the Pulitzer Prize for International Correspondence in 1966. Many say that he should have won more than one Pulitzer. An example of his reporting is the following account of one of the first engagements of the war involving U.S. units, printed in AP wireservice newspapers on August 19, 1965:

"VAN TUONG, Vietnam (AP)—The mission of U.S. Marine Supply Column 21 yesterday was simple: Get to the beachhead, resupply a line company and return to the 7th Fleet mother ship anchored a mile out in the bay.

"It never found the line company. And it never returned.

"Supply Column 21 was a formidable force made up of five steel-shod amtraks—35-ton amphibious vehicles—to carry food and ammunition—and two M-48 tanks to escort them once ashore.

"The column packed a total of 287 tons of steel. It was made up of 30 men.

"The paths that led to its destruction were paved with confusion.

"Failing to locate the designated line company immediately, Column 21 set out to look for it.

"But the huge amtraks, once out of the water, were unwieldy. They flopped from one rice paddy to another, with their crews calling at one battalion and then the next. No one seemed to pay much attention.

"At 11 A.M., Supply Column 21 was about 400 yards ahead of the nearest Marine riflemen. The vehicles were deep in Vietcong territory and, suddenly, were deep in trouble.

"Survivors said the Vietcong rose out of hedge rows and swamps.

"Lance Corporal Richard Pass of Homewood, Ill., said his amtrak veered aside as explosions erupted around them. The leading tank was hit with an

motivation, JUSPAO processed hundreds of these reporters in and out of the war zone, through the good offices of a fairly senior sergeant who handed out the plastic-coated accreditation cards and recorded their registration numbers on a small green blackboard behind his desk—a job held at one point by a brusque though soft-hearted marine gunnery sergeant famous for his evenhanded ways. "Hold on to your ass awhile," he once told a star television reporter. "You people from the electronic media don't scare me anymore."

The accreditation card was not only a sort of passport for travel in the war zone, but also a ticket. On the backside of this ID card the following appeared: "The bearer of this card should be accorded full cooperation and assistance . . . to assure the successful completion of his mission. Bearer is authorized rations and quarters on a reimbursable basis. Upon presentation of this card, bearer is entitled to air, water, and ground transportation under a priority of 3. . . ." This meant that he could eat in the mess halls at a minimal charge or, if out in the field, free of charge, partaking of whatever the GIs ate. Sleeping accommodations were also usually free if one was working outside the big base areas. Transportation on military helicopters and planes, for example, was free too.

There was no press censorship during the time American combat units were in South Vietnam. In past wars, American officials had made it a common practice. Vietnam was different. "As large numbers of American ground troops were committed, I seriously considered recommending press censorship," Westmoreland later wrote. "Yet I saw many obstacles. How, for example, to prevent reporters, including many from countries other than the United States, from filing their stories from some other country. . . . As for television, the very mechanics of censoring it was [sic] forbidding to contemplate. . . . In any event, in the final analysis, the decision on censorship was not mine to make but the President's." Interestingly enough, at least one distinguished correspondent thinks that press coverage might have been better in some respects had censorship been imposed. "On three trips to Vietnam," observes Drew Middleton, the *New York Times*'s senior military correspondent, "I found generals and everyone else far more wary of talking to reporters precisely because there was no censorship. Their usual line with a difficult or sensitive question was 'You must ask the public relations people about that.' The latter, usually of low rank, clammed up, and the reporter and the public got less. . . . Comparing the Second World War [in which he was a correspondent] and Vietnam, I think there was a hell of a lot more original reporting in the first."

Throughout the war zone, every large unit had a press staff made up of officers and enlisted men whose job was not only to work with reporters but also to report on the war themselves. Their stories were made available to the wire services, for example, and also published in military publications such as *7th Air Force News*. Military writers and photographers, most notably from *Stars and Stripes,* the military newspaper distributed to servicemen overseas, roamed the war zone just like their counterparts at any commercial outlet. Few reporters had problems with military press staffs in the field. In many cases, the war was impossible to cover without them; they characteristically facilitated the movement of reporters to stories involving their units. In fact, though reporters were not required to have military escort while covering a story, they often requested it.

Friction between reporters and press officers usually occurred only on the policy level — i.e., out of Saigon, where daily press briefings were conducted by officers representing the service branches and the embassy. "It could have rained frogs over Tan Son Nhut and they wouldn't have been upset," says Michael Herr, who covered the war for *Esquire*. These briefings were called the "Five O'Clock Follies," and it was there that the daily body counts were released, as well as much of the data on the air war. Euphemisms such as "friendly fire" (ours), "friendly casualties" (ours), "meeting engagement" (ambush), and "discreet burst" (machine-gun fire with a defined target) were first heard at these briefings.

Herr was in an unusual position to observe and write about the war because he never had to attend these briefings or get the obligatory interview with visiting VIPs. Not being a slave to daily deadlines, he could roam the war zone observing the daily goings-on wherever he pleased, and then later write to develop a broader perspective and a deeper feeling. His editors gave him almost unlimited space. ("*Esquire,* wow, *they* got a guy over here," exclaimed one GI

Corporal William Perkins (left background), a military combat photographer, records a medical evacuation only two hours before he was killed in action.

armor-piercing shell. Two men inside were wounded.

"The terraced paddies made maneuvering difficult and the supply men were not trained for it. Attempting to get in to good firing positions, three of the five amtraks backed into a deep paddy and bogged down.

"The other two edged toward the tanks for shelter. One didn't make it. A Vietcong knocked it out by dropping a grenade down its hatch, killing two Americans inside and wounding others.

"Mortar fire bounced off the vehicles and cannon put three holes in one tank. The wounded driver squeezed himself through the 18-inch wide escape hatch under his vehicle only to be riddled by bullets.

"Corporal Pass saw Vietcong with ammunition bandoliers, black pajama uniforms, and camouflaged steel helmets move right up to an amtrak 30 yards to his left.

"He said the doors of the vehicle clanged open as the two drivers tried to make a break to Pass's vehicle. One of the Americans was killed as he leaped out.

"The other was plunging through the paddyfield swinging his Marine knife when he went down. When pulled out dead today, he still had a knife clutched in his hand.

"Soon after noon, as the hot sun beat

down on the scurrying figures and the steel vehicles, the Vietcong knocked out a third amtrak. Survivors massed in the other two.

"Corporal Frank Guilford of Philadelphia said machine guns sliced into the guerrillas, but they kept coming.

"The men took turns as sharpshooters at peepholes on top of the vehicles. All were wounded in some degree.

"'I couldn't maneuver up there,' said Pfc. James Reef of Seattle, who escaped with a slight injury.

"A young corporal shouted, 'Okay, men, we're Marines. Let's do the job.'

"He started to climb out of the vehicle but never got his rifle to his shoulder. A bullet hit him between the eyes.

"Among those sweltering in the other amtrak was Staff Sgt. Jack Merino of Limita, Calif. He said he almost passed out from heat exhaustion. The men took turns splashing water over each other from resupply cans within the vehicle.

"Merino said that in midafternoon he heard a man outside whispering, 'Amtrak, amtrak.' He proved to be a wounded tank crewman. Merino and others pulled him inside.

"'It was a hair-raising moment but we managed it,' Merino said.

"The Marines continued with the nerve-wracking task of keeping off the attackers. The enemy bodies began piling up.

"In late afternoon, air strikes eased the pressure.

"By this time, a lieutenant had been killed and another wounded.

"Another tank joined the beleaguered group.

"At daybreak, a solitary helicopter landed at the scene. It had mistaken the landing zone.

"At the drone of the helicopter, the Americans surged from their amtraks like moths to a flame.

"Crouched, and with weapons at the ready, the Americans slipped past the bodies of their own and the enemy. They carried the wounded to the helicopter and left the dead.

upon reading the tag sewn above Herr's breast pocket. "What the fuck for, you tell 'em what we're wearing?") Actually, he wrote almost exclusively about the average soldier. The result, on one level, is some of the most poignant, powerful writing about the war's effect on the GI in the field. Herr's book *Dispatches* recreates the atmosphere of the Vietnam war as accurately as Erich M. Remarque's *All Quiet On the Western Front* caught the feeling of the First World War or Norman Mailer's *Naked and the Dead*, the Second.

Herr's writing also reveals much about how the Vietnam war was reported. Of the early popular image of the war, notably the movie *The Green Berets*, he wrote: "That wasn't really about Vietnam, it was about Santa Monica." Of the difficulty of reporting the war: "A lot of things had to be unlearned before you could learn anything at all, and even after you knew better you couldn't avoid the ways in which things got mixed, the war itself with those parts of the war that were just like the movies." Of reporting the war: "Conventional journalism could no more reveal this war than conventional firepower could win it, all it could do was view the most profound events of the American decade and turn it into a communications pudding, taking its most obvious, undeniable history and making it into a secret history." Of government reports about aircraft and helicopter losses: "...this was spoken of as an expensive equipment loss, as though our choppers were crewless entities that held to the sky by themselves, spilling nothing more precious than fuel when they crashed." On the difficulty of understanding what was going on from a continent away: "The jargon of Progress got blown into your head like bullets, and by the time you waded through all the Washington stories and all the Saigon stories, all the Other War stories and the corruption stories and the stories about brisk new gains in ARVN effectiveness, the suffering was somehow unimpressive. And after enough years of that, so many that it seemed to have been going on forever, you got to the point where you could sit there in the evening and listen to the man say that American casualties for the week had reached a six-week low, only eighty G.I.'s had died in combat, and you'd feel like you'd gotten a bargain."

And, finally, of the ultimate inability of the media to truly convey what the war was about:

". . . in back of every column of print you read about Vietnam there was a dripping, laughing death-face: it hid there in the newspapers and magazines and held to your television screens for hours after the set was turned off for the night, an afterimage that simply wanted to tell you at last what somehow had not been told yet."

It was also Herr's observation that of all the reporters who covered the Vietnam war, there were only about "fifty, who were gifted or honest or especially kind and who gave journalism a better name than it deserved." At the top of his and many others' list was AP's Peter Arnett, who was awarded one Pulitzer Prize for his reporting there and, it is said, should have been awarded others. Halberstam deems Arnett the best reporter of the war. Arnett and his colleague Horst Faas, a German photographer for AP who was one of the best in his field, were renowned for their courtesy to both GIs and new journalists in-country—a trait that Herr describes as "war-wise grace." Each was respected by both his colleagues and by the military. This was generally true of top newspeople, about whom Herr observed that "by some equation that was so wonderful that I've never stopped to work it out, the best and the bravest correspondents were also usually the most compassionate, the ones who were most in touch with what they were doing."

Because of his many years in Vietnam, Arnett was, of course, in a good position to himself judge the work of colleagues who covered the war for shorter periods. His list of the best reporters to cover the war includes many from the *New York Times,* the paper that in his view far surpassed the performance of any of its rival dailies. The *Times* reporters he mentions are Halberstam, Johnny Apple, Charlie Mohr, Gloria Emerson and Sydney Schanberg. He also names Bill Tuohy and Jack Foisie of the *Los Angeles Times,* Ward Just of the *Washington Post,* and Peter Kann of the *Wall Street Journal* for their outstanding work. From the wire services, Arnett lists reporter Neil Sheehan and photographers Kyoichi Sawada and David Kennerly of United Press; and reporters George Esper, John Wheeler and Hugh Mulligan and photographers Horst Faas, Henry Huet, Eddie Adams and Nick Ut from Associated Press. Other print media journalists he mentions are photographers Larry Burrows of *Life* and freelancer Catherine Leroy.

CBS dominated the television coverage much

"The helicopter came back once for more wounded.

"Ground forces arrived to relieve the others. In the interval they had scoured the nearby paddyfields and brush for Vietcong bodies. They found 18.

"Corporal Earle Eberly of Sycamore, Ill., said:

"'We don't like being here and killing people and being killed. But this is a job we've been told to do, we have to do it, and we're going to do it.'

"The fate of Supply Column 21 was sealed at noon.

"The men thought the disabled vehicles might be carted off and repaired. But an officer of the relief force told them:

"'Take your personal belongings out of the vehicles. We're going to blow them up.'

"The remains of the amtraks at Van Tuong will be a reminder of Supply Column 21."

Peter Arnett of Associated Press covered the entire war, arriving before the first American combat units and staying to observe North Vietnamese tanks roll down the streets of Saigon.

as the *New York Times* did that for newspapers. Arnett names CBS's best as being Morley Safer and Jack Laurence—with perhaps the latter being the best of all television journalists during the Vietnam war. He also cites CBS's Ed Bradley and NBC's Garrick Utley for their outstanding work.

There were other able journalists who covered the war but whose reputations were actually established elsewhere or later: Frances FitzGerald, who would write *Fire On the Lake;* NBC's Liz Trotta (now with CBS); CBS's Dan Rather, Ed Rabel, Richard Threlkeld (now with ABC), Gary Shephard (now with ABC), and husband and wife George and Gusta Syvertson, who between them spoke about ten languages fluently; ABC's Ted Koppel, Sam Donaldson, Steve Bell and Ken Kashiwahara, who first served in Vietnam as an air force press officer and returned to cover the fall of Saigon for the network.

Stories about the men and women of the press became part of Vietnam war folklore, both humorous and otherwise. There was the Portuguese novelist who showed up at Khe Sanh in sports clothes, thinking he could purchase fatigues at the besieged outpost. At the opposite extreme, photographer John Schneider, in the midst of a vicious firefight near Khe Sanh in early 1968, marched from the top of Hill 881 North back to the marine position on Hill 881 South while carrying a white flag; that episode became known as Schneider's March. CBS's Don Webster, who seemed totally insensitive to danger, was famous among press officers (who frequently trailed behind) for briskly marching off into the jungle, toward the sounds of battle, as if late for a press conference in Central Park. (Later, his fearlessness led to his being captured in a war in Africa; CBS and the U.S. government barely managed to get him released.) Photographer Dana Stone developed the habit of walking point; because of his longevity in the war zone, he was more adept at spotting enemy booby traps than almost any GI. Photographer Charlie Eggleston of UPI staged his own kamikaze-type attack on VC positions to avenge the deaths of four of his colleagues.

Page, Stone and their fellow photographer Sean Flynn, who had covered the first big army battle at Ia Drang and was the son of actor Errol Flynn, occasionally rode Honda motorcycles to the fighting. Page's activities, in fact, reached legendary proportions. "Hey, Page, there's

This photograph of South Vietnamese General Loan executing a suspected Viet Cong officer on February 1, 1968, during the height of the Tet fighting, became one of the most famous of the war. AP photographer Eddie Adams was awarded the Pulitzer Prize for taking it.

an airstrike looking for you," his friends used to say to him, so frequent were his brushes with death. "He was twenty-three when I first met him," Herr later wrote, "and I can remember wishing that I'd known him when he was still young." His first injury came from shrapnel in 1965. Later, he was in a coast guard cutter in the South China Sea getting photos of Market Time operations when allied aircraft mistook the small boat for an enemy craft. Machine-gun fire cut the boat in half, killing three and wounding eight; Page suffered more than two hundred wounds in that attack. The injury that finally put him out of action occurred near Cu Chi. He was riding in a helicopter that was ordered down to pick up some wounded. When it landed, Page jumped out with a sergeant to help. The latter stepped on a mine that blew both his legs off and sent a two-inch piece of shrapnel into Page's brain, entering just above his right eye. Before collapsing, Page changed lenses and took more photographs. Miraculously, he survived, though rendered a hemiplegic. His condition has greatly improved over the years and he now lives in London, where he grew up. Time-Life paid more than $100,000 for his rehabilitation, much of which took place at Walter Reed Army Hospital — an unusual accommodation given that he was both a civilian and a British subject.

Many other newsmen were not as fortunate as Page. His friends Dana Stone and Sean Flynn were killed in a helicopter crash during Lam Son, the South Vietnamese attack into Cambodia. George Syvertson died with CBS bureau chief Gerald Miller when an enemy rocket struck their jeep during the Cambodian incursion of 1970. Bernard Fall died after stepping on a land mine. Larry Burrows and François Sully were also killed. Eight newsmen died during the first five days of Tet 1968—four of them in the same jeep (the incident that prompted Eggleston's suicidal assault). The four had accidentally driven up a street in Cholon controlled by Viet Cong soldiers. They had yelled "bao chi, bao chi"—Vietnamese for "journalist"— over and over as the enemy approached, but they were machine-gunned anyway. A fifth in the jeep survived by playing dead. In all, fifty-nine reporters or photographers were killed or are missing in action as a result of covering the war.

No wonder the common soldier thought they were crazy to do what they did. "You mean you

Photographer Dana Stone, immediately in front of a U.S. tank, makes his way to Khe Sanh behind marines clearing mines from a rarely used road.

The press was not a monolithic group that shared one view about the war. For example, Jim Lucas (right) of Scripps-Howard Newspapers, a former military correspondent who saw action at Guadalcanal and Iwo Jima, publicly criticized colleagues in 1964 for not covering military operations in the field more frequently. Here Lucas poses with Congressman Basil Whitener of North Carolina (second from left) and two marines from the lawmaker's district.

During the 1968 election campaign, Johnson personally briefed both presidential candidates on Vietnam and other issues.

guys *volunteer* to come over here?" one asked Stone, Page, Flynn and Herr. "Oh, man, you got to be kidding me."

But most soldiers openly expressed their respect for anyone who shared their hardships. "You're all right, man, you guys are cool, you got balls." Others, however, were never able to get over the suspicion that the newsmen were the root of the problem—the cause of folks back home being so opposed to what they had been ordered to do. Their story must not be getting back, some of them thought. Surely no one who knew they were getting killed and maimed chasing Charlie up and down mountains and through jungles could fail to support them. The reporters must not be telling it straight. This suspicion was usually kept inside. But occasionally it burst forth from the lips of some forlorn GI, his uniform all wet with sweat, his body drained of energy and his hollow eyes betraying the fear he'd never get back home.

One such soldier, a marine, accosted Herr just as he was preparing to leave fierce fighting that had raged for weeks. Unlike Herr, the marine had been ordered in and ordered to stay. Finally, the thought of it all overwhelmed the soldier, who ran up to the reporter, grabbing him violently.

"Okay, man, you go on, you go on out of here, you cocksucker," he said, "but I mean it, you tell it! You tell it, man, if you don't tell it. . . ."

By 1969 the mutiny on the ship of state seemed complete. Students, blacks and a large segment of the general population had combined to throw Lyndon Johnson and his crew overboard. Surprisingly, the new captain of the ship was the old warrior Richard Nixon, who had helped to chart the present course. But he had represented himself as being for change, so, by the slimmest of margins, he had been chosen to lead.

But the deck of the old ship was a babel of sorts. Those who had taken control spoke the same language, but the meaning of the words varied from group to group. For a militant minority, the anti-Vietnam battle cry was a call for fundamental changes—a new course altogether for the country; however, the vast majority saw no need for such drastic action—they sought only new leadership, someone who would turn the ship around and retrace its course. As matters turned out, Nixon exploited the differences between the groups so as to keep the country on the same course for four more years.

Nixon apparently had not intended to do this. For reasons of overconfidence as much as anything, he at first believed that he could negotiate a quick end to the conflict. During his presidential campaign against Hubert Humphrey, he had explained his strategy to H. R. Haldeman, his future White House chief of staff. "I call it the Madman Theory," Nixon said, as the two walked down a foggy beach. "I want the North Vietnamese to believe I've reached the point where I might do *anything* to stop the war. We'll just slip the word to them that 'For God's sake, you know, Nixon is obsessed about Communism. We can't restrain him when he's angry—and he has his hand on the nuclear button.'

"They'll believe any threat of force that Nixon makes because it's Nixon," explained the future president as he characterized himself.

Within thirty days of taking office, Nixon took the first step in his Madman scenario. To signal Hanoi that he was prone to a dramatic escalation of force, he ordered the Strategic Air Command to begin bombing enemy staging areas in Cambodia.

The second step in the scenario followed Nixon's June 8 announcement that 25,000 American combat troops would be withdrawn by August 31. At that point, Nixon exchanged letters with Ho Chi Minh; Frenchmen Jean Sainteny, who had known the North Vietnamese leader for years, hand-carried Nixon's opening missive dated July 15, 1969. As a result it was agreed that the U.S. and North Vietnam would engage in secret negotiations while the very public Paris Peace Talks were in session. Henry Kissinger, the president's national security adviser, and Le Du Tho would meet to resolve matters between their countries. According to Melvin Laird, the defense secretary at the time, Nixon and Kissinger "entered into these negotiations with a great deal of confidence that they would have some sort of success."

The third step tied the threat of escalation to the negotiations. The North Vietnamese government was informed that if there was not a breakthrough in negotiations by November 1, 1969, Nixon would "regretfully" have to resort to "measures of great consequence and force."

Fate then intervened. Ho Chi Minh died in early September and his passing seemed to harden the North Vietnamese bargaining posi-

On the issue of Vietnam, Richard Nixon's views more closely coincided with those of Johnson than did those of Democrat Hubert Humphrey.

✻ One of the most unusual and dramatic protests against the Vietnam war was staged by two crewmen of the American cargo ship S.S. *Columbia Eagle* on March 13, 1970. The ship, loaded to the gunwales with 500- and 750-pound bombs destined for B-52s stationed in Thailand, was cruising in the Gulf of Siam when the captain of the ship ordered all hands to abandon ship. Fearing an explosion, twenty-four crewmen did so quickly and pushed away in lifeboats. About an hour later, to their wonderment, the *Columbia Eagle* steamed off; fortunately they were picked up within hours by another munitions ship. Unbeknown to these crew members left behind, steward Clyde McKay and stoker Alvin Glatowski had pulled a gun on the captain and taken control of the ship. McKay later explained that he perceived himself "in the position of a German sailor during World War II. . . . I should feel myself guilty if I were just to comply and be part of threatening the people of Asia."

Until the takeover, both seemed almost apolitical. They couldn't have distinguished Marx from Lenin, one of their fellow crewmen observed. Both McKay and Glatowski had grown up in military families; their mothers had divorced and remarried servicemen. McKay, twenty-five, had once tried to join the army, but had failed the physical. Glatowski had signed on to the ship's crew to earn more money because his wife was pregnant.

The two ordered the captain to change course from Thailand to Sihanoukville, Cambodia, where the ship anchored five miles offshore. At that point, no one—neither McKay and Glatowski, American officials nor the Cambodian government—knew exactly what to do. Complicating the problem was the overthrow of Prince Norodom Sihanouk by General Lon Nol just days before. The Communist press throughout the world reported that the episode was all part of an elaborate CIA

tion. Nixon and Kissinger repeated the threat of escalation; they even caused speculation to be printed in the press that the administration was considering a blockade of Haiphong Harbor and an invasion of North Vietnam. But the threats had no effect. There was absolutely no movement during four secret negotiation sessions in 1969.

In frustration, Nixon then decided to convince the North Vietnamese that the U.S. had sufficient resolve to see the war through. He was certain that a great "silent majority" of Americans did not favor a unilateral withdrawal from Vietnam. He also surmised that even the vast majority of those who wanted out of Vietnam also wanted to disassociate themselves from the more vocal elements of the anti--Vietnam war movement. By this time, the majority of Americans opposed the war (fifty-five percent, according to a Gallup poll taken in November 1969). However, they were divided even in their opposition. Some opposed the war on moral grounds. Most opposed it for pragmatic reasons—that our campaign there was not working, that our allies were not worth the cost in lives and money. Nixon correctly perceived that many of the latter group, and certainly most of those who supported the war, resented the intellectuals and students who generally opposed it for moral reasons. They were seen as children of privilege, decrying the country that had given them so much. The other, more militant, elements of the peace movement seemed threatening to the majority of the American public. Nixon launched a counterattack, using Spiro Agnew, his vice-president, as his chief instrument to divide the antiwar movement against itself and rally the rest of the country to his side.

The political conditions were perfect for such a plan. A conservative backlash had been building since the first disruptions at Berkeley in 1964. A major issue used by Republican candidate Ronald Reagan against the incumbent California governor, Edmund Brown, in the 1966 elections was the need to reassert control of the state's campuses. The challenger's message had great appeal; despite an all-out student movement to oppose him, Reagan won by more than a million votes. There were other notable conservative victors that year. Agnew had been elected governor of Maryland. Altogether Republicans won eight governorships and picked up three seats in the Senate, forty-seven in the House of

Representatives. Nixon had every reason to believe that the conservative trend was continuing. It seemed to be increasing almost in direct proportion to the campus unrest. And since the spring of 1969 was the most turbulent period yet on the campuses, he surmised that conservative sentiment had increased to its highest levels since the trend began.

Colleges across the country had experienced problems. At Rice University, a demonstration by a thousand students and two hundred faculty members forced the resignation of the school's president. Police were called to quell disturbances at, among other places, San Francisco State, Howard University, Penn State, and the University of Massachusetts. The home of the president of San Mateo State was firebombed. At the University of Wisconsin, the Black People's Alliance, an organization of black students, called a strike. When conservative students of the Young Americans for Freedom crossed the picket lines, fighting broke out. The Wisconsin governor sent in the national guard to restore order with fixed bayonets and tear gas. At the City College of New York, some Puerto Rican students locked themselves in a campus building and demanded that the school's enrollment reflect New York's racial balance. Before the disruption ran its course, a school auditorium was destroyed by fire, classes were disrupted for two extended periods, and the school president was forced to resign. At Harvard, students invaded University Hall and evicted the deans while demanding that ROTC be kicked off campus. School president Nathan Pusey called in the police, who arrested 197 for trespass.

The most dramatic student protest and reaction that spring occurred a few days after the events at Harvard. The location of the violence was where it all began—Cal-Berkeley. Students and other activists who lived in the area dug up a temporary parking lot owned by the university near the campus and turned it into what they called a "People's Park." They carted off asphalt and planted grass and a few trees. Immediately the project became a magnet for activists of every sort, including the Black Panthers. About three weeks later, school officials decided to reassert control over the property. At three o'clock in the morning hours of May 15, two hundred campus and city police converged on the area, arresting three people found in the park. Workers then quickly erected a fence

scheme to ship Lon Nol weapons. Such speculation ended when McKay and Glatkowski were granted political asylum in Phnom Penh, the ship was returned to U.S. control, and newsmen were allowed to board the ship to confirm that its cargo was untouched and entirely composed of bombs that were of no use to Lon Nol's soldiers.

At that point McKay and Glatowski began paying the price for their protest. Their asylum gradually evolved into a form of arrest. In October 1970, McKay managed to escape. He was last seen headed toward Communist forces at Siem Reap to join them. He was never heard from again. Glatowski tried to gain asylum at the Russian and Chinese embassies in Phnom Penh. Both refused him. In absentia, he and McKay were indicted by a federal grand jury in Los Angeles on charges of mutiny, kidnapping and assault. Glatowski eventually surrendered to the American embassy in Phnom Penh and was returned to the U.S. In 1972 he was convicted for the assault and mutiny charges and sentenced to ten years in the federal corrections institution at Lompoc, California. He was paroled after five years.

around it. At noon a campus women's rally turned into a larger event at which the student body president-elect exhorted the crowd: "We must show Heyns and the other bums who run this campus that the park belongs to the people. Take the park!"

A melee ensued. Rocks and bottles were thrown at police, who responded with tear gas and finally with bullets and shotgun blasts. More than thirty demonstrators were wounded; one later died.

Reagan then called out the national guard. The following week, the campus was an armed camp. Military helicopters flew over spraying CS gas, the same used in Vietnam to flush enemy soldiers from their tunnels and bunkers. Eight hundred students and street people were arrested during the period.

All these disturbances justifiably worried many Americans. And as if to confirm the coming storm, four hundred thousand young people gathered on Max Yasgur's farm, about seventy miles northwest of New York City, for a music happening called Woodstock during the weekend of August 15-17, 1969. For hours on end they listened to the troubadours of their time: the Jefferson Airplane, the Creedence Clearwater Revival, Sly and the Family Stone, Jimi Hendrix, Joan Baez and Janis Joplin. Overnight, they had created the third largest city in New York. It was an event that would define one generation and terrify all others.

So Nixon's plan in the fall of 1969 to strengthen his hand against the North Vietnamese by dividing the protest movement and polarizing the country was well timed. Given the decreased intensity of the fighting in Vietnam and the troop withdrawals under way, many Amerians were feeling a little better about Vietnam. And the first moon landing, on July 20, 1969, had made Americans feel better in general about their country. Nixon's standing in the polls reflected this mood. According to Gallup, his approval rating stood at a high of sixty-eight percent that November. He sensed that the public was in no mood for events like the October 15 antiwar moratorium, a huge gathering at which a message from North Vietnamese Premier Pham Van Dong was read: "May your offensive succeed splendidly."

The man who as a candidate said he had been much moved by a young girl's campaign poster plea to "Bring Us Together" now moved deci-

Thousands of college-age Americans gather near White Lake, New York, for the Woodstock Music Festival during the summer of 1969.

sively to do just the opposite. On November 3 the president himself set the plan in motion by delivering his famous "silent majority" speech, intended to rally support for the war. He then put Agnew to work speaking around the country. The vice-president described dissidents as "an effete corps of impudent snobs who characterize themselves as intellectuals." He called their political supporters "parasites of passion" and "ideological eunuchs." And then on November 13, 1969, during a speech in Des Moines, he took out after "the small group of men, numbering perhaps no more than a dozen anchormen, commentators and executive producers," who "settle upon the twenty minutes or so of film and commentary that is to reach the public." This "unelected elite," he said, was "a tiny and closed fraternity of privileged men . . . enjoying a monopoly sanctioned and licensed by the government." A week later he launched an assault on the print media, singling out the *New York Times* and the *Washington Post.* They were all part of the "eastern liberal establishment" that did not represent the views of most American people, he said.

So positive and immediate was the response that Nixon kept Agnew on the road for most of the next year. During 1970, the vice-president logged 17,240 miles in twenty-two states in twenty-three days. Presidential speechwriters William Safire and Patrick Buchanan poured out the words and phrases he would speak. Senate doves were called "solons of sellout" and "pampered prodigies." Democratic candidates for office were called "nattering nabobs of negativism," "pusillanimous pussyfooters," "vicars of vacillation," and "troglodytic leftists."

As the rhetoric suggests, the charges were vastly exaggerated. In the case of the networks, at least, the administration had little to complain about. The fighting was not being sensationalized on the air; in fact, for about a year, network executives had deliberately been cutting back on the amount of combat footage appearing on the evening news. During about a six-month period beginning with Tet 1968 and extending until sometime after the Democratic National Convention that summer, there had been great focus on Vietnam fighting. But after that, events at the convention had influenced the way television covered the news.

Thousands of convention viewers called the networks to blame them for the violence they

Nixon used Vice-President Spiro Agnew to polarize public opinion on Vietnam and rally what he called the "silent majority."

Portrait of a student protester...

John Khanlian was a graduate student at Columbia University's School of International Affairs when the photograph of him on page 404 was taken by freelancer Maury Englander in April 1968. Soon thereafter the photo was made into a poster. For thousands who purchased it, Khanlian's portrait became an enduring image of the period.

The vast majority of students who joined the antiwar movement were like Khanlian, more idealistic than anarchistic. But, Khanlian's pacifist roots ran deeper than those of most. His father, a history teacher, gave him the middle name of Fosdick in honor of the family minister, the Reverend Harry Emerson Fosdick of New York City's Riverside Church, who voiced strong pacifist views even during the Second World War. At age ten, Khanlian, after reading Fosdick's sermon on the unknown soldier, told his mother, tears rolling down his cheeks, "I made up my mind. I'll never take part in any war." For college, Khanlian went west, attending Earlham, a Quaker college in Richmond, Indiana. It was there in 1965 that he took part in his first anti-Vietnam war protest.

By the end of 1967 he had married and was attending Columbia, hoping eventually to go to work for the State Department. Though he was not a member of any radical group, protesting the war had become a regular part of his life. For an extended period, he attended school during the day and rallies at night.

The moment immortalized by the poster occurred after the turbulent forces of early 1968 swept across Columbia University's campus. SDS members had occupied a school building and for twenty-four hours held captive a dean whose office was inside. They were protesting CIA recruiting on campus and the school's research contracts

saw on the screen. Indeed, events in Chicago were so extraordinary and shocking that television executives immediately began wondering whether their coverage had indeed contributed to the situation by magnifying the intensity of it all. Perhaps their news divisions had gotten out too far ahead of the rest of the country—not just with domestic news coverage but with Vietnam coverage as well. Observations by independent observers reinforced this conclusion. Columnist Joseph Kraft, for example, wrote shortly afterwards: ". . . do we, as the supporters of Mayor Richard Daley and his Chicago police have charged, have a prejudice of our own? The answer, I think, is that Mayor Daley and his supporters have a point. Most of us in what is called the communications field are not rooted in the great mass of ordinary Americans—in Middle America. . . . It seems wise to exercise a certain caution, a prudent restraint, in pressing a claim for a plenary indulgence to be in all places at all times the agent of the sovereign public."

Reflecting this new, chastened attitude, television news executives began stepping cautiously —a year before Agnew's attacks. Less extensive coverage of Vietnam created the impression that the war was winding down. While that was true, thousands of American soldiers were still dying at a time when the emphasis on the air was on the reduction of combat activity.

Robert Northshield, the executive producer for the Huntley-Brinkley evening news on NBC from 1965 through 1968 (and now the executive producer of CBS's *Sunday Morning*), explains how the new mood changed policy: "The executive producer sits down every morning to plan his show. He aims at having five segments. He talks to Brinkley in Washington, to other guys. And very often his feeling is, 'Oh, God, not Vietnam again!' By early 1969 that feeling was very marked. The trend was away from Vietnam." This was true for all the networks. For example, when in March 1969, Av Westin became executive producer at ABC, he wrote a memo to all his correspondents that included the following: "I think the time has come to shift some of our focus from the battlefield . . . to themes and stories under the general heading: We Are on Our Way Out of Vietnam."

Thus, even the trial of William Calley and the release of the *Pentagon Papers* weren't enough to undo the indifference of most Americans at a time when they believed the war was drawing to a close.

Even the Smothers Brothers couldn't survive the new conservative mood at the networks. CBS fired them in November 1969 for encouraging guests to make flippant remarks about patriotism and the Vietnam war. The print media were also affected. The *New York Times* ended up hiring Safire as a columnist, though his background was in advertising. Good conservative commentators became hot properties.

In spite of these favorable conditions, Nixon's plan to use Agnew to isolate the more liberal and radical elements of the protest movement failed on several counts. First, it failed to impress the North Vietnamese. In April 1970 they rejected a five-point peace plan proposed by Nixon: "Our rejection is firm, total, and categorical," they said. Second, it actually increased the appeal of radical leaders among students. Agnew's harsh, maniacal rhetoric and Nixon's deliberate insensitivity helped legitimize demands for fundamental changes. A 1970 Harris survey revealed that seventy-six percent of a national sample of students believed that "basic changes in the system" were necessary. Third, it failed to develop any lasting political popularity for Nixon. His favorability rating dropped steadily from its high point in November 1969, partly because of economic problems such as unemployment and partly because the polarized environment contributed to the public's unease. Exactly one year later, conservative columnists Rowland Evans and Robert Novak wrote that "the Presidency of Richard Nixon . . . hit bottom." In elections during the fall of 1970, the Republicans lost eleven governorships; before the election, they led Democrats thirty-two to eighteen; afterward the Democrats led twenty-nine to twenty-one. Republican candidates did only slightly better on the national level. One Republican senatorial candidate who lost even with strong White House backing was George Bush of Texas.

Essentially, all that Agnew and Nixon had achieved was the creation of a dangerous climate of domestic hatred that manifested itself in several tragic ways during 1970. In late April of that year, Nixon's announcement of the invasion of Cambodian border areas caused what was, according to William Manchester, the "first general student strike in the country's history, and it was entirely spontaneous." By the end of May, four hundred and fifteen colleges and

for the Defense Department. Black militants protesting the planned construction of a school gymnasium in Harlem joined them and eventually kicked out the SDS members, who then occupied four other campus buildings, including Low Memorial Library in which school president Grayson Kirk's offices were located. The university was forced to shut down. The occupations continued for about a week. By the time Kirk acted to end it all, the siege had become somewhat institutionalized—the radicals in one building, moderates in another; in some cases, occupiers of different buildings had different pet causes. But opposition to the Vietnam war unified them.

Though not one of the original occupiers, Khanlian spent several hours one night in a building occupied by the moderates. And in the early morning hours of April 30, he was outside the library with hundreds of protesting students and faculty sympathizers, who had taken upon themselves to block entry to this and other occupied buildings. A university official read a statement ordering them to disperse or subject themselves to arrest. They refused to leave; instead, they locked arms. At that point, the police charged. Khanlian was hit on the head by one who wielded a blackjack, the blow knocking him to the ground. As he got up to leave, another policeman caught him with a right hook that landed squarely on his left eye. Khanlian was not arrested, however.

The events of April 30 profoundly affected Khanlian's life. He decided that he could never work for the State Department and perhaps be forced to espouse views with which he disagreed. He now works as an educational consultant, training teachers in techniques that can be used to acquaint their high school students with the practical applications of good citizenship—including how to make their opinions heard.

Ohio National Guard troops assemble on the campus of Kent State University on May 4, 1970, under the direction of Brigadier General Robert Canterbury (left, in civilian clothing).

Guardsmen advance toward Taylor Hall to disperse the crowd of students assembled during the noontime hours. The smoke is from tear gas canisters being lobbed back and forth.

At the top of the hill, the guardsmen opened fire, causing students to run for their lives.

universities had been disrupted; two hundred and eighty-six of these were still paralyzed at the end of the semester. Many of those that managed to reopen had empty classrooms.

In the polarized environment that Nixon and Agnew had largely created, some authorities reacted to the campus unrest as if dealing with hordes of anarchists rather than American citizens exercising a basic right of assembly to protest government policy. After police at Jackson State College, Mississippi, killed two students and wounded nine with buckshot, machine guns and armor-piercing bullets, a presidential commission headed by former Pennsylvania Governor William Scranton observed that although the reaction "was unreasonable" and "unjustified," people who "engage in civil disorders and riots . . . must expect to be injured or killed when law enforcement officers are required to reestablish order."

That view was shared by Brigadier General Robert Canterbury of the Ohio National Guard. His units had been called to the campus of Kent State University to quell an unruly protest that had been as much the result of police overreaction to an earlier incident as to the students' political passions. "These students are going to have to find out what law and order is all about," Canterbury told a press conference. A short time later, his troops knelt down on a grassy slope in the middle of the campus, took careful aim at students who were not even within rock-throwing distance, and fired, wounding nine and killing four. None of them were radicals in any sense. In fact, one of the students who was murdered was an ROTC cadet.

It was true that anarchists were at work in some parts of the country, including college campuses. At the University of Wisconsin, for example, a revolutionary planted a bomb in the Army Mathematics Research Center that killed a physicist, injured four and caused six million dollars in damage. However, the Nixon-Agnew polarization campaign categorized all protestors as dangerous. At the same time, it helped make radical leaders heroes rather than isolate them. In the state of rebellion that was rapidly evolving because of the war and because of the administration's inflamatory speech and action, the trials of radicals such as the Chicago Seven, the Harrisburg Seven, the Camden Seventeen, the Seattle Seven, the Kansas City Four, the Evanston Four and the Gainesville Eight, the

Soledad Brothers and Angela Davis became *causes célèbres* during the next couple of years. The burgeoning protest movement, in turn, fueled the paranoia of Nixon and members of his administration. Even J. Edgar Hoover loomed as a possible enemy in their minds: Nixon underlings had a list of administration-ordered wiretaps stolen out of Hoover's safe because they feared being blackmailed by the FBI director. They compiled an enemies list that included Carol Channing (she had sung the Lyndon Johnson campaign song set to the music of her hit "Hello, Dolly"), the president of Otis Elevator Company (the Otis elevator at San Clemente didn't work properly) and Daniel Schorr of CBS ("a real media enemy"). And then, finally, they set about breaking the law in wholesale fashion in order to stop government leaks to the press and to ensure Nixon's reelection. In search of information to discredit Daniel Ellsberg, who had released the *Pentagon Papers* to the *New York Times,* they ordered that the office of Ellsberg's psychiatrist be burglarized. To build a huge campaign war chest, special illegal deals were worked out to ensure large contributions. And then, of course, administration paranoia led burglars from CREEP (the Committee to Reelect the President) to the offices of the Democratic National Committee at the Watergate.

These illegal activities, which would lead to Nixon's resignation on August 9, 1974, had all come about, of course, because he had persisted with the war in order to find what he called an "honorable" way out. Lyndon Johnson had used the same adjective in the same context years before. "I am ready to go anywhere at any time, and meet with anyone wherever there is a promise of progress toward an honorable peace," he said on March 25, 1965, the same month the Rolling Thunder campaign began and the marines waded ashore at Nam O Beach. Both presidents' peace initiatives had consistently been frustrated by North Vietnamese intransigence.

In June of 1964, the Johnson administration had secretly called upon Canadian diplomat Blair Seaborn to sound out North Vietnamese officials on their willingness to negotiate. As Canada's delegate to the three-member International Control Commission appointed to supervise the Geneva Accords, Seaborn was a logical emissary to Hanoi. Seaborn met with Prime

Students tend to one of thirteen wounded by gunfire; four died. The victim closest to the guardsmen was seventy-one feet away; that farthest away was shot from a distance of 730 feet.

The freelance photographer at right was taken into custody by guardsmen for carrying a pistol. No demonstrators were found to have had guns, however. A presidential commission found the guards' action unwarranted.

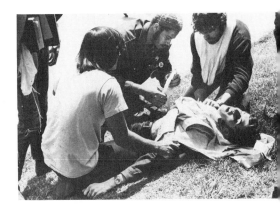

Students care for John Cleary, who was shot in the chest. He recovered.

Upon landing at Andrews Air Force Base on August 9, 1974, after a short helicopter trip from the White House, Richard Nixon flashes one last "V" sign as president. He then boarded "The Spirit of '76." His resignation became effective during his flight to San Clemente, California.

Minister Pham Van Dong, who informed him that if the U.S. wanted peace, Johnson should order the withdrawal of all American advisers so that the Vietnamese could settle the issue among themselves; only the NLF represented the true aspirations of Vietnamese in the south. Hanoi's attitude should not have been unexpected. The American bargaining position was extremely weak during those days when its South Vietnamese ally was being routed on the battlefield by the Viet Cong.

Another attempt to settle matters peacefully before involving U.S. combat troops came shortly after the Gulf of Tonkin reprisal strikes, and is still shrouded in mystery and confusion. In September of 1964, U Thant of Burma, secretary-general of the U.N. at the time, claimed that Ho had agreed to direct negotiations between North Vietnam and the U.S. in Rangoon. To win American approval, he contacted Adlai Stevenson, the U.S. ambassador to the U.N., who deemed the matter so sensitive that he informed only Dean Rusk. According to Chester Cooper, who was then on McGeorge Bundy's staff at the White House and was intimately involved in negotiation efforts during the Johnson years, "Rusk's reaction was negative, primarily because the proposal excluded the South Vietnamese Government." Rusk did not inform Johnson about U Thant's initiative. And Stevenson did not report the negative reaction to U Thant, presumably because he hoped to change Rusk's mind or talk to Johnson himself.

Weeks passed. Finally, in frustration, U Thant contacted Stevenson's deputies at the U.N., Charles Yost and Francis Plimpton, when Stevenson was vacationing in the Caribbean.

They knew nothing about the peace initiative. Upset and embarrassed, Yost actually called the State Department from U Thant's office. He reached the responsible assistant secretary of state, Harlan Cleveland, and demanded an explanation, but Cleveland didn't know anything either. Though there ensued a flurry of calls from Cleveland to Stevenson and Undersecretary of State George Ball (Rusk being away), and from Ball to McGeorge Bundy, the matter seems mysteriously to have languished again for several weeks, at which point U Thant apparently leaked the story to the *New York Times,* which put it on page one.

Johnson reacted angrily; he still knew nothing of U Thant's initiative. He called Bundy, who was away; in his boss's absence, Cooper, along with Bromley Smith, the executive secretary of the National Security Council, began searching the files for information. Like the president, neither of them was aware of the peace effort. Finally, a short, rather rough memo describing Ball's conversation with Bundy was found—a sort of "Did-you-know-that-U-Thant-told-Stevenson-that-he-could-set-up-a-meeting-in-Rangoon-with-Hanoi?" Cooper's interpretation of it was that "This by itself did not seem a very robust initiative." They so informed Johnson. Within hours, press secretary George Reedy was responding to the press: "There are no authorized negotiations under way with Mr. Thant or any other government. I am not going into any diplomatic chitchat that may be going forth, or way-out feelers. But authorized or meaningful negotiations—no."

The U Thant episode typified attempts at negotiations during the Johnson years. The North Vietnamese were very sure of what they wanted and what they were willing to do to get it. U.S. officials seemed much more confused. Eventually, however, each of the participants expressed its point of view in multipoint proposals. The NLF had a ten-point plan; the North Vietnamese, a four-point plan; the U.S., a fourteen-point plan. And in the spring of 1966, the administration encouraged Thieu to come up with South Vietnam's own multipoint plan.

The NLF's ten-point plan was first presented in 1960. Two of the points were of special relevance to U.S. interests; the others addressed internal reforms in South Vietnam and policies the NLF would institute as leaders of South Vietnam. The two, in summary, were as follows: "(1) Overthrow the camouflaged colonial regime of the American imperialists and . . . Ngo Dinh Diem . . . and institute a government of national democratic union. (9) Reestablish normal relations between the two zones, and prepare for the peaceful reunification of the country."

The American and North Vietnamese multipoint plans were first presented in 1965. In early April of that year, Marshal Josip Tito of Yugoslovia hosted a conference of seventeen nonaligned nations whose leaders made "an urgent appeal to the parties concerned to start . . . negotiations without . . . preconditions." The key word in their communiqué was *parties;* the clear implication was that the NLF be included in the talks. But the Johnson administration

✳ One of the most controversial allied programs of the war was called "Phoenix." Its purpose was to identify and "neutralize" the Viet Cong infrastructure (VCI). The idea for it came initially from Robert Komer, Westmoreland's civilian deputy, who developed the plan in close coordination with the CIA. In mid-1968 President Thieu endorsed the program and ordered it to begin. It was not a military program. It was run by the South Vietnamese working with American advisers. No troops were assigned to Phoenix. William Colby, who assumed Komer's position in late 1968, is the American most generally associated with it.

The principal effort of Phoenix was intelligence gathering; the chief task was coordinating the various levels of Vietnamese authority in all the jurisdictions. Three independent sources were required to identify a person as a VCI suspect. Once so identified, the targeted person could be neutralized in one of three ways—by persuasion, arrest or death.

Controversy associated with the Phoenix program arose out of charges that it was a death-squad operation. Colby denies the accusations. "To call it a program of murder is nonsense," he says.

That Thieu's government imposed quotas for the Phoenix program contributed to its bad image. Some American advisers say South Vietnamese authorities frequently counted enemy killed in normal military operations as Phoenix casualties so as to fill quotas. There were known abuses, of course. But documentation of widespread murder as part of Phoenix is absent.

In 1970, Komer described the Phoenix program as a "largely ineffective effort." Colby, by contrast, argued that it was fairly effective. His view was supported by Nguyen Co Thach, who after the war served as Vietnam's foreign minister. Phoenix "wiped out many of our bases," he says.

A network cameraman struggles through the water of a rice paddy to film a sweep operation by American troops. Reporting the war could be as dangerous and difficult as fighting in it.

was not willing to meet with NLF leaders for fear of implicitly conferring official recognition on the insurgent group by doing so. Furthermore, the U.S. was convinced that Hanoi leaders controlled all NLF activities in the south. On April 8, the Johnson administration officially responded: the U.S. was open to the idea of discussions with the "governments concerned"; only Hanoi, in other words. The day before, Johnson, during a speech delivered at Johns Hopkins University, had offered inducement for the North Vietnamese to begin these discussions. In a landmark presentation of administration policy, the president proposed that the U.S. spend a billion dollars for economic development in Southeast Asia, including North Vietnam. During speech preparations, a $500 million figure was originally proposed. But, typically, Johnson had opted for the billion-dollar gesture because it was a "nice, round dramatic figure."

The North Vietnamese countered with their four-point peace plan the day after Johnson's Johns Hopkins speech. It was as follows: "(1) The United States must withdraw its troops, weapons, and bases from South Vietnam and cease its 'acts of war' against North Vietnam; (2) Pending unification of the country, both North and South Vietnam must agree that no foreign bases or troops be allowed on their soil and that they will join no military alliances; (3) The internal affairs of South Vietnam must be settled in accordance with the program of the National Liberation Front; (4) The reunification of Vietnam must be settled by the Vietnamese themselves without outside interference." And then in a sweeping wrap-up statement, the North Vietnamese cemented these positions. Their four points were to be perceived as "*the* basis" for a settlement; "any approach contrary to the above-mentioned stand is inappropriate." The point Washington officials disliked most was the third because it "brushed aside the ideas and aspirations of any group other than the NLF."

Then the U.S. position also began to harden, as its troops took over the ground fight. Occasionally the administration made peace overtures, however. One type of overture was the bombing pauses, the first beginning on May 13, 1965, which lasted five days. (There were fourteen prior to March 31, 1968.) But all these failed because the U.S. refused to halt the bombing unconditionally, and the North

Vietnamese made this a precondition for negotiations.

The U.S. fourteen-point peace plan was written by Rusk himself in late 1965. It was the product of a "peace offensive" conducted during an extended bombing pause. A half-dozen top American officials hopscotched around the world trying to open up some avenues of influence with Hanoi and to arouse worldwide interest in a settlement. The Russians had suggested that Hanoi would be receptive. Averell Harriman made the most important trip. He traveled to twelve capitals, beginning with Warsaw. Of his fourteen-point plan, which Johnson, of course, approved, Rusk later observed, "We put everything into the basket except the surrender of South Vietnam." It included the following: "(1) The Geneva Agreements of 1954 and 1962 are an adequate basis for peace in Southeast Asia; . . . (3) We would welcome 'negotiations without pre-conditions,' as the 17 [nonaligned] nations put it; . . . (5) A cessation of hostilities could be the first order of business at a conference or could be the subject of preliminary discussions; . . . (7) We want no U.S. bases in Southeast Asia; (8) We do not desire to retain U.S. troops in South Viet-Nam after peace is assured; (9) We support free elections in South Viet-Nam to give the South Vietnamese a government of their own choice; (10) The question of reunification of Viet-Nam should be determined by the Vietnamese through their own free decision."

On January 24, 1966, Ho responded to the American initiative via letters to the heads of several governments. Ho's letter read in part: "If the U.S. government really wants a peaceful settlement, it must accept the four-point stand of the DRV Government and prove this by actual deeds; it must end unconditionally and for good all bombing raids and other war acts against the DRV."

From the peace offensive the administration drew one useful conclusion—that only subtle, quiet diplomacy had a chance of succeeding. But for seven more years even those attempts failed. In 1966, for example, U Thant tried working through the Russians to gain a settlement. The U.S. tried working through various Eastern European officials, such as the Poles and the Rumanians. Jean Sainteny was contacted about flying to Hanoi as a private citizen. (French President Charles de Gaulle would not allow it, though. He did not want France involved in any

Private First Class Frank Bunton tries to get into the Christmas spirit in spite of his surroundings. The lot of the soldier changed little during the long years of peace negotiations.

Senate Majority Leader Mike Mansfield
listens intently to LBJ. During the fifties
and early sixties, Mansfield had supported U.S. involvement in South
Vietnam; gradually he came to the conclusion that it was a mistake.

exploratory role, only in a final settlement.) In
early 1967 an attempt was made by British
Prime Minister Harold Wilson and Soviet Premier Aleksei Kosygin. They offered to mediate.
Wilson was the primary moving force; Kosygin's
state visit to London had precipitated the action.
Their efforts went for naught. Neither Hanoi nor
the U.S. seemed too eager for their ally's intervention. On another occasion that year the pope
became involved. Johnson also tried sending a
secret letter to Ho, who in response merely
reiterated Hanoi's position: "It is only after the
unconditional cessation of the U.S. bombing
raids and all other acts of war . . . that the
Democratic Republic of Vietnam and the United
States could enter into talks."

It was also in 1967 that Henry Kissinger
managed to get involved in the effort for the
first time. Still a private citizen, he met in Paris
with an old friend, a French doctor named M.
Marcovich, to discuss using Marcovich's close
friend M. Aubrac as an intermediary with the
North Vietnamese. Aubrac, a Resistance fighter
during the Second World War, was considered a
"good Frenchman" by Vietnamese. In 1946 he
had played host to Ho in Paris during the
implementation agreement negotiations. During
his stay, Ho became the godfather of Aubrac's
son. Marcovich thought Aubrac could reestablish contact with Ho. Kissinger immediately
inquired of friends in the State Department
whether they were interested. They were, but
the Aubrac-Marcovich mission to Hanoi would
have to be unofficial.

In late July 1967 the two Frenchmen arrived
in Hanoi and were promptly received by Ho and
Premier Pham Van Dong. The result was a
breakthrough, it seemed. The two North Vietnamese agreed to conduct "secret bilateral discussions with the United States on matters that
did not directly affect the internal situation in
South Vietnam." They were talking mostly about
the bombing of the north. They also "indicated
that Hanoi would not press for an early reunification of North and South Vietnam."

The administration reacted immediately. For
the first time the U.S. agreed to stop the
bombing in exchange for Honoi's agreement to
negotiate. The significance of this, says Cooper,
is that "we were no longer insisting on a substantial act of military reciprocity, although the
message did ask that Hanoi 'not take advantage'
of a bombing cessation." Cooper was ordered to

accompany Kissinger to Paris so that Aubrac and Marcovich would be assured that Kissinger was now acting as an official emissary.

But in direct contradiction to the administration's message, U.S. air forces began a major campaign at the same time to, in the words of Admiral Ulysses S. G. Sharp, "isolate Hanoi and Haiphong from each other and from the northern and southern logistic routes." Aubrac and Marcovitch were understandably worried that the intensified bombing had sent the wrong signal, but they reluctantly agreed to proceed. However, they were then denied visas on the grounds that Hanoi was unsafe. The two were asked to deliver their message instead to Mai Van Bo, the North Vietnamese representative in Paris.

Concurrent with this backdoor diplomatic move was the comprehensive reexamination of the war effort by Hanoi. Plans for Tet 1968 were the product of these deliberations. Perhaps Ho, through Aubrac and Marcovich, had been exploring an alternative to increased military activity, but had been convinced of the futility of negotiations by the U.S. bombing campaign. Whatever the case, the North Vietnamese had decided on the Tet offensive by September. On September 29, 1967, Johnson revealed publicly the new American position that had been delivered to Bo. It became known as the San Antonio formula—his speech discussing the subject had been delivered in that city. "As we have told Hanoi time and time and time again, the heart of the matter is really this: The United States is willing to stop all . . . bombardment of North Vietnam when this will lead promptly to productive discussions. We, of course, assume that while discussions proceed, North Vietnam would not take advantage of the bombing cessation." His "time and time again" reference was a subterfuge of sorts; the proposal was new.

Within a week, Hanoi's official newspaper denounced the San Antonio formula. Still, in retrospect, it seems clear that both sides were moving toward talks even though Hanoi was publicly strident about the American position. In fact, a short-term North Vietnamese objective of Tet seems to have been to improve its bargaining position.

Just how close they had come to the conference table became evident in January 1968, just days before Tet. On the first, Radio Hanoi reported on remarks by Foreign Minister Trinh

The president meets with Ambassador Ellsworth Bunker (left) and Secretary of Defense Clark Clifford (right) at Camp David during April 1968. National security adviser Walt Rostow is seated behind Clifford. By this time, Clifford had forced a thorough reappraisal of the administration's Vietnam policy.

Johnson first proposed a huge U.S.-funded economic development program for Southeast Asia, including North Vietnam, during a speech at Johns Hopkins University on April 7, 1965, but Ho Chi Minh would not accept Johnson's conditions. Seated (l-r) are college president Milton Eisenhower, and Lynda Bird and Lady Bird Johnson.

to a delegation from Mongolia. Trinh said that "after the United States had ended unconditionally the bombing and all other acts of war against the DRV, the DRV *will* hold talks with the United States on questions of concern." The word *will* had been substituted for the word *could* used in all previous announcements. The proposal was close to being the same as the San Antonio formula. Then, on January 25, another important step was taken. During testimony before the Senate Armed Services Committee, Secretary of Defense-designate Clark Clifford was asked to clarify the San Antonio formula—in particular, would the North Vietnamese be required to cease all military activities in return for a bombing halt? Clifford replied that he did not "expect them to stop their military activities. I would expect that they would start negotiations promptly and not take advantage of the pause." And by "take advantage," he said he meant that their flow of reinforcements and material down the Ho Chi Minh Trail would remain at "normal" levels.

At this point, both sides suffered through the bloodshed of Tet before Johnson himself took the final step. He halted the bombing of North Vietnam above the twentieth parallel (and at the same time announced his decision not to seek reelection); three days later, the North Vietnamese entered into peace talks. On May 3, 1968, Hanoi and Washington agreed that the first meeting would take place in Paris on May 10. The governments of South Vietnam, North Vietnam and the U.S. would be represented.

Many months passed before the parties agreed to anything. Hanoi wanted a cessation of all bombing of the north down to the seventeenth parallel, and they insisted on NLF participation in any agreement. There was also the problem of the shape of the table and seating. Johnson removed the biggest obstacle a few days before the U.S. presidential election when he ordered a halt to "all air, naval, and artillery bombardment of North Vietnam as of 8 A.M. November 1." The NLF was also allowed to be seated, but not as a separate delegation. All four parties would be arranged according to "our side—your side," the allies versus the Communists. Thieu balked at this arrangement initially, but finally agreed to sit down at the table.

Unfortunately, the latter symbolic issues were not resolved until January 16, 1969, when the first agreement was announced. The *New York*

Times reported that "Under the terms of the agreement, representatives of the United States, South Vietnam, North Vietnam and the National Liberation Front, or Vietcong, will sit at a circular table without nameplates, flags or markings. Two rectangular tables, measuring about 3 feet by 4½ feet, will be placed 18 inches from the circular table at opposite sides." Almost four years would pass before the opposing sides would reach another agreement. Nixon's own six-point peace plan (which reiterated Johnson's planned economic aid to North Vietnam after hostilities ceased), the formal Paris peace talks and Kissinger's secret talks would all prove futile during that time. The North Vietnamese would be as implacable in the conference room as on the battlefield. Nixon was inexorable himself, as the Cambodian incursion and the U.S.-sponsored South Vietnamese Army foray into Laos indicated. Criticism resulting from the lack of progress forced Nixon to announce in January 1972 that Kissinger had been meeting secretly with Le Duc Tho for two and a half years. His announcement would sound the death knell for the secret talks.

During that period, Kissinger made fifteen trips across the Atlantic for secret Paris rendezvous. Elaborate precautions were taken to keep the proceedings secret. "These trips were almost always on a weekend or on a holiday," says Kissinger assistant Winston Lord. "We had the presidential plane at our disposal and the close cooperation of the French.

"We'd usually go on a Saturday morning, drive out to Andrews Air Force Base to a special hangar, just three or four of us along with Kissinger; get on the plane, fly across the Atlantic all day Saturday, and land in central France, get out and transfer to a small French jet arranged by President Pompidou's office and fly from there to the outskirts of Paris where we'd be met by our military attaché at the Embassy who had rented a car under an anonymous name; drive to a safe haven apartment to get a night's sleep, negotiate with the Vietnamese on Sunday and with the time change we could fly back late Sunday and still go in the office the next morning as if nothing had happened. . . . It had its James Bond aspects."

But Le Duc Tho would only smile, never exactly saying yes or no to any proposal. With U.S. troops gradually being withdrawn and with domestic pressure building against Nixon, he

On May 8, 1968, Johnson led his delegation for the Paris peace talks to a meeting with the press on the White House grounds. The group included (l-r) Philip Habib, Cyrus Vance, Andrew Goodpaster, Averell Harriman and William Jorden.

Soldiers who helped in the turning...

"Son, I don't think what you're doing is good for the troops," the elderly lady said to the young man handing out antiwar leaflets in Washington, D.C., in April 1971.

"Lady," he answered, "we are the troops."

The young man was one of about two thousand members of an organization called the Vietnam Veterans Against the War—soldiers finally home from the war—who had come to the nation's capital to protest its continuation. Most ranged in age from twenty-one to twenty-five and had enlisted voluntarily. Dressed in the remnants of the fatigues, boots and headgear they had worn into battle, they paraded to Arlington National Cemetery (where they were denied entrance), to the Supreme Court (where one hundred and ten of them were arrested) and to the White House (where they lighted candles). They also conducted demonstrations, visited offices of congressmen and testified before congressional committees. After five days of activities, they broke camp, which was located on the mall between 3rd and 4th Streets in front of the Capitol, planted a tree there to commemorate the event, and returned home.

Their numbers were few but the impression they left was strong. Protesting students were one thing; protesting veterans were another—especially those who, at one emotional highpoint, marched together with combat medals in hand up the Capitol steps to unceremoniously give them back. After a middle-aged father wearing his dead son's fatigue jacket blew taps, they one by one hurled their Purple Heart ribbons, Silver Stars and Bronze Stars over a temporary fence erected by police to keep them back.

Another memorable moment during that siege of protest occurred at a

knew that time was on his side. Even major concessions failed to move the North Vietnamese. In May 1971, for example, Kissinger dropped the demand that as part of a settlement, North Vietnamese troops must be withdrawn from the South. They could keep them in place as of the cease-fire.

This concession might have had some effect on Communist strategy, according to Gareth Porter, author of *Peace Denied*, who believes that the object of the massive North Vietnamese invasion of the south beginning in March 1972 was to get as many troops in place in the south as possible. Indeed, fighting associated with the offensive ended in late July and within a couple of months Le Duc Tho requested another secret meeting with Kissinger. After an interim of almost a year, the two met on October 8, 1972, and the North Vietnamese politburo member proposed "a cease-fire in-place in return for the complete withdrawal of U.S. forces and exchange of prisoners. A 'National Council of Reconciliation' would deal with elections or the political settlement at some future time." This amounted to their agreeing to Kissinger's May 1971 proposal. It was more of a military settlement than a political settlement, but by then the Nixon administration thought that was the most that could be hoped for. Underlying that conclusion was the feeling that the U.S. had done enough militarily for the Saigon government over the years; if by then it was not strong enough to survive alone, it didn't deserve to. Given all the sacrifice and frustrations of the many years in Vietnam and the growing unrest at home, Nixon and Kissinger seized upon the proposal as if it were the Holy Grail. It was the honorable peace they had long sought—or, at least, honorable enough, given the circumstances. Tad Szulc, author of *The Illusion of Peace*, described it this way: "What the North Vietnamese were really giving the United States was the great face-saving device of letting Thieu remain in power, and inevitably their own calculation was, Okay, let's get the Americans out, let's sign the bloody peace treaty, let Thieu stay and let nature take its course; in the next year or two he will disappear—as he, indeed, did."

Not surprisingly, Thieu shared the North Vietnamese view of his government's chances for survival in the absence of American combat troops. Consequently, he balked when he learned of the settlement, the final details of which had been worked out during an intense ten-day period ending October 18, 1972. "In an exchange of cables, President Nixon and Prime Minister Pham Van Dong agreed to a limit on arms replacements after a cease-fire and the North agreed to a schedule for releasing the 566 American pilots held captive in Hanoi." The day these finalities were completed, Kissinger flew to Saigon to brief Thieu and win his approval. He had to work quickly; the signing date was set for October 31.

But Thieu refused to go along; after a couple of days of brooding, he told Kissinger, "I am not a yes-man. I am not a puppet. I will not agree with everything that the Americans would like to impose on our people."

Winston Lord accompanied Kissinger. "I'd have to say that this, for me, and I think probably for Kissinger, was one of the most painful episodes throughout these eight years [of the war]. We really thought that we had achieved an honorable peace, with just a few language details to be worked out. We thought that Thieu and the South Vietnamese would be so happy that after years the North Vietnamese had finally dropped their insistence on a coalition government, had agreed that we could continue supplying military equipment to South Vietnam after the cease-fire."

Thieu voiced two major reasons for opposing the tentative agreement: that the North Vietnamese troops were allowed to remain in place, and that the agreement was being pushed on him so quickly; he said he needed more time to prepare his people for such an agreement. Of course, neither Lord nor Thieu was being entirely candid. Thieu's real reason for opposing the agreement was his understanding that he could not survive without American troops; Lord had to know this.

Thieu formally rejected the treaty on October 22. On the twenty-fifth, Nixon cabled Pham Van Dong, explaining Thieu's objections and asking for more time to work things out. The North Vietnamese thought they had been duped for Nixon's political advantage at home. In a matter of days he would face reelection against Senator George McGovern. And so, in anger, the North Vietnamese made public on October 26 via Hanoi Radio the nearly consummated secret agreement. Their objective, no doubt, was to damage Nixon's reelection, but Nixon won by a landslide vote.

meeting of the Senate Foreign Relations Committee, when VVAW coordinator and former naval officer John Kerry delivered a short, eloquent statement that read, in part:

"We are also here to ask, and we are here to ask vehemently, where are the leaders of our country? Where is the leadership? We are here to ask where are McNamara, Rostow, Bundy, Johnson and so many others? Where are they now that we, the men whom they sent off to war, have returned?"
He accused them of "attempting to disown us."

He finished with these words:
"We wish that a merciful God could wipe away our own memories of that service as easily as this administration has wiped away their memories of us. But all that they have done and all that they can do by this denial is to make more clear than ever our last own determination to undertake one last mission—to search out and destroy the last vestige of this barbaric war, to pacify our own hearts, to conquer the hate and the fear that have driven this country these last ten years and more, so when thirty years from now our brothers go down the street without a leg, without an arm, or a face, and small boys ask why, we will be able to say 'Vietnam' and not mean a desert, not a filthy obscene memory, but mean instead the place where America finally turned and where soldiers like us helped in the turning."

In November 1984, Kerry was elected to the U.S. Senate by the people of Massachusetts.

Senator George McGovern, amid a crowd
of youthful supporters, campaigns in
New Brunswick, New Jersey. The promise of an immediate withdrawal from
Vietnam did the Democratic nominee
little good. Nixon won by what was then
the largest majority in American presidential election history.

After the election, Washington continued to
pursue a settlement. The administration requested another meeting and the North Vietnamese agreed to it. On November 20, in Paris,
Kissinger met again with Le Duc Tho and
proposed sixty changes and clarifications aimed
mostly at pleasing Thieu. The latter was also
placated by promises of increased military and
economic aid. At the same time, he was threatened with the total cut-off of U.S. aid if he didn't
go along.

Then the North Vietnamese became the recal-
citrant party. They began stalling, apparently
in expectation of an imminent move by the
American Congress to mandate an end to U.S.
fighting in South Vietnam. The talks collapsed
on December 13, 1972, and the final, ferocious
bombing campaign of the war followed. Before
long the Communists were bombed back to the
peace table. The final settlement was initialed
by Kissinger and Le Duc Tho in Paris at noon
on January 23, 1973. It was essentially the same
as that which was supposed to have been signed
on October 31. Its principal and most contested
provisions allowed Thieu to remain in power and
the 150,000 North Vietnamese troops in the
south to remain there. Thieu went along this
time, given U.S. concessions and threats; the
bombing campaign had also helped assure him
of continuing American resolve, says Lord. Practically speaking, Thieu had no choice, however.
The cease-fire went into effect at midnight, Green-
wich Mean Time, on January 27, 1973.

Kissinger and Le Duc Tho were later named
co-winners of the Nobel Peace Prize, though the
North Vietnamese refused to accept on the
grounds that peace had not returned to Vietnam—an omen of Communist intentions. But
Kissinger says that he and Nixon had never
misled themselves on that point. "We had no
illusions about Hanoi's long-range goal of subjugation of all of Indochina," he later wrote in his
memoirs.

That understanding was reinforced during
what Kissinger remembers as the "eerie" trip to
Hanoi. "For me," he says, "the sensation of
landing in Hanoi on February 10 [1973] was the
equivalent of stepping onto the moon." He had
been invited by Le Duc Tho. The North Vietnamese politburo was eager for him to visit.
Kissinger did not know exactly why. "Their
motive was elusive," he says. Whatever it was,
the trip had value for the administration: "I had

come to Hanoi in part to symbolize a commitment to national reconciliation at home."

The trip also included stops in Bangkok, Vientiane and Peking. At the same time, Agnew was traveling to Phnom Penh and Saigon. In 1954 Nixon had been the first sitting vice-president to visit South Vietnam; Agnew would be the last.

Kissinger landed at Noi Bai military airfield about fifty miles north of Hanoi in one of the presidential Boeing jets. The landscape had been pockmarked by B-52 bombing raids a few weeks before. Only the facade of the control tower stood. The runway had been cratered, but had been filled and smoothed sufficiently for the plane to land. Kissinger was greeted pleasantly by Le Duc Tho and the two departed for Hanoi aboard a smaller Soviet-built craft because the runway at Gia Lam International Airport near Hanoi was not long enough to accommodate their 707. The B-52s had left their calling cards at Gia Lam too, and, since the Doumer Bridge had been knocked out, the caravan of vehicles transporting Kissinger and Le Duc crossed the Red River separating Hanoi from Gia Lam on a pontoon bridge. "Once we reached Hanoi proper, however," says Kissinger, "the scene could not have been more peaceful. It was immediately evident (and confirmed by surprised journalists a few weeks later) that the city itself was practically undamaged by our bombing, contrary to the mythology of the alleged barbarity of our Christmas attacks." Kissinger's quarters during the stay was the elegant two-story structure that had once been the residence of the French governor-general of Tongking. Paul Doumer had walked its halls; Jean Sainteny had been kept there under house arrest during the turbulent days following the Second World War.

The next day he began meeting with Le Duc Tho and Pham Van Dong, who by that time had been prime minister for almost twenty years. Kissinger was chiefly interested in assurances that the Communists would abide by the Paris Accords. Pham Van Dong was primarily interested in the vast amounts of American aid that had been promised, contingent upon congressional approval. And, true to form, he was interested in testing his adversary's will. In the first meeting, held less than two weeks after the agreement had been signed, the North Vietnamese prime minister jarred the U.S. secretary of state with the observation that if a new

A car carrying Secretary of State Henry Kissinger crosses the Red River into Hanoi via a pontoon bridge before his February 1973 meetings with North Vietnamese leaders.

Kissinger walks through the gardens of his guest quarters in Hanoi with Le Duc Tho.

relationship between their two countries did not quickly develop, the accords would be "only a temporary stabilization of the situation, only a respite." The men then addressed three main issues — observance of the Paris Agreement, normalization of relations, and economic reconstruction. "No sooner had we turned to the first agenda item than we realized that Hanoi had no intention of making the Paris Accords the first agreement it had ever observed," Kissinger says. He had brought with him a list of more than two hundred truce violations that Communist forces had already perpetrated, such as the movement of 223 tanks through Laos and Cambodia, and the movement of 175 trucks through the DMZ on February 6, in violation of Article 15(a) of the agreement. Military equipment was supposed to be replenished only on a one-for-one basis and was to be monitored by the International Control Commission. The allegations were shrugged off; the trucks had not crossed the DMZ, it was claimed, and, besides, they were only carrying civilian goods (which, even so, would have amounted to a violation). But, according to Kissinger, the North Vietnamese leaders were their "most adamant (and obnoxious) about Laos and Cambodia." Article 20 had stipulated that all foreign troops were to be withdrawn from Laos and Cambodia; this included those of North Vietnam as well as those of the U.S. During the meetings, it became clear that the Communists had no intention of doing so. "They took the position that the required withdrawal, unconditional on its face, would have to await not only a cease-fire in Laos and Cambodia but also a political settlement in both those countries." This was not contemplated when the agreement was signed, and since it was impossible to effect, it afforded them a excuse, sufficient in their view, to remain.

Discussions about economic aid were informed by the same logic. Kissinger says that Nixon had instructed him "to reiterate to my interlocutors in Hanoi that aid depended on strict observance of the Paris Agreement, with special reference to withdrawal from Cambodia. . . . If the war did not end, the 'postwar' period could not begin."

"Pham Van Dong rejected this agreement," says Kissinger. "He advanced the startling view that asking Hanoi to observe a signed agreement was to attach 'political conditions.' Our aid was to be 'unconditional.' In other words, Hanoi was to be free to use American economic aid to complete its long-standing ambition of conquering Indochina."

The aid amounted to billions of dollars. The North Vietnamese looked upon it as war reparations; the U.S. viewed it as an inducement for its adversary to abide by the agreement. Nixon and Kissinger also hoped that the funds would develop the region's economy so that its politics would become more stable.

The monetary aid idea had first been broached by Johnson during his Johns Hopkins speech back in 1965, of course. Nixon had voiced his version of it on January 18, 1969, before the United Nations General Assembly. The President's Foreign Policy Report issued on February 9, 1972, had been more specific: "We are prepared to undertake a massive 7½ billion dollar five-year reconstruction program in conjunction with an overall agreement, in which North Vietnam could share up to two and a half billion dollars."

During the final days of negotiations in January 1973, Le Duc Tho had insisted on the entire $7.5 billion for North Vietnam. After considerable haggling, $3.25 billion was agreed to. And, says Kissinger, "In order to underline the fact that it was voluntary and distinct from the formal obligations of the Agreement, Le Duc Tho and I had agreed that the message announcing it [to the public] would be delivered on January 30, 1973, three days after the Agreement was signed, in exchange for a list of American prisoners held in Laos." The delay, which was Kissinger's idea, was meant to reinforce the American perception of the aid as a voluntary gesture of goodwill, not an obligation. That it was contingent upon North Vietnamese adherence to the rest of the agreement was clearly understood; that it was contingent upon congressional approval was explicitly noted. Kissinger also noted publicly that aid would be forthcoming only when "implementation [of the agreement] was well advanced." The dispute did not end agreeably. "I would like to express my suspicions. . . . I will speak very frankly and straightforwardly to you," said Pham Van Dong. "It is known to everyone that the U.S. has spent a great amount of money in regard to the war in Vietnam. It is said about $200 billion, and in conditions that one would say that the Congress was not fully agreeable to this war. When the war was going on, then the appropriation was so easy [he

Prime Minister Pham Van Dong greets his American visitor, as Le Duc Tho observes. Almost immediately, Pham Van Dong pressed for huge amounts of American aid as war reparations.

laughed at this point], and when we have to solve now a problem that is very legitimate . . . then you find it difficult." There followed inconclusive discussions about normalizing relations and convening an international conference to win worldwide endorsement of the agreement. But Hanoi did not want formal relations of any kind between the two countries, not even the establishment of offices "that fell short of full diplomatic status."

After these meetings, Kissinger says that he reboarded the Boeing 707 with a feeling of relief. "The soggy weather, the Spartan austerity, the palpable suspiciousness combined in Hanoi to produce the most oppressive atmosphere of any foreign capital I have ever visited," he remembers.

In the formal report of the meetings he delivered to Nixon, Kissinger wrote: "They have two basic choices which I frankly point out to them. . . . They can use the Vietnam agreement as an offensive weapon, nibbling at its edges, pressuring Saigon, confronting us with some hard choices. In this case they would carry out the release of our prisoners and wait till our withdrawals were completed before showing their real colors unambiguously; they would keep their forces in Laos and Cambodia through procrastination of negotiations or straightforward violations; and launch a big new attack soon. They would calculate that we would not have the domestic base or will to respond.

"Their other option is to basically honor the Agreement and seek their objectives through gradual evolution. . . . I emphasized that the first course would mean renewed confrontation with us and that they cannot have their aid and eat Indochina too."

The U.S. was caught on the horns of a serious dilemma, however, one that Kissinger described succinctly in the memoirs he published nine years later: "They had the capacity to damage us out of any proportion to what we could gain, by resuming the war or their assault on our domestic tranquility. But they could do nothing positive for us."

Looking back, he wrote: "To navigate the passage successfully would have proved very difficult in the best of circumstances. It required a united country and a strong, purposeful, disciplined American government capable of acting decisively and of maintaining the delicate balance of risks and incentives that constituted the Paris Agreement. Watergate soon ensured we

A major success of the Paris negotiations was the exchange of POWs. Above, some of the twenty-seven Americans held prisoner in the south disembark from a truck near Loc Ninh, about seventy-five miles from Saigon. Eight of the twenty-seven were civilians.

did not have it."

"It is 105 degrees and rising," said the announcer over the American-owned radio station at noon on the day of April 29, 1975, which, had it been true, would have been exceptionally hot weather even for Saigon. His selection of music—"White Christmas" by Bing Crosby—was repeated along with the temperature report every fifteen minutes. It was a bizarre format with very little entertainment value; however, few cared on this eventful day. Listeners were totally preoccupied with the thought of thousands of North Vietnamese troops massed on the outskirts of Saigon. In fact, the announcer's temperature reading and Christmas music were a prearranged signal to all Americans to flee while they could.

The end had come quickly. The Paris Accords had not brought peace to Indochina, only a brief respite before the fight to the finish. Almost exactly two years after Kissinger's plane had lifted off the end of the runway at Noi Bai, North Vietnamese army units had captured Phuoc Long Province. It was part of the final offensive, which Giap expected to take at least a couple of years; it was also a test of U.S. reaction. Richard Nixon had personally assured Thieu that American bombers would be back if necessary to save South Vietnam. But he was no longer president. The Watergate scandal had chased him from office. Furthermore, congressional action had precluded any reinvolvement in Indochina. All President Gerald Ford could do when Phuoc Long was overrun was posture a little (he ordered reconnaissance flights over the north resumed) and ask Congress for more military aid for Thieu's government ($300 million). But, in truth, he, like Congress and most Americans, was not interested in doing much more. "Our long national nightmare is over," he had told the nation upon taking over from Nixon. "Our constitution works. Our great republic is a government of laws and not of men." He wasn't just talking about Watergate. Watergate was only one part of the Vietnam nightmare, which after Phuoc Long had only one act to run. Saigon's control of South Vietnam quickly unraveled after that battle.

On March 11, 1975, a huge North Vietnamese force overran Ban Me Thuot, a city on the western edge of the central highlands. Hundreds of tanks and thousands of vehicles marshaled

The negotiations did not bring peace to South Vietnam. By the spring of 1975, the American ally was on the verge of collapse. American planes, such as these A-7E Corsairs aboard the U.S.S. *Enterprise,* were held in reserve, to be used only if needed to help rescue American personnel.

After many years of fighting, the end came quickly once the final Communist offensive began. Panic-stricken, some South Vietnamese tried reaching the safety of American ships offshore in helicopters. (Top) A South Vietnamese pilot leaps from his airborne chopper. (Middle) Another attempts a ditching at sea. (Bottom) American seamen push one of the fifteen helicopters that landed on the deck of the U.S.S. *Blue Ridge* into the sea to make room for others to land.

for the assault after traveling down the Ho Chi Minh Trail. On March 15, Thieu had panicked and ordered the entire central highlands region abandoned so as to consolidate his forces. It was the worst possible decision. The population of the region had panicked, too, clogging the roads and immobilizing a large part of the government army. Then, in a move that Westmoreland had long concerned himself about, the North Vietnamese invasion army under General Van Tien Dung raced across the south, cutting it in two. Turning north, part of it attacked Hue, which fell on March 25, and Danang, which fell on the thirtieth. Billions of dollars' worth of U.S. equipment were captured intact. The attacks on Hue and Danang created hundreds of thousands more refugees. Relatively few found avenues of escape. Some departed by boat; a handful boarded emergency flights out of Danang Air Base. Most took to the highways with all they could carry, a pitiful horde with no place to go.

Finally, on April 9, the last major battle of the war was joined. At Xuan Loc, about a hundred miles northeast of Saigon, government troops held the line courageously for twelve days. When eventually they were overwhelmed, Saigon's last defense line was breached. The war was lost for the allies; confirmation awaited only the evacuation of the seven thousand U.S. government civilian employees and fifty military advisers. On April 23, Ford prepared the American people for that occurrence. "Today America can regain a sense of pride that existed before Vietnam. But it cannot be achieved by refighting a war that is finished as far as America is concerned," he said.

On April 26, Thieu resigned and departed South Vietnam, flying out of Tan Son Nhut. "Thank you for all you've done," he told CIA agent Frank Snepp, who drove him to his plane, tears welling in his eyes. General Duong Van ("Big Minh") Minh replaced him. Graham Martin, the embattled last U.S. ambassador to South Vietnam, had helped engineer this, Minh being more acceptable to the Communists, it was hoped. Then, on April 28, to everyone's surprise, Minh, as his first act, ordered all Americans out of the country within twenty-four hours.

General Dung was of the same impatient disposition. That same day he gave Saigon twenty-four hours to surrender. And the next morning before dawn he ordered his artillery units to begin bombarding Tan Son Nhut. Within hours the airstrip was closed. During the preceding several weeks, tens of thousands had fled through its gates. Means of escape were now few, as the thousands of Vietnamese clambering over the wall of the U.S. embassy understood only too well. Many had worked for the United States for years and, if left behind—as they would be—faced a disturbing future.

Bing Crosby's voice and the high temperature reading had sent the Americans remaining in Saigon into their final frenzy. A bus loaded with reporters had raced to Tan Son Nhut, only to find it closed. As it raced back to the embassy through crowded streets, it ran over a child.

Helicopter evacuation was now the only way out. Thirteen Saigon rooftops had been designated pickup points. At midafternoon, sixty giant CH-34 Sea Knights from the carriers *Hancock, Okinawa* and *Midway* began plucking their eager passengers off these improvised LZs and transporting them two hundred miles out to a rescue fleet of forty ships. This last operation of the war was called "Operation Frequent Wind." Sporadic shelling made it dangerous. Some mortar rounds that landed on the edge of the defense attaché's compound that day hit the last two American ground troops to die in South Vietnam. Gradually, the rescue points dwindled to one — the embassy rooftop.

Informed that the Americans were leaving, Dung extended his deadline to 6 A.M., April 30, just enough time, as it turned out, for Ambassador Martin to leave. At 4:30 A.M., he, the last American official in South Vietnam, was still at his desk, on the phone to Washington awaiting permission to, of all things, extend the deadline for the evacuation, when a young helicopter pilot walked in and handed him a message scrawled on a notepad. "The President of the United States directs Ambassador Martin to come out on this helicopter," it read. It had been transmitted through the fleet. Graham put down the phone, walked to the helicopter and was off. Only a small contingent of American marines then remained. They departed at 7:53 A.M. after lowering the American flag flying over the embassy. Americans, having been at peace with the world for about two years, could now focus on coming to peace with themselves. That would take as much time as the war itself.

By the early morning hours of April 30, 1975, all American soldiers and government officials had fled South Vietnam. They were joined by most of that country's top leadership, including Nguyen Cao Ky (top photo, right) shown shortly after a helicopter had transported him to the deck of the U.S.S. *Midway.* (Bottom) For many South Vietnamese, this was the last image of the U.S. in their country—Americans fleeing from the rooftops of the embassy and the thirteen other Saigon buildings, like this one.

Chapter Notes

Chapter 1: Colony of Cruelty

(pages 6-29)

7 "exactly the same"; TDB. **8** "tends toward ruin": Karnow 76; "Cochinchina could exist": Buttinger 19; "of the natives": Buttinger 74; "Continuez": Buttinger 109; "famine and misery": Buttinger 56; domination of South Vietnam: *PP* 90; "war of liberation": *PP* 278; "as a guarantor": *PP* 255, 342. **10** to President Grant: O'Connor 166. **12** "Old Ironsides": Buttinger 1197; apologized to Thieu Tri: Karnow 69; "from the invader": Buttinger 127; bars found there: Buttinger 127. **14** to some degree: Buttinger 46; eighty percent could not: Buttinger 173; "positions to bureaucrats": Buttinger 80; 30 million Vietnamese: Buttinger 104; Vietnamese in government: Buttinger 18; budget for Indochina: Buttinger 448; took only ten: Buttinger 443. **15** loan to begin: Buttinger 26; Laotians and Cambodians: Buttinger 91. **16** "becomes a Red Sea": *PP* 128. **17** school of any kind: Buttinger 50. **18** "birth of Indochina": Buttinger 22; planned for Vietnam: Buttinger 28. **19** for miscellaneous expenditures: Buttinger 34; turbulent Red River: Buttinger 43; structure in Asia: Buttinger 33; due to overuse: *NYT Magazine* 10/30/83 27. **20** Bank of Indochina: Buttinger 545; and other sicknesses: Buttinger 30; was 35 million: Buttinger 24; average twelve percent: Buttinger 107. **22** during bad years: Buttinger 165; general budget revenue: Buttinger 60. **23** what they received: Buttinger 59; for salt fivefold: Buttinger 56; in the country: Buttinger 58; Burma and Thailand: Buttinger 166; new farming areas: Buttinger 163. **24** remainder lying fallow: Buttinger 172; declined thirty percent: Buttinger 171; "enough to eat": Buttinger 174. **25** three-year contract: Buttinger 178; rice-growing countries: Buttinger 172. **26** was so high: Buttinger 176. **27** of disposable income: Buttinger 184; of mistaken identity: TDB. **28** enterprise in Indochina: Buttinger 445; francs by 1940: Buttinger 190.

Chapter 2: The Diplomatic Puzzle

(pages 30-63)

31 of future fighting: Louis 20; "Or take Indochina?": Roosevelt 115. **24** "League of Nations": Louis 3; "the great powers": Louis 28. **33** "allowed to go on": Louis 38; "in the E. Indies?": Louis 40; "a sand bar": Louis 26; "does not govern": Buttinger 245; "many as you can": Buttinger 334; "form it may be": Buttinger 365; "if forced to": Buttinger 365. **34** Georges Catroux complied: Patti 32; stationed in Indochina: Buttinger 235; "the British flag": Louis 7; "imperialism is ended": Louis 155; "of the British Empire": Bartlett 924. **35** "New York and Washington": Louis 30. **36** "of the Annamite": Patti 33; Asia never recovered: Louis 7; "words nasally intoned": Louis 13. **37** "Southern United States": Louis 39; "favor of imperialism": Louis 166. **38** in Hanoi in 1940: White, *Search* 106; "evading the issue": Louis 441; Indochina from the French: Buttinger 286. **39** "circles in France": Louis 551; the northern Pacific: Louis 82. **40** "their own identity": Louis 44. **41** "China from France": Louis 40; "fate of the people": Buttinger 240. **42** POWs in the Saigon area: Patti 272. **43** "her own trustee": Louis 46. **45** "development towards independence": Louis 115; "colonies under trusteeship": Louis 117; "and military consequences": Louis 552; "of French control": Louis 552; "support French guerrillas": Patti 122; Ho's visa: Patti 46. **46** Wendell Willkie: Patti 51. **47** "bloodshed and agony": Schlesinger, *Heritage* 3; "a pipe-dream": Louis 551; Cal-Texaco's agent: Patti 44. **48** "named Ho Chih-chi(?)": Patti 46. **50** "Claire L. Chennault": Patti 55; "unusual destructive force": Manchester 379. **51** "world trade relations": Manchester 379. **53** "is so already": Buttinger 300. **54** Ho's declaration of independence: Patti 220; "question of weeks": Buttinger 325. **55** "kicked them out": Buttinger 327; "America in 1776": Patti 223. **56** the March uprising: Patti 315; in horrible fashion: Patti 332; under his command: Buttinger 337. **57** "would start again": Buttinger 337; on short rations: Buttinger 351; generals as bribes: Buttinger 356; "savior of the nation": Patti 250. **58** "maimed for life": Patti 317; the Yunnan railroad: Buttinger 362. **59** "the French Union": Buttinger 369; "out of Southeast Asia": Patti 320. **60** "by General Gracey": Patti 322; "visibly shaken": Patti 321;

"peoples of the world": Goulden, *Years* 250; "liberty and freedom": Goulden, *Years* 250; Russia after the war: Goulden, *Years* 249; "jointly assist": Goulden, *Years* 251. **61** "iron fense": Goulden, *Years* 254; "World War III": Goulden, *Years* 256; "to start negotiations": Patti 210. **62** rule the world: Goulden, *Years* 249; "even fraternal orders": Goulden, *Years* 226; $400 million in aid: Goulden, *Years* 268; "as political infiltration": Goulden, *Years* 268. **63** duties in Hanoi: Buttinger 432; control over Vietnam: *PP* 10.

Chapter 3: Emerging Enemies

(pages 64-109)

65 renewed fighting erupted: Buttinger 37. **66** "shall have it": Buttinger 431; "It's ours!": Fall, *Hell* 241; "blessing in disguise": Manchester 687; "than to fight": Buttinger 371; "Of French greatness": Buttinger 380; "Bank of Indochina": Buttinger 380; "no longer being one": Buttinger 435. **67** "a coup d'état": Buttinger 397; "tried to save": White, *History* 107. **68** section of the city: Buttinger 425; "Even that": Buttinger 427. **69** Vietnam People's Army: Buttinger 421. **70** "of the situation": Buttinger 427; "civilians was concerned": Buttinger 428; "A French soldier": Buttinger 431; according to Mus: Buttinger 433. **71** born in 1890: Fall, *Two* 83; some say 1894: Buttinger 1249; "toward the French": Buttinger 1250; "village aristocracy": Fall, *Two* 84; "well-trained": Patti 125; "impressive reception committee": Patti 127. **72** "cow in our honor": Patti 127; forty miles from Hanoi: Patti 167; such lowly employ: Fall, *Two* 87; "did the rest": Fall, *Two* 87; "socialism and Communism": Buttinger 1250. **73** "Paris XVIIth District": Fall, *Two* 88; the gilded palace: Buttinger 1250; several Indochinese dialects: Buttinger 1250; "Starved 2 Million People": Patti 171; "used against Americans": Patti 129. **74** "of abstract internationalism": Buttinger 1251; "an Aristophanic verve": Shaplen, *Reporter* 14. **75** "will grow again": Lacoture 239; "way to revolution": Fall, *Two* 92; returned to Indochina: Fall, *Two* 93; "support Vietnam's independence": Patti 373; "indebted to Moscow?": Patti 374. **76** "are always welcome": Patti 374; a Communist second: Patti 381; "always carefully prescribed": Shaplen, *Reporter* 15; "of the proletariat": Fall, *Two* 95. **77** "General Yeh Chien-ying": Fall, *Two* 98; in thirty years: Fall, *Two* 98; "rounds of ammunition": Patti 545; "latest American weapons": Patti 129; purchase American weapons: Patti 337. **78** "to a village": Fall, *Street* 273; "to the ground": Buttinger 135; began to flow: Fall, *Two* 99; fight the Japanese: Fall, *Two* 100; Vietnamese People's Army: Buttinger 277. **79** "illusions of splendour": Morris 462; 1945 and 1954: Buttinger 674; they would leave: Morris 488; "Operation Lea": Fall, *Street* 28. **80** "of French control": Buttinger 726. **81** December 1947: Buttinger 722; "devoted to the French": Buttinger 734. **82** "crab fishing": Buttinger 101; "of political propaganda": Buttinger 277. **83** was remarkably prophetic: Fall, *Street* 35; "their home towns": Fall, *Street* 257. **87** "in that mess": Fall, *Street* 65; "is a profession": Fall, *Street* 256. **86** and recoilless cannons: Fall, *Street* 93; eight hundred Molotovas: Fall, *Street* 94; recapture of Hanoi: Fall, *Street* 37. **87** water through rocks: Fall, *Street* 180; twenty-two hundred pillboxes: Fall, *Street* 180; and a sergeant: Fall, *Street* 176. **89** covered with jungle: Fall, *Street* 51; Red River Delta: Buttinger 760. **90** "in static duties": Buttinger 760. **91** miles from Laos: Fall, *Hell* 14; about fifteen thousand: Fall, *Hell* 52; seventy-five-mile valley: Fall, *Hell* 39; "or the Argonne": Manchester 681. "mooring point": Fall, *Hell* 37. **93** meat-grinder: Fall, *Hell* 49; the officers were: Fall, *Hell* x. **94** "human wave": Fall, *Hell* 99; $2,000 per month": Fall, *Hell* 328; "behalf of the French": Fall, *Hell* 241; refused to fly: Fall, *Hell* 265; that besieged outpost: Fall, *Street* 134; Lafayette in America: Fall, *Hell* 54. **95** "Dien Bien Phu to resist": Fall, *Hell* 106; "Dien Bien Phu at War": Fall, *Hell* 108; "we'll smash them": Fall, *Hell* 101; were indeed impressive: Fall, *Hell* 45; "I'm riding her in": Fall, *Street* 112. **96** "useful as crossbows": Manchester 679; in all Indochina: Fall, *Hell* 458; their combat aircraft: Fall, *Hell* 21; "an indescribable enthusiasm": Fall, *Hell* 128; out of the jungle: Fall, *Hell* 128; carried their loads: Fall, *Hell* 128; "Everything for victory": Fall, *Hell* 129. **97** along the road: Fall, *Hell* 130; fifty thousand troops: Fall, *Hell* 52; "the battle began": Fall, *Hell* 127; "the free world": Spector 200; "initiating allout war": Spector 201; with the Viet Minh: Fall, *Hell* 307. **99** "I'm leaving": Fall, *Hell* 156; "Rats of Nam Yum": Fall, *Hell* 453; "transmitted our messages": Fall, *Hell* 177; French army in Vietnam: Fall, *Hell* 135; die in the fighting: Fall, *Hell* 361; Whom were killed: Fall, *Hell* 225. **100** lasted fifty-six: Fall, *Hell* vu; 105mm artillery shells: Fall, *Hell* 143; the flak became: Fall, *Hell* 265. **102** kilograms of mustard: Fall, *Hell* 247; "a baseball field": Fall, *Hell* 372; "fine for that": Fall, *Hell* 407; "and to Win": Fall, *Hell* 155. **104** the Indochina problem: Buttinger 824; "and sovereign state": Buttinger 836. **106** "Gallacian Catholicism": Shaplen, *New Yorker*; three hundred villages: Buttinger 1254; "of Ho Chi Minh": Shaplen, *New Yorker*. **107** "independent": Buttinger 1255; Vatican in 1950: Buttinger 847; notable among them: Buttinger 847; Joseph

McCarthy: FitzGerald 111. **108** "French Union forces there": Cooper 134; "was a mistake": Fall, *Two* 240; "will take the risks": Shaplen, *New Yorker*; "to their implementation": Buttinger 1255. **109** "headed by Diem": Buttinger 847; "William O. Douglas": Buttinger 847; "full political power": Buttinger 1255; "and military powers": Buttinger 850; "the Eisenhower administration": Cooper 134; "omens of failure": Buttinger 927.

Chapter 4: Poles Apart

(pages **110-151**)
111 American advisers there: Goulden, *Years* 269; "that strategic load": Goulden, *Years* 268; Vandenberg of Virginia: Goulden, *Years* 268. **112** "throughout the world": Goulden, *Years* 270; "act of war": Goulden, *Years* 268; "Turkey and Greece": Goulden, *Years* 269. **113** "theoretically welcome revolution": Buttinger 806; "hammer away at them": Halberstam, *Best* 147; "most profound influences": Manchester 684; "is moving south": Doyle, *Stage* 77. **114** call to arms: Patti 134; "problem to suggest": *PP* 7; the report concluded: *PP* 8. **115** "French military forces": *PP* 9; "expansion in Asia": *PP* 9; "independence in Indochina": Buttinger 808; "self-government and independence": Manchester 680. **116** "not look back": Manchester 680; "condition of life": Buttinger 809. **117** "and possibly westward": *PP* 9; $10 million grant: *PP* 10; "with these forces": Buttinger 808. **118** "the Vietnam War": White, *Search* 345; Air Force support technicians: Manchester 680; "Indochina and Malaya": Eisenhower 64; "Japan and into China": Eisenhower 64. **119** "losing Southeast Asia": Halberstam, *Best* 173; "security of the U.S.": *PP* 10; "would automatically cease": *PP* 11; by Vietnamese troops: Manchester 682; was $815 million: Buttinger 808; "later, in Vietnam": White, *Search* 396; "to disciplinary action": Patti xviii. **120** culture of that country: White, *Search* 396; "trap for radiators": White, *Search* 395; "wished to hear": White, *Search* 396. **121** "material assistance in": Manchester 683; service the aircraft: Halberstam, *Best* 173; "with large units": Manchester 680; "will be decided": Fall, *Hell* 161; to the press: Spector 174; "initiative from the enemy": Spector 181; "psychology to the war": Spector 175. **122** "will improve rapidly": Spector 186; "capable of launching": Spector 187; "a successful conclusion": Spector 187; narrow in scope: Spector 176; 50-50 survival rating: Spector 183; "be resolute today": Manchester 683; placed on alert: Halberstam, *Best* 174. **123** "appalling political repercussions": Fall, *Hell* 305; "power in Indochina": Manchester 684; "fighting a war": Spector 175; almost any eventuality: Spector 181. **124** "service point of view": Spector 189; "operations" in Vietnam: Spector 189; his negative reporting: Spector 189; announced his support: Halberstam, *Best* 174; "when to deal": Halberstam, *Best* 172. **125** "raise my voice": Halberstam, *Best* 181; "the situation better": Halberstam, *Best* 174. **126** grant $100 million: Buttinger 904; "by Michigan State University": Buttinger 927; "facilities" and schools: Buttinger 928; "stay in the war": Fall, *Hell* 301; "from that lesson?": Fall, *Hell* 303. **127** "Chinese army personnel": *PP* 38. **128** "defeat by the Communists": *PP* 36; "from Communist control": *PP* 11; "action in Indochina": *PP* 40. **129** "such a decision": Manchester 685; "unlikely" he announced: Manchester 685; "declaration of support": Fall, *Hell* 309; "have Dien Bien Phu": Fall, *Hell* 310. **130** of Richard Nixon: White, *Search* 122; "under U.N. auspices": *PP* 41; "or to anyone else": *PP* 41; entered the picture: Halberstam, *Best* 176. **131** sustain the effort: Halberstam, *Best* 177. **132** "a shameful treaty": Dooley 45; "limited U.S. capabilities": *PP* 13. **133** "or territorial boundary": Buttinger 839; summer of 1956: *PP* 15; departed through Haiphong: *Newsweek* 11/23/59 106; "had communicable diseases": Dooley 157; crown of thorns: Dooley 164. **134** "into Communist teeth": Dooley 168; "birth of freedom": Dooley 169; "dialectical materialism": Dooley 172; "error of his ways": Dooley 173; "catastrophic and immoral": Buttinger 838; "loss of Southeast Asia": *PP* 14; "Far East Munich": *PP* 6. **135** "the next year": *PP* 6; "maintenance of armed forces": *PP* 14; "the Far East": *PP* 15; "Shake, Rattle and Roll": Dooley 173; a "tough" group: Dooley 174; "in Southeast Asia?": Dooley 174; "hard to sever": Dooley 174. **146** was terminally ill: *Newsweek* 11/23/59 106; "scriptural life span": *Newsweek* 1/30/61 70; "the People's Army": Fall, *Hell* 152. **137** no medical care: Buttinger 900; "of the colonial regime": Buttinger 897; gradually trailed away: Buttinger 901. **138** first official visitor: Buttinger 895; time of Dien Bien Phu: Buttinger 901; into the socialist economy: Buttinger 909; "tendency to capitalism": Buttinger 909. **140** Vietnamese with germs: Dooley 46; "with utmost ferocity": Buttinger 913; by the tribunals: Buttinger 914. **141** Troung Chinh was fired: Buttinger 913; arrested several thousand: Buttinger 915; secret *Pentagon Papers*: *PP* 15. **143** would certainly fall: Buttinger 960; perhaps considerably more: Buttinger 861; the leaflet's distribution: *PP* 17; Vietnamese agents there: *PP* 18. **148** French military equipment: *PP* 23. **149** to 30,000 men: Buttinger 887; of the votes: *PP* 21; "at his initiative": *PP* 22; "subverted in

advance": Cooper 150. **150** Scigliano in 1960: Buttinger 891; "subverted in advance": Cooper 150; in Pleiku Province: Buttinger 943; to mid-1959: Cooper 165; delegation at Geneva: Cooper 166; seventy-five percent of the land: *PP* 71; by two thousand people: Buttinger 855.

Chapter 5: Sharing the Sampan

(pages **152-203**)
152 to Henry Luce: Halberstam, *Best* 26. "moral reference point": Halberstam, *Best* 88; "for a long time": Halberstam, *Best* 97; "the Diem government": *PP* 172; "Chinese-Russian aggressor": Halberstam, *Best* 46. **156** "Pentagon were interchangeable": Halberstam, *Best* 64. **157** "and bitter peace": Manchester 890. **160** the senior prom?: TDB; and one hundred and four: TDB. **161** neutralism was immoral: Manchester 903; "produced Max Taylor": Halberstam, *Best* 53. **162** "on Foreign Relations": Halberstam, *Best* 55; "for sheriff once": Halberstam, *Best* 53. **163** to a friend: Halberstam, *Best* 98; the third one: Manchester 892. **164** in February 1961: *PP* 79; remembers Eisenhower saying: Halberstam, *Best* 109; before a congressional committee: Halberstam, *Best* 111; the opium trade: Halberstam, *Best* 110; "we're in trouble": Halberstam, *Best* 110. **165** the scene related: Cooper 172; in the Pacific: Halberstam, *Best* 113; "pillars will collapse": Halberstam, *Best* 113. **166** said Charles Bolte: Goulden, *Years* 62; "goal by five years": Goulden, *Years* 62; "and independent Laos": Cooper 172; the Laos settlement: Halberstam, *Best* 117; "the Communist line": Halberstam, *Best* 47; "safety of us all": Halberstam, *Best* 116. **167** on April 17, 1961: Manchester 895; "and morally defeated": Manchester 903; "lack of determination": Manchester 902. **168** "of the peril": Halberstam, *Best* 907; another world war: Halberstam, *Best* 909. **169** "Kennedy to Paris": Halberstam, *Best* 910. **170** "about the infantryman": Halberstam, *Best* 131. **171** "have to act": Manchester 911. **172** "pretext for war": Manchester 911; anaother 4,000: Manchester 912. **173** about thirty days: Manchester 912; "a billion Communists": Manchester 913; *Pentagon Papers* noted: *PP* 87. **174** hearts and minds: Buttinger 970; spent on military programs: Buttinger 970; "like the place": Manchester 913; "of that country": *PP* 88; "reforms in return": *PP* 88; "win this battle": *PP* 89; "possibly Southern China": *PP* 89. **175** for training purposes: *PP* 89; the summer of 1956: *PP* 89; the former goal: *PP* 91; "Austin, Texas, ever saw": Halberstam, *Best* 165. **176** "get out there": Halberstam, *Best* 167; "to San Francisco": *PP* 94; of Communist domination: *PP* 94; urging action there: Halberstam, *Best* 199; "WWR": *PP* 95. **177** "accepted by Diem": *PP* 95; response to Diem's letter: *PP* 95. **178** Interdepartmental Working Group: *PP* 174; "go from here?": *PP* 174; miles from Saigon: *PP* 96; "of the Vietcong": *PP* 97; "50-50 or so on": *PP* 98; "on external supplies": *PP* 98. **179** "forced to leave": *PP* 174; "Nhu-dominated government": *PP* 174; "winning the war": *PP* 174. **180** meeting ended inconclusively: *PP* 175; was a "disservice": Halberstam, *Best* 451; "to remain longer": *PP* 101; "a losing horse": *PP* 102; for American troops: *PP* 102; of U.S. ground units: *PP* 85; "to lay off SVN": *PP* 85. **181** "about 205,000 men": *PP* 85; "a careful examination": *PP* 85; "of his regime": *PP* 107; "the security situation": *PP* 107; "upset and brooding": *PP* 109; "over all else": *PP* 109; what later transpired: Halberstam, *Best* 451. **182** 5,576: *PP* 110; 16,732: *PP* 113; "more locally controlled": Buttinger 936. **184** "lifetime of extortion": Buttinger 951; David Halberstam observed: Buttinger 951; "rule and dictatorship": Buttinger 944. **186** "and national defense": Buttinger 944; "nor pro-Communist": Buttinger 977; Some were tortured: Buttinger 942; "700 persons kidnapped": Cooper 158; "Central Vietnam's economy": Buttinger 955. **187** to the peasants: Buttinger 933. **188** Lew Saris: Halberstam, *Best* 315; "matter die. Bob": Halberstam, *Best* 316. **190** the general population: Buttinger 956; "sentimental songs": Buttinger 957; the whole government: Cooper 210. **191** and wounding fourteen: *PP* 165. **192** Thich Quang Duc's example: Buttinger 994; to the press: *PP* 165; "supply the gasoline": *PP* 195; "has ever understood us": *PP* 225. **193** "accept us Irish?": Halberstam, *Best* 16; blaming the army: *PP* 166. **194** "central government mechanism": *PP* 168; "Request modification instruction": *PP* 169. **195** quickly informed Lodge: *PP* 169; "overrule the Ambassador": *PP* 177; "the plotting generals": *PP* 178. **196** "to tell you": *PP* 187. **197** Johnson told them: Halberstam, *Best* 365; "classic can-do President": Halberstam, *Best* 367; "Communists had done it": Halberstam, *Best* 364; White House associate: Miller 380; "never suggested it": Miller 380. **198** "Johnson took office": Miller 381; "the way China went": Halberstam, *Best* 364; "for Vietnam today?" Halberstam, *Best* 366. **199** "somewhat embarrassed": Halberstam, *Best* 364; "disregard than otherwise": Miller 381; "correctly in Vietnam": Miller 381. **200** "about his problems": Halberstam, *Best* 336; soldiers and pilots: *PP* 235; "by PT boats": *PP* 238. **201** "are probably accurate": *PP* 261; dead in the water: *PP* 259. **202** "we were voting on": Miller 385; the Plan 34A raids: *PP* 263. **203** "no wider war": *PP* 264; "defense of its freedom": *PP* 265.

Chapter 6: Down We Dive

(pages 204-271)

205 LeMay was upset: Halberstam, *Best* 558; North Vietnam was inevitable: *PP* 307. **206** "who you're killing": Halberstam, *Quagmire* 167; "what I'm doing": Halberstam, *Best* 511; "picking my targets": Halberstam, *Best* 200; their own terms: Halberstam, *Best* 559; "the Stone Age": Halberstam, *Best* 560. **208** Captain Chris Depaorte: TDB; is strategic bombing: Fallows 32; "population to persevere": Fallows 32; "unrestricted U.S. airpower": Momyer 34. **209** "productivity had declined": Fallows 33; "the Hanoi regime": Halberstam, *Best* 200. **210** our fledgling ally: Westmoreland 108; "in December 1972": Momyer 34. **211** to the pressure: Halberstam, *Best* 640; "bust their ass": Halberstam, *Best.* **212** "but a victory": Hurley 320; of keeping count: Halberstam, *Best* 515; route through Laos: Manchester 1030; "to enlarge the war": *PP* 311. **213** sixty-eight members: Halberstam, *Best* 591; he would say: Halberstam, *Best* 695. **214** Johnson only twice: Halberstam, *Best* 593; which he did not: Halberstam, *Best* 593. **215** in the south: *PP* 312; "Alice-in-Wonderland atmosphere": *PP* 391; "morale" in South Vietnam: *PP* 312. **216** air force airlift commanders: Bowers 31; upholding air force doctrine: Westmoreland 109; government of South Vietnam: *PP* 314; the group decided: *PP* 358; was Bill Moyers: Halberstam, *Best* 603; not to retaliate: *PP* 321. **218** "question" to them: *PP* 323; of ground troops: *PP* 309; only Ball favored light: *PP* 325; two-phased bombing campaign: *PP* 327. **219** rotten place to fight: Halberstam, *Best* 613; "united front": *PP* 329; "favorable to the U.S.": 329; "at its capabilities": *PP* 330; "the will of Hanoi": *PP* 331. **220** "North Vietnam population": *PP* 331; "of the concept": *PP* 332; "place to dismount": Halberstam, *Best* 604; "not a final act": Halberstam, *Best* 626. **221** enhance their influence: Halberstam, *Best* 628; calling their proposals: Halberstam, *Best* 607; "up my ass": Halberstam, *Best* 643; "to the poor": Halberstam, *Best* 614. **222** "get along fine": Halberstam, *Best* 643; White House in late 1964: Halberstam, *Best* 611. **223** "his pecker off": Halberstam, *Best* 503; "before we moved": *PP* 340. **224** "attrition targets": *PP* 342; "late January 1965": *PP* 342; Rusk told Taylor: *PP* 342; "to contain China": *PP* 342; was at hand: *PP* 343. **226** "goal of peace": Halberstam, *Best* 630; superpowers could control": Halberstam, *Best* 613. **227** personnel at each: Halberstam, *Best* 627; Reprisal in order: Halberstam, *Best* 631; for his reaction: Manchester 1047; "will do that": Halberstam, *Best* 631; "person or property": Halberstam, *Best* 638. **228** injuring twenty-one: Cooper 486; impact on Johnson: Halberstam, *Best* 624; "was historically necessary": Halberstam, *Best* 643. **230** time of attack: Hurley 334; over the north: Hurley 311; to Hanoi passed: Lavalle, *Bridges* 67. **232** "the manure piles": Halberstam, *Best* 560; heat-seeking missiles: Hurley 312; history of air warfare: Hurley 312; "to appease Hanoi": Westmoreland 154. **233** "absence of targets": Halberstam, *Best* 786; was grossly overbuilt: Lavalle, *Bridges* 38; Risner to lead: Lavalle, *Bridges* 31; "off like popcorn": TDB; only superficial damage: Lavalle, *Bridges* 37; the next day: Lavalle, *Bridges* 38. **235** the access roadways: TDB; encouraged the enemy: Lavalle, *Bridges* 42. **236** they were traveling: Rutledge 24; all Southeast Asia: Lavalle, *Bridges* 42. **237** from ground defenses: Lavalle, *Bridges* 71. **238** a single person: Lavalle, *Invasion* 36; Doumer Bridge was successful: Lavalle, *Bridges* 74; on March 31, 1968: Lavalle, *Bridges* 75. **239** of $1.1 billion: Halberstam, *Best* 782; "a sad failure": Hurley 313; 818 airmen killed: Maclear 286; conducted against it: *PP* 329. **240** "division in that area": Lavalle, *Invasion* 41; in early 1965: Westmoreland 498; "his old one: Halberstam, *Best* 506. **241** insurgency in the south: *PP* 102; "likes the gadget": Maclear 286; "to civilian neighborhoods": Maclear 287; "love to do that": Lavalle, *Invasion* 43. **242** "sick of it": Halberstam, *Best* 786; the twentieth parallel: Lavalle, *Bridges* 78; "within ninety days": Hubbell 435; the North Vietnamese: Hubbell 585; ever seen again: Fall, *Hell* 438. **244** basis of the code: Hubbell 44; not at all: Fall, *Hell* 438; then rebury them: Fall, *Hell* 434; "no international law": Rutledge 26; Code of Conduct: Nehring 154. **246** and then departed: Hubbell 366; of January 27, 1973: Hubbell 606. **247** life-giving pragmaticism: Hubbell 241; "I was nothing": Rutledge 125. **248** in windowless cells: Rutledge 94; of the audience: Hubbell 264; which to shave: Hubbell 476; before the cameras: Hubbell 177. **250** "confess their mistakes": Hubbell 519; "to the United States": Hubbell 599. **252** Captain Hilliard Wilbanks: Schneider 16; three miles from Danang: *PP* 401; kill the Viet Cong: *PP* 401; put into effect: *PP* 400; about 30,000: *PP* 400; was 46,500: Millett 144; was 74,500: Millett 145; to 148,300: Millett 145; 184,314: *PP* 385; "the transport plane": Hurley 314. **253** villages and cities: Hurley 314; "for ground artillery": Hurley 315. **254** fighter-bomber could carry: Hurley 315. **255** in house-to-house fighting: Lavalle, *Invasion:* 91. **256** "few Viet Cong": Hurley 316; "were fired upon": Hurley 316; "overused" in South Vietnam: Hurley 316; the nation's capitol: Buckingham 165; the Communist insurgency: Buckingham 10. **267** "tactic of war": Buckingham 21; "or biological warfare": Buckingham

15; value in Vietnam: Buckingham 16; endorsing their view: Buckingham 21; "had been created": Buckingham 21; approved defoliation missions: Buckingham 24; "violent men": Buckingham 39. **258** "not be disguised": Buckingham 28; southern South Vietnam: Buckingham 31; "will witness process": Buckingham 31; "or the soil": Buckingham 33; "in that country": Buckingham 163. **259** doses were administered: Buckingham 163; effects of spraying: Buckingham 169; Vietnam at the time: Buckingham 166; "range and pastures": Buckingham 166; operate and defend it: Buckingham 319. **260** "stockpiled in North Vietnam": Hurley 319. **261** the latter mission: Hurley 319; "relatively inefficient": Hurley 320; "about two more": Lavalle, *Invasion* 73. **262** for Commando Hunt 7: Hurley 319; "than Rolling Thunder": Hurley 320; was agreed to: Lavalle, *Invasion* 1; "U.S. ground forces": Lavalle, *Invasion* 1; Lavalle, three hundred fifty in 1969: Lavalle, *Invasion* 1. **263** fourth largest in the world: Hurley 323; dry season began: Lavalle, *Invasion* 3; to seventeen miles: Lavalle, *Invasion* 4; nine thousand troops: Lavalle, *Invasion* 4. **264** in the other: Lavalle, *Invasion* 6; "of the people: Lavalle, *Invasion* 9. **265** Guam and Thailand: Lavalle, *Invasion* 27; "From stateside air force bases": Lavalle, *Invasion* 26; thirty-six marine corps F-4s: Lavalle, *Invasion* 16; the Pacific Ocean: Lavalle, *Invasion* 29. **266** at Yankee Station: Lavalle, *Invasion* 17; open during daylight: Hurley 317; "everybody is shooting": Lavalle, *Invasion* 31; and B-52 strikes: Lavalle, *Invasion* 31; "monuments to airpower": Hurley 318; forward air controllers: Lavalle, *Invasion* 107. **267** targets near Haiphong: Hurley 320; "supplies it needs": Maclear 363. **268** North Vietnam during May: Hurley 321; "games in history": Maclear 363; all American forces: Maclear 365; pending Thieu's approval: Hurley 321. **269** 60.7 percent plurality: Maclear 367; "off the negotiations": Maclear 367; "away with this war": Maclear 368; Hanoi and Haiphong: Hurley 321; at thirty thousand feet: Maclear 369. **270** "I could see": McCarthy 134; one hundred eighty: Hurley 322; eleven, total: Maclear 369; captured by that time: Maclear 369; less predicatable tactics: Hurley 322; twenty missiles per night: Hurley 322; "apparently been broken": Hurley 322; capturing thirty-three: Maclear 369; in the Second World War: Hurley 322; the *New York Times:* Maclear 369; "changing its attitude": Maclear 370. **271** in South Vietnam: Hurley 322; "the American people": Hurley 322; "God bless America": Hubbell 600.

Chapter 7: War Without End, Amen

(pages 272-327)

273 "to take it": Halberstam, *Best* 85. **274** "crazier than hell: Hodgson 252; "I think forever": Hodgson 245; "hell I knew": Knightley 43; "a little war": Westmoreland 43; "seem hard indeed": Westmoreland 47. **275** "mutter on the battlefield": Westmoreland 43; terrain in Korea: Doughty 14; "artillery is today": Doughty 14; "type of war": Doughty 17. **277** Donovan Yeuell: Halberstam, *Best* 576. **278** "clean it all out": Halberstam, *Best* 578; "to be CINC World": Halberstam, *Best* 682; role in modern warfare: Doughty 16. **279** traditional infantry division: Doughty 17; "doctrine and organizations": Doughty 18; "is always wrong": Halberstam, *Best* 580; "confusion reigned": Doughty 26. **280** "Mao and Giap": Halberstam, *Best* 154; "scavengers of revolution": Halberstam, *Best* 154; pack on his back: Halberstam, *Best* 154; "tried it in 1951": Halberstam, *Best* 154. **281** "than I can read": Halberstam, *Best* 195; to television reception: Halberstam, *Best* 154; "cut to ribbons": Westmoreland 48; "country has benefited": Westmoreland 133. **282** to make decisions": Westmoreland 54. **283** wives and children: Westmoreland 54. **284** convince him to return: Westmoreland 80. **285** "Communist in 1958–60": Buttinger 977; "the Vietnamese countryside": Buttinger 982. **286** of the Viet Cong: Westmoreland 132; he withdraws, pursue: Doughty 33; "bow and arrow": Doughty 33. **287** occurred in Korea: Halberstam, *Best* 589. **288** "caserne mentality": Westmoreland 81; a cornered tiger: Westmoreland 129; "escaping almost unharmed": Buttinger 984; twenty to eighteen: Westmoreland 127. **289** "in European schools": Westmoreland 127; and Popular Forces: Westmoreland 127; for the future: Westmoreland 128; "this thing immediately": Westmoreland 83; "bottomless pit": Westmoreland 133. **290** "them was ours": Westmoreland 113; at Iwo Jima; Westmoreland 159. **291** "and two sergeants": Manchester 1048; "the gallant Marines": Westmoreland 159; French Expeditionary Corps: Westmoreland 160; firing nuclear shells: Westmoreland 160; "things bubbling", General": Halberstam, *Best* 684. **292** the bombing campaign: Halberstam, *Best* 594; protecting the bases: Westmoreland 165; "outcome of events": Westmoreland 166. **293** DePuy refused to listen: Halberstam, *Best* 657; military man in Vietnam: Westmoreland 678. **294** Nui Ba Dinh: Westmoreland 383. **295** twenty thousand combat troops: Westmoreland 168; soldiers were assigned: Westmoreland 168. **296** Wheeler in Honolulu: Westmoreland 169; effort to collapse: Westmoreland 180; "they cannot win": Westmoreland 180; "U.S. force requirements": Westmoreland 181. **297** South Vietnamese forces: Westmoreland 182; "sent as requested": Westmoreland 185. **298**

"inflationary snowball moving": Hodgson 250; "number of times": Westmoreland 183; "escalating stalemate": PP 472; the entire war: Westmoreland 359. **299** Humphrey asked: Halberstam, *Best* 180; envisioned three phases: PP 463; "end of 1967": Westmoreland 464; "national defense requirements": Hodgson 251; "schools and housing?" Halberstam, *Best* 740. more than six percent: Hodgson 253. **300** "by the Vietnam War": Hodgson 258; the war itself: Hodgson 258; fight in Vietnam: Hodgson 251; "world's monetary gold": Hodgson 255; been in 1949: Hodgson 256; "destroy enemy forces": Westmoreland 104; *Vietnam: A History:* Karnow 468; "their ancestral land": Halberstam, *Best* 641. **301** "reconnaissance in force": Westmoreland 105; "into the area": Doughty 32; *for Pacification support:* Scoville 3. **302** "to the people": Scoville 3; height of the war: Doyle, *Stage* 9; "was stay alive": Downs 113. **303** Communists to bargain: Westmoreland 165; "inkblot strategy": Shulimson 13; "villages and hamlets": Shulimson 11. **304** little black box: Westmoreland 379; "rich, populous lowlands": Shulimson 13; "among these mountains": Shulimson 13; "in persuading him": Shulimson 15; "town and hamlet": Shulimson 14; "broad arrow": Shulimson 14. **305** "among the population": Westmoreland 194. **306** "the high ground?": Westmoreland 194; "from 1965 to 1972": Doughty 40; use of helicopters: Doughty 29. **307** "cavalrymen in 1936": Doughty 27; range of artillery support: Doughty 37. **308** "know about tunnels": Herr, *Dispatches* 47; of floating craft: Westmoreland 271. **309** for long periods: Westmoreland 274; mines on the roads: Doughty 35; "hugging tactics": Doughty 34; "their job, too": Aronson 244. **310** and injure allied soldiers: Randolph A14; "under exceptional circumstances": Doughty 33; "to accommodate you": Halberstam, *Best* 808. **311** there were eight: Westmoreland 243; million tons per month: Westmoreland 245; such as warehouses: Westmoreland 243. **312** "sometime in 1968": Herr, *Dispatches* 46. **313** Filipino and Vietnamese: Westmorland 244. **314** Rome Plow: Westmoreland 367; Market Time: Westmoreland 214. **315** only ten percent: Westmoreland 241; "the fire brigade" period: Doughty 30. "Hitlers in Vietnam": Knightley 383; by government forces: Westmoreland 175; South Vietnamese battalions: Westmoreland 182. **317** "more flags": Westmoreland 170; his own name: Westmoreland 163. **318** "Valley of Death": Smith 56; start for American forces: Westmoreland 202; Summers *Strategy:* 21. **301** "the final balance": Clausewitz 234; Special Force troops: Westmoreland 203. **320** found the enemy: Westmoreland 204. **321** thirty-seven days: Johnson 578. **322** "Westmoreland's big-unit war": Westmoreland 191; too heavy-handed: Westmoreland 214. **323** huge Patton tanks: Westmoreland 233; called Operation Hastings: Westmoreland 258; "blow the lid off Washington": Randolph A14; "the initiative in the South": Randolph A14. **324** Operations Attleboro: Westmoreland 234; end of 1965: Millett 147; thirty miles from Saigon: Westmoreland 238; tons of Russian rockets: Westmoreland 238. **325** more without success: Westmoreland 236; and limited range: Westmoreland 239. **326** "red, white or blue": Westmoreland 239; "reversion to 1959": PP 472. **327** in North Vietnam: Halberstam, *Best* 751; no one was fooled: Shulimson 74. **328** show up for work: Shulimson 74; Hue radio station: Shulimson 81; "U.S. military justice": Shulimson 81. **329** "to prevent bloodshed": Shulimson 85. **330** sharply to his side: Shulimson 86; three hundred twenty-five surrendered: Shulimson 88. **331** and Ky's leadership: Westmoreland 246.

Chapter 8: Paying the Price, Bearing the Burden

(pages **332-403**)
333 "be won militarily": Mohr A24; "more U.S. forces": PP 473; "all of North Vietnam": PP 518. **334** service in Vietnam: PP 517; "rapid and violent": PP 519. **335** "lot of shit": Halberstam, *Best* 784; "dovish on me": Halberstam, *Best* 783; "him a murderer": Knightly 393; "called me 'nigger'": TDB; "to save it": Hodgson 356; by Rome Plows: Westmoreland 269. **337** battalions were involved: Westmoreland 269. **338** per American casualty: Doughty 31. **340** read the invitation: Halberstam, *Best* 786; shocked the American public: Doyle, *Stage* 9. **341** "final victory": Westmoreland 411; two hundred percent: Westmoreland 411; height of fighting: Doyle, *Stage* 9. **342** bar at home: Manchester 1273; throughout South Vietnam: Westmoreland 411; "is within reach": Westmoreland 412; "dark days ahead": Westmoreland 412; "considered particularly important": Westmoreland 422; "festival next Monday": Westmoreland 418; "and fifty hamlets": Westmoreland 431; finally overwhelmed them: Westmoreland 434. **344** killed the VC: Westmoreland 426; overwhelmed by the Viet Cong: Westmoreland 429; cotton mill nearby: Westmoreland 429. **345** the officers' barbershop: TDB. **346** soldiers were killed: Westmoreland 434; among the victims: Westmoreland 434; Chaisson once observed: Pisor 56. **347** Quang Tri and Hue: Westmoreland 195. **348** "Ho Chi Minh Trail": Pisor 25; had to be abandoned: Westmoreland 260. **349** M-16 rifles jammed: Pisor 5; "they will jam": Fallows 92; "not their fault": Fallows 92; "they considered worthless": Fallows 92; "80 rifles failed": Fallows 93; "on criminal negligence": Fallows 91. **350**

weapons during battle: Fallows 79; hand-to-hand combat: Westmoreland 264. **351** sent to investigate: Pisor 82. **352** for about $100: Fallows 90; favor of the latter: Fallows 85; "rifle ever invented": Fallows 77. **353** as forty thousand: Pisor 85; parts work together: Fallows 87; "weapon function indefinitely": Fallows 91. **354** the American combat base: Pisor 83; positions around Khe Sanh: Pisor 84; "from the northwest": Westmoreland 442. **355** shot to death: Pisor 83. **357** thirty-five wounded: Pisor 17. **358** the enemy soldier: Pisor 88. **359** noise of battle: Pisor 95. **360** a direct hit: Pisor 96; "extreme combat fatigue": Pisor 97; those rough findings: Pisor 98; had been destroyed: Pisor 99. **362** commitment in Vietnam: Doyle, *Stage* 8; had been delivered: Pisor 99; only 1,432: Pisor 98; "Kamikaze attacks": Manchester 379; assess the situation: Pisor 118. **363** "the Situation Room": Pisor 114; Khe Sanh could hold: Pisor 118; "any damn Dinbinfoos": Herr, *Dispatches* 121. **364** "application of airpower": Westmoreland 441; every three hours: Pisor 193; of 2,602 sorties: Westmoreland 446; sorties per day: Westmoreland 446; "decimated the base": Pisor 204. **365** "no apparent reason": Westmoreland 447; four soldiers inside: Pisor 162. **366** for a flagpole: Pisor 200. **367** Luke the Gook: Pisor 201; "all over them": Pisor 165. **369** forty-three marine replacements: Pisor 209. **370** "6,000 and 8,000 men": Pisor 210; was called Pegasus: Westmoreland 456; according to Westmoreland: Westmoreland 455; died at Khe Sanh: Westmoreland 456; "the presidential agenda": Kalb 209. **371** Walter Cronkite said: Pisor 206; "what we needed": Kalb 209; "we can give you": Kalb 209; "ask for them": Kalb 210. **372** "the dust first": Kalb 212; "under the circumstances": Kalb 212; "82nd Airborne Division": Kalb 212; "a plausible possibility": Westmoreland 465; "White House in 1967": Westmoreland 467. **373** "in the United States": Westmoreland 468; "three combat divisions": Kalb 216; "doesn't understand that?" Kalb 230; about $30 billion: Kalb 222. **375** five hundred to Vietnam: Kalb 204; "in 1967 than we?": Kalb 204; "for all time": Kalb 228; questions and answers: Kalb 233. **377** "going to win": Kalb 237; "in a stalemate": Kalb 235; "Mr. Average Citizen": Maclear 237. **378** "they're talking about": Kalb 235; "Get it ready": Kalb 226; "on your side": Kalb 238. **379** "success of liberty": Gardner 379. **380** "quite shocked": Kalb 245; Johnson asked angrily: Kalb 248; "futility of it all": Kalb 245; "United States apart": Kalb 246. **381** in March 1968: Kalb 247; "was called for": Kalb 247. **382** "lower your sights": Kalb 247; "lost their meaning": Kalb 248; "Vietnam and Southeast Asia": Kalb 250. **383** "completely their own": Halberstam, *Best* 807; "yourselves in Vietnam": Nixon 501; "throw of the dice": Halberstam, *Best* 808. **384** "with the war": Karnow 595; "the Johnsonian bog": Karnow 596. **385** "themselves as intellectuals": Karnow 599; "will I be affected": Karnow 599; "new respectability and popularity": Karnow 599; "business as usual": Karnow 599; "so do we": Lipsman 54. **386** "understand this war!": Lipsman 53; "such orders as this": Lipsman 54; the Korean war: Kalb 275. **287** "nitpicker I ever saw": Karnow 608; favorite movie, *Patton:* Westmoreland 513. **388** traps and mines: Bonds 34; "throughout the world": Nixon 559; "saw these supplies": Lipsman 167. **389** "down as regiments": Westmoreland 515. **390** each for $100: Knightley 391. **391** of sixteen children: Maclear 329; called My Khe: Lipsman 108; the official count: Maclear 330; "no big deal": Lipsman 108; "commission its Calleys": Maclear 330; was only 123,000: Lipsman 96.

Chapter 9: The Politics of Peace

(pages **404-471**)
405 "man in Saigon?": Halberstam, *Quagmire* 268. **406** "you kill today": Manchester 1055; "should be believed": Knightley 373; "they're killing us": Manchester 1215; "of happy childhoods": Herr, *Esquire* 183; "reality than it is": Salinger 328. **407** "survive another defeat": Aronson 185; "have no quarrel": Aronson 186; "esteem in Washington": Aronson 186. **408** "national suicide": Aronson 186; "the Communist threat": Aronson 187; "doughty little Diem": Aronson 187; "Diem in the United States": Aronson 183; "in Southeast Asia": Aronson 183. **409** "for the cause": Aronson 196; month plus expenses: Aronson 185. **410** palace were killed: Aronson 196; "real war in Southeast Asia": Salinger 320; Cable 1006: Aronson 182; "United States helicopters": Aronson 182. **411** "by the censors": Aronson 192; "days to go": Aronson 193; "if Diem failed us": Aronson 193. **412** "the young Turks": Aronson 196; "on the team": Aronson 195; should be "bigot": Aronson 195. **413** "the highminded crusaders": Aronson 204; "they are right": Aronson 204; "in February 1962": Aronson 196; "stuff like that": Halberstam, *Quagmire* 268. **414** "losing proposition": Aronson 196; "to both questions": Aronson 196; "your all-important task": Aronson 196; "brush-off": Mecklin 135. **415** "waste of time": Aronson 197; peasants' enthusiastic support: Aronson 200; "is being lost": Aronson 200; "better than ever": Aronson 201. **416** "counter-coup is doomed": Knightley 416; "heard of you": Knightley 417; "a bemused observer": Aronson 201. **417** "bloodstream of American life": Hodgson 169. **418** "people of Mississippi": Hodgson 211; "the whole society": Hodgson 209.

419 killing the three men: Hodgson 209. **420** Brancroft Way: Hodgson 292; five hundred should be: Hodgson 292; "the student revolution": Hodgson 293; "of unemployment": Hodgson 293. **421** the student movement: Hodgson 239; been guaranteeed immunity: Hodgson 294; eight hundred arrested: Hodgson 294; "use of force": Hodgson 295. **422** "equivocation and manipulation": Hodgson 281; "educate me politically": Hodgson 280; "the New Frontier": Hodgson 281; caused the turmoil: Hodgson 294; "for the cause": Hodgson 295; "on the subject": Hodgson 295; on March 1: Hodgson 296. **423** of the evening: Hodgson 285; March 7 and 9: Hodgson 286; "Plans Teach-In": Hodgson 286; "it was clear": Hodgson 281; Capital C, capital G!": Hodgson 282. "at any time": Hodgson 279; "the Democratic Party": Hodgson 282; "to stop it": Hodgson 286; called associates elsewhere: Hodgson 286; "small domestic pressure": Hodgson 274. **425** "to elect Johnson": Hodgson 284; "we shall overcome": Hodgson 220; "Nigger lover": Hodgson 219; was a mistake: Hodgson 318. **426** "refuse to serve": Shachtman 129; "profoundly influenced": Greene 142; "called me nigger": Greene 142; "and a result": Hodgson 264; "fulfill these rights": Hodgson 265; "this other thing": Hodgson 268. **427** people were killed: Hodgson 266; to reestablish order: Hodgson 431; the Washington rioting: Manchester 1128; the *Chicago Defender*: Hodgson 319; "my wholehearted support": Greene 142. **428** to $1.625 billion: Hodgson 271; "might have caused": Hodgson 272; "battlefields of Vietnam": Hodgson 319; emerge as a priority: Hodgson 11. **430** "poverty and education": Hodgson 11; "victories we win": Aronson 233. **432** "bombing communiqués": Aronson 255; "with each other": Aronson 233; "the American press": Aronson 233; "take us on": Aronson 231. **433** foreign news outlets: Aronson 224; "priming the pump": Aronson 225; "while we sleep": Aronson 233; he countered: Aronson 237; "and 405 wounded": Aronson 255; the Second World War: Aronson 257; "the national interest": Aronson 257; "by the Communists": Aronson 255; "With Viet Reds": Aronson 256; "New Propaganda Weapon": Aronson 256. **434** "is Ho's instrument": Aronson 256; "self-deceiving nonsense?": Aronson 257; "public military information": Aronson 235; a massive offensive: Herr, *Esquire* 101. **435** "past six years?": Aronson 233; "winning the war": Knightley 397; "our stubbornness there": Braestrup 188. **436** "decision on the battlefield": Braestrup 187; "yet unsatisfactory conclusion": Braestrup 188. **437** for fifteen dollars: Knightley 419. **438** "Supply Column 21": Hohenberg 271; "scare me anymore": Herr, *Esquire* 162; "priority of 3": Knightley 403. **439** "but the President's": Westmoreland 359. **439** "in the first": Knightley 423; "have been upset": Herr, *Esquire* 101. **440** "what we're wearing": Herr, *Esquire* 96; "about Santa Monica": Herr, *Esquire* 95; "like the movies": Herr, *Esquire* 100; "a secret history": Herr, *Esquire* 160; "when they crashed": Herr, *Esquire* 96; "gotten a bargain": Herr, *Esquire* 101. **441** "been told yet": Herr, *Esquire* 160; "than it deserved": Herr, *Esquire* 166; "warwise grace": Herr, *Esquire* 170; "they were doing": Herr, *Esquire* 168. **443** "brushes with death": Herr, *Esquire* 180; covering the war: Morgan 60. **444** "be kidding me": Herr, *Esquire* 98; "you got balls": Herr, *Esquire* 99; "don't tell it": Herr, *Esquire* 100. **445** "because it's Nixon": Haldeman 82; 'sort of success": Maclear 345; "consequence and force": Maclear 345. **446** *Columbia Eagle*: Lipsman 141; in November 1969: Hodgson 385. **447** 197 for trespass: Manchester 1168. **448** "Take the park!": Hodgson 303; "one later died": Hodgson 303; during the period: Hodgson 303; August 15–17, 1969: Manchester 1169; percent that November: Manchester 1218; "offensive succeed splendidly": Maclear 345. **449** "ideological eunuchs": Manchester 1165; "eastern liberal establishment": Manchester 1165; twenty-two states: Manchester 1220. **450** John Khanlian: Davis 444; "the sovereign public": Hodgson 375; "away from Vietnam": Hodgson 378; "Out of Vietnam": Hodgson 378. **451** "total and categorical": Manchester 1168; "hit bottom": Manchester 1221; "was entirely spontaneous": Manchester 1211. **452** "to reestablish order": Manchester 1212; a press conference: Manchester 1214; an ROTC cadet: Manchester 1215; dollars in damage: Manchester 1212. **453** "a real media enemy": Manchester 1235; "an honorable peace": Cooper 261. **454** "South Vietnamese Government": Cooper 327. **455** "very robust initiative": Cooper 328; "meaningful negotiations – no": Cooper 328; "of the country": Cooper 274; "get them alive": Lipsman 80; "largely ineffective effort": Lipsman 80; "of our bases": Karnow 602. **456** "round dramatic figure": Cooper 273; "without outside interference": Cooper 273; "than the NLF": Cooper 274. **457** "surrender of South Vietnam": Cooper 294; "own free decision": Cooper 293; "against the DRV": Cooper 294. **458** "enter the talks": Cooper 370; "North and South Vietnam": Cooper 378; "a bombing cessation": Cooper 379. **459** "southern logistic routes": Cooper 379; "the bombing cessation": Cooper 385. **460** "questions of concern": Cooper 384; "normal" levels: Cooper 385; "November 1": Cooper 404; "our side – your side": Cooper 405. **461** "at opposite sides": Cooper 407; made fifteen trips: Maclear 361; James Bond aspects": Maclear 361. **463** "we are the troops": Emerson 331; "some future time": Maclear 364; "he, indeed, did": Maclear 365. **463** "captive in Hanoi": Maclear 365; "impose on our people": Maclear 366; "after the cease-fire": Maclear 366. **464** "didn't go along": Maclear 368; to remain there: Maclear 370; "all of Indochina": Kissinger 11; "onto the moon": Kissinger 23; "motive was elusive": Kissinger 25. **465** "reconciliation at home": Kissinger 25; "our Christmas attacks": Kissinger 24. **466** "only a respite": Kissinger 29; "had ever observed": Kissinger 31; of 175 trucks: Kissinger 32; "could not begin": Kissinger 40. **467** "of conquering Indochina": Kissinger 40; "half billion dollars": Kissinger 38; "held in Laos": Kissinger 39; "was well advanced": Kissinger 40. **468** "find it difficult": Kissinger 41; "have ever visited": Kissinger 42; "eat Indochina too": Kissinger 43; "positive for us": Kissinger 26. **469** "did not have it": Kissinger 43; every fifteen minutes: Maclear 402. **470** fifty military advisers: Maclear 379; "America is concerned": Maclear 398; "all you've done": Snepp 436. **471** thirteen Saigon rooftops: Maclear 402.

Bibliography

Acheson, Dean. *Present at the Creation.* New York: Norton, 1969.

Aronson, James. *The Press and the Cold War.* Indianapolis: Bobbs-Merrill, 1970 (Boston: Beacon, 1973).

Berger, Carl, ed. *The United States Air Force in Southeast Asia, 1961–1973.* Washington, D.C.: Office of Air Force History, 1977.

Bonds, Ray, ed. *The Vietnam War.* New York: Crown, 1983 (London: Salamander, 1979).

Bowers, Ray L. *The United States Air Force in Southeast Asia: Tactical Airlift.* Washington, D.C.: Office of Air Force History, 1983.

Braestrup, Peter. *Big Story,* volume II. Boulder, Colo.: Westview, 1977.

Buckingham, William A., Jr. *Operation Ranch Hand: The Air Force and Herbicides in Southeast Asia, 1961–1971.* Washington, D.C.: Office of Air Force History, 1982.

Buttinger, Joseph. *Vietnam: A Dragon Embattled.* Volume I: *From Colonialism to the Vietminh;* volume II: *Vietnam at War.* New York: Praeger, 1967.

Cincinnatus. *Self-Destruction.* New York: Norton, 1981.

Clausewitz, Karl von. *On War.* Princeton, N.J.: Princeton University, 1984.

Clifford, Clark. "A Vietnam Reappraisal," *Foreign Affairs* (July 1969).

Cooper, Chester L. *The Lost Crusade.* New York: Dodd, Mead, 1970.

Davies, Peter. *The Truth About Kent State.* New York: Farrar Straus Giroux, 1973.

Davis, Peter. "The Unknown Nonsoldier," *Esquire* (December 1983).

Dooley, Thomas A. "Deliver Us from Evil," *Reader's Digest* (April 1956).

Dougan, Clark, ed. *The Vietnam Experience: Nineteen Sixty-Eight.* Boston: Boston Publishing Company, 1983.

Doughty, Robert A. *Leavenworth Papers.* Volume I: *The Evolution of U.S. Army Tactical Doctrine, 1946–76.* Fort Leavenworth, Kans.: Combat Studies Institute (U.S. Army Command and General Staff College), 1979.

Doyle, Edward, ed. *The Vietnam Experience: America Takes Over.* Boston: Boston Publishing Company, 1982.

_____. *The Vietnam Experience: Passing the Torch.* Boston: Boston Publishing Company, 1981.

_____. *The Vietnam Experience: Setting the Stage.* Boston: Boston Publishing Company, 1981.

Downs, Frederick. *The Killing Zone.* New York: Norton, 1978 (New York: Berkley, 1983).

Eisenhower, Dwight D. *Mandate for Change.* Garden City, N.Y.: Doubleday, 1963.

Fall, Bernard B. *Hell in a Very Small Place.* Philadelphia: Lippincott, 1967.

_____. *Street Without Joy.* New York: Schocken, 1972.

_____. *The Two Viet-Nams.* New York: Praeger, 1967.

Fallows, James. *National Defense.* New York: Random House, 1981.

FitzGerald, Frances. *Fire in the Lake.* Boston: Atlantic/Little, Brown, 1972.

Fulghum, David, ed. *The Vietnam Experience: South Vietnam on Trial.* Boston: Boston Publishing Company, 1983.

Futrell, Robert F. *The United States Air Force in Southeast Asia: The Advisory Years to 1965.* Washington, D.C.: Office of Air Force History, 1980.

Gardner, Gerald, ed. *The Quotable Mr. Kennedy.* New York: Popular Library, 1963.

Goulden, Joseph C. *The Best Years.* New York: Atheneum, 1976.

_____. *Truth Is the First Casualty.* Chicago: Rand McNally/Adler, 1969.

Greene, Bob. "Muhammad Ali Is the Most Famous Man in the World," *Esquire* (December 1983).

Gropman, Alan L. *Airpower and the Airlift Evacuation of Kham Duc.* Washington, D.C.: U.S. Government Printing Office, 1979.

Halberstam, David. *The Best and the Brightest.* New York: Random House, 1969 (New York: Fawcett, 1973).

_____. *The Making of a Quagmire.* New York: Random House, 1964.

Haldeman, H. R. *The Ends of Power.* New York: New York Times, 1978.

Hendrickson, Paul. "McNamara: The Advancing Pain," *Washington Post* (May 9, 1984).

Herr, Michael. *Dispatches.* New York: Knopf, 1977.

_____. "The War Correspondent: A Reappraisal," *Esquire* (April 1970).

Hilsman, Roger. *To Move a Nation.* Garden City, N.Y.: 1967.

Hodgson, Godfrey. *America In Our Time.* New York: Doubleday, 1976 (New York: Vintage, 1978).

Hohenberg, John, ed. *The Pulitzer Prize Story 1959–1980.* New York: Columbia University, 1980.

Hubbell, John G. *P.O.W.* New York: Reader's Digest/McGraw-Hill, 1976.

Hurley, Alfred F., and Robert C. Ehrhart, eds. *Air Power and Warfare.* Washington, D.C.: U.S. Government Printing Office, 1979.

Johnson, Lyndon B. *The Vantage Point.* New York: Holt, Rinehart & Winston, 1971.

Kalb, Marvin, and Elie Abel. *Roots of Involvement.* New York: Norton, 1971.

Karnow, Stanley. *Vietnam: A History.* New York: Viking, 1983.

Kearns, Doris. *Lyndon Johnson and the American Dream.* New York: Harper & Row, 1972.

Kennedy, John F. *A Compilation of Statements and Speeches Made During His Service in the United States Senate and House of Representatives.* Washington, D.C.: U.S. Government Printing Office, 1964.

Kissinger, Henry. *Years of Upheaval.* Boston: Little, Brown, 1982.

Knightley, Phillip. *The First Casualty.* New York: Harcourt Brace Jovanovich, 1975.

Lacoture, Jean. *Ho Chi Minh.* New York: Random House, 1968.

Lash, Joseph P. *Roosevelt and Churchill.* New York: Norton, 1976.

Lavalle, A. J. C., ed. *Airpower and the 1972 Spring Invasion.* Washington, D.C.: U.S. Government Printing Office, 1976.

_____. *The Tale of Two Bridges and the Battle for the Skies Over North Vietnam.* Washington, D.C.: U.S. Government Printing Office, 1976.

Lipsman, Samuel, ed. *The Vietnam Experience: Fighting for Time.* Boston: Boston Publishing Company, 1983.

Louis, William Roger. *Imperialism at Bay.* New York: Oxford University Press, 1978.

Maclear, Michael. *The Ten Thousand Day War.* New York: St. Martin's, 1981.

MacPherson, Myra. *Long Time Passing.* Garden City, N.J.: Doubleday, 1984.

Maitland, Terrence, ed. *The Vietnam Experience: A Contagion of War.* Boston: Boston Publishing Company, 1983.

_____. *The Vietnam Experience: Raising the Stakes.* Boston: Boston Publishing Company, 1982.

Manchester, William. *The Glory and the Dream.* Boston: Little, Brown, 1974 (New York: Bantam, 1975).

Marshall, S. L. A. *Vietnam: Three Battles.* New York: Dial, 1971 (New York: Da Capo, 1982).

Matusow, Allen J. *The Unraveling of America.* New York: Harper & Row, 1984.

McCarthy, James R., and George B. Allison. *Linebacker II: A View from the Rock.* Washington, D.C.: U.S. Government Printing Office, 1979.

Mecklin, John. *Mission in Torment.* Garden City, N.Y.: Doubleday, 1965.

Mersky, Peter B., and Norman Polmar. *The Naval Air War in Vietnam.* Annapolis: The Nautical and Aviation Publishing Company, 1981.

Miller, Merle. *Lyndon.* New York: Putnam, 1980.

Millett, Allan R., ed. *A Short History of the Vietnam War.* Bloomington: Indiana University, 1978.

Mohr, Charles. "McNamara on Record, Reluctantly, on Vietnam," *New York Times* (May 16, 1984).

Momyer, William W. *Air Power in Three Wars.* Washington, D.C.: U.S. Government Printing Office, 1978.

Morgan, Thomas B. "Reporters of the Lost War," *Esquire* (July 1984).

Morris, James. *Farewell the Trumpets.* New York: Harcourt Brace Jovanovich, 1978.

Morrocco, John, ed. *The Vietnam Experience: Thunder from Above.* Boston: Boston Publishing Company, 1983.

Nehring, John A., ed. *Contrails 1963–64.* U.S. Air Force Academy, Colo., 1963.

Newsweek, editors of. "Doctor of the Jungle," *Newsweek* (January 30, 1961).

_____. "The Doctor's Last Days," *Newsweek* (November 23, 1959).

Nixon, Richard M. *The Memoirs of Richard M. Nixon.* New York: Grosset & Dunlap, 1978 (New York: Warner, 1979).

Nolan, Keith William. *Battle for Hue.* Navato, Calif.: Presidio, 1983.

Oberdorfer, Don. *Tet!.* Garden City, N.Y.: Doubleday, 1971.

O'Connor, Richard. *Pacific Destiny.* Boston: Little, Brown, 1969.

Oliphant, Tom. "War in the Back Pages," *Ramparts* (November 1972).

Patti, Archimedes L. A. *Why Viet Nam?*. Berkeley: University of California, 1980.

Pentagon Papers. New York: New York Times/Bantam, 1971.

Pisor, Robert. *The End of the Line*. New York: Norton, 1982 (New York: Ballantine, 1983).

Porter, Gareth. *A Peace Denied*. Bloomington: Indiana University, 1975.

———. *Vietnam: A History in Documents*. New York: Meridian, 1981.

Randolph, Eleanor. "Westmoreland Told Not to Inform Media," *Washington Post* (October 19, 1984).

Risner, Robinson. *The Passing of the Night*. New York: Random House, 1973.

Roosevelt, Elliott. *As He Saw It*. New York: Duell, Sloan & Pearce, 1946.

Rutledge, Howard, and Phyllis Rutledge. *In the Presence of Mine Enemies*. Old Tappan, N.J.: Spire, 1973.

Ryan, Paul B. "U.S.S. *Constellation* Flare-up: Was it Mutiny?," *Proceedings of the United States Naval Institute* (January 1976).

Salinger, Pierre. *With Kennedy*. Garden City, N.Y.: Doubleday, 1966.

Scheer, Robert. *How the United States Got Involved in Vietnam*. Santa Barbara, Calif.: Center for Democratic Institutions, 1965.

Schlesinger, Arthur, Jr. *Robert Kennedy and His Times*. Boston: Houghton Mifflin, 1978.

———. *A Thousand Days*. Boston: Houghton Mifflin, 1965.

Schneider, Donald K. *Air Force Heroes in Vietnam*. Washington, D.C.: U.S. Government Printing Office, 1979.

Scoville, Thomas W. *Reorganizing for Pacification Support*. Washington, D.C.: Center for Military History (U.S. Army), 1982.

Schachtman, Tom. *Decade of Shocks*. New York: Poseidon, 1983.

Shaplen, Robert. "Diem," *The New Yorker* (September 22, 1962).

———. "The Enigma of Ho Chi Minh," *The Reporter*. (January 27, 1955).

———. *The Lost Revolution*. New York: Harper & Row, 1965.

Shawcross, William. *Sideshow*. New York: Washington Square, 1979.

Shulimson, Jack. *U.S. Marines in Vietnam 1966*. Washington, D.C.: History and Museums Division (U.S. Marine Corps), 1982.

Smith, Jack. "Death in the Ia Drang Valley," *Saturday Evening Post* (January 28, 1967).

Snepp, Frank. *Decent Interval*. New York: Random House, 1977.

Spector, Ronald H. *United States Army in Vietnam: Advice and Support – The Early Years*. Washington, D.C.: Center of Military History (U.S. Army), 1983.

Steel, Ronald. *Walter Lippmann and the American Century*. Boston: Little, Brown, 1980 (New York: Vintage, 1981).

Sully, François. "Vietnam: The Unpleasant Truth," *Newsweek* (August 22, 1962).

Summers, Harry G., Jr. *On Strategy*. Navato, Calif.: Presidio, 1982.

———. "The Bitter Triumph of Ia Drang," *American Heritage* (February-March 1984).

Szulc, Tad. *The Illusion of Peace*. New York: Viking, 1978.

Terry, Wallace. *Bloods*. New York: Random House, 1984.

Time, editors of. "Covering Viet Nam: Crud, Fret and Jeers," *Time* (June 10, 1966).

Tuchman, Barbara W. *The March of Folly*. New York: Knopf, 1984.

U.S. Senate Foreign Relations Committee. "The U.S. Government and the Vietnam War – Part 1: 1945–1961." Washington, D.C.: U.S. Government Printing Office, 1984.

Westmoreland, William C. *A Soldier Reports*. New York: Doubleday, 1976 (New York: Dell, 1980).

White, Theodore H. *In Search of History*. New York: Harper & Row, 1978 (New York: Warner, 1979).

———. *The Making of the President 1960*. New York: Atheneum, 1961 (New York: Mentor, 1967).

Photo Credits

Chapter 1: Colony of Cruelty

6 Collection Viollet **7** Wide World **9** Eastfoto **11** Mary Evans Library/Photo Researchers, Inc. **13** U.S.S. *Constitution* Museum **14** top, Collection D. Seylan; bottom, Collection Viollet **15** top, Historical Picture Service, Inc.; bottom, Collection Viollet **17** NYT Collection/National Archives **18** top, NYT Collection/National Archives; bottom, Collection D. Seylan **20** Collection D. Seylan **21** top, Collection D. Seylan; bottom, NYT Collection/National Archives **22** NYT Collection/National Archives **23** Tass from Sovfoto/Eastfoto **24** NYT Collection/National Archives **25** Collection D. Seylan **26** NYT Collection/National Archives **29** top, U.S. Army; bottom, NYT Collection/National Archives

Chapter 2: The Diplomatic Puzzle

30 Wide World **31** Wide World **32** Wide World **34** Wide World **35** Wide World **37** left, National Archives; right, State Department **40** Wide World **42** top, NYT Collection/National Archives; bottom, National Archives **43** top, U.S. Army; bottom, Archimedes Patti Collection **44** Wide World **46** National Archives **48** National Archives **49** U.S. Army **50** U.S. Army **51** National Archives **52** Defense Department **53** top, Eastfoto; bottom, National Archives **54** National Archives **55** Defense Department **57** Eastfoto **59** Defense Department **61** National Archives **62** National Archives

Chapter 3: Emerging Enemies

64 Wide World **65** USIA **66** Eastfoto **67** NYT Collection/National Archives **68** Wide World **69** NYT Collection/National Archives **70** NYT Collection/National Archives **73** Black Star **74** Ngo Vinh Long Collection **77** Archimedes Patti Collection **80** NYT Collection/National Archives **81** NYT Collection/National Archives **82** Eastfoto **83** Eastfoto **84** top, USIA; bottom, Eastfoto **85** USIA **86** NYT Collection/National Archives **87** USIA **88** NYT Collection/National Archives **89** USIA **90** NYT Collection/National Archives **91** top, USIA; bottom, NYT Collection/National Archives **92** NYT Collection/National Archives **93** top, French Army; bottom, USIA **95** French Army **98** NYT Collection/National Archives **99** French Army **100** National Archives **101** National Archives **102** Eastfoto **103** Eastfoto **104** top, USIA; bottom, Wide World **105** National Archives **106** National Archives **108** left, National Archives; right, John F. Kennedy Library **109** National Archives

Chapter 4: Poles Apart

110 Wide World **111** National Archives **112** top, Wide World; bottom, National Archives **113** State Department **115** State Department **116** U.S. Army **117** USIA **118** USIA **120** Wide World **122** U.S. Navy **123** USIA **124** Eastfoto **125** Eastfoto **127** State Department **128** USIA **129** USIA **131** U.S. Army **133** State Department **136** Eastfoto **137** Eastfoto **138** Eastfoto **139** Eastfoto **140** Eastfoto **141** USIA **142** Edward Lansdale Collection/Stanford University Library **144** U.S. Army **145** top, U.S. Army; middle, NYT Collection/National Archives; bottom, Wide World **146** NYT Collection/National Archives **147** top, USIA; bottom, Wide World **148** top, USIA; bottom, Wide World **149** USIA **151** top, State Department; middle, USIA; bottom, U.S. Army

Chapter 5: Sharing the Sampan

152 Wide World **153** USIA **154** left, National Archives; right, Time Inc. **155** clockwise: Abbie Rowe Collection/National Archives, U.S. Army, Abbie Rowe Collection/National Archives, Abbie Rowe Collection/National Archives **156** top, Abbie Rowe Collection/National Archives; middle: left, USIA, right, Defense Department; bottom, USIA **157** top and bottom, USIA; middle, U.S. Army **158** top, USIA; bottom, Abbie Rowe Collection/National Archives **159** USIA **160** USIA **162** UPI/Bettmann Archive, Inc. **163** top, NYT; middle and bottom, USIA **164**

165 Abbie Rowe Collection/National Archives **165** Abbie Rowe Collection/National Archives **167** top, USIA; middle, United Nations; bottom, Abbie Rowe Collection/National Archives **168** NYT **169** Abbie Rowe Collection/National Archives **171** USIA **172** USIA **173** United Nations **175** top, USIA; bottom, U.S. Army **176** top, U.S. Army; bottom, State Department **177** top, Abbie Rowe Collection/National Archives; bottom, USIA **179** Defense Department **180** University of South Carolina **182** U.S. Army **183** U.S. Army **184** U.S. Army **185** National Archives **186** USIA **187** top, U.S. Army; bottom, Michigan State University Archives and Historical Collections **188** top, U.S. Army; bottom, USIA **189** U.S. Army **190** Black Star **191** Wide World **192** top, National Archives; bottom, United Nations **193** U.S. Army **194** National Archives **195** National Archives **196** top, UPI/Bettmann Archive Inc.; bottom, Abbie Rowe Collection/National Archives **198** USIA **201** USIA **202** National Archives **203** top and middle, U.S. Navy; bottom, National Archives

Chapter 6: Down We Dive

204 Y.R. Okamoto/Lyndon Johnson Library **205** Eastfoto **207** U.S. Air Force **209** U.S. Air Force **211** U.S. Air Force **212** Wide World **213** Wide World **214** Defense Department **215** Defense Department **217** USIA **218** National Archives **219** Cecil Stoughton/Lyndon Johnson Library **220** U.S. Air Force **221** U.S. Air Force **222** top, Eastfoto; bottom, Defense Department **223** top, U.S. Navy; bottom, U.S. Air Force **224** U.S. Air Force **225** left, U.S. Air Force; right, National Archives **226** U.S. Air Force **227** U.S. Navy **228** top, U.S. Air Force; bottom, Eastfoto **229** U.S. Navy **230** top, Eastfoto; bottom, U.S. Air Force **231** Eastfoto **232** top, U.S. Air Force; bottom, Eastfoto **233** U.S. Air Force **234** top and middle, Eastfoto; bottom, U.S. Navy **235** top, Eastfoto; bottom, U.S. Air Force **236** top, U.S. Navy; bottom, Eastfoto **237** U.S. Air Force **238** U.S. Air Force **242** top, U.S. Air Force; bottom, U.S. Air Force **243** Eastfoto **245** Eastfoto **246** U.S. Navy **247** Phyllis Rutledge Collection **249** Defense Department **250** Eastfoto **251** top, Eastfoto; middle and bottom, U.S. Navy **253** U.S. Air Force **255** U.S. Air Force **256** U.S. Navy **257** U.S. Air Force **258** U.S. Air Force **259** U.S. Air Force **260** top, Eastfoto; bottom, U.S. Navy **262** U.S. Air Force **263** U.S. Air Force **264** U.S. Air Force **265** U.S. Air Force **266** top, White House; bottom, U.S. Air Force **267** U.S. Air Force **268** U.S. Air Force **269** U.S. Air Force **270** top, Eastfoto; bottom, U.S. Air Force **271** U.S. Marine Corps

Chapter 7: War Without End, Amen

272 U.S. Marines **273** U.S. Army **275** top, U.S. Marines; middle and bottom, U.S. Army **276** U.S. Army **277** Defense Department **278** U.S. Army **279** top and bottom, U.S. Army **280** U.S. Army **281** U.S. Army **282** Eastfoto **283** U.S. Army **285** Eastfoto **287** Eastfoto **288** U.S. Army **289** U.S. Army **290** top, U.S. Air Force; bottom, UPI/Bettmann Archive, Inc. **291** U.S. Marine Corps **292** U.S. Marine Corps **293** top, U.S. Marine Corps; bottom, U.S. Army **297** top, U.S. Marine Corps; bottom, U.S. Air Force **300** Frank Wolfe/Lyndon Johnson Library **301** top and bottom, U.S. Marine Corps; middle, U.S. Army **302** top, U.S. Army; middle and bottom, U.S. Marine Corps **303** U.S. Marine Corps **304** U.S. Marine Corps **305** U.S. Marine Corps **307** U.S. Marine Corps **308** U.S. Marine Corps **309** U.S. Marine Corps **310** Eastfoto **311** U.S. Air Force **312** top, U.S. Army; bottom, U.S. Marine Corps **313** U.S. Marine Corps **314** top, U.S. Army; bottom, U.S. Navy **315** top, U.S. Navy; bottom, U.S. Marine Corps **317** top, U.S. Marine Corps; bottom, Eastfoto **318** U.S. Marine Corps **321** Eastfoto **322** top, U.S. Marine Corps; middle, U.S. Army; bottom, Eastfoto **324** Eastfoto **325** top, U.S. Army; bottom, U.S. Marine Corps **326** U.S. Marine Corps **327** U.S. Marine Corps **328** U.S. Marine Corps **329** top, Y.R. Okamoto/Lyndon Johnson Library; bottom, U.S. Marine Corps **330** U.S. Marine Corps **331** U.S. Navy

Chapter 8: Paying the Price, Bearing the Burden

332 U.S. Marine Corps **333** U.S. Navy **334** Y.R. Okamoto/Lyndon Johnson Library **336** U.S. Marine Corps **337** U.S. Marine Corps **338** U.S. Marine Corps **339** U.S. Marine Corps **340** U.S. Marine Corps **341** U.S. Marine Corps **343** U.S. Marine Corps **344** U.S. Air Force **345** U.S. Air Force **346** top, USIA; bottom, U.S. Marine Corps **347** U.S. Marine Corps **348** top, U.S. Marine Corps; bottom, U.S. Army **350** U.S. Marine Corps **351** U.S. Marine Corps **353** U.S. Marine Corps **354** U.S. Marine Corps **355** U.S. Marine Corps **356** U.S. Marine Corps **357** U.S. Marine Corps **358** U.S. Marine Corps **359** U.S. Marine Corps **360** top, Robert Ellison/Black Star; bottom, U.S. Marine Corps **361** U.S. Marine Corps **362** U.S. Marine Corps **363** top, Y.R. Okamoto/Lyndon Johnson Library; middle and bottom, U.S. Navy **364** U.S. Marine Corps **365** U.S. Marine Corps **366** U.S. Marine Corps **367** U.S. Marine Corps **368** U.S. Marine Corps **369** U.S. Marine Corps **370** top, U.S. Marine Corps; bottom, Y.R.

Okamoto/Lyndon Johnson Library **371** Y.R. Okamoto/Lyndon Johnson Library **372** U.S. Air Force **373** Y.R. Okamoto/Lyndon Johnson Library **374** Y.R. Okamoto/Lyndon Johnson Library **376** U.S. Navy **377** U.S. Navy **378** Y.R. Okamoto/Lyndon Johnson Library **379** Y.R. Okamoto/Lyndon Johnson Library **380** Y.R. Okamoto/Lyndon Johnson Library **381** Y.R. Okamoto/Lyndon Johnson Library **382** Y.R. Okamoto/Lyndon Johnson Library **383** top, Y.R. Okamoto/Lyndon Johnson Library; bottom, U.S. Army **384** U.S. Army **384** U.S. Marine Corps **386** top, U.S. Marine Corps; bottom, U.S. Army **387** U.S. Marine Corps **388** U.S. Marine Corps **390** Wide World **391** U.S. Marine Corps **392** U.S. Marine Corps **393** U.S. Marine Corps **394** U.S. Marine Corps **396** U.S. Marine Corps **397** U.S. Marine Corps **400** U.S. Marine Corps **401** U.S. Marine Corps **403** Eastfoto

Chapter 9: The Politics of Peace

(pages **404-471**)

404 Wide World **405** Wide World **407** Archimedes Patti Collection **408** top, UPI/Bettmann Archive, Inc., bottom, U.S. Marine Corps **409** Michigan State University **410** Wide World **411** UPI/Bettmann Archive, Inc. **412** U.S. Marine Corps **413** U.S. Army **414** U.S. Marine Corps **415** U.S. Marine Corps **417** Y.R. Okamoto/Lyndon Johnson Library **418** Wide World **419** Wide World **420** University of California at Berkeley **427** Wide World **428** Y.R. Okamoto/Lyndon Johnson Library **429** Wide World **430** Y.R. Okamoto/Lyndon Johnson Library **431** Y.R. Okamoto/Lyndon Johnson Library **435** U.S. Marine Corps **436** U.S. Marine Corps **437** U.S. Marine Corps **439** U.S. Marine Corps **441** Wide World **442** Wide World **443** top and bottom, U.S. Marine Corps **444** top and bottom, Y.R. Okamoto/Lyndon Johnson Library **445** top and bottom, Y.R. Okamoto/Lyndon Johnson Library **448** Wide World **449** Wide World **452** Kent State University **453** Kent State University **454** Wide World **456** U.S. Marine Corps **457** U.S. Marine Corps **458** Y.R. Okamoto/Lyndon Johnson Library **459** Y.R. Okamoto/Lyndon Johnson Library **460** Y.R. Okamoto/Lyndon Johnson Library **461** Y.R. Okamoto/Lyndon Johnson Library **464** Wide World **465** State Department **466** Democratic Republic of Vietnam **467** Democratic Republic of Vietnam **468** U.S. Navy **469** U.S. Navy **470** U.S. Navy **471** top, U.S. Navy; bottom, UPI/Bettmann Archive, Inc.

Index